Evolution & Prehistory

9e

Evolution & Prehistory

The Human Challenge

WILLIAM A. HAVILAND
University of Vermont

DANA WALRATH
University of Vermont

HARALD E. L. PRINS
Kansas State University

BUNNY McBRIDE
Kansas State University

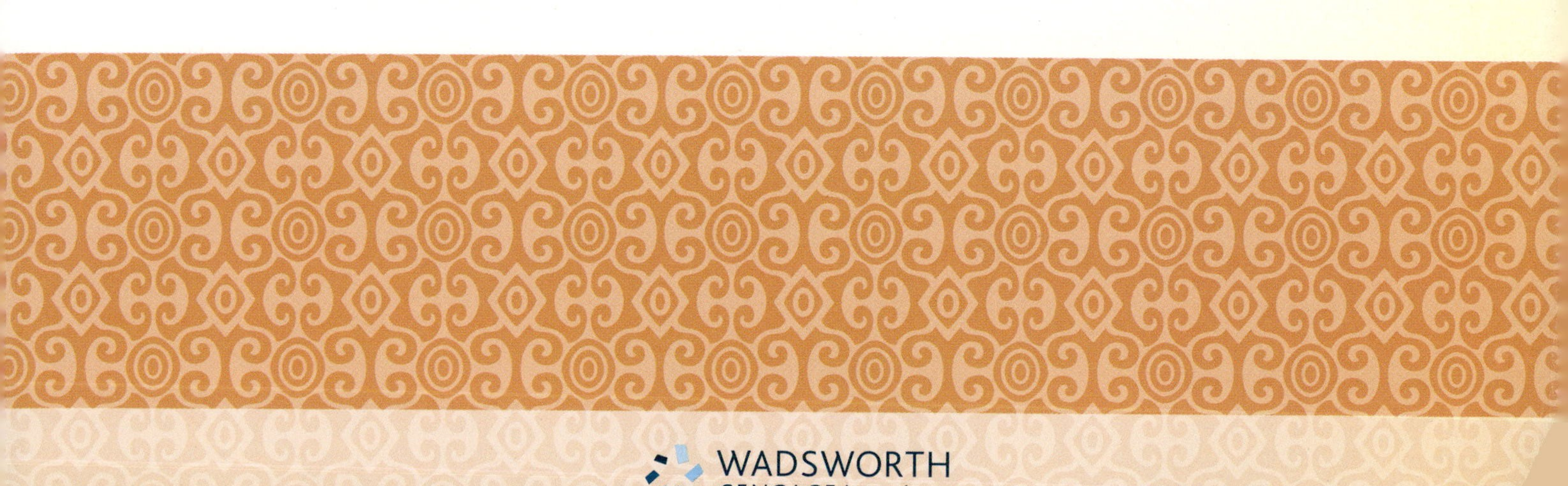

WADSWORTH
CENGAGE Learning

Australia • Brazil • Japan • Korea • Mexico • Singapore • Spain • United Kingdom • United States

***Evolution & Prehistory: The Human Challenge,* Nineth Edition**
William A. Haviland, Dana Walrath, Harald E. L. Prins, Bunny McBride

Anthropology Editor: Erin Mitchell
Developmental Editor: Lin Marshall Gaylord
Assistant Editor: Rachael Krapf
Editorial Assistant: Pamela Simon
Media Editor: Melanie Cregger
Marketing Manager: Andrew Keay
Marketing Coordinator: Dimitri Hagnéré
Marketing Communications Manager: Tami Strang
Content Project Manager: Samen Iqbal
Creative Director: Rob Hugel
Art Director: Caryl Gorska
Print Buyer: Karen Hunt
Rights Acquisitions Account Manager, Text: Roberta Broyer
Rights Acquisitions Account Manager, Image: Robyn Young
Production Service: Joan Keyes, Dovetail Publishing Services
Text Designer: Lisa Buckley
Photo Researchers: Billie Porter, Susan Kaprov
Copy Editor: Jennifer Gordon
Cover Designer: Lawrence R. Didona
Cover Images, clockwise from top right: stem cell: © SPL/Photo Researchers, Inc.; young orangutan: © Gerry Ellis/Photolibrary; Angkor Wat ruins, Bayon, Prasat Bayon, Khmer temple: © John Miles/Getty Images; Ona Nagast site excavation, Aksum, Ethiopia: © George Steinmetz/Corbis; skeletons at excavation site in Tyre, Lebanon: © Hassan Bahsoun/epa/Corbis; researcher examining DNA image: © Andrew Brookes/Corbis; Templo Mayor excavation, Mexico City, Mexico: © David Hiser/Getty Images
Compositor: Pre-PressPMG

Library of Congress Control Number: 2009941339

Student Edition:

ISBN-13: 978-0-495-81219-7

ISBN-10: 0-495-81219-6

Loose-leaf Edition:

ISBN-13: 978-0-8400-3332-1

ISBN-10: 0-8400-3332-X

Wadsworth
20 Davis Drive
Belmont, CA 94002-3098
USA

Cengage Learning is a leading provider of customized learning solutions with office locations around the globe, including Singapore, the United Kingdom, Australia, Mexico, Brazil, and Japan. Locate your local office at **www.cengage.com/global.**

Cengage Learning products are represented in Canada by Nelson Education, Ltd.

To learn more about Wadsworth, visit **www.cengage.com/wadsworth**

Purchase any of our products at your local college store or at our preferred online store **www.CengageBrain.com.**

Printed in the United States of America
1 2 3 4 5 6 7 14 13 12 11 10

Dedicated to our parents who provided each of us with a nourishing environment, inspiring guidance, and an appreciation for cultural heritage. All of them fostered in all of us an eagerness to explore, experience, and enjoy other cultures, past and present.

Putting the World in Perspective

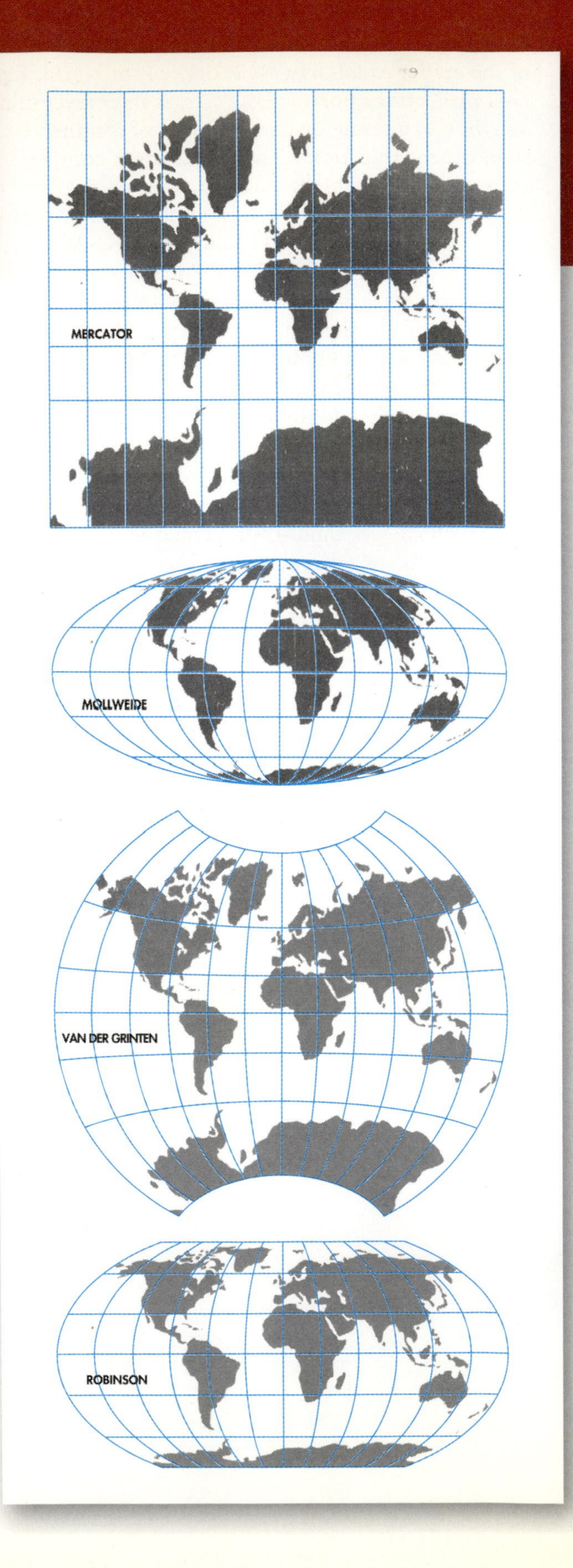

Although all humans that we know about are capable of producing accurate sketches of localities and regions with which they are familiar, **cartography** (the craft of map making as we know it today) had its beginnings in 16th-century Europe, and its subsequent development is related to the expansion of Europeans to all parts of the globe. From the beginning, there have been two problems with maps: the technical one of how to depict on a two-dimensional, flat surface a three-dimensional spherical object, and the cultural one of whose worldview they reflect. In fact, the two issues are inseparable, for the particular projection one uses inevitably makes a statement about how one views one's own people and their place in the world. Indeed, maps often shape our perception of reality as much as they reflect it.

In cartography, a **projection** refers to the system of intersecting lines (of longitude and latitude) by which part or all of the globe is represented on a flat surface. There are more than a hundred different projections in use today, ranging from polar perspectives to interrupted "butterflies" to rectangles to heart shapes. Each projection causes distortion in size, shape, or distance in some way or another. A map that correctly shows the shape of a landmass will of necessity misrepresent the size. A map that is accurate along the equator will be deceptive at the poles.

Perhaps no projection has had more influence on the way we see the world than that of Gerhardus Mercator, who devised his map in 1569 as a navigational aid for mariners. So well suited was Mercator's map for this purpose that it continues to be used for navigational charts today. At the same time, the Mercator projection became a standard for depicting landmasses, something for which it was never intended. Although an accurate navigational tool, the Mercator projection greatly exaggerates the size of landmasses in higher latitudes, giving about two thirds of the map's surface to the northern hemisphere. Thus the lands occupied by Europeans and European descendants appear far larger than those of other people. For example, North America (19 million square kilometers) appears almost twice the size of Africa (30 million square kilometers), while Europe is shown as equal in size to South America, which actually has nearly twice the landmass of Europe.

A map developed in 1805 by Karl B. Mollweide was one of the earlier *equal-area projections* of the world. Equal-area projections portray landmasses in correct relative size, but, as a result, distort the shape of continents more than other projections. They most often compress and warp lands in the higher latitudes and vertically stretch landmasses close to the equator. Other equal-area projections include the Lambert Cylindrical Equal-Area Projection (1772), the Hammer Equal-Area Projection (1892), and the Eckert Equal-Area Projection (1906).

The Van der Grinten Projection (1904) was a compromise aimed at minimizing both the distortions of size in the Mercator and the distortion of shape in equal-area maps such as the Mollweide. Although an improvement, the lands of the northern hemisphere are still emphasized at the expense of the southern. For example, in the Van der Grinten, the Commonwealth of Independent States (the former Soviet Union) and Canada are shown at more than twice their relative size.

The Robinson Projection, which was adopted by the National Geographic Society in 1988 to replace the Van der Grinten, is one of the best compromises to date between the distortions of size and shape. Although an improvement over the Van der Grinten, the Robinson Projection still depicts lands in the northern latitudes as proportionally larger at the same time that it depicts lands in the lower latitudes (representing most Third World nations) as proportionally smaller. Like European maps before it, the Robinson Projection places Europe at the center of the map with the Atlantic Ocean and the Americas to the left, emphasizing the cultural connection between Europe and North America, while neglecting the geographic closeness of northwestern North America to northeastern Asia.

The following pages show four maps that each convey quite different cultural messages. Included among them is the Peters Projection, an equal-area map that has been adopted as the official map of UNESCO (the United Nations Educational, Scientific, and Cultural Organization), and a map made in Japan, showing us how the world looks from the other side.

The Robinson Projection

The map below is based on the Robinson Projection, which is used today by the National Geographic Society and Rand McNally. Although the Robinson Projection distorts the relative size of landmasses, it does so much less than most other projections. Still, it places Europe at the center of the map. This particular view of the world has been used to identify the location of many of the cultures discussed in this text.

YUPIK
ESKIMO
RUSSIANS
SLOVAKIANS
SERBS
CHECHENS
MONGOLIANS
UYGHUR
TURKS
KURDS
UZBEK
TAJIK
KOHISTANI
JAPANESE
BAKHTIARI
PASHTUN
TIBETANS
HAN CHINESE
AWLAD ALI
BEDOUINS
BAHREIN
TAIWANESE
KAREN
MOSUO
TRUK
SHAIVITE
NUER
TIGREANS
AFAR
SOMALI
NAYAR
DINKA
KOTA AND
KURUMBA
VEDDA
AZANDE
MALDIVES
TODA AND
BADAGA
ACEH
PINGELAP ISLANDERS
TURKANA
WAPE
KAPAUKU
ENGA
MBUTI
NANDI
KIKUYU
MINANGKABAU
TSEMBAGA
HUTU
MAASAI
GUSII
TIRIKI
SOLOMON ISLANDERS
ARAPESH
BALINESE
HADZA
TROBRIANDERS
DOBU
ABORIGINAL
AUSTRALIANS
SWAZI
ZULU
BASUTO
MAORI
TASMANIANS

The Peters Projection

The map below is based on the Peters Projection, which has been adopted as the official map of UNESCO. While it distorts the shape of continents (countries near the equator are vertically elongated by a ratio of 2 to 1), the Peters Projection does show all continents according to their correct relative size. Though Europe is still at the center, it is not shown as larger and more extensive than the Third World.

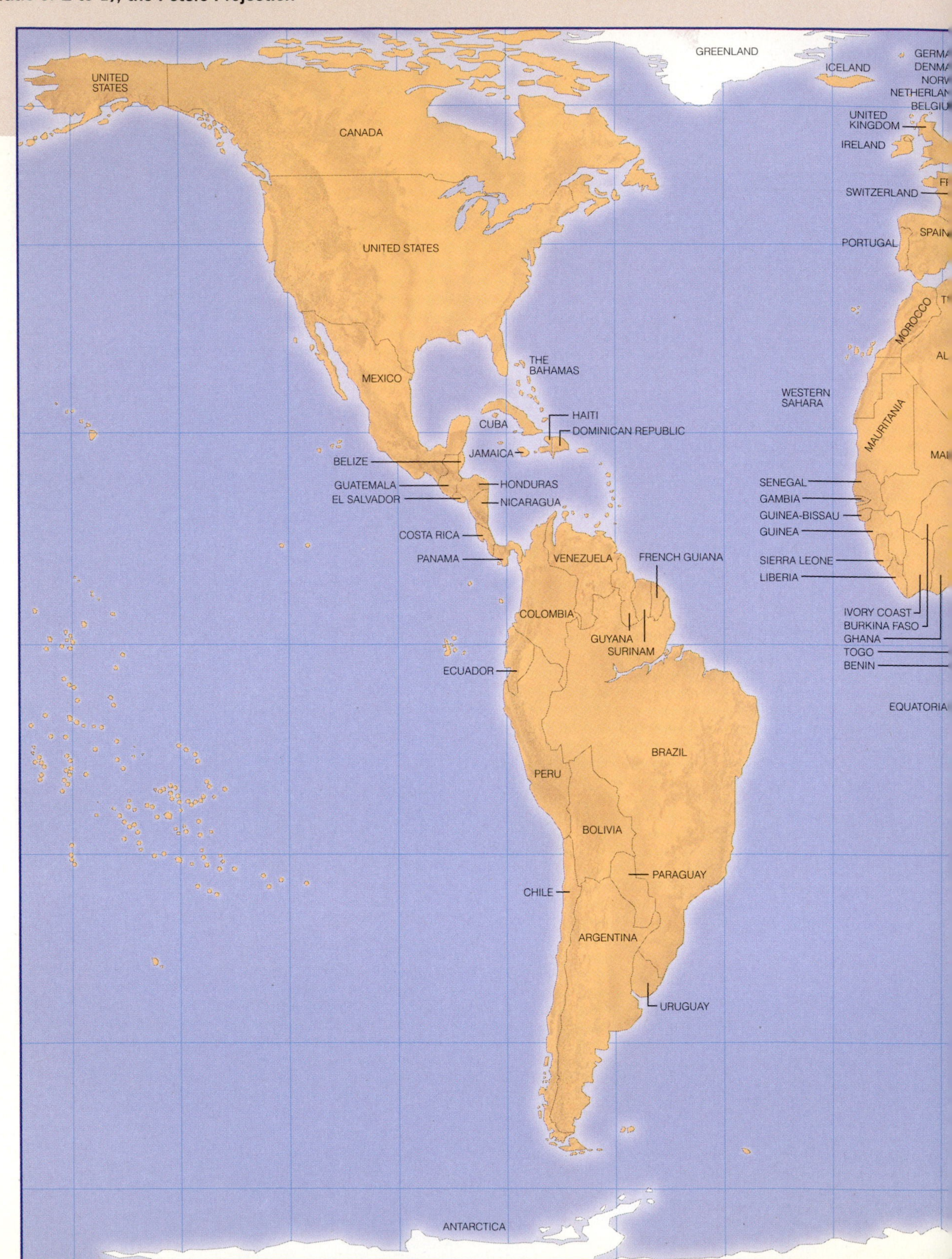

FINLAND
ESTONIA
LATVIA
LITHUANIA
BELARUS
ROMANIA
UKRAINE
MOLDOVA
SERBIA
BULGARIA
MONTENEGRO
MACEDONIA
ALBANIA
TURKEY
SYRIA
LEBANON
ISRAEL
JORDAN
EGYPT
AZERBAIJAN
ARMENIA
GEORGIA
RUSSIA
KAZAKHSTAN
KIRGHIZSTAN
TAJIKISTAN
UZBEKISTAN
TURKMENISTAN
MONGOLIA
NORTH KOREA
SOUTH KOREA
JAPAN
PEOPLE'S REPUBLIC OF CHINA
IRAQ
IRAN
AFGHAN-ISTAN
PAKISTAN
BAHRAIN
KUWAIT
QATAR
SAUDI ARABIA
OMAN
UNITED ARAB EMIRATES
YEMEN
NEPAL
BHUTAN
INDIA
MYANMAR
TAIWAN
BANGLA-DESH
LAOS
THAILAND
VIETNAM
CAMBODIA
PHILIPPINES
SUDAN
DJIBOUTI
ETHIOPIA
SOMALIA
SRI LANKA
BRUNEI
MALAYSIA
SINGAPORE
INDONESIA
PAPUA NEW GUINEA
CAMEROON
UGANDA
KENYA
TANZANIA
MALAWI
ZAMBIA
MADAGASCAR
ZIMBABWE
BOTS-WANA
MOZAMBIQUE
SWAZILAND
SOUTH AFRICA
AUSTRALIA
NEW ZEALAND
ANTARCTICA

Japanese Map

Not all maps place Europe at the center of the world, as this Japanese map illustrates. Besides reflecting the importance the Japanese attach to themselves in the world, this map has the virtue of showing the geographic proximity of North America to Asia, a fact easily overlooked when maps place Europe at their center.

GREENLAND
UNITED STATES
CANADA
UNITED STATES
MEXICO
THE BAHAMAS
HAITI
DOMINICAN REPUBLIC
CUBA
JAMAICA
BELIZE
GUATEMALA
EL SALVADOR
HONDURAS
NICARAGUA
COSTA RICA
PANAMA
VENEZUELA
FRENCH GUIANA
COLOMBIA
GUYANA
SURINAM
ECUADOR
BRAZIL
PERU
BOLIVIA
PARAGUAY
CHILE
ARGENTINA
URUGUAY
NEW ZEALAND
ANTARCTICA

The Turnabout Map

The way maps may reflect (and influence) our thinking is exemplified by the Turnabout Map, which places the South Pole at the top and the North Pole at the bottom. Words and phrases such as "on top," "over," and "above" tend to be equated by some people with superiority. Turning things upside-down may cause us to rethink the way North Americans regard themselves in relation to the people of Central America. © 1982 by Jesse Levine Turnabout Map™—Dist. by Laguna Sales, Inc., 7040 Via Valverde, San Jose, CA 95135

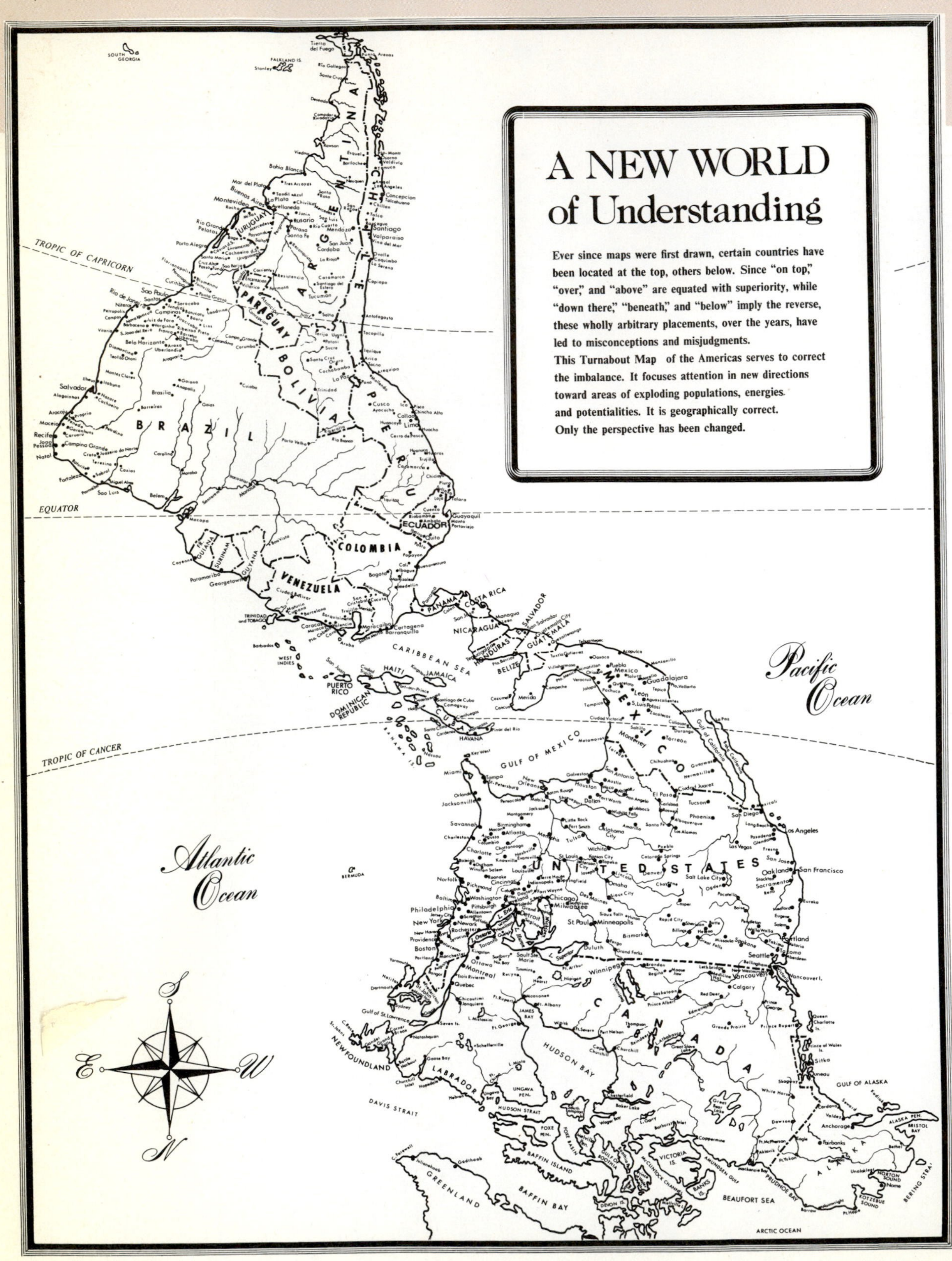
A NEW WORLD
of Understanding
Ever since maps were first drawn, certain countries have been located at the top, others below. Since "on top," "over," and "above" are equated with superiority, while "down there," "beneath," and "below" imply the reverse, these wholly arbitrary placements, over the years, have led to misconceptions and misjudgments.
This Turnabout Map of the Americas serves to correct the imbalance. It focuses attention in new directions toward areas of exploding populations, energies and potentialities. It is geographically correct.
Only the perspective has been changed.
TROPIC OF CAPRICORN
EQUATOR
TROPIC OF CANCER
ARGENTINA
CHILE
URUGUAY
PARAGUAY
BOLIVIA
BRAZIL
PERU
ECUADOR
COLOMBIA
VENEZUELA
GUYANA
SURINAM
FR. GUIANA
PANAMA
COSTA RICA
NICARAGUA
HONDURAS
EL SALVADOR
GUATEMALA
BELIZE
MEXICO
CUBA
HAITI
JAMAICA
DOMINICAN REPUBLIC
PUERTO RICO
CARIBBEAN SEA
GULF OF MEXICO
UNITED STATES
CANADA
ALASKA
GREENLAND
HUDSON BAY
BAFFIN ISLAND
BAFFIN BAY
DAVIS STRAIT
LABRADOR
NEWFOUNDLAND
GULF OF ALASKA
BEAUFORT SEA
ARCTIC OCEAN
BERING STRAIT
Pacific Ocean
Atlantic Ocean
S
E
W
N

Brief Contents

Features Contents

Anthropologists of Note

Anthropology Applied

Biocultural Connection

Globalscape

Original Study

Contents

Chapter 6 Macroevolution and the Early Primates 122

Chapter 7 The First Bipeds 144

Chapter 8 Early *Homo* and the Origins of Culture 172

Chapter 9 The Global Expansion of *Homo sapiens* and Their Technology 202

Preface

Working on this ninth edition of *Evolution and Prehistory* has proved to us how fortunate we are to have the opportunity to revisit our textbook multiple times with the ambition of reaching well beyond mere updating to making the narrative and images ever-more compelling, informative, and relevant to readers. Our efforts continue to be fueled by vital feedback from our students and from anthropology professors who have reviewed and used previous editions. Their input—combined with our own ongoing research and the surprisingly delightful task of rethinking familiar concepts that appear self-evident—has helped us bring fresh insight to classical themes.

Evolution and Prehistory is designed for introductory anthropology courses at the college level. While focusing on biological anthropology and archaeology, a four-field approach is central to this book. By emphasizing the fundamental connection between biology and culture, the archaeology student learns more about the biological basis of human cultural abilities and the many ways that culture has impacted human biology, past and present. Similarly, this combination provides more of the cultural context of human evolutionary history, the development of scientific thought, and present-day biological diversity than a student would get in a course restricted to biological anthropology. There has been much debate about the future of four-field anthropology. In our view, its future will be assured through collaboration among anthropologists with diverse backgrounds, as exemplified in this book.

With each new edition, we look anew at the archetypal examples of our discipline and weigh them against the latest innovative research methodologies, archaeological discoveries, genetic and other biological findings, linguistic insights, and ethnographic descriptions, theoretical revelations, and significant examples of applied anthropology. These considerations, combined with attention to compelling issues in our global theater, go toward fashioning a thought-provoking textbook that presents both classical and fresh material in ways that stimulate students' interest, stir critical reflection, and prompt "ah-ha" moments.

Our Mission

Time and time again, we have observed that most students enter an introductory anthropology class intrigued by the general subject but with little more than a vague sense of what it is all about. Thus the first and most obvious task of our text is to provide a thorough introduction to the discipline—its foundations as a domain of knowledge and its major insights into the rich diversity of humans as a culture-making species.

In doing this, we draw from the research and ideas of a number of traditions of anthropological thought, exposing students to a mix of theoretical perspectives and methodologies. Such inclusiveness reflects our conviction that different approaches offer distinctly important insights about human biology, behavior, and beliefs in the past and in the present.

If most students start out with only a vague sense of what anthropology is, they often have less clear and potentially more problematic views of the superiority of their own species and culture. A second task for this text, then, is to prod students to appreciate the rich complexity and breadth of human biology and behavior. Along with this is the aim of helping them understand why there are so many differences and similarities in the human condition, past and present.

Debates regarding globalization and notions of progress, the "naturalness" of the mother/father/child(ren) nuclear family, new genetic technologies, and how gender roles relate to biological variation all benefit greatly from the fresh and often fascinating insights gained through anthropology. This probing aspect of our discipline is perhaps the most valuable gift we can pass on to those who take our classes. If we, as teachers (and textbook authors), do our jobs well, students will gain a wider and more open-minded outlook on the world and a critical but constructive perspective on human origins and on their own biology and culture today. To borrow a favorite line from the famous poet T. S. Eliot, "the end of all our exploring will be to arrive where we started and know the place for the first time" (*Four Quartets*).

There has never been as great a need for students to acquire the anthropological tools to help them escape culture-bound ways of thinking and acting and to gain more tolerance for other ways of life. Thus we have written this text, in large part, to help students make sense of our increasingly complex world and to navigate through its interrelated biological and cultural networks with knowledge and skill, whatever professional path they take. We see the book as a guide for people entering the often bewildering maze of global crossroads in the 21st century.

A Distinctive Approach

Two key factors distinguish *Evolution and Prehistory* from other introductory anthropology texts: our integrative presentation of the discipline's four fields and a trio of unifying themes that tie the book together.

Integration of the Four Fields

Unlike traditional texts that present anthropology's four fields—archaeology, linguistics, cultural anthropology, and physical anthropology—as if they were relatively separate or independent, our book takes an integrative approach. This reflects the comprehensive character of our discipline, a domain of knowledge where members of our species are studied in their totality—as social creatures biologically evolved with the inherent capacity of learning and sharing culture by means of symbolic communication. This approach also reflects our collective experience as practicing anthropologists who recognize that we cannot fully understand humanity in all its fascinating complexity unless we appreciate the systemic interplay among environmental, physiological, material, social, ideological, psychological, and symbolic factors, both past and present.

For analytical purposes, of course, we have no choice but to discuss physical anthropology as distinct from archaeology, linguistics, and sociocultural anthropology. Accordingly, this text focuses primarily on biological anthropology and archaeology, but the links between biology and culture, past and present, are shown repeatedly. Among many examples of this integrative approach, Chapter 12, "Modern Human Diversity: Race and Racism," discusses the social context of "race" and recent cultural practices that have impacted the human genome. Similarly, material concerning linguistics appears not only in the chapter on living primates (Chapter 3), but also in the chapters on primate behavior (Chapter 4), on early *Homo* and the origins of culture (Chapter 8), and on the emergence of cities and states (Chapter 11). These chapters include material on the linguistic capabilities of apes, the emergence of human language, and the origin of writing. In addition, every chapter includes a Biocultural Connection feature to further illustrate the interplay of biological and cultural processes in shaping the human experience.

Unifying Themes

In our own teaching, we have come to recognize the value of marking out unifying themes that help students see the big picture as they grapple with the vast array of material involved with the study of human beings. In *Evolution and Prehistory* we employ three such themes:

1. We present anthropology as a study of humankind's responses through time to the fundamental **challenges of survival.** Each chapter is framed by this theme, opening with a Challenge Issue paragraph and photograph and ending with Questions for Reflection tied to that particular challenge.
2. We emphasize the integration of human culture and biology in the steps humans take to meet these challenges. The **Biocultural Connection** theme appears throughout the text—as a thread in the main narrative and in a boxed feature that highlights this connection with a topical example for each chapter.
3. We track the emergence of **globalization and its disparate impact on various peoples and cultures around the world.** While European colonization was a global force for centuries—leaving a significant, often devastating, footprint on the affected peoples in Asia, Africa, and the Americas—decolonization began about 200 years ago and became a worldwide wave in the mid-1900s. Since the 1960s, however, political and economic hegemony has taken a new and fast-paced form—namely, globalization (in many ways a concept that expands or builds on imperialism). Attention to both forms of global domination—colonialism and globalization—runs through *Evolution and Prehistory,* in our treatment of specific topics such as primate habitat destruction, ownership of the past, and the social distribution of health and disease.

Pedagogy

Evolution and Prehistory features a range of learning aids, in addition to the three unifying themes described above. Each pedagogical piece plays an important role in the learning process—from clarifying and enlivening the material to revealing relevancy and aiding recall.

Accessible Language and a Cross-Cultural Voice

What could be more basic to pedagogy than clear communication? In addition to our standing as professional anthropologists, all four co-authors have made a specialty of speaking to audiences outside of our profession. Using that experience in the writing of this text, we consciously cut through unnecessary jargon to speak directly to students. Manuscript reviewers have recognized this, noting that even the most difficult concepts are presented in prose that is straightforward and understandable for today's first- and second-year college students. Where technical terms are necessary, they appear in bold-faced type, are carefully defined in the narrative, and are presented again in the running glossary in simple, clear language; these terms also appear in the glossary at the end of the book.

To make the narrative more accessible to students, we have broken it up into smaller bites, shortening the length of the paragraphs. We have also inserted additional subheads to provide visual cues to help students track what has been read and what is coming next.

Accessibility involves not only clear writing enhanced by visual cues but also a broadly engaging voice or style. The voice of *Evolution and Prehistory* is distinct among introductory texts in the discipline, for it has been written from a cross-cultural perspective. We avoid the typical Western "we/they" voice in favor of a more inclusive one that will resonate with both Western and non-Western students and professors. Also, we highlight the theories and work of anthropologists from all over the world. Finally, we have drawn the text's cultural examples from industrial and postindustrial societies as well as nonindustrial ones. No doubt these efforts have played a role in the book's international appeal, evident in various translations and international editions.

Compelling Visuals

Haviland et al. texts repeatedly garner high praise from students and faculty for having a rich array of visuals, including maps, photographs, and figures. This is important since humans—like all primates—are visually oriented, and a well-chosen image may serve to "fix" key information in a student's mind. Unlike some competing texts, all of our visuals are in color, enhancing their appeal and impact. Notably, all maps and figures (many new to this edition) have been created with a color-blind sensitive palette.

PHOTOGRAPHS

Our pages feature a hard-sought collection of new and meaningful photographs. Large in size, many of them feature substantial captions that help students do a "deep read" of the image. Each chapter features at least fourteen pictures, and many chapters contain our popular Visual Counterpoints—side-by-side photos that effectively compare and contrast biological or cultural features.

MAPS

Map features include our "Putting the World in Perspective" map series, locator maps, and distribution maps that provide overviews of key issues such as pollution, endangered species, and fossil localities. Of special note are the Globalscape maps and stories, described in the boxed features section a bit further on.

Challenge Issues and Questions for Reflection

Each chapter opens with a Challenge Issue and accompanying photograph, which together carry forward the book's theme of humankind's responses through time to the fundamental challenges of survival within the context of the particular chapter. And each chapter closes with five Questions for Reflection, including one that relates back to the Challenge Issue presented in the chapter's opening. These questions are designed to stimulate and deepen thought, trigger class discussion, and link the material to the students' own lives.

Chapter Preview

Every chapter opening also presents three or four preview questions that mark out the key issues covered in the chapter. Beyond orienting students to the chapter contents, these questions provide study points useful when preparing for exams.

Integrated Gender Coverage

In contrast to many introductory texts, *Evolution and Prehistory* integrates rather than separates gender coverage. Thus material on gender-related issues is included in *every* chapter. The result of this approach is a measure of gender-related material that far exceeds the single chapter that most books contain.

Why is the gender-related material integrated? Because concepts and issues surrounding gender are almost always too complicated to remove from their context. Moreover, spreading this material through all of the chapters has a pedagogical purpose, for it emphasizes how considerations of gender enter into virtually everything people do. Further, integration of gender into the book's "biological" chapters allows students to grasp the analytic distinction between sex and gender, illustrating the subtle influence of gender norms on biological theories about sex difference. Gender-related material ranges from discussions of gender roles in evolutionary discourse and the ways that contemporary gender norms can shape biological theories to studies of varied sexual behavior in nonhuman primates and same-sex marriage. Through a steady drumbeat of such coverage, this edition avoids ghettoizing gender to a single chapter that is preceded and followed by resounding silence.

Glossary as You Go

The running glossary is designed to catch the student's eye, reinforcing the meaning of each newly introduced term. It is also useful for chapter review, as the student may readily isolate the new terms from those introduced in earlier chapters. A complete glossary is also included at the back of the book. In the glossaries, each term is defined in clear, understandable language. As a result, less class time is required for going over terms, leaving instructors free to pursue other matters of interest.

Special Boxed Features

Our text includes five types of special boxed features. Every chapter contains a Biocultural Connection, along with two of the following three features: an Original Study, Anthropology Applied, and Anthropologist of Note. In addition, about half of the chapters include a Globalscape. All of these boxed features are carefully placed and introduced within the main narrative to alert students to their importance and relevance.

BIOCULTURAL CONNECTIONS

Appearing in every chapter, this signature feature of the Haviland et al. textbooks illustrates how cultural and biological processes interact to shape human biology, beliefs, and behavior. It reflects the integrated biocultural approach central to the field of anthropology today. New to this edition is a critical thinking question to accompany each topic explored. The thirteen Biocultural Connection titles hint at the intriguing array of topics covered by this feature:

- "The Anthropology of Organ Transplantation"
- "The Social Impact of Genetics on Reproduction"
- "Why Red Is Such a Potent Color," by Meredith F. Small
- "Disturbing Behaviors of the Orangutan," by Anne Nacey Maggioncaldo and Robert M. Sapolsky
- "Kennewick Man"
- "Why 'Ida' Inspires Navel-Gazing at Our Ancestry," by Meredith F. Small
- "Evolution and Human Birth"
- "Sex, Gender, and Female Paleoanthropologists"
- "Paleolithic Prescriptions for the Diseases of Civilization"
- "Breastfeeding, Fertility, and Beliefs"
- "Perilous Pigs: The Introduction of Swine-Borne Disease to the Americas," by Charles C. Mann
- "Beans, Enzymes, and Adaptation to Malaria"
- "Picturing Pesticides"

ORIGINAL STUDIES

Written expressly for this text, or selected from ethnographies and other original works by diverse scholars, these studies present concrete examples that bring specific concepts to life and convey the passion of the authors. Each study sheds additional light on an important anthropological concept or subject area found in the chapter where it appears. Notably, these boxes are carefully integrated within the flow of the chapter narrative, signaling students that their content is not extraneous or supplemental. Appearing in thirteen chapters, Original Studies cover a wide range of topics, evident from their titles:

- "Fighting HIV/AIDS in Africa: Traditional Healers on the Front Line," by Suzanne Leclerc-Madlala
- "Ninety-Eight Percent Alike: What Our Similarity to Apes Tells Us about Our Understanding of Genetics, "by Jonathan Marks
- "Ethics of Great Ape Habituation and Conservation: The Costs and Benefits of Ecotourism," by Michele Goldsmith
- "Reconciliation and Its Cultural Modification in Primates," by Frans B. M. de Waal
- "Whispers from the Ice," by Sherry Simpson
- "Melding Heart and Head," by Sir Robert May
- "Ankles of the Australopithecines," by John Hawks
- "Humans as Prey," by Donna Hart
- "Paleolithic Paint Job," by Roger Lewin
- "History of Mortality and Physiological Stress," by Anna Roosevelt
- "Action Archaeology and the Community at El Pilar," by Anabel Ford
- "A Feckless Quest for the Basketball Gene," by Jonathan Marks
- "Dancing Skeletons: Life and Death in West Africa," by Katherine Dettwyler

ANTHROPOLOGY APPLIED

These succinct and compelling profiles illustrate anthropology's wide-ranging relevance in today's world and give students a glimpse into a variety of the careers anthropologists enjoy. Featured in seven chapters, they include

- "Forensic Anthropology: Voices for the Dead"
- "What It Means to Be a Woman: How Women Around the World Cope with Infertility," by Karen Springen
- "The Congo Heartland Project"
- "Cultural Resource Management," by John Crock
- "Stone Tools for Modern Surgeons"

- "The Real Dirt on Rainforest Fertility," by Charles C. Mann
- "Tell It to the Marines: Teaching the Troops about Cultural Heritage," by Jane C. Waldbaum

ANTHROPOLOGISTS OF NOTE

Profiling pioneering and contemporary anthropologists from many corners of the world, this feature puts the work of noted anthropologists in historical perspective and draws attention to the international nature of the discipline in terms of both subject matter and practitioners. This edition highlights eleven distinct anthropologists who reflect the intellectual and geographic diversity of the discipline: Berhane Asfaw, Franz Boas, Peter Ellison, Jane Goodall, Kinji Imanishi, Fatimah Jackson, Louis S. B. Leakey, Mary Leakey, Matilda Coxe Stevenson, Allan Wilson, and Xinzhi Wu.

GLOBALSCAPES

Appearing in about half of the chapters, this unique feature charts the global flow of people, goods, and services, as well as pollutants and pathogens. With a map, a story, and a photo, the feature shows how the world is interconnected through human activity with topics geared toward student interests. Each one ends with a Global Twister—a question that prods students to think critically about globalization. Globalscapes in this edition are

- "A Global Body Shop?," investigating human organ trafficking around the world
- "Gorilla Hand Ashtrays?," showing how mining for the cell phone component coltan is linked to gorilla habitat destruction
- "Whose Lakes Are These?," exploring the global and local impact of efforts to preserve places of shared cultural and natural importance through UNESCO's World Heritage List
- "Factory Farming Fiasco?," investigating the global industrial farming practices that have led to the current swine flu pandemic
- "Iraqi Artifacts in New York City?," exploring the effects of the Iraq War on the precious Mesopotamian artifacts that were housed in the National Museum in Baghdad
- "From Soap Opera to Clinic?," chronicling pioneering methods to disseminate life-changing public health information through radio and television dramas

Changes and Highlights in the Ninth Edition

The pedagogical features described above strengthen each of the thirteen chapters in *Evolution and Prehistory*, serving as threads that tie the text together and help students feel the holistic nature of the discipline. In addition, the engagingly presented concepts themselves provide students with a solid foundation in the principles and practices of anthropology today.

The text in hand has a significantly different feel to it than previous editions. All chapters have been revised extensively—the data, examples, and Suggested Readings updated, the chapter openers refreshed with new, up-to-date Challenge Issues and related photographs, and the writing further chiseled to make it all the more clear, lively, and engaging. Also, in addition to providing at least one new entry in the much-used Questions for Reflection at the end of the chapter, we have introduced a new question in each Biocultural Connection box.

Beyond these overall changes, each chapter has undergone specific modifications and additions. The inventory presented below provides brief previews of the chapter contents and changes in this edition.

CHAPTER 1: THE ESSENCE OF ANTHROPOLOGY

The book's opening chapter introduces students to the holistic discipline of anthropology, the unique focus of each of its fields, and the common philosophical perspective and methodological approaches they share. Touching briefly on fieldwork and the comparative method, along with ethical issues and examples of applied anthropology in all four fields, this chapter provides a foundation for understanding the methods shared by all four fields of anthropology. It also prepares students for the in-depth discussions of methods in primatology and the methods for studying the past shared by archaeology and paleoanthropology that follow in later chapters.

A new Challenge Issue question dealing with global aspects of surrogate births that demonstrates the ways that an integrated holistic anthropological perspective contributes to the ability to negotiate the new technologies and practices of our ever-more interconnected world. The updated descriptions of the anthropological fields that follow take into account the excellent suggestions of our reviewers. The section on linguistic anthropology has been expanded to include linguistic relativity, sociolinguistics, the work to save endangered languages, and the ways that languages continually change. The overview of physical anthropology was reorganized to improve the flow and includes an expanded discussion of developmental and physiological adaptation. Primate conservation issues are also highlighted. The archaeology section now includes historical archaeology and the work of James Deetz along with mention of other archaeological subspecializations. Technological innovations in archaeology such as GIS and GPR are included. Philippe Bourgois's work on the urban drug scene is included to illustrate range of the field sites open to ethnographers today.

The chapter also rejects the characterization of a liberal bias in anthropology, identifying instead the discipline's critical evaluation of the status quo. The ideological diversity among anthropologists is explored while emphasizing their shared methodology that avoids ethnocentrism. An expanded section on ethics includes the history of ethics, the changes of the AAA Code in response to classified or corporate fieldwork, and the effects of emergent technology. We emphasize the shared global environment in the section on globalization, with an updated Globalscape on organ trafficking.

CHAPTER 2: GENETICS AND EVOLUTION

This revised chapter on genetics and evolution grounds students in basic human biological processes including the evolutionary forces that worked over millennia to shape us into the species we are today. By moving some material to later chapters, we are able to add new concepts and diagrams that will serve to clarify and simplify the genetic mechanisms at work. The new Challenge Issue focusing on DNA fingerprinting, genetic determinism, and identity captures students' attention regarding the relevancy of genetics. The Chapter Preview questions have been expanded to make the genetic material more accessible. Sections on hominin taxonomy and altruism and other models of behavior have been moved to other chapters to make room for a more detailed but accessible discussion of genetics and evolution. This includes more on the background of the development of evolutionary theory including Cuvier's catastrophism, Lamarck's inheritance of acquired characteristics, and Lyell's principles of geology.

This edition includes a discussion of chromatids to clarify students' understanding of DNA replication, mitosis, and meiosis. Examples of classic Mendelian traits that students can explore with their relatives and thought questions accompanying the figures will help students master this material. New figures on Punnett squares, a karyotype illustrating the locus of a variety of common genes, and the alleles using sickle-cell disease as an example will make these concepts more accessible. The discussion of forces of evolution includes a new section illustrating genetic drift and founder effects featuring the achromotopsia on Pingelap Island in Micronesia. A new section on adaptation and physical variation introduces the concept of clines. Finally, a new Anthropology Applied feature on global infertility as a human rights issue features the work of Marcia Inhorn.

CHAPTER 3: LIVING PRIMATES

With this edition, our original chapter on the living primates was expanded into two separate chapters. This allowed for more material on the vital issue of primate conservation as we survey the living primates and the place of humans among them. Our expanded section on primate conservation includes the scope of the threat, description of diverse conservation methods, along with coverage of some of the some successes such as the recovery of golden lion tamarin populations. A new Anthropology Applied on primate conservation features the work of bonobo specialist Jef Dupain and the Congo Heartland Project of the African Wildlife Foundation. Michele Goldsmith explores the ethics of field research in the chapter's Original Study. The chapter's Globalscape connects cell phone recycling to the preservation of endangered gorilla habitats. A new figure presenting the biogeography of the primates includes the twenty-five most endangered primate species.

In terms of our survey of living primates, we include an in-depth discussion of primate taxonomy including the hot spots, alternate taxonomies, and controversies (tarsier question and hominid/hominin question). The clade/grade distinction is described, and the term *clade* is added to the discussion and running glossary. Our figure comparing the skeletons of bison and gorilla has been revised to help students understand how skeletal analyses are conducted. Moving primate behavior to its own chapter has allowed for more coverage of non-hominoid living primates (lemurs/lorises, tarsiers, Old and New World monkeys). Notably, Karen Strier's work with the muriqui is included in the discussion of New World monkeys that provides insights into field methods and primate demographics. A new Biocultural Connection by Meredith Small focuses on primate vision and the human affinity for the color red.

CHAPTER 4: PRIMATE BEHAVIOR

This new, beautifully illustrated chapter is devoted exclusively to primate behavior, allowing for an expanded treatment of the topic. The sophistication of primate behavior is framed by ethical questions regarding the use of primates in medical research that open and close the chapter. While the chapter emphasizes the great apes, examples from other anthropoid primates are included in this discussion. A new section critically discusses the use of baboon studies to reconstruct lifeways of our ancestors. New material on primate communication includes syntax in vervet monkeys and dialect in marmosets along with new material on social learning among macaques. Our discussion of communication also includes a discussion of altruism and an expanded section on the communication abilities of the bonobo Kanzi. Various forms of primate social organization are outlined along with their proposed links to biological features such as sexual dimorphism. These and other theories about primate reproductive biology are analyzed in terms of the potential influence of contemporary gender norms, an approach pioneered by primatologist Linda Fedigan. A new Biocultural Connection on arrested development in male orangutans by Anne Nacey Maggioncaldo and Robert M. Sapolsky complements this discussion. Along with many new, updated, and classic references, this chapter contains all new Questions for Reflection and Suggested Readings.

CHAPTER 5: FIELD METHODS IN ARCHAEOLOGY AND PALEOANTHROPOLOGY

This methods chapter clearly conveys the key methodological techniques employed by archaeologists and paleoanthropologists as they study human prehistory. We open with the question of shared cultural heritage and ownership of the past through a new Challenge Issue on the Bamiyan Buddhas of Afghanistan destroyed by the Taliban in 2001. We have streamlined this comprehensive chapter with this edition to make room for technological advances and the ethical issues that have arisen from these new technologies. The chapter contains a new figure to illustrate the concept of stratification and a complete description of the ecofacts and features used to study the past. We cover new technologies such as ground-penetrating radar (GPR), geographic information systems (GIS), remote sensing techniques, and an expanded section on underwater archaeology. We describe the use of CT scans in bioarchaeology, forensics, and paleoanthropology and make explicit the links between bioarchaeology and forensics. The chapter includes more coverage on the purpose of NAGPRA. We also explore the issues surrounding the digitization of human remains and aboriginal responses to museum efforts to do this in contexts without NAGPRA, as seen in the current controversy between the University of Vienna and the Ju/'hoansi people.

An Anthropology Applied box on cultural resource management by John Crock, an Original Study on the chance discovery of the skeleton of a young girl frozen in the ice of Barrow, Alaska, and a Biocultural Connection on Kennewick Man all provide insights into the complexities involved in investigating the past. They also explore the philosophical approach necessary for successful collaboration between scientists and local people.

CHAPTER 6: MACROEVOLUTION AND THE EARLY PRIMATES

Building on the evolutionary principles laid out in Chapter 2, this chapter provides an excellent overview of macroevolutionary mechanisms along with a concise discussion of mammalian primate evolution. While introducing students to concepts such as heterochrony, homeobox genes, anagenesis, and cladogenesis, through clear descriptions and diagrams, we also discuss the comparative approach employed by evolutionary scientists.

The Eocene specimen "Ida" (*Darwinius masillae*) discovered in 2009 is featured in a variety of contexts. The chapter's Challenge Issue discusses the recent popularity of human evolutionary studies in the media, asking how the self-correcting nature of science can function against a backdrop of "tweets," Google logos, and unprecedented prices for fossil specimens paid by museums to private collectors. A new Biocultural Connection by Meredith Small explores the significance of the "Ida" specimen.

Another chapter theme is the importance of understanding evolutionary processes for the survival of the planet. In a new Original Study, leading global ecologist Sir Robert May explores the relationship between human practices and the extinction of other species. Against this philosophical backdrop, we also consider the mechanics of the molecular regulation of variational change as well as punctuated change using recent discoveries regarding Darwin's finches. A new figure accompanies this discussion. Another new figure compares the skull shape and size of fossil prosimians and fossil anthropoids. A revised timeline and figure of the evolutionary relationships among the anthropoid primates take into account the potential new fossil gorilla evidence discovered in 2007 (*Chororapithecus abyssinicus*). More images of fossil specimens are included in the chapter compared to previous editions so that students can "see" as well as read about our mammalian primate heritage.

CHAPTER 7: THE FIRST BIPEDS

This up-to-date chapter explores bipedalism, the distinctive feature of the human evolutionary line, concentrating on the australopithecines and other species that inhabited Africa before the appearance of the genus *Homo*. It contains the new evidence and analyses published in 2009 suggesting that forest-dwelling *Ardipithecus* is the common ancestor to all later bipeds. It also integrates this notion into the hypotheses regarding the savannah adaptation of our ancestors. We introduce students to how paleoanthropologists go about reconstructing human evolutionary history. A new Original Study, "Ankles of the Australopithecines" by John Hawks, exemplifies how paleoanthropologists use comparative morphological studies to reconstruct the past. Chapter figures and glossary terms are linked to this Original Study.

Current ethical issues also find their way into the chapter, such as the controversy regarding the current U.S. tour of the 3.2-million-year-old "Lucy" fossils. A new figure compares gracile and robust australopithecines, and a revised figure also indicates all the major australopithecine sites. The Biocultural Connection on evolution and human birth explores the ways that contemporary Western practices influenced the paleoanthropological reconstruction of the human birth pattern. The Anthropologists of Note feature explores the extraordinary contributions of Louis and Mary Leakey to the discipline of paleoanthropology.

CHAPTER 8: EARLY *HOMO* AND THE ORIGINS OF CULTURE

This chapter traces the genus *Homo* from its origins 2.5 or so million years ago up until the Upper Paleolithic. Taking a "lumping" approach, it divides the fossil record into the three divisions of *Homo habilis*, *Homo erectus*, and archaic *Homo sapiens*. At the same time we explore the differences between lumping and splitting fossil specimens into numerous taxa and discuss the relationship between biological change and cultural change in human evolutionary history. The place of the Neandertals in this history closes the chapter. The chapter contains sufficient detail for an introductory course on human origins while streamlining the presentation from previous editions and avoiding redundancy.

Many new figures allow for material to be communicated clearly and efficiently. For example, the new figure comparing KNM ER 1470 and KNM ER 1813 illustrates the taxonomic issue of lumping or splitting in early *Homo*. The new discoveries from Gona, including the well-preserved pelvis, are included as is the newly discovered *Homo erectus* footprint trail from Kenya. Middle Paleolithic *Homo* from throughout the world is surveyed in this chapter while the question of modern human origins is saved for Chapter 9. A nuanced discussion of sex and gender in the fossil record is supported by a Biocultural Connection on the contributions of female paleoanthropologists to the discipline, along with the recent revisioning of the "man the hunter" hypothesis as "man the hunted" in the chapter's Original Study. The Anthropology Applied box demonstrates the unique strengths of stone tools through their use by modern-day surgeons.

CHAPTER 9: THE GLOBAL EXPANSION OF *HOMO SAPIENS* AND THEIR TECHNOLOGY

This chapter explores the fossil, genetic, and cultural evidence used in theories to account for modern human origins. It also explores the cultural explosion characteristic of the Upper Paleolithic and the spread of humans throughout the globe. To make space for an in-depth discussion of the multiregional continuity versus out of Africa models of modern human origins, we have streamlined and reorganized material to avoid redundancy. Rich with new and revised figures, the chapter also includes the latest discoveries such as the Venus figurine from Hohle Fels Cave as well as the flute from the same site. New research on cooking and brain metabolism is included as is recent research on the peopling of the Americas. A new section on gender and archaeology features Margaret Conkey's work as a feminist practicing archaeology and the contemporary projections of gender norms onto Venus figurines.

The chapter's boxed features chronicle paleoanthropology from throughout the globe. The Anthropologists of Note features Ethiopian paleoanthropologist Berhane Asfaw and Chinese paleoanthropologist Xinzhi Wu. The Biocultural Connection looks to contemporary hunter-gatherers, whose lifeways have not departed as glaringly from our Paleolithic template, in order to promote human health. The Original Study details the methods used by prehistoric artists to paint cave walls in southwestern France. A new Globalscape on World Heritage sites focuses on Willandra Lakes in Australia and the importance of this place to the Aboriginal people of the region, as well as to paleoanthropologists and the global community.

CHAPTER 10: THE NEOLITHIC REVOLUTION: THE DOMESTICATION OF PLANTS AND ANIMALS

Chapter 10 concentrates on the drastic cultural changes that occurred at the Neolithic transition with the domestication of plants and animals along with the development of permanent settlements in villages. The unexpected deleterious health consequences of this "Neolithic revolution" are explored throughout the chapter along with the complex relationship between food production and population growth.

The new Challenge Issue featuring a contemporary Hmong embroidery depicting the mythical origins of agriculture opens the chapter. The art illustrates that global food flows have a long history. We include a new section on primary and secondary innovation, as well as the recent discovery of the earliest pottery from Yuchanyan Cave, located in China's Hunan Province, and current research providing new dates for earliest dairying. Several revised figures, such as ones on the Fertile Crescent and the domestication of corn from teosinte, improve clarity and provide richer content.

Several sections of the chapter have been expanded. These include the contemporary application of *terra preta*, the rich black earth produced by Amazonian farmers and described in the chapter's Anthropology Applied box; the impact of colonialism on American Indian cultures; and the ongoing health consequences of the Neolithic transition. Table 10.1 has been updated to show the incidence of selected zoonotic diseases globally along with prevention strategies. A new Globalscape on swine flu and industrial farming practices illustrates the consequences of these large-scale operations.

CHAPTER 11: THE EMERGENCE OF CITIES AND STATES

This chapter draws parallels between ancient and modern cities and states while exploring the origins of this very human way of life. It contains a variety of new figures and examples that drive home the points about the beginnings of cities and states and the many facets, both positive and negative, of these social organizations that have endured to the present. Continuity is shown through factors ranging from social stratification, to the social distribution of sickness and health, to artisanal techniques.

Carneiro's theory on the development of states is described in more detail in this revised chapter. In terms of ancient sites, the figure of Teotihuacan is revised for clarity, and a new figure of Tikal shows the major monuments and causeways. The chapter's Original Study on El Pilar is revised and updated. We discuss the Cahokia mounds as an example of the both the presence of cities and the conscious choice by North American Indians not to engage in conquest relationships.

New figures on cuneiform writing and bronze lost-wax casting illustrate the details of these innovations. Sections on social stratification and disease are expanded to include both the impact within a given society and the effects of conquest. This expanded coverage includes the impact of infectious disease brought about by European colonizers of the Americas, we include a new Biocultural Connection from Charles Mann's book *1491*. The chapter's Anthropology Applied box and Globalscape both feature the link between contemporary military action and preservation of ancient cultural heritage.

CHAPTER 12: MODERN HUMAN DIVERSITY: RACE AND RACISM

This chapter gives an overview of race and racism, in the science of the past as well as current problems. With the politics of diversity changing globally, an understanding of the true nature of biological variation has become indispensable. The contributions of anthropology to debunking race as a biological category—starting with the work of Franz Boas and Ashley Montagu—are complemented by the contemporary work of cutting-edge biological anthropologists such as Jonathan Marks (Original Study) and Fatimah Jackson (Anthropologist of Note). We emphasize the interaction of the cultural and biological throughout the chapter in topics ranging from skin color to intelligence to G-6-PD deficiency as detailed in the Biocultural Connection.

With this edition, we include the history of the Mexican *casta* system and the contemporary tragedy of Rwandan genocide. The section on race and human evolution is expanded and includes a discussion of scientific and pseudo-scientific attempts to predict behavior by physical phenotypic characteristics. The section concludes with neurological research dealing with the brain and stereotypical thinking. Informative new illustrations include a demonstration of the differences between a normal female pelvis and one deformed by bone disease and a contemporary graphic artist's views on 19th- and early 20th-century racial hierarchies.

CHAPTER 13: HUMAN ADAPTATION TO A CHANGING WORLD

From battles between local farmers and multinational corporations for water rights in India to new findings on the toxic effects of plastics, this chapter continues to engage with the ways humans adapt to the human-made environment. The chapter weaves together the anthropological study of adaptation by biological and medical anthropologists with advanced work in evolutionary medicine and the political ecology of health and disease. It examines the way that human alteration of the environment is leading to disease in our species and how political and social forces impact the distribution of health and disease in human populations.

New to this chapter are global flows of HIV/AIDS and prevention strategies and a Globalscape concerning an initiative incorporating public health education into radio and television soap operas. This edition features a significantly expanded section on the impact of environmental estrogens on human disease. Our emphasis on the relationship between economics and fertility in women continues. Several of the straightforward biological adaptations also explored in this chapter are now supported with new figures, including an illustration of the relationship between altitude and partial pressure of oxygen and illustrations of Bergmann's rule and Allen's rule. In addition, a new section explores the highly topical issue of vaccinations and so-called pox parties.

The work of reproductive ecologist Peter Ellison linking human fertility to the environment is featured in the Anthropologist of Note box. Cross-cultural differences in sickness categories are featured in Katherine Dettwyler's stirring piece on infection, malnutrition, and Down syndrome. The Biocultural Connection features the impact of industrial farming pesticides on child development. Throughout this chapter, we explore the biocultural theme characteristic of the entire text as connections are drawn between human health and political and economic forces both globally and locally.

Supplements

Evolution and Prehistory comes with a comprehensive supplements program to help instructors create an effective learning environment both inside and outside the classroom and to aid students in mastering the material.

Supplements for Instructors

ONLINE INSTRUCTOR'S MANUAL AND TEST BANK

The Instructor's Manual offers detailed chapter outlines, lecture suggestions, key terms, and student activities such as video exercises and Internet exercises. In addition, there are over seventy-five chapter test questions including multiple choice, true/false, fill-in-the-blank, short answer, and essay.

POWERLECTURE WITH JOININ™ AND EXAMVIEW®

On CD or DVD, this one-stop class preparation tool contains ready-to-use Microsoft PowerPoint® slides, enabling you to assemble, edit, publish, and present custom lectures with ease. PowerLecture helps you bring together text-specific lecture outlines and art from Haviland's text along with videos and your own materials—culminating in powerful, personalized, media-enhanced presentations. The **JoinIn**™ content (for use with most "clicker" systems) available within PowerLecture delivers instant classroom assessment and active learning. Take polls and attendance, quiz, and invite students to actively participate while they learn. Featuring automatic grading,

ExamView® is also available within PowerLecture, allowing you to create, deliver, and customize tests and study guides (both print and online) in minutes. See assessments onscreen exactly as they will print or display online. Build tests of up to 250 questions using up to twelve question types and enter an unlimited number of new questions or edit existing questions. PowerLecture also includes the text's Instructor's Resource Manual and Test Bank as Word documents.

WEBTUTOR ON BLACKBOARD AND WEBCT

Jumpstart your course with customizable, rich, text-specific content within your Course Management System. Simply load a content cartridge into your course management system to easily blend, add, edit, reorganize, or delete content, all of which is specific to Haviland et al.'s *Evolution and Prehistory,* 9th edition, and includes media resources, quizzing, weblinks, discussion topics, and interactive games and exercises.

WADSWORTH ANTHROPOLOGY VIDEO LIBRARY

Qualified adopters may select full-length videos from an extensive library of offerings drawn from such excellent educational video sources as *Films for the Humanities and Sciences.*

ABC ANTHROPOLOGY VIDEO SERIES

This exclusive video series was created jointly by Wadsworth and ABC for the anthropology course. Each video contains approximately 60 minutes of footage originally broadcast on ABC within the past several years. The videos are broken into short 2- to 7-minute segments, perfect for classroom use as lecture launchers or to illustrate key anthropological concepts. An annotated table of contents accompanies each video, providing descriptions of the segments and suggestions for their possible use within the course.

AIDS IN AFRICA DVD

Southern Africa has been overcome by a pandemic of unparalleled proportions. This documentary series focuses on the new democracy of Namibia and the many actions there to control HIV/AIDS. Included in this series are four documentary films created by the Periclean Scholars at Elon University: (1) *Young Struggles, Eternal Faith,* which focuses on caregivers in the faith community; (2) *The Shining Lights of Opuwo,* which shows how young people share their messages of hope through song and dance; (3) *A Measure of Our Humanity,* which describes HIV/AIDS as an issue related to gender, poverty, stigma, education, and justice; and (4) *You Wake Me Up,* a story of two HIV-positive women and their acts of courage helping other women learn to survive. Cengage/Wadsworth is excited to offer these award-winning films to instructors for use in class. When presenting topics such as gender, faith, culture, poverty, and so on, the films will be enlightening for students and will expand their global perspective of HIV/AIDS.

Online Resources for Instructors and Students

ANTHROPOLOGY RESOURCE CENTER

This online center offers a wealth of information and useful tools for both instructors and students in all four fields of anthropology. It includes interactive maps, learning modules, video exercises, and breaking news in anthropology. For instructors, the Resource Center includes a gateway to time-saving teaching tools, such as image banks, sample syllabi, and more. Access to the website is available free when bundled with the text or for purchase at a nominal fee.

THE HAVILAND ET AL. COMPANION WEBSITE

The book's companion site includes chapter-specific resources for instructors and students. For instructors, the site offers a password-protected Instructor's Manual, Microsoft PowerPoint presentation slides, and more. For students, there are a multitude of text-specific study aids: tutorial practice quizzes that can be scored and e-mailed to the instructor, weblinks, flash cards, crossword puzzles, and much more!

INFOTRAC© COLLEGE EDITION

InfoTrac College Edition is an online library that offers full-length articles from thousands of scholarly and popular publications. Among the journals available are *American Anthropologist, Current Anthropology,* and *Canadian Review of Sociology and Anthropology.* Contact your local Cengage sales representative for details.

Supplements for Students

TELECOURSE STUDY GUIDE

The new distance learning course, **Anthropology: The Four Fields,** provides online and print companion study guide options that include study aids, interactive exercises, videos, and more.

Additional Student Resources

BASIC GENETICS FOR ANTHROPOLOGY CD-ROM: PRINCIPLES AND APPLICATIONS (STAND-ALONE VERSION), BY ROBERT JURMAIN AND LYNN KILGORE

This student CD-ROM expands on such biological concepts as biological inheritance (genes, DNA sequencing, and so on) and applications of that to modern human populations at the molecular level (human variation and adaptation—to disease, diet, growth, and development). Interactive animations and simulations bring these important concepts to life for students so they can fully understand the essential biological principles required for physical anthropology. Also available are quizzes and interactive flashcards for further study.

HOMINID FOSSILS CD-ROM: AN INTERACTIVE ATLAS, BY JAMES AHERN

The interactive atlas CD-ROM includes over seventy-five key fossils important for a clear understanding of human evolution. The QuickTime Virtual Reality (QTVR) "object" movie format for each fossil enables students to have a near-authentic experience of working with these important finds, by allowing them to rotate the fossil 360 degrees. Unlike some VR media, QTVR objects are made using actual photographs of the real objects and thus better preserve details of color and texture. The fossils used are high-quality research casts and real fossils. The organization of the atlas is nonlinear, with three levels and multiple paths, enabling students to see how the fossil fits into the map of human evolution in terms of geography, time, and evolution. The CD-ROM offers students an inviting, authentic learning environment, one that also contains a dynamic quizzing feature that will allow students to test their knowledge of fossil and species identification, as well as provide more detailed information about the fossil record.

VIRTUAL LABORATORIES FOR PHYSICAL ANTHROPOLOGY CD-ROM, FOURTH EDITION, BY JOHN KAPPELMAN

The new edition of this full-color, interactive CD-ROM provides students with a hands-on computer component for completing lab assignments at school or at home. Through the use of video clips, 3-D animations, sound, and digital images, students can actively participate in twelve labs as part of their physical anthropology and archaeology course. The labs and assignments teach students how to formulate and test hypotheses with exercises that include how to measure, plot, interpret, and evaluate a variety of data drawn from osteological, behavioral, and fossil materials.

Readings and Case Studies

CLASSIC AND CONTEMPORARY READINGS IN PHYSICAL ANTHROPOLOGY, EDITED BY M. K. SANDFORD WITH EILEEN M. JACKSON

This highly accessible reader emphasizes science—its principles and methods—as well as the historical development of physical anthropology and the applications of new technology to the discipline. The editors provide an introduction to the reader as well as a brief overview of the article so students know what to look for. Each article also includes discussion questions and Internet resources.

CASE STUDIES IN ARCHAEOLOGY, EDITED BY JEFFREY QUILTER

These engaging accounts of cutting-edge archaeological techniques, issues, and solutions—as well as studies discussing the collection of material remains—range from site-specific excavations to types of archaeology practiced.

EVOLUTION OF THE BRAIN MODULE: NEUROANATOMY, DEVELOPMENT, AND PALEONTOLOGY, BY DANIEL D. WHITE

The human species is the only species that has ever created a symphony, written a poem, developed a mathematical equation, or studied its own origins. The biological structure that has enabled humans to perform these feats of intelligence is the human brain. This module explores the basics of neuroanatomy, brain development, lateralization, and sexual dimorphism and provides the fossil evidence for hominid brain evolution. This module in chapter-like print format can be packaged for free with the text.

FORENSIC ANTHROPOLOGY MODULE: A BRIEF REVIEW, BY DIANE FRANCE

Diane France explores the myths and realities of forensic anthropology: the search for human remains in crime scenes, forensic anthropology in the courtroom, special challenges in mass fatality incident responses (such as plane crashes and terrorist acts), and what students should consider if they want to pursue a career in forensic anthropology.

MOLECULAR ANTHROPOLOGY MODULE, BY LESLIE KNAPP

Leslie Knapp explores how molecular genetic methods are used to understand the organization and expression of genetic information in humans and nonhuman primates. Students will learn about the common laboratory methods used to study genetic variation and evolution in molecular anthropology. Examples are drawn from up-to-date research on human evolutionary origins and comparative primate genomics to demonstrate that scientific research is an ongoing process with theories frequently being questioned and reevaluated.

HUMAN ENVIRONMENT INTERACTIONS: NEW DIRECTIONS IN HUMAN ECOLOGY, BY CATHY GALVIN

Cathy Galvin provides students with an introduction to the basic concepts in human ecology, before discussing cultural ecology, human adaptation studies, human behavioral ecology, and political ecology. The module concludes with a discussion of resilience and global change as a result of human–environment interactions today.

Acknowledgments

In this day and age, no textbook comes to fruition without extensive collaboration. Beyond the shared endeavors of our author team, this book owes its completion to a wide range of individuals, from colleagues in the discipline to those involved in the production process. We are particularly grateful for the comments received through an electronic survey as well as the remarkable group of manuscript reviewers listed below. They provided unusually detailed and thoughtful feedback that helped us to hone and re-hone our narrative.

Stewart Brewer, Dana College
Kendall Campbell, Washington State University
Jennifer Coe, Jamestown Community College
Julie David, Orange Coast College and California Baptist University
Rene M. Descartes, State University of New York at Cobleskill
Sylvia Grider, Texas A&M University
Susan H. Krook, Normandale Community College
Barbara J. Michael, University of North Carolina Wilmington
Renee B. Walker, SUNY College at Oneonta
Linda F. Whitmer, Hope International University
Holly E. Yatros, Oakland Community College and Macomb Community College

We carefully considered and made use of the wide range of comments provided by these individuals. Our decisions on how to utilize their suggestions were influenced by our own perspectives on anthropology and teaching, combined with the priorities and page limits of this text. Neither our reviewers nor any of the other anthropologists mentioned here should be held responsible for any shortcomings in this book. They should, however, be credited as contributors to many of the book's strengths.

Thanks, too, go to colleagues who provided material for some of the Original Study, Biocultural Connection, and Anthropology Applied boxes in this text: John Crock, Katherine Dettwyler, Frans B. M. de Waal, Anabel Ford, Michele Goldsmith, Donna Hart, John Hawks, Michael M. Horowitz, Suzanne Leclerc-Madlala, Roger Lewin, Anne Nacey Maggioncalda, Charles C. Mann, Jonathan Marks, Sir Robert May, Anna Roosevelt, Robert M. Sapolsky, Sherry Simpson, Meredith F. Small, Karen Springen, William Ury, and Jane C. Waldbaum, Among these individuals we particularly want to acknowledge our admiration, affection, and appreciation for our mutual friend and colleague Jim Petersen, whose life came to an abrupt and tragic end while returning from fieldwork in the Brazilian Amazon. Jim's work is featured in one of the pieces by Charles C. Mann.

We have debts of gratitude to office workers in our departments for their cheerful help in clerical matters: Debbie Hedrick, Karen Rundquist, Emira Smailagic, Katie Weaver, and Sheri Youngberg. And to research librarian extraordinaire Nancy Bianchi and colleagues Yvette Pigeon, Paula Duncan, Lajiri Van Ness-Otunnu, and Michael Wesch for engaging in lively discussions of anthropological and pedagogical approaches. Also worthy of note here are the introductory anthropology teaching assistants who, through the years, have shed light for us on effective ways to reach new generations of students.

Our thanksgiving inventory would be incomplete without mentioning individuals at Wadsworth Publishing who helped conceive this text and bring it to fruition. Special gratitude goes to acquisitions editor Erin Mitchell and to senior development editor Lin Marshall Gaylord for her vision, vigor, and anthropological knowledge. Our thanks also go out to Wadsworth's skilled and enthusiastic editorial, marketing, design, and production team: Andrew Keay (marketing manager), Melanie Cregger (media editor), Pamela Simon (editorial assistant), Rachel Krapf (assistant editor), as well as Jerilyn Emori (content project manager) and Caryl Gorska (art director).

In addition to all of the above, we have had the invaluable aid of several most able freelancers, including our photo researchers Billie Porter and Susan Krapov, who were always willing to go the extra mile to find the most telling and compelling photographs, and our skilled graphic designer Lisa Buckley. We are especially thankful to have had the opportunity to work once again with copy editor Jennifer Gordon and production coordinator Joan Keyes of Dovetail Publishing Services. Consummate professionals and generous souls, both of them keep track of countless details and bring calm efficiency and grace to the demands of meeting difficult deadlines. Their efforts and skills play a major role in making our work doable and pleasurable.

And finally, all of us are indebted to family members who have not only put up with our textbook preoccupation but cheered us on in the endeavor. Dana had the tireless support and keen eye of husband Peter Bingham—along with the varied contributions of their three sons Nishan, Tavid, and Aram Bingham. As co-author spouses under the same roof, Harald and Bunny have picked up slack for each other on every front to help this project move along smoothly. But the biggest debt of gratitude may be in Bill's corner for initiating this book more than three decades ago, building it into a leading introductory text used by hundreds of thousands of students around the world, and having the foresight to bring a trio of co-authors on board about a decade ago to maintain and build upon the established strengths of this long-term educational endeavor. Before putting together a team of co-authors several editions ago, he relied on the know-how of his spouse Anita de Laguna Haviland, whose varied skills played a vital role in this book's success.

About the Authors

Authors Bunny McBride, Dana Walrath, Harald Prins, and William Haviland.

All four members of this author team share overlapping research interests and a similar vision of what anthropology is (and should be) about. For example, all are true believers in the four-field approach to anthropology and all have some involvement in applied work.

WILLIAM A. HAVILAND is Professor Emeritus at the University of Vermont, where he founded the Department of Anthropology and taught for thirty-two years. He holds a PhD in anthropology from the University of Pennsylvania.

He has carried out original research in archaeology in Guatemala and Vermont; ethnography in Maine and Vermont; and physical anthropology in Guatemala. This work has been the basis of numerous publications in various national and international books and journals, as well as in media intended for the general public. His books include *The Original Vermonters*, co-authored with Marjorie Power, and a technical monograph on ancient Maya settlement. He also served as consultant for the award-winning telecourse, *Faces of Culture,* and is co-editor of the series *Tikal Reports,* published by the University of Pennsylvania Museum of Archaeology and Anthropology.

Besides his teaching and writing, Dr. Haviland has lectured to numerous professional as well as non-professional audiences in Canada, Mexico, Lesotho, South Africa, and Spain, as well as in the United States. A staunch supporter of indigenous rights, he served as expert witness for the Missisquoi Abenakis of Vermont in an important court case over aboriginal fishing rights.

Awards received by Dr. Haviland include being named University Scholar by the Graduate School of the University of Vermont in 1990; a Certificate of Appreciation from the Sovereign Republic of the Abenaki Nation of Missisquoi, St. Francis/Sokoki Band in 1996; and a Lifetime Achievement Award from the Center for Research on Vermont in 2006. Now retired from teaching, he continues his research, writing, and lecturing from the coast of Maine. His most recent book is *At the Place of the Lobsters and Crabs* (2009).

DANA WALRATH is Assistant Professor of Family Medicine at the University of Vermont and a Women's Studies-affiliated faculty member. She earned her PhD in anthropology from the University of Pennsylvania and is a medical and biological anthropologist with principal interests in biocultural aspects of reproduction, the cultural context of biomedicine, genetics, and evolutionary medicine. She founded and directed an innovative educational program at the University of Vermont's College of Medicine that brings anthropological theory and practice to first-year medical students. Before joining the faculty at the University of Vermont in 2000, she taught at the University of Pennsylvania and Temple University. Her research has been supported by the National Science Foundation, Health Resources and Services Administration, the Centers for Disease Control, and the Templeton Foundation. Dr. Walrath's publications have appeared in *Current Anthropology, American Anthropologist,* and *American Journal of Physical Anthropology.* An active member of the Council on the Anthropology of Reproduction, she has also served on a national committee to develop women's health-care learning objectives for medical education and works locally to improve health care for refugees and immigrants.

HARALD E. L. PRINS is a University Distinguished Professor of Anthropology at Kansas State University. Born in the Netherlands, he studied at universities in Europe and the United States. He has done extensive fieldwork among indigenous peoples in South and North America, published many dozens of articles in seven languages, authored *The Mi'kmaq: Resistance, Accommodation, and Cultural Survival* (1996), co-authored *Indians in Eden* (2009), and co-edited *American Beginnings* (1994) and other books. Also trained in film, he has made award-winning documentaries and served as president of the Society for

Visual Anthropology and visual anthropology editor of the *American Anthropologist*. Dr. Prins has won his university's most prestigious undergraduate teaching awards, held the Coffman Chair for University Distinguished Teaching Scholars (2004–05), and was selected as Professor of the Year for the State of Kansas by the Carnegie Foundation for the Advancement of Teaching in 2008. Active in human rights, he served as expert witness in Native rights cases in the U.S. Senate and various Canadian courts, and was instrumental in the successful federal recognition and land claims of the Aroostook Band of Micmacs (1991). Dr. Prins was appointed Research Associate at the National Museum of Natural History, Smithsonian Institution (2008–11), and served as guest professor at Lund University in Sweden (2010).

BUNNY MCBRIDE is an award-winning author specializing in cultural anthropology, indigenous peoples, international tourism, and nature conservation issues. Published in dozens of national and international print media, she has reported from Africa, Europe, China, and the Indian Ocean. Highly rated as a teacher, she served as visiting anthropology faculty at Principia College, the Salt Institute for Documentary Field Studies, and since 1996 as adjunct lecturer of anthropology at Kansas State University. McBride's many publications include *Women of the Dawn* (1999), *Molly Spotted Elk: A Penobscot in Paris* (1995), and *Indians in Eden: Wabanakis and Rusticators on Maine's Mount Desert Island, 1850s–1920s* (co-authored, 2009). The Maine State legislature awarded her a special commendation for significant contributions to Native women's history (1999). A community activist and researcher for the Aroostook Band of Micmacs (1981–91), McBride assisted this Maine Indian community in its successful efforts to reclaim lands, gain tribal status, and revitalize cultural traditions. She has curated various museum exhibits based on her research, most recently *Journeys West: The David & Peggy Rockefeller American Indian Art Collection* for the Abbe Museum in Bar Harbor, Maine. Currently she is working on a new book co-authored with Harald Prins (*From Indian Island to Omaha Beach: The Story of Charles Shay, Penobscot Indian War Hero,* 2010) and a series of museum exhibitions based on a two-volume study co-authored with Harald Prins for the National Park Service (*Asticou's Island Domain*, 2007). McBride also serves as oral history advisor for the Kansas Humanities Council and as board member and vice president of the Women's World Summit Foundation, based in Geneva, Switzerland.

Evolution & Prehistory

Challenge Issue It is a challenge to make sense of who we are. Where did we come from? Why are we so radically different from some animals and so surprisingly similar to others? Why do our bodies look the way they do? How do we explain so many different beliefs, languages, and customs? Why do we act in certain ways? What makes us tick? While some people answer these questions with biological mechanisms and others with social or spiritual explanations, scholars in the discipline of anthropology address them through a holistic, integrated approach. Anthropology considers human culture and biology, in all times and places, as inextricably intertwined, each affecting the other in important ways. This photograph, taken in a specialized maternity clinic in Gujarat, India, provides a case in point. Since commercial surrogacy—the practice of paying a woman to carry another's fetus to term—was legalized in 2002, wealthy childless parents from all over the globe have traveled to India for this service. Chosen by foreigners because of their healthy drug-free lifestyle and lower fees, Indian women take on extra biological risk to make it possible for others to reproduce their genes. Global politics and local cultural practices interact with the seemingly purely biological process of birth. Understanding humanity in all its biological and cultural variety, past and present, is the fundamental contribution of anthropology. In the era of globalization, this contribution is all the more important. Indeed, the holistic and integrative anthropological perspective has become essential to human survival.

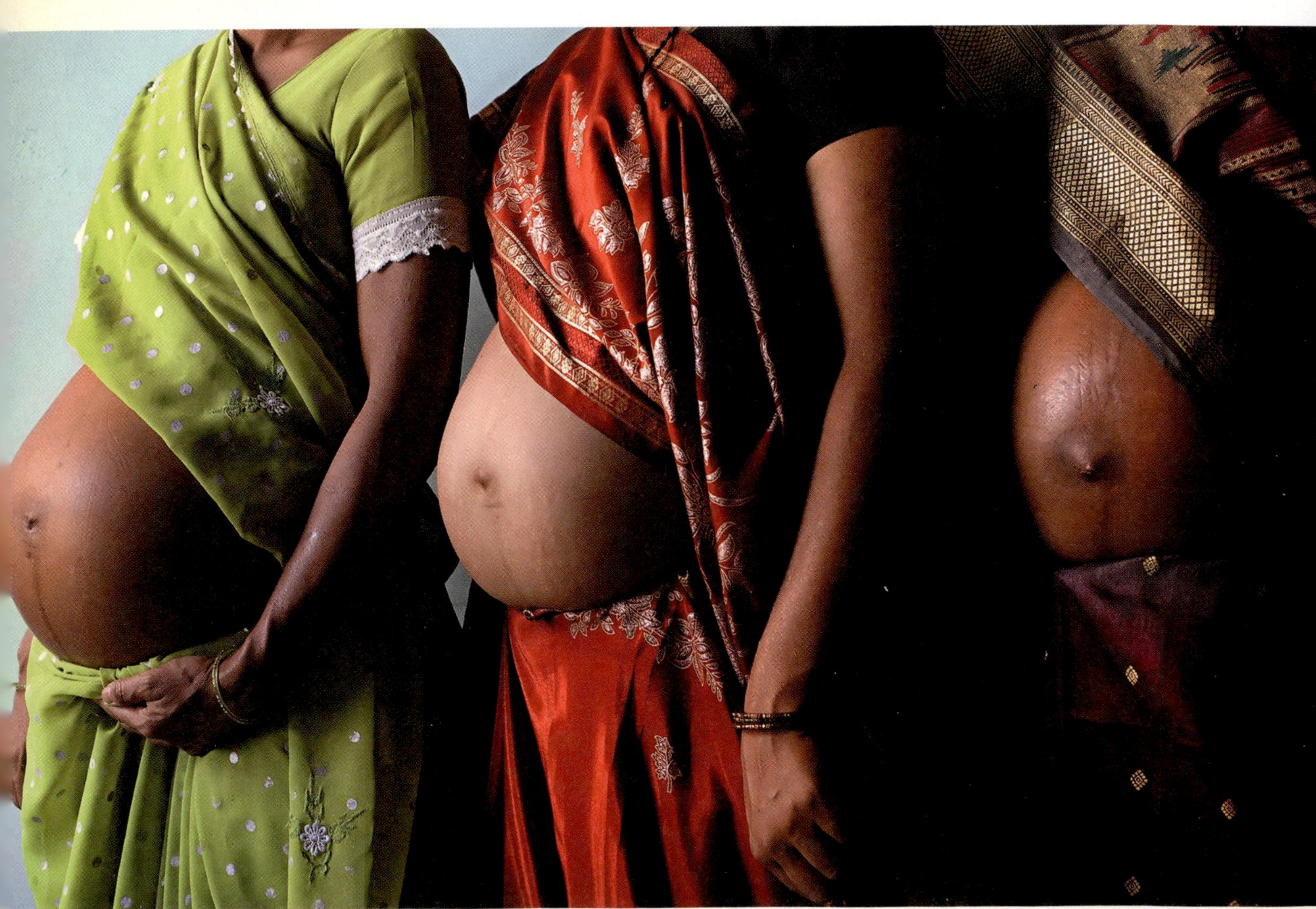

The Essence of Anthropology

Chapter Preview

What Is Anthropology?

Anthropology, the study of humankind everywhere throughout time, produces knowledge about what makes people different from one another and what we all have in common. Anthropologists work within four fields of the discipline. While physical anthropologists focus on humans as biological organisms (tracing evolutionary development and looking at biological variations), cultural anthropologists investigate the contrasting ways groups of humans think, feel, and behave. Archaeologists try to recover information about human cultures—usually from the past—by studying material objects, skeletal remains, and settlements. Meanwhile, linguists study languages—communication systems by which cultures are maintained and passed on to succeeding generations. Practitioners in all four fields are informed by one another's findings and united by a common anthropological perspective on the human condition.

How Does Anthropology Compare to Other Disciplines?

In studying humankind, early anthropologists came to the conclusion that to fully understand the complexities of human thought, feelings, behavior, and biology, it was necessary to study and compare all humans, wherever and whenever. More than any other feature, this comparative, cross-cultural, long-term perspective distinguishes anthropology from other social sciences. Anthropologists are not the only scholars who study people, but they are uniquely holistic in their approach, focusing on the interconnections and interdependence of all aspects of the human experience, past and present. This holistic and integrative outlook equips anthropologists to grapple with an issue of overriding importance for all of us today: globalization.

How Do Anthropologists Do What They Do?

Anthropologists, like other scholars, are concerned with the description and explanation of reality. They formulate and test hypotheses—tentative explanations of observed phenomena—concerning humankind. Their aim is to develop reliable theories—interpretations or explanations supported by bodies of data—about our species. These data are usually collected through fieldwork—a particular kind of hands-on research that gives anthropologists enough familiarity with a situation that they can begin to recognize patterns, regularities, and exceptions. It is also through careful observation, combined with comparison, that anthropologists test their theories.

For as long as we have been on earth, people have sought to understand who we are, where we come from, and why we act as we do. Throughout most of human history, though, people relied on myth and folklore for answers, rather than on the systematic testing of data obtained through careful observation. Anthropology, over the last 150 years, has emerged as a tradition of scientific inquiry with its own approaches to answering these questions. Simply stated, **anthropology** is the study of humankind in all times and places. While focusing primarily on *Homo sapiens*—the human species—anthropologists also study our ancestors and close animal relatives for clues about what it means to be human.

The Development of Anthropology

Although works of anthropological significance have a considerable antiquity—about 2,500 years ago the Greek historian Herodotus chronicled the many different cultures he encountered during extensive journeys through territories surrounding the Mediterranean Sea and beyond, and nearly 700 years ago far-roving North African Arab scholar Ibn Khaldun wrote a "universal history"—anthropology as a distinct field of inquiry is a relatively recent product of Western civilization. The first anthropology program in the United States, for example, was established at the University of Pennsylvania in 1886, and the first doctorate in anthropology was granted by Clark University in 1892. If people have always been concerned about their origins and those of others, then why did it take such a long time for a systematic discipline of anthropology to appear?

The answer to this is as complex as human history. In part, it relates to the limits of human technology. Throughout most of history, the geographic horizons of people have been restricted. Without ways to travel to distant parts of the world, observation of cultures and peoples far from one's own was a difficult—if not impossible—undertaking. Extensive travel was usually the privilege of an exclusive few; the study of foreign peoples and cultures could not flourish until improved modes of transportation and communication developed.

This is not to say that people have been unaware of the existence of others in the world who look and act differently from themselves. The Old and New Testaments of the Bible, for example, are full of references to diverse ancient peoples, among them Babylonians, Egyptians, Greeks, Jews, and Syrians. However, the differences among these people are slight in comparison to those among peoples of arctic Siberia, the Amazon rainforest, and the Kalahari Desert of southern Africa.

Anthropologists come from many corners of the world and carry out research in a huge variety of cultures all around the globe. Dr. Jayasinhji Jhala, pictured here, hails from the old city of Dhrangadhra in Gujarat, northwestern India. A member of the Jhala clan of Rajputs, an aristocratic caste of warriors, he grew up in the royal palace of his father, the maharaja. After earning a bachelor of arts degree in India, he came to the United States and earned a master's in visual studies from MIT, followed by a doctorate in anthropology from Harvard. Currently a professor and director of the programs of Visual Anthropology and the Visual Anthropology Media Laboratory at Temple University, he returns regularly to India with students to film cultural traditions in his own caste-stratified society.

The invention of the magnetic compass allowed seafarers on better-equipped sailing ships to travel to truly faraway places and to meet people who differed radically from themselves. The massive encounter with previously unknown peoples—which began 500 years ago as Europeans sought to extend their trade and political

anthropology The study of humankind in all times and places.

domination to all parts of the world—focused attention on human differences in all their amazing variety. With this attention, Europeans gradually came to recognize that despite all the differences, they might share a basic humanity with people everywhere. Initially, Europeans labeled these societies "savage" or "barbarian" because they did not share the same cultural values. Over time, however, Europeans acknowledged such highly diverse groups as fellow members of one species and therefore as relevant to an understanding of what it is to be human. This growing interest in human diversity coincided with increasing efforts to explain findings in scientific terms. It cast doubts on the traditional explanations based on religious texts such as the Torah, Bible, or Koran and helped set the stage for the birth of anthropology.

Although anthropology originated within the historical context of European cultures, it has long since gone global. Today, it is an exciting, transnational discipline whose practitioners come from diverse societies all around the world. Many professional anthropologists born and raised in Asian, African, Latin American, or American Indian cultures traditionally studied by European and North American anthropologists contribute substantially to the discipline. Their distinct non-Western perspectives shed new light not only on their own cultures but on those of others. It is noteworthy that in one regard diversity has long been a hallmark of the discipline: From its earliest days, women as well as men have entered the field. Throughout this text, we will be spotlighting individual anthropologists, illustrating the diversity of these practitioners and their work.

Anthropological Perspectives

Many academic disciplines are concerned in one way or another with our species. For example, biology focuses on the genetic, anatomical, and physiological aspects of organisms. Psychology is concerned primarily with cognitive, mental, and emotional issues, while economics examines the production, distribution, and management of material resources. And various disciplines in the humanities look into the historic, artistic, and philosophic achievements of human cultures. But anthropology is distinct because of its focus on the interconnections and interdependence of all aspects of the human experience in all places and times—both biological and cultural, past and present. It is this **holistic perspective** that best equips anthropologists to broadly address that elusive phenomenon we call human nature.

Anthropologists welcome the contributions of researchers from other disciplines and in return offer the benefit of their own findings. Anthropologists do not expect, for example, to know as much about the structure of the human eye as anatomists or as much about the perception of color as psychologists. As synthesizers, however, anthropologists are prepared to understand how these bodies of knowledge relate to color-naming practices in different human societies. Because they look for the broad basis of human ideas and practices without limiting themselves to any single social or biological aspect, anthropologists can acquire an especially expansive and inclusive overview of the complex biological and cultural organism that is the human being.

The holistic perspective also helps anthropologists stay keenly aware of ways that their own cultural ideas and values may impact their research. As the old saying goes, people often see what they believe, rather than what appears before their eyes. By maintaining a critical awareness of their own assumptions about human nature—checking and rechecking the ways their beliefs and actions might be shaping their research—anthropologists strive to gain objective knowledge about people. With this in mind, anthropologists aim to avoid the pitfalls of **ethnocentrism**, a belief that the ways of one's own culture are the only proper ones. Thus anthropologists have contributed uniquely to our understanding of diversity in human thought, biology, and behavior, as well as to our understanding of the many shared characteristics of humans.

To some, an inclusive, holistic perspective that emphasizes the inherent diversity within and among human cultures can be mistaken as shorthand for uniform liberal politics among anthropologists. This is not the case. Individual anthropologists are quite varied in their personal, political, and religious beliefs. At the same time, they apply a rigorous methodology for researching cultural practices from the perspective of the culture being studied—a methodology that requires them to check for the influences of their own biases. This is as true for an anthropologist analyzing the culture of the global banking industry as it is for one investigating trance dancing among contemporary hunter-gatherers. We might say that anthropology is a discipline concerned with unbiased evaluation of diverse human systems, including one's own. At times this requires challenging the status quo that is maintained and defended by the power elites of the system under study. This is true regardless of whether anthropologists focus on aspects of their own culture or on distant and different cultures.

holistic perspective A fundamental principle of anthropology: that the various parts of human culture and biology must be viewed in the broadest possible context in order to understand their interconnections and interdependence.

ethnocentrism The belief that the ways of one's own culture are the only proper ones.

Visual Counterpoint

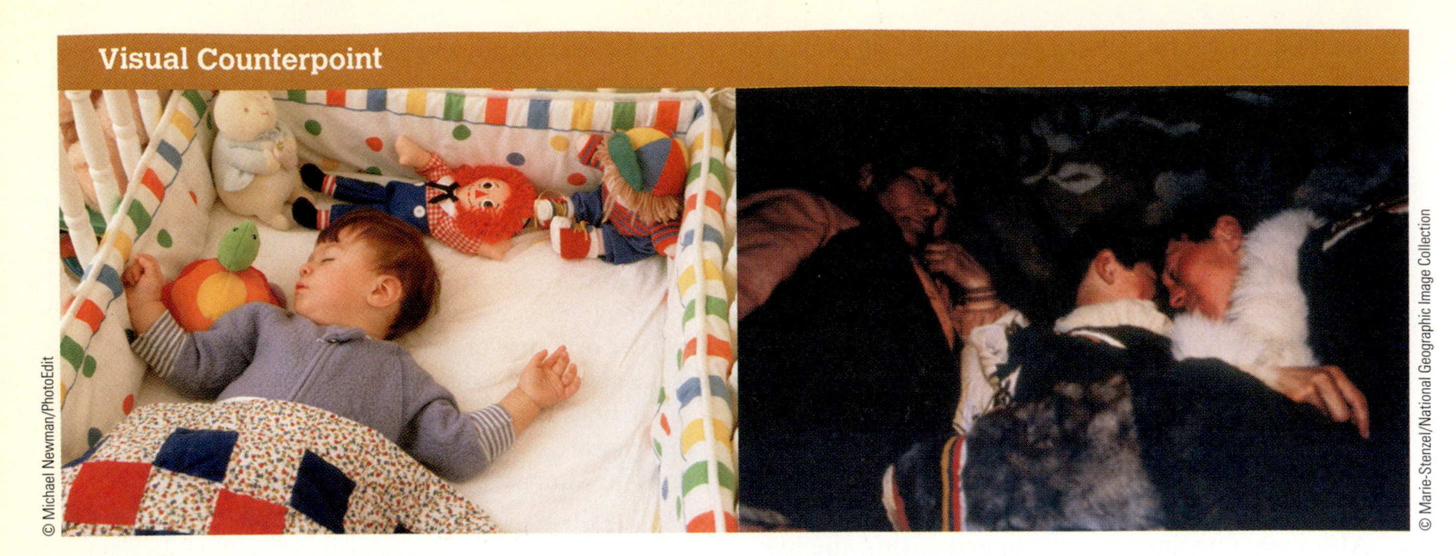

© Michael Newman/PhotoEdit

© Marie-Stenzel/National Geographic Image Collection

Although infants in the United States typically sleep apart from their parents, cross-cultural research shows that co-sleeping, of mother and baby in particular, is the rule. Without the breathing cues provided by someone sleeping nearby, an infant is more susceptible to sudden infant death syndrome (SIDS), a phenomenon in which a 4- to 6-month-old baby stops breathing and dies while asleep. The highest rates of SIDS are found among infants in the United States. The photo on the right shows a Nenet family sleeping together in their *chum* (reindeer-skin tent). Nenet people are arctic reindeer pastoralists living in Siberia.

While other social sciences have concentrated predominantly on contemporary peoples living in North American and European (Western) societies, historically anthropologists have focused primarily on non-Western peoples and cultures. Anthropologists work with the understanding that to fully access the complexities of human ideas, behavior, and biology, *all* humans, wherever and whenever, must be studied. Anthropologists work with a time depth that extends back millions of years to our pre-human ancestors. A cross-cultural, comparative, and long-term evolutionary perspective distinguishes anthropology from other social sciences. This all-encompassing approach also guards against **culture-bound** theories of human behavior: that is, theories based on assumptions about the world and reality that come from the researcher's own particular culture.

As a case in point, consider the fact that infants in the United States typically sleep apart from their parents. To people accustomed to multi-bedroom houses, cribs, and car seats, this may seem normal, but cross-cultural research shows that co-sleeping, of mother and baby in particular, is the norm. Further, the practice of sleeping apart favored in the United States dates back only about 200 years.

Recent studies have shown that separation of mother and infant has important biological and cultural consequences. For one thing, it increases the length of the infant's crying bouts. Some mothers incorrectly interpret the crying as indicating that the babies are receiving insufficient breast milk and consequently switch to feeding them bottled formula, proven to be less healthy. In extreme cases, a baby's cries may provoke physical abuse. But the benefits of co-sleeping go beyond significant reductions in crying: Infants who are breastfed receive more stimulation important for brain development, and they are apparently less susceptible to sudden infant death syndrome (SIDS or "crib death"). There are benefits to the mother as well: Frequent nursing prevents early ovulation after childbirth, it promotes loss of weight gained during pregnancy, and nursing mothers get at least as much sleep as mothers who sleep apart from their infants.[1]

Why do so many mothers continue to sleep separately from their infants? In the United States the cultural values of independence and consumerism come into play. To begin building individual identities, babies are provided with rooms (or at least space) of their own. This room also provides parents with a place for the toys, furniture, and other paraphernalia associated with "good" and "caring" childrearing in the United States.

Anthropology's historical emphasis on studying traditional, non-Western peoples has often led to findings that run

culture-bound Looking at the world and reality based on the assumptions and values of one's own culture.

[1] Barr, R. G. (1997, October). The crying game. *Natural History,* 47. Also, McKenna, J. J. (2002, September–October). Breastfeeding and bedsharing. *Mothering,* 28–37; and McKenna, J. J., & McDade, T. (2005, June). Why babies should never sleep alone: A review of the co-sleeping controversy in relation to SIDS, bedsharing, and breast feeding. *Pediatric Respiratory Reviews 6* (2), 134–152.

counter to generally accepted opinions derived from Western studies. Thus anthropologists were the first to demonstrate

> that the world does not divide into the pious and the superstitious; that there are sculptures in jungles and paintings in deserts; that political order is possible without centralized power and principled justice without codified rules; that the norms of reason were not fixed in Greece, the evolution of morality not consummated in England. . . . We have, with no little success, sought to keep the world off balance; pulling out rugs, upsetting tea tables, setting off firecrackers. It has been the office of others to reassure; ours to unsettle.[2]

Although the findings of anthropologists have often challenged the conclusions of sociologists, psychologists, and economists, anthropology is absolutely indispensable to them, as it is the only consistent check against culture-bound assertions. In a sense, anthropology is to these disciplines what the laboratory is to physics and chemistry: an essential testing ground for their theories.

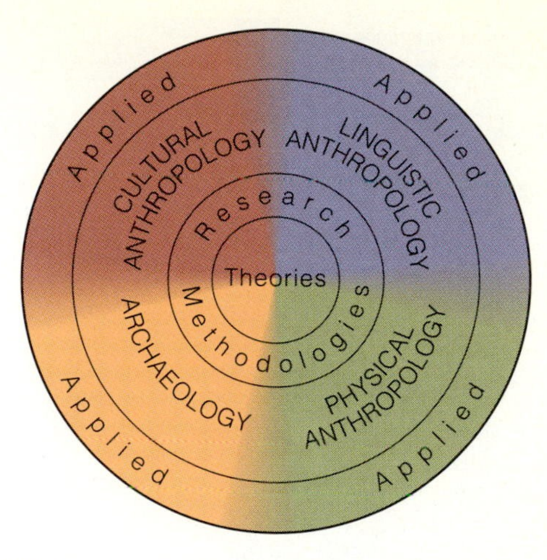

Figure 1.1 The four fields of anthropology. Note that the divisions among them are not sharp, indicating that their boundaries overlap.

Anthropology and Its Fields

Individual anthropologists tend to specialize in one of four fields or subdisciplines: physical (biological) anthropology, archaeology, linguistic anthropology, or cultural anthropology (Figure 1.1). Some anthropologists consider archaeology and linguistics as part of the broader study of human cultures, but archaeology and linguistics also have close ties to biological anthropology. For example, while linguistic anthropology focuses on the cultural aspects of language, it has deep connections to the evolution of human language and to the biological basis of speech and language studied within physical anthropology.

Each of anthropology's fields may take a distinct approach to the study of humans, but all gather and analyze data that are essential to explaining similarities and differences among humans, across time and space. Moreover, all of them generate knowledge that has numerous practical applications. Many scholars within each of the four fields practice **applied anthropology,** which entails using anthropological knowledge and methods to solve practical problems. Applied anthropologists do not offer their perspectives from the sidelines. Instead, they actively collaborate with the communities in which they work—setting goals, solving problems, and conducting research together. In this book, numerous specific examples of how anthropology contributes to solving a wide range of challenges appear in Anthropology Applied features.

One of the earliest contexts in which anthropological knowledge was applied to a practical problem was the international public health movement that began in the 1920s. This marked the beginning of **medical anthropology**—a specialization that combines theoretical and applied approaches from the fields of cultural and biological anthropology with the study of human health and disease. The work of medical anthropologists sheds light on the connections between human health and political and economic forces, both locally and globally. Examples of this specialization appear in many of the Biocultural Connections featured in this text, including the one presented in this chapter, "The Anthropology of Organ Transplantation."

Physical Anthropology

Physical anthropology, also called *biological anthropology,* focuses on humans as biological organisms. Traditionally, biological anthropologists concentrated on human evolution, primatology, growth and development, human adaptation, and forensics. Today, **molecular anthropology,** or the anthropological study of genes and genetic relationships, contributes significantly to the contemporary study of human biological diversity. Comparisons among groups

applied anthropology The use of anthropological knowledge and methods to solve practical problems, often for a specific client.

medical anthropology A specialization in anthropology that combines theoretical and applied approaches from cultural and biological anthropology with the study of human health and disease.

physical anthropology The systematic study of humans as biological organisms; also known as biological anthropology.

molecular anthropology A branch of biological anthropology that uses genetic and biochemical techniques to test hypotheses about human evolution, adaptation, and variation.

---

[2] Geertz, C. (1984). Distinguished lecture: Anti anti-relativism. *American Anthropologist 86,* 275.

Biocultural Connection

The Anthropology of Organ Transplantation

In 1954, the first organ transplant occurred in Boston when surgeons removed a kidney from one identical twin to place it inside his sick brother. Though some transplants rely upon living donors, routine organ transplantation depends largely upon the availability of organs obtained from individuals who have died.

From an anthropological perspective, the meanings of death and the body vary cross-culturally. While death could be said to represent a particular biological state, social agreement about this state's significance is of paramount importance. Anthropologist Margaret Lock has explored differences between Japanese and North American acceptance of the biological state of "brain death" and how it affects the practice of organ transplants.

Brain death relies upon the absence of measurable electrical currents in the brain and the inability to breathe without technological assistance. The brain-dead individual, though attached to machines, still seems alive with a beating heart and pink cheeks. North Americans find brain death acceptable, in part, because personhood and individuality are culturally located in the brain. North American comfort with brain death has allowed for the "gift of life" through organ donation and subsequent transplantation.

By contrast, in Japan, the concept of brain death is hotly contested and organ transplants are rarely performed. The Japanese do not incorporate a mind–body split into their models of themselves and locate personhood throughout the body rather than in the brain. They resist accepting a warm pink body as a corpse from which organs can be harvested. Further, organs cannot be transformed into "gifts" because anonymous donation is not compatible with Japanese social patterns of reciprocal exchange.

Organ transplantation carries far greater social meaning than the purely biological movement of an organ from one individual to another. Cultural and biological processes are tightly woven into every aspect of this new social practice.

BIOCULTURAL QUESTION

What criteria do you use for death, and is it compatible with the idea of organ donation? Do you think that donated organs are fairly distributed in your society or throughout the globe?

(For more on this subject, see Lock, M. (2001). Twice dead: Organ transplants and the reinvention of death. *Berkeley: University of California Press.)*

separated by time, geography, or the frequency of a particular gene can reveal how humans have adapted and where they have migrated. As experts in the anatomy of human bones and tissues, physical anthropologists lend their knowledge about the body to applied areas such as gross anatomy laboratories, public health, and criminal investigations.

PALEOANTHROPOLOGY

Paleoanthropology is the study of the origins and predecessors of the present human species; in other words, it is the study of human evolution. Paleoanthropologists focus on biological changes through time to understand how, when, and why we became the kind of organisms we are today. In biological terms, we humans are primates, one of the many kinds of mammals. Because we share a common ancestry with other primates, most specifically apes, paleoanthropologists look back to the earliest primates (65 or so million years ago) or even the earliest mammals (225 million years ago) to reconstruct the complex path of human evolution. Paleoanthropology, unlike other evolutionary studies, takes a **biocultural** approach, focusing on the interaction of biology and culture.

The fossilized skeletons of our ancestors allow paleoanthropologists to reconstruct the course of human evolutionary history. To do this, paleoanthropologists compare the size and shape of these fossils to one another and to the bones of living species. Each new fossil discovery brings another piece to add to the puzzle of human evolutionary history. Biochemical and genetic studies add considerably to the fossil evidence. As we will see in later chapters, genetic evidence establishes the close relationship between humans and ape species—chimpanzees, bonobos, and gorillas. Genetic analyses indicate that the distinctive human line originated 5 to 8 million years ago. Physical anthropology therefore deals with much greater time spans than the other branches of anthropology.

PRIMATOLOGY

Studying the anatomy and behavior of the other primates helps us understand what we share with our closest living relatives and what makes humans unique. Therefore, **primatology**, or the study of living and fossil primates, is a vital part of physical anthropology. Primates include the Asian and African apes, as well as monkeys, lemurs, lorises, and tarsiers.

Biologically, humans are members of the ape family—large-bodied, broad-shouldered primates with no tail. Detailed studies of ape behavior in the wild indicate that the sharing of learned behavior is a significant part of their social life. Increasingly, primatologists designate the shared, learned behavior of nonhuman apes as *culture*. For example, tool use and communication systems indicate the elementary basis of language in some ape societies. Primate studies offer scientifically grounded perspectives on the behavior of our ancestors, as well as greater appreciation and respect for the abilities of our closest

paleoanthropology The study of the origins and predecessors of the present human species; the study of human evolution.
biocultural Focusing on the interaction of biology and culture.
primatology The study of living and fossil primates.

Though Jane Goodall originally began her studies of chimpanzees to shed light on the behavior of our distant ancestors, the knowledge she has amassed through over forty years in the field has reinforced how similar we are. In turn, she has devoted her career to championing the rights of our closest living relatives.

living relatives. As human activity encroaches on all parts of the world, the habitats of many primate species are endangered, thereby threatening the survival of the species themselves. Primatologists often advocate for the preservation of primate habitats so that these remarkable animals will be able to continue to inhabit the earth with us.

HUMAN GROWTH, ADAPTATION, AND VARIATION

Another specialty of physical anthropologists is the study of human growth and development. Anthropologists examine biological mechanisms of growth as well as the impact of the environment on the growth process. For example, Franz Boas, a pioneer of American anthropology of the early 20th century (see the Anthropologists of Note feature in this chapter) compared the heights of immigrants who spent their childhood in the "old country" (Europe) to the increased heights reached by their children who grew up in the United States. Today, physical anthropologists study the impact of disease, pollution, and poverty on growth. Comparisons between human and nonhuman primate growth patterns can provide clues to the evolutionary history of humans. Detailed anthropological studies of the hormonal, genetic, and physiological bases of healthy growth in living humans also contribute significantly to the health of children today.

Studies of human adaptation focus on the capacity of humans to adapt or adjust to their material environment—biologically and culturally. This branch of physical anthropology takes a comparative approach to humans living today in a variety of environments. Humans are remarkable among the primates in that they now inhabit the entire earth. Though cultural adaptations make it possible for humans to live in some environmental extremes, biological adaptations also contribute to survival in extreme cold, heat, and high altitude.

Some of these biological adaptations are built into the genetic makeup of populations. The long period of human growth and development provides ample opportunity for the environment to shape the human body. *Developmental adaptations* are responsible for some features of human variation, such as the enlargement of the right ventricle of the heart to help push blood to the lungs among the Quechua Indians of the Andean highlands known as the *altiplano*. In contrast, *physiological adaptations* are short-term changes in response to a particular environmental stimulus. For example, a woman who normally lives at sea level will undergo a series of physiological responses, such as increased production of oxygen-carrying red blood cells, if she suddenly moves to a high altitude. All of these kinds of biological adaptation contribute to present-day human variation.

Human differences include visible traits such as height, body build, and skin color, as well as biochemical factors such as blood type and susceptibility to certain diseases. Still, we remain members of a single species. Physical anthropology applies all the techniques of modern biology to achieve fuller understanding of human variation and its relationship to the different environments in which people have lived. Physical anthropologists' research on human variation has debunked false notions of biologically defined races, a belief based on widespread misinterpretation of human variation.

Anthropology Applied

Forensic Anthropology: Voices for the Dead

Forensic anthropology is the analysis of skeletal remains for legal purposes. Law enforcement authorities call upon forensic anthropologists to use skeletal remains to identify murder victims, missing persons, or people who have died in disasters, such as plane crashes. Forensic anthropologists have also contributed substantially to the investigation of human rights abuses in all parts of the world by identifying victims and documenting the cause of their death.

Among the best-known forensic anthropologists is Clyde C. Snow. He has been practicing in this field for over forty years—first for the Federal Aviation Administration and more recently as a freelance consultant. In addition to the usual police work, Snow has studied the remains of General George Armstrong Custer and his men from the 1876 battle at Little Big Horn, and in 1985 he went to Brazil, where he identified the remains of the notorious Nazi war criminal Josef Mengele.

© AP Photo/Rodrigo Abd

The excavation of mass graves by the Guatemalan Foundation for Forensic Anthropology (Fernando Moscoso Moller, director) documents the human rights abuses committed during Guatemala's bloody civil war, a conflict that left 200,000 people dead and another 40,000 missing. In 2009, in a mass grave in the Quiche region, Diego Lux Tzunux uses his cell phone to photograph the skeletal remains believed to belong to his brother Manuel who disappeared in 1980. Genetic analyses allow forensic anthropologists to confirm the identity of individuals so that family members can know the fate of their loved ones. The analysis of skeletal remains provides evidence of the torture and massacre sustained by these individuals.

He was also instrumental in establishing the first forensic team devoted to documenting cases of human rights abuses around the world. This began in 1984 when he went to Argentina at the request of a newly elected civilian government to help with the identification of remains of the *desaparecidos,* or "disappeared ones," the 9,000 or more people who were eliminated by death squads during seven years of military rule. A year later, he returned to give expert testimony at the trial of nine junta members and to teach Argentineans how to recover, clean, repair, preserve, photograph, x-ray, and analyze bones. Besides providing factual accounts of the fate of victims to their surviving kin and refuting the assertions of revisionists that the massacres never happened, the work of Snow and his Argentinean associates was crucial in convicting several military officers of kidnapping, torture, and murder.

Since Snow's pioneering work, forensic anthropologists have become increasingly involved in the investigation of human rights abuses in all parts of the world, from Chile to Guatemala, Haiti, the Philippines, Rwanda, Iraq, Bosnia, and Kosovo. Meanwhile, they continue to do important work for more typical clients. In the United States these clients include the Federal Bureau of Investigation and city, state, and county medical examiners' offices.

Forensic anthropologists specializing in skeletal remains commonly work closely with forensic archaeologists. The relation between them is rather like that between a forensic pathologist, who examines a corpse to establish time and manner of death, and a crime scene

FORENSIC ANTHROPOLOGY

One of the many practical applications of physical anthropology is **forensic anthropology:** the identification of human skeletal remains for legal purposes. Although they are called upon by law enforcement authorities to identify murder victims, forensic anthropologists also investigate human rights abuses such as systematic genocide, terrorism, and war crimes. These specialists use details of skeletal anatomy to establish the age, sex, population affiliation, and stature of the deceased. Forensic anthropologists can also determine whether the person was right- or left-handed, exhibited any physical abnormalities, or had experienced trauma. While forensics relies upon differing frequencies of certain skeletal characteristics to establish population affiliation, it is nevertheless false to say that all people from a given population have a particular type of skeleton. (See the Anthropology Applied feature to read about the work of several forensic anthropologists and forensic archaeologists.)

forensic anthropology Applied subfield of physical anthropology that specializes in the identification of human skeletal remains for legal purposes.

investigator, who searches the site for clues. While the forensic anthropologist deals with the human remains—often only bones and teeth—the forensic archaeologist controls the site, recording the position of all relevant finds and recovering any clues associated with the remains. In 1995, for example, a team was assembled by the United Nations to investigate a mass atrocity in Rwanda; this group included archaeologists from the U.S. National Park Service's Midwest Archaeological Center. They performed the standard archaeological procedures of mapping the site; determining its boundaries; photographing and recording all surface finds; and excavating, photographing, and recording buried skeletons and associated materials in mass graves.[a]

In another example, Karen Burns of the University of Georgia was part of a team sent to northern Iraq after the 1991 Gulf War to investigate alleged atrocities. On a military base where there had been many executions, she excavated the remains of a man's body found lying on its side facing Mecca, conforming to Islamic practice. Although no intact clothing existed, two polyester threads typically used in sewing were found along the sides of both legs. Although the threads survived, the clothing, because it was made of natural fiber, had decayed. "Those two threads at each side of the leg just shouted that his family didn't bury him," said Burns.[b] Proper though his position was, no Islamic family would bury their own in a garment sewn with polyester thread; proper ritual would require a simple shroud.

In recent years New York City has been the site of two major anthropological analyses of skeletal remains. To deal with a present-day atrocity, Amy Zelson Mundorff, a forensic anthropologist for New York City's Office of the Chief Medical Examiner, supervised and coordinated the management, treatment, and cataloguing of people who lost their lives in the September 11 terrorist attack on the World Trade Center. Mundorff herself had been injured in the attack, but she was able to return to work two days after the towers fell.

And in 1991, just a short distance from the World Trade Center site, construction workers in lower Manhattan discovered an African burial ground from the 17th and 18th centuries. A bioarchaeological rather than strictly forensic approach allowed researchers to examine the complete cultural and historical context and lifeways of the entire population buried there. The African Burial Ground Project provided incontrovertible evidence of the horror of slavery in North America, in the busy northern port of New York City. The more than 400 individuals buried there, many of them children, were worked so far beyond their ability to endure that their spines were fractured. African American biological archaeologist Michael Blakey, who led the research team, noted the social impact of this work:

> Descendants of the enslaved in different parts of the world have the right to know about the past and the right to memorialize history so that it might not happen again. With the project, we knew that we were peeling off layers of obscurity. We were also doing something that scholars within the African diaspora have been doing for about 150 years and that is realizing that history has political implications of empowerment and disempowerment. That history is not just to be discovered but to be re-discovered, to be corrected, and that African-American history is distorted. Omissions are made in order to create a convenient view of national and white identity at the expense of our understanding our world and also at the expense of African-American identity. So that the project of history—in this case using archaeology and skeletal biology—is a project meant to help us understand something that has been systematically hidden from us.[c]

Thus several kinds of anthropologists analyze human remains for a variety of purposes, contributing to the documentation and correction of violence committed by humans of the past and present.

---

[a] Haglund, W. D., Conner, M., & Scott, D. D. (2001). The archaeology of contemporary mass graves. *Historical Archaeology 35* (1), 57–69.

[b] Cornwell, T. (1995, November 10). Skeleton staff. *Times Higher Education,* 20. http://www.timeshighereducation.co.uk/story.asp?storyCode=96035§ioncode=26.

[c] "Return to the African Burial Ground: An interview with physical anthropologist Michael L. Blakey." (2003, November 20). *Archaeology.* http://www.archaeology.org/online/interviews/blakey/.

Cultural Anthropology

Cultural anthropology (also called *social* or *sociocultural anthropology*) is the study of patterns of human behavior, thought, and feelings. It focuses on humans as culture-producing and culture-reproducing creatures. Thus in order to understand the work of the cultural anthropologist, we must clarify what we mean by **culture**—a society's shared and socially transmitted ideas, values, and perceptions, which are used to make sense of experience and generate behavior and are reflected in that behavior. These standards are socially learned, rather than acquired through biological inheritance. The manifestations of culture may vary considerably from place to place, but no person is "more cultured" in the anthropological sense than any other.

cultural anthropology Also known as social or sociocultural anthropology. The study of customary patterns in human behavior, thought, and feelings. It focuses on humans as culture-producing and culture-reproducing creatures.

culture A society's shared and socially transmitted ideas, values, and perceptions, which are used to make sense of experience and generate behavior and are reflected in that behavior.

© Jeff Schonberg 2009

Through his pioneering ethnographic studies of the culture of drug addicts and dealers, cultural anthropologist Philippe Bourgois opened up a new range of edgy field sites for cultural anthropologists. The insights from his detailed ethnographies about this world have been important not only for anthropological literature but for those concerned with the health of individuals and communities. Here Bourgois is pictured in one of his more recent field sites, a homeless encampment in North Philadelphia.

Cultural anthropology has two main components: ethnography and ethnology. An **ethnography** is a detailed description of a particular culture primarily based on **fieldwork,** which is the term all anthropologists use for on-location research. Because the hallmark of ethnographic fieldwork is a combination of social participation and personal observation within the community being studied, as well as interviews and discussions with individual members of a group, the ethnographic method is commonly referred to as **participant observation.** Ethnographies provide the information used to make systematic comparisons among cultures all across the world. Known as **ethnology,** such cross-cultural research allows anthropologists to develop anthropological theories that help explain why certain important differences or similarities occur among groups.

ETHNOGRAPHY

Through participant observation—eating a people's food, sleeping under their roof, learning how to speak and behave acceptably, and personally experiencing their habits and customs—the ethnographer seeks to gain the best possible understanding of a particular way of life. Being a participant observer does not mean that the anthropologist must join in battles to study a culture in which warfare is prominent; but by living among a warlike people, the ethnographer should be able to understand how warfare fits into the overall cultural framework. She or he must observe carefully to gain an overview without placing too much emphasis on one part at the expense of another. Only by discovering how *all* aspects of a culture—its social, political, economic, and religious practices and institutions—relate to one another can the ethnographer begin to understand the cultural system. This is the holistic perspective so basic to the discipline.

The popular image of ethnographic fieldwork is that it occurs among people who live in far-off, isolated places. To be sure, much ethnographic work has been done in the remote villages of Africa or South America, the islands of the Pacific Ocean, the Indian reservations of North America, the deserts of Australia, and so on. However, as the discipline has developed, Western industrialized societies have also become the focus of anthropological study. Some of this shift occurred as scholars from non-Western cultures became anthropologists. Ethnographic fieldwork has transformed from having expert Western anthropologists study people in "other" places to collaboration among anthropologists and the varied communities in which they work. Today, anthropologists from all around the globe employ the same research techniques that were used in the study of non-Western peoples to explore such diverse subjects as religious movements, street gangs, land rights,

ethnography A detailed description of a particular culture primarily based on fieldwork.

fieldwork The term anthropologists use for on-location research.

participant observation In ethnography, the technique of learning a people's culture through social participation and personal observation within the community being studied, as well as interviews and discussion with individual members of the group over an extended period of time.

ethnology The study and analysis of different cultures from a comparative or historical point of view, utilizing ethnographic accounts and developing anthropological theories that help explain why certain important differences or similarities occur among groups.

schools, marriage practices, conflict resolution, corporate bureaucracies, and health-care systems in Western cultures.

ETHNOLOGY

Largely descriptive in nature, ethnography provides the raw data needed for ethnology—the branch of cultural anthropology that involves cross-cultural comparisons and theories that explain differences or similarities among groups. Intriguing insights into one's own beliefs and practices may come from cross-cultural comparisons. Consider, for example, the amount of time spent on domestic chores by industrialized peoples and traditional food foragers (people who rely on wild plant and animal resources for subsistence). Anthropological research has shown that food foragers work far less time at domestic tasks and other subsistence pursuits compared to people in industrialized societies. Urban women in the United States who were not working for wages outside their homes put 55 hours a week into their housework—this despite all the "labor-saving" dishwashers, washing machines, clothes dryers, vacuum cleaners, food processors, and microwave ovens. In contrast, aboriginal women in Australia devoted 20 hours a week to their chores.[3] Nevertheless, consumer appliances have become important indicators of a high standard of living in the United States due to the widespread belief that household appliances reduce housework and increase leisure time.

By making systematic comparisons, ethnologists seek to arrive at scientific explanations concerning the function and operation of social practices and cultural features and patterns in all times and places. Today cultural anthropologists contribute to applied research in a variety of contexts—ranging from business to education to health care to government intervention to humanitarian aid.

Linguistic Anthropology

Perhaps the most distinctive feature of the human species is language. Although the sounds and gestures made by some other animals—especially apes—may serve functions comparable to those of human language, no other animal has developed a system of symbolic communication as complex as that of humans. Language allows people to preserve and transmit countless details of their culture from generation to generation.

The branch of anthropology that studies human languages is called **linguistic anthropology.** Although it shares data and methods with the more general discipline of linguistics, it differs in that it uses these to answer anthropological questions related to society and culture, such as language use within speech communities. When this field began, it emphasized the documentation of languages of cultures under ethnographic study—particularly those whose future seemed precarious. Mastery of Native American languages—with grammatical structures so different from the Indo-European and Semitic languages to which Euramerican scholars were accustomed—prompted the notion of *linguistic relativity.* This refers to the idea that linguistic diversity reflects not just differences in sounds and grammar but differences in ways of looking at the world. For example, the observation that the language of the Hopi Indians of the American Southwest had no words for *past, present,* and *future* led the early proponents of linguistic relativity to suggest that the Hopi people had a different conception of time.[4] Similarly, the observation that English-speaking North Americans use a number of slang words—such as *dough, greenback, dust, loot, bucks, change, paper, cake, moolah, benjamins,* and *bread*—to refer to money could be a product of linguistic relativity. The profusion of names helps to identify a thing of special importance to a culture. For instance, the importance of money within North American culture is evident in the association between money and time, production, and capital in phrases such as "time is money" and "spend some time."

Complex ideas and practices integral to a culture's survival can also be reflected in language. For example, among the Nuer, a nomadic group that travels with grazing animals throughout southern Sudan, a baby born with a visible deformity is not considered a human baby. Instead it is called a baby hippopotamus. This name allows for the safe return of the hippopotamus to the river where it belongs. Such infants would not be able to survive in this society, and so linguistic practice is compatible with the compassionate choice the Nuer have had to make.

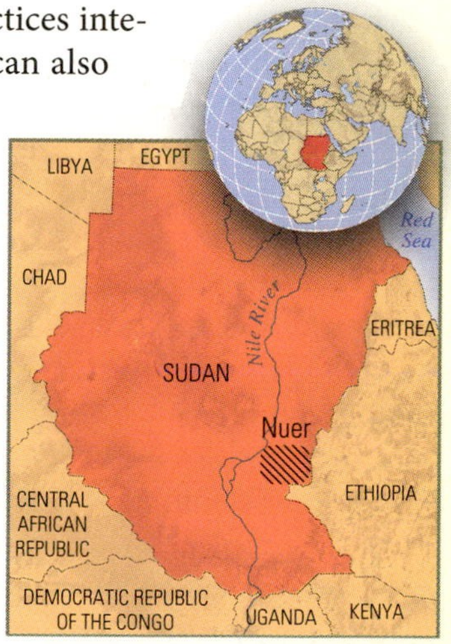

The notion of linguistic relativity has been challenged by theorists who propose that the human capacity for language is based on biological universals that underlie all human thought. Recently, Canadian cognitive scientist Stephen Pinker has even suggested that, at a fundamental

[3] Bodley, J. H. (1985). *Anthropology and contemporary human problems* (2nd ed., p. 69). Palo Alto, CA: Mayfield.

[4] Whorf, B. (1941). The relation of habitual thought and behavior to language. In L. Spier, A. I. Hallowell, & S. S. Newman (Eds.), *Language, culture, and personality: Essays in memory of Edward Sapir* (pp. 75–93). Menasha, WI: Sapir Memorial Publication Fund.

linguistic anthropology The study of human languages—looking at their structure, history, and relation to social and cultural contexts.

Linguistic anthropologist Gregory Anderson has devoted his career to saving indigenous languages. He founded and heads the Living Tongues Institute of Endangered Languages and works throughout the globe to preserve languages that are dying out at a shocking rate of about one every two weeks. Here he is working with Don Francisco Ninacondis and Ariel Ninacondis in Charazani, Bolivia, to preserve their language Kallawaya.

level, thought is nonverbal.[5] A holistic anthropological approach considers language to have both a universal biological basis and specific cultural patterning.

Researching questions about human relations through language can involve focusing on specific speech events.[6] Such events form a **discourse** or an extended communication on a particular subject. These speech events reveal how social factors such as financial status, age, or gender affect the way an individual uses its culture's language. The linguistic anthropologist might examine whether the tendency for females in the United States to end statements with an upward inflection, as though the statement were a question, reflects a pattern of male dominance in this society. Because members of any culture may use a variety of different registers and inflections, the ones they choose to use at a specific instance convey particular meanings.

As with the anthropological perspective on culture, language is similarly regarded as alive, malleable, and changing. Online tools such as Urban Dictionary track the changes in North American slang, and traditional dictionaries include new words and usages each year. The implications of these language changes help increase our understanding of the human past. By working out relationships among languages and examining their spatial distributions, linguistic anthropologists may estimate how long the speakers of those languages have lived where they do. By identifying those words in related languages that have survived from an ancient ancestral tongue, these linguistic anthropologists can also suggest not only where, but how, the speakers of the ancestral language lived. Such work has shown, for example, linguistic ties between geographically distant groups such as the people of Finland and Turkey.

Linguistic anthropology is practiced in a number of applied settings. For example, linguistic anthropologists have collaborated with ethnic minorities in the revival of languages suppressed or lost during periods of oppression by another ethnic group. This work has included helping to create written forms of languages that previously existed only orally. This sort of applied linguistic anthropology represents the true collaboration that is characteristic of anthropological research today.

Archaeology

Archaeology is the branch of anthropology that studies human cultures through the recovery and analysis of material remains and environmental data. Such material products include tools, pottery, hearths, and enclosures that remain as traces of cultural practices in the past, as well as human, plant, and marine remains, some of which date back 2.5 million years. The arrangement of these traces when recovered reflects specific human ideas and behavior. For example, shallow, restricted concentrations of charcoal that include oxidized earth, bone fragments, and charred plant remains, located near pieces of fire-cracked rock, pottery, and tools suitable for food preparation, indicate cooking and food processing. Such remains can reveal much about

[5] Pinker, S. (1994). *The language instinct: How the mind creates language.* New York: Morrow.

[6] Hymes, D. (1974). *Foundations in sociolinguistics: An ethnographic approach.* Philadelphia: University of Pennsylvania Press.

discourse An extended communication on a particular subject.
archaeology The study of human cultures through the recovery and analysis of material remains and environmental data.

a people's diet and subsistence practices. Together with skeletal remains, these material remains help archaeologists reconstruct the biocultural context of past human lifeways. Archaeologists organize this material and use it to explain cultural variability and culture change through time.

Because archaeology is explicitly tied to unearthing material remains in particular environmental contexts, a variety of innovations in the geographic and geologic sciences have been readily incorporated into archaeological research. Innovations such as geographic information systems (GIS), remote sensing, and ground penetrating radar (GPR) complement traditional explorations of the past through archaeological digs.

Archaeologists can reach back for clues to human behavior far beyond the mere 5,000 years to which historians are confined by their reliance on written records. Calling this time period "prehistoric" does not mean that these societies were less interested in their history or that they did not have ways of recording and transmitting history. It simply means that written records do not exist. That said, archaeologists are not limited to the study of societies without written records; they may study those for which historic documents are available to supplement the material remains. In most literate societies, written records are associated with governing elites rather than with farmers, fishers, laborers, or slaves, and therefore they include the biases of the ruling classes. In fact, according to James Deetz, a pioneer in historical archaeology of the Americas, in many historical contexts, "material culture may be the most objective source of information we have."[7]

ARCHAEOLOGICAL SUBSPECIALTIES

While archaeologists tend to specialize in particular culture zones or time periods, connected with particular regions of the world, a number of topical subspecialties also exist. **Bioarchaeology,** for instance, is the archaeological study of human remains, emphasizing the preservation of cultural and social processes in the skeleton. For example, mummified skeletal remains from the Andean highlands in South America not only preserve this burial practice but also provide evidence of some of the earliest brain surgery ever documented. In addition, these bioarchaeological remains exhibit skull deformation techniques that distinguish nobility from other members of society. Other archaeologists specialize in *ethnobotany,* studying how people of a given culture made use of indigenous plants. Still others specialize in *zooarchaeology,* tracking the animal remains recovered in archaeological excavations.

Although most archaeologists concentrate on the past, some of them study material objects in contemporary settings. One example is the Garbage Project, founded by William Rathje at the University of Arizona in 1973. This anthropological study of household waste of Tucson residents produced a wide range of thought-provoking information about contemporary social issues. For example, when surveyed by questionnaires, only 15 percent of households reported consuming beer, and no household reported consuming more than eight cans a week. Analysis of garbage from the same area showed that some beer was consumed in over 80 percent of the households, and 50 percent of households discarded more than eight cans per week.

In addition to providing actual data on beer consumption, the Garbage Project has tested the validity of research survey techniques, upon which sociologists, economists, other social scientists and policymakers rely heavily. The tests show a significant difference between what people *say* they do and what the garbage analysis shows they *actually* do. Therefore, ideas about human behavior based on simple survey techniques may be seriously in error.

In 1987, the Garbage Project began a program of excavating landfills in different parts of the United States and Canada. From this work came the first reliable data on what materials actually go into landfills and what happens to them there. And once again, common beliefs turned out to be at odds with the actual situation. For example, when buried in deep compost landfills, biodegradable materials such as newspapers take far longer to decay than anyone had expected. This kind of information is a vital step toward solving waste disposal problems.[8]

Ranging from technical to philosophical, the impact of the Garbage Project has been profound. Data from its landfill studies on hazardous waste and rates of decay of various materials play a major role in landfill regulation and management today. In terms of philosophy, the data gathered from the Garbage Project underscored the dire need for public recycling and composting that is now an accepted part of mainstream U.S. culture.

CULTURAL RESOURCE MANAGEMENT

While archaeology may conjure up images of ancient pyramids and the like, much archaeological fieldwork is carried out as **cultural resource management**. What

[7] Deetz, J. (1977). *In small things forgotten: The archaeology of early American life* (p. 160). Garden City, NY: Anchor/Doubleday.

[8] Details regarding the Garbage Project's history and legacy can be found at http://traumwerk.stanford.edu:3455/17/174.

bioarchaeology The archaeological study of human remains, emphasizing the preservation of cultural and social processes in the skeleton.

cultural resource management A branch of archaeology tied to government policies for the protection of cultural resources and involving surveying and/or excavating archaeological and historical remains threatened by construction or development.

distinguishes this work from traditional archaeological research is that it is specifically charged with preserving important aspects of a country's prehistoric and historic heritage. For example, in the United States, if the transportation department of a state government plans to replace an inadequate highway bridge, the state must first contract with archaeologists to identify and protect any significant prehistoric or historic resources that might be affected.

Since passage of the Historic Preservation Act of 1966, the National Environmental Policy Act of 1969, the Archaeological and Historical Preservation Act of 1974, and the Archaeological Resources Protection Act of 1979, cultural resource management is required for any construction project that is partially funded or licensed by the U.S. government. As a result, the field of cultural resource management has flourished. Many archaeologists are employed by such agencies as the Army Corps of Engineers, the National Park Service, the U.S. Forest Service, and the U.S. Natural Resource Conservation Service to assist in the preservation, restoration, and salvage of archaeological resources. Countries such as Canada and the United Kingdom have programs very similar to that of the United States, and from Chile to China, various governments use archaeological expertise to protect and manage their cultural heritage.

When cultural resource management work or other archaeological investigation unearths Native American cultural items or human remains, federal laws come into the picture again. The Native American Graves Protection and Repatriation Act (NAGPRA), passed in 1990, provides a process for the return of these remains to lineal descendants, culturally affiliated Indian tribes, and Native Hawaiian organizations. NAGPRA has become central to the work of anthropologists who study Paleo-Indian cultures in the United States. It has also been the source of controversy, such as that regarding Kennewick Man, a 9,300-year-old skeleton discovered near Kennewick, Washington, in 1996.

In addition to working in all the capacities mentioned, archaeologists also consult for engineering firms to help them prepare environmental impact statements. Some of these archaeologists operate out of universities and colleges, while others are on the staff of independent consulting firms. When state legislation sponsors any kind of archaeological work, it is referred to as *contract archaeology*.

empirical Based on observations of the world rather than on intuition or faith.

hypothesis A tentative explanation of the relationships between certain phenomena.

Anthropology, Science, and the Humanities

With its broad scope of subjects and methods, anthropology has sometimes been called the most humane of the sciences and the most scientific of the humanities—a designation that most anthropologists accept with pride. Given their intense involvement with people of all times and places, anthropologists have amassed considerable information about human failure and success, weakness and greatness—the real stuff of the humanities. While anthropologists steer clear of a cold, impersonal scientific approach that reduces people and the things they do and think to mere numbers, their quantitative studies have contributed substantially to the scientific study of the human condition. But even the most scientific anthropologists always keep in mind that human societies are made up of individuals with rich assortments of emotions and aspirations that demand respect.

Beyond this, anthropologists remain committed to the proposition that one cannot fully understand another culture by simply observing it; as the term *participant observation* implies, one must *experience* it as well. This same commitment to fieldwork and to the systematic collection of data, whether qualitative or quantitative, is also evidence of the scientific side of anthropology. Anthropology is an **empirical** social science based on observations or information about humans taken in through the senses and verified by others rather than on intuition or faith. But anthropology is distinguished from other sciences by the diverse ways in which scientific research is conducted within the discipline.

Science, a carefully honed way of producing knowledge, aims to reveal and explain the underlying logic, the structural processes that make the world tick. In their search for explanations, scientists do not assume that things are always as they appear on the surface. After all, what could be more obvious to the scientifically uninformed observer than the earth staying still while the sun travels around it every day? The creative scientific endeavor seeks testable explanations for observed phenomena, ideally in terms of the workings of hidden but unchanging principles or laws. Two basic ingredients are essential for this: imagination and skepticism. Imagination, though having the potential to lead us astray, helps us recognize unexpected ways phenomena might be ordered and to think of old things in new ways. Without it, there can be no science. Skepticism allows us to distinguish fact (an observation verified by others) from fancy, to test our speculations, and to prevent our imaginations from running wild.

Like other scientists, anthropologists often begin their research with a **hypothesis** (a tentative explanation or hunch) about the possible relationships between certain observed facts or events. By gathering various kinds of data that seem

Anthropologists of Note

Franz Boas (1858–1942) ▪ *Matilda Coxe Stevenson (1849–1915)*

Franz Boas was not the first to teach anthropology in the United States, but it was Boas and his students, with their insistence on scientific rigor, who made anthropology courses common in college and university curricula. Born and raised in Germany where he studied physics, mathematics, and geography, Boas did his first ethnographic research among the Inuit (Eskimos) in arctic Canada in 1883 and1884. After a brief academic career in Berlin, he came to the United States where he worked in museums interspersed with ethnographic research among the Kwakiutl (Kwakwaka'wakw) Indians in the Canadian Pacific. In 1896, he became a professor at Columbia University in New York City. He authored an incredible number of publications, founded professional organizations and journals, and taught two generations of great anthropologists, including numerous women and ethnic minorities.

Franz Boas on a sailing ship circa 1925.

As a Jewish immigrant, Boas recognized the dangers of ethnocentrism and especially racism. Through ethnographic fieldwork and comparative analysis, he demonstrated that white supremacy theories and other schemes ranking non-European peoples and cultures as inferior were biased, ill-informed, and unscientific. Throughout his long and illustrious academic career, he promoted anthropology not only as a human science but also as an instrument to combat racism and prejudice in the world.

Among the founders of North American anthropology were a number of women who were highly influential among women's rights advocates in the late 1800s. One such pioneering anthropologist was **Matilda Coxe Stevenson,** who did fieldwork among the Zuni Indians of Arizona. In 1885, she founded the Women's Anthropological Society in Washington, DC, the first professional association for women scientists. Three years later, hired by the Smithsonian's Bureau of American Ethnology, she became one of the first women in the world to receive a full-time official position in science.

Mathilda Cox Stevenson in New Mexico around 1600.

The tradition of women being active in anthropology continues. In fact, since World War II more than half the presidents of the now 12,000-member American Anthropological Association have been women.

Recording observations on film as well as in notebooks, Stevenson and Boas were also pioneers in visual anthropology. Stevenson used an early box camera to document Pueblo Indian religious ceremonies and material culture, while Boas photographed Inuit (Eskimos) in northern Canada in 1883 and Kwakiutl Indians from the early 1890s for cultural as well as physical anthropological documentation. Today, these old photographs are greatly valued not only by anthropologists and historians, but also by indigenous peoples themselves.

to ground such suggested explanations on evidence, anthropologists come up with a **theory**—an explanation supported by a reliable body of data. In their effort to demonstrate links between *known* facts or events, anthropologists may discover *unexpected* facts, events, or relationships. An important function of theory is that it guides us in our explorations and may result in new knowledge. Equally important, the newly discovered facts may provide evidence that certain explanations, however popular or firmly believed, are unfounded. When the evidence is lacking or fails to support the suggested explanations, promising hypotheses or attractive hunches must be dropped. In other words, anthropology relies on empirical evidence. Moreover, no scientific theory—no matter how widely accepted by the international community of scholars—is beyond challenge.

It is important to distinguish between scientific theories—which are always open to future challenges born of new evidence or insights—and doctrine. A **doctrine**, or dogma, is an assertion of opinion or belief formally handed down by an authority as true and indisputable. For instance, those who accept a creationist doctrine on the origin of the human species as recounted in sacred texts or myths do so on the basis of religious authority;

theory In science, an explanation of natural phenomena, supported by a reliable body of data.

doctrine An assertion of opinion or belief formally handed down by an authority as true and indisputable.

they concede that their views may be contrary to explanations derived from genetics, geology, biology, or other sciences. Such doctrines cannot be tested or proved one way or another: They are accepted as matters of faith.

Straightforward though the scientific approach may seem, its application is not always easy. For instance, once a hypothesis has been proposed, the person who suggested it is strongly motivated to verify it, and this can cause one to unwittingly overlook negative evidence and unanticipated findings. This is a familiar problem in all science as noted by paleontologist Stephen Jay Gould: "The greatest impediment to scientific innovation is usually a conceptual lock, not a factual lock."[9] Because culture provides and shapes our very thoughts, it can be challenging to frame hypotheses or to develop interpretations that are not culture-bound. But by encompassing both humanism and science, the discipline of anthropology can draw on its internal diversity to overcome conceptual locks.

Fieldwork

All anthropologists think about whether their culture may have shaped the scientific questions they ask. In so doing, they rely heavily on a technique that has been successful in other disciplines: They immerse themselves in the data to the fullest extent possible. In the process, anthropologists become so thoroughly familiar with even the smallest details that they begin to recognize underlying patterns in the data, many of which might have been overlooked. Recognition of such patterns enables the anthropologist to frame meaningful hypotheses, which then may be subjected to further testing or validation in the field. Within anthropology, fieldwork provides additional rigor to the concept of total immersion in the data.

While fieldwork was introduced above in connection with cultural anthropology, it is characteristic of *all* the anthropological subdisciplines. Archaeologists and paleoanthropologists excavate in the field. A biological anthropologist interested in the effects of globalization on nutrition and growth will live in the field among a community of people to study this question. A primatologist might live among a group of chimpanzees or baboons just as a linguist would study the language of a culture by living in that community. Fieldwork, being fully immersed in another culture, challenges the anthropologist to be aware of the ways that cultural factors influence the research questions. Anthropological researchers monitor themselves by constantly checking their own biases and assumptions as they work; they present these self-reflections along with their observations, a practice known as *reflexivity*.

The validity or the reliability of a researcher's conclusions is established through the replication of observations and/or experiments by another researcher. Thus it becomes obvious if one's colleague has "gotten it right." But traditional validation by others is uniquely challenging in anthropology because observational access is often limited. Contact with a particular research site can be constrained by a number of factors. Difficulties of travel, obtaining permits, insufficient funding, or other conditions can interfere with access; also, what may be observed in a certain context at a certain time may not be observable at others. Thus one researcher cannot easily confirm the reliability or completeness of another's account. For this reason, anthropologists bear a special responsibility for accurate reporting. In the final research report, she or he must be clear about several basic issues: Why was a particular location selected as a research site? What were the research objectives? What were the local conditions during fieldwork? Which local individuals played a role in conducting the research? How were the data collected and recorded? How did the researcher check his or her own biases? Without such background information, it is difficult for others to judge the validity of the account and the soundness of the researcher's conclusions.

On a personal level, fieldwork requires the researcher to step out of his or her cultural comfort zone into a world that is unfamiliar and sometimes unsettling. Anthropologists in the field are likely to face a host of challenges—physical, social, mental, political, and ethical. They may have to deal with the physical challenge of adjusting to unaccustomed food, climate, and hygiene conditions. Typically, anthropologists in the field struggle with such mental challenges as being lonely, feeling like a perpetual outsider, being socially clumsy and clueless in their new cultural setting, and having to be alert around the clock because anything that is happening or being said may be significant to their research. Political challenges include the possibility of unwittingly letting oneself be used by factions within the community, or being viewed with suspicion by government authorities who may suspect the anthropologist is a spy. And there are ethical dilemmas as well: What does the anthropologist do if faced with a cultural practice he or she finds troubling, such as female circumcision? How does one deal with demands for food supplies and/or medicine? And is the fieldworker ever justified in using deception to gain vital information? Many such ethical questions arise in anthropological fieldwork.

At the same time, fieldwork often leads to tangible and meaningful personal, professional, and social rewards, ranging from lasting friendships to vital knowledge and insights concerning the human condition that make positive contributions to people's lives. Something of the meaning of anthropological fieldwork—its usefulness and its impact

[9] Gould, S. J. (1989). *Wonderful life* (p. 226). New York: Norton.

on researcher and subject—is conveyed in the following Original Study by Suzanne Leclerc-Madlala, an anthropologist who left her familiar New England surroundings about twenty-five years ago to do AIDS research among Zulu-speaking people in South Africa. Her research interest has changed the course of her own life, not to mention the lives of individuals who have AIDS/HIV and the type of treatment they receive.

Original Study

Fighting HIV/AIDS in Africa: Traditional Healers on the Front Line

by Suzanne Leclerc-Madlala

In the 1980s, as a North American anthropology graduate student at George Washington University, I met and married a Zulu-speaking student from South Africa. It was the height of apartheid, and upon moving to that country I was classified as "honorary black" and forced to live in a segregated township with my husband. The AIDS epidemic was in its infancy, but it was clear from the start that an anthropological understanding of how people perceive and engage with this disease would be crucial for developing interventions. I wanted to learn all that I could to make a difference, and this culminated in earning a PhD from the University of Natal on the cultural construction of AIDS among the Zulu. The HIV/AIDS pandemic in Africa became my professional passion.

Faced with overwhelming global health-care needs, the World Health Organization passed a series of resolutions in the 1970s promoting collaboration between traditional and modern medicine. Such moves held a special relevance for Africa where traditional healers typically outnumber practitioners of modern medicine by a ratio of 100 to 1 or more. Given Africa's disproportionate burden of disease, supporting partnership efforts with traditional healers makes sense. But what sounds sensible today was once considered absurd, even heretical. For centuries Westerners generally viewed traditional healing as a whole lot of primitive mumbo jumbo practiced by witchdoctors with demonic powers who perpetuated superstition. Yet, its practice survived. Today, as the African continent grapples with an HIV/AIDS epidemic of crisis proportion, millions of sick people who are either too poor or too distant to access modern health care are proving that traditional healers are an invaluable resource in the fight against AIDS.

Of the world's estimated 40 million people currently infected by HIV, 70 percent live in sub-Saharan Africa, and the vast majority of children left orphaned by AIDS are African. From the 1980s onward, as Africa became synonymous with the rapid spread of HIV/AIDS, a number of prevention programs involved traditional healers. My initial research in South Africa's KwaZulu-Natal province—where it is estimated that 36 percent of the population is HIV infected—revealed that traditional Zulu healers were regularly consulted for the treatment of sexually transmitted disease (STD). I found that such diseases, along with HIV/AIDS, were usually attributed to transgressions of taboos related to birth, pregnancy, marriage, and death. Moreover, these diseases were often understood within a framework of pollution and contagion, and like most serious illnesses, ultimately believed to have their causal roots in witchcraft.

In the course of my research, I investigated a pioneer program in STD and HIV education for traditional healers in the province. The program aimed to provide basic biomedical knowledge about the various modes of disease transmission, the means available for prevention, the diagnosing of symptoms, the keeping of records, and the making of patient referrals to local clinics and hospitals.

Interviews with the healers showed that many maintained a deep suspicion of modern medicine. They perceived AIDS education as a one-way street intended to press them into formal health structures and convince them of the superiority of modern medicine. Yet, today, few of the 6,000-plus KwaZulu-Natal

Medical anthropologist Suzanne Leclerc-Madlala visits with "Doctor" Koloko in KwaZulu-Natal, South Africa. This Zulu traditional healer proudly displays her official AIDS training certificate.

CONTINUED

CONTINUED

healers who have been trained in AIDS education say they would opt for less collaboration; most want to have more.

Treatments by Zulu healers for HIV/AIDS often take the form of infusions of bitter herbs to "cleanse" the body, strengthen the blood, and remove misfortune and "pollution." Some treatments provide effective relief from common ailments associated with AIDS such as itchy skin rashes, oral thrush, persistent diarrhea, and general debility. Indigenous plants such as *unwele (Sutherlandia frutescens)* and African potato *(Hypoxis hemerocallidea)* are well-known traditional medicines that have proven immuno-boosting properties.

Both have recently become available in modern pharmacies packaged in tablet form. With modern anti-retroviral treatments still well beyond the reach of most South Africans, indigenous medicines that can delay or alleviate some of the suffering caused by AIDS are proving to be valuable and popular treatments.

Knowledge about potentially infectious bodily fluids has led healers to change some of their practices. Where porcupine quills were once used to give a type of indigenous injection, patients are now advised to bring their own sewing needles to consultations. Patients provide their own individual razor blades for making incisions on their skin, where previously healers reused the same razor on many clients. Some healers claim they have given up the practice of biting clients' skin to remove foreign objects from the body. It is not uncommon today, especially in urban centers like Durban, to find healers proudly displaying AIDS training certificates in their inner-city "surgeries" where they don white jackets and wear protective latex gloves.

Politics and controversy have dogged South Africa's official response to HIV/AIDS. But back home in the waddle-and-daub, animal-skin-draped herbariums and divining huts of traditional healers, the politics of AIDS holds little relevance. Here the sick and dying are coming in droves to be treated by healers who have been part and parcel of community life (and death) since time immemorial. In many cases traditional healers have transformed their homes into hospices for AIDS patients. Because of the strong stigma that still plagues the disease, those with AIDS symptoms are often abandoned or sometimes chased away from their homes by family members. They seek refuge with healers who provide them with comfort in their final days. Healers' homes are also becoming orphanages as healers respond to what has been called the "third wave" of AIDS destruction: the growing legions of orphaned children.

The practice of traditional healing in Africa is adapting to the changing face of health and illness in the context of HIV/AIDS. But those who are suffering go to traditional healers not only in search of relief for physical symptoms. They go to learn about the ultimate cause of their disease—something other than the immediate cause of a sexually transmitted "germ" or "virus." They go to find answers to the "why me and not him" questions, the "why now" and "why this." As with most traditional healing systems worldwide, healing among the Zulu and most all African ethnic groups cannot be separated from the spiritual concerns of the individual and the cosmological beliefs of the community at large. Traditional healers help to restore a sense of balance between the individual and the community, on one hand, and between the individual and the cosmos, or ancestors, on the other hand. They provide health care that is personalized, culturally appropriate, holistic, and tailored to meet the needs and expectations of the patient. In many ways it is a far more satisfactory form of healing than that offered by modern medicine.

Traditional healing in Africa is flourishing in the era of AIDS, and understanding why this is so requires a shift in the conceptual framework by which we understand, explain, and interpret health. Anthropological methods and its comparative and holistic perspective can facilitate, like no other discipline, the type of understanding that is urgently needed to address the AIDS crisis.

Adapted from: Leclerc-Madlala, S. (2002). Bodies and politics: Healing rituals in the democratic South Africa. In V. Faure (Ed.), Les cahiers de 'l'IFAS, *no. 2. Johannesburg: The French Institute. (Leclerc-Madlala now works for USAID.)*

Anthropology's Comparative Method

The end product of anthropological research, if properly carried out, is a coherent statement about a people that provides an explanatory framework for understanding the beliefs, behavior, or biology of those who have been studied. And this, in turn, is what permits the anthropologist to frame broader hypotheses about human beliefs, behavior, and biology. A single instance of any phenomenon is generally insufficient for supporting a plausible hypothesis. Without some basis for comparison, the hypothesis grounded in a single case may be no more than a particular historical coincidence. On the other hand, a single case may be enough to cast doubt on, if not refute, a theory that had previously been held to be valid. For example, the discovery in 1948 that Aborigines living in Australia's northern Arnhem Land put in an average workday of less than 6 hours, while living well above a bare-sufficiency level, was enough to call into question the widely accepted notion that food-foraging peoples are so preoccupied with finding scarce food that they lack time for any of life's more pleasurable activities. The observations made in the Arnhem Land study have since been confirmed many times over in various parts of the world.

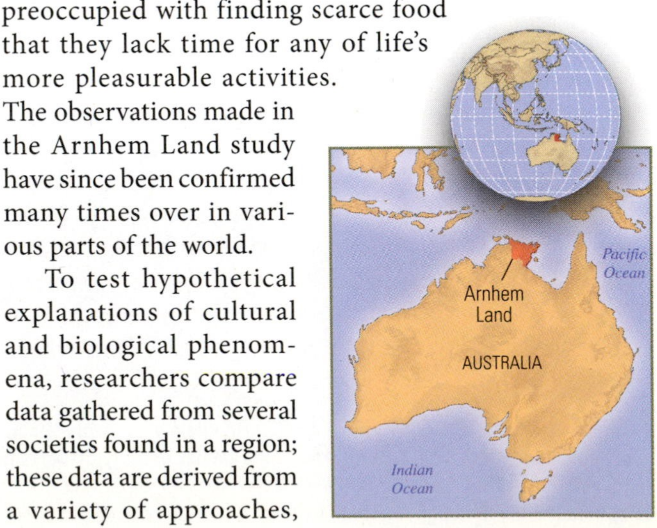

To test hypothetical explanations of cultural and biological phenomena, researchers compare data gathered from several societies found in a region; these data are derived from a variety of approaches, including archaeology, biology, linguistics, history, and ethnography. Carefully controlled comparison provides a broader basis for drawing general conclusions about humans than does the study of a single culture or population.

Ideally, theories in anthropology are generated from worldwide comparisons or comparisons across species or through time. The cross-cultural researcher examines a global sample of societies in order to discover whether hypotheses proposed to explain cultural phenomena or biological variation are universally applicable. The cross-cultural researcher depends upon data gathered by other scholars as well as his or her own. These data can be in the form of written accounts, artifacts and skeletal collections housed in museums, published descriptions of these collections, or recently constructed databases that allow for cross-species comparisons of the molecular structure of specific genes or proteins.

Questions of Ethics

The kinds of research carried out by anthropologists, and the settings within which they work, raise a number of important moral questions about the potential uses and abuses of our knowledge. In the early years of the discipline, many anthropologists documented traditional cultures they assumed would disappear due to disease, warfare, or acculturation imposed by colonialism, growing state power, or international market expansion. Some worked as government anthropologists, gathering data used to formulate policies concerning indigenous peoples or even to help predict the behavior of enemies during wartime. After the colonial era ended in the 1960s, anthropologists began to establish a code of ethics to ensure their research did not harm the groups they studied.

Today, this code grapples with serious questions: Who will utilize our findings and for what purposes? Who decides what research questions are asked? Who, if anyone, will profit from the research? For example, in the case of research on an ethnic or religious minority whose values may be at odds with the dominant mainstream society, will government or corporate interests use anthropological data to suppress that group? And what of traditional communities around the world? Who is to decide what changes should, or should not, be introduced for community "betterment"? And who defines what constitutes betterment—the community, a national government, or an international agency like the World Health Organization? What are the limits of cultural relativism when a traditional practice is considered a human rights abuse globally?

Today, many universities require that anthropologists, like other researchers, communicate in advance the nature, purpose, and potential impact of the planned study to individuals who provide information—and obtain their **informed consent,** or formal recorded agreement to participate in the research. Of course, this requirement is easier to fulfill in some societies or cultures than in others. When it is a challenge to obtain informed consent, or even impossible to precisely explain the meaning and purpose of this concept and its actual consequences, anthropologists may protect the identities of individuals, families, or even entire communities by altering their names and locations. For example, when Dutch anthropologist Anton Blok studied the Sicilian mafia, he did not obtain the informed consent of this violent secret group but opted not to disclose their real identities.[10]

Anthropologists deal with matters that are private and sensitive, including things that individuals would prefer not to have generally known about them. How does one write about such important but delicate issues and at the same time protect the privacy of the individuals who have shared their stories?

The dilemma facing anthropologists is also recognized in the preamble to the code of ethics of the American Anthropological Association (AAA), which was formalized in 1971 and revised in 1998 and again in 2009. This document outlines the various ethical responsibilities and moral obligations of anthropologists, including this central maxim: "Anthropological researchers must do everything in their power to ensure that their research does not harm the safety, dignity, or privacy of the people with whom they work, conduct research, or perform other professional activities." The recent healthy round of debates regarding this code has focused on the potential ethical breaches if anthropologists undertake classified contract work for the military, as some have in Afghanistan, or work for corporations. Some argue that in both cases the required transparency to the people studied cannot be maintained under these circumstances.

The AAA ethics statement is an educational document that lays out the rules and ideals applicable to anthropologists in all the subdisciplines. While the AAA has no legal authority, it does issue policy statements on research ethics questions as they come up. For example, recently the AAA recommended that field notes from medical settings should be protected and not subject to subpoena in malpractice lawsuits. This honors the ethical imperative to protect the privacy of individuals who have shared their stories with anthropologists.

---

[10] Blok, A. (1974). *The mafia of a Sicilian village 1860–1960: A study of violent peasant entrepreneurs.* New York: Harper & Row.

informed consent Formal recorded agreement to participate in research; federally mandated for all research in the United States and Europe.

The consumption habits of people in more temperate parts of the world are threatening the lifestyle of people from circumpolar regions. As global warming melts the polar ice caps, traditional ways of life, such as building an igloo, may become impossible. This Inuit man—in Iqaluit, the capital of the Canadian territory of Nunavut—may not be able to construct an igloo much longer. Therefore, the Inuit people consider global warming a human rights issue.

Emerging technologies have ethical implications that impact anthropological inquiry. For example, the ability to sequence and patent particular genes has led to debates about who has the right to hold a patent—the individuals from whom the particular genes were obtained or the researcher who studies the genes? Given the radical changes taking place in the world today, a scientific understanding of the past has never been more important. Do ancient remains belong to the scientist, to the people living in the region under scientific investigation, or to whoever happens to have possession of them? Market forces convert these remains into very expensive collectibles and lead to systematic mining of archaeological and fossil sites. Collaboration between local people and scientists not only preserves the ancient remains from market forces but also honors the connections of indigenous people to the places and remains under study.

To sort out the answers to the all of the above questions, anthropologists recognize that they have special obligations to three sets of people: those whom they study, those who fund the research, and those in the profession who rely on published findings to increase our collective knowledge. Because fieldwork requires a relationship of trust between fieldworkers and the community in which they work, the anthropologist's first responsibility clearly is to the people who have shared their stories and the greater community. Everything possible must be done to protect their physical, social, and psychological welfare and to honor their dignity and privacy.

This task is frequently complex. For example, telling the story of a people gives information both to relief agencies who might help them and to others who might take advantage of them. While anthropologists regard a people's right to maintain their own culture as a basic premise, any connections with outsiders can endanger the cultural identity of the community being studied. To surmount these obstacles, anthropologists frequently collaborate with and contribute to the communities in which they are working, allowing the people being studied to have some say about how their stories are told.

globalization Worldwide interconnectedness, evidenced in global movements of natural resources, trade goods, human labor, finance capital, information, and infectious diseases.

Anthropology and Globalization

A holistic perspective and a long-term commitment to understanding the human species in all its variety are the essence of anthropology. Thus anthropology is well equipped to grapple with an issue that has overriding importance for all of us at the beginning of the 21st century: **globalization.** This term refers to worldwide interconnectedness, evidenced in global movements of natural resources, trade goods, human labor, finance capital, information, and infectious diseases. Although worldwide travel, trade relations, and information flow have existed for several centuries, the pace and magnitude of these

Globalscape

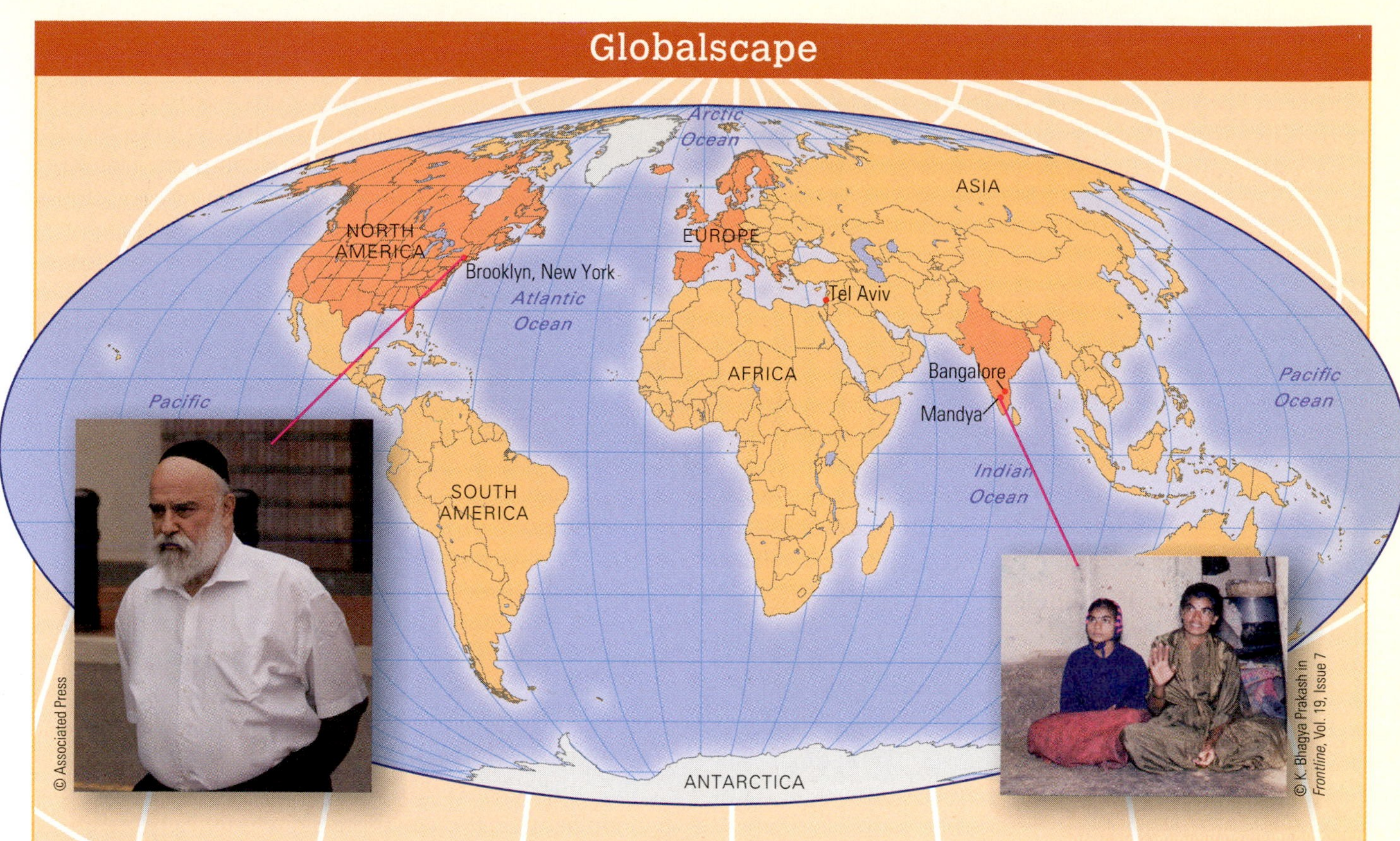

© Associated Press

© K. Bhagya Prakash in *Frontline*, Vol. 19, Issue 7

A Global Body Shop?
Lakshmamma, a mother in southern India's rural village of Holalu, near Mandya, has sold one of her kidneys for about 30,000 rupees ($650). This is far below the average going rate of $6,000 per kidney in the global organ transplant business. But the broker took his commission, and corrupt officials needed to be paid as well. Although India passed a law in 1994 prohibiting the buying and selling of human organs, the business is booming. In Europe and North America, kidney transplants can cost $200,000 or more, plus the waiting list for donor kidneys is long, and dialysis is expensive. Thus "transplant tourism," in India and several other countries, caters to affluent patients in search of "fresh" kidneys to be harvested from poor people like Lakshmamma, pictured here with her daughter.

The global trade network in organs has been documented by Israeli filmmaker Nick Rosen, who sold his own kidney for $15,000 through a broker in Tel Aviv to a Brooklyn, New York, dialysis patient. Rosen explained to the physicians at Mt. Sinai Hospital in New York City that he was donating his kidney altruistically. Medical anthropologist Nancy Scheper-Hughes has taken on the criminal and medical aspects of global organ trafficking for the past twenty years or so. She also co-founded Organs Watch in Berkeley, California, an organization working to stop the illegal traffic in organs.

The well-publicized arrest of Brooklyn-based organ broker Levy Izhak Rosenbaum in July 2009—part of an FBI sting operation that also led to the arrest of forty-three other individuals, including several public officials in New Jersey—represents progress made in combating illegal trafficking of body parts. According to Scheper-Hughes, "Rosenbaum wasn't the tip of an iceberg, but the end of something."[a] International crackdowns and changes in local laws are beginning to bring down these illegal global networks.

Global Twister Considering that $650 is a fortune in a poor village like Holalu, does medical globalization benefit or exploit people like Lakshmamma who are looked upon as human commodities? What factors account for the different values placed on the two donated kidneys?

[a] http://www.npr.org/templates/story/story.php?storyId=106997368.

long-distance exchanges have picked up enormously in recent decades; the Internet, in particular, has greatly expanded information exchange capacities.

The powerful forces driving globalization are technological innovations, cost differences among countries, faster knowledge transfers, and increased trade and financial integration among countries. Touching almost everybody's life on the planet, globalization is about economics as much as politics, and it changes human relations and ideas as well as our natural environments. Even geographically remote communities are quickly becoming interdependent through globalization.

Doing research in all corners of the world, anthropologists are confronted with the impact of globalization on human communities wherever they are located. As participant observers, they describe and try to explain how individuals and organizations respond to the massive changes confronting them. Anthropologists may also find out how local responses sometimes change the global flows directed at them. Dramatically increasing every year, globalization can be a two-edged sword. It may generate economic growth and prosperity, but it also undermines long-established institutions. Generally, globalization has brought significant gains to higher-educated groups in wealthier countries, while doing little to boost developing countries and actually contributing to the erosion of traditional cultures. Upheavals due to globalization are key causes for rising levels of ethnic and religious conflict throughout the world.

Since all of us now live in a global village, we can no longer afford the luxury of ignoring our neighbors, no matter how distant they may seem. In this age of globalization, anthropology may not only provide humanity with useful insights concerning diversity, but it may also assist us in avoiding or overcoming significant problems born of that diversity. In countless social arenas, from schools to businesses to hospitals to emergency centers, anthropologists have done cross-cultural research that makes it possible for educators, businesspeople, doctors, and humanitarians to do their work more effectively.

For example, in the United States today, discrimination based on notions of race continues to be a serious issue affecting economic, political, and social relations. Far from being the biological reality it is supposed to be, anthropologists have shown that the concept of race (and the classification of human groups into higher and lower racial types) emerged in the 18th century as an ideological vehicle for justifying European dominance over Africans and American Indians. In fact, differences of skin color are simply surface adaptations to different climactic zones and have nothing to do with physical or mental capabilities. Indeed, geneticists find far more biologic variation *within* any given human population than *among* them. In short, human "races" are divisive categories based on prejudice, false ideas of differences, and erroneous notions of the superiority of one's own group. Given the importance of this issue, race and other aspects of biologic variation will be discussed further in upcoming sections of the text.

A second example of the impact of globalization involves the issue of same-sex marriage. In 1989, Denmark became the first country to enact a comprehensive set of legal protections for same-sex couples, known as the Registered Partnership Act. At this writing, more than a half-dozen other countries and a growing number of individual U.S. states have passed similar laws, variously named, and numerous countries around the world are considering or have passed legislation providing people in homosexual unions the benefits and protections afforded by marriage.[11] In some societies—including Belgium, Canada, the Netherlands, Norway, South Africa, Spain, and Sweden—same-sex marriages are considered socially acceptable and allowed by law, even though opposite-sex marriages are far more common. The same is true for several U.S. states including Connecticut, Iowa, Massachusetts, New Hampshire, and Vermont.

As individuals, countries, and states struggle to define the boundaries of legal protections they will grant to same-sex couples, the anthropological perspective on marriage is useful. Anthropologists have documented same-sex marriages in human societies in various parts of the world, where they are regarded as acceptable under appropriate circumstances. Homosexual behavior occurs in the animal world just as it does among humans.[12] The key difference between people and other animals is that human societies possess beliefs regarding homosexual behavior, just as they do for heterosexual behavior. An understanding of global variation in marriage patterns and sexual behavior does not dictate that one pattern is more right than another. It simply illustrates that all human societies define the boundaries for social relationships.

A final example relates to the common confusion of *nation* with *state*. Anthropology makes an important distinction between these two: States are politically organized territories that are internationally recognized, whereas nations are socially organized bodies of people who share ethnicity—a common origin, language, and cultural heritage. For example, the Kurds constitute a nation, but their homeland is divided among several states: Iran, Iraq, Turkey, and Syria. The international boundaries among these states were drawn up after World War I, with little regard for the region's ethnic groups or nations. Similar processes have taken place throughout the world, especially in Asia and Africa, often making political conditions in these countries inherently unstable. As we will see in later chapters, states and nations rarely coincide—nations being split among different states, and states typically being controlled by members of one nation who commonly use their control to gain access to the land, resources, and labor of other nationalities within the state. Most of the armed conflicts in the world today, such as the many-layered conflicts in the Caucasus Mountains of Russia's

---

[11] Merin, Y. (2002). *Equality for same-sex couples: The legal recognition of gay partnerships in Europe and the United States*. Chicago: University of Chicago Press; "Court says same-sex marriage is a right." (2004, February 5). *San Francisco Chronicle;* current overviews and updates on the global status of same-sex marriage are posted on the Internet by the Partners Task Force for Gay & Lesbian Couples at www.buddybuddy.com.

[12] Kirkpatrick, R. C. (2000). The evolution of human homosexual behavior. *Current Anthropology 41,* 384.

southern borderlands, are of this sort and are not mere acts of "tribalism" or "terrorism," as commonly asserted.

As these examples show, ignorance about other cultures and their ways is a cause of serious problems throughout the world, especially now that our interactions and interdependence have been transformed by global information exchange and transportation advances. Anthropology offers a way of looking at and understanding the world's peoples—insights that are nothing less than basic skills for survival in this age of globalization.

Questions for Reflection

1. Anthropology uses a holistic approach to explain all aspects of human beliefs, behavior, and biology. How might anthropology challenge your personal perspective on the following questions: Where did we come from? Why do we act in certain ways? Does the example of legalized paid surrogacy, featured in the chapter opener, challenge your worldview?

2. From the holistic anthropological perspective, humans have one leg in culture and the other in nature. Are there examples from your life that illustrate the interconnectedness of human biology and culture?

3. Globalization can be described as a two-edged sword. How does it foster growth and destruction simultaneously?

4. The textbook definitions of *state* and *nation* are based on scientific distinctions between both organizational types. However, this distinction is commonly lost in everyday language. Consider, for instance, the names *United States of America* and *United Nations.* How does confusing the terms contribute to political conflict?

5. The Biocultural Connection in this chapter contrasts different cultural perspectives on brain death, while the Original Study features a discussion about traditional Zulu healers and their role in dealing with AIDS victims. What do these two accounts suggest about the role of applied anthropology in dealing with cross-cultural health issues around the world?

Suggested Readings

Bonvillain, N. (2007). *Language, culture, and communication: The meaning of messages* (5th ed.). Upper Saddle River, NJ: Prentice-Hall.

An up-to-date text on language and communication in a cultural context.

Fagan, B. M. (2005). *Archaeology: A brief introduction* (9th ed.). New York: Longman.

This primer offers an overview of archaeological theory and methodology, from field survey techniques to excavation to analysis of materials.

Kedia, S., & Van Willigen, J. (2005). *Applied anthropology: Domains of application.* New York: Praeger.

Compelling essays by prominent scholars on the potential, accomplishments, and methods of applied anthropology in domains including development, agriculture, environment, health and medicine, nutrition, population displacement and resettlement, business and industry, education, and aging. The contributors show how anthropology can be used to address today's social, economic, health, and technical challenges.

Marks, J. (2009). *Why I am not a scientist: Anthropology and modern knowledge.* Berkeley: University of California Press.

With his inimitable wit and deep philosophical insights, biological anthropologist Jonathan Marks shows the immense power of bringing an anthropological perspective to the culture of science.

Peacock, J. L. (2002). *The anthropological lens: Harsh light, soft focus* (2nd ed.). New York: Cambridge University Press.

This lively and innovative book gives the reader a good understanding of the diversity of activities undertaken by cultural anthropologists, while at the same time identifying the unifying themes that hold the discipline together. Additions to the second edition include such topics as globalization, gender, and postmodernism.

Challenge Issue The genetics revolution has given new meaning to human identity. Police identify criminals through DNA fingerprinting and maintain DNA databases of convicts and suspects for solving crimes in the future. Others wrongfully imprisoned for many years have been freed after genetic testing. But the thornier issue in genetics is whether genes can predispose an individual to criminal behavior. Do our genes determine our actions? Some scientists argue that biology controls behavior because of hints found in the genome, the complete sequence of human DNA. These new theories are dangerously similar to those proposed in the late 19th and early 20th centuries, as they do not take into account the social and political environments in which genes are ultimately expressed. As we learn more about the human genetic code, will we reshape our understanding of what it means to be human? How much of our lives are dictated by the structure of DNA? And what will be the social consequences of depicting people as beings programmed by their DNA? Individuals and societies can answer these challenging questions using an anthropological perspective, which emphasizes the connections between human biology and culture.

CHAPTER 2

Genetics and Evolution

Chapter Preview

What Is Evolution?

Although all living creatures ultimately share a common ancestry, they have come to differ from one another through the process of evolution. Biological evolution refers to genetic change over successive generations. The process of change is characterized by descent with modification, as descendant populations diverge from ancestral ones. As a population's genetic variation changes from one generation to another, genetic change is reflected in visible differences between organisms. With sufficient genetic change, a new species can appear. Thus, the process of evolution provides a mechanism to account for the diversity of life on earth.

What Is the Molecular Basis of Evolution?

Scientists began to understand the mechanics of heredity and how evolution works in populations long before molecular biologists identified the genetic basis of evolutionary change. With the discovery of DNA (deoxyribonucleic acid) molecules in 1953, scientists came to understand how genetic information is stored in the chromosomes of a cell. Genes, specific portions of DNA molecules, direct the synthesis of the protein molecules upon which all living organisms depend. Through the process of biological reproduction, each of us inherits a combination of genes from our biological parents that creates a unique new individual.

What Are the Forces Responsible for Evolution?

Four evolutionary forces—mutation, genetic drift, gene flow, and natural selection—account for change in the genetic composition of populations. Random mutations introduce new genetic variation into individual organisms. Gene flow (the introduction of new gene variants from other populations), genetic drift (random changes in frequencies of gene variants in a population), and natural selection shape genetic variation at the population level. Natural selection is the mechanism of evolution that results in adaptive change, favoring individuals with genetic variants relatively better adapted to the conditions of local environments.

The mythology of most peoples includes a story explaining the appearance of humans on earth. The account of creation recorded in Genesis in the Bible, for example, explains human origins. A vastly different example, serving the same function, is the traditional belief of the Nez Perce, American Indians native to eastern Oregon and Idaho. For the Nez Perce, humanity is the creation of Coyote, a trickster-transformer inhabiting the earth before humans. Coyote chased the giant beaver monster Wishpoosh over the earth, leaving a trail to form the Columbia River. When Coyote caught Wishpoosh, he killed him, dragged his body to the riverbank, and cut it into pieces, each body part transforming into one of the various peoples of this region. The Nez Perce were made from Wishpoosh's head, thus conferring on them great intelligence and horsemanship.[1]

Creation stories depict the relationship between humans and the rest of the natural world, sometimes reflecting a deep connection among people, other animals, and the earth. In the traditional Nez Perce creation story, groups of people derive from specific body parts—each possessing a special talent and relationship with a particular animal. By contrast, the story of creation in the Book of Genesis emphasizes human uniqueness and the concept of time. Creation is depicted as a series of actions occurring over the course of six days. God's final act of creation is to fashion the first human from the earth in his own image before the seventh day of rest.

This linear creation story from Genesis—shared by Jews, Christians, and Muslims—differs from the cyclical creation stories characteristic of Hinduism, which emphasize reincarnation and the cycle of life, including creation and destruction. For Hindus, the diversity of life on earth comes from three gods—Lord Brahma, the creator; Lord Vishnu, the preserver; and Lord Shiva, the destroyer and re-creator—all of whom are part of the Supreme One. When Lord Brahma sleeps the world is destroyed, then re-created again when he awakes. Similarly, according to the Intelligent Design movement—proposed by a conservative think tank called the Discovery Institute in Seattle, Washington—creation is the result of some sort of supreme intelligent being.

Like creation stories, evolution, the major organizing principle of the biological sciences, accounts for the diversity of life on earth. Theories of evolution provide explanations for how it works and for how the variety of organisms, both in the past and today, came into being. However, evolution differs from creation stories in that it explains the diversity of life in consistent scientific language, using testable ideas (hypotheses). Contemporary scientists make comparisons among living organisms to test hypotheses drawn from evolutionary theory. Through their research, scientists have deciphered the molecular basis of evolution and the mechanisms through which evolutionary forces work on populations of organisms. Though scientific theories of evolution treat humans as biological organisms, at the same time historical and cultural processes also shape evolutionary theory and our understanding of it.

The Classification of Living Things

Examining the development of biology and its central concept, evolution, provides an excellent example of the ways that historical and cultural processes can shape scientific thought. As the exploration of foreign lands by European seafarers, including Columbus, changed the prevailing European approach to the natural world, the discovery of new life forms challenged the previously held notion of fixed, unchanging life on earth. As well, the invention of instruments, such as the microscope to study the previously invisible interior of cells, led to new appreciation of life's diversity.

Before this time, Europeans organized living things and inanimate objects alike into a ladder or hierarchy known as the Great Chain of Being—an approach to nature first developed by the great philosopher Aristotle in ancient Greece over 2,000 years ago. The categories were based upon visible similarities, and one member of each category was considered its "primate" (from the Latin *primus*), meaning the first or best of the group. For example, the primate of rocks was the diamond, and the primate of birds was the eagle, and so forth. Humans were at the very top of the ladder, just below the angels.

This classificatory system was in place until Carl von Linné (using the Latin-form name Carolus Linnaeus) developed the *Systema Naturae*, or system of nature, in the 18th century to classify the living things that were being brought back to Europe on seafaring vessels from all parts of the globe. Linnaeus's compendium reflected a new understanding of life on earth and of the place of humanity among the animals.

Linnaeus noted the similarity among humans, monkeys, and apes, classifying them together as **primates.** Not the first or the best of the animals on earth, primates are just one of several kinds of **mammal,** animals having body hair or fur who suckle or nurse their young. In other

[1] Clark, E. E. (1966). *Indian legends of the Pacific Northwest* (p. 174). Berkeley: University of California Press.

primate The group of mammals that includes lemurs, lorises, tarsiers, monkeys, apes, and humans.

mammal The class of vertebrate animals distinguished by bodies covered with fur, self-regulating temperature, and, in females, milk-producing mammary glands.

Lindauer Bilderbogen no 5, edited by Friedrich Boer. Jan Thorbecke Verlag. Sigmaringen, West Germany

A professor of medicine and botany in Sweden, Carolus Linnaeus, who created the first comprehensive system of living things, also prepared and prescribed medicinal plants, as did other physicians of the time. He arranged for his students to join the major European voyages, such as Captain James Cook's first round-the-world voyage, so they could bring back new medicinal plants and other life forms. Through his observation of the bloom times of some plant species, Linnaeus proposed a "flower clock" that could show the time of day according to whether blossoms of particular species were open or shut.

words, Linnaeus classified living things into a series of categories that are progressively more inclusive on the basis of internal and external visual similarities. **Species**, the smallest working units in biological classificatory systems, are reproductively isolated populations or groups of populations capable of interbreeding to produce fertile offspring. Species are subdivisions of a larger, more inclusive group, called a **genus** (plural, **genera**). Humans, for example, are classified in the genus *Homo* and species *sapiens*. This binomial nomenclature, or two-part naming system, mirrors the naming patterns in many European societies where individuals possess two names—one personal and the other reflecting their membership in a larger group of related individuals.

Linnaeus based his classificatory system on the following criteria:

1. *Body structure:* A Guernsey cow and a Holstein cow are the same species because, unlike a cow and a horse, they have identical body structure.
2. *Body function:* Cows and horses give birth to live young. Although they are different species, they are closer than either cows or horses are to chickens, which lay eggs and have no mammary glands.
3. *Sequence of bodily growth:* At the time of birth—or hatching out of the egg—young cows and chickens resemble their parents in their body plan. They are therefore more closely related to each other than either one is to the frog, whose tadpoles undergo a series of changes before attaining the basic adult form.

Modern **taxonomy,** or the science of classification (from the Greek for naming divisions), while retaining the structure of the Linnaean system, is based on more than body structure, function, and growth. Today, scientists also compare protein structure and genetic material to construct the relationships among living things. Such molecular comparisons can even be aimed at parasites, bacteria, and viruses, allowing scientists to classify or trace the origins of particular diseases, such as swine flu, SARS (sudden acute respiratory syndrome), or HIV (human immunodeficiency virus). An emphasis on genetics rather than morphology has led to a reworking of taxonomic designation in the human family, among others, as is described in Table 2.1. Alternative taxonomies based on genetics compared to body form in the primate order will be discussed in detail in the next chapter.

Cross-species comparisons identify anatomical features of similar function as **analogies,** while anatomical features that have evolved from a common ancestral feature are called **homologies.** For example, the hand of a human and the wing of a bat evolved from the forelimb of a common ancestor, though they have acquired different functions: The human hand and bat wing are homologous structures. During their early embryonic development, homologous structures arise in a similar fashion and pass through similar stages before differentiating. The wings of birds and butterflies look similar and have a similar function (flying): These are analogous, but not homologous, structures because they do not follow the same

species The smallest working units in the system of classification. Among living organisms, species are populations or groups of populations capable of interbreeding and producing fertile viable offspring.

genus (genera, pl.) In the system of plant and animal classification, a group of like species.

taxonomy The science of classification.

analogies In biology, structures possessed by different organisms that are superficially similar due to similar function, without sharing a common developmental pathway or structure.

homologies In biology, structures possessed by two different organisms that arise in similar fashion and pass through similar stages during embryonic development though they may possess different functions.

Table 2.1 Classification of Humans

Taxonomic Category	Category to Which Humans Belong	Biological Features Used to Define and Place Humans in This Category
Kingdom	Animalia	Humans are animals. We do not make our own food (as plants do) but depend upon the consumption of other organisms.
Phylum	Chordata	Humans are chordates. We have a **notochord** (a rodlike structure of cartilage) and nerve chord running along the back of the body as well as gill slits in the embryonic stage of our life cycle.
Subphylum*	Vertebrata	Humans are vertebrates possessing an internal backbone, with a segmented spinal column.
Class	Mammalia	Humans are mammals, warm-blooded animals covered with fur, possessing mammary glands for nourishing their young after birth.
Order	Primates	Humans are primates, a kind of mammal with a generalized anatomy, relatively large brains, and grasping hands and feet.
Suborder	Anthropoidea	Humans are anthropoids—social, daylight-active primates. (An alternative suborder taxonomic system is discussed in Chapter 3.)
Superfamily	Hominoidea	Humans are hominoids with broad flexible shoulders and no tail. Chimps, bonobos, gorillas, orangutans, gibbons, and siamangs are also hominoids.
Family Subfamily	Hominidae Homininae	Humans are hominids. We are hominoids from Africa, genetically more closely related to chimps, bonobos, and gorillas than to hominoids from Asia. Some scientists use "hominid" to refer only to humans and their ancestors. Others include chimps and gorillas in this category, using the subfamily "hominin" to distinguish humans and their ancestors from chimps and gorillas and their ancestors. (The alternative taxonomies at the subfamily level are explored further in Chapter 3.)
Genus Species	*Homo sapiens*	Humans have large brains and rely on cultural adaptations to survive. Ancestral fossils are placed in this genus and species depending upon details of the skull shape and interpretations of their cultural capabilities. Genus and species names are always italicized.

*Most categories can be expanded or narrowed by adding the prefix "sub" or "super." A family could thus be part of a superfamily and in turn contain two or more subfamilies.

Visual Counterpoint

An example of homology: The same bones of the mammalian forelimb differentiate into the human arm and hand and the bat wing. These structures have the same embryonic origin but come to take on different functions.

Visual Counterpoint

An example of analogy: The wings of birds and butterflies are both used for flight and share similar appearance due to their common function. However, the course of their development and their structure differ.

developmental sequence. Only homologies are relevant for constructing evolutionary relationships.

Through careful comparison and analysis of organisms, Linnaeus and his successors have grouped species into genera and into even larger groups such as families, orders, classes, phyla, and kingdoms. Each taxonomic level is distinguished by characteristics shared by all the organisms in the group.

The Discovery of Evolution

Just as European seafaring and exploration brought about an awareness of the diversity of life across the earth, construction and mining, which came with the onset of industrialization in Europe, led to an awareness of change in life forms through time. As work like cutting railway lines or quarrying limestone became commonplace, fossils, or preserved remains, of past life forms were brought into the light.

At first, the fossilized remains of elephants and giant saber-toothed tigers in Europe were interpreted according to religious doctrine. For example, the early 19th-century theory of *catastrophism*, championed by French paleontologist and anatomist Georges Cuvier, invoked natural events like the supposed Great Flood chronicled in Genesis to account for the disappearance of these species in European lands. Another French scientist, Jean-Baptiste Lamarck, was among the first to suggest a mechanism to account for diversity among living creatures that did not rely upon scriptures. His theory of the "inheritance of acquired characteristics" proposed that behavior brought about changes in organisms' forms. The famed example was that the first giraffe gained its long neck by stretching to reach the leaves on the highest treetop branches and in turn passed this acquired long neck onto its offspring. While Lamarck's theory has long since been disproved as a mechanism to account for biological change, his proposal seems likely as a change mechanism for cultural inheritance, and he is credited with making the connection between organisms and the environments they inhabit.

During this same time, British geologist Sir Charles Lyell championed *uniformitarianism*—a theory that accounts for variation in the earth's surface. According to Lyell, these variations are the result of gradual changes over extremely long periods of time; although the changes are not obvious at the moment, they are caused by the same natural processes, such as erosion, that are immediately observable. Because the time span required for uniformitarianism is so long, this theory was incompatible with literal interpretations of the Bible, in which the earth is believed to be only about 6,000 years old.

With industrialization, however, Europeans became generally more comfortable with the ideas of change and progress. In hindsight, it seems inevitable that someone would hit upon the scientific concept of evolution. So it was that, by the start of the 19th century, many naturalists

notochord A rodlike structure of cartilage that, in vertebrates, is replaced by the vertebral column.

had come to accept the idea that life had evolved, even though they were not clear about how it happened. It remained for Charles Darwin (1809–1882) to formulate a theory that has withstood the test of time.

Grandson of Erasmus Darwin (a physician, scientist, poet, and originator of a theory of evolution himself), Charles Darwin began studying medicine at the University of Edinburgh, Scotland. Finding himself unfit for this profession, he went to Christ's College, Cambridge University, to study theology. He then left Cambridge to take the position of companion to British Royal Navy Captain Robert FitzRoy on the *H.M.S. Beagle*, which was about to embark on a scientific expedition to explore various poorly mapped parts of the world. The voyage lasted for almost five years, taking Darwin along the coasts of South America, to the Galapagos Islands, across the Pacific to Australia, and then across the Indian and Atlantic Oceans to South America before returning to England in 1836.

Observing the tremendous diversity of living creatures as well as the astounding fossils of extinct animals, Darwin began to note that species varied according to the environments they inhabited. The observations he made on this voyage, his readings of Lyell's *Principles of Geology* (1830), and the arguments he had with the orthodox and dogmatic FitzRoy all contributed to the ideas culminating in Darwin's most famous book, *On the Origin of Species*. This book, published in 1859, over twenty years after he returned from his voyage, described a theory of evolution accounting for change within species and for the emergence of new species in purely naturalistic terms.

Darwin added observations from English farm life and intellectual thought to the ideas he began to develop on the *Beagle*. He paid particular attention to domesticated animals and farmers' practice of breeding their stock to select for specific traits. Darwin's theoretical breakthrough derived from an essay by economist Thomas Malthus (1766–1834), which warned of the potential consequences of increased human population, particularly of the poor. Malthus observed that animal populations, unlike human populations, remained stable, due to an overproduction of young followed by a large proportion of animal offspring not surviving to maturity. Darwin wrote in his autobiography, "It at once struck me that under these circumstances favourable variations would tend to be preserved, and unfavourable ones to be destroyed. The results of this would be the formation of a new species. Here, then I had at last got a theory by which to work."[2]

[2] Darwin, C. (1887). *Autobiography*. Reprinted in F. Darwin (Ed.). (1902), *The life and letters of Charles Darwin*. London: John Murray.

natural selection The evolutionary process through which factors in the environment exert pressure, favoring some individuals over others to produce the next generation.

Today Darwinian **natural selection** can be defined as the evolutionary process through which factors in the environment exert pressure, favoring some individuals over others to produce the next generation. Darwin combined his observations into the theory of evolution as follows: All species display a range of variation, and all have the ability to expand beyond their means of subsistence. It follows that, in their "struggle for existence," organisms with variations to help them survive in a particular environment will reproduce with greater success than others. Thus, as generation succeeds generation, nature selects the most advantageous variations and species evolve. So obvious did the idea seem in hindsight that Thomas Henry Huxley, one of the era's most prominent scientists, remarked, "How extremely stupid of me not to have thought of that."[3]

As often happens in the history of science, Darwin was not alone in authoring the theory of natural selection. A Welshman, Alfred Russel Wallace, independently came up with the same idea at the same time while on a voyage to the Malay Archipelago in Southeast Asia to collect specimens for European zoos and museums. According to his autobiography, a theory came to Wallace while he was in a feverish delirium from malaria. He shared excitedly his idea with other scientists in England, including Darwin, whose own theory was yet unpublished. The two scientists jointly presented their findings.

However straightforward the idea of evolution by natural selection may appear, the theory was (and has continued to be) a source of considerable controversy. Darwin avoided the most contentious question of human origins, limiting his commentary in the original work to a single sentence near the end: "much light will be thrown on the origin of man and his history." The feisty Thomas Henry Huxley, however, took up the subject of human origins explicitly through comparative anatomy of apes and humans and an examination of the fossils in his book, *On Man's Place in Nature*, published in 1863.

Two problems plagued Darwin's theory throughout his career: First, how did variation arise in the first place? Second, what was the mechanism of heredity by which variable traits could be passed from one generation to the next? Ironically, some of the information Darwin needed, the basic laws of heredity, were available by 1866, through the experimental work of Gregor Mendel (1822–1884), a Roman Catholic monk, working in the monastery gardens in Brno, a city in today's Czech Republic.

Mendel, who was raised on a farm, possessed two particular talents: a flair for mathematics and a passion for gardening. As with all farmers of his time, Mendel had an intuitive

[3] Darwin, C. (1887). *Autobiography*. Reprinted in F. Darwin (Ed.). (1902), *The life and letters of Charles Darwin*. London: John Murray. [3] Quoted in Durant, J. C. (2000, April 23). Everybody into the gene pool. *New York Times Book Review*, 11.

understanding of biological inheritance. He went a step farther, though, in that he recognized the need for theoretical explanations, so at age 34, he began careful breeding experiments in the monastery garden, starting with pea plants.

Over eight years, Mendel planted over 30,000 plants—controlling their pollination, observing the results, and figuring out the mathematics behind it all. This allowed him to predict the outcome of hybridization, or breeding that combined distinct varieties of the same species, over successive generations, in terms of basic laws of heredity. Though his findings were published in 1866 in a respected scientific journal, no one seemed to recognize the importance of Mendel's work during his lifetime.

Interestingly, a copy of this journal was found in Darwin's own library with the pages still uncut (journals were printed on long continuous sheets of paper and then folded into pages to be cut by the reader), an indication that the journal had never been read. In 1900, cell biology had advanced to the point where appreciation of Mendel's laws was inevitable, and in that year three European botanists, working independently of one another, rediscovered not only the laws but also Mendel's original paper. With this recognition, the science of genetics began. Still, it would be another fifty-three years before the molecular mechanisms of heredity and the discrete units of inheritance would be discovered. Today, a comprehensive understanding of heredity, molecular genetics, and population genetics supports evolutionary theory.

British scientist Rosalind Franklin's pioneering work in x-ray crystal photography played a vital role in unlocking the secret of the genetic code in 1953. Without her permission, Franklin's colleague Maurice Wilkins showed one of her images to James Watson. In his book *The Double Helix*, Watson wrote, "The instant I saw the picture my mouth fell open and my pulse began to race." While her research was published simultaneously in the prestigious journal *Nature* in 1953 alongside that of James Watson, Francis Crick, and Maurice Wilkins, only the gentlemen received the Nobel Prize for the double-helix model of DNA in 1962.

Heredity

In order to understand how evolution works, one has to have some understanding of the mechanics of heredity, because heritable variation constitutes the raw material for evolution. Our knowledge of the mechanisms of heredity is fairly recent; most of the fruitful research into the molecular level of inheritance has taken place in the past five decades. Although some aspects remain puzzling, the outlines by now are reasonably clear.

The Transmission of Genes

Today we define a **gene** as a portion of the DNA molecule containing a sequence of base pairs that encodes a particular protein; however, the molecular basis of the gene was not known at the turn of the 20th century when biologists coined the term from the Greek word for "birth." Mendel had deduced the presence and activity of genes by experimenting with garden peas to determine how various traits are passed from one generation to the next. Specifically, he discovered that inheritance was *particulate*, rather than *blending*, as Darwin and many others thought. That is, the units controlling the expression of visible traits come in pairs, one from each parent, and retain their separate identities over the generations rather than blending into a combination of parental traits in offspring. This was the basis of Mendel's first **law of segregation,** which states that pairs of genes separate and keep their individuality and are passed on to the next generation, unaltered. Another of his laws—**independent assortment**—states that different traits (under the control of distinct genes) are inherited independently of one another.

Mendel based his laws on statistical frequencies of observed characteristics, such as color and texture in generations of plants. His inferences about the mechanisms of inheritance were confirmed through the discovery of the cellular and molecular basis of inheritance in the first half of the 20th century. When **chromosomes,** the cellular structures containing the genetic information, were discovered at the start of the 20th century, they provided a visible vehicle for transmission of traits proposed in Mendel's laws.

It was not until 1953 that James Watson and Francis Crick found that genes are actually portions of molecules

gene A portion of the DNA molecule containing a sequence of base pairs that is the fundamental physical and functional unit of heredity.

law of segregation The Mendelian principle that variants of genes for a particular trait retain their separate identities through the generations.

law of independent assortment The Mendelian principle that genes controlling different traits are inherited independently of one another.

chromosomes In the cell nucleus, the structures visible during cellular division containing long strands of DNA combined with a protein.

of deoxyribonucleic acid **(DNA)**—long strands of which form chromosomes. DNA is a complex molecule with an unusual shape, rather like two strands of a rope twisted around each other with ladderlike steps between the two strands. X-ray crystallographic photographs of the DNA molecule created by British scientist Rosalind Franklin contributed significantly to deciphering the molecule's structure. Alternating sugar and phosphate molecules form the backbone of these strands connected to each other by four base pairs: adenine, thymine, guanine, and cytosine (usually written as A, T, G, and C). Connections between the strands occur between so-called complementary pairs of bases (A to T, G to C; Figure 2.1). Sequences of three complementary bases specify the sequence of amino acids in protein synthesis. This arrangement allows genes to replicate or make exact copies of themselves. The term **chromatid** refers to one half of the "X" shape of chromosomes visible once replication is complete. Sister chromatids are exact copies of each other.

How is the DNA recipe converted into a protein? Through a series of intervening steps, each three-base sequence of a gene, called a **codon,** specifies production of a particular amino acid, strings of which build proteins. Because DNA cannot leave the cell's nucleus (Figures 2.2), the

DNA Deoxyribonucleic acid. The genetic material consisting of a complex molecule whose base structure directs the synthesis of proteins.

chromatid One half of the "X" shape of chromosomes visible once replication is complete. Sister chromatids are exact copies of each other.

codon Three-base sequence of a gene that specifies a particular amino acid for inclusion in a protein.

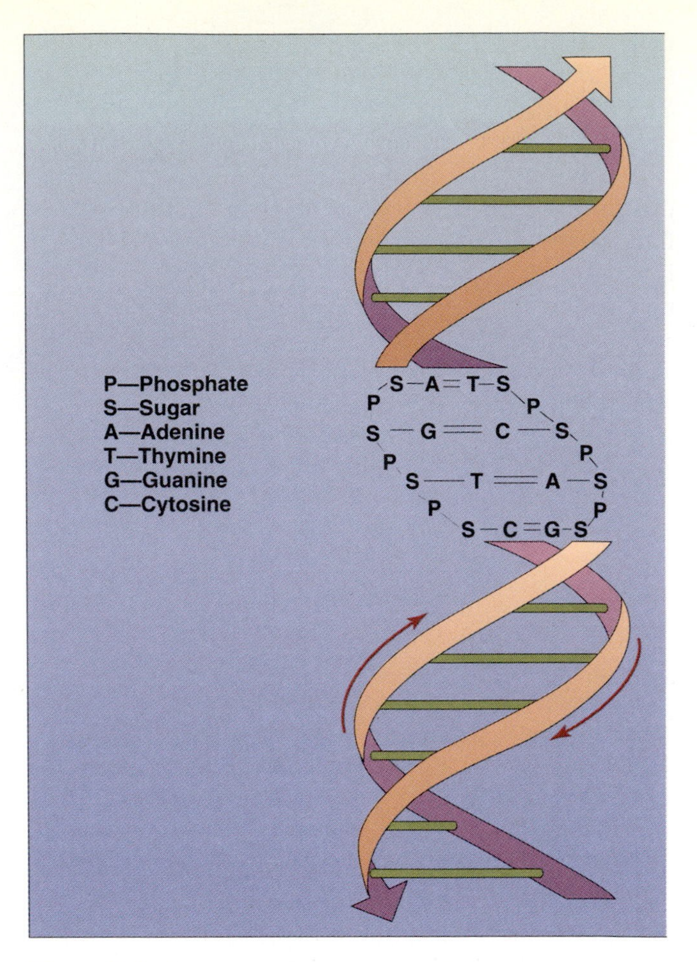

Figure 2.1 This diagrammatic representation of a portion of deoxyribonucleic acid (DNA) illustrates its twisted ladderlike structure. Alternating sugar and phosphate groups form the structural sides of the ladder. The connecting "rungs" are formed by pairings between complementary bases—adenine with thymine and cytosine with guanine.

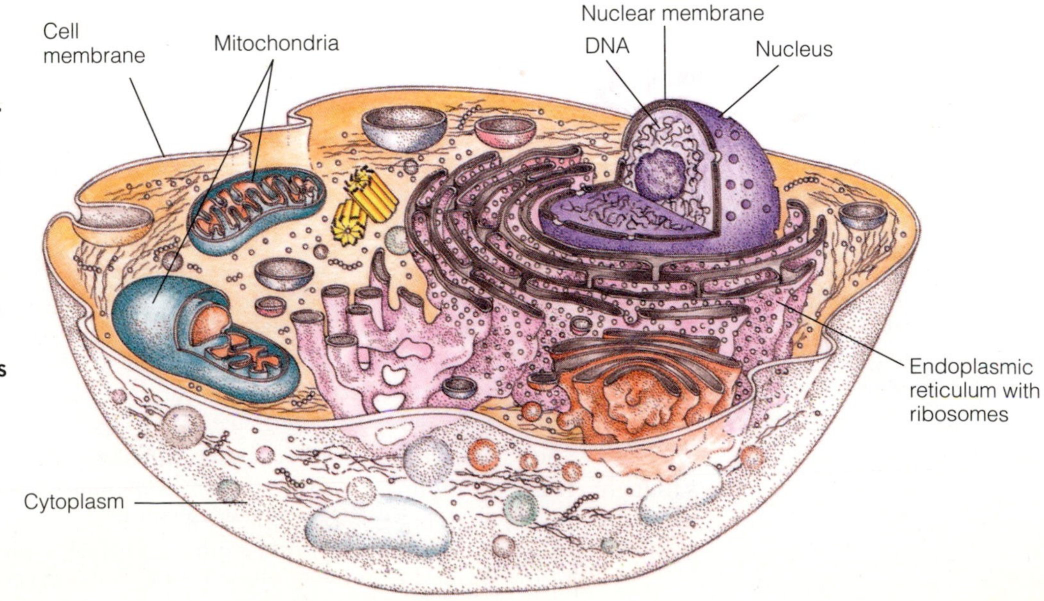

Figure 2.2 Structure of a generalized eukaryotic, or nucleated, cell, illustrating the cell's three-dimensional nature. DNA is located in the nucleus. Because DNA cannot leave the nucleus, genes must first be transcribed into RNA, which carries genetic information to the ribosomes, where protein synthesis occurs. Note also the mitochondria, which contain their own circular chromosomes and mitochondrial DNA.

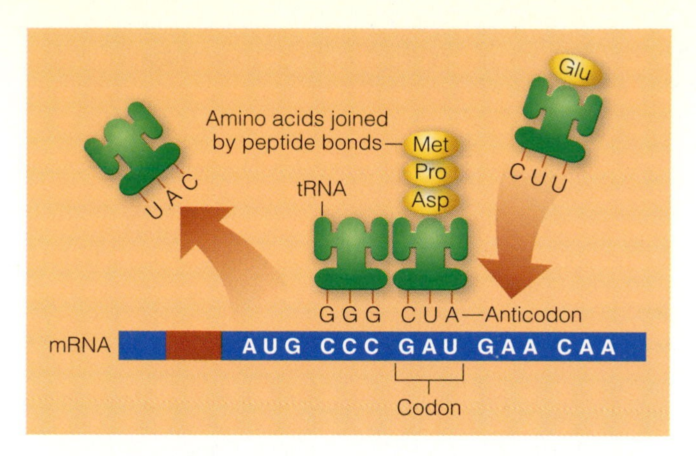

Figure 2.3 **Codons of DNA (a sequence of three bases) are transcribed into the complementary codons of a kind of RNA called messenger RNA (mRNA) in order to leave the nucleus. In the ribosomes, these codons are translated into proteins by transfer RNA (tRNA), which strings the amino acids together into particular chains. Can you think of the bases that would have been found in the DNA that correspond to the section of mRNA pictured here?**

directions for a specific protein are first converted into ribonucleic acid or **RNA** in a process called **transcription**. RNA differs from DNA in the structure of its sugar phosphate backbone and in the presence of the base uracil rather than thymine. Next, the RNA (called *messenger RNA* or *mRNA*) travels to the **ribosomes**, the cellular structure (Figure 2.3) where **translation** of the directions found in the codons into proteins occurs. Anti-codons of transfer RNA (tRNA) transport the individual amino acids to the corresponding mRNA codons, and the amino acids are joined together by peptide bonds to form polypeptide chains. For example, the sequence of AUG specifies the amino acid methionine, CCC proline, GAU aspartic acid, and so on.

There are twenty amino acids, which are strung together in different amounts and sequences to produce an almost infinite number of different proteins. This is the so-called **genetic code,** and it is the same for every living thing, whether a worm or a human being. In addition to the genetic information stored in the chromosomes of the nucleus, complex organisms also possess cellular structures called *mitochondria,* each of which has a single circular chromosome. The genetic material known as *mitochondrial DNA* or *mtDNA* has figured prominently in human evolutionary studies. On the other end of the spectrum, simple living things without nucleated cells, such as the retrovirus that causes AIDS, contain their genetic information only as RNA.

Genes and Alleles

A sequence of chemical bases on a molecule of DNA (a gene) constitutes a recipe for making proteins. As science writer Matt Ridley puts it, "Proteins . . . do almost every chemical, structural, and regulatory thing that is done in the body: they generate energy, fight infection, digest food, form hair, carry oxygen, and so on and on."[4] Almost everything in the body is made of or by proteins.

There are alternate forms of genes, known as **alleles.** For example, the gene for a human blood type in the A-B-O system refers to a specific portion of a DNA molecule on chromosome 9 that in this case is 1,062 letters long (a medium-sized gene). This gene specifies the production of an **enzyme,** a kind of protein that initiates and directs a chemical reaction. This particular enzyme causes molecules involved in immune responses to attach to the surface of red blood cells. Alleles correspond to alternate forms of this gene (changes in the base pairs of the DNA) that determine the specific blood type (the A allele and B allele). Genes, then, are not really separate structures, as had once been imagined, but locations, like dots on a map. These genes provide the recipe for the many proteins that keep us alive and healthy.

The human **genome**—the complete sequence of human DNA—contains 3 billion chemical bases, with 20,000 to 25,000 genes, a number similar to that found in most mammals. Of the 3 billion bases, humans and mice are about 90 percent identical. Both species have three times as many genes as does the fruit fly but half the number of genes found in the rice plant. In other words, the number of genes or base pairs does not explain every difference among organisms. At the same time, those 20,000 to 25,000 human genes account for only 1 to 1.5 percent of the entire genome, indicating that scientists still have far more to learn about how genes work. Frequently, genes themselves are split by long stretches of DNA that is not part of the known protein code; for example, the 1,062 bases of the A-B-O blood-group gene are interrupted by five such stretches. In the course of protein production,

[4] Ridley, M. (1999). *Genome: The autobiography of a species in 23 chapters* (p. 40). New York: HarperCollins.

RNA Ribonucleic acid; similar to DNA but with uracil substituted for the base thymine. Transcribes and carries instructions from DNA from the nucleus to the ribosomes, where it directs protein synthesis. Some simple life forms contain RNA only.

transcription Process of conversion of instructions from DNA into RNA.

ribosomes Structures in the cell where translation occurs.

translation Process of conversion of RNA instructions into proteins.

genetic code The sequence of three bases (a codon) that specifies the sequence of amino acids in protein synthesis.

alleles Alternate forms of a single gene.

enzyme Protein that initiates and directs chemical reactions.

genome The complete structure sequence of DNA for a species.

Biocultural Connection

The Social Impact of Genetics on Reproduction

While pregnancy and childbirth have been traditional subjects for cultural anthropology, the advances in genetics are raising new questions for the biocultural study of reproduction. At first glance, the genetics revolution has simply expanded biological knowledge. Individuals today, compared to a hundred years ago, can see their own genetic makeup, even down to the base-pair sequence level. But this new biological knowledge also has the capacity to profoundly transform cultures, and in many places new genetic information has dramatically affected the social experience of pregnancy and childbirth.

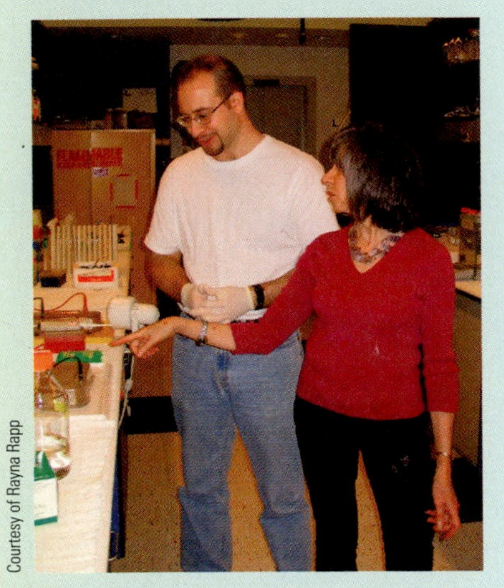
Courtesy of Rayna Rapp

Medical anthropologist Rayna Rapp has conducted fieldwork in genetics laboratories and genetic counseling centers as part of her ethnographic study of the social impact of genetic testing.

New reproductive technologies allow for the genetic assessment of fertilized eggs and embryos (the earliest stage of animal development), with far-reaching social consequences. These technologies have also become of interest to cultural anthropologists who are studying the social impact of biological knowledge. For nearly twenty-five years, anthropologist Rayna Rapp has examined the social influence of prenatal genetic testing in North America.[a] Her work illustrates that biological facts pertaining to reproduction do not exist outside of an interpretive framework provided by the culture.

Prenatal genetic testing is conducted most frequently through amniocentesis, a technique developed in the 1960s through which fluid, containing cells from the developing embryo, is drawn from the womb of a pregnant woman. The chromosomes and specific genes are then analyzed for abnormalities. Rapp has traced the development of amniocentesis from an experimental procedure to one routinely used in pregnancy in North America. For example, today pregnant women over the age of 35 routinely undergo this test because certain genetic conditions are associated with older maternal age. Trisomy 21 or Down syndrome, in which individuals have an extra 21st chromosome, can be easily identified through amniocentesis.

Through ethnographic study, Rapp has shown that a biological fact (such as an extra 21st chromosome) is open to diverse interpretations and reproductive choices by "potential parents." She also illustrates how genetic testing may lead to the labeling of certain people as "undesirable," pitting women's reproductive rights against the rights of the disabled—born or unborn. Generally, during the first two trimesters, women in the United States have a constitutionally protected right to decide whether to terminate or continue a pregnancy for any reason at all, including the diagnosis of a genetic anomaly. Following this window, federal law protects the rights of disabled individuals with these same anomalies.

Individual women must negotiate a terrain in which few rules exist to guide them. New reproductive technology, which reveals genetic anomalies, has created an utterly novel social situation. Rapp's anthropological investigation of the social impact of amniocentesis illustrates the complex interplay between biological knowledge and cultural practices.

BIOCULTURAL QUESTION

What do you think about prenatal genetic testing for diseases? Would you like to know if you carry the recessive allele for a harmful condition?

[a] Rapp, R. (1999). *Testing women, testing the fetus: The social impact of amniocentesis in America.* New York: Routledge.

these stretches of DNA are metaphorically snipped out and left on the cutting room floor.

Some of this seemingly useless, noncoding DNA (often called *junk DNA*) has been inserted by retroviruses. *Retroviruses* are some of the most diverse and widespread infectious entities of vertebrates—responsible for AIDS, hepatitis, anemias, and some neurological disorders.[5] Other junk DNA consists of decaying hulks of once-useful but now functionless genes: damaged genes that have been "turned off." As cells divide and reproduce, junk DNA, like known genes, also replicates. Mistakes can occur in the replication process, adding or subtracting repeats of the four bases: A, C, G, and T. This happens with some frequency and differently in every individual. As these "mistakes" accumulate over time, each person develops his or her unique DNA fingerprint.

Cell Division

In order to grow and maintain good health, the cells of an organism must divide and produce new cells. Cell division is initiated when the chromosomes replicate, forming a second pair that duplicates the original pair of chromosomes in the nucleus. To do this, the DNA "unzips" between the base pairs—adenine from thymine and

[5] Amábile-Cuevas, C. F., & Chicurel, M. E. (1993). Horizontal gene transfer. *American Scientist 81*, 338.

guanine from cytosine—and then each base on each now-single strand attracts its complementary base, reconstituting the second half of the double helix. Each new pair is surrounded by a membrane and becomes the nucleus that directs the activities of a new cell. This kind of cell division is called **mitosis.** As long as no errors are made in this replication process, cells within organisms can divide to form daughter cells that are exact genetic copies of the parent cell.

Like most animals, humans reproduce sexually. One reason sex is so popular, from an evolutionary perspective, is that it provides opportunity for genetic variation. All animals contain two copies of each chromosome, having inherited one from each parent. In humans this involves twenty-three pairs of chromosomes. Sexual reproduction can bring beneficial alleles together, purge the genome of harmful ones, and allow beneficial alleles to spread without being held back by the baggage of disadvantageous variants of other genes. While human societies have always regulated sexual reproduction in some ways, the science of genetics has had a tremendous impact on social aspects of reproduction, as seen in this chapter's Biocultural Connection.

Sexual reproduction increases genetic diversity, which in turn has contributed to a multitude of adaptations among sexually reproducing species such as humans. When new individuals are produced through sexual reproduction, the process involves the merging of two cells, one from each parent. If two regular body cells, each containing twenty-three pairs of chromosomes, were to merge, the result would be a new individual with forty-six pairs of chromosomes; such an individual surely could not survive. But this increase in chromosome number does not occur, because the sex cells that join to form a new individual are the product of a different kind of cell division, called **meiosis.**

Although meiosis begins like mitosis, with the replication and doubling of the original genes in chromosomes through the formation of sister chromatids, it proceeds to divide that number into four new cells rather than two (Figure 2.4). Thus each new cell has only half the number of chromosomes compared to the parent cell. Human eggs and sperm, for example, have twenty-three single chromosomes (half of a pair), whereas body cells have twenty-three pairs, or forty-six chromosomes.

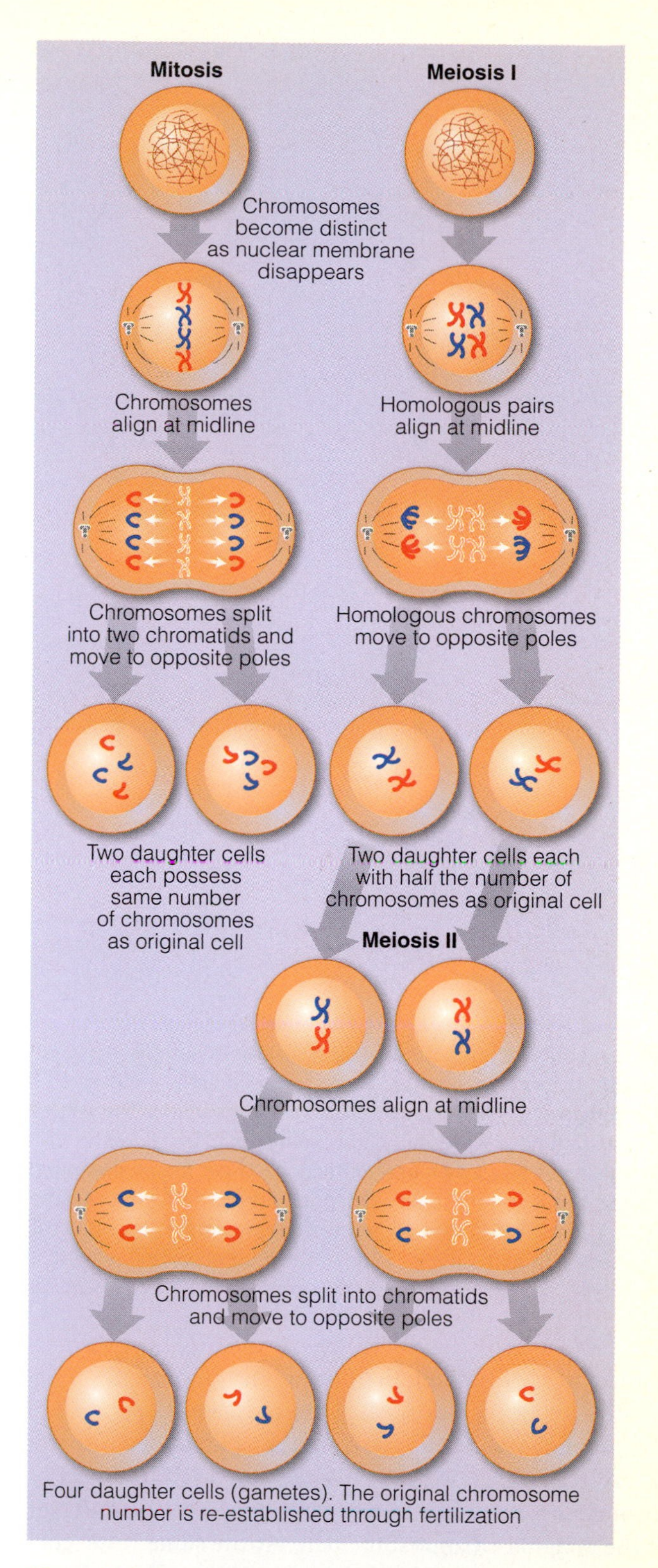

Figure 2.4 **Each chromosome consists of two sister chromatids, which are exact copies of each other. During mitosis, these sister chromatids separate into two identical daughter cells. In meiosis, the cell division responsible for the formation of gametes, the first division halves the chromosome number. The second meiotic division is essentially like mitosis and involves the separation of sister chromatids. Chromosomes in red came from one parent; those in blue came from the other. Meiosis results in four daughter cells that are not identical.**

mitosis A kind of cell division that produces new cells having exactly the same number of chromosome pairs, and hence copies of genes, as the parent cell.

meiosis A kind of cell division that produces the sex cells, each of which has half the number of chromosomes found in other cells of the organism.

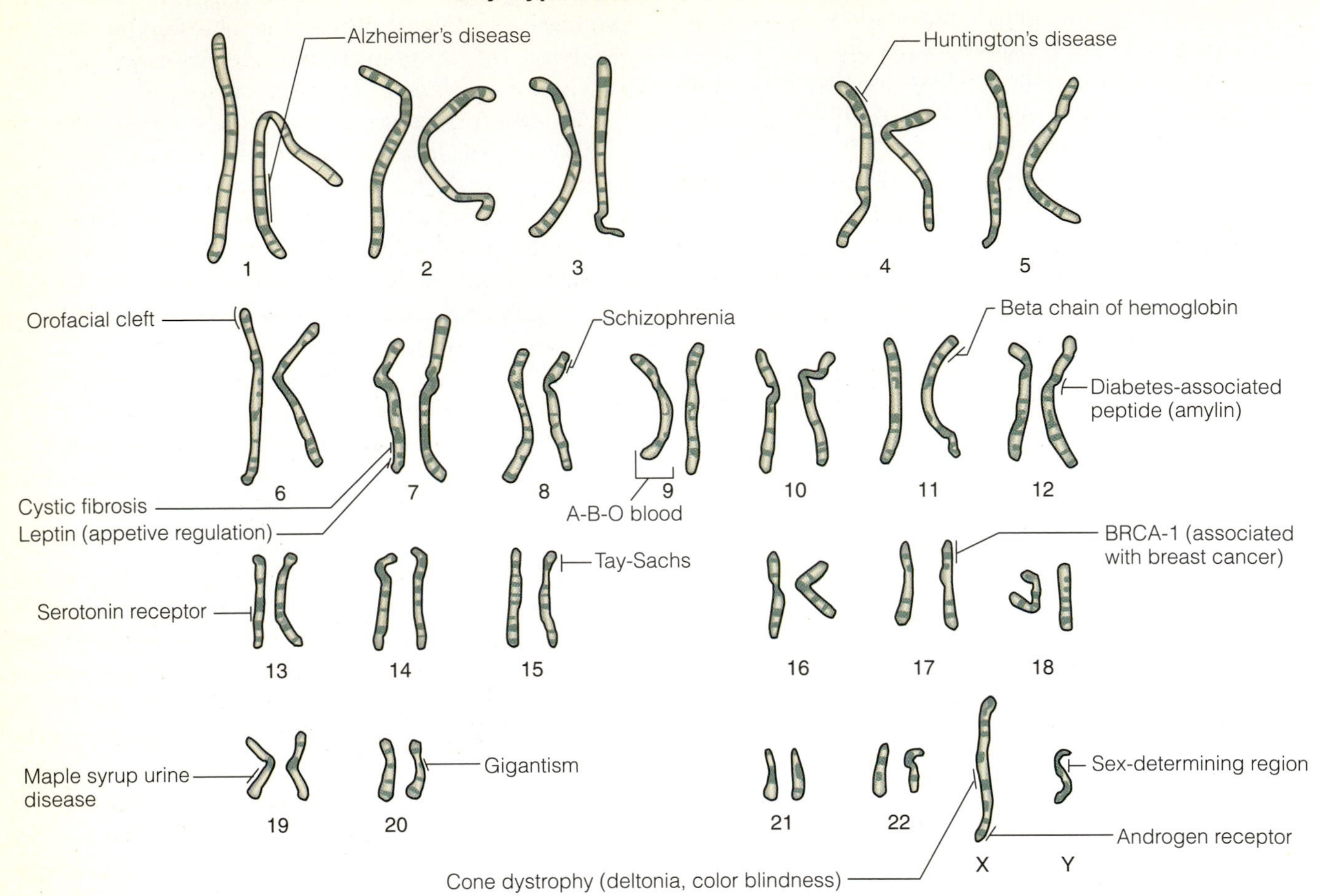

Figure 2.5 The twenty-three pairs of chromosomes humans possess include twenty-two pairs of somatic or body chromosomes plus one pair of sex chromosomes for a total of forty-six chromosomes. Of each pair, one is inherited from the individual's mother and the other from the father. Each pair of chromosomes has a characteristic size and shape. The genes coding for specific traits are located on specified places on each chromosome as indicated here. In the lower right corner is the pair of sex chromosomes typically found in males: a larger X chromosome (left) and smaller Y. Females typically possess two X chromosomes. Offspring inherit an X chromosome from their mother but either an X or a Y from their father, resulting in approximately equal numbers of male and female offspring in subsequent generations. Though the Y chromosome is critical for differentiation into a male phenotype, compared to other chromosomes the Y is tiny and carries little genetic information.

The process of meiotic division has important implications for genetics. Because paired chromosomes are separated, two different types of new cells will be formed; two of the four new cells will have one half of a pair of chromosomes, and the other two will have the second half of the original chromosome pair. At the same time, corresponding portions of one chromosome may "cross over" to the other one, somewhat scrambling the genetic material compared to the original chromosomes.

Sometimes the original pair is **homozygous,** possessing identical alleles for a specific gene. For example, if in both chromosomes of the original pair the gene for A-B-O blood type is represented by the allele for type A blood, then all new cells will have the A allele. But if the original pair is **heterozygous,** with the A allele on one chromosome and the allele for type B blood on the other, then half of the new cells will contain only the B allele; the offspring have a 50-50 chance of getting either one. It is impossible to predict any single individual's **genotype,** or genetic composition, but (as Mendel originally discovered) statistical probabilities can be established (see Figure 2.5).

homozygous Refers to a chromosome pair that bears identical alleles for a single gene.

heterozygous Refers to a chromosome pair that bears different alleles for a single gene.

genotype The alleles possessed for a particular gene.

What happens when a child inherits the allele for type O blood from one parent and that for type A from the other? Will the child have blood of type A, O, or some mixture of the two? Figure 2.6 illustrates some of the possible outcomes. Many of these questions were answered by Mendel's original experiments.

Mendel discovered that certain alleles are able to mask the presence of others; one allele is dominant, whereas the other is recessive. Actually, it is the traits that are dominant or recessive, rather than the alleles themselves; geneticists merely speak of dominant and recessive alleles for the sake of convenience. Among your biological relatives you can trace classic examples of visible traits governed by simple dominance such as a widow's peak (dominant), attached earlobes (recessive), or the presence of hair on the back of the middle section of each finger (dominant). A person with a widow's peak may be either homozygous or heterozygous because the presence of one allele will mask the allele for an un-peaked hairline. Similarly, one might speak of the allele for type A blood as being dominant to the one for type O. An individual whose blood-type genes are heterozygous, with one A and one O allele, will have type A blood. In other words, the heterozygous condition (AO) will show exactly the same physical characteristic, or **phenotype,** as the homozygous (AA), even though the two have a somewhat different genetic composition, or genotype. Only the homozygous recessive genotype (OO) will show the phenotype of type O blood.

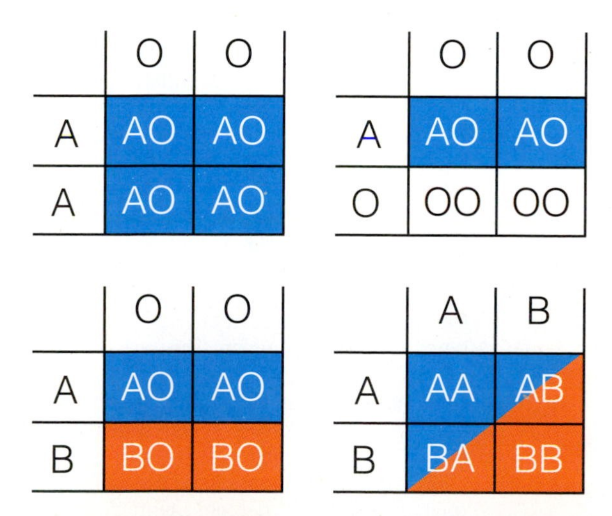

Figure 2.6 These four Punnett squares (named for British geneticist Reginald Punnett) illustrate some of the possible phenotypes and genotypes of offspring within the A-B-O system. Each individual possesses two alleles within this system, and together these two alleles constitute the individual's genotype. "Phenotype" refers to the physical characteristics expressed by the individual. The alleles of one parent are listed on the left-hand side of the square while the other parent's alleles are listed across the top. The potential genotypes of offspring are listed in the colored squares by letter. Phenotypes are indicated by color: Blue indicates the type A phenotype; orange indicates the B phenotype. Individuals with one A and one B allele have the AB phenotype and make both blood antigens. Individuals with the O phenotype have two O alleles.

The **dominance** of one allele does not mean that the **recessive** one is lost or in some way blended. A type A heterozygous parent (AO) will produce sex cells containing both A and O alleles. (This is an example of Mendel's law of segregation—that alleles retain their separate identities.) Recessive alleles can be handed down for generations before they are matched with another recessive in the process of sexual reproduction and show up in the phenotype. The presence of the dominant allele simply masks the expression of the recessive allele.

All of the traits Mendel studied in garden peas showed this dominant–recessive relationship, and so for some years it was believed that this was the only relationship possible. Later studies, however, have indicated that patterns of inheritance are not always so simple. In some cases, neither allele is dominant; they are both co-dominant. An example of co-dominance in human heredity can be seen in the inheritance of blood types. Type A is produced by one allele; type B by another. A heterozygous individual will have a phenotype of AB, because neither allele can dominate the other.

The inheritance of blood types points out another complexity of heredity. Although each of us has at most two alleles for any given gene, the number of *possible* alleles is by no means limited to two. Certain traits have three or more allelic forms. For example, over a hundred alleles exist for **hemoglobin,** the blood protein that carries oxygen. Only one allele can appear on each of the two homologous chromosomes, so each individual is limited to two genetic alleles.

Polygenetic Inheritance

So far, we have spoken as if all the traits of organisms are determined by just one gene. However, most physical traits—such as height, skin color, or liability to disease—are controlled by multiple genes. In such cases, we speak of **polygenetic inheritance,** where the

phenotype The observable characteristic of an organism that may or may not reflect a particular genotype due to the variable expression of dominant and recessive alleles.

dominance The ability of one allele for a trait to mask the presence of another allele.

recessive An allele for a trait whose expression is masked by the presence of a dominant allele.

hemoglobin The protein that carries oxygen in red blood cells.

polygenetic inheritance When two or more genes contribute to the phenotypic expression of a single characteristic.

respective alleles of two or more genes influence phenotype. For example, several individuals may have the exact same height, but because there is no single gene for determining an individual's height, we cannot neatly unravel the genetic underpinnings of 5 feet 3 inches or 160 centimeters.

Characteristics subject to polygenetic inheritance exhibit a continuous range of variation in their phenotypic expression that does not correspond to simple Mendelian rules. As biological anthropologist Jonathan Marks demonstrates in the following Original Study, the relationship between genetics and continuous traits remains a mystery.

Original Study

Ninety-Eight Percent Alike: What Our Similarity to Apes Tells Us about Our Understanding of Genetics *by Jonathan Marks*

It's not too hard to tell Jane Goodall from a chimpanzee. Goodall is the one with long legs and short arms, a prominent forehead, and whites in her eyes. She's the one with a significant amount of hair only on her head, not all over her body. She's the one who walks, talks, and wears clothing.

A few decades ago, however, the nascent field of molecular genetics recognized an apparent paradox: However easy it may be to tell Jane Goodall from a chimpanzee on the basis of physical characteristics, it is considerably harder to tell them apart according to their genes.

More recently, geneticists have been able to determine with precision that humans and chimpanzees are over 98 percent identical genetically, and that figure has become one of the most well-known factoids in the popular scientific literature. It has been invoked to argue that we are simply a third kind of chimpanzee, together with the common chimp and the rarer bonobo; to claim human rights for nonhuman apes; and to explain the roots of male aggression.

Using the figure in those ways, however, ignores the context necessary to make sense of it. Actually, our amazing genetic similarity to chimpanzees is a scientific fact constructed from two rather more mundane facts: our familiarity with the apes and our unfamiliarity with genetic comparisons.

To begin with, it is unfair to juxtapose the differences between the bodies of people and apes with the similarities in their genes. After all, we have been comparing the bodies of humans and chimpanzees for 300 years, and we have been comparing DNA sequences for less than 20 years.

Now that we are familiar with chimpanzees, we quickly see how different they look from us. But when the chimpanzee was a novelty, in the 18th century, scholars were struck by the overwhelming similarity of human and ape bodies. And why not? Bone for bone, muscle for muscle, organ for organ, the bodies of humans and apes differ only in subtle ways. And yet, it is impossible to say just how physically similar they are. Forty percent? Sixty percent? Ninety-eight percent? Three-dimensional beings that develop over their lifetimes don't lend themselves to a simple scale of similarity.

Genetics brings something different to the comparison. A DNA sequence is a one-dimensional entity, a long series of A, G, C, and T subunits. Align two sequences from different species and you can simply tabulate their similarities; if they match 98 out of 100 times, then the species are 98 percent genetically identical.

But is that more or less than their bodies match? We have no easy way to tell, for making sense of the question "How similar are a human and a chimp?" requires a frame of reference. In other words, we should be asking: "How similar are a human and a chimp, compared to what?" Let's try and answer the question. How similar are a human and a chimp, compared to, say, a sea urchin? The human and chimpanzee have limbs, skeletons, bilateral symmetry, a central nervous system; each bone, muscle, and organ matches. For all intents and purposes, the human and chimpanzee aren't 98 percent identical, they're 100 percent identical.

By Jonathan Marks (2000)

A true four-fielder, biological anthropologist Jonathan Marks is at the grave of Emile Durkheim, the French sociologist who profoundly influenced the founding of cultural anthropology.

On the other hand, when we compare the DNA of humans and chimps, what does the percentage of similarity mean? We conceptualize it on a linear scale, on which 100 percent is perfectly identical, and 0 percent is totally different. But the structure of DNA gives the scale a statistical idiosyncrasy.

Because DNA is a linear array of those four bases—A, G, C, and T—only four possibilities exist at any specific point in a DNA sequence. The laws of chance tell us that two random sequences from species that have no ancestry in common will match at about one in every four sites.

Thus, even two unrelated DNA sequences will be 25 percent identical, not 0 percent identical. (You can, of course, generate sequences more different than that, but greater differences would not occur randomly.) The most different two DNA sequences can be, then, is 75 percent different.

Now consider that all multicellular life on earth is related. A human, a chimpanzee, and the banana the chimpanzee is eating share a remote common ancestry, but a common ancestry nevertheless. Therefore, if we compare any particular DNA sequence in a human and a banana, the sequence would have to be more than 25 percent identical.

For the sake of argument, let's say 35 percent. In other words, your DNA is over one-third the same as a banana's. Yet, of course, there are few ways other than genetically in which a human could be shown to be one-third identical to a banana.

That context may help us to assess the 98 percent DNA similarity of humans and chimpanzees. The fact that our DNA is 98 percent identical to that of a chimp is not a transcendent statement about our natures, but merely a decontextualized and culturally interpreted datum.

Moreover, the genetic comparison is misleading because it ignores qualitative differences among genomes. Genetic evolution involves much more than simply replacing one base with another. Thus, even among such close relatives as human and chimpanzee, we find that the chimp's genome is estimated to be about 10 percent larger than the human's; that one human chromosome contains a fusion of two small chimpanzee chromosomes; and that the tips of each chimpanzee chromosome contain a DNA sequence that is not present in humans.

In other words, the pattern we encounter genetically is actually quite close to the pattern we encounter anatomically. In spite of the shock the figure of 98 percent may give us, humans are obviously identifiably different from, as well as very similar to, chimpanzees. The apparent paradox is simply a result of how mundane the apes have become, and how exotic DNA still is.

Evolution, Individuals, and Populations

At the level of the individual, the study of genetics shows how traits are transmitted from parent to offspring, enabling a prediction about the chances that any given individual will display some phenotypic characteristic. At the level of the group, the study of genetics takes on additional significance, revealing how evolutionary processes account for the diversity of life on earth.

A key concept in genetics is that of the **population,** or a group of individuals within which breeding takes place. **Gene pool** refers to all the genetic variants possessed by members of a population. It is within populations that natural selection takes place, as some members contribute a disproportionate share of the next generation. Over generations, the relative proportions of alleles in a population change (biological evolution) according to the varying reproductive success of individuals within that population. In other words, at the level of population genetics, **evolution** can be defined as changes in allele frequencies in populations. This is also known as *microevolution.* Four evolutionary forces—mutation, gene flow, genetic drift, and natural selection—are responsible for the genetic changes that underlie the biological variation present in species today. As we shall see, variation is at the heart of evolution. These evolutionary forces create and pattern diversity.

In theory, the characteristics of any given population should remain stable. For example, generation after generation, the bullfrogs in a farm pond look much alike, have the same calls, and exhibit the same behavior when breeding. The gene pool of the population—the genetic variation available to that population—appears to remain stable over time.

Although some alleles may be dominant over others, recessive alleles are not just lost or destroyed. Statistically, an individual who is heterozygous for a particular gene with one dominant (A) and one recessive (a) allele has a 50 percent chance of passing on the dominant allele and a 50 percent chance of passing on the recessive allele. Even if another dominant allele masks the presence of the recessive allele in the next generation, the recessive allele nonetheless will continue to be a part of the gene pool.

Because alleles are not "lost" in the process of reproduction, the frequency of the different alleles within a population should remain exactly the same from one generation to the next in the absence of evolution. In 1908, the English mathematician G. H. Hardy (1877–1947) and the German obstetrician W. Weinberg (1862–1937) worked this idea into a mathematical formula called the **Hardy-Weinberg principle.** The principle algebraically demonstrates that the percentages of individuals homozygous for the dominant allele, homozygous for the recessive allele, and heterozygous will remain the same from one generation to the next provided that certain specified conditions are met. Among the conditions are these: Mating is entirely random; the population is sufficiently

population In biology, a group of similar individuals that can and do interbreed.

gene pool All the genetic variants possessed by members of a population.

evolution Changes in allele frequencies in populations; also known as microevolution.

Hardy-Weinberg principle Demonstrates algebraically that the percentages of individuals that are homozygous for the dominant allele, homozygous for the recessive allele, and heterozygous should remain constant from one generation to the next, provided that certain specified conditions are met.

In evolutionary terms, mutations serve as the ultimate source of all new genetic variation. A generally positive force, most mutations have minimal effect or are neutral. Nevertheless, human-produced mutagens—such as pollutants, preservatives, cigarette smoke, radiation, and even some medicines—increasingly threaten people in industrial societies. While the negative effects of mutation are evident in the clear link between cigarette smoke and cancer, the positive side of mutation has been fictionalized in the special talents of the X-Men.

20th Century Fox/The Kobal Collection/Hayes, Kerry

large for a statistical average to express itself; no new variants will be introduced into the population's gene pool; and all individuals are equally successful at surviving and reproducing. These four conditions are equivalent to the absence of evolution. Geographic, physiologic, and social factors may favor mating between certain individuals over others.

Thus changes in the gene pools of populations, without which there could be no evolution, can and do take place. The mechanisms by which these changes might lead to the formation of new species will be discussed in detail in Chapter 6.

Evolutionary Forces

Mutation

The ultimate source of evolutionary change is **mutation** of genes because mutation constantly introduces new variation. Although some mutations may be harmful or beneficial to individuals, most mutations are neutral. But in an evolutionary sense, random mutation is inherently positive, as it provides the ultimate source of new genetic variation. New body plans—such as walking on two legs compared to knuckle-walking like our closest relatives, chimpanzees and gorillas—ultimately depended on genetic mutation. A random mutation might create a new allele that creates a modified protein making a new biological task possible. Without the variation brought in through random mutation, populations could not change over time in response to changing environments.

mutation Chance alteration of genetic material that produces new variation.

For sexually reproducing species like humans, the only mutations of any *evolutionary* consequence are those occurring in sex cells, since these cells form future generations. Mutations may arise whenever copying mistakes are made during cell division. This may involve a change in a single base of a DNA sequence or, at the other extreme, relocation of large segments of DNA, including entire chromosomes. As you read this page, the DNA in each cell of your body is being damaged.[6] Fortunately, DNA repair enzymes constantly scan for mistakes, slicing out damaged segments and patching up gaps. These repair mechanisms prevent diseases like cancer and ensure that we get a faithful copy of our parental inheritance. Genes controlling DNA repair therefore form a critical part of any species' genetic makeup.

Because no species has perfect DNA repair, new mutations arise continuously, so that all species continue to evolve. Geneticists have calculated the rate at which various types of mutant genes appear. In human populations, they run from a low of about five mutations per million sex cells formed, in the case of a gene abnormality that leads to the absence of an iris in the eye, to a high of about a hundred per million, in the case of a gene involved in a form of muscular dystrophy. The average is about thirty mutants per million. Environmental factors may increase the rate at which mutations occur. These include certain dyes,

[6]Culotta, E., & Koshland, D. E., Jr. (1994). DNA repair works its way to the top. *Science 266*, 1926.

antibiotics, and chemicals used in the preservation of food. Radiation, whether industrial or solar, represents another important cause of mutation. There is even evidence that stress can raise mutation rates, increasing the diversity necessary for selection if successful adaptation is to occur.[7]

In humans, as in all multicellular animals, the very nature of genetic material ensures that mutations will occur. For instance, the fact that a gene can be split by stretches of DNA that are not part of that gene increases the chances that a mistake in the process of copying DNA will cause mutations. To cite one example, no fewer than fifty such segments of DNA fragment the gene for collagen—the main structural protein of the skin, bones, and cartilage. One possible benefit of this seemingly inefficient situation is that it allows the gene segments themselves to be shuffled like a deck of cards, sometimes creating new proteins with new functions. So although individuals may suffer as a result, mutations also confer versatility at the population level, making it possible for an evolving species to adapt more quickly to environmental changes. Remember, however, that mutations occur randomly and thus do not arise out of need for some new adaptation.

Genetic Drift

Another evolutionary force is **genetic drift,** or the chance fluctuations of allele frequencies in the gene pool of a population. These changes at the population level come about due to random events at the individual level. Over the course of its lifetime, each individual is subject to a number of random events affecting its survival. For example, an individual squirrel in good health and possessed of a number of advantageous traits may be killed in a chance forest fire; a genetically well-adapted baby cougar may not live longer than a day if its mother gets caught in an avalanche, whereas the weaker offspring of a mother that does not die may survive. In a large population, such accidents of nature are unimportant; the accidents that preserve individuals with certain alleles will be balanced out by the accidents that destroy them. However, in small populations such averaging out may not be possible. Some alleles may become overrepresented in a population due to chance events.

Because today human populations are large, we might suppose that human beings are unaffected by genetic drift. But a chance event, like a rock slide that kills five people from a small town, say a population of 1,000, could significantly alter the frequencies of alleles in the local gene pool.

A particular kind of genetic drift, known as **founder effects,** may occur when an existing population splits up into two or more new ones, especially if one of these new populations is founded by a small number of individuals. In such cases, it is unlikely that the gene frequencies of the smaller population will be representative of those of the larger one. Isolated island populations may possess limited variability due to founder effects.

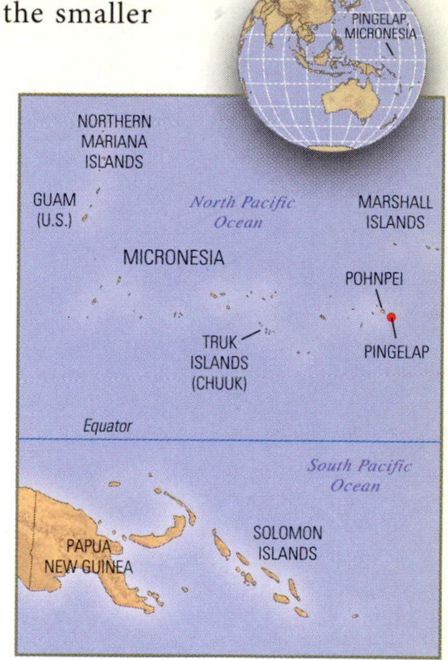

An interesting example can be seen on the Pacific Ocean island of Pingelap in Micronesia, where 5 percent of the population is completely color-blind, a condition known as *achromotopsia.* This is not the "normal" red-green color blindness that affects 8 to 20 percent of males in most populations but rather a complete inability to see color. The high frequency of achromotopsia occurred sometime around 1775 after a typhoon swept through the island, reducing its total population to only twenty individuals. Among the survivors was a single individual who was heterozygous for this condition. After a few generations, this gene became fully embedded in the expanding population. Today a full 30 percent of the island's inhabitants are carriers compared to a mere .003 percent seen in the United States.[8]

Genetic drift is likely to have been an important factor in human evolution, because until 10,000 years ago all humans were food foragers generally living in relatively small communities. Whenever biological variation is observed, whether it is the distant past or the present, it is always possible that chance events of genetic drift are responsible for it.

Gene Flow

Another factor that brings change to the gene pool of a population is **gene flow,** or the introduction of new alleles from nearby populations. Interbreeding allows

[7]Chicurel, M. (2001). Can organisms speed their own evolution? *Science 292,* 1824–1827.

[8]Sacks, O. (1998). *Island of the colorblind.* New York: Knopf.

genetic drift Chance fluctuations of allele frequencies in the gene pool of a population.

founder effects A particular form of genetic drift deriving from a small founding population not possessing all the alleles present in the original population.

gene flow The introduction of alleles from the gene pool of one population into that of another.

Anthropology Applied

What It Means to Be a Woman: How Women Around the World Cope with Infertility *by Karen Springen*

As anthropologists study the social consequences of infertility throughout the globe, their findings help reduce the social stigma surrounding this condition and make new biomedical technologies more available. In some developing countries, the consequences of infertility—which can include ostracism, physical abuse, and even suicide—are heartbreaking. "If you are infertile in some cultures, you are less than a dog," says Willem Ombelet of the Genk Institute for Fertility Technology in Belgium. Women are often uneducated, so their only identity comes from being moms. "It [infertility] is an issue of profound human suffering, particularly for women," says Marcia Inhorn, professor of anthropology and international affairs at Yale University. "It's a human-rights issue."

© Marcia Inhorn

Marcia C. Inhorn at one of her research site—an IVF clinic in the United Arab Emirates—where she studies reproductive tourism in the Arab world.

The stigma that infertile women face can infiltrate every aspect of life. They may not even be invited to weddings or other important gatherings. "People see them as having a 'bad eye' that will make you infertile, too. Infertile women are considered inauspicious," says Inhorn. Other people simply "don't want to have them around at joyous occasions," says Frank van Balen, co-author (with Inhorn) of "Infertility Around the Globe" and a professor in the department of social and behavioral sciences at the University of Amsterdam. Their reasoning: "they could spoil it," he says.

Often the female takes the blame even when the problem lies with the man, says Inhorn. The women often keep their husband's secret and bear the insults. In Chad, a proverb says, "A woman without children is like a tree without leaves." If women don't bear children, their husbands may leave them or take new wives with society's blessing. In some Muslim places, women can't go on the street on their own. "If they have a child with them, they can do their errands," says van Balen.

Childlessness can also be an enormous economic problem in developing countries where Social Security, pensions, and retirement-savings plans are not the norm. "If you don't have your children, no one looks after you," says Guido Pennings, professor of philosophy and moral science at Belgium's Ghent University. Religion shapes attitudes, too. In the Hindu religion, a woman without a child, particularly a son, can't go to heaven. Sons perform death rituals. Infertile couples worry that without a child, who will mourn for them and bury them? In China and Vietnam, the traditional belief is that the souls of childless people can't easily rest. In India, the eldest son traditionally lights the funeral pyre. In Muslim cultures, the stigma follows childless women even after death: Women without children aren't always allowed to be buried in graveyards or sacred grounds.

In Western countries, it has become much more socially acceptable to be childless, and more American women are hitting their 40s without kids, according to the latest census data. By contrast, in many developing countries, women have no careers—just motherhood—to give them their identity. "The notion of child-free living is not considered an acceptable thing for a married couple," says Inhorn. And particularly in Muslim and Hindu areas, she says, adoption "is not an immediate second path."

Legal adoption is "bureaucratically onerous" and often not socially acceptable, says Elizabeth Roberts, assistant professor of anthropology at the University of Michigan, who studied the people of Ecuador. So it's not surprising that even extremely poor people may go into debt trying to conceive. "A family is only a family if there are children, basically," says Roberts. "The biggest stumbling block is money."

Many couples may waste valuable years resorting to "black magic," says

"road-tested" genes to flow into and out of populations, thus increasing the total amount of variation present within the population. Migration of individuals or groups into the territory occupied by others may lead to gene flow.

Geographic factors also can affect gene flow. For example, if a river separates two populations of small mammals, preventing interbreeding, these populations will begin to accrue random genetic differences due to their isolation. If the river changes course and the two populations can interbreed freely, new alleles that may have been present in only one population will now be present in both populations due to gene flow.

Among humans, social factors—such as mating rules, intergroup conflict, and our ability to travel great distances—affect gene flow. For example, the last 500 years have seen the introduction of Spanish and African alleles into Central and South American populations from Spanish colonists and African slaves. More recent migrations of people from East Asia have added to this mix. When gene flow is present, variation within populations increases. Throughout the history of life on earth, gene flow has kept human populations from developing into separate species.

Natural Selection

Although gene flow and genetic drift may produce changes in the allele frequency in a population, that change would not necessarily make the population better adapted to its

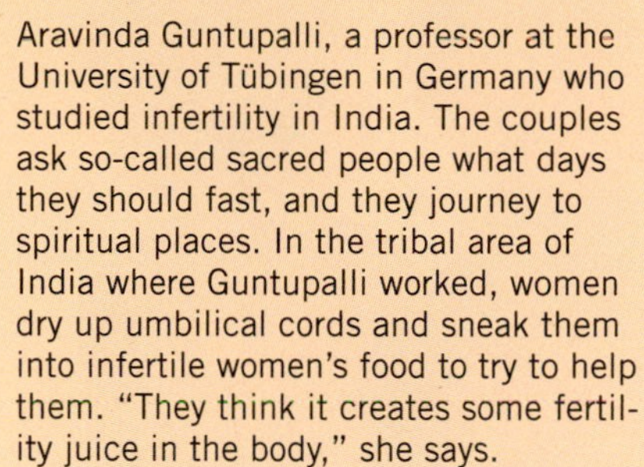

Aravinda Guntupalli, a professor at the University of Tübingen in Germany who studied infertility in India. The couples ask so-called sacred people what days they should fast, and they journey to spiritual places. In the tribal area of India where Guntupalli worked, women dry up umbilical cords and sneak them into infertile women's food to try to help them. "They think it creates some fertility juice in the body," she says.

Not surprisingly, infertility treatments are rarely covered by insurance or by government aid. "How do you provide what is clearly a highly technological, sophisticated procedure in a place that doesn't have a lot of money?" says Adamson, a member of the not-for-profit International Committee Monitoring Assisted Reproductive Technologies, a technical adviser to the World Health Organization. Leaders of countries struggling with dirty drinking water, tuberculosis, malaria, and AIDS may find IVF expenditures hard to justify.

Infertile couples in developing countries don't publicize the fact that they need help even if they can afford treatment. Children are seen as a gift of the gods, so failure to conceive may be perceived as an indication that someone has sinned or is unworthy. "People aren't willing to go up on [the equivalent of] Oprah Winfrey and say, 'Yes, I'm infertile, and I'm getting treatment,'" says Dr. Aniruddha Malpani, an Ob-Gyn who runs the Malpani Infertility Clinic in Mumbai with his wife. "People have actually traveled [for treatment], telling people they're going on holiday," says Inhorn.

Even for couples who do have access to fertility clinics, there are challenges. For example, some cultures consider masturbation evil. Yet it's traditionally the way doctors get semen samples to check a man's sperm count and then to perform IVF. In some cases, doctors can offer condoms that allow a couple to have intercourse and save the sperm. Another cultural hurdle: The Muslim world does not accept egg or sperm donation. "Each child should have a known father and a known mother," explains Inhorn. "Every child must know his own heritage." Adds Adamson: "It's very important to honor and respect the fact that people have these values."

One important approach is to focus on preventing, rather than curing, infertility. A major cause of infertility is untreated reproductive tract infections such as chlamydia and gonorrhea. In places like Africa, the cost of condoms, and taboos against them, contribute to the STD problem. Infection from female genital mutilation adds to the problem. And in some countries, 90 percent of women do not deliver in hospitals, which can also cause complications. And the hospitals they use for birth or abortions aren't always sanitary. Some doctors also believe sperm quality has suffered from toxins like lead, high in Mexico City and Cairo, and dioxin sprayed on crops.

In the developed world, there's sometimes little sympathy for the problem, since the common view is that developing countries are suffering from overpopulation and don't need any more babies. The United Nations projects that the world population will balloon from its current 6.7 billion to 9.1 billion by 2050. But the picture is more complicated than it seems. "We have a fertility paradox in Africa—high fertility rates and high infertility rates," says Dr. Silke Dyer, an Ob-Gyn in Cape Town and a member of the European Society for Human Reproduction and Embryology task force on developing countries and infertility. (Infertility treatment proponents note that IVF doesn't contribute to overpopulation any more than saving lives with vaccinations does. And both alleviate suffering.)

The good news is that interest in treating infertility around the globe is growing. In 2004, the World Health Organization said people should have access to high-quality services for family planning, including infertility services. Doctors hope to provide $200 to $500 IVF cycles, with cheaper drugs and simplified laboratories, by the end of the year in places like Cape Town and Cairo. Their goal: more happy birth stories.

Adapted from Springen, K. (2008, September 15). What it means to be a woman: How women around the world cope with infertility. *Newsweek Web Exclusive. http://www.newsweek.com/id/158625.*

biological and social environment. Natural selection, the evolutionary force described by Darwin, accounts for adaptive change. **Adaptation** is a series of beneficial adjustments to the environment. Adaptation is not an active process but rather the outcome of natural selection. As we will explore throughout this textbook, humans can adapt to their environment through culture as well as biology. When biological adaptation occurs at a genetic level, natural selection is at work.

As described earlier in the chapter, natural selection refers to the evolutionary process through which genetic variation at the population level is shaped to fit local environmental conditions. In other words, instead of a completely random selection of individuals whose traits will be passed on to the next generation, there is selection by the forces of nature. In the process, the frequency of genetic variants for harmful or nonadaptive traits within the population is reduced while the frequency of genetic variants for adaptive traits is increased. Over time, changes in the genetic structure of the population are visible in the biology or behavior of a population, and such genetic changes can result in the formation of new species.

In popular writing, natural selection is often thought of as "survival of the fittest," a phrase coined by British philosopher Herbert Spencer (1820–1903). The phrase implies that the physically weak, being unfit, are

adaptation A series of beneficial adjustments to the environment.

Across the globe, newborn babies weigh on average between 5 and 8 pounds. Stabilizing selection seems to be operating here to keep infant size well matched to the size of the human birth canal for successful childbirth. Natural selection can promote stability as well as change.

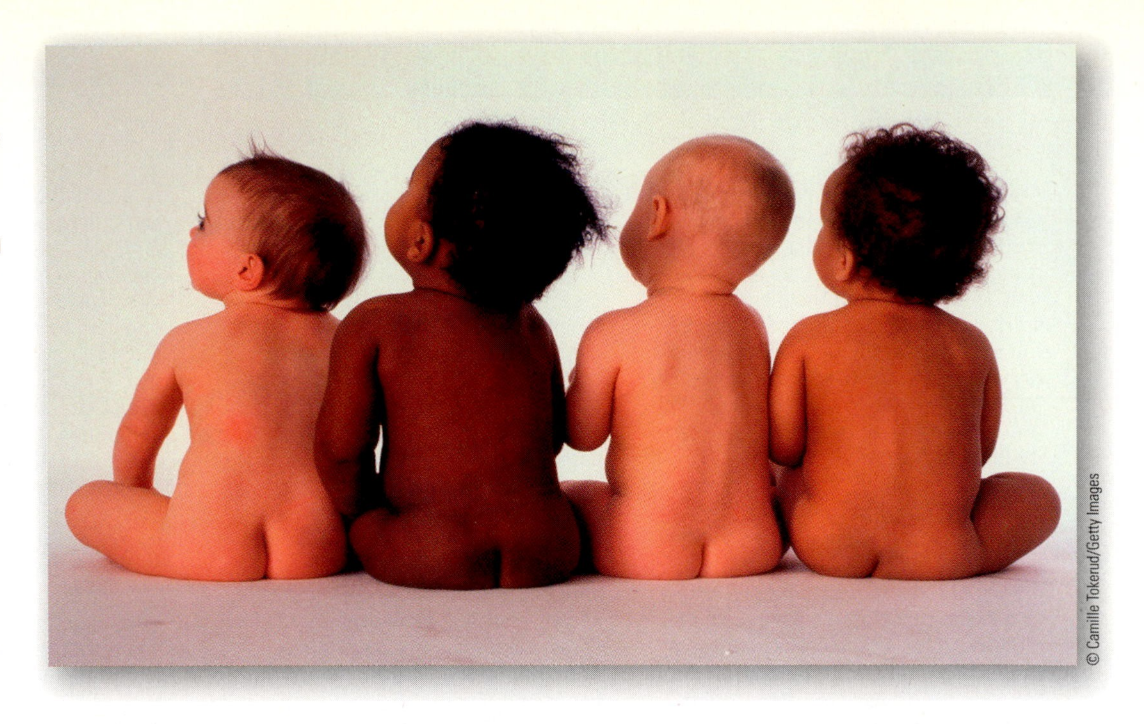

eliminated from the population by disease, predation, or starvation. Obviously, the survival of the fittest has some bearing on natural selection. But there are many cases in which "less fit" individuals survive, and even do quite well, but do not reproduce. They may be incapable of attracting mates, or they may be sterile, or they may produce offspring that do not survive after birth. For example, among the Uganda kob, a kind of antelope native to East Africa, males that are unable to attract females form bachelor herds in which they live out their lives. As members of a herd, they are reasonably well protected against predators, and so they may survive to relatively old ages. They do not, however, pass on their genes to succeeding generations.

Ultimately, all natural selection is measured in terms of **reproductive success**—mating and production of viable offspring who will in turn carry on one's genes. Reproductive success is also a powerful social phenomenon in some human societies where a woman's social worth is assessed in terms of her ability to bear children. In these contexts infertility becomes a human rights issue, as described in the Anthropology Applied feature.

The change in genetic variants in human populations can be very slow. For example, if an environment changed such that a recessive allele that had been present in humans at a modest frequency suddenly became lethal, this allele's frequency would still decrease only gradually. Even with complete selection against those homozygous for this allele, the allele would persist in the offspring of heterozygotes. In the first several generations, the frequency of the allele would decrease at a relatively rapid rate. However, with time, as the frequency of the recessive allele drops, the probability of forming a recessive homozygote also drops, so that it would take many generations to realize even a small decrease in allele frequency. This is compounded by the fact that a human generation takes about twenty-five years (forty generations would span over a thousand years). Nevertheless, even such small and slow changes can have a significant cumulative impact on both the genotypes and phenotypes of any population.

As a consequence of the process of natural selection, populations generally become well adapted to their environments. For example, consider the plants and animals that survive in the deserts of the western United States. Members of the cactus family have extensive root networks close to the surface of the soil, enabling them to soak up the slightest bit of moisture; they are able to store large quantities of water whenever it is available; they are shaped so as to expose the smallest possible surface to the dry air and are generally leafless as mature plants, thereby preventing water loss through evaporation; and a covering of spines discourages animals from chewing into the juicy flesh of the plant. Desert animals are also adapted to their environment. The kangaroo rat can survive without drinking water; many reptiles live in burrows where the temperature is lower; most animals are nocturnal or active only in the cool of the night. By

reproductive success The relative production of fertile offspring by a genotype. In practical terms, the number of offspring produced by individual members of a population is tallied and compared to that of others.

extrapolation, biologists assume that the same adaptive mechanisms also work on behavioral traits. These theories and how they influence the evolution of humans will be discussed in Chapter 4.

Natural selection may also promote stability, rather than change. **Stabilizing selection** occurs in populations that are already well adapted or where change would be disadvantageous. In cases where change is disadvantageous, natural selection will favor the retention of allele frequencies more or less as they are. However, the evolutionary history of most life forms is not one of constant change, proceeding as a steady, stately progression over vast periods of time; rather, it is one of prolonged periods of relative stability or gradual change punctuated by shorter periods of more rapid change (or extinction) when altered conditions require new adaptations or when a new mutation produces an opportunity to adapt to some other available environment. According to the fossil record, most species survive between 3 and 5 million years.[9]

Although it is true that all living organisms have many adaptive characteristics, it is not true that all characteristics are adaptive. All male mammals, for example, possess nipples, even though they serve no useful purpose. To female mammals, however, nipples are essential to reproductive success, which is why males have them. The two sexes are not separate entities, shaped independently by natural selection, but are variants upon a single body plan, elaborated in later embryology. Precursors of mammary glands are built in all mammalian fetuses, enlarging later in the development of females, but remaining small and without function in males.

Nor is it true that current utility is a reliable guide to historical origin or future use. For one thing, traits that seem nonadaptive may be co-opted for later use, and traits that appear adaptive might have come about due to unrelated changes in the pattern of growth and development. For instance, the unusually large size of a kiwi's egg enhances the survivability of kiwi chicks, in that they are particularly large and capable when hatched. Nevertheless, kiwi eggs probably did not evolve to this large size because the size is adaptive. Rather, kiwis evolved from an ancestor that was the size of an ostrich, and in birds, egg size reduces at a slower rate than does body size. Therefore, the outsized eggs of kiwi birds seem to be no more than a developmental byproduct of a reduction in body size.[10]

Similarly, an existing adaptation may come under strong selective pressure for some new purpose, as did

This x-ray showing the unusually large size of a kiwi egg illustrates that evolution does not continue by preplanned design but rather by a process of tinkering with preexisting body forms.

insect wings. These did not arise so that insects might fly, but rather as structures that were used to "row," and later skim, across the surface of the water.[11] Later, the larger ones by chance proved useful for purposes of flight. In both the kiwi eggs and the insect wings, what we see is natural selection operating as "a creative scavenger, taking what is available and putting it to new use."[12]

The adaptability of organic structures and functions, no matter how much a source of wonder and fascination, nevertheless falls short of perfection. This is so because natural selection can only work with what the existing store of genetic variation provides; it cannot create something entirely new. In the words of one evolutionary biologist, evolution is a process of tinkering, rather than design. Often tinkering involves balancing beneficial and harmful effects of a specific allele, as the case of sickle-cell anemia illustrates.

The Case of Sickle-Cell Anemia

Among human beings, **sickle-cell anemia** is a particularly well-studied case of adaptation (Figure 2.7). This painful disease, in which the oxygen-carrying red blood cells

[9] Thompson, K. S. (1997). Natural selection and evolution's smoking gun. *American Scientist 85*, 516.

[10] Gould, S. J. (1991). *Bully for brontosaurus* (pp. 109–123). New York: Norton.

[11] Kaiser, J. (1994). A new theory of insect wing origins takes off. *Science 266*, 363.

[12] Dorit, R. (1997). Molecular evolution and scientific inquiry, misperceived. *American Scientist 85*, 475.

stabilizing selection Natural selection acting to promote stability rather than change in a population's gene pool.

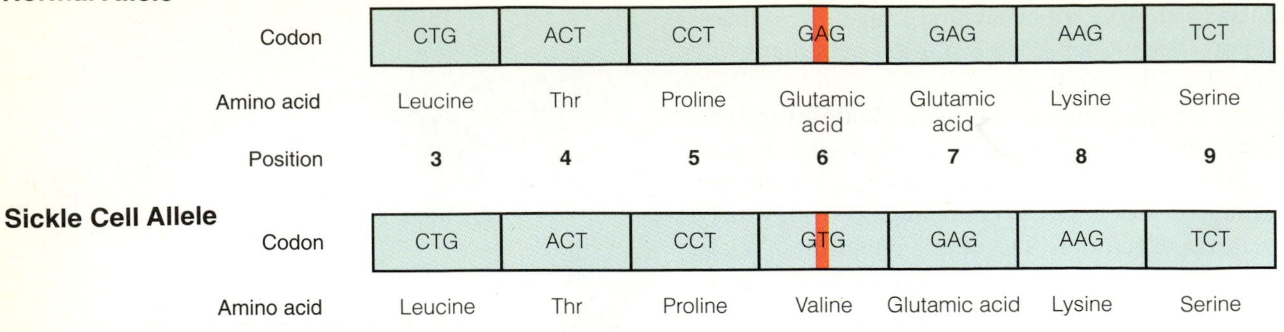

Figure 2.7 **Mutation of a single base of DNA can result in a dramatically different protein. Pictured here are codons 3 through 9 for the beta chain of hemoglobin, the protein that carries oxygen in red blood cells and the amino acids these codons specify. The top row depicts the normal allele, and in the bottom row is the single substitution that makes the red blood cells bend into a sickle shape (clogging the capillary beds and causing great pain, which is what occurs with sickle-cell anemia). Sickling occurs because the amino acid valine, compared to glutamic acid in the normal allele, gives the hemoglobin molecule different properties. The beta chain is 146 amino acids long. A simple mutation (the substitution of thymine for adenine in position 6 as indicated in red) has dramatic and tragic consequences.**

change shape (sickle) and clog the finest parts of the circulatory system, is caused by a mutation in the gene coding for hemoglobin, the protein responsible for oxygen transport. This disorder first came to the attention of geneticists in Chicago when it was observed that most North Americans who suffer from it are of African ancestry. Investigation traced the abnormality to populations that live in a clearly defined belt across tropical Central Africa where the sickle-cell allele is found at surprisingly high frequencies. Geneticists were curious about why such a harmful hereditary disability persisted in these populations.

According to the theory of natural selection, any alleles that are harmful will tend to disappear from the group, because the individuals who are homozygous for the abnormality generally die—are "selected out"—before they are able to reproduce. Why, then, had this seemingly harmful condition remained in populations from tropical Central Africa?

The answer to this mystery began to emerge when it was noticed that the areas with high rates of sickle-cell anemia are also areas in which a particularly deadly form of malaria (falciparum) is common (Figure 2.8). This severe form of malaria causes many deaths or, in those who survive, high fever that significantly interferes with the victims' reproductive abilities. Moreover, it was discovered that hemoglobin abnormalities are also found in people living in parts of the Arabian Peninsula, Greece, Algeria, Syria, and India, all regions where malaria is (or was) common.

Further research established that while individuals with hemoglobin abnormalities can still contract malaria, hemoglobin abnormalities are associated with an increased ability to survive the effects of the malarial parasite; it seems that the effects of the abnormal hemoglobin in limited amounts were less injurious than the effects of the malarial parasite. Thus selection favored heterozygous individuals with normal and sickling hemoglobin (Hb^AHb^S). The loss of alleles for abnormal hemoglobin

sickle-cell anemia An inherited form of anemia caused by a mutation in the hemoglobin protein that causes the red blood cells to assume a sickle shape.

Sickle-cell anemia is caused by a genetic mutation in a single base of the hemoglobin gene resulting in abnormal hemoglobin, called hemoglobin S. Those afflicted by the disease are homozygous for the S allele, and all their red blood cells "sickle." Co-dominance is observable with the sickle and normal alleles. Heterozygotes make 50 percent normal hemoglobin and 50 percent sickle hemoglobin. Shown here is a sickle hemoglobin red blood cell among normal red blood cells.

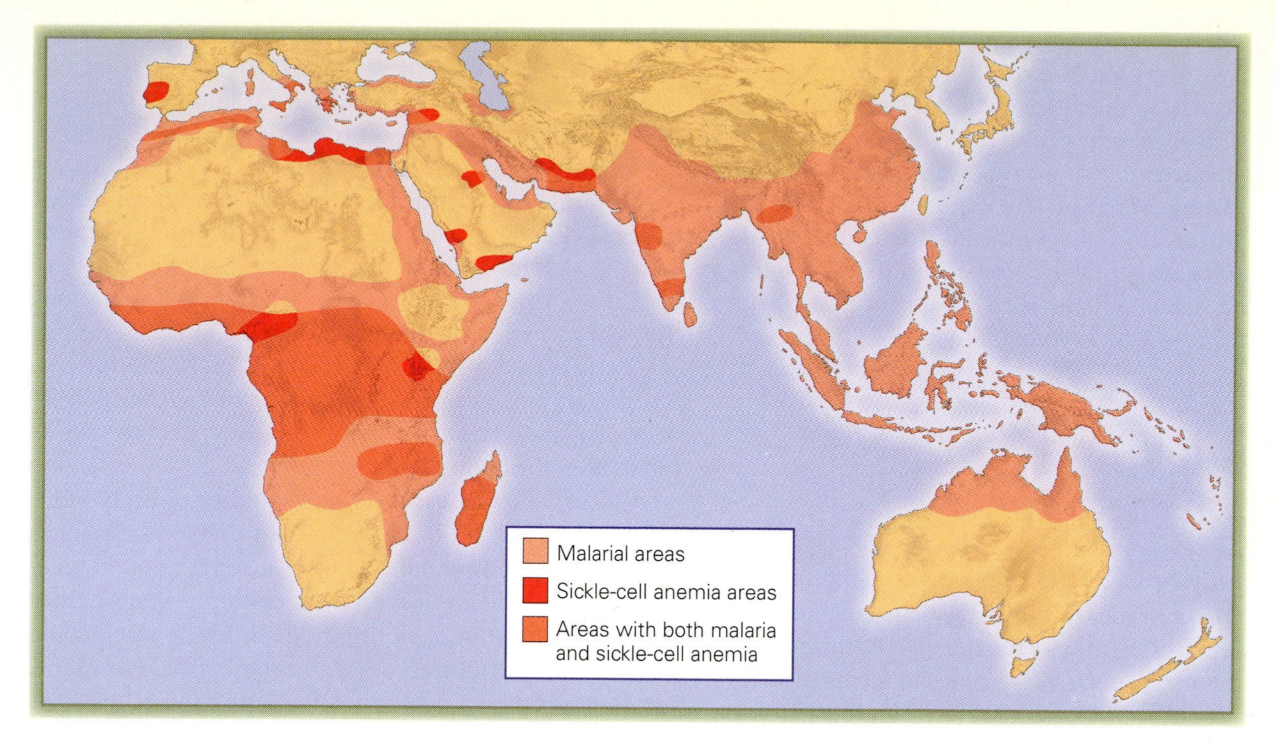

Figure 2.8 The allele that, in homozygotes, causes sickle-cell anemia makes heterozygotes resistant to falciparum malaria. While falciparum malaria is also found is tropical Latin America, the sickle cell allele is most common in populations native to regions of the Old World where this strain of malaria originated.

caused by the death of those homozygous for it (from sickle-cell anemia) was balanced out by the loss of alleles for normal hemoglobin, as those homozygous for normal hemoglobin were more likely to die from malaria and to experience reproductive failure.

Expression of normal versus sickle hemoglobin in a heterozygous individual represents an example of incomplete dominance. The mutation that causes hemoglobin to sickle consists of a change in a single base of DNA, so it can arise readily by chance (see Figure 2.7). The resulting mutant allele codes for an amino acid substitution in the beta chain of the hemoglobin protein that leads red blood cells to take on a characteristic sickle shape. In homozygous individuals with two sickle-hemoglobin alleles, collapse and clumping of the abnormal red cells block the capillaries and create tissue damage—causing the symptoms of sickle-cell disease. Afflicted individuals commonly die before reaching adulthood.

The homozygous dominant condition (Hb^AHb^A—normal hemoglobin is known as hemoglobin A, not to be confused with blood type A) produces only normal molecules of hemoglobin whereas the heterozygous condition (Hb^AHb^S) produces some percentage of normal and some percentage of abnormal hemoglobin. Except under low oxygen or other stressful conditions, such individuals suffer no ill effects. The heterozygous condition can actually improve individuals' resilience to malaria relative to the "normal" homozygous condition.

This example also points out that adaptation tends to be specific; the abnormal hemoglobin was an adaptation to the environment in which the malarial parasite flourished. When individuals who had adapted to malarial regions came to regions relatively free of malaria, what had been an adaptive characteristic became an injurious one. In environments without malaria, the abnormal hemoglobin becomes comparatively disadvantageous. Although the rates of the sickle-cell trait are still relatively high among African Americans—about 9 percent show the sickling trait—this represents a significant decline from the approximately 22 percent who are estimated to have shown the trait when African captives were shipped across the Atlantic and sold as slaves. A further decline over the next several generations is to be expected, as selection relaxes for the frequency of the sickle-cell allele.

This example also illustrates the important role culture may play even with respect to biological adaptation. In Africa, the severe form of malaria was not a significant problem until humans abandoned food foraging for farming a few thousand years ago. In order to farm, people had to clear areas of the natural forest cover. In the forest, decaying vegetation on the forest floor made the ground absorbent, so the heavy rain rapidly soaked into the soil. But once stripped of its natural vegetation, the soil lost this quality. Also, without the forest canopy to break the force of the rainfall, strong rains compacted the soil further. As a result, stagnant puddles commonly formed after downpours, providing the perfect breeding environment for the type of mosquito that hosts the malarial parasite. These mosquitoes began to flourish and transmit the malarial parasite to humans. Thus humans unwittingly created the environment that made a previously disadvantageous trait, the abnormal hemoglobin associated with sickle-cell anemia, advantageous. While the biological process of evolution accounts for the frequency of the sickle-cell allele, cultural processes shape the environment to which humans adapt.

Adaptation and Physical Variation

The relationship between sickle-cell disease and malaria provides us with a neat example of a genetic adaptation to a particular environment, but we can also examine continuous traits controlled by many genes in terms of adaptation to a particular environment. However, this tends to be more complex. Because specific examples of adaptation can be difficult to prove, scientists sometimes suggest that scenarios about adaptation may resemble Rudyard Kipling's fantastic "Just So Stories."

Anthropologists study biological diversity in terms of **clines,** or the continuous gradation in the frequency of a trait or allele over space. The spatial distribution or cline for the sickle-cell allele allowed anthropologists to identify the adaptive function of this gene in a malarial environment. Clinal analysis of a continuous trait such as body shape, which is controlled by a series of genes, allows anthropologists to interpret human global variation in body build as an adaptation to climate.

Generally, people long native to regions with cold climates tend to have greater body bulk (not to be equated with fat) relative to their extremities (arms and legs) than do people native to regions with hot climates, who tend to be relatively tall and slender. Interestingly, tall, slender bodies show up in human evolution as early as 2 million years ago. A person with larger body bulk and relatively shorter extremities may suffer more from summer heat than someone whose extremities are relatively long and whose body is slender. But the bulkier person will conserve needed body heat under cold conditions because this body type has less surface area relative to volume. In hot, open country, by contrast, people benefit from a long, slender body that can get rid of excess heat quickly. A small, slender body can also promote heat loss due to a high surface area to volume ratio.

clines Gradual changes in the frequency of an allele or trait over space.

In addition to these sorts of very long-term effects that climate may have imposed on human variation, climate can also contribute to human variation by influencing growth and development (developmental adaptation). For example, some of the physiological mechanisms for withstanding cold or dissipating heat have been shown to vary depending upon the climate an individual experiences as a child. Individuals spending their youth in very cold climates develop circulatory system modifications that allow them to remain comfortable at temperatures people from warmer climates cannot tolerate. Similarly, hot climate promotes the development of a higher density of sweat glands, creating a more efficient system for sweating to keep the body cool.

Cultural processes complicate studies of body build and climatic adaptation. For example, dietary differences particularly during childhood will cause variation in body shape through their effect on the growth process. Another complicating factor is clothing. Much of the way people adapt to cold is cultural rather than biological. For example, Inuit peoples of northern Canada live in a region that is very cold for much of the year. To cope with this, they long ago developed efficient clothing to keep their bodies warm. Thus the Inuit and other Eskimos are provided with an artificial tropical environment inside their clothing. Such cultural adaptations allow humans to inhabit the entire globe.

Some anthropologists have suggested that variation in certain features, such as face and eye shape, relate to climate. For example, biological anthropologists once proposed that the flat facial profile and round head, common in populations native to East and Central Asia, as well as arctic North America, derive from adaptation to very cold environments. Though these features tend to be more common in Asian and Native American populations, considerable physical variation exists within each population. Some individuals who spread to North America from Asia have a head shape that is more common among Europeans.

In biological terms, evolution is responsible for all that humans share as well as the broad array of human diversity. Evolution is also responsible for the creation of new species over time. Dutch primatologist Frans de Waal has said, "Evolution is a magnificent idea that has won over essentially everyone in the world willing to listen to scientific arguments."[13] We will return to the topic of human evolution in chapters that follow, but first we will look at the other living primates in order to understand the kinds of animals they are, what they have in common with humans, and what distinguishes the various forms.

---

[13]de Waal, F.B.M. (2001). Sing the song of evolution. *Natural History 110* (8), 77.

Questions for Reflection

1. Have scientific understandings of the human genetic code and technologies such as DNA fingerprinting challenged your conception of what it means to be human? How much of your life, or of the lives of the people around you, is dictated by the structure of DNA?

2. The social meanings of science can test other belief systems. Is it possible for spiritual and scientific models of human nature to coexist? How do you personally reconcile science and religion?

3. The four evolutionary forces—mutation, genetic drift, gene flow, and natural selection—all affect biological variation. Some are at work in individuals while others function at the population level. Compare and contrast these evolutionary forces, outlining their contributions to biological variation.

4. The frequency of the sickle-cell allele in populations provides a classic example of adaptation on a genetic level. Describe the benefits of this deadly allele. Are mutations good or bad?

5. Why is the evolution of continuous traits more difficult to study than the evolution of a trait controlled by a single gene?

Suggested Readings

Alper, J. S., et al. (Eds.). (2002). *The double-edged helix: Social implications of genetics in a diverse society.* Baltimore: John Hopkins University Press.

This collection of essays examines the social consequences of the new genetics in topics ranging from the discovery of a "gay" gene to the social history of the unsuccessful genetic testing programs for sickle-cell disease among African Americans.

Berra, T. M. (1990). *Evolution and the myth of creationism.* Stanford, CA: Stanford University Press.

Written by a zoologist, this book is a basic guide to the facts in the debate over evolution. It is not an attack on religion but a successful effort to assist in understanding the scientific basis for evolution.

Eugenides, J. (2002). *Middlesex: A novel.* New York: Farrar, Straus and Giroux.

This fascinating novel explores the lives of a family carrying a recessive allele that results in hermaphroditic phenotype in the third generation. It demonstrates the intersection of genetics and culture, deals with age-old questions of nature versus nurture, and explores the importance of the cultural meaning given any phenotypic state.

Gould, S. J. (1996). *Full house: The spread of excellence from Plato to Darwin.* New York: Harmony.

In this highly readable book, Gould explodes the misconception that evolution is inherently progressive. In the process, he shows how trends should be read as changes in variation within systems.

Rapp, R. (1999). *Testing women, testing the fetus: The social impact of amniocentesis in America.* New York: Routledge.

This beautifully written, meticulously researched book provides an in-depth historical and sophisticated cultural analysis, as well as a personal account of the geneticization of reproduction in America. It demonstrates the importance of cultural analyses of science without resorting to an anti-scientific stance.

Ridley, M. (1999). *Genome: The autobiography of a species in 23 chapters.* New York: HarperCollins.

Written just as the mapping of the human genome was about to be announced, this book made *The New York Times* best-seller list. The twenty-three chapters discuss DNA on each of the twenty-three human chromosomes. A word of warning, however: The author uncritically accepts some ideas (one example relates to IQ). Still, there is much food for thought here.

Challenge Issue Other primates have long fascinated humans owing to our many shared anatomical and behavioral characteristics. Our similarities, especially to the other great apes such as this bonobo, can be readily seen not just in our basic body shape but also in gestures and facial expressions. Our differences have had devastating consequences for our closest living relatives in the animal world. No primates other than humans threaten the survival of others on a large scale. Over a decade of civil war in the Democratic Republic of Congo, the natural habitat of bonobos, and genocide in neighboring Rwanda have drastically threatened the survival of this peace-loving species. These violent times have prompted the hunting of bonobos to feed starving people and the illegal capture of baby bonobos to be sold as pets. In the 21st century, humans face the challenge of making sure that other primates do not go extinct due to human actions.

CHAPTER 3

Living Primates

Chapter Preview

What Is the Place of Humanity among the Other Animals?

Biologists classify humans as belonging to the primate order, a mammalian group that also includes lemurs, lorises, tarsiers, monkeys, and apes. Among the primates, humans are most closely related to the apes, particularly to chimpanzees, bonobos, and gorillas. A common evolutionary history is responsible for the characteristics shared by humans and other primates. By studying the anatomy, physiology, and molecular structure of the other primates, we can gain a better understanding of what human characteristics we owe to our general primate ancestry and what traits are uniquely human.

Why Is Primate Conservation of Vital Importance to Anthropologists Today?

Anthropologists study other primates because their biology and behavior are so close to those of humans. Yet it is human behavior—politically and economically—that threatens primates throughout their natural ranges. Today, as a result of human destruction of primate habitats and the hunting of primates for bushmeat or souvenirs, nearly 50 percent of the known 634 primate species and subspecies are threatened with extinction in the next decade. Anthropological perspectives contribute significantly to preventing the extinction of our primate cousins.

What Are the Characteristics of the Primates Inhabiting the World Today?

Compared to other mammals, primates possess a relatively unspecialized anatomy, while their behavioral patterns are diverse and flexible. Although the earliest primates were active at night and tree dwelling, relatively few of the living primates still behave in this way. Most primate groups today live in social groups and are quite active in the day. Brain expansion and development of visual acuity in place of a reliance on sense of smell accompanied this behavioral shift. While some primates still live in the trees, many species today are ground dwelling; some move into the trees only to forage or to sleep at night.

The diversity of life on earth attests to the fact that living organisms solve the challenge of survival in many ways. In evolutionary terms, survival means reproducing subsequent generations of the species and avoiding extinction. Over the course of countless generations, each species has followed its own unique journey, an evolutionary history including random turns as well as patterned adaptation to the environment. Because new species are formed as populations diverge, closely related species resemble one another due to recent common ancestry. In other words, closely related species have shared part of their evolutionary journey together. With each step living creatures can only build on what already exists, making today's diversity a product of tinkering with ancestral body plans, behaviors, and physiology.

In this chapter we will look at the diversity of living primates, the group of animals to which humans belong. By doing so, we will gain a firmer understanding of those characteristics we share with other primates, as well as those that distinguish us from them and make us distinctively human. Figure 3.1 shows the natural global distribution of living and fossil primates. It also indicates where the twenty-five most endangered primate species are struggling to survive. Among them is the Tonkin snub-nosed monkey in northern Vietnam, with only 150 individuals remaining in the wild.

Methods and Ethics in Primatology

Just as anthropologists employ diverse methods to study humans, primatologists today use a variety of methods to study the biology, behavior, and evolutionary history of our primate cousins. Some primatologists concentrate on the comparative anatomy of ancient skeletons, while others trace evolutionary relationships by studying the comparative physiology and genetics of living species. Primatologists study the biology and behavior of living primates both in their natural habitats and in captivity in zoos, primate research colonies, and learning laboratories.

The classic image of a primatologist is someone like Jane Goodall, a world-renowned British researcher who

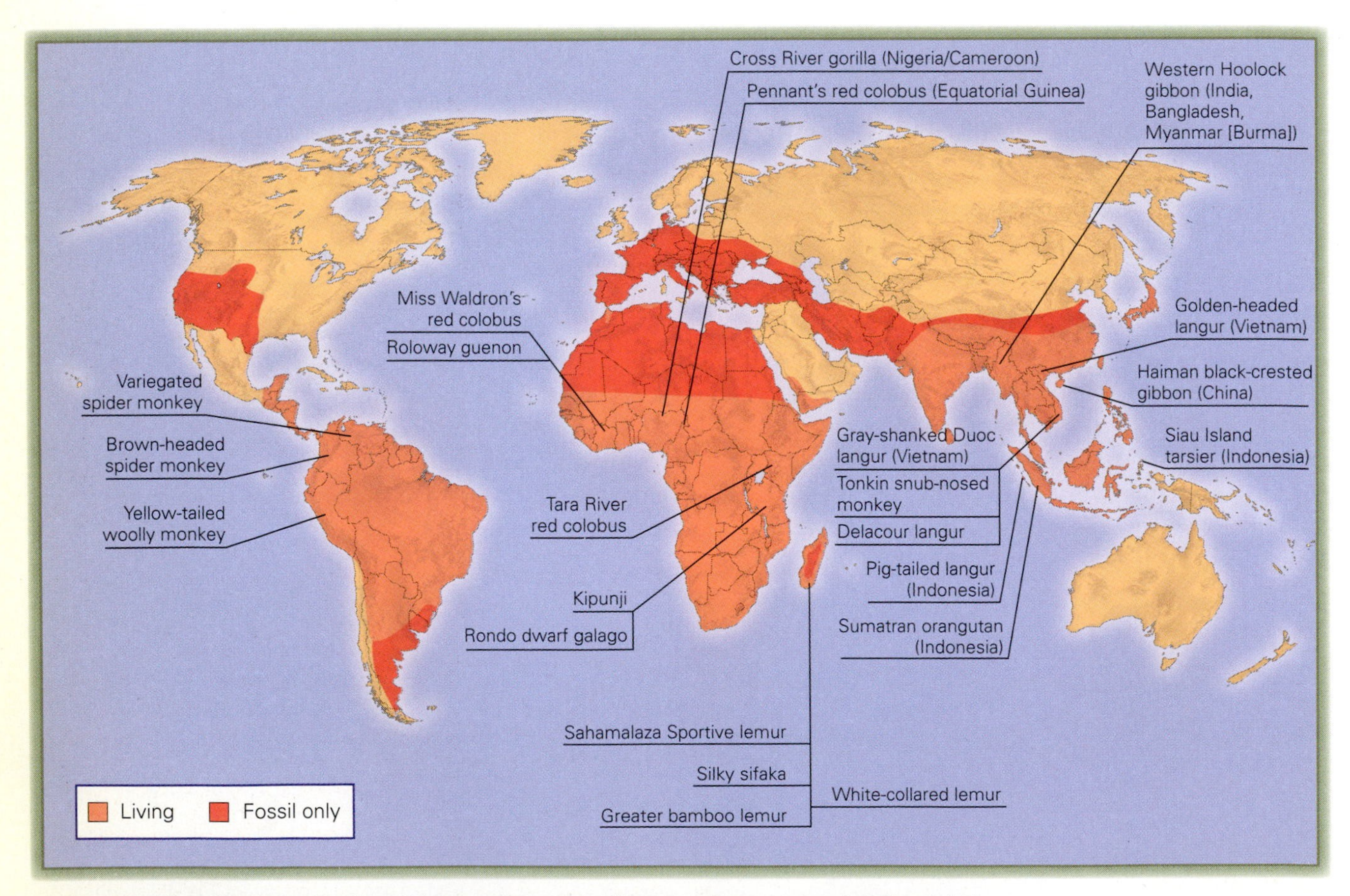

Figure 3.1 The global distribution of living and fossil nonhuman primates, showing the global distribution of living and fossil nonhuman primates. In the past, when more of the world was covered by tropical forests, the range of primates was far greater than it is now. Today, human activity threatens our primate cousins throughout the globe. The figure also shows the location of the twenty-five most endangered primate species today.

has devoted her career to in-depth observation of chimpanzees in their natural habitat. While documenting the range and nuance of chimpanzee behavior, she has also championed primate habitat conservation and humane treatment of primates in captivity. This philosophy of conservation and preservation has led to further innovations in primate research methods. For example, primatologists have developed a number of noninvasive methods that allow them to link primate biology and behavior in the field, while minimizing physical disruption. Primatologists gather hair, feces, or other body secretions left by the primates in the environment for later analysis in the laboratory. These analyses provide valuable information about characteristics such as dietary habits or genetic relatedness among a group of individuals.

Work with captive animals provides more than knowledge about the basic biology of primates. It has also allowed primatologists to document the "humanity" of our closest living relatives. Many of the amazing linguistic and conceptual abilities of primates became known through captive animal studies. Individual primatologists have devoted their careers to working with primates in captivity, teaching them to communicate through pictures on a computer screen or with American Sign Language. Of course, even compassionate captivity imposes stress on primates. Still, the knowledge gained through these studies will contribute ultimately to primate conservation and survival.

At first glance it might seem that it is inherently more humane to work with animals in the field than in captivity. But even field studies raise important ethical issues for primatologists to consider. Primatologists must maintain an awareness of how their presence affects the behavior of the group. For example, does becoming tolerant of human observers make the primates more vulnerable? Primates habituated to humans commonly range beyond established wilderness preserves and come in close contact with other humans who may be more interested in hunting than observation. Contact between animals and humans can also expose endangered primates to infectious diseases carried by humans. Whether working with primates in captivity or in the field, primatologists seriously consider the well-being of the primates they study. Primalotogist Michelle Goldsmith explores these issues in depth in this chapter's Original Study.

Original Study

Ethics of Great Ape Habituation and Conservation: The Costs and Benefits of Ecotourism *by Michele Goldsmith*

For the past ten years I have been studying the impact of habituation for the purpose of ecotourism on mountain gorillas living in Bwindi Impenetrable National Park, Uganda. "Habituation" refers to the acceptance by wild animals of a human observer as a neutral element in their environment. Habituation allows the natural behavior of a species to be observed and documented. Although information from habituated primates has been instrumental in providing a wealth of information for research and conservation, little attention has been given to the costs these animals bear when their fear of humans is removed. As a behavioral ecologist, great ape researcher, and conservationist, I am interested in how their lack of fear of humans influences both their behavior and their well-being.

Michele L. Goldsmith/Photograph © Katherine Hope

Primatologist Michele Goldsmith making observations of gorillas in the field.

All great apes are listed as "endangered species," and some subspecies (such as the mountain gorilla or *Gorilla gorilla beringei*) are "critically endangered."[a] Therefore, attempts at research and conservation, such as ecotourism, should improve local population numbers and conditions.

Although I study how habituation influences primate behavior, it is important to note that even the habituation process itself impacts primate behavior. For example, during the habituation process, a group of western lowland gorillas exhibited fear in their vocalizations, increased their aggressive behavior, and changed their daily ranging pattern.[b] Such stress can lead to loss of reproductive function and a weakened immune system. The process can also be dangerous to the people performing the habituation process as many of them have been charged, bitten, and hit.

Unfortunately, gorillas are still hunted for a number of reasons. Gorillas who have lost their fear of humans are especially vulnerable. Five Bwindi gorillas habituated for research were killed by poachers in order to capture a young infant gorilla. Babies are sold through illegal trade channels. In addition, humans have also brought great instability and warfare to areas where gorilla populations live. Sudden evacuation of research and tourist sites leaves behind habituated gorillas who become easy targets for the poacher's gun.

With regard to long-term changes in ecology and behavior, my research has shown that the diet, nesting, and ranging patterns of habituated gorilla groups are different from other "wild" gorillas in the same study area. The Nkuringo group, habituated in 1998 for tourism that started in 2004, lives near the edge

CONTINUED

CONTINUED

of the protected preserve. These gorillas spend close to 90 percent of their time outside the national park, in and around human-inhabited areas and farms. These behavioral changes have many costs to the gorillas, such as increased contact with humans and human waste, conflict with farmers that could result in injury, increased exposure to hunting as these areas are mostly open fields, and increased risk of disease transmission.

Another effect on behavior may be an artificial increase in group size. For example, a group of some forty-four animals now exist in the Virunga Mountains [along the border of Rwanda, the Democratic Republic of Congo, and Uganda] where the average group size is usually ten individuals. Furthermore, it is thought that, due to their fear of humans, nonhabituated adult male gorillas that would normally challenge other dominant males are either deterred from presenting a challenge or are less successful in their challenge against habituated groups.

Perhaps the biggest threat to habituated great apes is disease. There are over nineteen viruses and eighteen parasites that are known to infect both great apes and humans. These diseases have been responsible for between sixty-three and eighty-seven ape deaths in habituated groups (both research and tourist groups) in the Virungas, Bwindi, Mahale, Tai, and Gombe.[c] As for the gorillas in Bwindi, it has been shown that the prevalence of parasites such as *Crytopsporidium* and *Giardia* are most prevalent in habituated groups living near humans along the border of the park.

In highlighting the costs of habituation in field primatology, as a great ape primatologist, I know full well the benefits that have come out of this process. Weighing these costs and benefits as a biological anthropologist, I wonder if primatological field studies on endangered great apes for the sake of understanding humans is still a viable option. Perhaps primatologists should study apes only when it directly benefits the welfare and conservation of the study animals, rather than our interest or curiosity in learning more ourselves. Ethical considerations are crucial as the numbers of great apes in the wild continue to dwindle. Habituation may not be an ape's salvation.

---

[a]International Union for Conservation of Nature and Natural Resources (IUCN). (2000).

[b]Blom, A., et al. (2001). A survey of the apes in the Dzanga-Ndoki National Park, Central African Republic. *African Journal of Ecology 39*, 98–105.

[c]Butynski, T. M. (2001). Africa's great apes. In B. Beck et al. (Eds.), *Great apes and humans: The ethics of co-existence* (pp. 3–56). Washington, DC: Smithsonian Institution Press.

Primates as Mammals

Biologists classify humans within the primate order, a subgroup of the class Mammalia. The other primates include lemurs, lorises, tarsiers, monkeys, and apes. Humans—together with chimpanzees, bonobos, gorillas, orangutans, gibbons, and siamangs—form the hominoids, colloquially known as apes, a superfamily within the primate order. Biologically speaking, as hominoids, humans are apes.

The primates are only one of several different kinds of mammals, such as rodents, carnivores, and ungulates (hoofed mammals). Primates, like other mammals, are intelligent animals, having more in the way of brains than reptiles or other kinds of vertebrates. This increased brain power, along with the mammalian pattern of growth and development, forms the biological basis of the flexible behavior patterns typical of mammals. In most species, the young are born live, the egg being retained within the womb of the female until the embryo achieves an advanced state of growth.

Once born, the young receive milk from their mother's mammary glands, the physical feature from which the class Mammalia gets its name. During this period of infant dependency, young mammals learn many of the things they will need for survival as adults. Primates in general, and apes in particular, have a very long period of infant and childhood dependency in which the young learn the ways of their social group. Thus, mammalian primate biology is central to primate behavioral patterns.

Relative to other members of the animal kingdom, mammals are highly active. This activity is made possible by a relatively constant body temperature, an efficient respiratory system featuring a separation between the nasal and mouth cavities (allowing them to breathe while they eat), a diaphragm to assist in drawing in and letting out breath, and a four-chambered heart that prevents mixing of oxygenated and deoxygenated blood.

Mammals possess a skeleton in which the limbs are positioned beneath the body, rather than out at the sides. This arrangement allows for direct support of the body and easy flexible movement. The bones of the limbs have joints constructed to permit growth in the young while simultaneously providing strong, hard joint surfaces that will stand up to the stresses of sustained activity. Mammals stop growing when they reach adulthood, while reptiles continue to grow throughout their lives.

Mammals and reptiles also differ in terms of their teeth. Reptiles possess identical, pointed, peglike teeth while mammals have teeth specialized for particular purposes: incisors for nipping, gnawing, and cutting; canines for ripping, tearing, killing, and fighting; premolars that may either slice and tear or crush and grind (depending on the kind of animal); and molars for crushing and grinding (Figure 3.2). This enables mammals to eat a wide variety of food—an advantage to them, since they require more food than reptiles to sustain their high activity level. But they pay a price: Reptiles have unlimited tooth replacement throughout their lives, whereas mammals are limited to two sets. The first set serves the immature animal and is

Nursing their young is an important part of the general mammalian tendency to invest high amounts of energy into rearing relatively few young at a time. The reptile pattern is to lay many eggs, with the young fending for themselves. Interestingly, ape mothers, such as this one, tend to nurse their young for four or five years. The practice of bottle-feeding infants in the United States and Europe is a massive departure from the ape pattern. Although the health benefits for mothers (such as lowered breast cancer rates) and children (strengthened immune systems) are clearly documented, cultural norms have presented obstacles to breastfeeding. Across the globe, however, women nurse their children on average for about three years.

replaced by the permanent or adult teeth. The specializations of mammalian teeth allow species and evolutionary relationships to be identified through dental comparisons.

Evidence from ancient skeletons indicates the first mammals appeared over 200 million years ago as small **nocturnal** (active at night) creatures. The earliest primate-like creatures came into being about 65 million years ago when a new mild climate favored the spread of dense tropical and subtropical forests over much of the earth. The change in climate and habitat, combined with the sudden extinction of dinosaurs, favored mammal diversification, including the evolutionary development of **arboreal** (tree-living) mammals from which primates evolved.

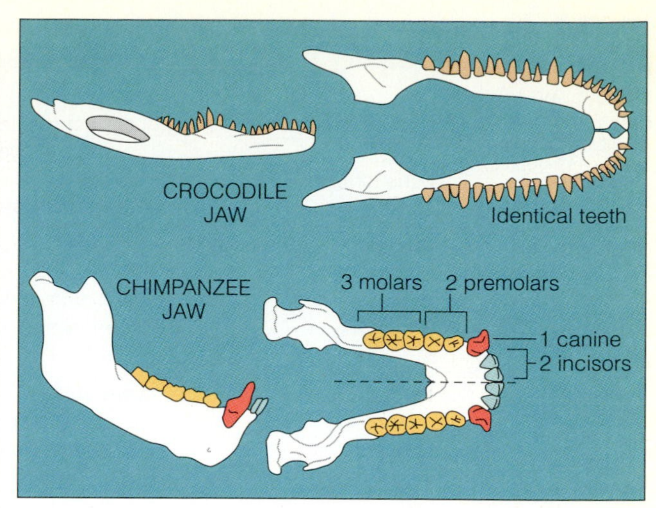

Figure 3.2 The crocodile jaw, like the jaw of all reptiles, contains a series of identical teeth. If a tooth breaks or falls out, a new tooth will emerge in its place. Mammals, by contrast, possess precise numbers of specialized teeth, each with a particular shape characteristic of the group, as indicated on the chimpanzee jaw: Incisors in front are shown in blue, canines behind in red, followed by two premolars and three molars in yellow (the last being the wisdom teeth in humans).

The ancestral primates possessed biological characteristics that allowed them to adapt to life in the forests. Their relatively small size enabled them to use tree branches not accessible to larger competitors and predators. Arboreal life opened up an abundant new food supply. The primates were able to gather leaves, flowers, fruits, insects, bird eggs, and even nesting birds, rather than having to wait for them to fall to the ground. Natural selection favored those who judged depth correctly and gripped the branches tightly. Those individuals who survived life in the trees passed on their genes to the succeeding generations.

Although the earliest primates were nocturnal, today most primate species are **diurnal** (active in the day). The transition to diurnal life in the trees involved important biological adjustments that helped shape the biology and behavior of humans today.

Primate Taxonomy

Taxonomies are ways of organizing the natural world. Because taxonomies reflect scientists' understanding of the evolutionary relationships among living things, these classificatory systems are continually under construction. With new scientific discoveries, taxonomic categories have

nocturnal Active at night and at rest during the day.
arboreal Living in the trees.
diurnal Active during the day and at rest at night.

Table 3.1 Two Alternative Taxonomies for the Primate Order: Differing Placement of Tarsiers

Suborder	Infraorder	Superfamily (family)	Location
I.			
Prosimii (lower primates)	Lemuriformes	Lemuroidea (lemurs, indriids, and aye-ayes)	Madagascar
	Lorisiformes	Lorisoidea (lorises)	Asia and Africa
		Tarsioidea (tarsiers)	Asia
Anthropoidea (higher primates)	Platyrrhini (New World monkeys)	Ceboidea	Tropical Americas
	Catarrhini	Cercopithecoidea (Old World monkeys)	Africa and Asia
		Hominoidea (apes and humans)	Africa and Asia (humans worldwide)
II.			
Strepsirhini	Lemuriformes	Lemuroidea (lemurs, indriids, and aye-ayes)	Madagascar
	Lorisiformes	Lorisoidea (lorises)	Asia and Africa
Haplorhini	Tarsiiformes	Tarsioidea (tarsiers)	Asia
	Platyrrhini (New World monkeys)	Ceboidea	Tropical Americas
	Catarrhini	Cercopithecoidea (Old World monkeys)	Africa and Asia
		Hominoidea (apes and humans)	Africa and Asia (humans worldwide)

to be redrawn, and scientists often disagree about these categorical distinctions.

There are two hot spots in the classification of primates where scientists argue for alternate taxonomies: one at the level of dividing the primate order into two suborders and the other at the level of the human family and subfamily. In both cases, the older classificatory systems, dating back to the time of Linnaeus, are based on shared visible physical characteristics. By contrast, the newer taxonomic systems depend upon genetic analyses. Molecular evidence has confirmed the close relationship between humans and other primates, but genetic comparisons have also challenged evolutionary relationships that had been inferred from physical characteristics. Laboratory methods involving genetic comparisons range from scanning species' entire genomes to comparing the precise sequences of base pairs in DNA, RNA, or amino acids in proteins.

Both genetic and morphological (body form and structure) data are useful. Biologists refer to the overall similarity of body plans within taxonomic groupings as a **grade.** The examination of shared sequences of DNA and RNA allows researchers to establish a **clade,** a taxonomic grouping that contains a single common ancestor and all of its descendants. Genetic analyses allow for precise quantification, but it is not always clear what the numbers mean (recall the Original Study from Chapter 2). When dealing with fossil specimens, paleoanthropologists begin their analyses by comparing the specific shape and size of the bones with which they work.

grade A general level of biological organization seen among a group of species; useful for constructing evolutionary relationships.

clade A taxonomic grouping that contains a single common ancestor and all of its descendants.

Prosimii A suborder of the primates that includes lemurs, lorises, and tarsiers.

Anthropoidea A suborder of the primates that includes New World monkeys, Old World monkeys, and apes (including humans).

The Linnaean system divides primates into two suborders: the **Prosimii** (from the Latin for "before monkeys"), which includes lemurs, lorises, and tarsiers, and the **Anthropoidea** (from the Greek for "humanlike"), which includes monkeys, apes, and humans. The prosimians have also been called the lower primates because they resemble the earliest fossil primates. On the whole, most prosimians are cat-sized or smaller, although some larger forms existed in the past. The prosimians also retain certain features common among nonprimate mammals that are not retained by the anthropoids, such as claws and moist, naked skin on their noses.

In Asia and Africa, all prosimians are nocturnal and arboreal creatures—again, like the fossil primates. The isolated but large island of Madagascar, off the coast of Africa, however, is home to a variety of diurnal ground-dwelling prosimians. In the rest of the world, the diurnal primates are all anthropoids. This group is sometimes called the higher primates, because they appeared later in evolutionary history and because of a lingering belief that the group including humans was more "evolved." From a contemporary biological perspective, no species is more evolved than any other.

Molecular evidence led to the proposal of a new primate taxonomy (Table 3.1). A close genetic relationship was discovered between the tarsiers—nocturnal tree dwellers who resemble lemurs and lorises—and monkeys and apes.[1] The taxonomic scheme reflecting this genetic relationship places lemurs and lorises in the suborder **Strepsirhini** (from the Greek for "turned nose"). In turn, the suborder **Haplorhini** (Greek for "simple nose") contains the tarsiers, monkeys, and apes. Tarsiers are separated from monkeys and apes at the infraorder level in this taxonomic scheme. Although this classificatory scheme accurately reflects genetic relationships, comparisons between grades, or general levels of organization, in the older prosimian and anthropoid classification make more sense when examining morphology and lifeways.

Using the older taxonomic scheme, the anthropoid suborder is further divided into two infraorders: the **Platyrrhini**, or New World monkeys, and the **Catarrhini**, consisting of the superfamilies Cercopithecoidea (Old World monkeys) and Hominoidea (apes). Although the terms *New World* and *Old World* reflect a Eurocentric vision of history (whereby the Americas were considered new only to European explorers and not to the indigenous people already living there), these terms have evolutionary and geologic relevance with respect to primates, as we will see in Chapter 6. Old World monkeys and apes, including humans, have a 40-million-year shared evolutionary history in Africa distinct from the course taken by anthropoid primates in the tropical Americas. "Old World" in this context represents the evolutionary origins of anthropoid primates rather than a political or historical focus on Europe.

In terms of human evolution, however, most taxonomic controversy derives from relationships established by the molecular evidence among the hominoids. Humans are placed in the **hominoid** or ape superfamily—with gibbons, siamangs, orangutans, gorillas, chimpanzees, and bonobos—due to physical similarities such as broad shoulders, absent tail, and long arms. Human characteristics such as bipedalism (walking on two legs) and culture led scientists to think that all the other apes were more closely related to one another than any of them were to humans. Thus humans and their ancestors were classified in the **hominid** family to distinguish them from the other apes.

Advances in molecular analysis of blood proteins and DNA later demonstrated that humans are more closely related to African apes (chimps, bonobos, and gorillas) than we are to orangutans and the smaller apes (siamangs and gibbons). Some scientists then proposed that African apes should be included in the hominid family, with humans and their ancestors distinguished from the other African hominoids at the taxonomic level of subfamily, as **hominins** (Figure 3.3).

Although all scientists today agree about the close relationship among humans, chimpanzees, bonobos, and gorillas, they differ as to whether they use the term *hominid* or *hominin* to describe the taxonomic grouping of humans and their ancestors. Museum displays and much of the popular press tend to retain the old term *hominid*, emphasizing the visible differences between humans and the other African apes. Scientists and publications using *hominin* (such as *National Geographic*) are emphasizing the importance of genetics in establishing relationships among species. These word choices are more than

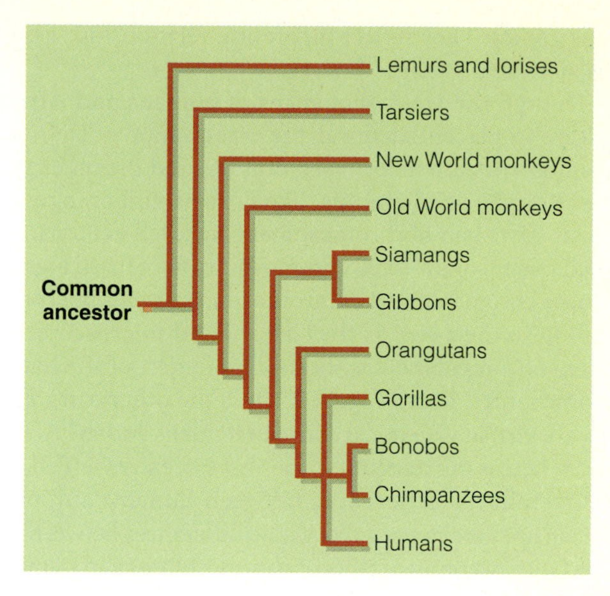

Figure 3.3 Based on molecular evidence, a relationship can be established among various primate groups. This evidence shows that tarsiers are more closely related to monkeys and apes than to the lemurs and lorises that they resemble physically. Present thinking is that the split between the human and African ape lines took place between 5 and 8 million years ago.

[1] Goodman, M., et al. (1994). Molecular evidence on primate phylogeny from DNA sequences. *American Journal of Physical Anthropology 94*, 7.

Strepsirhini In the alternate primate taxonomy, the suborder that includes the lemurs and lorises without the tarsiers.

Haplorhini In the alternate primate taxonomy, the suborder that includes tarsiers, monkeys, apes, and humans.

Platyrrhini A primate infraorder that includes New World monkeys.

Catarrhini A primate infraorder that includes Old World monkeys, apes, and humans.

hominoid The taxonomic division superfamily within the Old World primates that includes gibbons, siamangs, orangutans, gorillas, chimpanzees, bonobos, and humans.

hominid African hominoid family that includes humans and their ancestors. Some scientists, recognizing the close relationship of humans, chimps, bonobos, and gorillas, use the term *hominid* to refer to all African hominoids. They then divide the hominid family into two subfamilies: the Paninae (chimps, bonobos, and gorillas) and the Homininae (humans and their ancestors).

hominin The taxonomic subfamily or tribe within the primates that includes humans and our ancestors.

name games: They reflect theoretical relationships among closely related species.

Though the DNA sequences of humans and African apes are 98 percent identical, the organization of DNA into chromosomes differs between humans and the other great apes. Bonobos and chimps, like gorillas and orangutans, have an extra pair of chromosomes compared to humans, in which two medium-sized chromosomes have fused together to form chromosome 2. (Chromosomes are numbered according to their size as they are viewed microscopically, so that chromosome 2 is the second largest of the human chromosomes. Recall Figure 2.4.) Of the other pairs, eighteen are virtually identical between humans and the African apes, whereas the remaining ones have been reshuffled.

Overall, the differences between humans and other African apes are not as great as the differences between gibbons (with twenty-two pairs of chromosomes) and siamangs (twenty-five pairs of chromosomes)—closely related species that, in captivity, have produced live hybrid offspring. Although some studies suggest a closer relationship between the two species in the genus *Pan* (chimps and bonobos) and humans than either has to gorillas, others disagree; the safest course at the moment is to regard all three genera—*Pan*, humans, and gorillas—as having an equal degree of relationship. (Chimps and bonobos are, of course, more closely related to each other than either is to gorillas or humans.)[2]

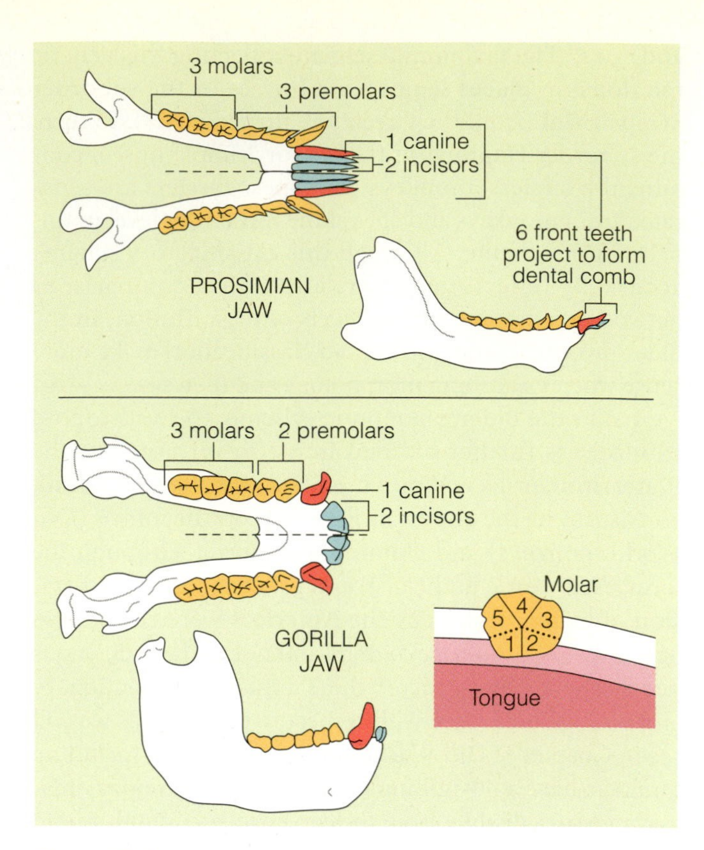

Figure 3.4 **Because the exact number and shape of the teeth differ among primate groups, teeth are frequently used to identify evolutionary relationships and group membership. Prosimians (top), with a dental formula of 2-1-3-3, possess two incisors, one canine, three premolars, and three molars on each side of their upper and lower jaws. Also, lower canines and incisors project forward, forming a "dental comb," which is used for grooming. A dental formula of 2-1-2-3, typical of Old World monkeys and apes, can be seen in the gorilla jaw (bottom). Note the large projecting canines. On one of the molars, the cusps are numbered to illustrate the Y5 pattern found in hominoids.**

Primate Characteristics

While the living primates are a varied group of animals, they do share a number of features. We humans, for example, can grasp, throw, and see in three dimensions because of shared primate characteristics. Compared to other mammals, primates possess a relatively unspecialized anatomy while their behavioral patterns are diverse and flexible.

Many primate characteristics are useful to arboreal animals, although (as any squirrel knows) they are not essential to life in the trees. For animals preying upon the many insects living on the fruit and flowers of trees and shrubs, however, primate characteristics such as dexterous hands and keen vision would have been enormously adaptive. Life in the trees, along with the visual predation of insects, played a role in the evolution of primate biology.

Primate Teeth

The varied diet available to arboreal primates—shoots, leaves, insects, and fruits—did not require the specialization of teeth seen in other mammals. In most primates (humans included), on each side of each jaw, in front, are two straight-edged, chisel-like broad teeth called incisors (Figure 3.4). Behind each incisor is a canine tooth, which in many mammals is large, flaring, and fanglike. The canines are used for defense as well as for tearing and shredding food.

In humans, canine tooth size is relatively small, although it has an oversized root, suggestive of larger canines some time back in our ancestry. Behind the canines are the premolars and molars (the "cheek teeth") for grinding and chewing food. Molars erupt through the gums while a young primate is maturing (6-year molars, 12-year molars, and wisdom teeth in humans). Thus the functions of grasping, cutting, and grinding were served by different kinds of teeth. The exact number of premolars and molars and the shape of individual teeth differ among primate groups (Table 3.2).

[2] Rogers, J. (1994). Levels of the genealogical hierarchy and the problem of hominid phylogeny. *American Journal of Physical Anthropology 94*, 81.

Table 3.2 Primate Anatomical Variation and Specialization

Primate Group	Skull and Face	Dental Formula and Specializations	Locomotor Pattern and Morphology	Tail and Other Skeletal Specializations
Earliest fossil primates	Eye not fully surrounded by bone	2-1-4-3		
Prosimians	Complete ring of bone surrounding eye Upper lip bound down to the gum Long snout	2-1-3-3 Dental comb for grooming	Hind leg dominance for vertical clinging and leaping	Tail present
Anthropoids	Forward-facing eyes fully enclosed in bone Free upper lip Shorter snout			
New World monkeys		2-1-3-3	Quadrupedal	Prehensile (grasping) tail in some
Old World monkeys		2-1-2-3 Four-cusped molars	Quadrupedal	Tail present
Apes		2-1-2-3 Y5 molars on lower jaw	Suspensory hanging apparatus	No tail

The evolutionary trend for primate dentition has been toward a reduction in the number and size of the teeth. The ancestral **dental formula,** or pattern of tooth type and number in mammals, consisted of three incisors, one canine, five premolars, and three molars (expressed as 3-1-5-3) on each side of the jaw, top and bottom, for a total of forty-eight teeth. In the early stages of primate evolution, one incisor and one premolar were lost on each side of each jaw, resulting in a dental pattern of 2-1-4-3 in the early fossil primates. This change differentiated primates from other mammals.

Over the millennia, as the first and second premolars became smaller and eventually disappeared altogether, the third and fourth premolars grew larger and added a second pointed projection, or cusp, thus becoming "bicuspid." In humans, all eight premolars are bicuspid, but in other Old World anthropoids, the lower first premolar is not bicuspid. Instead, it is a specialized, single-cusped tooth with a sharp edge to act with the upper canine as a shearing mechanism. The molars, meanwhile, evolved from a three-cusp pattern to one with four and even five cusps. The five-cusp pattern is characteristic of the lower molars of living and extinct hominoids (see Figure 3.4). Because the grooves separating the five cusps of a hominoid lower molar looks like the letter Y, hominoid lower molars are said to have a Y5 pattern. In humans there has been some departure from the Y5 pattern associated with the reduction in tooth and jaw size such that the second and third molars generally have only four cusps. Four- and five-cusp molars economically combined the functions of grasping, cutting, and grinding in one tooth.

The evolutionary trend for human dentition has generally been toward economy, with fewer, smaller, more efficient teeth doing more work. Thus our own thirty-two teeth (a 2-1-2-3 dental formula shared with the Old World monkeys and apes) are fewer than the teeth of some primates and more generalized than those of most primates. However, this trend does not indicate that species with more teeth are less evolved; it only shows that their evolutionary history followed different trends.

The canines of most primates develop into long, daggerlike teeth that enable them to rip open tough husks of fruit and other foods. In many species, males possess larger canine teeth compared to females. This sex difference is an example of **sexual dimorphism**—differences between the sexes in the shape or size of a feature. These large canines are used frequently for social communication. All an adult male gorilla, baboon, or mandrill needs to do to get a youngster to be submissive is to raise his upper lip to display his large, sharp canines.

Primate Sensory Organs

The primates' adaptation to arboreal life involved changes in the form and function of their sensory organs. The sense of smell was vital for the earliest ground-dwelling, night-active

dental formula The number of each tooth type (incisors, canines, premolars, and molars) on one half of each jaw. Unlike other mammals, primates possess equal numbers on their upper and lower jaws so the dental formula for the species is a single series of numbers.

sexual dimorphism Within a single species, differences between males and females in the shape or size of a feature not directly related to reproduction, such as body size or canine tooth shape and size.

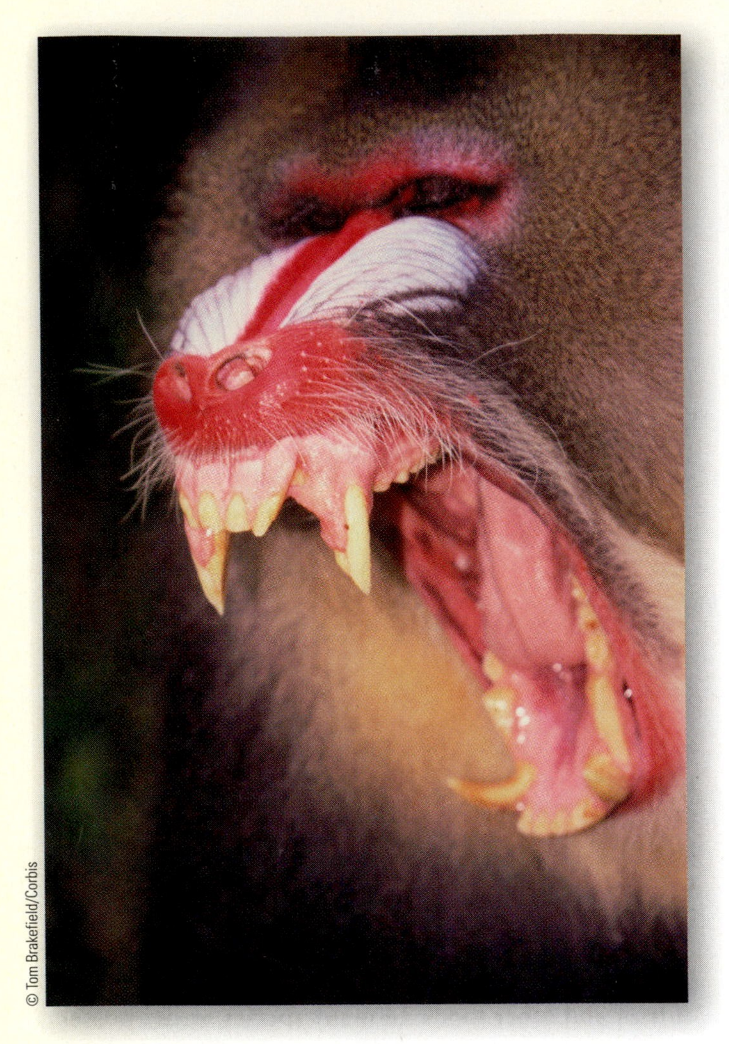

© Tom Brakefield/Corbis

Though the massive canine teeth of some male primates are serious weapons, they are more often used to communicate rather than to draw blood. Raising his lip to flash his canines, this mandrill will get the young members of his group in line right away. Over the course of human evolution, overall canine size decreased, as did differences in canine size between males and females.

mammals. It enabled them to operate in the dark, to sniff out their food, and to detect hidden predators. However, for active tree life during daylight, good vision is a better guide than smell in judging the location of the next branch or tasty morsel. Accordingly, the sense of smell declined in primates, while vision became highly developed.

Travel through the trees demands judgments concerning depth, direction, distance, and the relationships of objects hanging in space, such as vines or branches. Monkeys, apes, and humans achieved this through binocular stereoscopic color vision (Figure 3.5), the ability to see the world in the three dimensions of height, width, and depth. **Binocular vision** (in which two eyes sit next to each other on the same plane so that their visual fields overlap) and nerve connections that run from each eye to both sides of the brain confer complete depth perception characteristic of three-dimensional or **stereoscopic vision**. This arrangement allows nerve cells to integrate the images derived from each eye. Increased brain size in the visual area in primates, and a greater complexity at nerve connections, also contribute to stereoscopic color vision.

Visual acuity, however, varies throughout the primate order in terms of both color and spatial perception. Prosimians, most of whom are nocturnal, lack color vision. The eyes of lemurs and lorises (but not tarsiers) are capable of reflecting light off the retina, the surface where nerve fibers gather images in the back of the eye to intensify the limited light available in the forest at night. In addition, prosimian vision is binocular without the benefits of stereoscopy. Their eyes look out from either side of their muzzle or snout. Though there is some overlap of visual fields, their nerve fibers do not cross from each eye to both halves of the brain.

binocular vision Vision with increased depth perception from two eyes set next to each other, allowing their visual fields to overlap.

stereoscopic vision Complete three-dimensional vision (or depth perception) from binocular vision and nerve connections that run from each eye to both sides of the brain, allowing nerve cells to integrate the images derived from each eye.

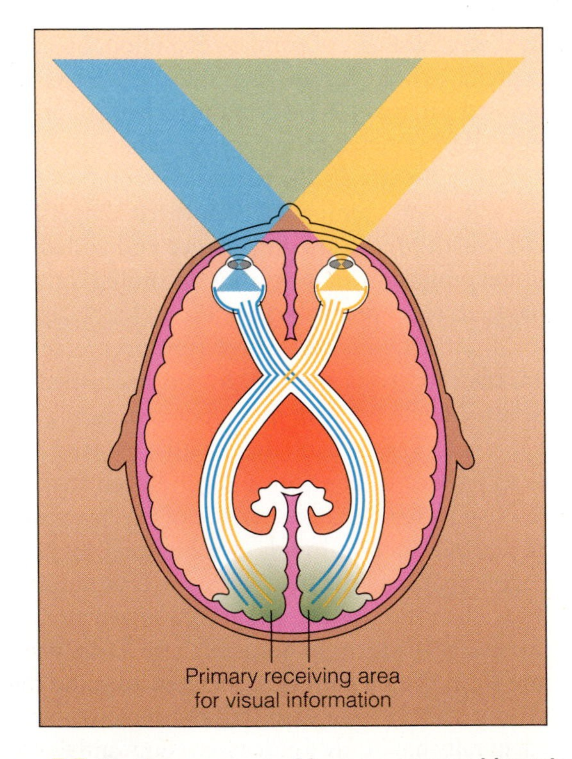

Figure 3.5 Monkeys, apes, and humans possess binocular stereoscopic vision. Binocular vision refers to overlapping visual fields due to forward-facing eyes. Three-dimensional or stereoscopic vision comes from binocular vision and the transmission of information from each eye to both sides of the brain.

Biocultural Connection

Why Red Is Such a Potent Color *by Meredith F. Small*

The Olympic athletes have been parading around like fashionistas in an array of colorful outfits, and we, their adoring public, can't resist commenting on the style and color of their high-end athletic wear. My favorite was the faux silk, faux embroidered, slinky red leotards of the Chinese women's gymnasts.

Apparently, as researchers have recently discovered, the choice of red for those leotards might also have given the Chinese gymnasts an advantage. But why is the color red so impressive?

The answer lies in our tree-living past.

The human response to the color red may well be rooted in our anthropoid heritage. Could this have given the Chinese gymnastic team an edge? It is certain that our ape ancestry contributes to the human range of motion. While we are all not able to move in the same ways that these talented gymnasts can, the human ability to grasp, swing, stretch, and throw things derives from characteristics of the hands and shoulders inherited from our ape ancestors.

In the back of the vertebrate eyeball are two kinds of cells called rods and cones that respond to light. Cones take in a wide range of light, which means they recognize colors, and they are stimulated best during daylight. Rods respond to a narrower range of light (meaning only white light) but notice that light from far away and at night.

Isaac Newton was the first person to hold up a prism and refract white light into a rainbow of colors and realize that there might be variation in what the eye can see. Color comes at us in electromagnetic waves. When the wavelength of light is short we perceive purple or blue. Medium wavelengths of lights tickle the cones in another way and we think green. Short light wavelengths make those cones stand up and dance as bright spots of yellow, orange, and red.

Various animals distinguish only parts of that rainbow because their cones respond in different ways. Butterflies, for example, see into the ultraviolet end of the rainbow, which allows them to see their own complex markings better than we can. Foxes and owls are basically color-blind and it doesn't matter because they are awake at night when the light spectrum is limited anyway.

Humans are lucky enough to be primates, animals with decent color vision, and we can thank monkeys for this special ability.

Long ago, primitive primates that resemble today's lemurs and lorises saw only green and blue, the longer wavelengths of color. But when monkeys evolved, around 34 million years ago, their cones became sensitive to even shorter wavelengths of color and they saw red.

And what a difference. With red, the forest comes alive. Instead of a blanket of bluish-green leaves, the world is suddenly accented with ripe red, yellow, and orange fruits, and even the leaves look different.

For a monkey leaping through the forest canopy, color vision would be an essential advantage. Unripe fruit doesn't have enough carbs to sustain a hungry primate and they taste really sour. Unripe leaves not only taste bad, they are toxic and indigestible.

For the first humans foraging about the forest and savannah around 5 million years ago, it would have been be much more efficient to spot a ripe fruit or tuber than bite into a zillion just to get the right one. And so humans ended up with color vision even though we no longer live in trees.

But color is more than wavelengths, more than an indicator of ripeness, to us.

Color has become symbolic, meaning it has meaning, and that meaning is highly cultural.

Chinese athletes and Chinese brides wear red because red is considered lucky. The U.S. athletes also wear red because that bright color is in the U.S. flag, and because designers of athletic wear, as well as scientists, know that red gets you noticed.

BIOCULTURAL QUESTION

While the vast majority of humans see color as described here, 8 to 20 percent of human males have red-green color blindness. Do you know someone who is color-blind? What could a conversation with a color-blind person reveal about the anthropological perspective? What colors besides red have particular meanings? Do these meanings derive from biology or culture?

Adapted from Small, M. F. (2008, August 15). Why red is such a potent color. Live Science. *http://www.livescience.com/culture/080815-hn-color-red.html.*

By contrast, monkeys, apes, and humans possess both color and stereoscopic vision. Color vision markedly improves the diet of these primates compared to most other mammals. The ability to distinguish colors allows anthropoid primates to choose ripe fruits or tender immature leaves due to their red rather than green coloration. See this chapter's Biocultural Connection to see how our primate ancestry affects our response to color.

In addition to color vision, anthropoid primates possess a unique structure called the **fovea centralis,** or central pit, in the retina of each eye. Like a camera lens, this feature enables the animal to focus on a particular object

fovea centralis A shallow pit in the retina of the eye that enables an animal to focus on an object while maintaining visual contact with its surroundings.

for acutely clear perception without sacrificing visual contact with the object's surroundings.

The primates' emphasis on visual acuity came at the expense of their sense of smell. Smells are processed in the forebrain, a part of the brain that projects into the snout of animals depending upon smells. A large protruding snout, however, may interfere with stereoscopic vision. But smell is an expendable sense to diurnal tree-dwelling animals in search of insects; they no longer needed to live a "nose to the ground" existence, sniffing the ground in search of food. The anthropoids especially have the least-developed sense of smell of all land animals. Though our sense of smell allows humans to distinguish perfumes, and even to distinguish family members from strangers, our brains have come to emphasize vision rather than smell. Prosimians, by contrast, still rely more on smell than on vision, possessing numerous scent glands for marking objects in their territories.

Arboreal primates also possess an acute sense of touch. An effective feeling and grasping mechanism helps prevent them from falling and tumbling while speeding through the trees. The early mammals from which primates evolved possessed tiny touch-sensitive hairs at the tips of their hands and feet. In primates, sensitive pads backed up by nails on the tips of the animals' fingers and toes replaced these hairs.

The Primate Brain

These changes in sensory organs have corresponding changes to the primate brain. In addition, an increase in brain size, particularly in the cerebral hemispheres—the areas supporting conscious thought—occurred in the course of primate evolution. In monkeys, apes, and humans, the cerebral hemispheres completely cover the cerebellum, the part of the brain that coordinates the muscles and maintains body balance.

One of the most significant outcomes of this development is the flexibility seen in primate behavior. Rather than relying on reflexes controlled by the cerebellum, primates constantly react to a variety of features in the environment. Messages from the hands and feet, eyes and ears, as well as from the sensors of balance, movement, heat, touch, and pain, are simultaneously relayed to the cerebral cortex. Obviously the cortex had to evolve considerably in order to receive, analyze, and coordinate these impressions and transmit the appropriate response back down to the motor nerves. The enlarged, responsive cerebral cortex provides the biological basis for flexible behavior patterns found in all primates, including humans.

There are many reasons for the increased learning capacity of the primate brain, but it likely started as the earliest primates, along with many other mammals, began to carry out their activities in the daylight hours. Prior to 65 million years ago, mammals seem to have been nocturnal in their habits. The extinction of the dinosaurs and climate change at that time opened new **ecological niches**—a species' way of life considered in the full context of its environment, including other species, geology, climate, and so on. With the change to a diurnal life, the sense of vision took on greater importance, and so visual acuity was favored by natural selection. Unlike reptile vision, where the information-processing neurons are in the retina, mammalian vision is processed in the brain, permitting integration with information received through other senses such as sound, touch, taste, and smell.

If the evolution of visual acuity led to larger brains, it is likely that the primates' insect predation in an arboreal setting also played a role in enlargement of the brain. This would have required great agility and muscular coordination, favoring development of the brain centers. Thus it is of interest that much of the higher mental faculties are apparently developed in an area alongside the motor centers of the brain.[3]

Another related hypothesis that may help account for primate brain enlargement involves the use of hands as tactile instruments to replace the teeth and jaws or snout. The hands assumed some of the grasping, tearing, and dividing functions of the jaws, again requiring development of the brain centers for more complete coordination.

The Primate Skeleton

The skeleton gives animals with internal backbones, or **vertebrates,** their basic shape or silhouette, supports the soft tissues, and helps protect vital internal organs (Figure 3.6). In primates, for example, the skull protects the brain and the eyes. A number of factors are responsible for the shape of the primate skull as compared with those of most other mammals: changes in dentition, changes in the sensory organs of sight and smell, and increased brain size.

The primate braincase, or **cranium,** tends to be high and vaulted. A solid partition exists in anthropoid primates between the eye and the temple, affording maximum protection to the eyes from the contraction of the chewing muscles positioned directly next to the eyes.

ecological niche A species' way of life considered in the full context of its environment, including factors such as diet, activity, terrain, vegetation, predators, prey, and climate.

vertebrate An animal with a backbone, including fish, amphibians, reptiles, birds, and mammals.

cranium The braincase of the skull.

[3]Romer, A. S. (1945). *Vertebrate paleontology* (p. 103). Chicago: University of Chicago Press.

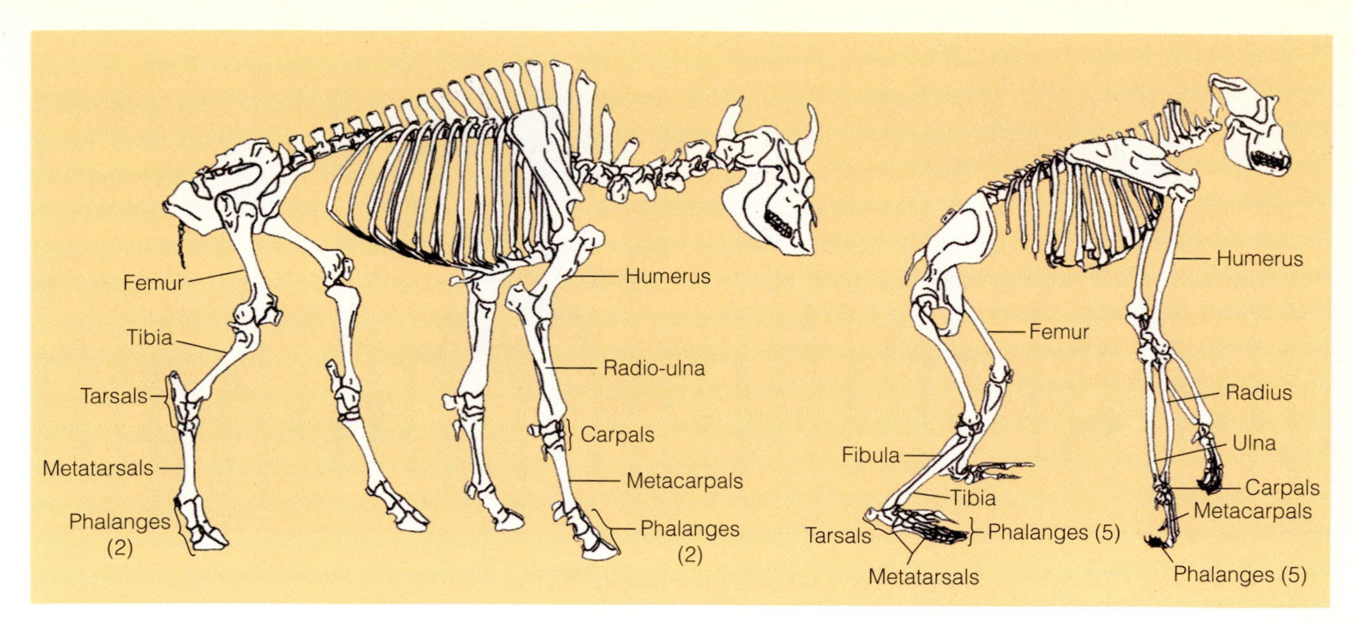

Figure 3.6 All primates possess the same ancestral vertebrate limb pattern seen in reptiles and amphibians, consisting of a single upper long bone, two lower long bones, and five radiating digits (fingers and toes), as seen in this gorilla (right) skeleton. Other mammals such as bison (left) have a modified version of this pattern. In the course of evolution, bison have lost all but two of their digits, which form their hooves. The second long bone in the lower part of the limb is reduced. Note also the joining of the skull and vertebral column in these skeletons. In bison (as in most mammals) the skull projects forward from the vertebral column, but in semi-erect gorillas, the vertebral column is further beneath the skull.

The **foramen magnum** (the large opening at the base of the skull through which the spinal cord passes and connects to the brain) is an important clue to evolutionary relationships. In most mammals, as in dogs and horses, this opening faces directly backward, with the skull projecting forward from the vertebral column. In humans, by contrast, the vertebral column joins the skull toward the center of its base, thereby placing the skull in a balanced position as required for habitual upright posture. Other primates, though they frequently cling, sit, or hang with their bodies upright, are not as fully committed to upright posture as humans, and so their foramen magnum is not as far forward.

In anthropoid primates, the snout or muzzle portion of the skull reduced as the acuity of the sense of smell declined. The smaller snout offers less interference with stereoscopic vision; it also enables the eyes to take a frontal position. As a result, primates have flatter faces than some other mammals.

Below the primate skull and the neck is the **clavicle,** or collarbone, a bone found in ancestral mammals though lost in mammals such as cats. The size of the clavicle is reduced in quadrupedal primates like monkeys that possess a narrow sturdy body plan. In the apes, by contrast, it is broad, orienting the arms at the side rather than at the front of the body and forming part of the **suspensory hanging apparatus** of this group (see Table 3.2). The clavicle also supports the **scapula** (shoulder blade) and allows for the muscle development that is required for flexible yet powerful arm movement—permitting large-bodied apes to hang suspended below tree branches and to **brachiate**, or swing from tree to tree.

The limbs of the primate skeleton follow the same basic ancestral plan seen in the earliest vertebrates. Other animals possess limbs specialized to optimize a particular behavior, such as speed. In each primate arm or leg, the upper portion of the limb has a single long bone, the lower portion two long bones, and then hands or feet with five radiating digits (phalanges). Their grasping feet and hands have sensitive pads at the tips of their digits, backed up (except in some prosimians) by flattened nails. This unique

foramen magnum A large opening in the skull through which the spinal cord passes and connects to the brain.

clavicle The collarbone connecting the sternum (breastbone) with the scapula (shoulder blade).

suspensory hanging apparatus The broad powerful shoulder joints and muscles found in all the hominoids, allowing these large-bodied primates to hang suspended below the tree branches.

scapula The shoulder blade.

brachiation Using the arms to move from branch to branch, with the body hanging suspended beneath the arms.

Visual Counterpoint

Wherever there is competition from the anthropoid primates, prosimian species, such as this loris on the right, retain the arboreal nocturnal patterns of the earliest fossil primates. Notice its large eyes, long snout, and moist split nose—all useful in its relatively solitary search for food in the trees at night. In contrast, only on the large island of Madagascar off the eastern coast of Africa, where no anthropoids existed until humans arrived, have prosimians come to occupy the diurnal ground-dwelling niche as do these ring-tailed lemurs. While all prosimians still rely on scent, marking their territory and communicating through smelly messages, daytime activity allowed the prosimians on Madagascar to become far less solitary. Also notice the difference in the size of the eyes in these two groups. Just as it would be incorrect to think of prosimians as "less evolved" than anthropoid primates because they bear a closer resemblance to the ancestral primate condition, it is also incorrect to think of lorises as less evolved compared to lemurs.

combination of pad and nail provides the animal with an excellent **prehensile** (grasping) device for use when moving from branch to branch. The structural characteristics of the primate foot and hand make grasping possible; the digits are extremely flexible, the big toe is fully **opposable** to the other digits in all but humans and their immediate ancestors, and the thumb is opposable to the other digits to varying degrees.

The retention of the flexible vertebrate limb pattern in primates was a valuable asset to evolving humans. It was, in part, having hands capable of grasping that enabled our own ancestors to manufacture and use tools and to embark on the evolutionary pathway that led to the revolutionary ability to adapt through culture.

To sum up, what becomes apparent when humans are compared to other primates is how many of the characteristics we consider distinctly human are not in fact uniquely ours; rather, they are variants of typical primate traits. We humans look the way we do because we are primates, and the differences between us and others of this order—especially the apes—are more differences of degree than differences of kind.

prehensile Having the ability to grasp.

opposable Able to bring the thumb or big toe in contact with the tips of the other digits on the same hand or foot in order to grasp objects.

Living Primates

Except for a few species of Old World monkeys who live in temperate climates and humans who inhabit the entire globe, living primates inhabit warm areas of the world. We will briefly explore the diversity of the five natural groupings of living primates: lemurs and lorises, tarsiers, New World monkeys, Old World monkeys, and apes. We will examine each group's distinctive habitat, biological features, and behavior.

Lemurs and Lorises

Although the natural habitat of lemurs is restricted to the large island of Madagascar (off the east coast of Africa), lorises range from Africa to southern and eastern Asia. Only on Madagascar, where there was no competition from anthropoid primates until humans arrived, are lemurs diurnal, or active during the day; lorises, by contrast, are all nocturnal and arboreal.

All these animals are small, with none larger than a good-sized dog. In general body outline, they resemble rodents and insectivores, with short pointed snouts, large pointed ears, and big eyes. In the anatomy of the upper lip and snout, lemurs and lorises resemble nonprimate mammals in that the upper lip is bound down to the gums, thus limiting their range of facial expression. The naked skin on the nose around the nostrils is moist and split, which facilitates a keen sense of smell. Most also have long tails, with that of a ring-tail lemur somewhat like the tail of a raccoon.

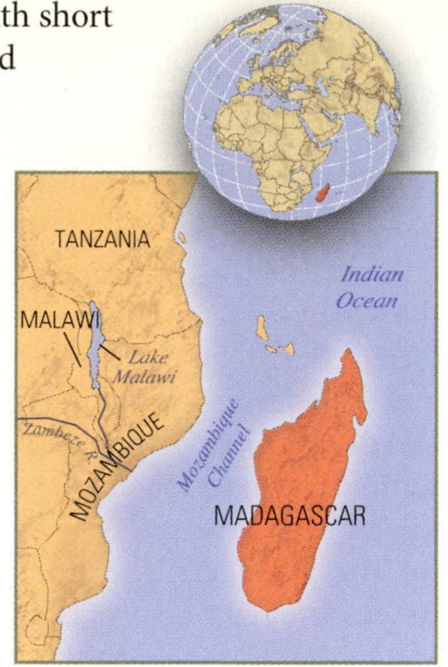

Lemurs and lorises have typical primate "hands," although they use them in pairs, rather than one at a time. Their fingers and toes are particularly strong. Sensitive pads and flattened nails are located at the tips of the fingers and toes, although they retain a claw on their second toe, sometimes called a grooming claw, which they use for scratching and cleaning. Lemurs and lorises possess another unique structure for grooming: a dental comb made up of the lower incisors and canines that projects forward from the jaw and that can be run through the fur. Behind the incisors and canines, lemurs and lorises have three premolars and molars, resulting in a dental formula of 2-1-3-3.

Lemurs and lorises have scent glands at their wrists, under their arms, and/or in their anal regions that they use for communication. Individuals leave smelly messages for one another by rubbing their scent glands on tree branches or some other fixture of the environment. Through such olfactory clues, lemurs and lorises can recognize distinct individuals within their own group as well as pinpoint their location and physical state. They also use scent to mark their territory, thus communicating to members of other groups.

The hind legs of lemurs and lorises are longer than their front legs, and when they move on all fours, the forelimbs are in a palms-down position. Some species can also move from tree to tree by vertical clinging and leaping. First they hang onto the trunk of one tree in an upright position, with their long legs curled up tightly like springs and their heads twisted to look in the direction they are moving. They propel themselves into the air, do a "180," and land facing the trunk on their tree of choice.

With their distinctive mix of characteristics, lemurs and lorises appear to occupy a place between the anthropoid primates and insectivores, the mammalian order that includes moles and shrews.

Tarsiers

Outwardly, tarsiers resemble lemurs and lorises. Molecular evidence, however, indicates a closer relationship to monkeys, apes, and humans. The head, eyes, and ears of these kitten-sized arboreal creatures are huge in proportion to the body. They have the remarkable ability to turn their heads 180 degrees, so they can see where they have been as well as where they are going. Their digits end in platelike adhesive discs.

Tarsiers are named for the elongated tarsal, or foot bone, that provides leverage for jumps of 6 feet or more. Tarsiers are mainly nocturnal insect eaters and so occupy a niche that is similar to that of the earliest ancestral primates. In the structure of the nose and lips and in the part of the brain governing vision, tarsiers resemble monkeys.

With their large eyes, tarsiers are well adapted for nocturnal life. If humans possessed eyes proportionally the same size as tarsiers relative to the size of our faces, our eyes would be approximately the size of oranges. In their nocturnal habit and outward appearance, tarsiers resemble lemurs and lorises. Genetically, however, they are more closed related to monkeys and apes, causing scientists to rework the suborder divisions in primate taxonomy to reflect this evolutionary relationship.

Grasping hands and three-dimensional vision enable primates like this South American monkey to lead an active life in the trees. In some New World monkey species, a grasping or prehensile tail makes tree life even easier. The naked skin on the underside of the tail resembles the sensitive skin found at the tips of our fingers and is even covered with whorls like fingerprints. This sensory skin allows New World monkeys to use their tails as a fifth limb.

New World Monkeys

New World monkeys live in tropical forests of South and Central America. In outward body plan they closely resemble Old World monkeys, except that New World monkeys are characterized by flat noses with widely separated, outward-flaring nostrils. Their infraorder name platyrrhine (from the Greek for "flat-nosed") comes from this characteristic. There are five different families of New World monkeys, and they range in size from less than a pound to over 30 pounds.

There are two reasons why New World monkeys have not been studied as extensively as other primates. The first is that an emphasis on human origins in primatology meant that Old World species were favored by researchers. The second is that nearly all New World species are arboreal, which makes it more difficult for researchers to observe them. In recent decades, however, primatologists have conducted numerous long-range field studies on a variety of species.

For example, anthropologist Karen Strier has studied the woolly spider monkey, or muriqui, in the state of Minas Gerais, Brazil, for close to three decades. Her field studies progressed from examining muriqui diet, social structure, and **demographics** (population characteristics such as the number of individuals of each age and sex) to tracking the reproductive cycles and health of these large, peaceful forest dwellers. She pioneered a noninvasive method to measure reproductive hormone levels and the presence of parasites through analysis of the feces of individual animals. Her fieldwork included waiting to catch feces (in a gloved hand) the moment it was dropping from the trees or quickly retrieving it from the ground. Through analysis of these samples, Strier was able to document correlations between diet and fertility.

Strier also documented a reduced parasite load in muriquis that consumed certain plants—apparently for their medicinal/therapeutic value. Amazonian peoples have been known to use some of these plants for the same reason. As these human populations become increasingly removed from their traditional lifeways due to globalization and modernization, the muriqui may become a valuable source to reclaim knowledge of the forest. According to Strier, "While traditional peoples of the Amazon have survived long enough to impart some of their knowledge of forest plants, the indigenous human societies of the Atlantic forest are long gone. The muriqui and other monkeys may provide humans with their best guides to the forest's medicinal values."[4] Field studies like Strier's not only have contributed to our understanding of the behavior and biology of New World monkeys but have also played a major role in bringing back a number of species from the brink of extinction.

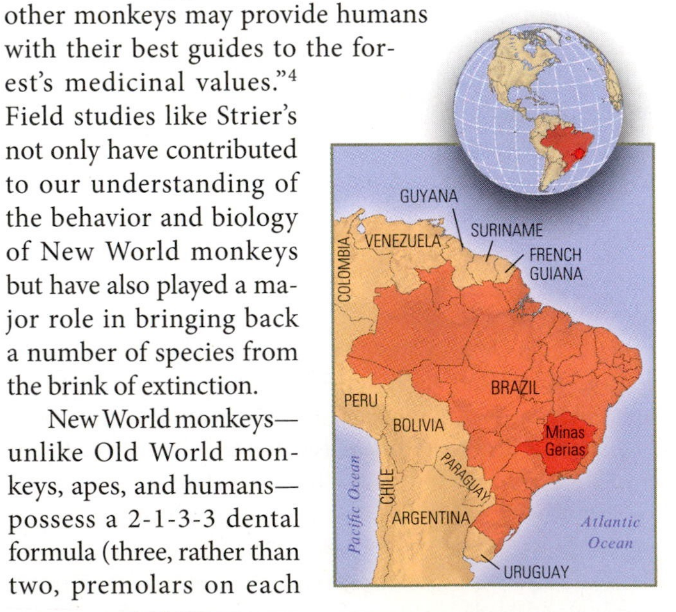

New World monkeys—unlike Old World monkeys, apes, and humans—possess a 2-1-3-3 dental formula (three, rather than two, premolars on each

demographics Population characteristics such as the number of individuals of each age and sex.

[4] Strier, K. (1993, March). Menu for a monkey. *Natural History*, 42.

While all Old World monkeys share certain features like a narrow body plan, a non-prehensile tail, and a 2-1-2-3 dental formula, some unusual specializations are also seen. The proboscis monkey, found in the mangrove swamps of Borneo, is known for its unusual protruding nose, which provides a chamber for extra resonance for its vocalizations. When a monkey is alarmed, the nose fills with blood so that the resonating chamber becomes even more enlarged.

side of each jaw). This is not as much a functional distinction as it is a difference in evolutionary path. The common ancestor of Old World anthropoids and New World anthropoids possessed this 2-1-3-3 dental pattern. In the New World this pattern remained, while in Old World species a molar was lost.

Like Old World monkeys, New World monkeys have long tails. All members of one group, the family Atelidae, possess prehensile or grasping tails that they use as a fifth limb. The naked skin on the underside of their tail resembles the sensitive skin found at the tips of our fingers and is even covered with whorls like fingerprints.

Platyrrhines walk on all fours with their palms down and scamper along tree branches in search of fruit, which they eat sitting upright. Although New World monkeys spend much of their time in the trees, they rarely hang suspended below the branches or swing from limb to limb by their arms and have not developed the extremely long forelimbs and broad shoulders characteristic of the apes.

Old World Monkeys

Old World or catarrhine (from the Greek for "sharp-nosed") primates are divided from the apes at the superfamily taxonomic level. They resemble New World monkeys in their basic body plan, but their noses are distinctive, with closely spaced, downward-pointing nostrils. Divided into two subfamilies, the Cercopithecinae and the Colobinae, which contain eleven and ten genera, respectively, Old World monkeys are very diverse and occupy a broader range of habitats compared to New World monkey species, which occupy only tropical forests.

Some Old World monkeys are known for their unusual coloring, such as mandrills (pictured on page 62) with their brightly colored faces and genitals. Others, like proboscis monkeys, have long droopy noses. They all possess a 2-1-2-3 dental formula (two, rather than three, premolars on each side of each jaw) and tails that are never prehensile. They may be either arboreal or terrestrial, using a quadrupedal pattern of locomotion on the ground or in the trees in a palms-down position. Their body plan is narrow with hind limbs and forelimbs of equal length, a reduced clavicle (collarbone), and relatively fixed and sturdy shoulder, elbow, and wrist joints.

The arboreal species include the colubus guereza monkey—a species known to have been hunted by chimpanzees. Some are equally at home on the ground and in the trees, such as the macaques, of which some nineteen species range from tropical Africa and Asia to Gibraltar on the southern coast of Spain to Japan. At the northernmost portions of their range, these primates are living in temperate rather than strictly tropical environments.

Baboons, a kind of Old World monkey, have been of particular interest to paleoanthropologists because they live in environments similar to those in which humans may have originated. These baboons have abandoned trees (except for sleeping and refuge) and are largely terrestrial, living in the savannahs, deserts, and highlands of Africa. Somewhat dog-faced, they have long muzzles and a fierce look and eat a diet of leaves, seeds, insects, lizards, and small mammals. They live in large, well-organized troops comprised of related females and adult males that have transferred out of other troops.

Other Old World species also have much to tell us. For example, over the past several decades primatologists

While all apes or hominoids possess a suspensory hanging apparatus that allows them to hang from the branches of the forest canopy, only the gibbon is a master of brachiation—swinging from branch to branch. The nonhuman hominoids can also walk bipedally for brief periods of time when they need their arms free for carrying, but they cannot sustain bipedal locomotion for more than 50 to 100 yards. Hominoid anatomy is better adapted to knuckle-walking and hanging in the trees.

have documented primate social learning and innovation in colonies of macaques in Japan. Similarly, field studies of vervet monkeys in eastern and southern Africa have revealed that these Old World monkeys possess sophisticated communication abilities. In short, wherever primatologists study primates they make fascinating new discoveries. These discoveries contribute not only to the disciplines of primatology, evolutionary biology, and ecology but also to deepening our understanding of who we are as primates. Chapter 4 includes more on the behavior of baboons and a variety of other Old World monkey species.

Small and Great Apes

The apes of the hominoid superfamily are our closest cousins in the animal world. Like us, apes are large, wide-bodied primates with no tails. As described earlier, apes possess a shoulder anatomy specialized for hanging suspended below tree branches. All apes have this suspensory hanging apparatus, though among apes only small, lithe gibbons and talented gymnasts swing from branch to branch in the pattern known as *brachiation*. At the opposite extreme are gorillas, which generally climb trees, using their prehensile hands and feet to grip the trunk and branches. While smaller gorillas may swing between branches, in large individuals swinging is limited to leaning outward while reaching for fruit and clasping a limb for support. Still, most of their time is spent on the ground. All apes except humans and their immediate ancestors possess arms that are longer than their legs.

In moving on the ground, African apes "knuckle-walk" on the backs of their hands, resting their weight on the middle joints of the fingers. They stand erect when reaching for fruit, looking over tall grass, or doing any activity where they find an erect position advantageous. The semierect position is natural in apes when on the ground because the curvature of their vertebral column places their center of gravity, which is high in their bodies, in front of their hip joint. Thus they are both "top heavy" and "front heavy." Though apes can walk on two legs, or bipedally, for short distances, the structure of the ape pelvis is not well suited to support the weight of the torso and limbs for more than several minutes.

Gibbons and siamangs, the small apes that are native to Southeast Asia and Malaya, have compact, slim bodies with extraordinarily long arms compared to their short legs and stand about 3 feet high. Although their usual form of locomotion is brachiation, they can run erect, holding their arms out for balance. Gibbon and siamang males and females are similar in size, living in family groups of two parents and offspring.

Orangutans, found in Borneo and Sumatra, are divided into two distinct species. They are considerably taller than gibbons and siamangs and are much heavier, with the bulk characteristic of the great apes. In the closeness of the eyes and facial prominence, an orangutan looks very humanlike. The people of Sumatra gave orangutans their name, "person of the forest," using the Malay term *oran,* which means "person." On the ground, orangutans walk with their forelimbs in a fists-sideways or a palms-down position. They are, however, more arboreal than the African apes. Although sociable by nature, the orangutans of upland Borneo spend most of their time alone (except in the case of females with young), as they have to forage over a wide area to obtain sufficient food. By contrast, fruits and insects are sufficiently abundant in the swamps of Sumatra to sustain groups of adults and permit coordinated group travel. Thus gregariousness is a function of habitat productivity.[5]

---

[5] Normile, D. (1998). Habitat seen as playing larger role in shaping behavior. *Science 279*, 1454.

This male orangutan was photographed along the Gohong River on the island of Kaja, Borneo. A resident of a preserve where captive animals are rehabituated into the wild, the young male copied this hunting behavior by watching humans spear fishing along the same river. Although so far the orangutan has been unable to nab a fish with his spear tip, his intent is clear. This rare photograph, along with the first photograph of a swimming orangutan, appears in the beautiful book titled *Thinkers of the Jungle,* by Gerd Schuster, Willie Smits, and photographer Jay Ullal.

Gorillas, found in equatorial Africa, are the largest of the apes; an adult male can weigh over 450 pounds, with females about half that size. Scientists distinguish between two gorilla species: the lowland and mountain varieties. The body is covered with a thick coat of glossy black hair, and mature males have a silvery gray upper back. There is a strikingly human look about the face, and like humans, gorillas focus on things in their field of vision by directing the eyes rather than moving the head.

Gorillas are mostly ground dwellers, but the lighter females and young may sleep in trees in carefully constructed nests. Because of their weight, adult males spend less time in the trees but raise and lower themselves among the tree branches when searching for fruit. Gorillas knuckle-walk, using all four limbs with the fingers of the hand flexed, placing the knuckles instead of the palm of the hand on the ground. They stand erect to reach for fruit, to see something more easily, or to threaten perceived sources of danger with their famous chest-beating displays. Though known for these displays to protect the members of their troop, adult male silverback gorillas are the gentle giants of the forest. As vegetarians, gorillas devote a major portion of each day to eating volumes of plant matter to sustain their massive bodies. Although gorillas are gentle and tolerant, bluffing aggression is an important part of their behavioral repertoire.

Chimpanzees and bonobos are two closely related species of the same genus (*Pan*), pictured frequently throughout this chapter. Bonobos are restricted in their distribution to the rainforests of the Democratic Republic of Congo. The common chimpanzee, by contrast, is widely distributed in the forested portions of sub-Saharan Africa. Chimpanzees and bonobos are probably the best known of the apes and have long been favorites in zoos and circuses. In the past, bonobos were thought to be the same species. When bonobos were recognized as a distinct species in 1929, their common name was "pygmy chimpanzee." "Bonobo" replaced this term because not only does their size range overlap with that of chimpanzees, but as we will explore in the next chapter, this feature is not the most characteristic difference between the two groups.

Although thought of as particularly quick and clever, all four great apes are of equal intelligence, despite some differences in cognitive styles. More arboreal than gorillas but less so than orangutans, chimpanzees and bonobos forage on the ground much of the day, knuckle-walking like gorillas. At sunset, they return to the trees, where they build their nests.

Primate Conservation

The above survey of living primates illustrates the diversity of our closest living relatives. To ensure that they will continue to share the planet with us, primate conservation has become an issue of vital importance. Nearly 50 percent of the known primate species and subspecies face extinction in the next decade.[6]

In Asia, the statistics are even more alarming, with more than 70 percent of species threatened and at least 80 percent at risk in Indonesia and Vietnam. Included among them are all of the great apes, as well as such formerly widespread and adaptable species as rhesus macaques. In the wild these animals are threatened by habitat destruction caused by

[6] Kaplan, M. (2008, August 5). Almost half of primate species face extinction. doi:10.1038/news.2008.1013.

Globalscape

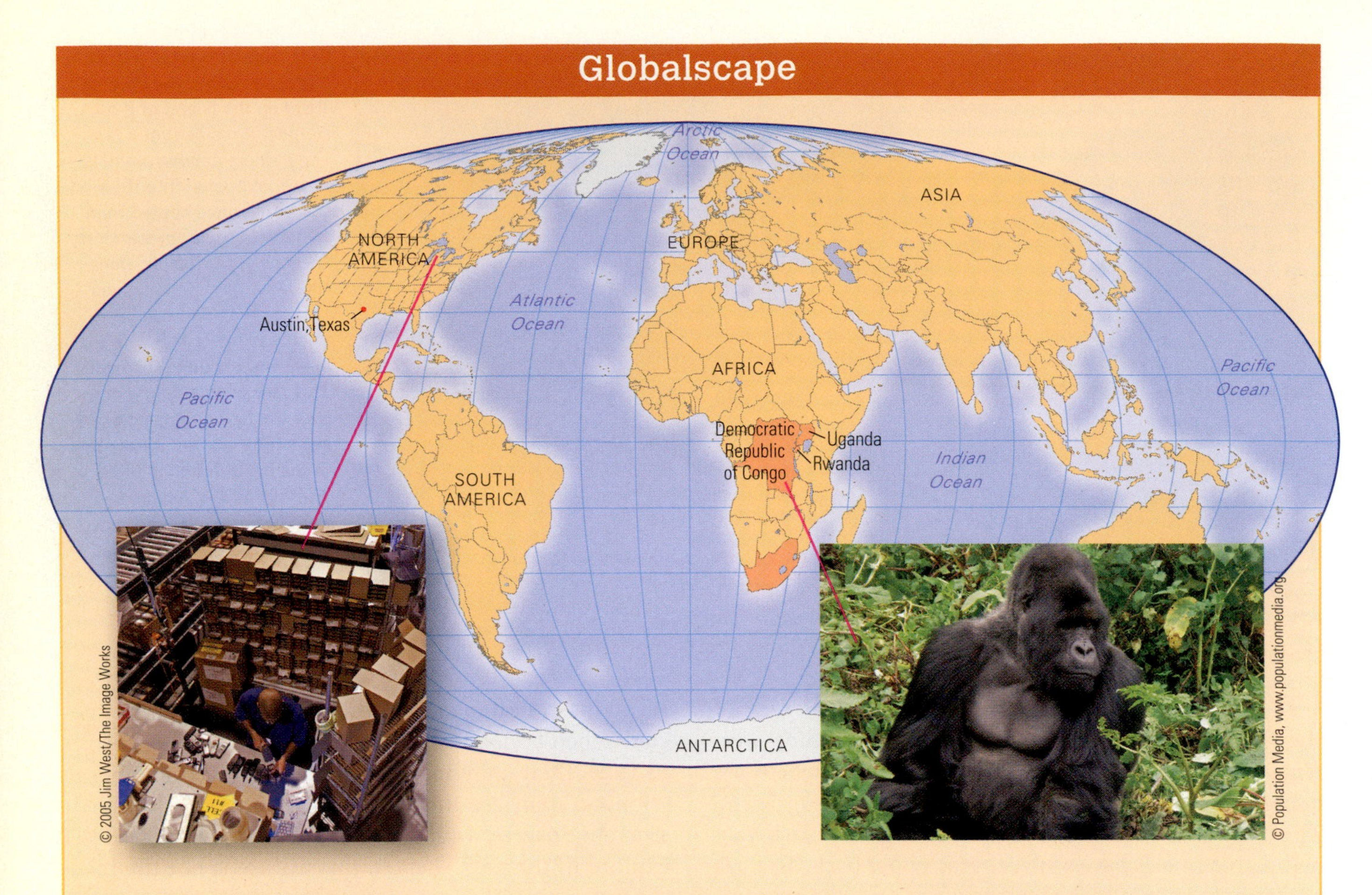

© 2005 Jim West/The Image Works

© Population Media, www.populationmedia.org

Gorilla Hand Ashtrays?
Tricia, a 20-year-old from Austin, Texas, blogs: "At that party did you meet the guy from South Africa that looked like an exact replica of Dave Matthews (only skinnier) who was talking about gorilla hand ashtrays?"[a] The unnamed guy was talking about one of the many real threats to gorillas in the wild. With no natural enemies, human actions alone are responsible for the shrinking population of gorillas in their natural habitats in Rwanda, Uganda, and the Democratic Republic of Congo. Despite conservation work, begun by the late primatologist Dian Fossey, who pioneered field studies of the gorillas in the 1970s, gorilla hand ashtrays and heads remain coveted souvenirs for unsavory tourists. A poacher can sell these body parts and the remaining bushmeat for a handsome profit.

Today, not only do logging and mining in gorilla habitats destroy these forests, but roads make it easier for poachers to access the gorillas. Local governments of Rwanda and Uganda in partnership with the Fossey Fund and the Bush Meat Project have set up poaching patrols and community partnerships to protect the endangered gorillas. Thousands of miles away, Tricia and her friends can also help by recycling their cell phones. The mineral coltan that is found in cell phones is mined primarily from gorilla habitats in the Democratic Republic of Congo. Recycling, as pictured here in a Michigan cell phone recycling plant, will reduce the amount of new coltan needed.

Global Twister Encouraging recycling of cell phones and discouraging poaching both will impact gorilla survival. How would you go about convincing average cell phone users or poachers to change their habits or livelihood to protect endangered gorillas?

---

[a] http://profile.myspace.com/index.cfm?fuseaction=user.viewprofile&friendid=40312227. (accessed July 3, 2006)

economic development (farming, lumbering, cattle ranching, rubber tapping), as well as by hunters and trappers who pursue them for food, trophies, research, or as exotic pets. Primatologists have long known the devastating effects of habitat destruction through slash-and-burn agriculture.

Further, it is not just traditional practices, such as the burning and clearing of tropical forests, that are destroying primate habitats. War also impacts primate habitats significantly, even after a war has ended. Hunters may use the automatic weapons left over from human conflicts in their pursuit of bushmeat. Also, because monkeys and apes are so closely related to humans, they are regarded as essential for biomedical research. While most primates in laboratories are bred in captivity, an active trade in live primates still threatens their local extinction. Globalization also exerts a profound impact on local conditions. This chapter's Globalscape illustrates how cell phones are impacting gorilla habitats and the survival of this species.

Because of their vulnerability, the conservation of primates has become a matter of urgency. Traditional conservation efforts have emphasized habitat preservation above all else, but primatologists are now expanding their efforts to include educating local communities and discouraging the hunting of primates for food and medical purposes. Some primatologists are even looking for alternative economic strategies for local peoples so that human and primate populations can return to the successful coexistence that prevailed before colonialism and globalization contributed to the destabilization of tradition homelands. This chapter's Anthropology Applied looks at these economic development efforts in the Democratic Republic of Congo.

In direct conservation efforts, primatologists work to maintain some populations in the wild, either by establishing preserves where animals are already living or by moving populations to suitable habitats. These approaches require constant monitoring and management to ensure that sufficient space and resources remain available. As humans encroach on primate habitats, translocation of primates to protected areas is an viable strategy for primate conservation, and the field studies by primatologists for such relocations are invaluable.

For example, when the troop of free-ranging baboons that primatologist Shirley Strum had been studying for fifteen years in Kenya began raiding people's crops and garbage on newly established farms, she was instrumental in successfully moving this troop and two other local troops—130 animals in all—to more sparsely inhabited country 150 miles away. Knowing their habits, Strum was able to trap, tranquilize, and transport the animals to their new home while preserving the baboons' vital social relationships. Strum's careful work allowed for a smooth transition. With social relations intact, the baboons did not abandon their new homes nor did they block the transfer of new males, with their all-important knowledge of local resources, into the troop. The success of her effort, which had never been tried with baboons, proves that translocation is a realistic technique for saving endangered primate species. However, this conservation effort depends first on available land, where preserves can be established to provide habitats for endangered primates.

A second strategy has been developed to help primates that have been illegally trapped—either for market as pets or for biomedical research. This approach involves returning these recovered animals to their natural habitats. Researchers have established orphanages in which specially trained human substitute mothers support the young primates so that they can gain enough social skills to return to living with their own species.

A third strategy to preventing primate extinction is to maintain breeding colonies in captivity. These colonies encourage psychological and physical well-being, as well as reproductive success. Primates in zoos and laboratories do not successfully reproduce when deprived of such amenities as opportunities for climbing, materials for nest building, others with whom to socialize, and places for privacy. While such features contribute to the success of breeding colonies in captivity, ensuring the survival of our primate cousins in suitable natural habitats is a far greater challenge that humans must meet in the years to come.

Because of their exceptional beauty, golden lion tamarin monkeys (or golden marmosets) have been kept as pets since colonial times. More recently, they have also been threatened by development, as they reside in the tropical forest habitats around the popular tourist destination of Rio de Janeiro, Brazil. A major conservation effort, initiated in the 1980s to save these monkeys, included planting wildlife corridors to connect the remaining forest patches and releasing animals bred in captivity into these newly created environments. Today live wild births have increased steadily, and the golden lion tamarin population is recovering from the threat of extinction.

The good news is the results of conservation efforts are beginning to show. For example, due to intense conservation programs, the population size of the mountain gorilla (*Gorilla beringei beringei*) is increasing, even with the political chaos of Rwanda, Uganda, and the Democratic Republic of Congo. Western lowland gorilla populations (*Gorilla gorilla*) are also on the rise. Similarly, tamarin monkey populations in Brazil have stabilized despite being on the brink of extinction thirty years ago, demonstrating the effectiveness of the conservation initiatives put into place. According to primatologist Sylvia Atsalis, "The presence alone of scientists has been shown to protect primates, acting as a deterrent to habitat destruction and hunting. The more people we can send, the more we can help to protect endangered primates."[7]

[7] Ibid.

Anthropology Applied

The Congo Heartland Project

Under the leadership of Belgian primatologist Jef Dupain, the African Wildlife Foundation has embarked on a number of projects to support the continued survival of bonobos and mountain gorillas in the Democratic Republic of Congo (DRC). Called the Congo Heartland Project, this work is designed to support the local human populations devastated by a decade of civil war in the Congo itself as well as the impact of the massive influx of refugees from war and genocide in neighboring Rwanda.

The rich rainforest habitats of the tributaries of the mighty Congo River in the DRC are the only natural habitats for bonobos in the world. Mountain gorillas can be found in the DRC and in neighboring Uganda and Rwanda. Primatological fieldwork thrived in sites established during the 1970s until the mid-1990s when war and genocide led to the forced removal of primatologists. While many left the region, Dupain stayed and monitored the kinds of bushmeat brought into the markets in Kinshasa. With the human population desperate and starving and the poachers armed with automatic weapons outnumbering the few park rangers charged with protecting the great apes, many primates perished. Since a fragile peace was achieved in 2003, initiatives of the Congo Heartland Project have been reestablished, including involving local communities in agricultural practices to protecting the Congo River and its tributaries and to preserve their precious animal populations.

Congo Heartland Project initiatives typically empower local communities in development efforts using a participative, interactive, and transparent approach. For example, a range of different ethnic groups, including those who are marginalized such as Pygmies and women, met with local authorities to reestablish the management policies of Dupain's field site (the Lomako Yokokala Faunal Reserve) as it reopened for researchers and ecotourists. Forty percent of the income generated in park revenues is to return to the local communities. According to Dupain, success for these projects is defined as follows:

> Local communities take part in decision making on how the protected area will be managed, on how revenue will be shared, and as a result, local communities take up the defense of their protected area. In time, densities of bonobo, bongo, forest elephant, Congo peacock, leopard, Allen's swamp monkey, black and white colobus, and many others will increase, more tourists and researchers will come and will be willing to pay for this environmental service, local communities will have increased access to education, medical treatment, electricity, clean water . . . the list goes on.

The African Wildlife Foundation team in the Congo Heartland. The Lomako Conservation Research Center provides jobs for local families and serves as an anchor for research, conservation, and microenterprise activities in the largely undisturbed Lomako Forest while also securing the habitat of the bonobo, a rare great ape that lives in the Lomako Forest.

Mange Bofaso put it best: "In Katanga they have diamonds. Here in Lomako, we have bonobos."[a]

The Congo Heartland Project also includes encouraging a variety of alternative economic practices in communities bordering existing wildlife preserves. For example, around the Virunga National Park, home to the endangered mountain gorilla, Congolese Enterprise Officer Wellard Makambo encourages and monitors bee keeping and a women's mushroom farm collective. He also advises members of a conflict resolution team dealing with gorillas that have left the wildlife preserve to raid human crops. Local communities require reassurance and restitution, while gorillas need to be returned safely to the park. When Makambo made his first trip back to the Bukima Ranger Station after the war, he wrote,

> While I was standing on the hill surveying the amazing Bukima view I felt like a mighty silverback gorilla looking at his bountiful bamboo kingdom. One whose life would be hopeless if this kingdom is destroyed. I tried to measure the effects of the war on people and on our activities and projects. It was tough getting my head around it: how to re-start things when you realise effort alone is not sufficient. You need stability as well, which is slowly coming back to this area.

These economic development projects are playing a crucial role in restoring the stability in the region required for the continued survival of bonobos and mountain gorillas.

[a]African Wildlife Foundation, Facebook blog. http://www.facebook.com/pages/African-Wildlife-Foundation/11918108948. (accessed June 13, 2009)

[b]Ibid.

Questions for Reflection

1. Does knowing more about the numerous similarities among the primates including humans motivate you personally to want to meet the challenge of preventing the extinction of our primate cousins? How would you go about doing this?

2. Considering some of the trends seen among the primates, such as increased brain size or reduced tooth number, why is it that we cannot say that some primates are more evolved than others? What is wrong with the statement that humans are more evolved than chimpanzees?

3. Two systems exist for dividing the primate order into suborders because of difficulties with classifying tarsiers. Should classification systems be based on genetic relationships or based on the biological concept of grade? Is the continued use of the older terminology an instance of inertia or a difference in philosophy? How do the issues brought up by the "tarsier problem" translate to the hominoids?

4. What aspects of mammalian primate biology do you see reflected in yourself or in other humans you know?

5. Many primate species are endangered today. What human factors are causing endangerment of primates, and how can we prevent the extinction of our closest living relatives?

Suggested Readings

de Waal, F.B.M. (2001). *The ape and the sushi master*. New York: Basic.

This masterful discussion of the presence of culture among apes moves this concept from an anthropocentric realm and ties it instead to communication and social organization. In an accessible style, Frans de Waal, one of the world's foremost experts on bonobos, demonstrates ape culture while challenging human intellectual theories designed to exclude animals from the "culture club."

de Waal, F.B.M. (2003). *My family album: Thirty years of primate photography*. Berkeley: University of California Press.

This book expertly blends scientific theories with photographs. De Waal illustrates the emotional intelligence, personality, and diverse social behaviors of the apes and Old World monkeys he has encountered in the field.

Fossey, D. (1983). *Gorillas in the mist*. Burlington, MA: Houghton Mifflin.

The late Dian Fossey is to gorillas what Jane Goodall is to chimpanzees. Fossey devoted years to the study of gorilla behavior in the field. This book is about the first thirteen years of her study; as well as being readable and informative, it is well illustrated.

Galdikas, B. (1995). *Reflections on Eden: My years with the orangutans of Borneo*. New York: Little, Brown.

Biruté Galdikas is the least known of the trio of young women sent by Louis Leakey in 1971 to study apes in the wild. Her work with the orangutans of Borneo, however, is magnificent. In this book she presents rich scientific information as well as her personal reflections on a life spent fully integrated with orangutans and the culture of Borneo.

Goodall, J. (1990). *Through a window: My thirty years with the chimpanzees of Gombe*. Boston: Houghton Mifflin.

This fascinating book is a personal account of Jane Goodall's early experiences studying wild chimpanzees in Tanzania. A pleasure to read and a fount of information on the behavior of these apes, the book is profusely illustrated as well.

Goodall, J. (2000). *Reason for hope: A spiritual journey*. New York: Warner.

Jane Goodall's memoir linking her monumental life's work with the chimpanzees of Gombe to her spiritual convictions. She clearly states her commitment to conferring on chimpanzees the same rights and respect experienced by humans through the exploration of difficult topics such as environmental destruction, animal abuse, and genocide. She expands the concept of humanity while providing us with powerful reasons to maintain hope.

Rowe, N., & Mittermeier, R. A. (1996). *The pictorial guide to the living primates*. East Hampton, NY: Pogonias.

Filled with dynamic photographs of primates in nature, this book also provides concise descriptions (including anatomy, taxonomy, diet, social structure, maps, and so on) for 234 species of primates. The book is useful for students and primatologists alike.

Challenge Issue Biological similarities among humans, apes, and Old World monkeys have led to the extensive use of nonhuman primate species in biomedical research aimed at preventing or curing disease in humans. These research animals are subjected to procedures that would be considered morally questionable if done on humans. Mickey, for example, was one of the hundreds of chimps who spent decades of her life alone in a concrete-and-steel windowless cage in a private research facility in New Mexico run by Frederick Coulston. After years of testing the effects of various infectious diseases, cosmetics, drugs, and pesticides on chimps like Mickey, the Coulston laboratory finally closed in 2002 when government research funding was withdrawn due to repeated violations of the Animal Welfare Act. But after years of abuse and neglect, research chimpanzees lack the skills to participate in chimpanzee social life. Furthermore, research animals have often been infected with deadly diseases such as HIV or hepatitis and cannot be released into the wild. Fortunately, Mickey and the other research chimps were given sanctuary through Save the Chimps, one of several organizations that rescue research animals. The human challenge for the future will be to use our abundant intelligence and social conscience, traits that our closest relatives also possess, to make the development of alternative research methods a top priority, so that nonhuman primates no longer have to be victimized by biomedical research.

Courtesy of Save the Chimps, the world's largest sanctuary for rescued chimpanzees; www.savethechimps.org

Primate Behavior

Chapter Preview

Why Do Anthropologists Study the Social Behavior of Primates?

The study of the social behavior of primates has contributed significantly to ecology and evolutionary theory. In addition, analysis of the behavior of monkeys and apes living today—especially those most closely related to us—provides important clues from which to reconstruct the adaptations and behavior patterns involved in the emergence of our earliest ancestors. The more we know about our nearest living relatives, the more it becomes clear that many of the differences between apes and humans reflect differences in degree of expression of shared characteristics.

What Determines the Behavior of Nonhuman Primates?

Diet, type of social organization, reproductive patterning, differences between the sexes, and the particular ecosystem a group of primates inhabits all contribute to the behavior of nonhuman primates. For many years primate behavior was seen as environmentally determined and tied to a certain diet and characteristics of the ecosystem. Today primatologists have established a strong socially learned component to primate behavior. Compared to other mammals, primates are characterized by a relatively long growth and development period that allows young primates to learn the behaviors of their social group. Some of these behaviors are influenced by the biology of the species while other behaviors derive from the traditions of the group.

Do Nonhuman Primates Possess Culture?

The more we learn of the behavior of our nearest primate cousins, the more we become aware of the importance of learned, socially shared practices and knowledge among the homonoids. This raises the question of whether chimpanzees, bonobos, and the other apes have culture. The answer appears to be yes. Detailed study of ape behavior has revealed variation among groups in use of tools and patterns of social engagement; these differences seem to derive from the traditions of the group rather than a biologically determined script. Humans share with the other apes an ability to learn the complex but flexible patterns of behavior particular to a social group during a long period of childhood dependency.

er 1960, the young Jane Goodall sent word back mentor, paleoanthropologist Louis Leakey, that she observed two chimps turning sticks into tools for fish- g termites out of nesting mounds (or termitarias). Leakey replied, "Now we must redefine tool, redefine Man, or accept chimpanzees as humans."[1] Field studies of primates by Western scientists have always contained a degree of anthropocentrism and a focus on what nonhuman primates can tell us about ourselves. How and why did humans develop as we did during the course of our evolutionary history? Because culture, tool use, and language were thought to be uniquely human, perhaps studies of primate behavior might unravel an old nature–nurture question: How much of human behavior is biologically determined and how much of it derives from culture?

Research into primate behavior has shown again and again the behavioral sophistication of our closest living relatives—the anthropoid primates in general and the hominoids in particular. Certainly, biology plays a role in primate behavior, but there are times that behavior is determined by the social traditions of the groups. Of course, as with humans, nature and nurture are linked. Primates require more time to reach adulthood compared to many other mammals. During their lengthy growth and development, young primates learn the behaviors of their social group.

While Goodall was originally criticized for giving names to the chimps she studied (David Greybeard and Goliath were the two chimps she first observed stripping twigs of their leaves to fish for termites), field studies have documented that primates know one another as individuals and can vary their behavior accordingly. The same is true of many other long-lived social mammals, such as elephants and dolphins. Observations of primates in their natural habitats over the past decades have shown that social interaction, organization, learning, reproduction, care of the young, and communication among our primate relatives are similar to human behavior.

Primates as Models for Human Evolution

As we will explore in the human evolution chapters to come, the human line split from a common ancestor that we share with the African apes. Although this split occurred millions of years ago, paleoanthropologists in the mid-20th century were hopeful that observations made among the living apes might shed light on the lifeways of the fossil species they were discovering. Louis Leakey encouraged Jane Goodall to begin her research with chimpanzees in Gombe Stream Chimpanzee Reserve (now a national park) on the eastern shores of Lake Tanganyika in Tanzania for this reason.

But the forest ape behavior model appeared flawed to the paleoanthropologists of the past. The fossil evidence indicated that the earliest human ancestors inhabited a grassy savannah environment rather than the tropical forests inhabited by the apes. Instead, paleoanthropologists turned to baboons: a group of Old World monkey species that inhabit the savannah environments of eastern Africa where the richest fossil evidence of our ancestors had also been found. While the savannah environment has certainly been important in human evolution, recent fossil discoveries and analyses have lead paleoanthropologists back into the forest. The earliest two-legged ancestors inhabited a forested environment and have lead paleoanthropologists to investigate the human origins in terms of the transition from forest to savannah.

Though baboons differ considerably from our two-legged ancestors, their survival strategies provide some clues as to how our ancestors adapted to the savannah environment. Members of the genus *Papio,* baboons are among the largest of the Old World monkeys. Fully terrestrial, troops of baboons can be seen sitting together on the dry savannah earth to forage for corms (thick, nutritious underground reproductive parts of plants). They keep a watchful eye out for predators while feeding. At the first sight or sound of danger, alarm calls by members of the troop will signal for all the individuals to retreat to safety.

Baboons live in groups that vary dramatically in size, from under ten to hundreds of individuals. In some species the groups are multi-male multi-female while others are made up of a series of harems—one male with several females that he dominates. Sexual dimorphism—anatomical differences between males and females—is high in baboons, and therefore males can use their physical advantages to overpower females easily. But the degree to which males choose to do so varies from group to group.

Extrapolating from baboons to theories about our ancestors poses problems. To use the words of primatologists Shirley Strum and William Mitchell, these baboon "models" often became baboon "muddles."[2] Paleoanthropologists

---

[1] Jane Goodall Institute. http://www.janegoodall.org/jane/study-corner/Jane/bio.asp. (accessed June 16, 2009)

[2] Strum, S., & Mitchell, W. (1987). Baboon models and muddles. In W. Kinsey (Ed.), *The evolution of human behavior: Primate models.* Albany: State University of New York Press.

The behavior of baboons, a type of Old World monkey, has been particularly well studied. There are several distinct species of baboon, each with their own social rules. In troops of hamadryas baboons (pictured), the sacred baboons of ancient Egypt, each male has a harem of females over which he dominates. Female hamadryas baboons, if transferred to a troop of olive baboons, where females are less submissive, maintain the passive behaviors learned in their original troop. But a female olive baboon placed in the hamadryas troop quickly learns submissive behaviors in order to survive.

did not expect our ancestors to possess tails or **ischial callosities**—the hardened, nerveless buttock pads that allow baboons to sit for long periods of time. Tails are strictly a monkey characteristic, not an ape one, and among the hominoids, only gibbons and siamangs possess ischial callosities. Instead, paleoanthropologists looking for evolutionary information were trying to piece together examples of *convergence*—of behaviors that might appear in large-bodied, dimorphic primates living in large multi-male multi-female groups in a savannah environment.

The upside of paleoanthropology's "baboon hypothesis" is that it led to many excellent long-term field studies of baboons that have yielded fascinating data on their social organization, omnivorous diet, mating patterns and other reproductive strategies, communication, and so forth. As with most primate field studies, the evolutionary questions remain in the background while the rich repertoire of primate behavior takes center stage.

Primate Social Organization

Primates are social animals, living and traveling in groups that vary in size and composition from species to species. Different environmental and biological factors have been linked to the group's size, and all the possible organizational forms appear in various primate species. For example, gibbons live in small nuclear family units consisting of a pair of bonded adults and their offspring. Orangutans tend to lead solitary existences, males and females coming together only to mate. Young orangutans stay with their mothers until they reach adult status.

Chimps and bonobos live in large multi-male multi-female groups. Among chimps and bonobos, the largest social organizational unit is the **community,** composed of fifty or more individuals who collectively inhabit a large geographic area. Rarely, however, are all these animals together at one time. Instead, they are usually found ranging singly or in small subgroups consisting of adult males together, females with their young, or males and females together with young. In the course of their travels, subgroups may join forces and forage together, but sooner or later these subgroups break up again into smaller units. When they do, some individuals split off and others join, so that the new subunits may be different in their composition from the ones that initially came together.

ischial callosities Hardened, nerveless pads on the buttocks that allow baboons and other primates to sit for long periods of time.

community A unit of primate social organization composed of fifty or more individuals who inhabit a large geographic area together.

The gorilla group is a "family" of five to thirty individuals led by a mature silver-backed male and including younger (black-backed) males, females, the young, and occasionally other silverbacks. Subordinate males, however, are usually prevented by the dominant male from mating with the group's females. Thus young, sexually mature males, who take on the characteristic silver color at the end of the sexual maturation process (about 11 to 13 years of age), are forced to leave their **natal group**—the community they have known since birth—by the dominant silverback. After some time as a solitary male in the forest, a young silverback may find the opportunity to start his own social group by winning outside females. In the natal group, if the dominant male is weakening with age, one of his sons may remain with the group to succeed to his father's position. Alternatively, an outside male may take over the group. With the dominant male controlling the group, gorillas rarely fight over food, territory, or sex, but they will fight fiercely to maintain the integrity of the group.

In many primate species, including humans, adolescence is a time during which individuals change the relationships they have had with their natal group. Among primates this change takes the form of migration to new social groups. In many species, females constitute the core of the social system. For example, offspring tend to remain with the group to which their mother, rather than their father, belongs. Among gorillas, male adolescents leave their natal groups more frequently than females. However, adolescent female chimpanzees and bonobos are frequently the ones to migrate.

In two Tanzanian chimpanzee communities studied, about half the females may leave the community they have known since birth to join another group.[3] Other females may also temporarily leave their group to mate with males of another group. Among bonobos, adolescent females appear to always transfer to another group, where they promptly establish bonds with females of their new group. While biological factors such as the hormonal influences on sexual maturity play a role in adolescent migration, the variation across species, and within the chimpanzees in dispersal patterns, indicates that differences may also derive from the learned social traditions of the group.

Home Range

Primates usually move about within a circumscribed area, or **home range,** which varies in size depending on the group and on ecological factors such as availability of food. Ranges often change seasonally, and the number of miles traveled by a group in a day varies. Some areas, known as *core areas,* are used more often than others. Core areas typically contain water, food sources, resting places, and sleeping trees. The ranges of different groups may overlap, as among bonobos, where 65 percent of one community's range may overlap with that of another.[4] By contrast, chimpanzee territories, at least in some regions, are exclusively occupied and will be defended from intrusion (Figure 4.1).

Gorillas do not defend their home range against incursions of others of their kind, although they will defend their group if it is in any way threatened. In the lowlands of Central Africa, it is not uncommon to find several families feeding in close proximity to one another.[5] In encounters with other communities, bonobos will defend their immediate space through vocalizations and displays but rarely through fighting. Usually, they settle down and feed side by side, not infrequently grooming, playing, and engaging in sexual activity between groups as well.

Chimpanzees, by contrast, have been observed patrolling their territories to ward off potential trespassers. Moreover, Jane Goodall (see Anthropologists of Note) has recorded the destruction of one chimpanzee community by another invading group. This sort of deadly intercommunity interaction has never been observed among bonobos. Some have interpreted the apparent territorial behavior as an expression of the supposedly violent nature of chimpanzees. However, another interpretation is that the violence that Goodall witnessed was a response to crowding as a consequence of human activity.[6]

[3] Moore, J. (1998). Comment. *Current Anthropology 39,* 412.

[4] Parish, A. R. (1998). Comment. *Current Anthropology 39,* 414.

[5] Parnell, R. (1999). Gorilla exposé. *Natural History 108* (8), 43.

[6] Power, M. G. (1995). Gombe revisited: Are chimpanzees violent and hierarchical in the "free" state? *General Anthropology 2* (1), 5–9.

natal group The group or the community an animal has inhabited since birth.

home range The geographic area within which a group of primates usually moves.

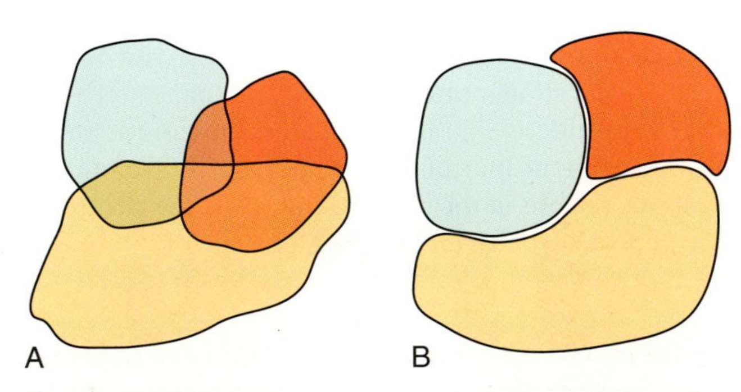

Figure 4.1 Home ranges illustrated in A can be overlapping. When members of the same species meet one another in the shared parts of the range, there might be some tension, deference, or peaceful mingling. Some groups maintain clear territories (B) that are strictly defended from any intrusion by members of the same species.

Anthropologists of Note

Jane Goodall (b. 1934) ▪ *Kinji Imanishi (1902–1992)*

In July 1960, **Jane Goodall** arrived with her mother at the Gombe Chimpanzee Reserve on the shores of Lake Tanganyika in Tanzania. Goodall was the first of three women Kenyan anthropologist Louis Leakey sent out to study great apes in the wild (the others were Dian Fossey and Birutė Galdikas, who studied gorillas and orangutans, respectively); her task was to begin a long-term study of chimpanzees. Little did she realize that, more than forty years later, she would still be at it.

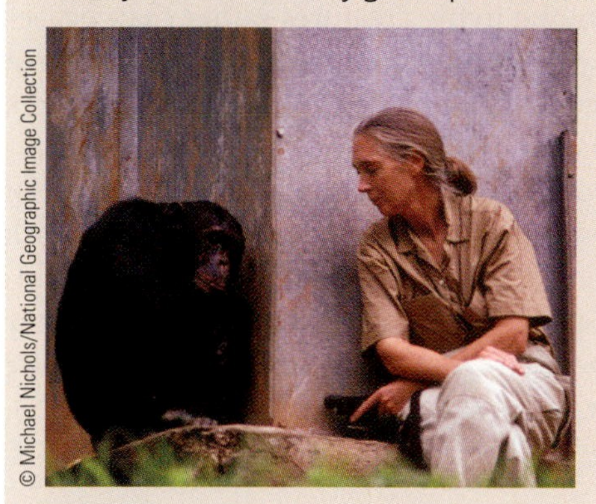

© Michael Nichols/National Geographic Image Collection

Born in London, Goodall grew up and was schooled in Bournemouth, England. As a child, she dreamed of going to live in Africa, so when an invitation arrived to visit a friend in Kenya, she jumped at the opportunity. While in Kenya, she met Leakey, who gave her a job as an assistant secretary. Before long, she was on her way to Gombe. Within a year, the outside world began to hear the most extraordinary things about this pioneering woman: tales of tool-making apes, cooperative hunts by chimpanzees, and what seemed like exotic chimpanzee rain dances. By the mid-1960s, her work had earned her a doctorate from Cambridge University, and Gombe was on its way to becoming one of the most dynamic field stations for the study of animal behavior anywhere in the world.

Although Goodall is still very much involved with chimpanzees, she spends a good deal of time these days lecturing, writing, and overseeing the work of other researchers. She is heavily committed to primate con-servation. Goodall is also passionately dedicated to halting illegal trafficking in chimps as well as fighting for the humane treatment of captive chimps.

Kinji Imanishi—naturalist, explorer, and mountain climber—profoundly influenced primatology in Japan and throughout the world. Like all Japanese scholars, he was fully aware of Western methods and theories but developed a radically different approach to the scientific study of the natural world.

© Bunataro Imanishi

He dates his transformation to a youthful encounter with a grasshopper: "I was walking along a path in a valley, and there was a grasshopper on a leaf in a shrubbery. Until that moment I had happily caught insects, killed them with chloroform, impaled them on pins, and looked up their names, but I realized I knew nothing at all about how this grasshopper lived in the wild."[a] In his most important work, *The World of Living Things*, first published in 1941, Imanishi developed a comprehensive theory about the natural world rooted in Japanese cultural beliefs and practices.

Imanishi's work challenged Western evolutionary theory in several ways. First, Imanishi's theory, like Japanese culture, does not emphasize differences between humans and other animals. Second, rather than focusing on the biology of individual organisms, Imanishi suggested that naturalists examine "specia" (a species society) to which individuals belong as the unit of analysis. Rather than focusing on time, Imanishi emphasized space in his approach to the natural world. He highlighted the harmony of all living things rather than conflict and competition among individual organisms.

Imanishi's research techniques, now standard worldwide, developed directly from his theories: long-term field study of primates in their natural societies using methods from ethnography. With his students, Imanishi conducted pioneering field studies of African apes and Japanese and Tibetan macaques, long before Louis Leakey sent the first Western primatologists into the field. Japanese primatologists were the first to document the importance of kinship, the complexity of primate societies, patterns of social learning, and the unique char-acter of each primate social group. Because of the work by Imanishi and his students, we now think about the distinct cultures of primate societies.

---

[a] Heita, K. (1999). Imanishi's world view. *Journal of Japanese Trade and Industry 18* (2), 15.

Social Hierarchy

Relationships among individuals within ape communities are relatively harmonious. In the past, primatologists believed that male **dominance hierarchies** (the pattern seen in baboons), in which some animals outrank and may dominate others, formed the basis of primate social structures. The researchers noted that physical strength and size play a role in determining an animal's rank. By this measure males generally outrank females. However, the gender bias of the humans studying these animals may have contributed disproportionately to this theory, with its emphasis on domination through superior size and strength. Male dominance hierarchies seemed "natural" to the early primatologists who, after all, were coming from human social systems organized according to similar principles.

With the benefit of detailed field studies over the last forty years, many of which were pioneered by female primatologists

dominance hierarchies Observed ranking systems in primate societies ordering individuals from high (alpha) to low standing corresponding to predictable behavioral interactions including domination.

like Goodall, the nuances of primate social behavior and the importance of female primates have been documented. High-ranking (alpha) females may dominate low-ranking males. In groups such as bonobos, females dominate overall. While strength and size contribute to an animal's rank, other important factors include the rank of its mother and effectiveness at creating alliances with other individuals. For males, drive or motivation to achieve high status also influences rank. For example, in the community studied by Goodall, one male chimp hit upon the idea of incorporating noisy kerosene cans into his charging displays, thereby intimidating all the other males.[7] As a result, he rose from relatively low status to the number one (alpha) position.

Among bonobos, female–female bonds play an important role in determining rank. Further, the strength of the bond between mother and son may interfere with the ranking among males. Not only do bonobo males defer to females in feeding, but alpha females have been observed chasing high-ranking males. Alpha males even yield to low-ranking females, and groups of females form alliances in which they may cooperatively attack males, to the point of inflicting blood-drawing injuries.[8] Thus instead of the male dominance characteristic of chimps, one sees female dominance.

Western primatologists' focus on social rank and attack behavior may be a legacy of the individualistic, competitive nature of the societies in which evolutionary theory originated. To a certain degree, natural selection relies upon a struggle among living creatures rather than peaceful coexistence. By contrast, noted Japanese primatologist Kinji Imanishi (see Anthropologists of Note) developed a harmonious theory of evolution and initiated field studies of bonobos that have demonstrated the importance of social cooperation rather than competition. As the work of Dutch primatologist Frans de Waal illustrates in the following Original Study, reconciliation after an attack may be even more important from an evolutionary perspective than the actual attack.

[7] Goodall, J. (1986). *The chimpanzees of Gombe: Patterns of behavior* (p. 424). Cambridge, MA: Belknap.

[8] de Waal, F. B. M., Kano, T., & Parish, A. R. (1998). Comments. *Current Anthropology 39,* 408, 410, 413.

Original Study

Reconciliation and Its Cultural Modification in Primates *by Frans B. M. de Waal*

Despite the continuing popularity of the struggle-for-life metaphor, it is increasingly recognized that there are drawbacks to open competition, hence that there are sound evolutionary reasons for curbing it. The dependency of social animals on group life and cooperation makes aggression a socially costly strategy. The basic dilemma facing many animals, including humans, is that they sometimes cannot win a fight without losing a friend.

This photo shows what may happen after a conflict—in this case between two female bonobos. About 10 minutes after their fight, the two females approach each other, with one clinging to the other and both rubbing their clitorises and genital swellings together in a pattern known as genito-genital rubbing, or GG-rubbing. This sexual contact, typical of bonobos, constitutes a so-called reconciliation. Chimpanzees, which are closely related to bonobos (and to us: bonobos and chimpanzees are our closest animal relatives), usually reconcile in a less sexual fashion, with an embrace and mouth-to-mouth kiss.

© Amy Parish/Anthro-Photo

Two adult female bonobos engage in so-called GG-rubbing, a sexual form of reconciliation typical of this species.

There is now evidence for reconciliation in more than twenty-five different primate species, not just in apes but also in many monkeys. The same sorts of studies have been conducted on human children in the schoolyard, and of course children show reconciliation as well. Researchers have even found reconciliation in dolphins, spotted hyenas, and some other nonprimates. Reconciliation seems widespread: a common mechanism found whenever relationships need to be maintained despite occasional conflict.[a,b]

The definition of reconciliation used in animal research is a friendly reunion between former opponents not long after a conflict. This is somewhat different from definitions in the dictionary, primarily because we look for an empirical definition that is useful in observational studies—in our case, the stipulation that the reunion happen not long after the conflict. There is no intrinsic reason that a reconciliation could not occur after hours or days, or, in the case of humans, generations.

Let me describe two interesting elaborations on the mechanism of reconciliation. One is *mediation*. Chimpanzees are the only animals to use mediators in conflict resolution. In order to be able to mediate conflict, one needs to understand relationships outside of oneself, which may be the reason why other animals fail to show this aspect of conflict resolution. For example, if two male chimpanzees have been involved in a fight, even on a very large island as where I did my studies, they can easily avoid each other, but instead they will sit opposite from each other, not too far apart, and avoid eye contact. They can sit like this for a long time. In this situation, a third party, such as an older female, may move in and try to solve the issue. The female will approach one of the males and groom him for a brief while. She then gets up and walks slowly to the other male, and the first male walks right behind her.

We have seen situations in which, if the first male failed to follow, the female turned around to grab his arm and make him follow. So the process of getting the two males in proximity seems intentional on the part of the female. She then begins grooming the other male, and the first male grooms her. Before long, the female disappears from the scene, and the males continue grooming: She has in effect brought the two parties together.

There exists a limited anthropological literature on the role of conflict resolution, a process absolutely crucial for the maintenance of the human social fabric in the same way that it is crucial for our primate relatives. In human society, mediation is often done by high-ranking or senior members of the community, sometimes culminating in feasts in which the restoration of harmony is celebrated.[c]

The second elaboration on the reconciliation concept is that it is not purely instinctive, not even in our animal relatives. It is a learned social skill subject to what primatologists now increasingly call "culture" (meaning that the behavior is subject to learning from others as opposed to genetic transmission).[d] To test the learnability of reconciliation, I conducted an experiment with young rhesus and stumptail monkeys. Not nearly as conciliatory as stumptail monkeys, rhesus monkeys have the reputation of being rather aggressive and despotic. Stumptails are considered more laid-back and tolerant. We housed members of the two species together for 5 months. By the end of this period, they were a fully integrated group: They slept, played, and groomed together.

After 5 months, we separated them again, and measured the effect of their time together on conciliatory behavior.

The research controls—rhesus monkeys who had lived with one another, without any stumptails—showed absolutely no change in the tendency to reconcile. Stumptails showed a high rate of reconciliation, which was also expected, because they also do so if living together. The most interesting group was the experimental rhesus monkeys, those who had lived with stumptails. These monkeys started out at the same low level of reconciliation as the rhesus controls, but after they had lived with the stumptails, and after we had segregated them again so that they were now housed only with other rhesus monkeys who had gone through the same experience, these rhesus monkeys reconciled as much as stumptails do. This means that we created a "new and improved" rhesus monkey, one that made up with its opponents far more easily than a regular rhesus monkey.[e]

This was in effect an experiment on social culture: We changed the culture of a group of rhesus monkeys and made it more similar to that of stumptail monkeys by exposing them to the practices of this other species. This experiment also shows that there exists a great deal of flexibility in primate behavior. We humans come from a long lineage of primates with great social sophistication and a well-developed potential for behavioral modification and learning from others.

[a]de Waal, F.B.M. (2000). Primates: A natural heritage of conflict resolution. *Science 28,* 586–590.

[b]Aureli, F., & de Waal, F.B.M. (2000). *Natural conflict resolution.* Berkeley: University of California Press.

[c]Reviewed by Frye, D. P. (2000). Conflict management in cross-cultural perspective. In F. Aureli & F.B.M. de Waal, *Natural conflict resolution* (pp. 334–351). Berkeley: University of California Press.

[d]For a discussion of the animal culture concept, see de Waal, F.B.M. (2001). *The ape and the sushi master.* New York: Basic.

[e]de Waal, F.B.M., & Johanowicz, D. L. (1993). Modification of reconciliation behavior through social experience: An experiment with two macaque species. *Child Development 64*, 897–908.

Individual Interaction and Bonding

The social sophistication characteristic of primates is evident in behaviors that at first glance might seem wholly practical. For example, **grooming,** the ritual cleaning of another animal to remove parasites and other matter from its skin or coat, is a common pastime for both chimpanzees and bonobos. The grooming animal deftly parts the hair of the one being groomed and removes any foreign object, often eating it. But besides serving hygienic purposes, it can be a social gesture of friendliness, closeness, appeasement, reconciliation, or even submission.

Bonobos and chimpanzees have favorite grooming partners. Group sociability, an important behavioral trait undoubtedly also found among human ancestors, is further expressed in embracing, touching, and the joyous welcoming of other members of the ape community.

Interestingly, different chimp communities have different styles of grooming. In one East African group, for example, the two chimps groom each other face to face, with one hand, while clasping their partner's free hand. In another group 90 miles distant, the hand clasp is unknown. In East Africa, all communities incorporate leaves in their grooming, but in West Africa they do not.

Gorillas, though gentle and tolerant, are also aloof and independent, and individual interaction among

grooming The ritual cleaning of another animal's coat to remove parasites and other matter.

Grooming is an important activity among all catarrhine primates, as shown here in a group of chimps grooming each other in a pattern known as the Domino Effect. Such activity is important for strengthening bonds among individual members of the group.

adults tends to be quite restrained. Friendship or closeness between adults and infants is more evident. Among bonobos, chimpanzees, gorillas, and orangutans, as among most other primates, the mother–infant bond is the strongest and longest lasting. It may endure for many years—commonly for the lifetime of the mother. Gorilla infants share their mothers' nests but have also been seen sharing nests with mature, childless females. Bonobo, chimpanzee, and gorilla males are attentive to juveniles and play a role in their socialization. Bonobo males even carry infants on occasion. Their interest in a youngster does not elicit the nervous reaction from the mother that it does among chimps; chimp mothers may be reacting to the occasional infanticide on the part of chimpanzee males, a behavior never observed among bonobos.

Sexual Behavior

Most mammals mate only during specified breeding seasons occurring once or twice a year. While some primates have a fixed breeding season tied to a simultaneous increase in body fat, or to the consumption of specific plant foods, many primate species are able to breed at any time during the course of the year. Among the African apes, as with humans, no fixed breeding season exists. In chimps, frequent sexual activity—initiated by either the male or the female—occurs during **estrus,** the period when the female is receptive to impregnation. In chimpanzees, estrus is signaled by vivid swelling of the skin around the genitals. Bonobo females, by contrast, appear as if they are fertile at all times due to their constantly swollen genitals and interest in sex. Gorillas appear to show less interest in sex compared to either chimps or bonobos.

By most human standards, the sexual behavior of chimps is promiscuous. A dozen or so males have been observed to have as many as fifty copulations in one day with a single female in estrus. For the most part, females mate with males of their own group. Dominant males try to monopolize females in full estrus, although cooperation from the female is usually required for this to succeed. In addition, an individual female and a lower-ranking male sometimes form a temporary bond, leaving the group together for a few "private" days during the female's fertile period. Interestingly, the relationship between reproductive success and social rank differs for males and females. In the chimpanzee community studied by Goodall, about half the infants were sired by low- or mid-level males. Although for females high rank is linked with successful reproduction, social success for males—achieving alpha status—does not translate neatly into the evolutionary currency of reproductive success.

In contrast to chimpanzees, bonobos (like humans) do not limit their sexual behavior to times of female fertility. The constant genital swelling of bonobos, in effect, conceals the females' **ovulation,** or moment when an egg released into the womb is receptive for fertilization.

estrus In some primate females, the time of sexual receptivity during which ovulation is visibly displayed.

ovulation Moment when an egg released from the ovaries into the womb is receptive for fertilization.

Because geladas spend far more time sitting than upright, signaling ovulation through genital swelling is nowhere near as practical as signaling it through the reddening of a patch of furless skin on their chests. This way it is easy for other members of the group to see that they are fertile even while they are foraging.

Ovulation is also concealed in humans, by the absence of genital swelling at all times.

Concealed ovulation in humans and bonobos may play a role in separating sexual activity for social and pleasurable reasons from the purely biological task of reproduction. In fact, among bonobos (as among humans) sexuality goes far beyond male–female mating for purposes of biological reproduction. Primatologists have observed virtually every possible combination of ages and sexes engaging in a remarkable array of sexual activities, including oral sex, tongue-kissing, and massaging each other's genitals.[9] Male bonobos may mount each other, or one may rub his scrotum against that of the other. They have also been observed "penis fencing"—hanging face to face from a branch and rubbing their erect penises together as if crossing swords. Among females, genital rubbing is particularly common.

As described in this chapter's Original Study, the primary function of most of this sex, both hetero- and homosexual, is to reduce tensions and resolve social conflicts. Bonobo sexual activity is very frequent but also very brief, lasting only 8 to 10 seconds. Since the documentation of sexual activities among bonobos, field studies by primatologists are now recording a variety of sexual behaviors among other species as well. This chapter's Biocultural Connection describes a variation on sexuality in orangutans that has been described as disturbing.

In gorilla families, the dominant silverback tends to have exclusive breeding rights with the females, although he will sometimes tolerate the presence of a young adult male and allow him occasional access to a low-ranking female. Generally by the time a young male becomes a silverback he must leave "home," luring partners away from other established groups, in order to have reproductive success.

Field studies have revealed variation in the typical gorilla pattern of a single dominant male. There are gorilla groups in Uganda and Rwanda in which there are multiple silverback males. Still, in one gorilla group with more than one adult male studied in Rwanda, a single dominant male fathered all but one of ten juveniles.[10]

Although the vast majority of primate species are not **monogamous**—bonded exclusively to a single sexual partner—in their mating habits, many smaller species of New World monkeys, a few island-dwelling populations of leaf-eating Old World monkeys, and all of the smaller apes (gibbons and siamangs) appear to mate for life with a single individual of the opposite sex. None of these species is closely related to human beings, nor do monogamous species ever display the degree of sexual dimorphism—anatomical differences between males and females—that is characteristic of our closest primate relatives or that was characteristic of our own ancient ancestors.

Evolutionary biologists, dating back to Charles Darwin himself,[11] have proposed that sexual dimorphism (for example, larger male size in apes, beautiful feathers in peacocks) relates to competition among males for access to females. Females only evolved by what Canadian primatologist Linda Fedigan has called the "coat-tails theory"

[9] de Waal, F. B. M. (2001). *The ape and the sushi master* (pp. 131–132). New York: Basic.

[10] Gibbons, A. (2001). Studying humans—and their cousins and parasites. *Science 292*, 627.

[11] Darwin, C. (1936). *The descent of man and selection in relation to sex.* New York: Random House (Modern Library). (orig. 1871)

monogamous Mating for life with a single individual of the opposite sex.

Biocultural Connection

Disturbing Behaviors of the Orangutan

by Anne Nacey Maggioncalda and Robert M. Sapolsky

An adult male orangutan is an impressive sight. The animal has a pair of wide cheek pads, called flanges, and a well-developed throat sac used for emitting loud cries known as long calls. The mature male also has long, brightly colored hair on its body and face. These are secondary sexual characteristics, the flamboyant signals that male orangutans flaunt to proclaim their fertility and fitness to the opposite sex. The features emerge during orangutan adolescence: Males reach puberty at around 7 to 9 years of age, then spend a few years in a far-from-impressive "subadult" stage, during which they are about the same size as mature females. The males reach their adult size and develop secondary sexual traits by ages 12 to 14. Or at least that's what primate researchers used to think.

As stable social groups of orangutans were established in zoos, however, it became clear that an adolescent male could remain a subadult, in a state of arrested development, until his late teens. In the 1970s, studies of orangutans in the rainforests of Southeast Asia by Biruté M. F. Galdikas . . . and others produced the same finding: Sometimes males were arrested adolescents for a decade or more, about half their potential reproductive lives. Variability of this magnitude is fascinating—it is like finding a species in which pregnancy could last anywhere from six months to five years.

Biologists are keenly interested in studying cases of arrested development because they often shed light on the processes of growth and maturation. . . . Environmental factors can . . . slow or halt an organism's development. For instance, food shortages delay maturation in humans and many other animals. This response is logical from an evolutionary standpoint—if it is unclear whether you will survive another week, it makes no sense to waste calories by adding bone mass or developing secondary sexual characteristics. Gymnasts and ballet dancers who exercise to extremes and anorexics who starve themselves sometimes experience delayed onset of puberty.

Among male orangutans, though, the cause of arrested development seems to lie in the animals' social environment. The presence of dominant adult males appears to delay the maturation of adolescent males in the same vicinity. Until recently, researchers believed that they were observing a stress-induced pathology—that is, the adolescent orangutans stopped developing because the adult males bullied and frightened them. Over the past few years, however, we have conducted studies (by measuring stress, growth, and reproductive hormone levels in urine) suggesting that arrested development among orangutans is not a pathology but an adaptive evolutionary strategy. The arrested adolescent males are capable of impregnating females, and by staying small and immature (in terms of secondary sexual features) they minimize the amount of food they need and lower the

© Danita Delimont/Alamy

© John Giustina

The male orangutan on the right has retained his adolescent physique even though his primary sex characteristics are fully mature, allowing him to father offspring. The male on the left has developed the secondary sexual characteristics typical of the adult male orangutan. These two individuals might be very close to the same age.

risk of serious conflict with adult males. But the strategy of these arrested adolescents has a disquieting aspect: They copulate forcibly with females. In other words, they rape.

These findings overturned some long-held assumptions about orangutans. Apparently, arrested adolescents are neither stressed nor reproductively suppressed. What is going on? It turns out that there is more than one way for a male orangutan to improve his chances of reproducing.

A cornerstone of modern evolutionary theory is that animal behavior has evolved not for the good of the species or the social group but to maximize the number of gene copies passed on by an individual and its close relatives. For a long time, the study of primates was dominated by simplistic models of how animals achieve this goal. According to these models, male behavior consists of virtually nothing but aggression and competition to gain access to females. If only one female is sexually receptive in a group with many males, this competition would result in the highest-ranking male mating with her; if two females are receptive, the males ranking first and second in the hierarchy would mate with them, and so on.

But this kind of behavior is rarely seen among social primates. Instead male primates can choose alternative strategies to maximize their reproductive success. Why should there be alternatives? Because the seemingly logical strategy—developing powerful muscles and dramatic secondary sexual characteristics to excel at male–male competition—has some serious drawbacks. In many species, maintaining those secondary characteristics requires elevated testosterone levels, which have a variety of adverse effects on health. The aggression that comes with such a strategy is not great for health either.

Furthermore, increased body mass means greater metabolic demands and more pressure for successful food acquisition. During famines, the bigger primates are less likely to survive. For an arboreal species such as the orangutan, the heavier body of the mature male also limits which trees and branches can be accessed for food. And the development of secondary sexual characteristics makes a male more conspicuous, both to predators and to other males that view those characteristics as a challenge.

In contrast, the key impression that a developmentally arrested male communicates to an adult male is a lack of threat or challenge, because the immature male looks like a kid. Arrested male orangutans are apparently inconspicuous enough to be spared a certain amount of social stress. What is more, the "low profile" of these animals may actually give them a competitive advantage when it comes to reproduction. In many primate species, the low-ranking males are actually doing a fair share of the mating. Genetic paternity testing of these primates has shown that the subordinate males are quite successful in passing on their genes. . . .

The great majority of adult female orangutans are sexually receptive only to mature males. So how do the arrested males mate? Observations of orangutans both in the wild and in captive populations have indicated that the arrested males forcibly copulate with females. Rape is an apt term for these copulations: The adult females usually resist the arrested adolescents fiercely, biting the males whenever they can and emitting loud, guttural sounds (called rape grunts) that are heard only under these circumstances. Adult males sometimes rape, too, but not nearly as often as the arrested males.

Thus, two reproductive strategies appear to have evolved for adolescent male orangutans. If no fully mature males are nearby, the adolescent will most likely develop quickly in the hopes of attracting female attention. When adult males are present, however, a strategy of arrested development has its advantages. If the social environment changes—say, if the nearby adult males die off or migrate—the arrested males will rapidly develop secondary sexual features and change their behavior patterns. Researchers are now trying to determine exactly how the presence or absence of adult males triggers hormonal changes in the adolescents.

What are the lessons we can learn from the male orangutan? First, a situation that seems stressful from a human's perspective may not necessarily be so. Second, the existence of alternative reproductive strategies shows that the optimal approach can vary dramatically in different social and ecological settings. There is no single blueprint for understanding the evolution of behavior. Third, although the recognition of alternative strategies built around female choice has generally met with a receptive audience among scientists, the rape-oriented strategy of arrested male orangutans is not so pleasing. But the study of primates has demonstrated time and again that the behavior of these animals is far from Disney-esque.

One must be cautious, however, in trying to gain insights into human behavior by extrapolating from animal studies. There is a temptation to leap to a wrongheaded conclusion: Because forcible copulation occurs in orangutans and something similar occurs in humans, rape has a natural basis and is therefore unstoppable. This argument ignores the fact that the orangutan is the only nonhuman primate to engage in forcible copulation as a routine means of siring offspring. Furthermore, close observations of orangutan rape show that it is very different from human rape: For example, researchers have never seen a male orangutan injure a female during copulation in an apparently intentional manner. Most important, the orangutan's physiology, life history, and social structure are completely unlike those of any other primate. Orangutans have evolved a unique set of adaptations to survive in their environment, and hence it would be the height of absurdity to draw simpleminded parallels between their behaviors and those of humans.

BIOCULTURAL QUESTION

While primatologists call the forced copulations by arrested male orangutans "rape," how does this differ from rape in humans?

Adapted from Maggioncalda, A. N., & Sapolsky, R. M. (2002). Disturbing behaviors of the orangutan. Scientific American 286 *(6), 60–65.*

of evolution.[12] She points out that evolutionary theories about sexual dimorphism and reproductive behaviors are particularly susceptible to becoming "gendered." That is, the gender norms of the scientists can easily creep their way (subconsciously, of course) into the theories they are creating. Darwin's era, despite the reign of Queen Victoria, was firmly patriarchal, and male–male competition prevailed in British society. Women of Darwin's time were denied basic rights like the right to vote and own property. Inheritance laws favored first-born male heirs. Feminist analyses such as Fedigan's have contributed substantially to the developing discipline of primatology.

Primate field studies have revealed that male–male competition is just one of many factors playing a role in primate reproduction. A broad range of social processes contribute to reproductive success, with as much variation as the numerous biological factors that contribute to body size. For example, in baboons, which are a very sexually dimorphic species, the female's choice of mate is as important as male–male competition. Females frequently choose to mate with lower-ranking males that show strong male–female **affiliative** actions (tending to promote social cohesion) and good parental behavior.[13]

In orangutans, the avoidance of male–male competition has become biologically evident in the male pattern of growth and development. Unlike gorillas that develop their silver backs at the same time as they become sexually active, orangutan males become sexually mature before they develop the secondary sex characteristics that would mark their adult status. Described in detail in this chapter's Biocultural Connection, this state of arrested development allows these lower-ranking males to have sexual alliances with females. Thus they optimize their personal reproductive success while simultaneously avoiding the stresses and costs of male–male competition.

Among baboons, paternal involvement has been shown to have distinct advantages for offspring, including more rapid growth in baboon infants if they receive attention from their fathers. In addition, adult males will also intercede on their offspring's behalf when the young ones are involved in fights. In short, choosing a good mate can optimize the reproductive success of female baboons.

Reproduction and Care of Young

The average adult female monkey or ape spends most of her adult life either pregnant or nursing her young, times at which she is not sexually receptive. Apes generally nurse each of their young for about four to five years. After her infant is weaned, she will come into estrus periodically, until she becomes pregnant again.

Among primates, as among some other mammals, females generally give birth to one infant at a time. Natural selection may have favored single births among primate tree dwellers because the primate infant, which has a highly developed grasping ability (the grasping reflex can also be seen in human infants), must be transported about by its mother, and more than one clinging infant would interfere with movement in the trees. Only among the smaller nocturnal prosimians, the primates closest to the ancestral condition, are multiple births common. Among the anthropoids, only the true marmoset, a kind of New World monkey, has a pattern of habitual twinning. Other species like humans will twin occasionally. In marmosets, both parents share infant care, with fathers doing most of the carrying.

Primates follow a pattern of bearing few young but devoting more time and effort to the care of each individual offspring. Compared to other mammals such as mice, which pass from birth to adulthood in a matter of weeks, primates spend a great deal of time growing up. As a general rule, the more closely related to humans the species is, the longer the period of infant and childhood dependency (Figure 4.2). For example, a lemur is dependent upon its mother for only a few months after birth, while an ape is dependent for four or five years. A chimpanzee infant cannot survive if its mother dies before it reaches the age of 4 at the very least. During the juvenile period, young primates are still dependent on the larger social group rather than on their mothers alone, using this period for learning and refining a variety of behaviors. If a juvenile primate's mother dies, he or she may be adopted by an older male or female member of the social group. Among bonobos, a juvenile who has lost his or her mother has very little social standing in the group.

The long interval between births, particularly among the apes, results in small population size. A female chimpanzee, for example, does not reach sexual maturity until about the age of 10, and once she produces her first live offspring, there is a period of five or six years before she will bear another. So, assuming that none of her offspring die before adulthood, a female chimpanzee must survive for at least twenty or twenty-one years just to maintain the status quo in chimpanzee population. In fact, chimpanzee infants and juveniles do die from time to time, and not all females live full reproductive lives. This is one reason why apes are far less abundant in the world today than are monkeys.

A long slow period of growth and development, particularly among the hominoids, also provides opportunities. Born without built-in responses dictating specific behavior in complex situations, the young monkey or ape, like the young human, learns how to strategically interact

[12] Fedigan, L. M. (1992). *Primate paradigms: Sex roles and social bonds.* Chicago: University of Chicago Press.

[13] Sapolsky, R. (2002). *A primate's memoir: Love, death, and baboons in East Africa.* New York: Vintage.

affiliative Tending to promote social cohesion.

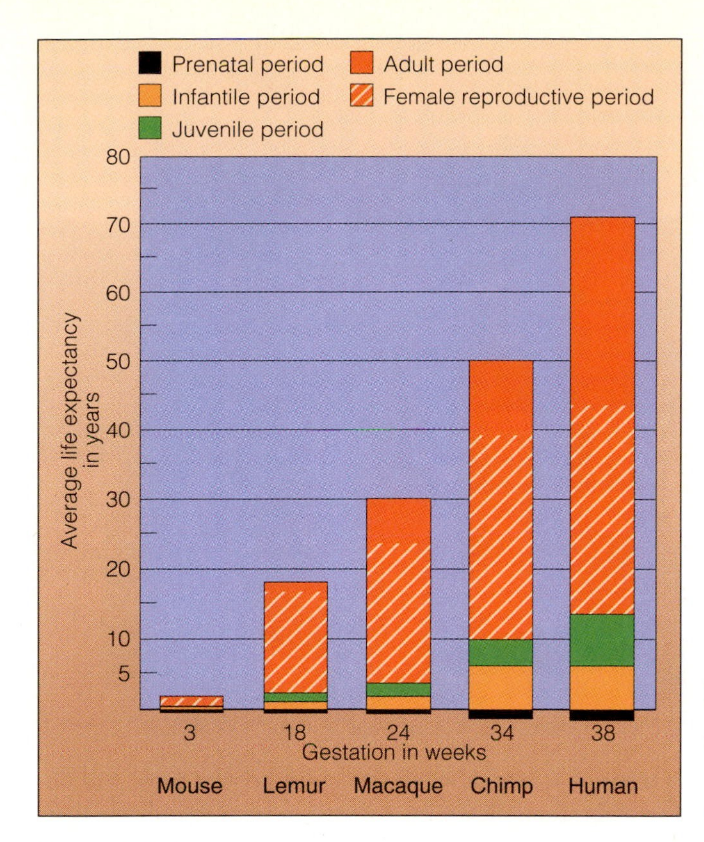

Figure 4.2 **A long life cycle, including a long period of childhood dependency, is characteristic of the primates. In biological terms, infancy ends when young mammals are weaned, and adulthood is defined as sexual maturation. In many species, such as mice, animals become sexually mature as soon as they are weaned. Among primates, a juvenile period for social learning occurs between infancy and adulthood. For humans, the biological definitions of infancy and adulthood are modified according to cultural norms.**

with others and even to manipulate them for his or her own benefit—by trial and error, observation, imitation, and practice. Young primates make mistakes along the way, learning to modify their behavior based on the reactions of other members of the group. Each member of the community has a unique physical appearance and personality. Youngsters learn to match their interactive behaviors according to each individual's social position and temperament. Anatomical features common to all monkeys and apes—such as a free upper lip (unlike lemurs and cats, for example)—allow for varied facial expression, contributing to communication between individuals. Much of this learning takes place through play.

For primate infants and juveniles, play is more than a way to pass the hours. It is a vital means of finding out about the environment, learning social skills, and testing a variety of behaviors. Chimpanzee infants mimic the food-getting activities of adults, "attack" dozing adults, and "harass" adolescents. Observers have watched young gorillas do somersaults, wrestle, and play various organized games, such as jostling for position on the top of a hillside or following and mimicking a single youngster. One juvenile, becoming annoyed at repeated harassment by an infant, picked it up, climbed a tree, and deposited it on a branch from which it was unable to get down on its own; eventually, its mother came to retrieve it.

Communication and Learning

Primates, like many animals, vocalize. They have a great range of calls that are often used together with movements of the face or body to convey a message. Observers have not yet established the meaning of all the sounds, but a good number have been distinguished, such as warning calls, threat calls, defense calls, and gathering calls. The behavioral reactions of other animals hearing the call have also been studied. Among bonobos, chimpanzees, and gorillas, most vocalizations communicate an emotional state rather than information. Much of the communication of these species takes place by using specific gestures and postures. Indeed, a number of these, such as kissing and embracing, are used universally among humans, as well as apes.

Primatologists have classified numerous chimpanzee vocalizations and visual communication signals. Facial expressions convey emotional states such as distress, fear, or excitement. Distinct vocalizations or calls have been associated with a variety of sensations. For example, chimps will smack their lips or clack their teeth to express

Many ape nonverbal communications are easily recognized by humans, as we share the same gestures.

© Bob Willingham

Athletes who have been blind since birth use the same body gestures to express victory and defeat as sighted athletes. Because they do this without ever having seen an "end zone" celebration, this indicates that these body gestures are hardwired into humans and presumably derive from our primate heritage.

pleasure with sociable body contact. Calls called "pant-hoots," which are used to announce the arrival of individuals or to inquire, can be differentiated into specific types. Together, these facilitate group protection, coordination of group efforts, and social interaction in general.

To what degree are various forms of communication universal and to what degree are they specific to a given group? On the group- specificity side, primatologists have recently documented within-species dialects of calls that appear as groups are isolated in their habitats. Social factors, genetic drift, and habitat acoustics could all contribute to the appearance of these distinct dialects.[14]

Smiles and embraces have long been understood to be universal among humans and our closest relatives. But recently some additional universals have been documented. Blind athletes use the same gestures to express submission or victory that sighted athletes use at the end of a match, though they have never seen such gestures themselves.[15] This raises interesting questions about whether primate communications are biologically hardwired or learned.

Visual communication can also take place through objects. Bonobos do so with trail markers. When foraging, the community breaks up into smaller groups, rejoining again in the evening to nest together. To keep track of each party's whereabouts, those in the lead, at the intersections of trails or where downed trees obscure the path, will deliberately stomp down the vegetation so as to indicate their direction or rip off large leaves and place them carefully for the same purpose. Thus they all know where to come together at the end of the day.[16]

Primatologists have also found that primates can communicate specific threats through their calls. Researchers have documented that vervet monkey alarm calls communicate on several levels of meaning to elicit specific responses from others in the group.[17] The calls designated types of predators (birds of prey, big cats, snakes) and where the threat might arise. Further, they have documented how young vervets go about learning the appropriate use of the calls. If the young individual has uttered the correct call, it will be repeated by adults, and the appropriate escape behavior will follow (heading into the trees to get away from a cat or into brush to be safe from an eagle). But if an infant utters the cry for an eagle in response to a leaf falling from the sky or in response to a nonthreatening bird, no adult calls will follow.

From an evolutionary perspective, scientists have been puzzled about behaviors such as these vervet alarm calls. Biologists assume that the forces of natural selection work on behavioral traits just as they do on genetic traits. It seems reasonable that individuals in a group of vervet

[14] de la Torre, S., & Snowden, C. T. (2009). Dialects in pygmy marmosets? Population variation in call structure. *American Journal of Primatology 71* (4), 333–342.

[15] Tracy, J. L., & Matsumoto, D. (2008). The spontaneous expression of pride and shame: Evidence for biologically innate nonverbal displays. *Proceedings of the National Academy of Sciences 105* (33), 11655–11660.

[16] Recer, P. (1998, February 16). Apes shown to communicate in the wild. *Burlington Free Press*, 12A.

[17] Seyfarth, R. M., Cheney, D. L., & Marler, P. (1980). Vervet monkey alarm calls: Semantic communication in a free-ranging primate. *Animal Behavior 28* (4), 1070–1094.

monkeys capable of warning one another of the presence of predators would have a significant survival advantage over those without this capability. However, these warning situations are enigmatic to evolutionary biologists because they would expect the animals to act in their own self-interest, with survival of self paramount. By giving an alarm call, an individual calls attention to itself, thereby becoming an obvious target for the predator. How, then, could **altruism,** or concern for the welfare of others, evolve so that individuals place themselves at risk for the good of the group? One biologist's solution substitutes money for reproductive fitness to illustrate how such cooperative behavior may have come about:

> You are given a choice. Either you can receive $10 and keep it all or you can receive $10 million if you give $6 million to your next door neighbor. Which would you do? Guessing that most selfish people would be happy with a net gain of $4 million, I consider the second option to be a form of selfish behavior in which a neighbor gains an incidental benefit. I have termed such selfish behavior benevolent.[18]

Natural selection of beneficial social traits was probably an important influence on human evolution, since in the primates some degree of cooperative social behavior became important for food-getting, defense, and mate attraction. Indeed, anthropologist Christopher Boehm argues, "If human nature were merely selfish, vigilant punishment of deviants would be expected, whereas the elaborate prosocial prescriptions that favor altruism would come as a surprise."[19]

Evolution has shaped primates to be social creatures, and communication is thus integral to our order. Experiments with captive apes, carried out over several decades, reveal that their communicative abilities exceed what they make use of in the wild. In some of these experiments, bonobos and chimpanzees have been taught to communicate using symbols, as in the case of Kanzi, a bonobo who uses a visual keyboard. Other chimpanzees, gorillas, and orangutans have been taught American Sign Language.

Although this research is controversial, in part because it challenges notions of human uniqueness, it has become evident that apes are capable of understanding language quite well, even using rudimentary grammar. They are able to generate original utterances, ask questions, distinguish naming something from asking for it, develop original ways to tell lies, coordinate their actions, and spontaneously teach language to others. Even though they cannot literally *speak,* it is now clear that all of the great ape species can develop *language skills* to the level of a 2- to 3-year-old human child.[20] Interestingly, a Japanese research team led by primatologist Tetsuro Matsuzawa recently demonstrated that chimps can outperform college students at a computer-based memory game. The researchers propose that human brains have lost some of the spatial skill required to master this game to allow for more sophisticated human language.[21]

Observations of monkeys and apes have shown learning abilities remarkably similar to those of humans. Numerous examples of inventive behavior have been observed among monkeys, as well as among apes. The snow monkeys or macaques of the research colony on Koshima Island, Japan, are particularly famous for demonstrating that individuals can invent new behaviors that then get passed on to the group through imitation.

The Great Ape Trust, photo courtesy of Sue Savage-Rumbaugh

Kanzi, the 23-year-old bonobo at the Great Ape Trust of Iowa, communicates with primatologist Sue Savage-Rumbaugh by pointing to visual images called lexigrams. With hundreds of lexigrams, Kanzi can communicate thoughts and feelings he wishes to express. He also understands spoken language and can reply in a conversation with the lexigrams. Kanzi began to learn this form of communication when he was a youngster, tagging along while his mother had language lessons. Though he showed no interest in the lessons, later he spontaneously began to use lexigrams himself.

[18] Nunney, L. (1998). Are we selfish because are we nice, or are we nice because we are selfish? *Science 281,* 1619.

[19] Boehm, C. (2000). The evolution of moral communities. *School of American Research, 2000 Annual Report,* 7.

[20] Lestel, D. (1998). How chimpanzees have domesticated humans. *Anthropology Today 12* (3); Miles, H. L. W. (1993). Language and the orangutan: The "old person" of the forest. In P. Cavalieri & P. Singer (Eds.), *The Great Ape Project* (pp. 45–50). New York: St. Martin's.

[21] Inoue, S., Matsuzawa, T. (2007). "Working Memory of Numerals in Chimpanzees." *Current Biology, 17* (23), 1004–1005.

altruism Concern for the welfare of others expressed as increased risk undertaken by individuals for the good of the group.

In the 1950s and early 1960s, one particularly bright young female macaque named Imo (Japanese primatologists always considered it appropriate to name individual animals) started several innovative behaviors in her troop. She figured out that grain could be separated from sand if it was placed in water. The sand sank and the grain floated clean, making it much easier to eat. She also began the practice of washing the sweet potatoes that primatologists provided—first in fresh water but later in the ocean, presumably because of the pleasant taste the saltwater added. In each case, these innovations were initially imitated by other young animals; Imo's mother was the lone older macaque to embrace the innovations right away.

One newly discovered example is a technique of food manipulation on the part of captive chimpanzees in the zoo of Madrid, Spain. It began when a 5-year-old female rubbed apples against a sharp corner of a concrete wall in order to lick the mashed pieces and juice left on the wall. From this youngster, the practice of "smearing" spread to her peers, and within five years most group members were performing the operation frequently and consistently. The innovation has become standardized and durable, having transcended two generations in the group.[22]

In the same way that young Imo got her troop to begin washing sweet potatoes in saltwater, at Kyoto University's Koshima Island Primatology Research Preserve another young female macaque recently taught other macaques to bathe in hot springs. In the Nagano Mountains of Japan, this macaque, named Mukbili, began bathing in the springs. Others followed her, and now this is an activity practiced by all members of the group.

Another dramatic example of learning is afforded by the way chimpanzees in West Africa crack open oil-palm nuts. For this they use tools: an anvil stone with a level surface on which to place the nut and a good-sized hammer stone to crack it. Not any stone will do; it must be of the right shape and weight, and the anvil may require leveling by placing smaller stones beneath one or more edges. Nor does random banging away do the job; the nut has to be hit at the right speed and the right trajectory, or else the nut simply flies off into the forest. Last but not least, the apes must avoid mashing their fingers, rather than the nut. According to fieldworkers, the expertise of the chimps far exceeds that of any human who tries cracking these hardest nuts in the world.

Youngsters learn this process by staying near to adults who are cracking nuts, where their mothers share some of the food. This teaches them about the edibility of the nuts but not how to get at what is edible. This they learn by observing and by "aping" (copying) the adults. At first they play with a nut or stone alone; later they begin to randomly combine objects. They soon learn, however, that placing nuts on anvils and hitting them with a hand or foot gets them nowhere.

Only after three years of futile effort do they begin to coordinate all of the multiple actions and objects, but even then it is only after a great deal of practice, by the age of 6 or 7 years, that they become proficient in this task. They do this for over a thousand days. Evidently, it is social motivation that accounts for their perseverance after at least three years of failure, with no reward to reinforce their effort. At first, they are motivated by a desire to act like the

[22] Fernandez-Carriba, S., & Loeches, A. (2001). Fruit smearing by captive chimpanzees: A newly observed food-processing behavior. *Current Anthropology 42*, 143–147.

mother; only later does the desire to feed on the tasty nutmeat take over.[23]

Use of Objects as Tools

A **tool** may be defined as an object used to facilitate some task or activity. The nut cracking just discussed is the most complex tool-use task observed by researchers in the wild, involving both hands, two tools, and exact coordination. It is not, however, the only case of tool use among apes in the wild. Chimpanzees, bonobos, and orangutans make and use tools.

Here, a distinction must be made between simple tool use, as when one pounds something with a convenient stone when a hammer is not available, and tool making, which involves deliberate modification of some material for its intended use. Thus otters that use unmodified stones to crack open clams may be tool users, but they are not toolmakers. Not only do chimpanzees modify objects to make them suitable for particular purposes, but chimps also modify these objects into regular and set patterns. They pick up and even prepare objects for future use at some other location, and they can use objects as tools to solve new problems. Thus chimps have been observed using stalks of grass, twigs that they have stripped of leaves, and even sticks up to 3 feet long that they have smoothed down to "fish" for termites. They insert the modified stick into a termite nest, wait a few minutes, pull the stick out, and eat the insects clinging to it, all of which requires considerable dexterity. Chimpanzees are equally deliberate in their own nest building. They test the vines and branches to make sure they are usable. If they are not, the animal moves to another site.

Other examples of chimpanzee use of tools involve leaves, used as wipes or as sponges, to get water out of a hollow to drink. Large sticks may serve as clubs or as missiles (as may stones) in aggressive or defensive displays. Twigs are used as toothpicks to clean teeth as well as to extract loose baby teeth. They use these dental tools not just on themselves but on other individuals as well.[24]

In the wild, bonobos have not been observed making and using tools to the extent seen in chimpanzees. However, the use of large leaves as trail markers may be considered a form of tool use. That these animals do have further capabilities is exemplified by a captive bonobo who has figured out how to make tools of stone that are remarkably like the earliest such tools made by our own ancestors.[25]

Chimps use a variety of tools in the wild. Here a chimp is using a long stick stripped of its side branches to fish for termites. Chimps will select a stick when still quite far from a termite mound and modify its shape on the way to the snacking spot.

Chimpanzees also use plants for medicinal purposes, illustrating their selectivity with raw materials, a quality related to tool manufacture. Chimps that are ill by outward appearance have been observed to seek out specific plants of the genus *Aspilia.* They will eat the leaves singly without chewing them, letting the leaves soften in their mouths for a long time before swallowing. Primatologists have discovered that the leaves pass through the chimp's digestive system whole and relatively intact, having scraped parasites off the intestine walls in the process.

tool An object used to facilitate some task or activity. Although tool making involves intentional modification of the material of which it is made, tool use may involve objects either modified for some particular purpose or completely unmodified.

[23] de Waal, *The ape and the sushi master.*

[24] McGrew, W. C. (2000). Dental care in chimps. *Science 288,* 1747.

[25] Toth, N., et al. (1993–2001). Pan the tool-maker: Investigations into the stone tool-making and tool-using capabilities of a bonobo (*Pan panisicus*). *Journal of Archaeological Science 20* (1), 81–91.

Although gorillas (like bonobos and chimps) build nests, they are the only one of the four great apes that have not been observed to make and use other tools in the wild. The reason for this is probably not that gorillas lack the intelligence or skill to do so; rather, their easy diet of leaves and nettles makes tools of no particular use.

Hunting

Prior to the 1980s most primates were thought to be vegetarian while humans alone were considered meat-eating hunters. Among the vegetarians, *folivores* were thought to eat only leaves while *frugivores* feasted on fruits. Though some primates do have specialized adaptations—such as a complex stomach and shearing teeth to aid in the digestion of leaves or an extra-long small intestine to slow the passage of juicy fruits so they can be readily absorbed—primate field studies have revealed that the diets of monkeys and apes are extremely varied.

Many primates are *omnivores* who eat a broad range of foods. Goodall's fieldwork among chimpanzees in their natural habitat at Gombe Stream demonstrates that these apes supplement their primary diet of fruits and other plant foods with insects and meat. Even more surprising, she found that in addition to killing small invertebrate animals for food, they also hunt and eat monkeys. Goodall observed chimpanzees grabbing adult red colobus monkeys and flailing them to death. Since her pioneering work, other primatologists have documented hunting behavior in baboons and capuchin monkeys, among others.

Chimpanzee females sometimes hunt, but males do so far more frequently. When on the hunt, they may spend hours watching, following, and chasing intended prey. Moreover, in contrast to the usual primate practice of each animal finding its own food, hunting frequently involves teamwork to trap and kill prey, particularly when hunting for baboons. Once a potential victim has been isolated from its troop, three or more adult chimps will carefully position themselves so as to block off escape routes while another pursues the prey. Following the kill, most who are present get a share of the meat, either by grabbing a piece as chance affords or by begging for it.

Whatever the nutritional value of meat, hunting is not done purely for dietary purposes, but for social and sexual reasons as well. Anthropologist Craig Stanford, who has been doing fieldwork among the chimpanzees of Gombe since the early 1990s, found that these sizable apes (100-pound males are common) frequently kill animals weighing up to 25 pounds and eat much more meat than previously believed. Their preferred prey is the red colobus monkey that shares their forested habitat. Annually, chimpanzee hunting parties at Gombe kill about 20 percent of these monkeys, many of them babies, often shaking them out of the tops of 30-foot trees. They may capture and kill as many as seven victims in a raid. These hunts usually take place during the dry season when plant foods are less readily available and when females display genital swelling, which signals that they are ready to mate. On average, each chimp at Gombe eats about a quarter-pound of meat per day during the dry season. For female chimps, a supply of protein-rich food helps support the increased nutritional requirements of pregnancy and lactation.

Somewhat different chimpanzee hunting practices have been observed in West Africa. At Tai National Park in the Ivory Coast, for instance, chimpanzees engage in highly coordinated team efforts to chase monkeys hiding in very tall trees in the dense tropical forest. Individuals who have especially distinguished themselves in a successful hunt see their contributions rewarded with more meat.

Recent research shows that bonobos in Congo's rainforest also supplement their diet with meat obtained by means of hunting. Although their behavior resembles that of chimpanzees, there are crucial differences. Among bonobos, hunting is primarily a female activity. Also, female hunters regularly share carcasses with other females, but less often with males. Even when the most dominant male throws a tantrum nearby, he may still be denied a share of meat.[26] Female bonobos behave in much the same way when it comes to sharing other foods such as fruits.

While it had long been assumed that male chimpanzees were the primary hunters, primatologist Jill Pruetz and her colleagues researching in Fongoli, Senegal, documented habitual hunting by groups of young female and male chimpanzees using spears.[27] The chimps took spears they had previously prepared and sharpened to a point and jabbed them repeatedly into the hollow parts

[26] Ingmanson, E. J. (1998). Comment. *Current Anthropology 39,* 409.

[27] Pruetz, J. D., & Bertolani, P. (2007, March 6). Savanna chimpanzees, *Pan troglodytes verus,* hunt with tools. *Current Biology 17,* 412–417.

of trees where small animals, including primates, might be hiding. The primatologists even observed the chimps extract bush babies from tree hollows with the spears. Because this behavior is practiced primarily by young chimpanzees, with one adolescent female the most frequently exhibiting the behavior, spear hunting seems to be a relatively recent innovation in the group. Just as the young female Japanese macaques mentioned above were the innovators in those groups, this young female chimp seems to be leading this behavior in Senegal. Further, the savannah conditions of the Fongoli Reserve make these observations particularly interesting in terms of human evolutionary studies, which have tended to suggest that males hunted while females gathered.

The Question of Culture

The more we learn of the behavior of our nearest primate relatives, the more we become aware of the importance of learned, socially shared practices and knowledge in these creatures. Do chimpanzees, bonobos, and the other apes have culture? The answer appears to be yes. The detailed study of ape behavior has revealed varied use of tools and patterns of social engagement that seem to derive from the traditions of the specific group rather than a biologically determined script. Humans share with the other apes an ability to learn the complex but flexible patterns of behavior particular to a social group during a long period of childhood dependency.

If we agree that these other primates possess culture, does this demand a reorientation in how humans behave toward them, such as stopping the use of monkeys and apes in biomedical research? Jane Goodall argues vehemently for this change. She emphasizes that cultural processes determine the place of animals within biomedical research, and she advocates eliminating the cultural distinction between humans and our closest relatives for research purposes. Some governments are responding to her calls as seen by the 2008 approval by the Spanish Parliament of the "Declaration on Great Apes," which extends some human rights to gorillas, chimpanzees, bonobos, and orangutans.[28]

Some biomedical research disturbs animals minimally. For example, DNA can be extracted from the hair naturally shed by living primates, allowing for cross-species comparisons of disease genes. To facilitate this process, cell repositories have been established for researchers to obtain samples of primate DNA. Other biomedical research is far more invasive to the individual primate. For example, to document the infectious nature of kuru, a disease closely related to mad cow disease, extract from the brains of sick humans was injected into the brains of living chimpanzees. A year and a half later, the chimpanzees began to sicken. They had the same classic features of kuru—uncontrollable spasticity, seizures, dementia, and ultimately death.

The biological similarities of humans and other primates leading to such research practices derive from a long, shared evolutionary history. By comparison, the cultural rules that allow our closest relatives to be the subjects of biomedical research are relatively recent. As Goodall has said, "Surely it should be a matter of moral responsibility that we humans, differing from other animals mainly by virtue of our more highly developed intellect and, with it, our greater capacity for understanding and compassion, ensure that the medical progress slowly detaches its roots from the manure of non-human animal suffering and despair. Particularly when this involves the servitude of our closest relatives."[29]

But there are powerful social barriers that work against the well-being of our animal relatives. In Western societies there has been an unfortunate tendency to erect what paleontologist Stephen Jay Gould refers to as "golden barriers" that set us apart from the rest of the animal kingdom.[30] Sadly, this mindset blinds us to the fact that a continuum exists between "us" and "them" (animals). We have already seen that the physical differences between humans and apes are largely differences of degree, rather than kind. It now appears that the same is true with respect to behavior. As primatologist Richard Wrangham put it,

> Like humans, [chimpanzees] laugh, make up after a quarrel, support each other in times of trouble, medicate themselves with chemical and physical remedies, stop each other from eating poisonous foods, collaborate in the hunt, help each other over physical obstacles, raid neighboring groups, lose their tempers, get excited by dramatic weather, invent ways to show off, have family traditions and group traditions, make tools, devise plans, deceive, play tricks, grieve, and are cruel and are kind.[31]

[28] O'Carroll, E. (2008, June 27). Spain to grant some human rights to apes. *Christian Science Monitor.*

[29] Goodall, J. (1990). *Through a window: My thirty years with the chimpanzees of Gombe.* Boston: Houghton Mifflin.

[30] Quoted in de Waal, *The ape and the sushi master,* p. 235.

[31] Quoted in Mydens, S. (2001, August 12). He's not hairy, he's my brother. *New York Times,* sec. 4, 5.

This is not to say that we are "just" another ape; obviously, degree does make a difference. Nevertheless, the continuities between us and our primate kin reflect a common evolutionary heritage and a responsibility to help our cousins today. Because of our shared evolutionary heritage, the biology and behavior of the other living primates, like the contemporary study of genetics, provide valuable insight into our understanding of human origins. The methods scientists use to recover data directly from fossilized bones and preserved cultural remains in order to study the human past are the subject of the next chapter.

Questions for Reflection

1. Those who fully support the use of nonhuman primates in biomedical research argue that using a limited number of chimpanzees or rhesus macaques to lessen human suffering and spare human lives is justified. Do you agree or disagree? What kinds of alternatives might be developed to replace nonhuman primates in biomedical research?
2. What kinds of communication systems have been observed in primates? How do these differ from human language?
3. This chapter describes several instances of scientists revising their paradigms when it appeared that their work was overly influenced by their own cultural norms, such as prevailing gender roles. Can you think of ways that this might still be occurring? How do researchers prevent this from happening?
4. Given the variation seen in the specific behaviors of chimp, bonobo, and gorilla groups, is it fair to say that these primates possess culture?
5. As we explored in the previous chapter, many primate species are endangered today. What features of ape biology may be responsible for apes' limited population size? Do these biological limitations pertain to humans? Why or why not?

Suggested Readings

Cavalieri, P., & Singer, P. (1994). *The Great Ape Project: Equality beyond humanity.* New York: St. Martin's.

This edited volume brings together leading primatologists, ethicists, animal rights activists, field biologists, and psychologists to make the case for extending the rights guaranteed to humans to the other great apes. This book was the first initiative of the Great Ape Project, a worldwide initiative to protect chimpanzees, bonobos, gorillas, and orangutans.

Cheney, D. L., & Seyfarth, R. M. (2007). *Baboon metaphysics: The evolution of a social mind.* Chicago: University of Chicago Press.

Through in-depth field studies extending over years, primatologists Cheney and Seyfarth examine the degree to which baboon behavior indicates thought compared to instinct. Their fascinating analysis written in an engaging style responds to the statement Charles Darwin made: "He who understands baboons would do more towards metaphysics than Locke."

de Waal, F. B. M., & Lanting, F. (1998). *Bonobo: The forgotten ape.* Berkeley: University of California Press.

This book perfectly blends photographs and text to allow the reader to immediately see the inherent humanity of the bonobos.

Fedigan, L. (1992). *Primate paradigms: Sex roles and social bonds.* Chicago: University of Chicago Press.

Fedigan uses a broad intellectual framework to connect the study of sex differences in primates to feminist theory as well as to the sciences of psychology, neurobiology, endocrinology, and biology. Her perspectives have helped shape primatology as it is practiced today.

Sapolsky, R. (2002). *A primate's memoir: Love, death, and baboons in East Africa.* New York: Vintage.

This book will take the reader from Sapolsky's childhood in New York City to his years working with a troop of baboons in Kenya, with his fascinating work as a neuroendocrinologist thrown in for good measure. Sapolsky is witty, cynical, and emotional as he tells his story and that of the baboons and the other humans who were part of this journey.

Challenge Issue Given the radical changes taking place in the world today, a scientific understanding of the past has never been more important. But investigating ancient remains challenges us to solve the complex question of who owns the past. For example, pictured here is the Bamiyan Valley, located along a section of the ancient Silk Road, which was a network of trade routes that stretched from eastern Asia to the Mediterranean. Before the Islamic invasion of the 9th century, this place of great natural beauty, located within the Hazarajat region of central Afghanistan, was a Buddhist homeland. There were several Buddhist monasteries, thousands of painted caves, and two colossal statues of Buddha, carved into the cliffs at the valley's edge and dating back some 1,500 years. In March 2001, the Taliban destroyed these two Buddhas on the grounds that they were idolatrous and an insult to Islam. Today, the niches that once held these grand sculptures are hauntingly empty. A huge international outcry has led to cooperative efforts to rebuild and preserve this archaeological site, and already the results have been impressive. In 2008 a team of Japanese, European, and U.S. researchers demonstrated that the Bamiyan cave wall images are the oldest oil paintings in the world. To whom do such ancient remains belong—to the local government, to the global community, to researchers or scientific institutions, to people living in the region, to those who happen to have possession at the moment? The archaeological perspective holds that for the collective benefit of local peoples and the global community alike, these questions must be answered with an eye to long-term preservation, cooperation, and peace.

Field Methods in Archaeology and Paleoanthropology

Chapter Preview

How Are the Physical and Cultural Remains of Past Humans Investigated?

Archaeologists and paleoanthropologists investigate the past by excavating sites where biological and cultural remains are found. Unfortunately, excavation results in the site's destruction. Thus every attempt is made to excavate in such a way that the location and context of everything recovered, no matter how small, are precisely recorded. Through careful analysis of the physical and cultural remains recovered through excavation, scientists make sense of the data and enhance our knowledge of the biology, behavior, and beliefs of our ancestors. The success of an excavation also depends upon cooperation and respect between anthropologists who are investigating the past and the living people connected to the sites and remains being studied.

Are Human Physical and Cultural Remains Always Found Together?

Archaeological sites are places containing the cultural remains of past human activity. Sites are revealed by the presence of artifacts as well as soil marks, changes in vegetation, and irregularities of the earth's surface. While skeletons of recent peoples are frequently associated with their cultural remains, as we go back in time, the association of physical and cultural remains becomes less likely. Fossils are defined as any surviving trace or impression of an organism from the past. Fossils sometimes accompany archaeological sites, but many of them predate the first stone tools or other cultural artifacts. The human cultural practice of burying the dead, starting about 100,000 years ago, changed the nature of the fossil record, providing relatively complete skeletons as well as information about this cultural practice.

How Are Archaeological or Fossil Remains Dated?

Calculating the age of physical and cultural remains is an essential aspect of interpreting the past. Remains can be dated by noting their stratigraphic position, by measuring the chemicals contained in fossil bones, or by association with other plant, animal, or cultural remains. More precise dating methods rely upon advances in the disciplines of chemistry and physics that use properties such as rates of decay of radioactive elements. These elements may be present in the remains themselves or in the surrounding soil. By comparing dates and remains across a variety of sites, anthropologists can make inferences about human origins, migrations, and technological developments. Sometimes the development of a new dating technique leads to an entirely new interpretation of physical and cultural remains.

Paleoanthropology and archaeology are the anthropological specialties most concerned with our past. They share a focus on **prehistory,** a conventional term used to refer to the period of time before written records. For some people, the term *prehistoric* might conjure up images of "primitive" cavemen and cavewomen, but it does not imply a lack of history or any inferiority—merely a lack of written history. Archaeologists also focus on the cultural remains of peoples living since the invention of writing, such as the makers of the Bamiyan Buddhas and the oil paintings buried in caves behind them as described in the chapter opener.[1] The next several chapters of this book focus on the past; this chapter examines the methods archaeologists and paleoanthropologists use to study that past.

Most of us are familiar with some kind of archaeological material: a coin dug out of the earth, a fragment of an ancient pot, a spear point used by some ancient hunter. Finding and cataloguing such objects are often thought to be the chief goal of archaeology. This was true up until the early 20th century, when professional and amateur archaeologists alike collected cultural treasures, but the situation changed by the mid-20th century. Today, the aim is to use archaeological remains to reconstruct the culture and worldview of past human societies. Archaeologists examine every recoverable detail from past societies, including all kinds of structures (not just palaces and temples), hearths, garbage dumps, bones, and plant remains. Although it may appear that archaeologists are digging up *things,* they are really digging up human biology, behavior, and beliefs.

Similarly, paleoanthropologists who study the physical remains of our ancestors and other ancient primates do more than find and catalogue old bones. Paleoanthropologists recover, describe, and organize these remains to see what they can tell us about human biological evolution. It is not so much a case of finding the ancient bones but finding out what the bones mean.

[1] Bonn-Muller, E. (2009). Oldest oil paintings: Bamiyan, Afghanistan. *Archaeology 62* (1); Cotte, M. (2008). *Journal of Analytical Atomic Spectrometry.* doi: 10.1039/b801358f.

prehistory A conventional term used to refer to the period of time before the appearance of written records; does not deny the existence of history, merely of *written* history.

artifact Any object fashioned or altered by humans.

material culture The durable aspects of culture, such as tools, structures, and art.

ecofact The natural remains of plants and animals found in the archaeological record.

feature A non-portable element such as a hearth or an architectural element such as a wall that is preserved in the archaeological record.

Recovering Cultural and Biological Remains

Archaeologists and paleoanthropologists face a dilemma. The only way to thoroughly investigate our past is to excavate sites where biological and cultural remains are found. Unfortunately, excavation results in the site's destruction. Thus researchers strive to excavate in such a way that the location and context of everything recovered, no matter how small, are precisely recorded. These records help scientists make sense of the data and enhance our knowledge of the past. Knowledge that can be derived from physical and cultural remains diminishes dramatically if accurate and detailed records of the excavation are not kept. As anthropologist Brian Fagan has put it,

> The fundamental premise of excavation is that all digging is destructive, even that done by experts. The archaeologist's primary responsibility, therefore, is to record a site for posterity as it is dug because there are no second chances.[2]

Archaeologists work with **artifacts,** any object fashioned or altered by humans—a flint scraper, a basket, an axe, or such things as house ruins or walls. An artifact expresses a facet of human culture. Because it is something that someone made, archaeologists like to say that an artifact is a product or representation of human behavior and beliefs, or, in more technical terms, artifacts are **material culture.**

Artifacts are not considered in isolation; rather, they are integrated with biological and ecological remains. Such **ecofacts,** the natural remains of plants and animals found in the archaeological record, convey much about associated artifacts. Archaeologists also focus on **features**—non-portable elements such as hearths and architectural elements such as walls—that are preserved in the archaeological record. Just as important as the artifacts and physical remains is the way they were left in the ground. For example, what people do with the things they have made, how they dispose of them, and how they lose them reflect important aspects of human culture. In other words, context allows archaeologists to understand the cultures of the past.

Similarly, context provides important information about biological remains. It provides information about which fossils are earlier or later in time than other fossils. Also, by noting the association of ancient human fossils with the remains of other species, the paleoanthropologist may make significant progress in reconstructing environmental settings of the past.

[2] Fagan, B. M. (1995). *People of the earth* (8th ed., p. 19). New York: HarperCollins.

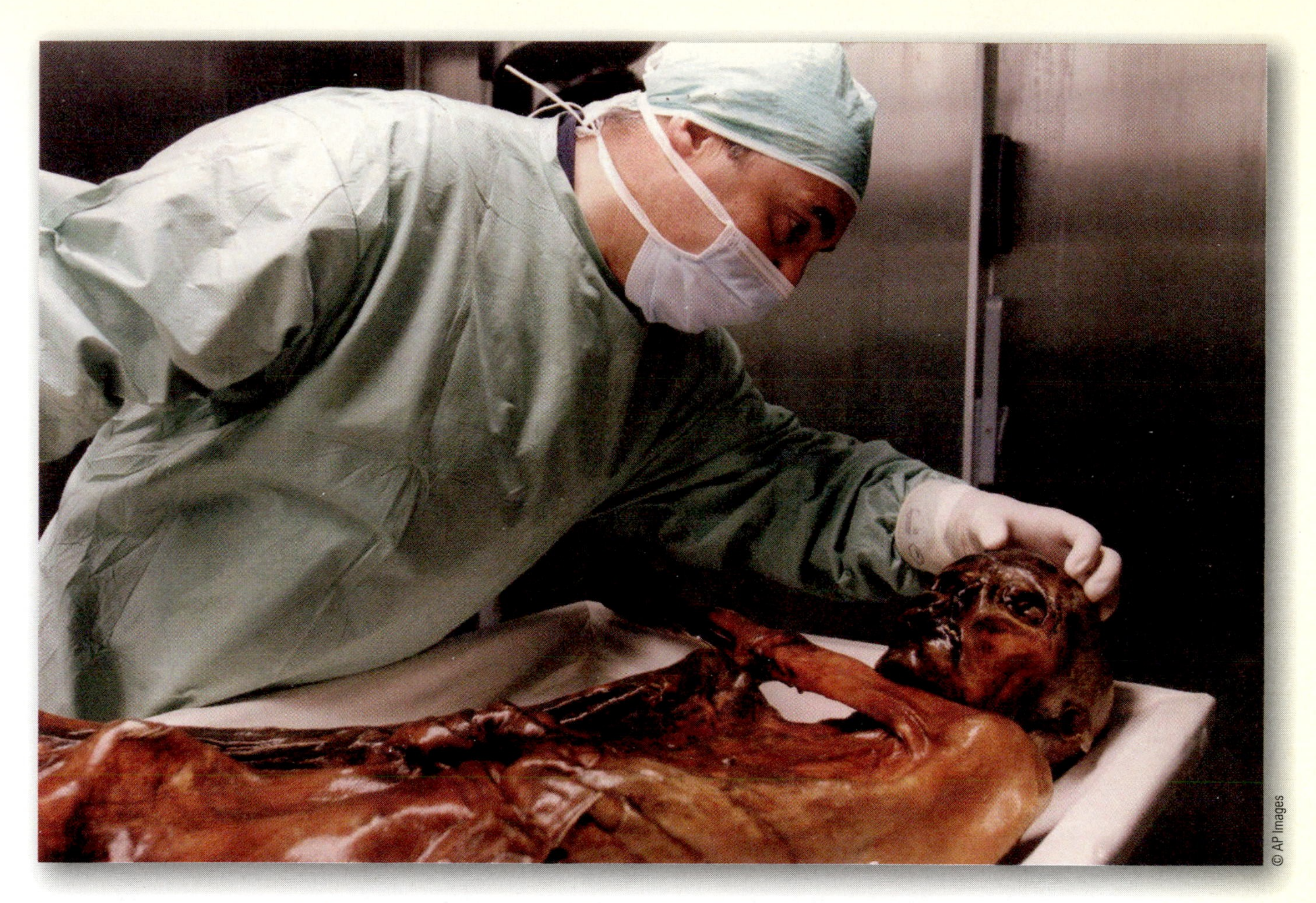

In rare circumstances, human bodies are so well preserved that they could be mistaken for recent corpses. Such is the case of "Ötzi," the 5,200-year-old "Ice Man," exposed by the melting of an alpine glacier in the Tyrolean Alps in 1991. Both the Italian and the Austrian governments felt they had legitimate claims on this rare find, and they mounted legal, geographic, and taphonomic arguments for housing the body. These arguments continued as the specimen, just released from the ice, began to thaw.

Cultural and physical remains represent distinct kinds of data, but the fullest interpretation of the human past requires the integration of ancient human biology and culture. Often paleoanthropologists and archaeologists work together to systematically excavate and analyze fragmentary remains, placing scraps of bone, shattered pottery, and scattered campsites into broad interpretive contexts.

The Nature of Fossils

Broadly defined, a **fossil** is any mineralized trace or impression of an organism that has been preserved in the earth's crust from past geologic time. Fossilization typically involves the hard parts of an organism. Bones, teeth, shells, horns, and the woody tissues of plants are the most successfully fossilized materials. Although the soft parts of an organism are rarely fossilized, casts or impressions of footprints, brains, and even whole bodies are sometimes found. Because dead animals quickly attract meat-eating scavengers and bacteria that cause decomposition, they rarely survive long enough to become fossilized. For an organism to become a fossil, it must be covered by some protective substance soon after death.

An organism or part of an organism may be preserved in a number of ways. The whole animal may be frozen in ice, like the famous mammoths found in Siberia, safe from the forces of predators, weathering, and bacteria. Or it may be enclosed in a natural resin exuding from evergreen trees, later becoming hardened and fossilized as amber. Specimens of spiders and insects dating back millions of years have been preserved in the Baltic Sea area in northeastern Europe, which is rich in resin-producing evergreens such as pine, spruce, or fir trees.

fossil Any mineralized trace or impression of an organism that has been preserved in the earth's crust from past geologic time.

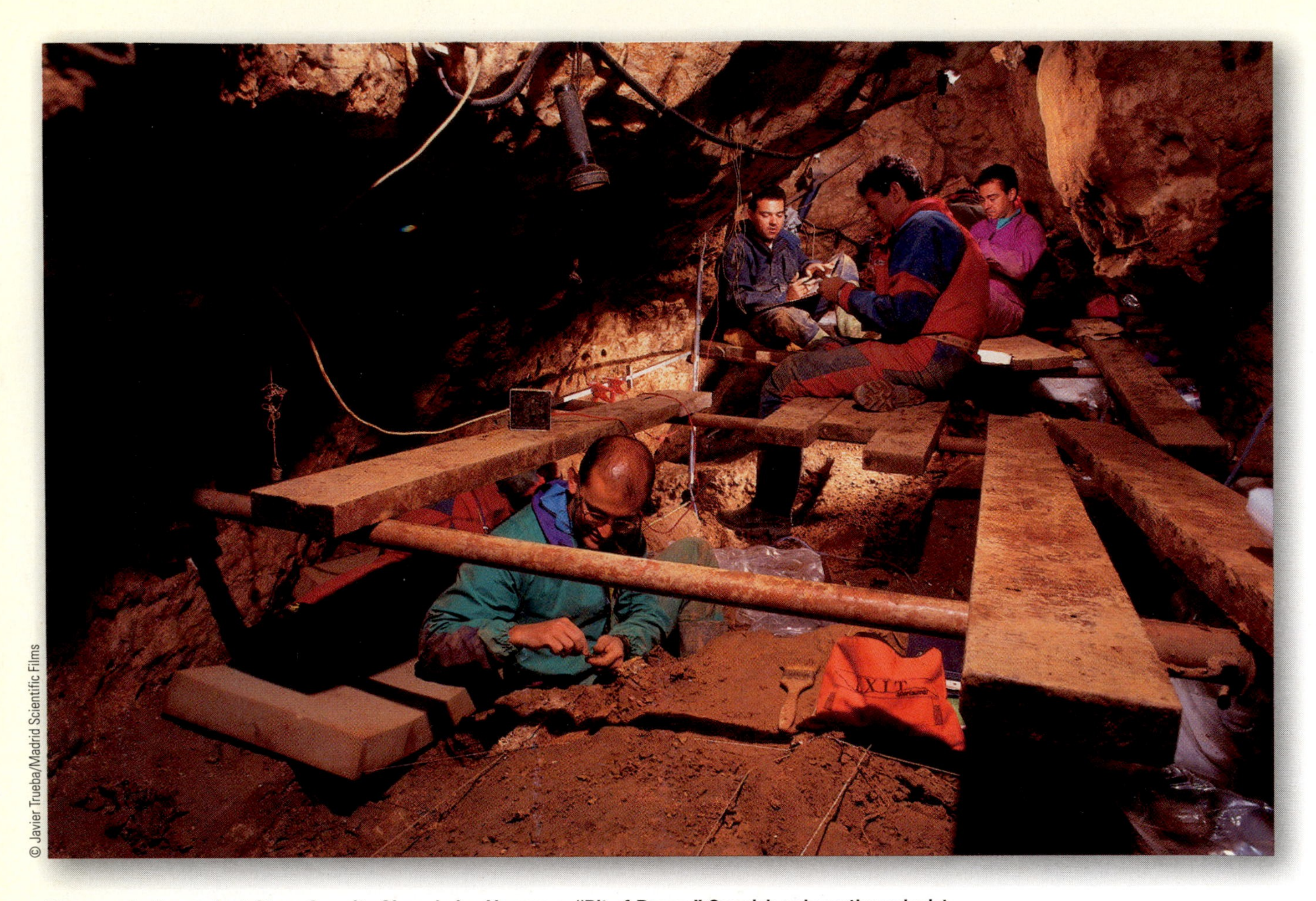

To excavate the ancient Stone Age site Sima de los Huesos or "Pit of Bones," Spanish paleoanthropologist Juan Luis Arsuaga and his team spend nearly an hour each day traveling underground through a narrow passage to a small enclosed space, rich with human remains. Here, fossils are excavated with great care and transported back to the laboratory, where the long process of interpretation and analysis begins.

An organism may be preserved in the bottoms of lakes and sea basins, where the body or body part may be quickly covered with sediment. An entire organism may also be mummified or preserved in tar pits, peat, oil, or asphalt bogs, in which the chemical environment prevents the growth of decay-producing bacteria.

It is especially rare to find an entire organism fossilized, let alone a human one. Fossils generally consist of scattered teeth and fragments of bones found embedded in rock deposits. Most have been altered in some way in the process of becoming fossilized. **Taphonomy** (from the Greek for "tomb"), the study of the biologic and geologic processes by which dead organisms become fossils, provides systematic understanding of the fossilization process vital for the scientific interpretations of the fossils themselves.

taphonomy The study of how bones and other materials come to be preserved in the earth as fossils.

Fossilization is most apt to occur among marine animals and other creatures living near water. Concentrations of shells and other parts of organisms are covered and completely enclosed by the soft waterborne sediments that eventually harden into shale and limestone in the following fashion: As the remains of organisms accumulate on shallow sea, river, or lake bottoms, they become covered by sediment and silt, or sand. These materials gradually harden, forming a protective shell around the skeleton of the organism. The internal cavities of bones or teeth and other parts of the skeleton fill in with mineral deposits from the sediment immediately surrounding the specimen. Then the external walls of the bone decay and are replaced by calcium carbonate or silica.

Unless protected in some way, the bones of a land dweller are generally scattered and exposed to the deteriorating influence of the elements, predators, and scavengers. Occasionally, terrestrial animals living near lakes or rivers become fossilized if they die next to or in the water. A land dweller may also become fossilized if it happens to die in a cave, or if some other meat-eating animal drags its remains to a site protected from erosion and decay. In caves, conditions are often excellent for fossilization, as minerals contained in water dripping from the ceiling may harden over bones left on the cave floor. In northern China, for example, many fossils of *Homo erectus* (discussed in Chapter 8) and other animals were found in a cave near a village called Zhoukoudian, in deposits of consolidated clay and rock that had fallen from the cave's limestone ceiling. The cave had been frequented by both humans and predatory animals, which left remains of many a meal there.

Burial of the Dead

It is quite rare to find entirely preserved fossil skeletons dating to before the cultural practice of burial began about 100,000 years ago. The human fossil record from before this time consists primarily of fragmentary remains. The fossil record for many other primates is even poorer, because organic materials decay rapidly in the tropical forests where they lived. The records are much more complete for primates (such as evolving humans) that lived on the grassy plains or in savannah environments, where conditions were far more favorable to the formation of fossils. This was particularly true in places where ash deposited from volcanic eruptions or waterborne sediment along lakes and streams could quickly cover organisms that died there. At several localities in Ethiopia, Kenya, and Tanzania in East Africa, numerous fossils important for our understanding of human evolution have been found near ancient lakes and streams, often sandwiched between layers of volcanic ash.

In more recent times, such complete remains, although not common, are often quite spectacular and may be particularly informative. As an example, consider the recovery in 1994 of an Eskimo girl's remains in Barrow, Alaska, described in the Original Study. As seen in this case study, successful exploration of the past depends upon cooperation and respect between anthropologists and the living people with ancestral connections to the physical and cultural remains being studied.

Original Study

Whispers from the Ice *by Sherry Simpson*

People grew excited when a summer rainstorm softened the bluff known as Ukkuqsi, sloughing off huge chunks of earth containing remains of historic and prehistoric houses, part of the old village that predates the modern community of Barrow. Left protruding from the slope was a human head. Archaeologist Anne Jensen happened to be in Barrow buying strapping tape when the body appeared. Her firm, SJS Archaeological Services, Inc., was closing a field season at nearby Point Franklin, and Jensen offered the team's help in a kind of archaeological triage to remove the body before it eroded completely from the earth.

The North Slope Borough hired her and Glenn Sheehan, both associated with Pennsylvania's Bryn Mawr College, to conduct the work. The National Science Foundation, which supported the 3-year Point Franklin Project, agreed to fund the autopsy and subsequent analysis of the body and artifacts. The Ukkuqsi excavation quickly became a community event. In remarkably sunny and calm weather, volunteers troweled and picked through the thawing soil, finding trade beads, animal bones, and other items. Teenage boys worked alongside grandmothers. The smell of sea mammal oil, sweet at first then corrupt, mingled with ancient organic odors of decomposed vegetation. One man searched the beach for artifacts that had eroded from the bluff, discovering such treasures as two feather parkas. Elder Silas Negovanna, originally of Wainwright, visited several times, "more or less out of curiosity to see what they have in mind," he said. George Leavitt, who lives in a house on the bluff, stopped by one day while carrying home groceries and suggested a way to spray water to thaw the soil without washing away valuable artifacts. Tour groups added the excavation to their rounds.

"This community has a great interest in archaeology up here just because it's so recent to their experience," says oral historian Karen Brewster, a tall young woman who interviews elders as part of her work with the North Slope Borough's division of Inupiat History, Language, and Culture. "The site's right in town, and everybody was really fascinated by it."

Slowly, as the workers scraped and shoveled, the earth surrendered its historical hoard: carved wooden bowls, ladles, and such clothing as a mitten made from polar bear hide, bird-skin parkas, and mukluks. The items spanned prehistoric times, dated in Barrow to before explorers first arrived in 1826.

The work prompted visiting elders to recall when they or their parents lived in traditional sod houses and relied wholly on the land and sea for sustenance.

CONTINUED

CONTINUED

Some remembered sliding down the hill as children, before the sea gnawed away the slope. Others described the site's use as a lookout for whales or ships. For the archaeologists, having elders stand beside them and identify items and historical context is like hearing the past whispering in their ears. Elders often know from experience, or from stories, the answers to the scientists' questions about how items were used or made. "In this instance, usually the only puzzled people are the archaeologists," jokes archaeologist Sheehan.

A modern town of 4,000, Barrow exists in a cultural continuum, where history is not detached or remote but still pulses through contemporary life. People live, hunt, and fish where their ancestors did, but they can also buy fresh vegetables at the store and jet to other places. Elementary school classes include computer and Inupiaq language studies. Caribou skins, still ruddy with blood, and black brant carcasses hang near late-model cars outside homes equipped with television antennas. A man uses power tools to work on his whaling boat. And those who appear from the earth are not just bodies, but relatives. "We're not a people frozen in time," says Jana Harcharek, an Inupiat Eskimo who teaches Inupiaq and nurtures her culture among young people. "There will always be that connection between us [and our ancestors]. They're not a separate entity."

The past drew still closer as the archaeologists neared the body. After several days of digging through thawed soil, they used water supplied by the local fire station's tanker truck to melt through permafrost until they reached the remains, about 3 feet below the surface. A shell of clear ice encased the body, which rested in what appeared to be a former meat cellar. With the low-pressure play of water from the tanker, the archaeologists teased the icy casket from the frozen earth, exposing a tiny foot. Only then did they realize they had uncovered a child. "That was kind of sad, because she was about my daughter's size," says archaeologist Jensen.

The girl was curled up beneath a baleen toboggan and part of a covering that Inupiat elder Bertha Leavitt identified as a kayak skin by its stitching. The child, who appeared to be 5 or 6, remained remarkably intact after her dark passage through time. Her face was cloaked by a covering that puzzled some onlookers. It didn't look like human hair, or even fur, but something with a feathery residue. Finally they concluded it was a hood from a feather parka made of bird skins. The rest of her body was delineated muscle that had freeze-dried into a dark brick-red color. Her hands rested on her knees, which were drawn up to her chin. Frost particles coated the bends of her arms and legs.

"We decided we needed to go talk to the elders and see what they wanted, to get some kind of feeling as to whether they wanted to bury her right away, or whether they were willing to allow some studies in a respectful manner—studies that would be of some use to residents of the North Slope," Jensen says. Working with community elders is not a radical idea to Jensen or Sheehan, whose previous work in the Arctic has earned them high regard from local officials who appreciate their sensitivity. The researchers feel obligated not only to follow community wishes, but to invite villagers to sites and to share all information through public presentations. In fact, Jensen is reluctant to discuss findings with the press before the townspeople themselves hear it.

© Courtesy of Anne Jensen and Glenn Sheehan

In the long cool days of the Alaska summer, archaeologist Anne Jensen and her team excavate artifacts that will be exhibited at the Inupiat Heritage Center in Barrow, Alaska. In addition to traditional museum displays honoring the past, the center actively promotes the continuation of Inupiat Eskimo cultural traditions through innovations such as the elder-in-residence program.

"It seems like it's a matter of simple common courtesy," she says. Such consideration can only help researchers, she points out. "If people don't get along with you, they're not going to talk to you, and they're liable to throw you out on your ear." In the past, scientists were not terribly sensitive about such matters, generally regarding human remains—and sometimes living natives—as artifacts themselves. Once, the girl's body would have been hauled off to the catacombs of some university or museum, and relics would have disappeared into exhibit drawers in what Sheehan describes as "hit-and-run archaeology."

"Grave robbers" is how Inupiat Jana Harcharek refers to early Arctic researchers. "They took human remains and their burial goods. It's pretty gruesome. But, of course, at the time they thought they were doing science a big favor. Thank goodness attitudes have changed."

Today, not only scientists but municipal officials confer with the Barrow Elders Council when local people find skeletons from traditional platform burials out on the tundra, or when bodies appear in the house mounds. The elders appreciate such consultations, says Samuel Simmonds, a tall, dignified man known for his carving. A retired Presbyterian minister, he presided at burial ceremonies of the famous "frozen family," ancient Inupiats discovered in Barrow [about twenty years ago]. "They were part of us, we know that," he says simply, as if the connection between old bones and bodies and living relatives is self-evident. In the case of the newly discovered body, he says, "We were concerned that it was reburied in a respectful manner. They were nice enough to come over and ask us."

The elders also wanted to restrict media attention and prevent photographs of the body except for a few showing her position at the site. They approved a limited autopsy to help answer questions about the body's sex, age, and state of health. She was placed in an orange plastic body bag in a stainless steel morgue with the temperature turned down to below freezing.

With the help of staff at the Indian Health Service Hospital, Jensen sent the girl's still-frozen body to Anchorage's

Providence Hospital. There she assisted with an autopsy performed by Dr. Michael Zimmerman of New York City's Mount Sinai Hospital. Zimmerman, an expert on prehistoric frozen bodies, had autopsied Barrow's frozen family in 1982, and was on his way to work on the prehistoric man recently discovered in the Alps.

The findings suggest the girl's life was very hard. She ultimately died of starvation, but also had emphysema caused by a rare congenital disease—the lack of an enzyme that protects the lungs. She probably was sickly and needed extra care all her brief life. The autopsy also found soot in her lungs from the family's sea mammal oil lamps, and she had osteoporosis, which was caused by a diet exclusively of meat from marine mammals. The girl's stomach was empty, but her intestinal tract contained dirt and animal fur. That remains a mystery and raises questions about the condition of the rest of the family. "It's not likely that she would be hungry and everyone else well fed," Jensen says.

That the girl appears to have been placed deliberately in the cellar provokes further questions about precontact burial practices, which the researchers hope Barrow elders can help answer. Historic accounts indicate the dead often were wrapped in skins and laid out on the tundra on wooden platforms, rather than buried in the frozen earth. But perhaps the entire family was starving and too weak to remove the dead girl from the house, Jensen speculates. "We probably won't ever be able to say, 'This is the way it was,'" she adds. "For that you need a time machine."

The scientific team reported to the elders that radiocarbon dating places the girl's death in about AD 1200. If correct—for dating is technically tricky in the Arctic—the date would set the girl's life about 100 years before her people formed settled whaling villages, Sheehan says.

Following the autopsy and the body's return to Barrow . . . , one last request by the elders was honored. The little girl, wrapped in her feather parka, was placed in a casket and buried in a small Christian ceremony next to the grave of the other prehistoric bodies. Hundreds of years after her death, an Inupiat daughter was welcomed back into the midst of her community.

The "rescue" of the little girl's body from the raw forces of time and nature means researchers and the Inupiat people will continue to learn still more about the region's culture. Sheehan and Jensen returned to Barrow in winter 1994 to explain their findings to townspeople. "We expect to learn just as much from them," Sheehan said before the trip. A North Slope Cultural Center . . . will store and display artifacts from the dig sites.

Laboratory tests and analyses also will contribute information. The archaeologists hope measurements of heavy metals in the girl's body will allow comparisons with modern-day pollution contaminating the sea mammals that Inupiats eat today. The soot damage in her lungs might offer health implications for Third World people who rely on oil lamps, dung fires, and charcoal for heat and light. Genetic tests could illuminate early population movements of Inupiats. The project also serves as a model for good relations between archaeologists and Native people. "The larger overall message from this work is that scientists and communities don't have to be at odds," Sheehan says. "In fact, there are mutual interests that we all have. Scientists have obligations to communities. And when more scientists realize that, and when more communities hold scientists to those standards, then everybody will be happier."

Adapted from Simpson, S. (1995, April). Whispers from the ice. Alaska, *23–28.*

Searching for Artifacts and Fossils

Where are artifacts and fossils found? Places containing archaeological remains of previous human activity are known as *sites*. There are many kinds of sites, and sometimes it is difficult to define their boundaries, for remains may be strewn over large areas. Sites are even found under water. Some examples of sites identified by archaeologists and paleoanthropologists are hunting campsites, from which hunters went out to hunt game; kill sites, in which game was killed and butchered; village sites, in which domestic activities took place; and cemeteries, in which the dead, and sometimes their belongings, were buried.

While skeletons of recent peoples are frequently associated with their cultural remains, archaeological sites may or may not contain any physical remains. As we go back in time, the association of physical and cultural remains becomes less likely. Physical remains dating from before 2.5 to 2.6 million years ago are found in isolation. This is not proof of the absence of material culture. It simply indicates that the earliest forms of material culture were not preserved in the archaeological record. It is likely that the earliest tools were made of organic materials (such as the termiting sticks used by chimpanzees) that were much less likely to be preserved. Similarly, fossils are found only in geologic contexts where conditions are known to have been right for fossilization. By contrast, archaeological sites may be found just about anywhere, perhaps because many date from more recent periods.

Site Identification

The first task for the archaeologist is actually finding sites to investigate. Archaeological sites, particularly very old ones, frequently lie buried underground, covered by layers of sediment deposited since the site was in use. Most sites are revealed by the presence of artifacts. Chance may play a crucial role in the site's discovery, as in the case discussed in Barrow, Alaska. Usually, however, the archaeologist will have to survey a region in order to plot the sites available for excavation.

A survey can be made from the ground, but more territory can be covered from the air. Aerial photographs

Some archaeological features are best seen from the air, such as this massive figure of a monkey made in prehistoric times on the Nazca Desert of Peru. Ancient people selectively removed the top layer of reddish stones thus exposing the light-colored earth below.

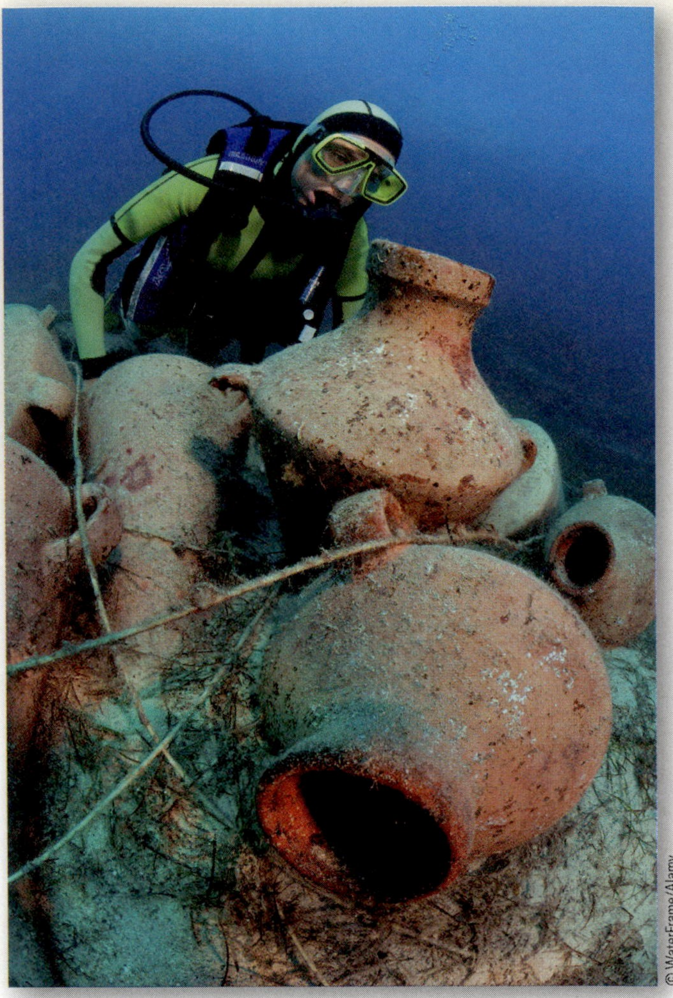

Here a diver recovers antique amphorae (the traditional containers for transporting wine, olives, olive oil, grain, and other commodities) from the site of a shipwreck in the Mediterranean Sea near the village of Kas, Turkey. The shipwreck dates back to the time of the Trojan War (over 3,000 years ago). Underwater archaeologists—led in this expedition by George Bass from the Institute of Nautical Archaeology of Texas A & M University collaborating with the Bodrum Museum of Underwater Archaeology in Istanbul, Turkey—can reconstruct facets of the past, ranging from ancient trade routes and and shipbuilding techniques, through the analysis of such remains.

have been used by archaeologists since the 1920s and are widely used today. Among other things, such photographs were used for the discovery and interpretation of the huge geometric and zoomorphic (from Latin for "animal-shaped") markings on the coastal desert of Peru. More recently a variety of innovations in the geographic and geologic sciences have been incorporated into archaeological surveys and other aspects of research. Innovations such as geographic information systems (GIS), remote sensing, and ground penetrating radar (GPR) complement traditional archaeological exploration methods.

High-resolution aerial photographs, including satellite imagery, resulted in the astonishing discovery of over 500 miles of prehistoric roadways connecting sites in the four-corners region of the United States (where Arizona, New Mexico, Colorado, and Utah meet) with other sites in ways that archaeologists had never suspected. This discovery led to a new understanding of prehistoric Pueblo Indian economic, social, and political organization. Evidently, large centers in this region governed a number of smaller satellite communities, mobilized labor for large public works, and allowed for the distribution of goods over substantial distances.

More obvious sites, such as the human-made mounds or *tells* of the Middle East, are easier to spot from the ground, for the country is open. But it is more difficult to locate ruins, even those that are well above ground, where there is a heavy forest cover. Thus the discovery of archaeological sites is strongly affected by local geography and climate.

Some sites may be spotted by changes in vegetation. For example, the topsoil of ancient storage and refuse pits is often richer in organic matter than that of the surrounding areas, and so it grows distinctive vegetation. At Tikal, an ancient Maya site in Guatemala, breadnut trees usually grow near the remains of ancient houses, so archaeologists can use these trees as guideposts.

On the ground, sites can be spotted by **soil marks,** or stains, showing up on the surface of recently plowed fields. Soil marks led archaeologists to many of the Bronze Age burial mounds in northern Hertfordshire and southwestern Cambridgeshire, England. The mounds hardly rose out of the ground, yet each was circled at its core by chalky soil marks. Sometimes the very presence of a particular chalky rock is significant.

Documents, maps, and folklore are also useful to the archaeologist. Heinrich Schliemann, the famous and controversial 19th-century German archaeologist, was led to the discovery of Troy after a reading of Homer's *Iliad.* He assumed that the city described by Homer as Ilium was really Troy. Place names and local lore often are an indication that an archaeological site is to be found in the area. Archaeological surveys therefore often depend upon amateur collectors and local people who are usually familiar with the history of the land.

Sometimes natural processes, such as soil erosion or droughts, expose sites or fossils. For example, in eastern North America erosion along the coastlines and river banks has exposed prehistoric refuse mounds known as shell **middens** (the general term for a trash deposit), which are filled with the remains of mussels and/or oysters, indicating that shellfish consumption was common. Similarly, a whole village of stone huts was exposed at Skara Brae in Scotland's Orkney Islands by the action of wind as it blew away sand.

Though natural forces sometimes expose fossils and sites, human physical and cultural remains are more often accidentally discovered. In Chapter 2 we noted how construction and quarrying work in Europe led to the discovery of fossils of extinct animals, which then played a role in the development of evolutionary theory. Similarly, limestone quarrying at a variety of sites in South Africa early in the 20th century led to the discovery of the earliest humanlike fossils from millions of years ago (see Chapter 7). Disturbances of the earth on a smaller scale, such as plowing, sometimes turn up bones, fragments of pots, and other archaeological objects.

Because construction projects do uncover archaeological remains so frequently, in many countries, including the United States, construction projects require government approval in order to ensure the identification and protection of archaeological remains. Cultural resource management, introduced in Chapter 1, is routinely included in the environmental review process for federally funded or licensed construction projects in the United States, as it is in Europe. This chapter's Anthropology Applied feature takes a closer look at cultural resource management.

Archaeological Excavation

Once a researcher identifies a site likely to contribute to his or her research agenda, the next step is to plan and carry out excavation. Obtaining permission to excavate from a variety of local and national authorities is a critical part of this planning. To begin, the land is cleared, and the places to be excavated are plotted as a **grid system** (Figure 5.1). The surface of the site is divided into squares of equal size, and each square is numbered and marked with stakes. Each object found may then be located precisely in the square from which it came. (Remember, context is everything!) The starting point of a grid system, which is located precisely in three dimensions, may be a large rock, the edge of a stone wall, or an iron rod sunk into the ground; this point is also known as the reference or **datum point.**

At a large site covering several square miles, the plotting may be done in terms of individual structures, numbered according to the square of a "giant grid" in which they are found. In a gridded site, each square is dug separately with great care. (In the photo on page 106, note how the grid system is used even in underwater archaeology.) Trowels are used to scrape the soil, and screens are used to sift all the loose soil so that even the smallest artifacts, such as flint chips or beads, are recovered.

A technique employed when looking for very fine objects, such as fish scales or very small bones, is called **flotation.** Flotation consists of immersing soil in water, causing the particles to separate. Some will float, others will sink to the bottom, and the remains can be easily retrieved.

If the site is **stratified**—that is, if the remains lie in layers one upon the other—each layer, or stratum, will be dug separately. Each layer, having been settled during a particular span of time, will contain artifacts deposited at the same time and belonging to the same culture (Figure 5.2). Cultural change can be traced through the order in which artifacts were deposited—deeper layers reveal older artifacts. But, archaeologists Frank Hole and Robert F. Heizer suggest,

> because of difficulties in analyzing stratigraphy, archaeologists must use the greatest caution in drawing conclusions. Almost all interpretations of time, space, and culture contexts depend on stratigraphy. The refinements of laboratory techniques for

soil mark A stain that shows up on the surface of recently plowed fields that reveals an archaeological site.

middens A refuse or garbage disposal area in an archaeological site.

grid system A system for recording data in three dimensions for an archaeological excavation.

datum point The starting point, or reference, for a grid system.

flotation An archaeological technique employed to recover very tiny objects by immersion of soil samples in water to separate heavy from light particles.

stratified Layered; term used to describe archaeological sites where the remains lie in layers, one upon another.

Anthropology Applied

Cultural Resource Management *by John Crock*

In the United States and Europe, cultural resource management or "regulatory" archaeology employs more archaeologists than universities and museums combined. This work is mandated by laws like Section 106 of the National Historic Preservation Act, which requires a cultural resources review for federally funded or regulated development projects, like the construction of new highways. These federal requirements have provided the funds for me and many other archaeologists to do what we love the best: to reconstruct the lives of people in the past through excavation of the material traces they have left behind.

For example, the Vermont Agency of Transportation's Missisquoi Bay Bridge Project at the northern end of Lake Champlain resulted in the discovery of one of the most significant archaeological sites ever found in Vermont. The initial Phase I survey sampling for the project included the excavation of small shovel test pits across the level field that would one day become the new bridge approach. Seven of the initial fifty-seven pits contained evidence of an archaeological site, including a total of just eight artifacts. Fortunately, this limited evidence was enough to document the presence of a pre-contact Native American habitation, later named the Bohannon site after the landowner.

To determine its size and significance, we conducted a Phase II evaluation of the site. Native American deposits were recovered from thirty-nine of the additional sixty-seven Phase II test pits excavated. The majority of the artifacts recovered are small fragments of clay pottery, including a portion of a turtle head effigy from a pipe or vessel. It was this artifact, the likes of which had never before been excavated in Vermont, which helped indicate the site was significant and eligible for the National Register of Historic Places. The effigy, and the style and thickness of pottery shards, indicated the site dated to the late pre-contact or contact period, between about 1400 and 1700. Since the site could not be avoided during construction, Phase III data recovery excavations were necessary to salvage a sample of the endangered site.

It was only during this final phase of work that the true size and significance of the Bohannon site was revealed. Excavation of large areas uncovered a substantial sample of decorated clay pipes and jars. Paleobotanist Nancy Sidell identified corn kernels and parts of corn plants in hearth and trash pit features at the site, indicating that the residents of the site grew corn close by. Zooarchaeologist Nanny Carder identified twenty-four different species in bone refuse from the same features, revealing a broad diet of animals ranging from flying squirrel to black bear. Living floors, trash pits, and the former location of house posts also were identified.

To salvage as much information as possible from the site before construction, an acre of the project area was stripped of topsoil to try to determine more about the layout of the site. Hundreds of post "mold" stains were revealed, from which portions of several longhouses have been reconstructed. A sample of corn kernels found was radiocarbon dated using accelerator mass spectrometry (AMS) to around AD 1600. Other dates and their error ranges place the site occupation between 1450 and 1650.

We believe the site was occupied just prior to 1609, when the first Europeans entered the region, based on the style of the pottery, the radiocarbon dates, and the fact that no European artifacts were recovered. The decorated clay pipes and pottery jars from the site are identical to material that has been found at late pre-contact village sites along the St. Lawrence River in Quebec. The inventory of artifacts, food resources, and house patterns from the site all suggest that the people at the Bohannon site were closely related to the St. Lawrence Iroquoians, a First Nations people who lived in what is now Quebec and Ontario.

From its humble identification in the early stages of archaeological survey for the new bridge, the Bohannon site has yielded an incredible amount of information; it represents the first St. Lawrence Iroquoian village discovered in Vermont.

Located on a relatively unobtrusive piece of land along an existing road, the first St. Lawrence Iroquoian village was discovered only because federal law mandated archaeological exploration before a road and bridge expansion project.

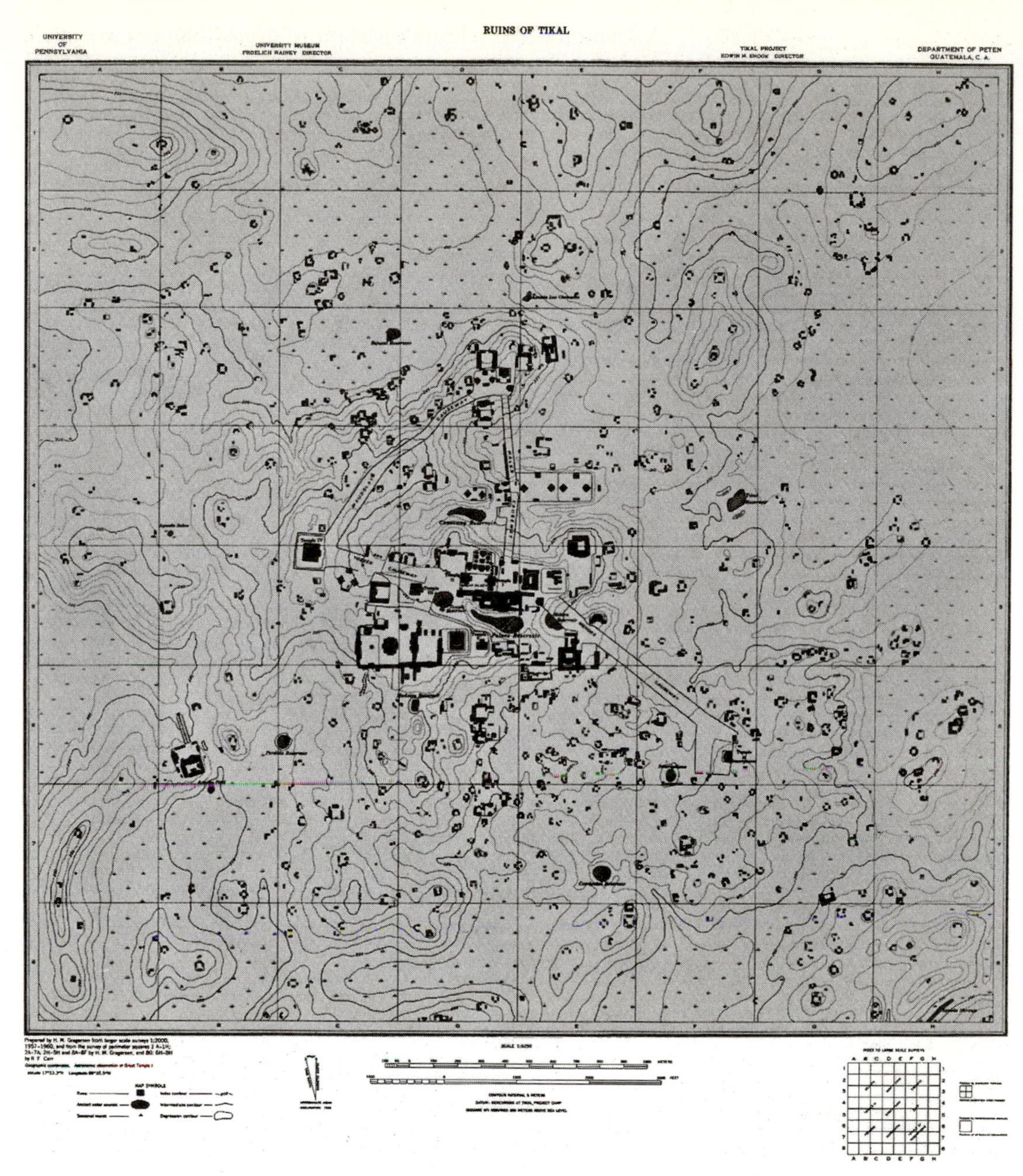

Figure 5.1 At large sites covering several square miles, a giant grid is constructed, as shown in this map of the center of the ancient Maya city of Tikal. Each square of the grid is one quarter of a square kilometer; individual structures are numbered according to the square in which they are found.

analysis are wasted if archaeologists cannot specify the stratigraphic position of their artifacts.[3]

If no stratification is present, then the archaeologist digs by arbitrary levels. Each square must be dug so that its edges and profiles are straight; walls between squares are often left standing to serve as visual correlates of the grid system.

Fossil Excavation

Although fossil excavation is similar to archaeological excavation, there are some key differences. The paleoanthropologist must be particularly skilled in the techniques of geology, or have ready access to geologic expertise, because a fossil is of little value unless its place in the sequence of rocks that contain it can be determined.

In order to provide all the necessary expertise, paleoanthropological expeditions today generally are made up of teams of experts in various fields in addition to physical anthropology. Surgical skill and caution are required to remove a fossil from its burial place without damage. Unusual tools and materials are found in the kit of the paleoanthropologist—pickaxes, dental instruments, enamel coating, burlap for bandages, and sculpting plaster.

To remove newly discovered bones, the paleoanthropologist begins uncovering the specimen, using pick and shovel for initial excavation, then small camel-hair brushes and dental picks to remove loose and easily detachable debris surrounding the bones. Once the entire specimen has been uncovered (a process that may take days of backbreaking, patient labor), the bones are covered with shellac

[3] Hole, F., & Heizer, R. F. (1969). *An introduction to prehistoric archeology* (p. 113). New York: Holt, Rinehart & Winston.

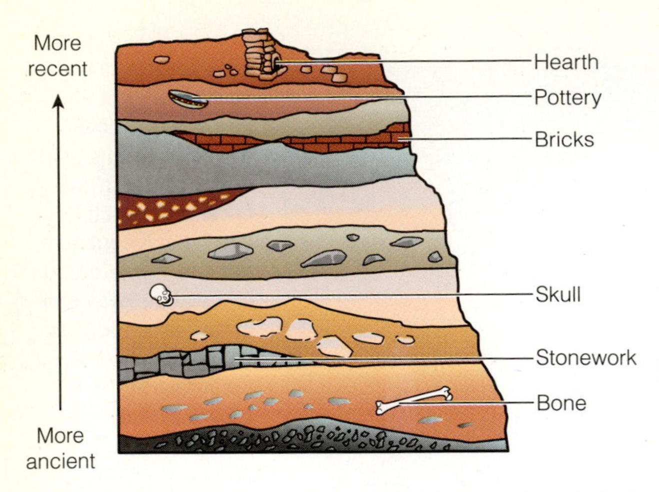

Figure 5.2 Some sites are stratified, in that archaeological remains lie in layers stacked one on top of the other; older layers are lower down, and more recent layers are on top. Geologic processes will result in strata of different depths in different places. Careful mapping of each stratum using the grid system is essential for interpretation of the site.

and tissue paper to prevent cracking and damage during further excavation and handling.

Both the fossil and the earth immediately surrounding it, or the *matrix,* are prepared for removal as a single block. The bones and matrix are cut out of the earth (but not removed), and more shellac is applied to the entire block to harden it. The bones are covered with burlap bandages dipped in plaster. Then the block is enclosed in more plaster and burlap bandages, perhaps splinted with tree branches and allowed to dry overnight. After it has hardened, the entire block is carefully removed from the earth, ready for packing and transport to a laboratory. Before leaving the discovery area, the investigator makes a thorough sketch map of the terrain and pinpoints the find on geologic maps to aid future investigators.

State of Preservation of Archaeological and Fossil Evidence

The results of an excavation depend greatly on the condition of the remains. Inorganic materials such as stone and metal are more resistant to decay than organic ones such as wood and bone. Sometimes the anthropologist discovers an assemblage—a collection of artifacts—made of durable inorganic materials, such as stone tools, and traces of organic ones long since decomposed, such as woodwork (Figure 5.3), textiles, or food.

Climate, local geologic conditions, and cultural practices also play a role in the state of preservation. For example, our knowledge of ancient Egyptian culture stems not only from their burial practices but from the effects of climate and soil on preservation. The ancient Egyptians believed that eternal life could be achieved only if the dead person were buried with his or her worldly possessions. Hence, their tombs are usually filled with a wealth of artifacts, including the skeletons of other humans owned by dynastic rulers.

Under favorable climatic conditions, even the most perishable objects may survive over vast periods of time. The earliest Egyptian burials, consisting of shallow pits in the sand with bodies buried long before mummification was practiced, often yield well-preserved corpses. Their preservation can only be the result of rapid desiccation, or complete drying out, in the warm desert climate. The elaborate tombs of the rulers of dynastic Egypt often contain wooden furniture, textiles, flowers, and written scrolls on paper made from papyrus reeds, barely touched by time, seemingly as fresh looking as they were when deposited in the tombs as long as 5,000 years ago—a consequence of the region's arid climatic conditions. Of course, the ancient Egyptian burial practices selectively preserved more information about the elite members of society than the average individual.

The dryness of certain caves is also a factor in the preservation of **coprolites,** the scientific term for fossilized human or animal feces. Coprolites provide information on prehistoric diet and health. From the analysis of elements preserved in coprolites such as seeds, insect skeletons, and tiny bones from fish or amphibians, archaeologists and paleoanthropologists can directly determine diets from the past. This information, in turn,

coprolites Preserved fecal material providing evidence of the diet and health of past organisms.

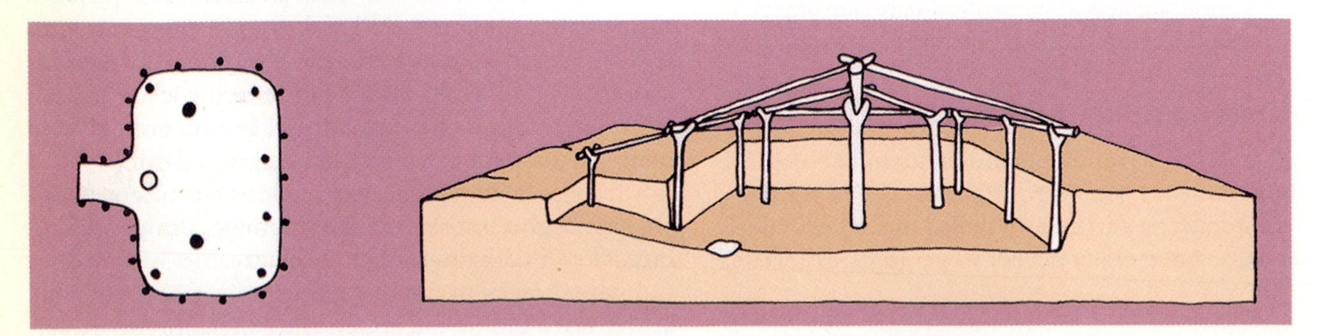

Figure 5.3 Although the wooden posts of a house may have long since decayed, their positions may still be marked by discoloration of the soil. The plan shown on the left—of an ancient post-hole pattern and depression at Snaketown, Arizona—permits the hypothetical house reconstruction on the right.

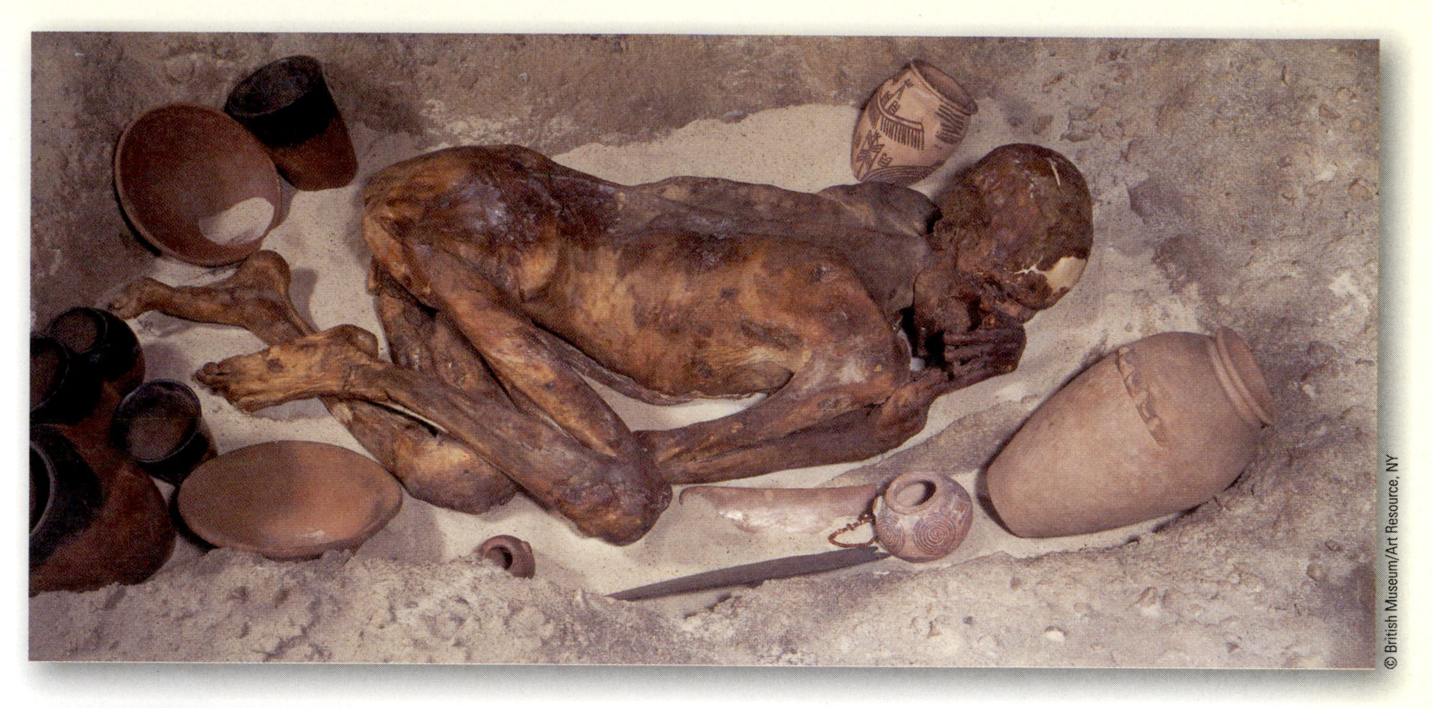

The preservation of archaeological remains is dependent upon the environment. Even before the invention of mummification technologies, buried bodies were very well preserved in Egypt because they dried so quickly in the extremely arid environment.

At the Maya site of Tikal, these intricately carved figures, originally made of wood, were recovered from a king's tomb by pouring plaster into a cavity in the soil, left when the original organic material decayed.

can shed light on overall health. Because many sources of food are available only in certain seasons, it is even possible to tell the time of year in which the food was eaten.

Certain climates can obliterate all evidence of organic remains. Maya ruins found in the tropical rainforests of Mesoamerica (the region encompassing central and southern Mexico and northern Central America) are often in a state of collapse—notwithstanding that many are massive structures of stone—as a result of the pressure exerted upon them by the heavy forest vegetation. The rain and humidity soon destroy almost all traces of woodwork, textiles, or basketry. Fortunately, impressions of these artifacts can sometimes be preserved in plaster, and some objects made of wood or plant fibers are depicted in stone carvings and pottery figurines. Thus even in the face of substantial decay of organic substances, something may still be learned about them.

Sorting Out the Evidence

Excavation records include a scale map of all the features, the stratification of each excavated square, a description of the exact location and depth of every artifact or bone unearthed, and photographs and scale drawings of the objects. This is the only way archaeological evidence can later be pieced together so as to arrive at a plausible reconstruction of a culture. Although the archaeologist or paleoanthropologist may be interested only in certain kinds of remains, every aspect of the site must be recorded, whether it is relevant to the particular investigation or not, because such evidence may be useful to others and would otherwise be lost forever. In sum, archaeological sites are nonrenewable resources. The disturbance of the arrangement of artifacts, even by proper excavation, is permanent.

Sometimes sites are illegally looted, which can result in loss not only of the artifacts themselves but of the site. Although looting has long been a threat to the archaeological record, it has become a high-tech endeavor today. Avid collectors and fans of archaeological sites unwittingly

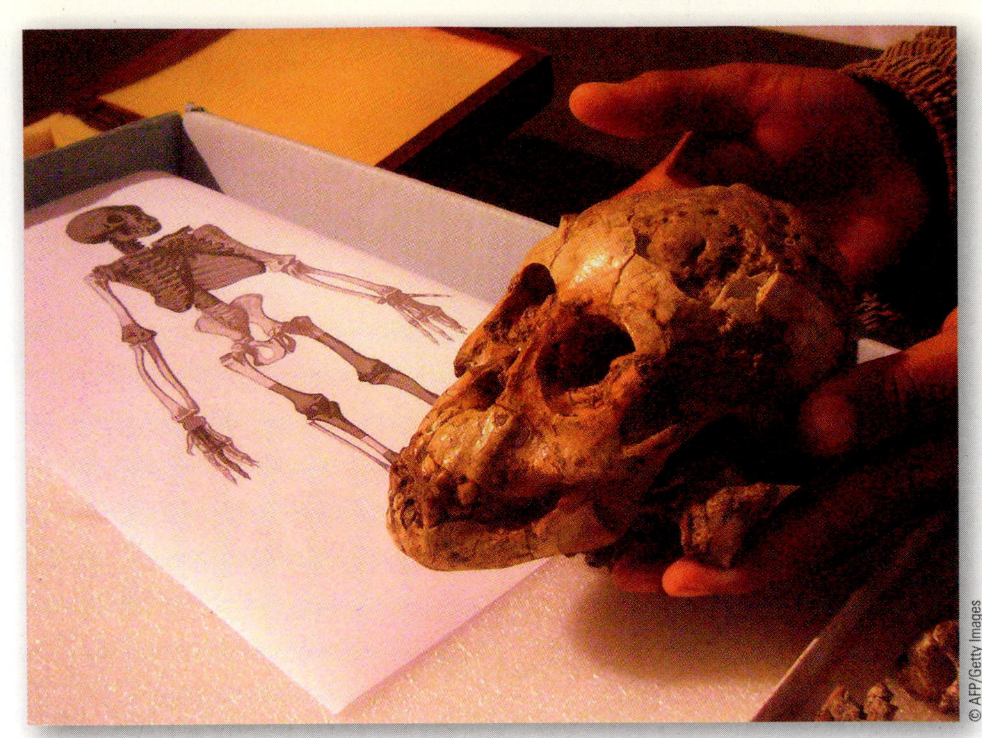

In September 2006, researchers announced the discovery of a spectacular new fossil—the skeleton of a young child dated to 3.3 million years ago. The fossil was actually discovered in the Dikika area of northern Ethiopia in 2000. Since then, researchers worked on careful recovery and analysis of the fossilized remains so that when the announcement was made, a great deal was already known about the specimen. Their analyses have determined that this child, a little girl about 3 years old who likely died in a flash flood, was a member of *Australopithecus afarensis,* the same species as the famous Lucy specimen (see Chapter 7). Due to the importance of this find, some scientists have referred to this child as "Lucy's baby" though the child lived about 150,000 years before Lucy.

aid looting through sharing site and artifact location information on the Internet, which has also provided a market for artifacts.

Once the artifact or fossil has been freed from the surrounding matrix, a variety of other laboratory methods come into play. Generally, archaeologists and paleoanthropologists plan on at least three hours of laboratory work for each hour of fieldwork. In the lab, artifacts that have been recovered must first be cleaned and catalogued—often a tedious and time-consuming job—before they are ready for analysis. From the shapes of the artifacts as well as from the traces of manufacture and wear, archaeologists can usually determine their function. For example, the Russian archaeologist S. A. Semenov devoted many years to the study of prehistoric technology. In the case of a flint tool used as a scraper, he was able to determine, by examining the wear patterns of the tool under a microscope, that the prehistoric individuals who used it began to scrape from right to left and then scraped from left to right, and in so doing avoided straining the muscles of the hand.[4] From the work of Semenov and others, we now know that right-handed individuals made most stone tools preserved in the archaeological record, a fact that has implications for brain structure. The relationships among populations can also be traced through material remains (Figure 5.4).

Dental specimens are frequently analyzed under the microscope to examine markings on teeth that might provide clues about diet in the past. Specimens are now regularly scanned using computed tomography (CT) to analyze structural details of the bone. Imprints or **endocasts** of the insides of skulls are taken to determine the size and shape of ancient brains.

Advances in genetic technology are now applied to ancient human remains. Anthropologists extract genetic material from skeletal remains in order to perform DNA comparisons among the specimen, other fossils, and living people. Small fragments of DNA are amplified or copied repeatedly using **polymerase chain reaction (PCR)**

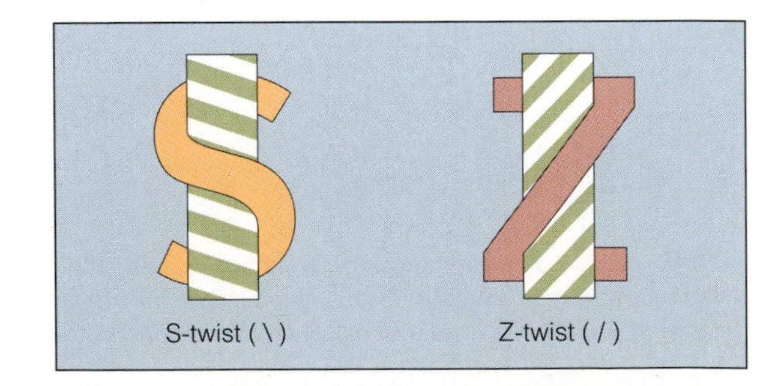

Figure 5.4 In northern New England, prehistoric pottery was often decorated by impressing the damp clay with a cord-wrapped stick. Examination of cord impressions reveals that coastal people twisted fibers used to make cordage to the left (Z-twist), while those living inland did the opposite (S-twist). The nonfunctional differences reflect motor habits so deeply ingrained as to seem completely natural to the cordage makers. From this, we may infer two distinctively different populations.

[4] Semenov, S. A. (1964). *Prehistoric technology.* New York: Barnes & Noble.

endocast A cast of the inside of a skull; used to help determine the size and shape of the brain.

polymerase chain reaction (PCR) A technique for amplifying or creating multiple copies of fragments of DNA so that it can be studied in the laboratory.

technology to provide a sufficient amount of material to perform these analyses. However, unless DNA is preserved in a stable material such as amber, it will decay over time. Therefore, analyses of DNA extracted from specimens older than about 50,000 years become increasingly unreliable due to the decay of DNA.

As defined in Chapter 1, *bioarchaeology,* which seeks to understand past cultures through analysis of skeletal remains, is a growing area within anthropology. It combines the biological anthropologists' expertise in skeletal biology with the archaeological reconstruction of human cultures. Examination of human skeletal material provides important insights into ancient peoples' diets, gender roles, social status, and patterns of activity. For example, analysis of human skeletons shows that elite members of society had access to more nutritious foods, allowing them to reach their full growth potential.[5]

Gender roles in a given society can be assessed through skeletons as well. In fully preserved adult skeletons, the sex of the deceased individual can be determined with a high degree of accuracy, allowing for comparisons of male and female life expectancy, mortality, and health status (Figure 5.5). These analyses can help establish the social roles of men and women in past societies.

Forensics, bioarchaeology's cousin discipline, also examines skeletal remains to determine characteristics of a deceased or injured individual. As with archaeological research, this information is integrated with material remains. New biomedical technology also plays a role in the investigation of remains from both the past and the present. For example, CT scans have added new information

[5] Haviland, W. (1967). Stature at Tikal, Guatemala: Implications for ancient Maya, demography, and social organization. *American Antiquity 32,* 316–325.

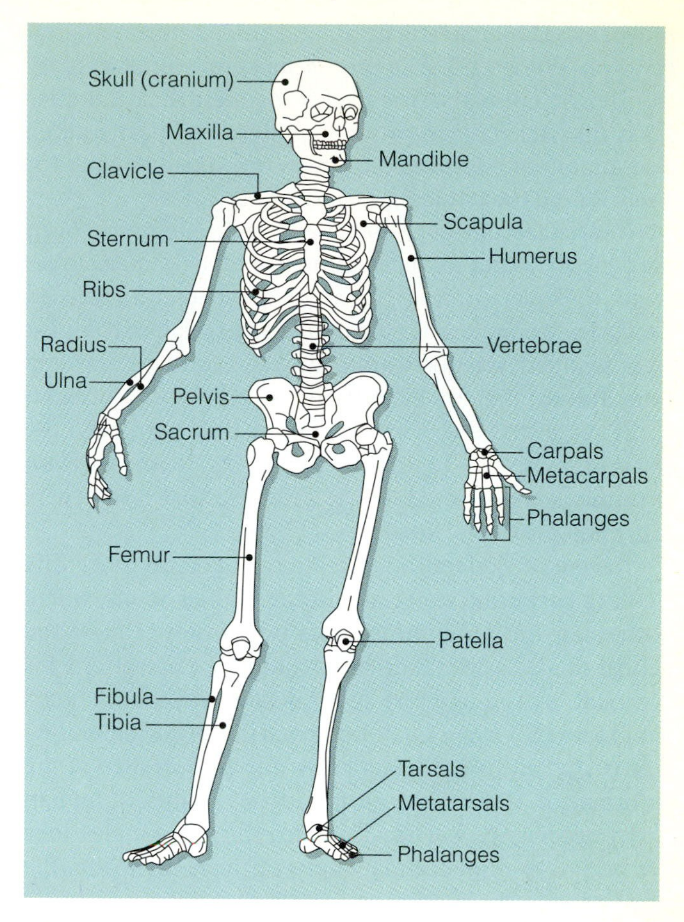

Figure 5.5 **The complete male and female skeletons differ on average in some consistent ways that allow skeletal biologists to identify the sex of the deceased individual. In addition to noting some of these features labeled above, learning the basic skeleton will be useful in the chapters ahead as we trace the history of human evolution.**

Skulls from peoples of the Tiwanaku empire, who tightly bound the heads of their children. The shape of the skull distinguished people from various parts of the empire that flourished in the Andes mountains of South America between AD 550 and 950.

in forensic, bioarchaeological, and paleoanthropological contexts. While a CT scan cannot substitute for an autopsy in forensic contexts, it is useful for identification after mass disasters. It can provide evidence of past trauma that might not be revealed from an investigation aimed at determining the immediate cause of death.[6]

In archaeological contexts, CT technology has been particularly useful for determining whether damage to remains took place during excavation or whether it preceded death. For example, after the remains of Egyptian King Tut were scanned, scientists uniformly agreed that the young king did not die of a head injury as previously thought; some suggested that a broken femur may have been the cause of his death.[7] To minimize handling, these rare fossil specimens are scanned one at a time so that researchers can study the digital images.

Recently, skeletal analyses have become more difficult to carry out, especially in the United States, where American Indian communities now often request the return of skeletons from archaeological excavations for reburial, as required by federal law. Anthropologists find themselves in a quandary over this requirement. As scientists, anthropologists know the importance of the information that can be gleaned from studies of human skeletons, but as scholars subject to ethical principles, they are bound to respect the feelings of those for whom the skeletons possess cultural and spiritual significance.

New techniques, such as 3D digital images of Native American skeletons, help to resolve this conflict as they allow for both rapid repatriation and continued study of skeletal remains. But globally, aboriginal groups are questioning the practice of digitizing remains of their people without permission. For example, the University of Vienna in Austria has been challenged by representatives of the Ju/'hoansi people of southern Africa because the remains that its ethnological museum has in its possession were not donated; rather, they were taken early in the century by Rudolf Pöch, a Viennese anthropologist whose writings about racial hierarchies were used as part of Nazi Germany's eugenics movement. According to Roger Chennells, the South African legal advisor for the Ju/'hoansi, their position is: "We have not been consulted, and we do not support any photographic archiving of our people's remains—we are opposed to it."[8]

By the standards of the 1990 Native American Graves Protection and Repatriation Act (NAGPRA), the Ju/'hoansi would have legal decision-making authority over the fate of these remains; but the equivalent of NAGPRA has not yet been codified as international law. Even with NAGPRA in place, the handling of remains is still often controversial. Scientists and American Indians sometimes have been unable to move beyond their conflicting views as seen with Kennewick Man, a 9,300-year-old skeleton that was dislodged by the Columbia River in Washington State in 1996. This chapter's Biocultural Connection focuses on how this controversy has been playing out in the federal courts.

Dating the Past

With accurate and detailed records of their excavations in hand, archaeologists and paleoanthropologists are able to deal with a crucial research issue: the question of age. As we have seen, analysis of physical and cultural remains is dependent on knowledge about the age of the artifacts or specimens. How, then, are the materials retrieved from excavations reliably dated? Calculating the age of physical and cultural remains is an essential aspect of interpreting the past. Because archaeologists and paleoanthropologists often deal with peoples and events from long ago, the traditional calendar of historic times is of little use to them.

Remains can be dated by noting their position in the earth, by measuring the amount of chemicals contained in fossil bones, or by association with other plant, animal, or cultural remains. These are known as **relative dating** techniques because they do not establish precise dates for specific remains but rather their relationship to a series of remains. Methods of **absolute** or **chronometric dating** (from the Latin for "measuring time") provide actual dates calculated in years "before the present" (BP). These methods rely on chemical and physical properties such as rates of decay of radioactive elements, which may be present in the remains themselves or in the surrounding soil. Absolute dating methods scientifically establish actual dates for the major events of geologic and evolutionary history. By comparing dates and remains across a variety of sites, anthropologists can reconstruct human origins, migrations, and technological developments.

Many relative and chronometric techniques are available. However, most of these techniques are applicable only for certain time spans and in certain environmental contexts. Bear in mind that each of the chronometric dating techniques also has a margin of error. Ideally, archaeologists

[6] Leth, P. M. (2007). The use of CT scanning in forensic autopsy. *Forensic Science, Medicine, and Pathology 3* (1), 65–69.

[7] Handwerk, B. (2005, March 8). King Tut not murdered violently, CT scans show. *National Geographic News*, 2.

[8] Scully, T. (2008). Online anthropology draws protest from aboriginal group. *Nature 453*, 1155. doi:10.1038/4531155a.

relative dating In archaeology and paleoanthropology, designating an event, object, or fossil as being older or younger than another.

absolute or chronometric dating In archaeology and paleoanthropology, dating recovered material based on solar years, centuries, or other units of absolute time.

Biocultural Connection

Kennewick Man

The "Ancient One" and "Kennewick Man" both refer to the 9,300-year-old skeletal remains that were found in 1996 below the surface of Lake Wallula, part of the Columbia River, in Kennewick, Washington State. This discovery has been the center of continuing controversy since it was made. Who owns these human remains? Who can determine what shall be done with them? Do the biological characteristics preserved in these remains play a role in determining their fate?

This particular conflict involves three major parties. Because the skeleton was found on a location for which the U.S. Army Corps of Engineers is responsible, this federal agency first took possession of the remains. Appealing to a 1990 federal law, the Native American Graves Protection and Repatriation Act (NAGPRA), a nearby American Indian group named the Confederated Tribes of the Umatilla Indian Reservation (representing the region's Umatilla, Cayuse, and Walla Walla nations) claimed the remains. Because Kennewick Man was found within their ancestral homeland, they argue that they are "culturally affiliated" with the individual they refer to as the Ancient One. Viewing these human bones as belonging to an ancestor, they wish to return them to the earth in a respectful ceremony.

This claim was challenged in federal court by a group of scientists, including some archaeologists and biological anthropologists. They view these human remains, among the oldest ever discovered in the western hemisphere, as scientifically precious, with potential to shed light on the earliest population movements in the Americas. The scientists do not want to "own" the remains but want the opportunity to study them. By means of DNA analysis, for instance, these scientists expect to determine possible prehistoric linkages between this individual and ancient human remains found elsewhere, including Asia. Moreover, scientific analysis may determine whether there actually exists any biological connection between these remains and currently living Native peoples, including individuals residing on the Umatilla Indian Reservation.

Fearing the loss of a unique scientific specimen, the scientists filed a lawsuit in federal court to prevent reburial before these bones were researched and analyzed. Their legal challenge is not based on "cultural affiliation," which is a very difficult concept when it concerns such ancient human remains, but focuses on the fact that the region's Native peoples cannot prove they are direct lineal descendants. Unless such ties have been objectively established, they argue, Kennewick Man should be released for scientific study.

In 2004 federal court rulings permitted initial scientific investigations. Just as these investigations were wrapping up in July 2005, the Senate Indian Affairs Committee heard testimony on a proposal by Arizona Senator John McCain to expand NAGPRA so that remains such as these would be once again prohibited from study. Congress adjourned without this bill becoming law, and the remains have been studied continually since then.

Doug Owsley, the forensic anthropologist from the Smithsonian Institution leading the research team, has said that scientific investigation is yielding even more information than expected. Because conflicting worldviews are at the center of this controversy, it is unlikely that it will be easily resolved.

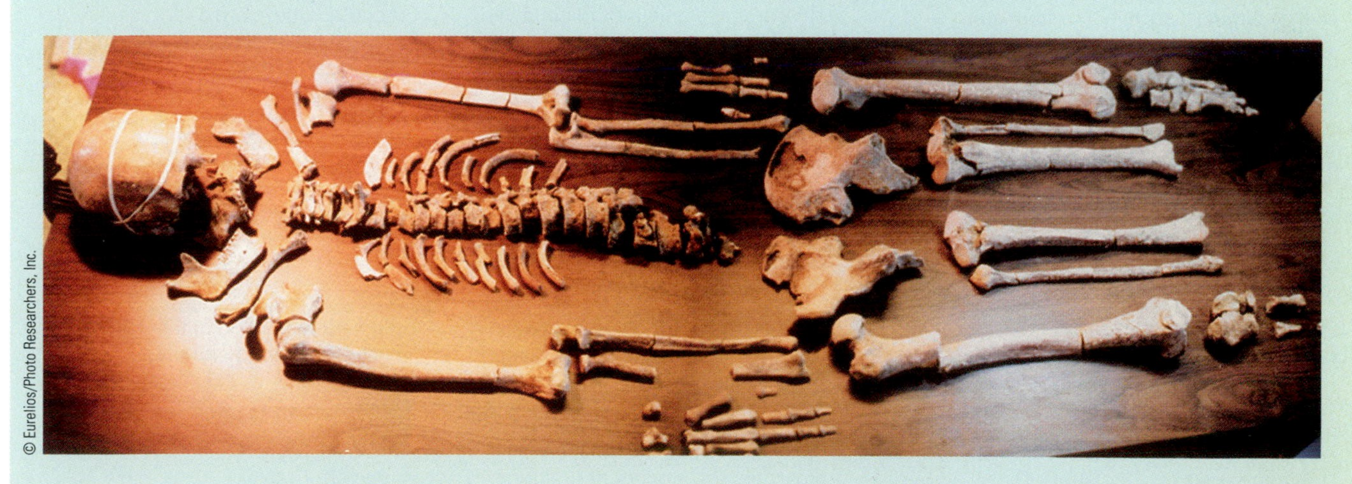

and paleoanthropologists utilize as many methods as are appropriate, given the materials available and the funds at their disposal. By doing so, they significantly reduce the risk of error. Several of the most frequently employed dating techniques are presented in Table 5.1.

Relative Dating

Of the many relative dating techniques available, **stratigraphy** is probably the most reliable (recall Figure 5.2). Stratigraphy is based on the simple principle that the oldest layer, or stratum, was deposited first (it is the deepest) whereas the newest layer was deposited last (in undisturbed situations, it lies at the top). Similarly, archaeological evidence is usually deposited in chronological order. The lowest stratum contains the oldest artifacts and/or fossils whereas the uppermost stratum contains the most recent ones. Thus even in the

stratigraphy In archaeology and paleoanthropology, the most reliable method of relative dating by means of strata.

Table 5.1 Absolute and Relative Dating Methods

Dating Method	Time Period	Method's Process	Drawbacks
Stratigraphy	Relative only	Based on the law of superposition, which states that lower layers or strata are older than higher layers	Site specific; natural forces, such as earthquakes, and human activity, such as burials, disturb stratigraphic relationships
Fluorine analysis	Relative only	Compares the amount of fluorine from surrounding soil absorbed by specimens after deposition	Site specific
Faunal and floral series	Relative only	Sequencing remains into relative chronological order based on an evolutionary sequence established in another region with reliable absolute dates; called *palynology* when done with pollen grains	Dependent upon known relationships established elsewhere
Seriation	Relative only	Sequencing cultural remains into relative chronological order based on stylistic features	Dependent upon known relationships established elsewhere
Dendrochronology	About 3,000 years BP maximum	Compares tree-growth rings preserved in a site with a tree of known age	Requires ancient trees of known age
Radiocarbon	Accurate less than 50,000 years BP	Compares the ratio of radioactive carbon 14 (^{14}C) (with a half-life of 5,730 years) to stable carbon 12 (^{12}C) in organic material	Increasingly inaccurate when assessing remains from more than 50,000 years ago
Potassium argon (K-Ar)	More than 200,000 years BP	Compares the amount of radioactive potassium (^{40}K) (with a half-life of 1.3 billion years) to stable argon (^{40}Ar)	Requires volcanic ash; requires cross-checking due to contamination from atmospheric argon
Amino acid racemization	40,000–180,000 years BP	Compares the change in the number of proteins in a right- versus left-sided three-dimensional structure	Amino acids leached out from soil variably cause error
Thermoluminescence	Possibly up to 200,000 years BP	Measures the amount of light given off due to radioactivity when sample heated to high temperatures	Technique developed for recent materials such as Greek pottery; not clear how accurate the dates are for older remains
Electron spin resonance	Possibly up to 200,000 years BP	Measures the resonance of trapped electrons in a magnetic field	Works with tooth enamel—not yet developed for bone; problems with accuracy
Fission track	Wide range of times	Measures the tracks left in crystals by uranium as it decays; good cross-check for K-Ar technique	Useful for dating crystals only
Paleomagnetic reversals	Wide range of times	Measures orientation of magnetic particles in stones and links them to whether magnetic field of earth pulled toward the north or south during their formation	Large periods of normal or reversed magnetic orientation require dating by some other method; some smaller events known to interrupt the sequence
Uranium series	40,000–180,000 years BP	Measures the amount of uranium decaying in cave sites	Large error range

absence of precise dates, one knows the *relative* age of objects in one stratum compared with the ages of those in other strata. However, defining the stratigraphy of a given site can be complicated by geologic activities such as earthquakes that shift the position of stratigraphic layers.

Another method of relative dating is the **fluorine** method. It is based on the fact that the amount of fluorine deposited in bones is proportional to the amount of time they have been in the earth. The oldest bones contain the greatest amount of fluorine and vice versa. The fluorine test is useful in dating bones that cannot be ascribed with certainty to any particular stratum. A shortcoming of this

fluorine dating In archaeology or paleoanthropology, a technique for relative dating based on the fact that the amount of fluorine in bones is proportional to their age.

Some ancient societies devised precise ways of recording dates that archaeologists have been able to correlate with our own calendar. Here is the tomb of an important ruler, Siyaj Chan K'awil II, at the ancient Maya city of Tikal. The glyphs painted on the wall give the date of the burial in the Maya calendar, which is the same as March 18, AD 457, in the Gregorian calendar.

method is that the amount of naturally occurring fluorine is not constant but varies from region to region, making it difficult to validate cross-site comparisons of fluorine values. This method was vital for exposing the infamous Piltdown hoax in England, in which a human skull and orangutan jaw were placed together in the earth as false evidence for an early human ancestor (see Chapter 7).

Relative dating can also be done by **seriation,** a method of establishing sequences of plant, animal, or even cultural remains. With seriation, the order of appearance of a succession (or series) of plants, animals, or artifacts provides relative dates for a site based on a series established in another area. An example of seriation based on cultural artifacts is the Stone–Bronze–Iron Age series used by prehistorians (see Chapter 11). Within a given region, sites containing artifacts made of iron are generally more recent than sites containing only stone tools. In well-investigated culture areas, series have even been developed for particular styles of pottery.

Similar inferences are made with animal or faunal series. For example, very early North American Indian sites have yielded the remains of mastodons and mammoths—animals now extinct—and on this basis the sites can be dated to a time before these animals died out, roughly 10,000 years ago. For dating some of the earliest African fossils in human evolution, faunal series have been developed in regions where accurate chronometric dates can be established. These series can then be used to establish relative sequences in other regions. Similar series have been established for plants, particularly using grains of pollen. This approach has become known as **palynology.** The kind of pollen found in any geologic stratum depends on the kind of vegetation that existed at the time that stratum was deposited. A site or locality can therefore be dated by determining what kind of pollen was found associated with it. In addition, palynology also helps to reconstruct the environments in which prehistoric people lived.

Chronometric Dating

Chronometric dating methods apply chemistry and physics to calculate the ages of physical and cultural remains. Several methods use naturally occurring radioactive elements that are present either in the remains themselves or in the surrounding soil.

One of the most widely used methods of absolute dating is **radiocarbon dating.** This method uses the fact that while they are alive, all organisms absorb radioactive carbon (known as carbon 14 or ^{14}C) as well as ordinary carbon 12 (^{12}C) in proportions identical to those found in the atmosphere. Absorption of ^{14}C ceases at the time of death, and the ratio between the two forms of carbon begins to change as the unstable radioactive element ^{14}C begins to "decay." Each radioactive element decays, or transforms into a stable nonradioactive form, at a specific rate. The amount of time it takes for one half of the material originally present to decay is expressed as the "half-life." In the case of ^{14}C, it takes 5,730 years for half of the amount of ^{14}C present to decay to stable nitrogen 14. In another

seriation In archaeology and paleoanthropology, a technique for relative dating based on putting groups of objects into a sequence in relation to one another.

palynology In archaeology and paleoanthropology, a technique of relative dating based on changes in fossil pollen over time.

radiocarbon dating In archaeology and paleoanthropology, a technique of chronometric dating based on measuring the amount of radioactive carbon (^{14}C) left in organic materials found in archaeological sites.

5,730 years (11,460 years total), half of the remaining amount will also decay to nitrogen 14 so that only one quarter of the original amount of ^{14}C will be present. Thus the age of an organic substance such as charcoal, wood, shell, or bone can be measured through determining the changing proportion of ^{14}C relative to the amount of stable ^{12}C.

Though scientists can measure the amount of radioactive carbon left in even a few milligrams of a given organic substance of a recent specimen, the amount of carbon 14 present in remains from the distant past is so small that accurate detection is difficult. The radiocarbon method can adequately date organic materials up to about 50,000 years old, but dating older material is far less reliable.

Of course, one has to be sure that the organic remains were truly contemporaneous with the archaeological materials. For example, charcoal found on a site may have gotten there from a recent forest fire rather than a more ancient activity, or wood found at a site may have been retrieved by the people who lived there from some older context.

Because there is always a certain amount of error involved, radiocarbon dates (like all chronometric dating methods) are not as absolute as is sometimes thought. This is why any stated date always has a plus-or-minus (±) factor attached to it corresponding to one standard deviation above and below the mean value. For example, a date of 5,200 ± 120 years ago means that there is about a 2 out of 3 chance (or a 67 percent chance) that the true date falls somewhere between 5,080 and 5,320 radiocarbon years ago. The qualification "radiocarbon years" is used because radiocarbon years are not precisely equivalent to calendar years.

The discovery that radiocarbon years are not precisely equivalent to calendar years was made possible by another method of absolute dating: **dendrochronology** (derived from *dendron*, a Greek word meaning "tree"). Originally devised for dating Pueblo Indian sites in the North American Southwest, this method is based on the fact that in the right kind of climate, trees add one (and only one) new growth ring to their trunks every year. The rings vary in thickness, depending upon the amount of rainfall received in a year, so that climatic fluctuation is registered in the growth ring. By taking a sample of wood, such as a beam from a Pueblo Indian house, and by comparing its pattern of rings with those in the trunk of a tree of known age, archaeologists can date the archaeological material.

dendrochronology In archaeology and paleoanthropology, a technique of chronometric dating based on the number of rings of growth found in a tree trunk.

potassium-argon dating In archaeology and paleoanthropology, a technique of chronometric dating that measures the ratio of radioactive potassium to argon in volcanic debris associated with human remains.

Dendrochronology is applicable only to wooden objects. Furthermore, it can be used only in regions in which trees of great age, such as the giant sequoias and the bristlecone pine, are known to grow. Radiocarbon dating of wood from bristlecone pines dated by dendrochronology allows scientists to correct the carbon 14 dates so as to bring them into agreement with calendar dates.

Potassium-argon dating, another commonly used method of absolute dating, is based on a technique similar to that of radiocarbon analysis. Following intense heating, as from a volcanic eruption, radioactive potassium decays at a known rate to form argon—any previously existing argon having been released by the heating of the molten lava. The half-life of radioactive potassium is 1.3 billion years. Deposits that are millions of years old can now be dated by measuring the ratio of potassium to argon in a given rock.

Volcanic debris at various localities in East Africa is routinely dated by potassium-argon analysis, indicating when the volcanic eruption occurred. If fossils or artifacts are found sandwiched between layers of volcanic ash, as they are at Olduvai and other sites in East Africa, they can be dated with some precision. As with radiocarbon dates, there are limits to that precision, and potassium-argon dates are always stated with a plus-or-minus margin of error attached. The precision of this method is limited to time periods older than about 200,000 years ago.

Though radiocarbon and potassium-argon methods are extremely valuable, neither technique works well during the time period dating from about 50,000 years ago to about 200,000 years ago. Because this same time period happens to be very important in human evolutionary history, scientists have developed a number of other methods to obtain accurate dates during this critical period.

One such method, *amino acid racemization,* is based on the fact that amino acids trapped in organic materials gradually change, or racemize, after death, from left-handed forms to right-handed forms. Thus the ratio of left- to right-handed forms should indicate the specimen's age. Unfortunately, in substances like bone, moisture and acids in the soil can leach out the amino acids, thereby introducing a serious source of error. However, ostrich eggshells have proved immune to this problem, the amino acids being so effectively locked up in a tight mineral matrix that they are preserved for thousands of years. Because ostrich eggs were widely used as food and the shells were used as containers in Africa and the Middle East, they provide a powerful means of dating sites of the later parts of the Old Stone Age (Paleolithic), between 40,000 and 180,000 years ago.

Electron spin resonance, which measures the number of trapped electrons in bone, and *thermoluminescence,* which measures the amount of light emitted from a specimen when heated to high temperatures, are two additional methods that have been developed to fill in prehistoric time gaps. Dates derived from these two methods changed the interpretation of key sites in present-day Israel vital for reconstructing human origins (see Chapters 8 and 9).

A few other chronometric techniques rely on the element uranium. *Fission track dating,* for example, counts radiation damage tracks on mineral crystals. Like amino acid racemization, all these methods have problems: They are complicated and tend to be expensive, many can be carried out only on specific kinds of materials, and some are so new that their reliability is not yet unequivocally established. It is for these reasons that they have not been as widely used as radiocarbon and potassium-argon dating techniques.

Paleomagnetic reversals contribute another interesting dimension to absolute dating methodologies by providing a method to cross-check dates (Figure 5.6). This method is based on the shifting magnetic pole of the earth—the same force that controls the orientation of a compass needle. Today, a compass points to the north because we are in a period defined as the geomagnetic "normal." Over the past several million years, there have been extended periods of time during which the magnetic field of the earth pulled toward the South Pole. Geologists call these periods *geomagnetic reversals.* Iron particles in stones will be oriented into positions determined by the dominant magnetic pole at the time of their formation, allowing scientists to derive broad ranges of dates for them. Human evolutionary history contains a geomagnetic reversal starting 5.2 million years ago that ended 3.4 million years ago, followed by a normal period until 2.6 million years ago; then a second reversal began, lasting until about 700,000 years ago when the present normal period began. This paleomagnetic sequence can be used to date sites to either normal or reversed periods and can be correlated with a variety of other dating methods to cross-check their accuracy.

Establishment of dates for human physical and cultural remains is a vital part of understanding our past. For example, as paleoanthropologists reconstruct human evolutionary history and the movement of the genus *Homo* out of Africa, dates determine the story told by the bones. In the next chapters we will see that many of the theories about human origins are dependent upon dates. Similarly, as archaeologists dig up material culture, interpretations of the movement and interactions of past peoples depend on dating methods to provide a sequence to the cultural remains.

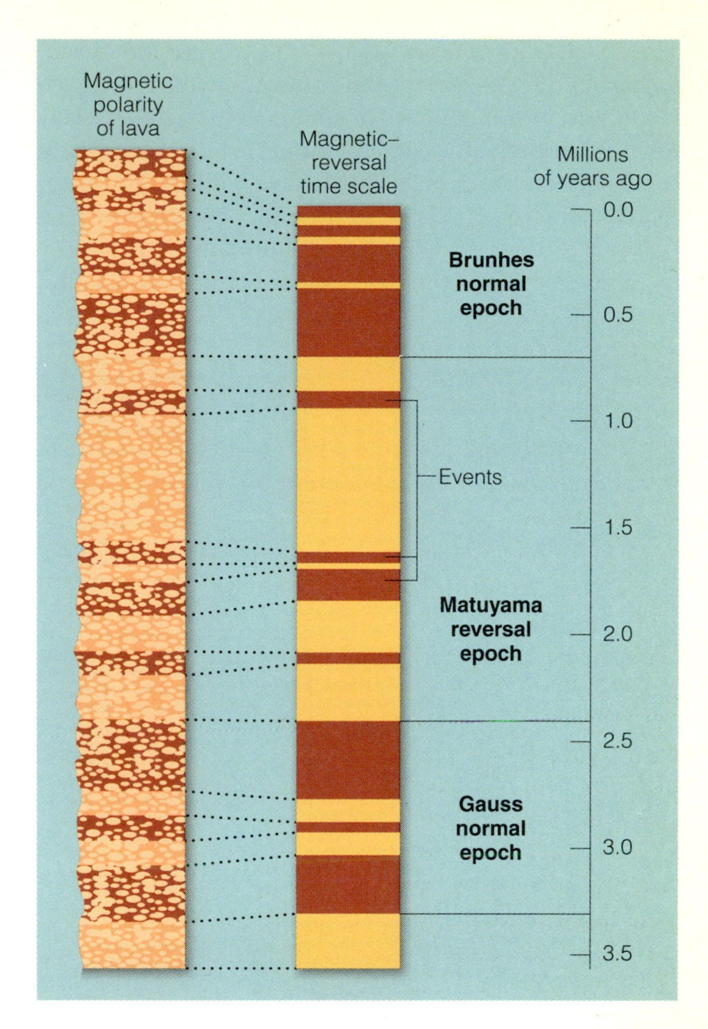

Figure 5.6 Scientists have documented a geomagnetic polarity time scale in which the changes in the earth's magnetic force—to north or south—have been calibrated. This geomagnetic time scale provides scientists with opportunities to cross-check other dating methods.

Chance and Study of the Past

Archaeological and fossil records are imperfect. Chance circumstances of preservation have determined what has and what has not survived the ravages of time. Thus the biology and culture of our ancestors are reconstructed on the basis of incomplete and possibly unrepresentative samples of physical and cultural remains. This is further compounded by the role that chance continues to play in the discovery of prehistoric remains. Remains may come to light due to factors ranging from changing sea level, vegetation, or even a local government's decision to build a highway.

Ancient cultural processes have also shaped the archaeological and fossil record. We know more about the past due to the cultural practice of deliberate burial. We know more about the elite segments of past societies because they have left more material culture behind. However, as archaeologists have shifted their focus from gathering treasures to the reconstruction of human behavior, they have gained a more complete picture of ancient societies. Similarly, paleoanthropologists no longer simply catalogue fossils; they interpret data about our ancestors in order to reconstruct the biological processes responsible for who we are today. The challenge of reconstructing our past will be met by a continual process of reexamination and modification as anthropologists discover new evidence in the earth, among living people, and in the laboratory leading to new understanding of human origins.

Questions for Reflection

1. How would you decide who owns the past? Have there been any examples of contested ownership in your community?
2. The cultural practice of burial of the dead altered the fossil record and provided valuable insight into the beliefs and practices of past cultures. The same is true today. What beliefs are reflected in the traditions for treatment of the dead in your culture?
3. Controversy has surrounded Kennewick Man since this skeleton was discovered on the banks of the Columbia River in Washington in 1996. Scientists and American Indians both feel they have a right to these remains. What kinds of evidence support these differing perspectives? How should this controversy be resolved?
4. Why is dating so important for paleoanthropologists and archaeologists? Would an interpretation of physical or cultural remains change depending upon the date assigned to the remains?
5. How have random events as well as deliberate cultural practices shaped both the fossil and archaeological records? Why do we know more about some places and peoples than others?

Suggested Readings

Fagan, B. M., Beck, C., & Silberman, N. A. (1998). *The Oxford companion to archaeology.* New York: Oxford University Press.

This encyclopedia of archaeology and prehistory contains 700 entries written in an engaging style by over 300 experts in the field. Topics range from fossils to historic sites, conveying the field's critical transition from an amateur to a scientific discipline.

Feder, K. L. (2008). *Frauds, myths, and mysteries: Science and pseudoscience in archaeology* (6th ed.). New York: McGraw-Hill.

This very readable book enlightens readers about the many pseudoscientific and even crackpot theories about past cultures that all too often have been presented to the public as solid archaeology.

Joukowsky, M. (1980). *A complete field manual of archaeology: Tools and techniques of fieldwork for archaeologists.* Englewood Cliffs, NJ: Prentice-Hall.

This book, encyclopedic in its coverage, explains for the novice and professional alike all of the methods and techniques used by archaeologists in the field.

Loubser, J. H. N. (2003). *Archaeology: The comic.* Lanham, MD: Altamira.

Taking advantage of the graphic novel format (a story line and constant illustrations), this book conveys complex technical aspects of archaeology and provides an excellent introduction to the field.

Sharer, R. J., & Ashmore, W. (2007). *Archaeology: Discovering our past* (4th ed.). New York: McGraw-Hill.

One of the best presentations of the methods, techniques, and theories that most archaeologists accept as fundamental to their discipline. The authors confine themselves to the operational modes, guiding strategies, and theoretical orientations of anthropological archaeology in a manner well designed to lead the beginner into the field.

Shipman, P. (1993). *Life history of a fossil: An introduction to taphonomy and paleoecology.* Cambridge, MA: Harvard University Press.

In order to understand what a fossil has to tell us, one must know how it came to be where the paleoanthropologist found it (taphonomy). In this book, anthropologist-turned-science writer Pat Shipman explains how animal remains are acted upon and altered from death to fossilization.

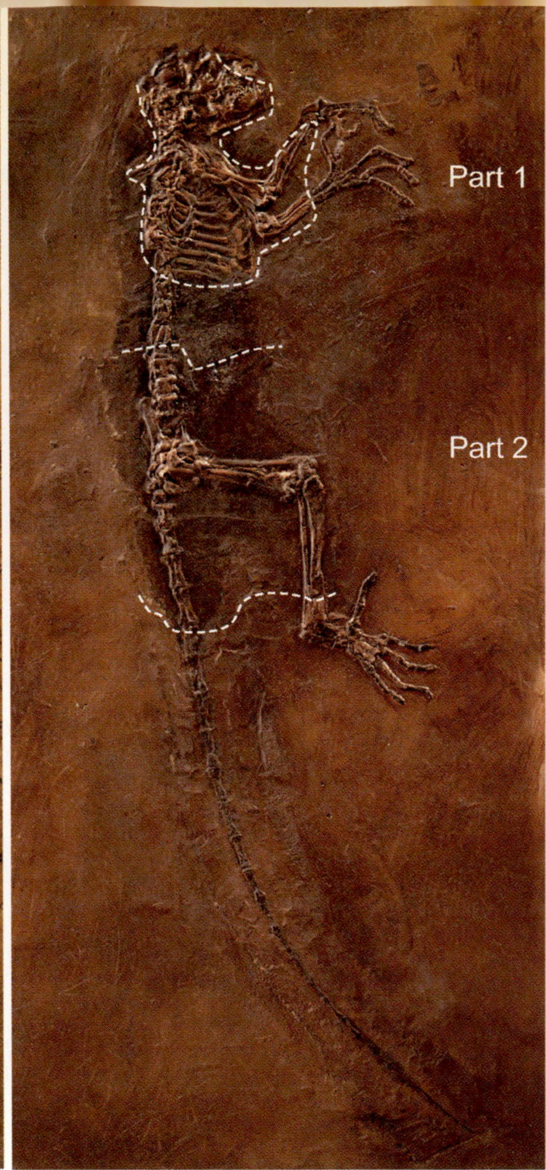

Challenge Issue The recent popularity of human evolutionary studies in the media has brought with it new challenges. How can the self-correcting nature of science function against a backdrop of "tweets," Google logos, and unprecedented sale prices for fossil specimens paid by museums to private collectors. Consider the case of "Ida," an entirely complete juvenile skeleton as well as some soft tissue and gut contents of a 47-million-year-old fossil primate who defined a new fossil primate species: *Darwinius masillae*.

Ida was actually discovered nearly thirty years ago but her remains were separated and sold to two different collections: one a museum and the other private. In 2006, the better-preserved part of Ida, pictured on the left, was reported to have been sold by a private collector to the Natural History Museum of Oslo for an unprecedented $750,000.

Once the two sections of Ida were reunited, the process of careful scientific scrutiny could begin. Various anatomical features led some scientists to suggest that Ida is a "missing link," one of the ancestors in the evolutionary line leading to humans. The notion that Ida could be a "missing link," perhaps along with her high sticker price, captured the media's attention and led to a book deal, a planned documentary, and even a logo on Google.

While all scientists agree that Ida is a remarkable find other scientists have disputed Ida's place on the human line suggesting instead that she is ancestral to the lemurs. Ida's story illustrates the kinds of commercial and public relations challenges scientists and the public alike face as media hype has come to play a role in the study and interpretation of fossil specimens.

CHAPTER 6

Macroevolution and the Early Primates

Chapter Preview

What Is Macroevolution?

While microevolution refers to changes in the allele frequencies of populations, macroevolution focuses on the formation of new species (speciation) and on the evolutionary relationships among groups of species. Speciation may proceed in a branching manner, as when reproductive isolation of populations prevents gene flow between them, leading to the formation of separate species. Alternatively, in the absence of isolation, a species may evolve without branching in response to environmental changes. The accumulation of small changes from generation to generation may transform an ancestral species into a new one.

When and Where Did the First Primates Appear, and What Were They Like?

Fossil evidence indicates that the earliest primates began to develop around 65 million years ago (mya), when the mass extinction of the dinosaurs opened new ecological opportunities for mammals. By 55 mya, primates inhabited North America and Eurasia, which at that time were joined together as the supercontinent Laurasia and separated from Africa. The earliest primates were small nocturnal insect eaters adapted to life in the trees.

When Did the First Monkeys and Apes Appear, and What Were They Like?

By the late Eocene epoch, about 40 mya, diurnal anthropoid primates appeared. Many of the Old World anthropoid species became ground dwellers. By the Miocene epoch (beginning 23.5 mya), apes were widespread in Asia, Africa, and Europe. While some of these hominoids were relatively small, others were larger than present-day gorillas. Sometime between 5 and 8 mya, a branch of the African hominoid line became bipedal, beginning the evolutionary line that later produced humans.

Today, humans are the only primate existing globally. We inhabit every continent, including areas as inhospitable as the icy Antarctic or the scorching Sahara Desert. This extended geographic range reflects the adaptability of *Homo sapiens*. By comparison, our relatives in the hominoid superfamily live in very circumscribed areas of the Old World tropical rainforest. Chimpanzees, bonobos, and gorillas can be found only in portions of Central, East, and West Africa. Orangutans are limited to the trees on the Southeast Asian islands of Sumatra and Borneo. Gibbons and siamangs swing through the branches of a variety of Southeast Asian forests.

Such comparisons between humans and the other primates appear natural to biologists and anthropologists today, because they accept that modern humans, apes, and monkeys are descended from the same prehistoric ancestors. However, a century and a half ago, when Charles Darwin published *On the Origin of Species* (1859), this notion was so controversial that Darwin limited himself to a single sentence on the subject. Today, anthropologists, as well as the global scientific community in general, accept that human origins are revealed in the evolutionary history of the primates. We now know that much of who we are, as culture-bearing biological organisms, derives from our mammalian primate heritage.

Although many of the primates discussed in this chapter no longer exist, their descendants (as we discussed in Chapters 3 and 4) now live in South and Central America, Africa, Asia, and Gibraltar at the southern tip of Spain, and in zoos and laboratories all over the world. The successful adaptation of the primates largely reflects their intelligence, a characteristic that provides for behavioral flexibility. Other physical traits, such as stereoscopic vision and a grasping hand, have also been instrumental in the success of the primates.

Why do paleoanthropologists attempt to recreate primate evolutionary history from ancient evidence? The study of these ancestral primates gives us a better understanding of the physical forces that caused these early creatures to evolve into today's primates. It gives us a fuller knowledge of the processes through which an insect-eating, small-brained mammal evolved into a toolmaker, a thinker, a human being. In addition, the continued survival of our species and of our world now depends on understanding evolutionary processes and the way all organisms interact with their environment.

macroevolution Evolution above the species level.

speciation The process of forming new species.

isolating mechanism A factor that separates breeding populations, thereby preventing gene flow, creating divergent subspecies and ultimately (if maintained) divergent species.

cladogenesis Speciation through a branching mechanism whereby an ancestral population gives rise to two or more descendant populations.

Macroevolution and the Process of Speciation

While microevolution refers to changes in the allele frequencies of populations, **macroevolution** focuses on the formation of new species (**speciation**) and on the evolutionary relationships among groups of species. To understand how the primates evolved, we must first look at how the evolutionary forces discussed in Chapter 2 can lead to macroevolutionary change. As noted in that chapter, the term *species* is usually defined as a population or group of populations that is capable of interbreeding and producing fertile, viable offspring. In other words, species are reproductively isolated. This definition, however, is not altogether satisfactory, because in nature isolated populations may be in the process of evolving into different species, and it is hard to tell exactly when they become biologically distinct without conducting breeding experiments. Furthermore, this definition can only be tested among living groups. Breeding experiments cannot be conducted with sets of fossilized bones.

Certain factors, known as **isolating mechanisms,** can separate breeding populations and lead to the appearance of new species. Because isolation prevents gene flow, changes that affect the gene pool of one population cannot be introduced into the gene pool of the other. Random mutation may introduce new alleles in one of the isolated populations but not in the other. Genetic drift and natural selection may affect the two populations in different ways. Over time, as the two populations come to differ from each other, speciation occurs in a branching fashion known as **cladogenesis** (Figure 6.1) (from the Greek *klados*, meaning "branch" or "shoot").

Some isolating mechanisms are geographic—preventing contact, hence gene flow, between members of separated populations. Biologic aspects of organisms can also serve as isolating mechanisms. For example, early miscarriage of the hybrid offspring or sterility of the hybrid offspring, as in the case of closely related species such as horses and donkeys (producing sterile mules), serve as mechanisms to keep populations reproductively isolated from one another.

Isolating mechanisms may also be social rather than physical. Speciation due to this mechanism is particularly common among birds. For example, cuckoos (birds that do not build nests of their own but lay their eggs in other birds' nests) attract mates by mimicking the song of the bird species in whose nests they place their eggs.

Visual Counterpoint

© David Bygott/Kybuyu Partners

© Nishan Bingham

Regulatory genes turn other genes on and off. A mere change in their timing can cause significant evolutionary change because these genes can alter the course of an individual organism's development. This may have played a role in differentiating chimps and humans; for example, adult humans retain the flat facial profile of juvenile chimps. Within primate species in which sexual dimorphism is high, females tend to retain the juvenile traits more than males.

Thus cuckoos that are physically capable of mating may be isolated due to differences in courtship song behavior, which effectively isolates them from other cuckoos singing different tunes. Though social rules about marriage might be said to impose reproductive isolation among humans,

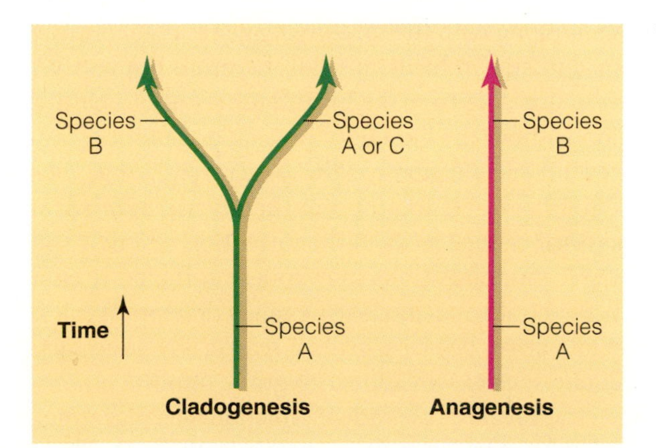

Figure 6.1 Cladogenesis occurs as different populations of an ancestral species become reproductively isolated. Through drift and differential selection, the number of descendant species increases. By contrast, anagenesis can occur through a process of variational change that takes place as small differences in traits that, by chance, are advantageous in a particular environment accumulate in a species' gene pool. Over time, this may produce sufficient change to transform an old species into a new one. Genetic drift may also account for anagenesis.

these social barriers have no biological counterpart. For humans, there are no sufficiently absolute or long-lasting barriers to gene flow.

Because speciation is a process, it can occur at various rates. Speciation through the process of adaptive change to the environment as proposed in Darwin's *Origin of Species* is generally considered to occur at a slow rate. In this model, speciation may occur as organisms become more adapted to their environmental niche. Sometimes, however, speciation can occur quite rapidly. For example, a genetic mutation, such as one involving a key regulatory gene, can lead to the formation of a new body plan. Such genetic accidents may involve material that is broken off, transposed, or transferred from one chromosome to another.

Genes that regulate the growth and development of an organism can have a major effect on its adult form. Developmental change in the timing of events, a phenomenon known as **heterochrony** (from Latin for "different time"), is often responsible for changes in the shape or size of a body part. A kind of heterochrony called *neotony,* in which juvenile traits are retained in the adult state, may be responsible for some of the visible differences between

heterochrony Change in the timing of developmental events that is often responsible for changes in the shape or size of a body part.

Sometimes mutations in a single gene can cause reorganization of an organism's body plan. Here the "bithorax" homeobox gene has caused this fruit fly to have two thoraxes and two sets of wings. Another homeobox gene, "antennepedia," caused legs to develop in the place of antennae on the heads of fruit flies.

humans and chimps. Scientists have discovered certain key genes called **homeobox genes** that are responsible for large-scale effects on the growth and development of the organism. If a new body plan happens to be adaptive, natural selection will maintain this new form for long periods of time rather than promoting change.

Paleontologists Stephen Jay Gould and Niles Eldred proposed that speciation occurs in a pattern of **punctuated equilibria**—the alternation between periods of rapid speciation and times of stability. Often this conception of evolutionary change is contrasted with speciation through adaptation, sometimes known as *Darwinian gradualism.* A close look at genetic mechanisms and the fossil record indicates that both models of evolutionary change are important.

homeobox gene A gene responsible for large-scale effects on growth and development that are frequently responsible for major reorganization of body plans in organisms.

punctuated equilibria A model of macroevolutionary change that suggests evolution occurs via long periods of stability or stasis punctuated by periods of rapid change.

anagenesis A sustained directional shift in a population's average characteristics.

All working evolutionary scientists—including Gould, the champion of the punctuated equilibrium model—recognize the importance of both rapid change and gradual Darwinian processes. Gould describes Darwinian evolution as *variational* change that occurs

> by the twofold process of producing copious and undirected variation within a population and then passing along only a biased (selected) portion of this variation to the next generation. In this manner, the variation within a population at any moment can be converted into differences in mean values (average size, average braininess) among successive populations through time.[1]

He states that this kind of change is unsettling because it is not predictable and does not proceed according to simple natural laws such as gravity. Instead,

> the sensible and explainable but quite unpredictable nature of the outcome (dependent upon complex and contingent changes in local environments), the nonprogressive character of the alteration (adaptive only to these unpredictable local circumstances and not inevitably building a "better" organism in any cosmic or general sense)—flow from the variational basis of natural selection.[2]

Genetic mechanisms underlie both rapid and gradual changes because mutations can have small or large effects. It is particularly interesting to see how molecular genetics supports Darwinian evolutionary change. For example, the tailoring of beak size and shape to diet among finches on the Galapagos Islands, in the Pacific Ocean west of Ecuador, constituted Darwin's classic example of natural selection (Figure 6.2). Recently scientists identified two proteins along with the underlying genes that control beak shape and size in birds. It is all the more impressive that Darwin was able to make his inferences about natural selection without the benefit of molecular genetics.

A fundamental puzzle in the fossil record is that scientists have not been able to pinpoint the precise moment when variational change leads to the formation of a new species. More recent populations may appear sufficiently changed from ancestral populations to be called different species. The difficulty arises because, given a reasonably good fossil record, one species will appear to grade into the other without a clear break. This gradual directional change over time, called **anagenesis,** can occur within a single line, without any evident branching (see Figure 6.1). Speciation is inferred as organisms take on a different appearance over time.

---

[1] Gould, S. J. (2000). What does the dreaded "E" word mean anyway? *Natural History 109* (1), 34–36.

[2] Ibid.

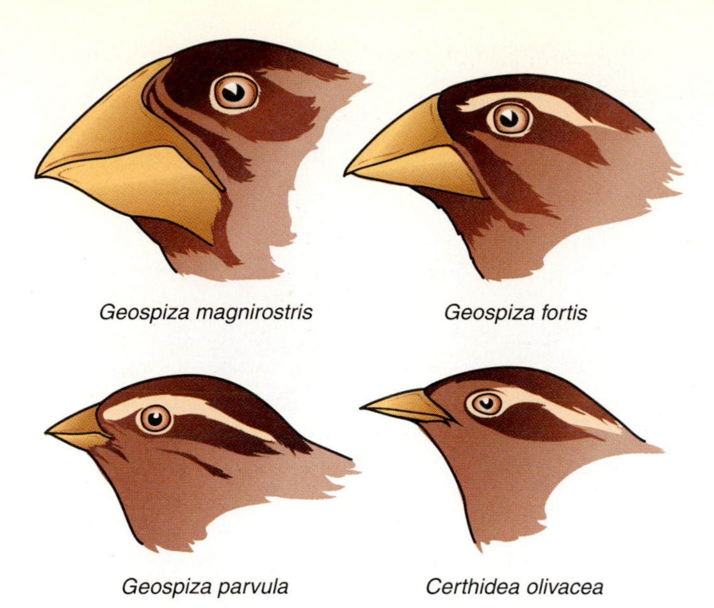

Figure 6.2 Scientists have begun to unravel the genetic mechanisms controlling beak shape and size of finches studied by Darwin on the Galapagos Islands. Darwin noted how beak size and shape were related to each species' diet and used the birds to illustrate adaptation to a particular ecological niche. Finches with blunt crushing beaks are seed eaters while others with long probing beaks pick between cactus thorns for food or use the beaks to get insects.

It may be difficult to determine whether variation preserved in the fossil record presents evidence of separate species. How can we tell whether two sets of fossilized bones represent organisms capable of interbreeding and producing viable fertile offspring? Paleoanthropologists use as many data sources as possible, checking the proposed evolutionary relationships in order to approximate an answer to this question. Today, paleoanthropologists use genetic data as well as observations about the biology and behavior of living groups to support theories about speciation in the past. Thus reconstructing evolutionary relationships draws on much more than bones alone. Fossil finds are always interpreted against the backdrop of scientific discoveries as well as prevailing beliefs and biases. Fortunately, the self-correcting nature of scientific investigation allows evolutionary lines to be redrawn in light of all new discoveries and more compelling explanations.

Constructing Evolutionary Relationships

In addition to designating species in the fossil record, paleoanthropologists and paleontologists construct evolutionary relationships among fossil groups. Scientists pay particular attention to features appearing more recently in evolutionary history that are unique to a line, calling these features **derived.** The counterparts to derived traits are **ancestral** characteristics, which occur not only in the present-day species but in ancestral forms as well. For example, bilateral symmetry, a body plan in which the right and left sides of the body are mirror images of each other, is an ancestral trait in humans. Because it is a characteristic of all vertebrates including fish, reptiles, birds, and mammals, bilateral symmetry does not contribute to the reconstruction of evolutionary relationships among fossil primates. Instead, paleoanthropologists pay particular attention to recently evolved derived features in order to construct evolutionary relationships among fossil groups. For example, because changes in bones associated with bipedalism are present only in the human line, these derived features can be used to separate humans and their ancestors from other hominoids.

Sorting out evolutionary relationships among fossil species may be complicated by a phenomenon called **convergent evolution,** in which two more distant forms develop greater similarities. The classic examples of convergence involve analogies discussed in Chapter 2, such as the wings of birds and butterflies, which resemble each other because these structures serve similar functions. Convergent evolution occurs when an environment exerts similar pressures on distantly related organisms causing these species to resemble each other. Distinguishing the physical similarities produced by convergent evolution from those resulting from shared ancestry may be difficult, complicating the reconstruction of the evolutionary history of any given species.

Among more closely related groups, convergence of homologous structures can occur, as when an identical structure present within several distinct species takes on a similar form in distantly related groups. Among the primates, an example is hind-leg dominance in both lemurs and humans. In most primates, the hind limbs are either shorter or of the same length as the forelimbs. Lemurs and humans are not as closely related to each other as are humans and chimps, for example, but both have longer hind limbs related to their patterns of locomotion. Humans are bipedal while lemurs use their long legs to push off and propel them from tree to tree. Hind-leg dominance appeared separately in these two groups and is not indicative of a close evolutionary relationship. Only shared derived features can be used to establish relationships among groups of species.

The Nondirectedness of Macroevolution

In the nonscientific community, evolution is often seen as leading in a predictable and determined way from one-celled organisms, through various multicelled forms, to

derived Characteristics that define a group of organisms and that did not exist in ancestral populations.

ancestral Characteristics that define a group of organisms that are due to shared ancestry.

convergent evolution In biological evolution, a process by which unrelated populations develop similarities to one another due to similar function rather than shared ancestry.

Visual Counterpoint

© Wolfgang Kaehler/Corbis

© Pete Saloutos/Corbis

The characteristic long legs of prosimians and humans are not the result of a close evolutionary relationship. This is instead the result of convergence of homologous structures. The long legs of prosimians allow them to follow their characteristic pattern of locomotion, called vertical clinging and leaping. On rare occasions for the briefest periods of time, they are also capable of taking a bipedal step or two.

humans, who occupy the top rung of a ladder of progress. However, even though one-celled organisms appeared long before multicellular forms, single-celled organisms were not replaced by multicellular descendants. Single-celled organisms exist in greater numbers and diversity than all forms of multicellular life and live in a greater variety of habitats.[3]

As for humans, we are indeed recent arrivals in the world (though not as recent as some new strains of bacteria). Our appearance—like that of any kind of organism—was made possible only as a consequence of a whole string of accidental happenings in the past. To cite but one example, about 65 million years ago the earth's climate changed drastically. Evidence suggests that a meteor or some other sort of extraterrestrial body slammed into earth where the Yucatan Peninsula of Mexico now exists, cooling global temperatures to such an extent as to cause the extinction of the dinosaurs (and numerous other species as well). For 100 million years, dinosaurs had dominated most terrestrial environments available for vertebrate animals and would probably have continued to do so were it not for this event. Although mammals appeared at about the same time as reptiles, they existed as small, inconspicuous creatures that an observer who came to earth from outer space would probably have dismissed as insignificant.

But with the demise of the dinosaurs, all sorts of opportunities became available, allowing mammals to begin their great expansion into a variety of species including our own ancestors, the earliest primates. Therefore, an essentially random event—the collision with a comet or asteroid—made our own existence possible. Had it not happened, or had it happened at some other time (before the existence of mammals), we would not be here.[4]

The history of any species is an outcome of many such occurrences. At any point in the chain of events, had any one element been different, the final result would be markedly different. As Gould puts it, "All evolutionary sequences include . . . a fortuitous series of accidents with respect to future evolutionary success. Human brains and bodies did not evolve along a direct and inevitable ladder, but by a circuitous and tortuous route carved by adaptations evolved for different reasons, and fortunately suited to later needs."[5]

Given that humans arrived here by chance relatively late in the history of life on earth, the drastic changes humans have imposed on the environment and on the other species with which we share this earth are particularly shocking. As described in this chapter's Original Study by Australian zoologist Sir Robert May, it is now time for humans to create solutions.

---

[3] Gould, S. J. (1996). *Full house: The spread of excellence from Plato to Darwin* (pp. 176–195). New York: Harmony.

[4] Gould, S. J. (1985). *The flamingo's smile: Reflections in natural history* (p. 409). New York: Norton.

[5] Ibid., p. 410.

Original Study

Melding Heart and Head

by Sir Robert May

Today we are living at a very special time in the history of the Earth. It is a time which might come in the history of any inhabited planet, when the activities of one particular species—in this case, ourselves—come to rival the scale and scope of the natural processes which built, and which maintain, the planet's biosphere.

It is easy to be skeptical of such dramatic claims, which are often voiced around millennia or other years with many zeros in them. But there are objective facts which demonstrate just how special our own time is. For one thing, humans today take for their own use somewhere between a quarter and a half of all plant material that grows on earth each year. For another—from the tropical rainforests, across the grain fields of America, Europe and Asia, to the Arctic tundra—fully half of all the atoms of nitrogen and of phosphorous annually fixed in new plants come from human intervention in the form of fertilizers rather than natural cycles. Turning to the sea, we take 10 percent of all its production each year, and larger amounts (around 30 percent) in rich areas of nutrient upwelling.

But all this represents bad news for the diverse populations of invertebrates, birds, and other creatures that share the countryside with us. *The State of the UK's Birds 1999*, recently published by the Royal Society for the Protection of Birds (RSPB) and the British Trust for Ornithology (BTO), for example, documents declines in populations of 41 species of woodland birds (on average down 20 percent from the mid-1970s) and of 20 species of farmland birds (down 40 percent over the same period).

More broadly, the outcome of intensification of agriculture, around the world, is an ever more Silent Spring. Documented extinctions of bird and mammal species over the past century or so are at a rate roughly 1,000 times faster than the rates seen, on average, over the half-billion-year sweep of the fossil record. The various causes are habitat destruction, unsustainably excessive harvesting and other exploitation, adverse impacts by introduced alien species, and—more often—combinations of all three.

Projections of future extinction rates are more difficult to make. Four different lines of argument, ranging from one which applies generally to all plants and animals, through to others which generalize from particular families of birds, reptiles, and mammals, all suggest a roughly tenfold increase in extinction rates over the coming few centuries. These are sober, analytic estimates, free of the rhetorical exaggerations which sometimes afflict the subject. These estimates make it clear that we are currently on the breaking tip of a sixth great wave of extinction in the history of life on Earth, fully comparable with the Big Five in the fossil record, such as the one that extinguished the dinosaurs.

Diminishing Gains

Toward the end of this century, estimates which I rate as rather optimistic suggest that—barring catastrophes—our descendants will live in a world of 10 billion people. How will they be fed? The Green Revolution, underpinned as it is by massive and unsustainable inputs of fossil fuel energy, already shows signs of diminishing gains. Just as we could not feed today's global population with yesterday's agriculture, I do not believe we can feed tomorrow's population with today's.

But if we seek only further intensification of agriculture—a further ratcheting up in the spirit of the Green Revolution—then we may feed tomorrow's world, but it will be biologically impoverished, and I doubt its sustainability. If, on the other hand, we use our increasing understanding of the molecular machinery of life, along with other cultural changes, to produce an agriculture that works with the grain of nature—rather than using fossil fuel subsidies to wrench nature to our crops—then I hope we can achieve Conway's Doubly Green Revolution.

Harnessing Impulse

Part of the motive for all this must be a more sustainable way of doing things. But a related part of the motive must come from our natural impulses of concern, and even affection, for the other creatures we share the world with. Too often, however, such concern expresses itself through a disproportionate focus on large mammals and colourful birds: "charismatic megafauna." Although understandable and effective in engaging a wider public, particularly in the developed world, these targets are not necessarily those that would be chosen in an analytic quest to preserve the maximum amount of the planet's evolutionary history, as written in the genetic richness and variability within today's living species. Although our emotions may relate most easily to the big mammals and the interesting birds, the smaller invertebrates and the diverse plant kingdom are more important for the functioning of many ecosystems, and they also carry more of the record of how life evolved on our planet. The justification that by saving charismatic megafauna we necessarily save large areas of habitat, and thence a host of less emotionally resonant invertebrates and plants, does not always survive close examination: such studies as do exist suggest that "hot spots" for birds are often weakly correlated with "hot spots" for particular plant and insect groups.

To summarize, I believe the challenge of the century is to emphasize valid emotional and ethical arguments for conserving biological diversity, but also to combine them with analytic approaches that ask questions—often cold and difficult ones—about which actions will, in the long run, be most effective in sustaining as much as possible of the biological riches and the unaccounted ecosystem services we have inherited. This melding of heart and head will, I think, pose tough challenges and choices. It is not an easy recipe for a new beginning to a new millennium.

Adapted from May, R. (2000). Melding heart and head. Beyond 2000. *New York: United Nations Environment Programme. http://www.unep.org/ourplanet/imgversn/111/may.html*

Continental Drift and Geologic Time

As described in Chapter 5, context and dating are vital for the interpretation of fossils. Because primate evolution extends so far back in time, paleoanthropologists reconstruct this evolution in conjunction with information about the geologic history of the earth.

The geologic time scale is unfamiliar because few people deal with hundreds of millions of anything, let alone years, on a regular basis. To understand this type of scale, astronomer Carl Sagan correlated the geologic time scale for the history of the earth to a single calendar year. In this "cosmic calendar," the earth itself originates on January 1, the first organisms appear approximately 9 months later around September 25, followed by the earliest vertebrates around December 20, mammals on December 25, primates on December 29, hominoids at 10:15 AM on New Year's Eve, bipeds at 9:30 PM, with our species appearing in the last minutes before midnight. In this chapter, we will consider human evolutionary history beginning with the December 25 appearance of the mammals in the Mesozoic era, roughly 245 million years ago.

Over such vast amounts of time, the earth itself has changed considerably. During the past 200 million years, the position of the continents has shifted through a process called **continental drift,** which accounts for the rearrangement of adjacent landmasses through the theory of plate tectonics. According to this theory, the continents, embedded in platelike segments of the earth, move their positions as the edges of the underlying plates are created or destroyed (Figure 6.3). Plate movements are also responsible for geologic phenomena such as earthquakes, volcanic activity, and mountain formation. Continental drift is important for understanding the distribution of fossil primate groups whose history we will now explore.

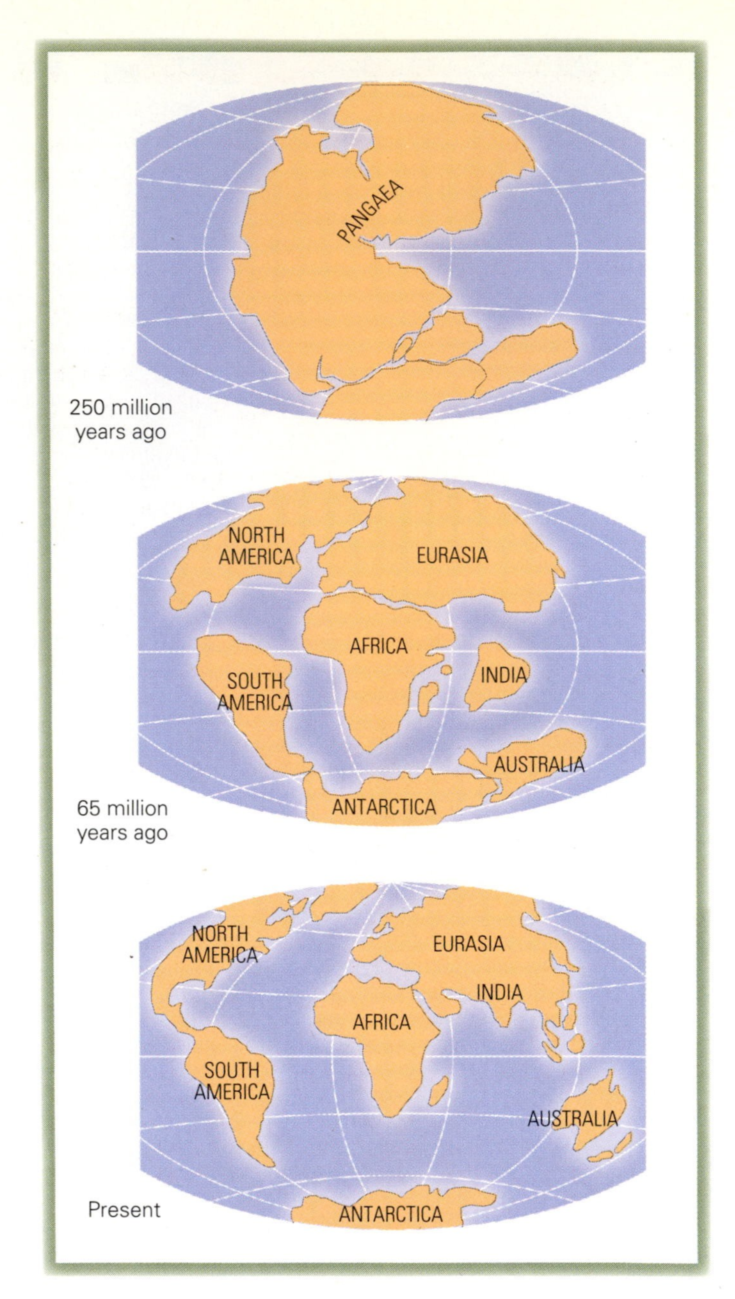

Figure 6.3 Continental drift is illustrated by the position of the continents during several geologic periods. At the time of the extinction of the dinosaurs 65 million years ago, the seas opened up by continental drift, creating isolating barriers between major landmasses. About 23 million years ago, at the start of the time period known as the Miocene epoch, African and Eurasian landmasses reconnected.

Early Mammals

By 190 million years ago—the end of what geologists call the Triassic period—true mammals were on the scene. Mammals from the Triassic, Jurassic (135–190 mya), and Cretaceous (65–135 mya) periods are largely known from hundreds of fossils, especially teeth and jaw parts. Because teeth are the hardest, most durable structures, they often outlast other parts of an animal's skeleton. Fortunately, investigators often are able to infer a good deal about the total animal on the basis of only a few teeth found lying in the earth.

For example, as described in Chapter 3, unlike the relatively homogeneous teeth of reptiles, mammals possess

continental drift According to the theory of plate tectonics, the movement of continents embedded in underlying plates on the earth's surface in relation to one another over the history of life on earth.

distinct tooth types, the structure of which varies by species. Knowledge of the way the teeth fit together indicates the arrangement of muscles needed to operate the jaws. Reconstruction of the jaw muscles, in turn, indicates how the skull must have been shaped to provide a place for these muscles to attach. The shape of the jaws and details of the teeth also suggest the type of food that these animals consumed. Thus a mere jawbone fragment with a few teeth contains a great deal of information about the animal from which it came.

An interesting observation about the evolution of the mammals is that the diverse forms with which we are familiar today, including the primates, are the products of an **adaptive radiation:** the rapid increase in number of related species following a change in their environment. This did not begin until after mammals had been present on the earth for over 100 million years. With the mass extinction of many reptiles at the end of the Cretaceous, however, a number of existing *ecological niches,* or functional positions in their habitats, became available to mammals. A species' niche incorporates factors such as diet, activity, terrain, vegetation, predators, prey, and climate.

The story of mammalian evolution starts as early as 230 to 280 mya (Figure 6.4). From deposits of this period, which geologists call the Permian, we have the remains of reptiles with features pointing in a distinctly mammalian direction. These mammal-like reptiles were slimmer than most other reptiles and were flesh eaters. Graded fossils demonstrate trends toward a mammalian pattern such as a reduction in the number of bones, the shifting of limbs underneath the body, the development of a separation between the mouth and nasal cavity, differentiation of the teeth, and so forth.

Eventually these creatures became extinct, but not before some of them developed into true mammals by the Triassic period. During the Jurassic period that followed, dinosaurs and other large reptiles dominated the earth, and mammals remained tiny, inconspicuous creatures occupying a nocturnal niche.

By chance, mammals were **preadapted**—possessing the biological equipment to take advantage of the new opportunities available to them through the mass extinction of the dinosaurs and other reptiles 65 million years ago. As **homeotherms,** mammals possess the ability to maintain a constant body temperature, a trait that appears to have promoted the adaptive radiation of the mammals. Mammals can be active at a wide range of environmental temperatures, whereas reptiles, as **isotherms** that take their body temperature from the surrounding environment, become progressively sluggish as the surrounding temperature drops. Cold global temperatures 65 mya appear to be responsible for the mass extinction of dinosaurs and some other reptiles, while mammals, as homeotherms, were preadapted for this climate change.

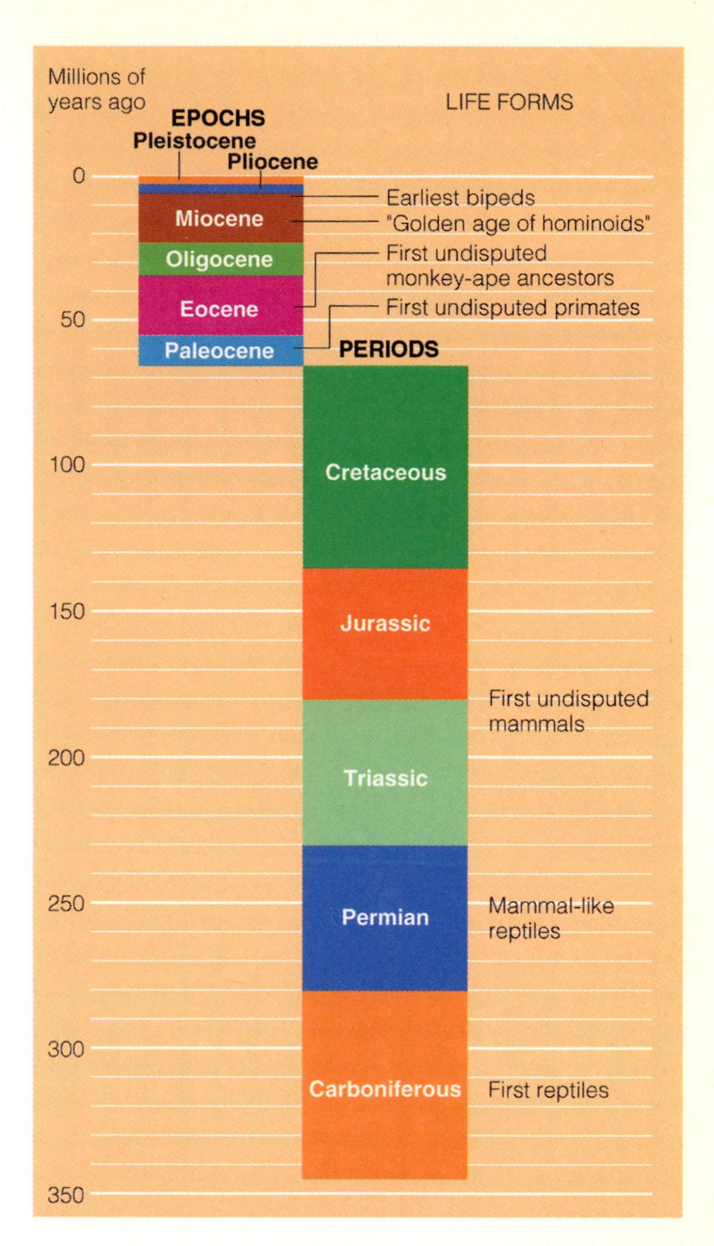

Figure 6.4 This timeline highlights some major milestones in the course of mammalian primate evolution that ultimately led to humans and their ancestors. The Paleocene, Eocene, Oligocene, and Miocene epochs are subsets of the Tertiary period. The Quaternary period begins with the Pleistocene and continues today.

adaptive radiation Rapid diversification of an evolving population as it adapts to a variety of available niches.

preadapted Possessing characteristics that, by chance, are advantageous in future environmental conditions.

homeotherm An animal that maintains a relatively constant body temperature despite environmental fluctuations.

isotherm An animal whose body temperature rises or falls according to the temperature of the surrounding environment.

Though popular media depict the coexistence of humans and dinosaurs, in reality the extinction of the dinosaurs occurred 65 mya, while the first bipeds ancestral to humans appeared between 5 and 8 mya.

The appearance of the true seed plants (the angiosperms) provided not only highly nutritious fruit seeds and flowers but also a host of habitats for numerous edible insects and worms—just the sorts of food required by mammals with their higher metabolism. For species like mammals to continue to survive, a wide diversity of plants, insects, and even single-celled organisms needs to be maintained. In ecosystems these organisms are dependent upon one another.

However, the mammalian trait of maintaining constant body temperature requires a diet high in calories. Based on evidence from their teeth, scientists know that early mammals ate foods such as insects, worms, and eggs. As animals with nocturnal habits, mammals have well-developed senses of smell and hearing relative to reptiles. Although things cannot be seen as well in the dark as they can in the light, they can still be heard and smelled.

The mammalian pattern also differs from reptiles in terms of how they care for their young. Compared to reptiles, mammalian species are **k-selected.** This means that they produce relatively few offspring at a time, providing them with considerable parental care. A universal feature of how mammals care for their young is the production of food (milk) via the mammary glands. Reptiles are relatively **r-selected,** which means that they produce many young at a time and invest little effort caring for their young after they are born. Though among mammals some species are relatively more k- or r-selected, the high energy requirements of mammals, entailed by parental investment and the maintenance of a constant body temperature, demand more nutrition than required by reptiles. During their adaptive radiation, the fruits, nuts, and seeds of flowering plants that became more common in the late Cretaceous period provided mammals with high-quality nutrition.

k-selected Reproduction involving the production of relatively few offspring with high parental investment in each.

r-selected Reproduction involving the production of large numbers of offspring with relatively low parental investment in each.

arboreal hypothesis A theory for primate evolution that proposes that life in the trees was responsible for enhanced visual acuity and manual dexterity in primates.

The Rise of the Primates

Early primates began to emerge during this time of great global change at the start of the Paleocene epoch. The distribution of fossil primates on earth makes sense only when one understands that the positions of the continents today differ tremendously from what was found in the past (see Figure 6.3). As noted earlier, during this period North America and Eurasia were connected in the supercontinent called Laurasia. South America, Africa, Antarctica, Australia, and the Indian subcontinent—previously joined together as the supercontinent Gondwanaland—were beginning to separate from one another through continental drift. Africa was separated from Eurasia by a narrow body of water.

On land, dinosaurs had become extinct, and mammals were undergoing the great adaptive radiation that ultimately led to the development of the diverse forms with which we are familiar today. At the same time, the newly evolved grasses, shrubs, and other flowering plants proliferated enormously. This diversification, along with a milder climate, favored the spread of dense, lush tropical and subtropical forests over the earth, including North and South America and much of Eurasia and Africa. With the spread of these huge belts of forest, the stage was set for the movement of some mammals into the trees. Forests would provide our early ancestors with the ecological niches in which they would flourish. Fossil evidence of primatelike mammals from the Paleocene forests has been found in North America and Eurasia. See Figure 6.5 for a full timeline of primate evolution.

One theory for primate evolution, the **arboreal hypothesis,** proposes that life in the trees was responsible for enhanced visual acuity and manual dexterity in primates. Misjudgments and errors of coordination, leading to

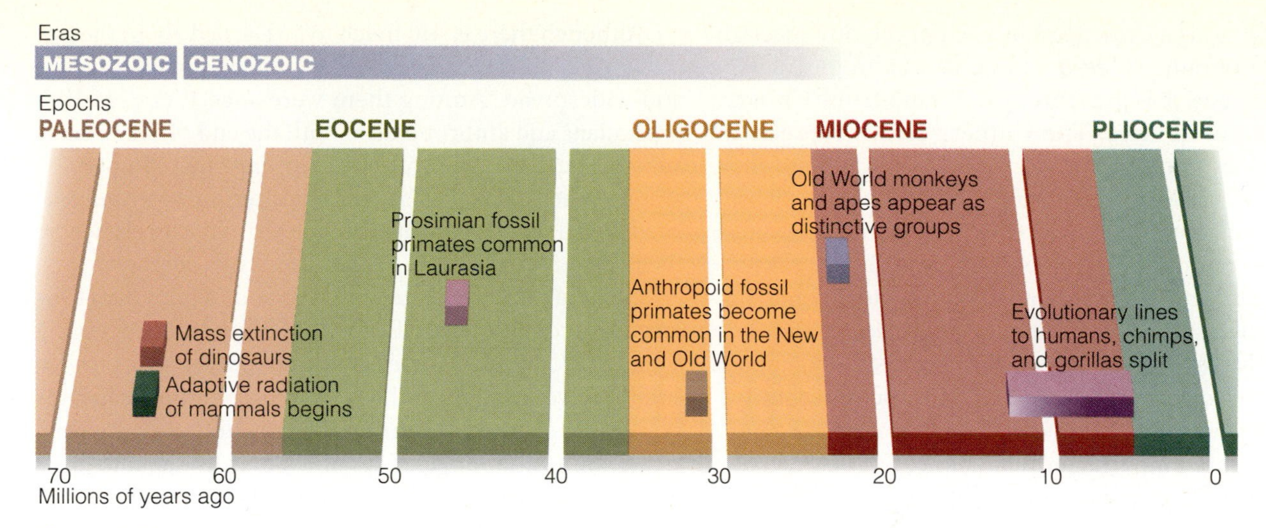

Figure 6.5 This timeline depicts some of the major events of primate evolution.

falls that injured or killed the individuals poorly adapted to arboreal life, may have been a part of initial forays into the trees. Natural selection would favor those that judged depth correctly and gripped the branches strongly. Early primates that took to the trees were probably in some measure pre-adapted by virtue of behavioral flexibility, better vision, and more dexterous fingers than their contemporaries.

Primatologist Matt Cartmill further suggests that primate visual and grasping abilities were also promoted through the activity of hunting for insects by sight. His **visual predation hypothesis** accounts for the observation that other tree-dwelling species and hunting species do not necessarily possess the same combination of visual and manual abilities possessed by the primates. The relatively small size of the early primates allowed them to make use of the smaller branches of trees; larger, heavier competitors, and most predators, could not follow. The move to the smaller branches also gave them access to an abundant food supply; the primates were able to gather insects, leaves, flowers, and fruits directly rather than waiting for them to fall to the ground.

The strong selection in a new environment led to an acceleration in the rate of change of primate characteristics. Paradoxically, these changes eventually made possible a return to the ground by some primates, including the ancestors of the genus *Homo.*

True Primates

The first well-preserved "true" primates appeared by about 55 mya at the start of the Eocene epoch. During this time period, an abrupt warming trend began on earth, causing many older forms of mammals to become extinct, to be replaced by recognizable forerunners of some of today's forms. Among the latter was an adaptive radiation of prosimian primates, of which over fifty fossil genera are known. Fossils of these creatures have been found in Africa, North America, Europe, and Asia, where the warm, wet conditions of the Eocene sustained extensive rainforests. Relative to ancestral primatelike mammals, these early primate families had enlarged braincases, slightly reduced snouts, and a somewhat forward position of the eye orbits, which, though not completely walled in, are surrounded by a complete bony ring called a *postorbital bar* (Figure 6.6).

During the Eocene, the first signs of anthropoid primates also begin to appear in the fossil record. Until

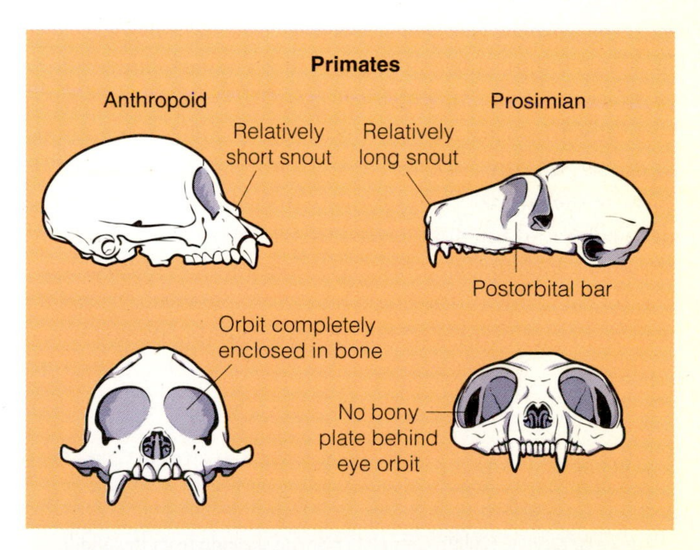

Figure 6.6 Ancestral features seen in Eocene and Oligocene primates are still seen in prosimians today. Like modern lemurs, these fossil prosimians have a postorbital bar, a bony ring around the eye socket that is open in the back. Anthropoid primates have orbits completely enclosed in bone. Note also the difference in the relative size of the snout in these two groups. Paleoanthropologists make these kinds of comparisons as they reconstruct our evolutionary history.

visual predation hypothesis A theory for primate evolution that proposes that hunting behavior in tree-dwelling primates was responsible for their enhanced visual acuity and manual dexterity.

recently, the earliest evidence consisted of the tiny species *Eosimias* (pronounced "ee-o-sim-ee-us"; Latin for "dawn of the monkeys"), represented by fossils from China, dated to about 45 mya. The Chinese fossils represent several species of tiny, insect-eating animals and are the smallest primates ever documented.[6] Some scientists have challenged whether these tiny fossils are truly anthropoids as they are reconstructed largely from foot bones rather than skulls or teeth. As described in the chapter opener, in 2009, controversy and media attention swirled around the spectacularly well-preserved 47-million-year-old potential anthropoid nicknamed "Ida."[7,8,9,10] Initially discovered thirty years ago through a mining and drilling operation at an old quarry near the southern German hamlet of Messel, Ida's remains were separated and sold to different collections. In Ida's time, the Messel region was a tropical forest with a lake and volcano. Fossils from this region are embedded into flaky layers of rock that split open into "plates." Now that the two plates that constitute Ida have been reunited, scientists can debate whether Ida is indeed the earliest anthropoid or not. This distinction, which would place her on the line leading to humans, captures our imaginations as described in this chapter's Biocultural Connection by anthropologist-primatologist Meredith Small.

More recent than Ida and well into the Oligocene epoch, rich deposits of primate fossils have been found in Fayum, Egypt. These fossils include a diverse range of species including some of the earliest to possess a dental comb. But more relevant to human ancestry are the early anthropoid primate species from Fayum, identified through dental, cranial, and postcranial (the rest of the skeleton) remains. Some possess the ancestral dental formula (2-1-3-3) seen in New World monkeys and prosimians, while others have the derived dental formula shared by Old World monkeys and apes: two incisors, a canine, two premolars, and three molars on each side of the jaw. The eye orbits have a complete wall, the latter being a feature of anthropoid primates.[11]

[6] Gebo, D. L., et al. (2001). Middle Eocene primate tarsals from China: Implications for haplorhine evolution. *American Journal of Physical Anthropology 116*, 83–107.

[7] Franzen, J. L., et al. (2009). Complete primate skeleton from the middle Eocene of Messel in Germany: Morphology and paleobiology. *PLoS ONE 4* (5), e5723.

[8] Dalton, R. (2009). Fossil primate challenges Ida's place: Controversial German specimen is related to lemurs, not humans, analysis of an Egyptian find suggests. Published online 21 October 2009, *Nature 461*, 1040, doi:10.1038/4611040a; Editorial. Media frenzy. *Nature 459*, 484, doi:10.1038/459484a; Published online 27 May 2009.

[9] Simons, E. L., et al. (2009). Outrage at high price paid for a fossil. *Correspondence Nature 460*, 456, doi:10.1038/460456a; Published online 22 July 2009.

[10] Seiffert, E. R., et al. (2009). Convergent evolution of anthropoid-like adaptations in Eocene adapiform primates. *Nature 461*, 1118–1121, doi:10.1038/nature08429; Received 11 July 2009; Accepted 18 August 2009.

[11] Simons, E. L. (1995). Skulls and anterior teeth of *Catopithecus* (Primates: Anthropoidea) from the Eocene and anthropoid origins. *Science 268*, 1885–1888.

Although there is still much to be learned about the Eocene primates, it is clear that they were abundant, diverse, and widespread. Among them were ancestors of today's prosimians and anthropoids.[12] With the end of the Eocene, substantial changes took place among the primates, as among other mammals. In North America, now well isolated from Eurasia, primates became extinct, and elsewhere their range seems to have been reduced considerably.

Climate change affected primate and mammalian evolution. Through the late Eocene, climates were becoming somewhat cooler and drier, but then temperatures took a sudden dive, triggering the formation of an ice cap over previously forested Antarctica. The result was a marked reduction in the range of suitable environments for primates. At the same time, cold climate led to lower sea levels through the formation of ice caps, perhaps changing opportunities for migration of primates.

Oligocene Anthropoids

During the Oligocene epoch, from about 23 to 34 mya, the anthropoid primates diversified and expanded their range. Fossil evidence from Egypt's Fayum region has yielded sufficient fossils (more than 1,000) to reveal that by 33 mya, Old World anthropoid primates existed in considerable diversity. Moreover, the cast of characters is growing, as new fossils continue to be found in the Fayum, as well as in newly discovered localities in Algeria (North Africa) and Oman (Arabian Peninsula). At present, we have evidence of at least sixty genera included in two families. During the Oligocene, prosimian fossil forms became far less prominent than anthropoids. Only on the large island of Madagascar (off the coast of East Africa), which was devoid of anthropoids until humans arrived, is prosimian diversity still evident. In their isolation, they underwent a further adaptive radiation.

Fossil evidence indicates that these Old World anthropoids were quadrupeds who were diurnal, as evidenced by their smaller orbits (eyes). Many of these Oligocene species possess a mixture of monkey and ape features. Of particular interest is the genus *Aegyptopithecus* (pronounced "Egypt-o-pith-ee-kus"; Greek for "Egyptian ape"), an Oligocene anthropoid that has sometimes been called a monkey with an ape's teeth. *Aegyptopithecus* possessed a mosaic of monkey and ape features as well as features shared by both groups. Its lower molars have the five cusps of an ape, and the upper canine and lower first premolar exhibit the sort of shearing surfaces found in monkeys and apes. Its skull has eye sockets that are in a forward position and completely protected by a bony wall, as is typical of modern monkeys and apes. The endocast of its skull indicates that it had a larger visual cortex than that found in prosimians. Relative to its body

[12] Kay, R. F., Ross, C., & Williams, B. A. (1997). Anthropoid origins. *Science 275*, 803–804.

Biocultural Connection

Why "Ida" Inspires Navel-Gazing at Our Ancestry

by Meredith F. Small

One long line of evidence that supports evolution is the ongoing discovery of "transitional" fossils that bridge the gap between one obvious kind of species and another. Nowhere are these transitional animals more interesting than when looking backwards through time at the human lineage.

This week, scientists from the University of Oslo announced the discovery (or re-discovery since the fossil was dug up in 1983) of a 47-million-year-old female primate known as Ida. This almost complete female animal appears to represent the transition between what are often called "primitive" primates, such as lemurs and lorises (known as prosimians), and the more "lofty" monkey, apes, and humans. And even more interesting, this transition was in place long before anyone realized.

We love this stuff because humans are a self-interested species, and some of that navel-gazing has been directed toward our ancient past. Luckily for us, we have living examples of our history still with us today.

Usually, the cycle of life involves repeated speciation, extinction, and survival of modified forms, so that what we see today is not anything like what came before. But as the human lineage went through a prosimian phase, then a monkey phase, then an ape phase over time, those branches didn't completely die off. Instead, representatives of every historical stage can still be found in forests, savannahs, and zoos around the world.

The ancient forms, of course, have been modified by natural selection during the millions of years they have survived, and their reign is not what it used to be. Prosimian primates were once found all across North America and Europe, and now they have retreated to specialized niches in Africa (especially Madagascar) and Asia. Monkeys ruled the Earth 34 million years ago during the Oligocene, but now they mostly rule forests that cling to the equator. And during the Miocene, about 23 million years ago, apes were all over the place until they fell from grace leaving only four endangered species.

That kind of ancestral mirroring is not so common. If, for example, we were modern horses, we wouldn't be able to find decent representatives of the various stages of horse evolution galloping across a field. We'd have to deduce everything about our horsy past from the fossils that happened to be preserved and unearthed.

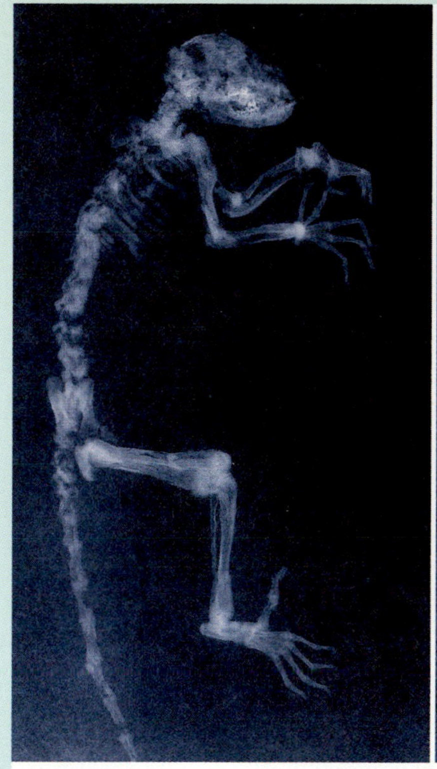
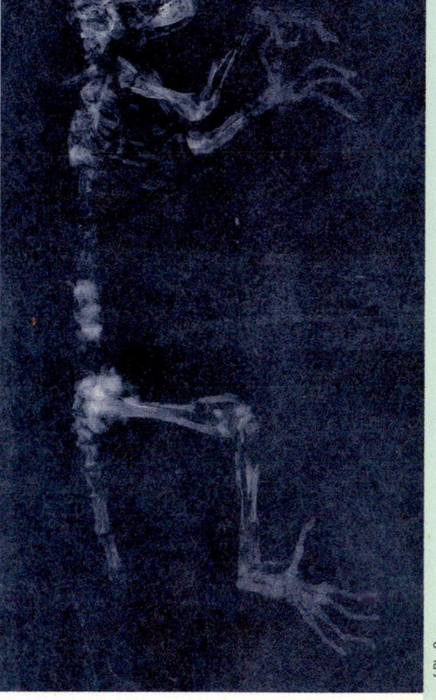

Due to the fragility of Ida's remains, scientists have been using CT scan technology to study her. The radiographic image in Plate B reveals that parts of this image have been forged (compare it to the chapter opener photo). Only the true remains show up as white because the mineralized bones and teeth in fossils, as in living creatures, are opaque in an x-ray.

But we humans have these living primate templates and so we know something about how the long line of our ancestors not only looked in the flesh, we also have an idea of how they behaved, ate, socialized, and mated.

And that's also why Ida is such a special find. She seems to be covering the entire history of primate anatomical evolution all on her own. She was the size and build of modern lemurs but lacked the "tooth comb" that prosimians use to clear their fur, which makes her more like a monkey. Ida also had the flat face of monkey, and, oddly, she had the heel bone of a human.

Ida seems to be cobbled together by evolution and looks like she could take off in any and all species directions.

The mishmash of Ida's features is a reminder that although we have living examples of our past, the story might be more complicated than we think. Sometimes it takes an animal that was buried long ago, had the unusual experience of becoming a fossil, was unearthed in Germany in 1983, sold off in parts, put back together, and then presented as the biological Rosetta stone for the Primate Order to make us take another look, and revaluate, our past.

BIOCULTURAL QUESTION

What cultural factors make the biology of the Ida specimen capture our collective imaginations?

Adapted from Small, M. F. (2009, May 15). Why "Ida" inspires navel-gazing at our ancestry. Live Science. *http://www.livescience.com/history/090520-hn-ida.html*

size, the brain of *Aegyptopithecus* was smaller than that of more recent anthropoids. Still, this primate seems to have had a larger brain than any prosimian, past or present. Possessed of a monkeylike skull and body, and fingers and toes capable of powerful grasping, it evidently moved about in a quadrupedal, monkeylike manner.[13]

The teeth of *Aegyptopithecus* suggest that this species may be closely related to an ancestor of humans and modern apes. Although no bigger than a modern house cat, *Aegyptopithecus* was nonetheless one of the larger Oligocene primates. Differences between males and females include larger body size, more formidable canine teeth, and deeper mandibles (lower jaws) in the males. In modern anthropoids, such sexual dimorphism correlates with social systems in which competition among males is high.

New World Monkeys

The earliest evidence of primates in Central and South America dates from this time. These fossil primates are certainly anthropoid monkeys, with the eyes fully encased in bone and limb bones for quadrupedal locomotion. Scientists hypothesize that these primates came to South America from Africa, because the earliest fossil evidence of anthropoids is from the Old World.

Some of the African anthropoids arrived in South America, which at the time was not attached to any other landmass, probably by means of floating masses of vegetation of the sort that originate even today in the great rivers of West and Central Africa. In the Oligocene, the distance between the two continents was far less than it is today; favorable winds and currents could easily have carried "floating islands" of vegetation to South America within a period of time that New World monkey ancestors could have survived.[14] Nearly all living and fossil New World primates possess the ancestral dental formula (2-1-3-3) of prosimians compared to the derived pattern (2-1-2-3) found in Old World anthropoids.

Miocene Apes

True apes first appeared in the fossil record during the Miocene epoch, 5 to 23 mya. It was also during this time period that the African and Eurasian landmasses made direct contact. For most of the preceding 100 million years, the Tethys Sea—a continuous body of water that joined what are now the Mediterranean and Black Seas to the Indian Ocean—created a barrier to migration between Africa and Eurasia. Once joined through the region of what is now the Middle East and Gibraltar, Old World primates, such as the apes, could extend their range from Africa into Eurasia. Miocene ape fossil remains have been found everywhere from the caves of China, to the forests of France, to East Africa, where scientists have recovered the oldest fossil remains of bipeds.

So varied and ubiquitous were the fossil apes of this period that the Miocene has even been labeled by some as the "golden age of the hominoids." The word *hominoid* comes from the Latin roots *homo* and *homin* (meaning "human being") and the suffix *oïdes* ("resembling"). As a group, the hominoids get their name from their resemblance to humans.

In addition to the Old World anthropoid dental formula of 2-1-2-3 and Y5 molars, hominoids can be characterized by the derived characteristics of Y5 molars, having no tail, and having broad flexible shoulder joints. As described in Chapters 3 and 4, the likeness between humans and the other apes bespeaks an important evolutionary relationship that makes other living hominoids vulnerable to human needs in today's world. In the distant past, one of the Miocene apes is the direct ancestor of the human line. Exactly which one is a question still to be resolved.

An examination of the history of the contenders for direct human ancestor among the Miocene apes demonstrates how reconstruction of evolutionary relationships draws on much more than simply bones. Scientists interpret fossil finds by drawing on existing beliefs and knowledge. With new discoveries, interpretations change.

The first Miocene ape fossil remains were found in Africa in the 1930s and 1940s by the British archaeologist A. T. Hopwood and the renowned Kenyan paleoanthropologist Louis Leakey. These fossils turned up on one of the many islands in Lake Victoria, the 27,000-square-mile lake where Kenya, Tanzania, and Uganda meet. Impressed with the chimplike appearance of these fossil remains, Hopwood suggested that the new species be named *Proconsul*, combining the Latin root for "before" (*pro*) with the stage name of a chimpanzee who was performing in London at the time.

Dated to the early Miocene 17 to 21 million years ago, *Proconsul* has some of the classic hominoid features, lacking a tail and having the characteristic pattern of Y5 grooves in the lower molar teeth. However, the adaptations of the upper body seen in later apes (including humans) were absent. These included a skeletal structure adapted for hanging suspended below tree branches. In other words, *Proconsul* had some apelike features as well as some features of four-footed Old World monkeys (Figure 6.7). This mixture of ape and monkey features makes *Proconsul* a contender for a missing link between monkeys and apes but not as a connection between Miocene apes and later-appearing bipeds.

At least seven fossil hominoid groups besides *Proconsul* have been found in East Africa from the early to middle Miocene. But between 5 and 14 mya this fossil record thins out. It is not that all the apes suddenly moved from

---

[13] Ankel-Simons, F., Fleagle, J. G., & Chatrath, P. S. (1998). Femoral anatomy of *Aegyptopithecus zeuxis*, an early Oligocene anthropoid. *American Journal of Physical Anthropology 106*, 421–422.

[14] Houle, A. (1999). The origin of platyrrhines: An evaluation of the Antarctic scenario and the floating island model. *American Journal of Physical Anthropology 109*, 554–556.

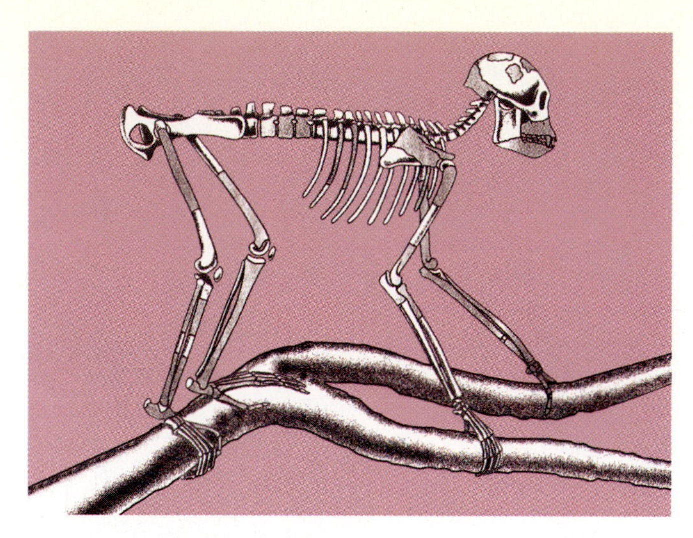

Figure 6.7 **Reconstructed skeleton of *Proconsul*. Note the apelike absence of a tail but monkeylike limb and body proportions. *Proconsul*, however, was capable of greater rotation of forelimbs than monkeys.**

Africa to Eurasia, but that the environmental conditions made it less likely that any of the African remains would fossilize. Tropical forests inhabited by chimps and gorillas today constitute unfavorable conditions for the preservation of bones. As mentioned in Chapter 5, in order to become a fossil, bones must be quickly incorporated into the earth before any rotting or decomposition occurs. In tropical forests, the heat, humidity, and general abundance of life make this unlikely. The bones' organic matrix is consumed by other creatures before it can be fossilized.

Nevertheless, the scarcity of African fossil evidence from this time period fits well with notions about human origins that prevailed in the past. Two factors conspired to take the focus away from Africa. First, investigators initially did not consider that humans were any more closely related to the African apes than they were to the other intelligent great ape—the Asian orangutan. Chimps, bonobos, gorillas, and orangutans were thought to be more closely related to one another than any of them were to humans. The construction of evolutionary relationships still relied upon visual similarities among species, much as it did in the mid-1700s when Linnaeus developed the taxonomic scheme that grouped humans with other primates. Chimps, bonobos, gorillas, and orangutans all possess the same basic body plan, adapted to hanging by their arms from branches or knuckle-walking on the ground. Humans and their ancestors had an altogether different form of locomotion: walking upright on two legs. On an anatomical basis, the first Miocene ape to become bipedal could have come from any part of the vast Old World range of the Miocene apes.

The second factor drawing attention away from African origins was more subtle; it was not embedded in the bones from the earth but in the subconscious minds of the scientists: It was hard for these Eurocentric researchers to imagine

For many years paleoanthropologists considered the European wood ape *Dryopithecus* to be an important ancestor to humans. Fossil remains had been discovered in Europe as early as the 1850s. Eurocentrism allowed researchers to emphasize the European fossil record and to explain away the evidence from Africa.

that humans originated entirely in Africa. European scientists in the early 20th century therefore concentrated on the various species of European ape—all members of the genus *Dryopithecus* (pronounced "dry-o-pith-ee-kus"). They believed that humans evolved where "civilization" developed and that these apes could be the missing link to humans.

As we will see in the next chapter, it took many years for the first bipedal fossils discovered in South Africa in the 1920s to be accepted by the scientific community as key evidence of the human line. Instead, human origins were imagined to involve a close link between those who invented the first tools and those responsible for Western civilization.

During the 1960s, it appeared as though this Miocene human ancestor lived in the Siwaliks, the foothills of the majestic Himalayan Mountains along the northern borders of India and Pakistan, near the ruins of the later Indus Valley civilization. The Himalayas are some of the youngest mountains of the world. They began forming during the Miocene when the Indian subcontinent collided with the rest of Eurasia, and they have been becoming taller ever since.

In honor of the Hindu religion practiced in the region where the fossils were found, the contender was given the name *Ramapithecus,* after the Indian deity Rama and the Greek word for "ape," *pithekos.* Rama is the physical embodiment, or incarnation, of the major Hindu god Vishnu, the preserver. He is meant to portray what a perfect human can be. He is benevolent, protects the weak, and exemplifies all noble human characteristics. Features like the relative delicacy and curvature of the jaw and palate as well as thick tooth enamel led paleoanthropologists David Pilbeam and Elwyn Simons to suggest that this was the first hominoid to become part of the direct human line. They suggested that *Ramapithecus* was a bipedal tool user—the earliest human ancestor. With these qualities, *Ramapithecus* was perfectly named.

Other Miocene apes were also present in the foothills of the Himalayas. *Sivapithecus* was named after the Hindu deity Shiva, the god of destruction and regeneration. In the Hindu religion Lord Shiva is depicted as an asocial hermit who, when provoked, reduces his enemies to smoldering ashes in fits of rage. Though never considered a human ancestor, *Sivapithecus* also had the humanlike characteristic of thick molar tooth enamel (unlike the African apes but like the orangutans). *Sivapithecus* also had large projecting canine teeth more suitable to a destroyer than to a human ancestor. The *Sivapithecus* and *Ramapithecus* fossils were dated to between 7 and 12 mya.

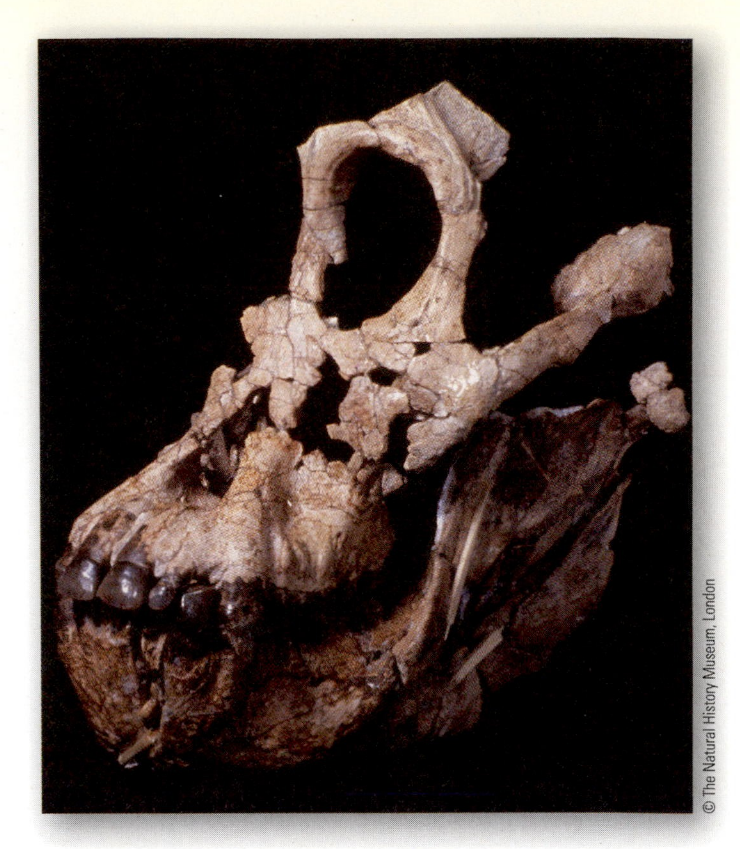

In the 1960s scientists identified two distinct species of Miocene ape from the foothills of the Himalayas: *Sivapithecus* and *Ramapithecus*. The smaller one, *Ramapithecus,* was proposed as a tool-using species ancestral to humans. Molecular investigations along with new fossil finds demonstrate that these specimens were actually the male and female of the same species and ancestral to orangutans. This well-preserved specimen from the Potwar Plateau of Pakistan proved that *Sivapithecus* was ancestral to the orangutan.

The interpretation of these fossils changed with discoveries in the laboratory. By the 1970s, scientists had begun using biochemical and genetic evidence to establish evolutionary relationships among species. Vince Sarich, a biochemist at the University of California, Berkeley, was working in the laboratory of Allan Wilson (see Anthropologist of Note) and developed the revolutionary concept of a **molecular clock.** Such clocks help detect when the branching of related species from a common ancestor took place in the distant past.

Sarich used a molecular technique that had been around since the beginning of the 20th century: comparison of the blood proteins of living groups. He worked on serum albumin, a protein from the fluid portion of the blood (like the albumin that forms egg whites) that can be precipitated out of solution. *Precipitation* refers to the chemical transformation of a substance dissolved in a liquid back into its solid form. One of the forces that will cause such precipitation is contact of this protein with antibodies directed against it. Antibodies are proteins produced by organisms as part of an immune response to an infection. The technique relies on the notion that the stronger the biochemical reaction between the protein and the antibody (the more precipitate), the closer the evolutionary relationship. The antibodies and proteins of closely related species resemble one another more than the antibodies and proteins of distant species.

molecular clock The hypothesis that dates of divergences among related species can be calculated through an examination of the genetic mutations that have accrued since the divergence.

Sarich made immunological comparisons between a variety of species and suggested that he could establish dates for evolutionary events by calculating a molecular rate of change over time. By assuming a constant rate of change in the protein structure of each species over time, Sarich used these results to predict times of divergence between related groups. Each molecular clock needs to be set, or calibrated, by the dates associated with a known event, such as the divergence between prosimian and anthropoid primates or Old World monkeys and apes, as established by absolute dating methods.

Using this technique, Sarich proposed a sequence of divergence for the living hominoids showing that human, chimp, and gorilla lines split roughly 5 mya. He boldly stated

Anthropologist of Note

Allan Wilson (1934–1991)

Though a biochemist by training, New Zealander **Allan Wilson** has made key contributions to anthropology through his pioneering work in applying the principles of biochemistry to human evolutionary questions. Wilson forged a new "hybrid science," combining fossil and molecular evidence with groundbreaking results. Because the molecular evidence required rethinking long-held theories about the relationships among fossil groups, Wilson's work has been surrounded by controversy. According to those close to Wilson, he enjoyed his role as an outsider—being on the edges of anthropology and shaking things up.

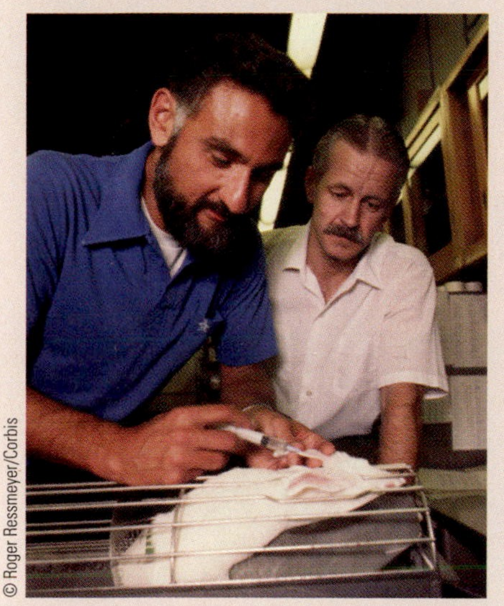

Allan Wilson (right) observes as a laboratory rabbit is injected.

Wilson was born in Ngaruwahia, New Zealand, and grew up on a farm in Pukekohe. After attending school in New Zealand and Australia, he was invited to study biochemistry at the University of California, Berkeley, in 1955. His father was reluctant to have his son travel so far from home, but his mother saw this as an opportunity for him and encouraged him to head to California.

Wilson stayed at Berkeley for the next thirty-five years, running one of the world's most creative biochemistry labs. In the 1960s, Berkeley was a center of academic liberalism and social protest. Wilson's highly original work was conducted with a similar revolutionary spirit, garnering him a MacArthur "genius" award, two Guggenheim fellowships, and a place on the short list for the Nobel Prize.

He developed the notion of a "molecular clock" with his graduate student Vince Sarich and published the groundbreaking paper "Immunological Time-Scale for Human Evolution" in the journal *Science* in 1967. The molecular clock proposes that evolutionary events such as the split between humans and apes can be dated through an examination of the number of genetic mutations that accumulated since two species diverged from a common ancestor. In the 1980s, his laboratory (including Rebecca Cann and Mark Stoneking) was also responsible for seminal work with the mitochondrial Eve hypothesis that continues to be widely debated today (see Chapters 8 and 9).

Wilson died from leukemia at the age of 56. Joseph Felsenstein, one of his biographers, stated in his obituary in the journal *Nature*, "while others concentrated on what evolution could tell them about molecules, Wilson always looked for ways that molecules could say something about evolution."

that it was impossible to have a separate human line before 7 mya "no matter what it looked like." In other words, anything that old would also have to be ancestral to chimps and gorillas as well as humans. Because *Ramapithecus,* even with its humanlike jaws, was dated to between 7 and 12 mya, it could no longer be considered a human ancestor.

In the meantime, Pilbeam continued fossil hunting in the Himalayan foothills. Further specimens began to indicate that *Ramapithecus* was actually a smaller, perhaps female version of *Sivapithecus.*[15] Eventually all the specimens referred to as *Ramapithecus* were "sunk" or absorbed into the *Sivapithecus* group, so that today *Ramapithecus* no longer exists as a valid name for a Miocene ape. Instead of two distinct groups, one of which went on to evolve into humans, they are considered males and females of the sexually dimorphic genus *Sivapithecus.* Pilbeam found a spectacular complete specimen in the Potwar Plateau of Pakistan, showing that *Sivapithecus* was undoubtedly the ancestor of orangutans. This conclusion matched well with the molecular evidence that the separate line to orangutans originated 10 to 12 mya.

All of these changes reflect the fact that paleoanthropologists participate in an unusual kind of science. Paleoanthropology, like all paleontology, is a science of discovery. As new fossil discoveries come to light, interpretations inevitably change, making for better understanding of our evolutionary history. Today, discoveries can occur in the laboratory as easily as on the site of an excavation. Molecular studies since the 1970s provide a new line of evidence much the same way that fossils provide new data as they are unearthed. A discovery in the laboratory, like molecular clocks (now calibrating the split between 5 and 8 mya), can drastically change the interpretation of the fossil evidence.

The converse is also true. Fossil discoveries can raise new interpretations of the course of evolutionary history. The discovery of a 10-million-year-old ape in Ethiopia in 2007, thought to be ancestral to gorillas, provides a case in point.[16] Genetic evidence had pointed to a split between humans and the other African apes sometime between 5 and 8 mya. The scientists who found the nine fossil teeth that resulted in the naming of the species claim

[15] Pilbeam, D. R. (1987). Rethinking human origins. In R. L. Ciochon & J. G. Fleagle (Eds.), *Primate evolution and human origins* (p. 217). Hawthorne, NY: Aldine.

[16] Suwa, G., et al. (2007, August 23). A new species of great ape from the late Miocene epoch in Ethiopia. *Nature 448*, 921–924.

that it indicates that the gorilla lineage had become distinct 2 to 4 million years earlier than that. The species is called *Chororapithecus abyssinicus*, after Chorora, the local area where the fossil was found, and Abyssinia, the ancient name of Ethiopia. While Ethiopia has been the home for numerous spectacular fossil specimens that are part of the human lineage, this is the first fossil ape discovery from this region. Other scientists do not concur, however, and feel more fossil evidence is warranted before pushing back the timing of the split.

Miocene Apes and Human Origins

As described above, determining which Miocene apes were directly ancestral to humans is one of the key questions in primate evolution. Molecular evidence directs our attention to Africa between 5 and 8 mya (Figure 6.8). Though any fossil discoveries in Africa from this critical time period

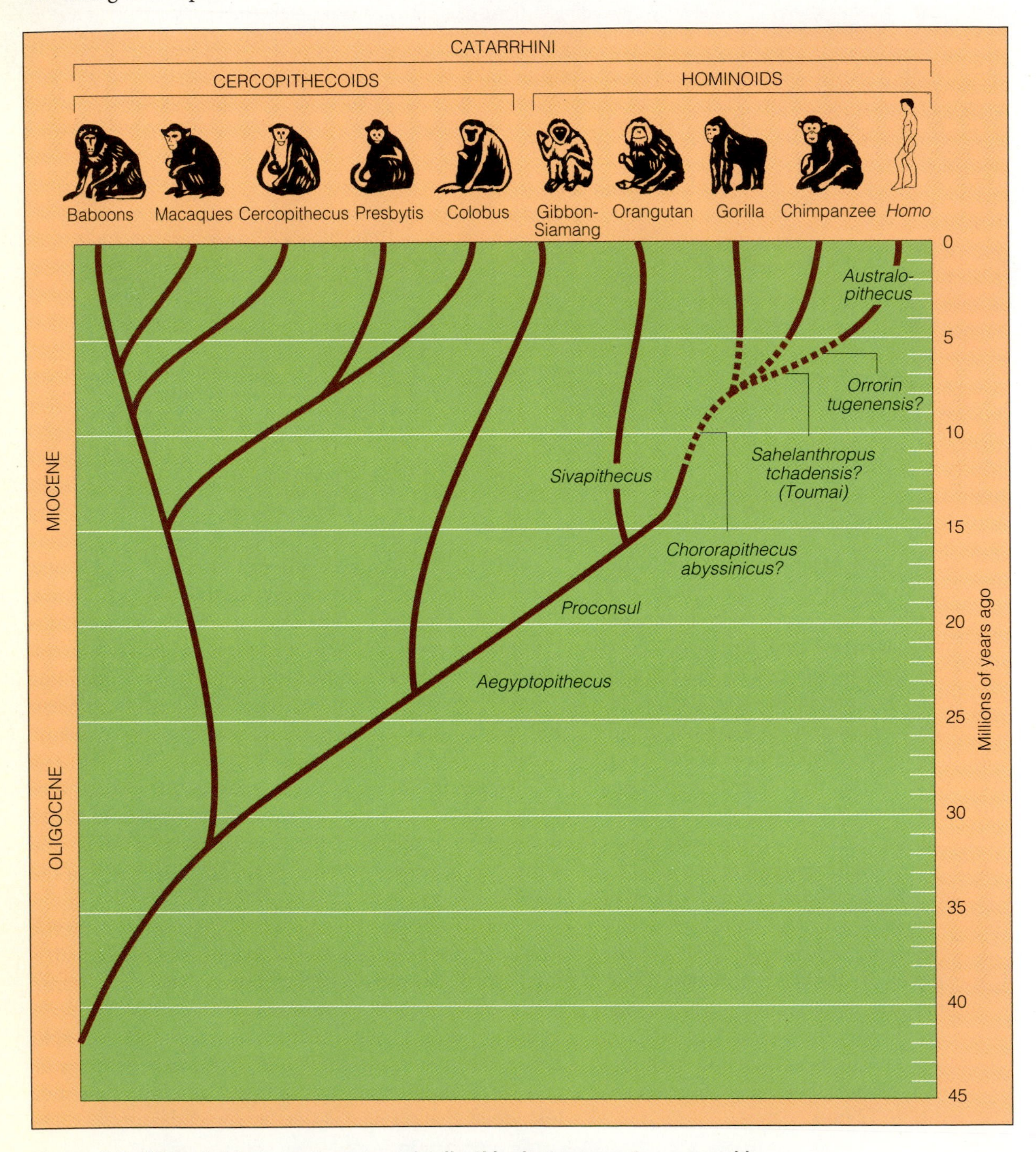

Figure 6.8 Although debate continues over details, this chart represents a reasonable reconstruction of evolutionary relationships among the Old World anthropoid primates. (Extinct evolutionary lines are not shown.) The 2007 discovery of a fossil ancestor to gorillas has suggested a new interpretation of the timing and nature of the split between humans and the African apes.

The spectacular skull from Chad nicknamed "Toumai" ("hope for life") has been proposed as the earliest direct human ancestor. While the 6- to 7-million-year-old specimen is beautifully preserved and has some derived features, some paleoanthropologists feel that alone, it does not establish bipedalism, the derived trait characteristic of the human line.

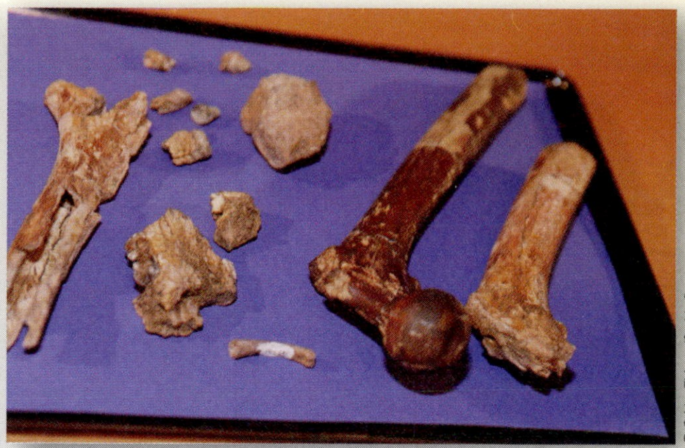

These 6-million-year-old fossils, discovered in Kenya in 2001, represent a new species, *Orrorin tugenensis,* which has also been proposed as the earliest human ancestor. Like Toumai, these bones are surrounded by controversy. The thigh bones (femora) strongly suggest bipedalism, and the upper arm bone (humerus) may be more like that of humans than it is like some of the later bipeds. More discoveries and scientific comparisons will solve controversies surrounding both *Orrorin* and Toumai.

have the potential to be the missing link between humans and the other African ape species, the evidence from this period has been, until recently, particularly scrappy. Controversy surrounds the interpretation of many of these new fossil finds.

For example, in Chad in the summer of 2002, a team of international researchers led by Michel Brunet of France unearthed a well-preserved skull dated to between 6 and 7 mya.[17] Calling their find *Sahelanthropus tchadensis* ("Sahel man of Chad," referring to the Sahel—a belt of semi-arid land bordering the southern edge of the Sahara Desert)—the researchers suggested that this specimen represented the earliest known ancestor of humans, or earliest biped. Nicknamed "Toumai," from the region's Goran-language word meaning "hope for life" (a name typically given to babies born just before the dry season), this specimen is the only skull from this time period.

Considering that bipedalism is the derived characteristic that indicates inclusion in the human subfamily, some paleoanthropologists argue that the relationship of this specimen to humans cannot be established from skull bones alone. The research team argues that derived features, such as a reduced canine tooth, can be seen in the face of the Toumai specimen, indicating its status as a member of the human evolutionary line. Whether or not this specimen proves to be a direct human ancestor, as the only skull from this time period it is nevertheless a very important find.

In 2001, 6-million-year-old fossils discovered in Kenya by French and British researchers Brigitte Senut and Martin Pickford were also reported as human ancestors.[18] Officially given the species name *Orrorin tugenensis* (*Orrorin* meaning "original man" and *tugenensis* meaning "from the Tugen Hills") but nicknamed "Millennium Man," these specimens have also been surrounded by controversy.

The evidence for *Orrorin* consists of fragmentary arm and thigh bones, a finger bone, some jaw fragments, and teeth of at least five individuals. The thigh bones demonstrate possible but not definite bipedalism. Unfortunately, the distal or far ends of the thigh bone that would prove this are not fully preserved. The humerus (upper arm) appears to be more like that of humans than it is like the later bipedal species we will explore in the next chapter. Also *Orrorin* appears to be larger in size than some of these later bipeds. The methods that paleoanthropologists use to determine bipedalism from the fossil record will be fully described in Chapter 7.

---

[17] Brunet, M., et al. (2002). A new hominid from the Upper Miocene of Chad, Central Africa. *Nature 418,* 145–151.

[18] Senut, B., et al. (2001). First hominid from the Miocene (Lukeino Formation, Kenya). *Comptes Rendus de l'Académie de Sciences 332,* 137–144.

Questions for Reflection

1. How can evolutionary studies attract public attention while avoiding getting caught up in a media blitz? Did the current popularity of fossils in the media influence you personally?

2. Why are shared derived characteristics more important than shared ancestral characteristics in evolutionary reconstructions? Using the Miocene apes and humans, think about the ways that conclusions about evolution would change if ancestral rather than derived characteristics were used to figure out evolutionary relationships among species.

3. As we discussed, species are populations or groups of populations that are capable of interbreeding and producing fertile, viable offspring. Why is this biological definition of species difficult to apply to the fossil record?

4. The interpretation of fossil material changes with the discovery of new specimens and with findings in the laboratory. How has that happened? Can you imagine a different conception of human evolutionary history in the future?

5. An understanding of the changing position of the earth's continents through the past several hundred million years is important for the reconstruction of primate evolutionary history. Do you think the evolutionary history of the primates can be understood without knowledge of continental drift?

Suggested Readings

Carroll, S. B. (2005). *Endless forms most beautiful: The new science of evo devo.* NewYork: Norton.

The individual development of an organism from a single fertilized egg to its multibillion-celled complexity and its evolutionary history have been linked in the minds of scientists since Darwin's time. Today the burgeoning field of evolutionary development harnesses the power of molecular genetics to map out the ways that evolution and development are connected. Carroll's engaging book is an excellent introduction to one of the hottest areas of evolutionary biology.

Fleagle, J. (1998). *Primate adaptation and evolution.* New York: Academic.

This beautifully illustrated book is an excellent introduction to the field of primate evolution, synthesizing the fossil record with primate anatomical and behavioral variation.

Hartwig, W. C. (2002). *The primate fossil record.* New York: Cambridge University Press.

This book contains an up-to-date and comprehensive treatment of the discovery and interpretation of primate fossils.

Jones, S., Martin, R., & Pilbeam, D. (1994). *The Cambridge encyclopedia of human evolution.* New York: Cambridge University Press.

This comprehensive introduction to the human species covers genetics, primatology, and fossil evidence as well as a detailed exploration of contemporary human ecology, demography, and disease. Over seventy scholars from throughout the world contributed to this encyclopedia.

Mayr, E., & Diamond, J. (2002). *What evolution is.* New York: Basic.

Written for a general educated audience, this engaging book provides a comprehensive treatment of evolutionary theory.

Challenge Issue In the fall of 2009, a dramatic paleoanthropological find was announced: a remarkably complete skeleton of a putative human ancestor dated to 4.4 million years ago. Only a half-dozen partially complete fossil skeletons on the human line older than 1 million years have ever been discovered, and this one is the oldest. Nicknamed "Ardi," short for the new species, *Ardipithecus ramidus,* the fossil remains themselves were first discovered between 1992 and 1995. All the fine cracks visible in this close up of Ardi's lower jaw shows how fragile these ancient bones are. Features such as the small size of Ardi's canine tooth led paleoanthropologists to determine that she is a female. Early analyses of the Ardi remains in the early 1990s also established that there were forest rather than savannah dwellers on the human line. For the following fifteen-plus years, an international team of forty-seven scientists conducted painstaking excavation, reconstruction, and analysis to create a complete picture of the lifeways of this new species; through this process Ardi has become "personified." A series of research papers in the prestigious journal *Science,* along with a Discovery Channel documentary about how the scientists went about their work, reveal not only the importance of the find but how Ardi has captured our collective imagination. Sophisticated computer graphics allow scientists to simulate how regulatory genes might have shaped the development of Ardi's bones that caused her to move in a more humanlike fashion. Gymnasts were tapped to mimic her gait for scientific analysis, and advances in physics and chemistry were incorporated in the reconstruction of the ancient forested environment she inhabited. In the coming years, as scientists debate how the Ardi discovery influences theories about the human evolutionary line, these ancient bones that we know as the individual Ardi challenge us to think about what it means to be human.

CHAPTER 7

The First Bipeds

Chapter Preview

What Is the Anatomy of Bipedalism, and How Is It Preserved in the Fossil Record?

Bipedalism is the shared derived characteristic used to establish whether a fossilized hominoid is part of the evolutionary line that produced humans. Evidence for bipedalism is preserved literally from head to toe. Bipedalism can be inferred from the forward position of the large opening in the base of the skull, a series of curves in the spinal column, the basin-shaped structure of the pelvis, the angle of the lower limbs from the hip joint to the knees, and the shape of the foot bones. Thus even fragmentary evidence can prove bipedalism, providing the right fragment is preserved. Several groups from between 4 and 7 million years ago (mya) have been proposed as the earliest bipedal human ancestor. Some of these, such as 4.4 mya *Ardipithecus* specimens, preserve evidence of facultative bipedalism, or an intermediate form of upright walking, and may be the link between earlier and later hominins.

What Role Did Bipedalism Play in Human Evolutionary History?

Numerous theories stressing adaptation have been proposed to account for the appearance of bipedalism in human evolutionary history. These theories range from the adaptive advantage of having hands free to carry young or wield weapons to adapting to the danger of too much heat in the brain from direct exposure to the sun in a hot, treeless environment. While bipedalism was present in the earliest forest-dwelling hominins, this way of movement may have conferred an adaptive advantage on bipeds as the environment became increasingly arid over the course of the Pliocene. Bipedalism appeared in human evolutionary history several million years before brain size expanded.

Who Were the First Bipeds, and What Were They Like?

The fossil record indicates that around the time of the Miocene to Pliocene transition, between 5 and 6 mya, the first confirmed bipeds appeared in Africa. The recently discovered genus *Ardipithecus* (4.4 to 5.8 mya) may be ancestral to the genus *Australopithecus,* a group of fossil bipeds known since the early 20th century. Australopithecines include a diverse group of fully bipedal species still possessing relatively small-sized brains in proportion to their body size. Some of the later australopithecines, known as "robust" forms, possessed particularly large teeth, jaws, and chewing muscles and represent an evolutionary dead end, disappearing from the fossil record completely by 1 mya. One of the other australopithecine species, though it is not clear which one, appears to be a direct ancestor of the genus *Homo*.

Though genetic evidence established that the human line diverged from those leading to chimpanzees and gorillas between 5 and 8 mya, for a long time the fossil evidence of the early st[illegible]ution was both sparse and t[illegible]ral interesting specimens fi[illegible]t period. Inclusion of any fo[illegible]volutionary line depends up[illegible] (also called *bipedality*), th[illegible]e human line. The possib[illegible] ancestors from the Miocene recently found in Chad (*Sahelanthropus tchadensis*) and Kenya (*Orrorin tugenensis*), dated 6 to 7 mya, were described in the last chapter. In this chapter, we will pick up our story with a diverse array of fossil bipeds from the Pliocene—the geological epoch that began around 5 mya beginning with *Ardipithecus* from the chapter opener.[1]

Before focusing on the fossils, however, let's look at the anatomy of **bipedalism**—the shared derived characteristic distinguishing humans and their ancestors from the other African apes.

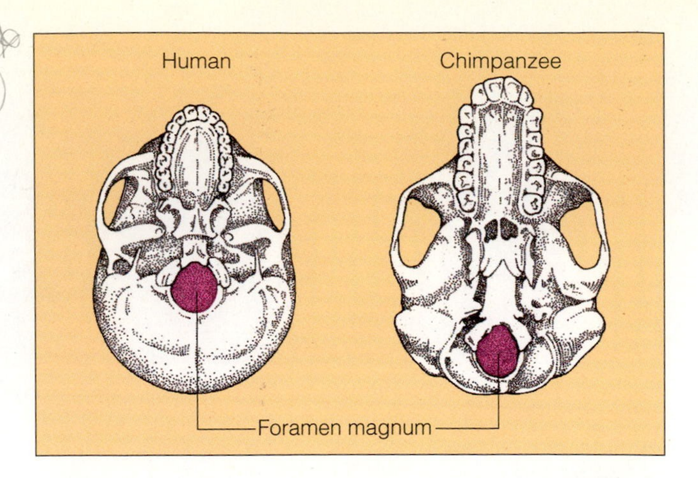

Figure 7.1 **Bipedalism can be inferred from the position of the foramen magnum, the large opening at the base of the skull. Note its relatively forward position on the human skull (left) compared to the chimp skull.**

The Anatomy of Bipedalism

For a hominoid fossil to be definitively classified as part of the human evolutionary line, certain evidence of bipedalism is required. Bipedalism is associated with anatomical changes literally from head to toe.

Bipedalism can even be preserved in the skull (Figure 7.1) because balancing the head in an upright posture requires a skull position relatively centered above the spinal column. The spinal cord leaves the skull at its base through an opening called the *foramen magnum* (Latin for "big opening"). In a knuckle-walker like a chimp, the foramen magnum is placed more toward the back of the skull while in a biped it is in a more forward position.

Extending down from the skull of a biped, the spinal column makes a series of convex and concave curves that together maintain the body in an upright posture by positioning the body's center of gravity above the legs rather than forward. The curves correspond to the neck (cervical), chest (thoracic), lower back (lumbar), and pelvic (sacral) regions of the spine, respectively. In a chimp, the shape of the spine follows a single arching curve (Figure 7.2). Interestingly, at birth the spines of human babies have a single arching curve as seen in adult apes. As humans mature the curves characteristic of bipedalism appear, the cervical curve at about 3 months on average and the lumbar curve at around 12 months—a time when many babies begin to walk.

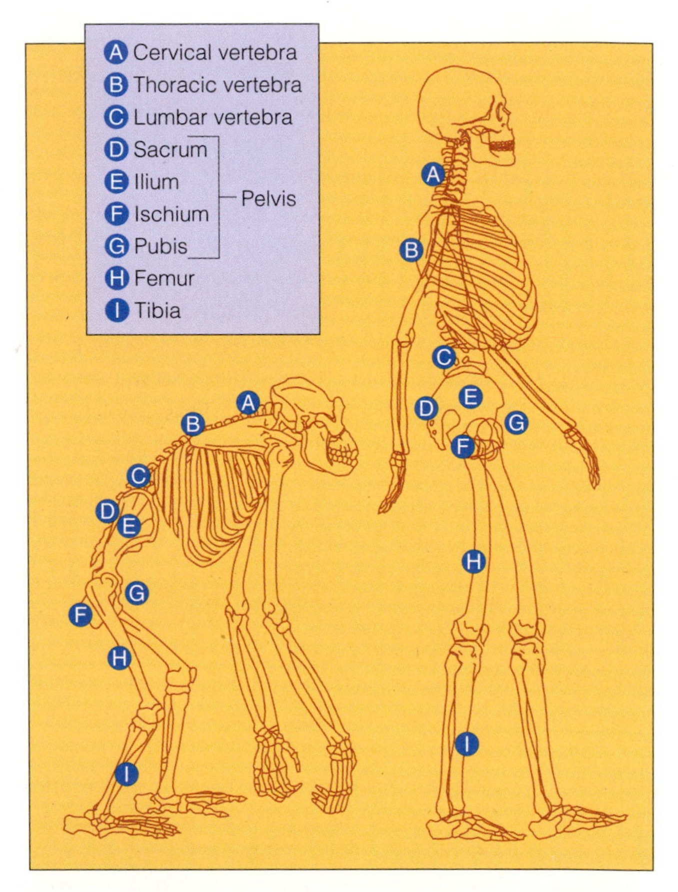

Figure 7.2 **Differences between skeletons of chimps and humans reflect their mode of locomotion.**

[1] White, T. D., et al. (2009, October). *Ardipithecus ramidus* and the paleobiology of early hominids. *Science 326* (5949), 64, 75–86; see also the entire October 2, 2009, issue of *Science*.

bipedalism The mode of locomotion in which an organism walks upright on its two hind legs, characteristic of humans and their ancestors; also called bipedality.

Fossilized footprints were preserved in volcanic ash at the 3.6-million-year-old Tanzanian site of Laetoli. As shown here, the foot of a living human fits right inside this ancient footprint, which shows the characteristic pattern of bipedal walking. The actual trail of footprints is 24 meters (80 feet) long.

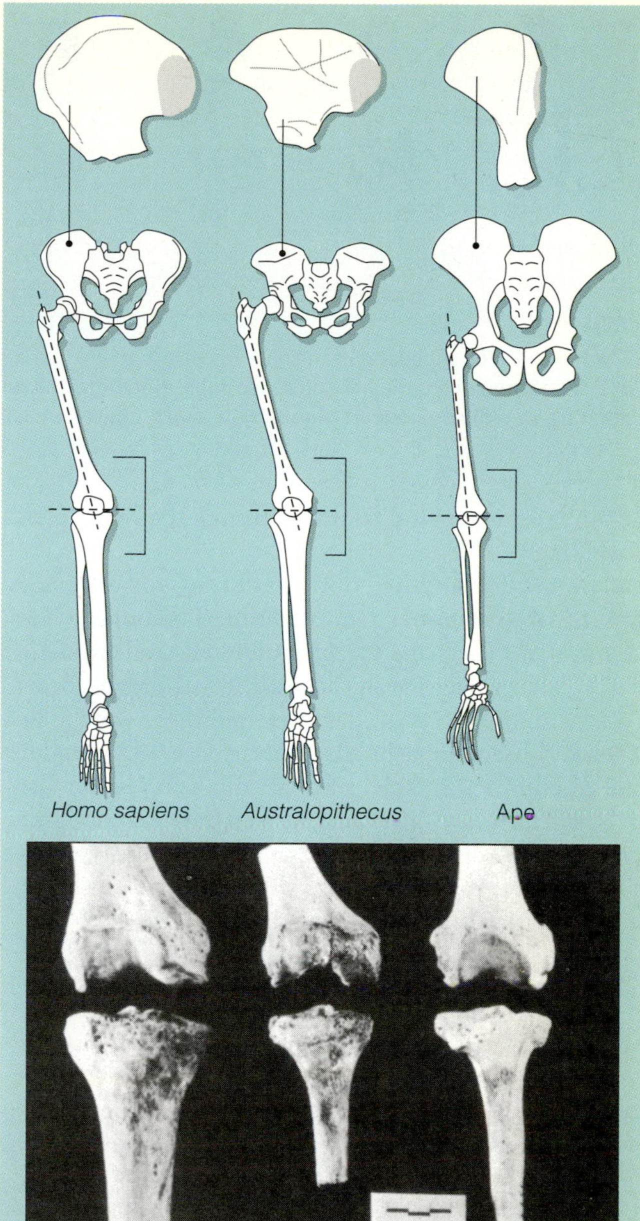

Figure 7.3 Examination of the upper hip bones and lower limbs of (from left) *Homo sapiens, Australopithecus*, and an ape can be used to determine means of locomotion. The similarities between the human and australopithecine bones are striking and are indicative of bipedal locomotion.

The shape of the pelvis also differs considerably between bipeds and other apes. Rather than an elongated shape following the arch of the spine as seen in chimps, the biped pelvis is wider and foreshortened so that it can provide structural support for the upright body. With a wide bipedal pelvis, the lower limbs would be oriented away from the body's center of gravity if the thigh bones (femora) did not angle in toward each other from the hip to the knee, a phenomenon described as "kneeing-in." (Notice how your own knees and feet can touch when standing while your hip joints remain widely spaced.) This angling does not continue past the knee to the shin bones (tibia), which are oriented vertically. The resulting knee joint is not symmetrical, allowing the thigh and shin bones to meet despite their different orientations (Figure 7.3).

Another characteristic of bipeds is their stable arched feet and the absent opposable big toe. The ape big toe is in an **abducted** position (sticking out away from the midline) while the human big toe is pulled in toward the midline (**adducted**). In general, humans and their ancestors possess shorter toes than the other apes.

These anatomical features allow paleoanthropologists to "diagnose" bipedal locomotion even in fragmentary remains such as the top of the shin bone or the base of a skull. In addition, bipedal locomotion can also be established through fossilized footprints, preserving not so much the shape of foot bones but the characteristic stride used by humans and their ancestors. In fact, bipedal locomotion is a process of shifting the body's weight from one foot to the other as the nonsupporting foot swings forward. While the body is supported in a one-legged stance, a biped takes a stride by swinging the other leg forward. The heel of the foot is the first part of the swinging leg to hit the ground. Then as the biped continues to move forward, he or she rolls from the heel toward the toe, pushing or "toeing off" into the next swing phase of the stride (Figure 7.4). While one leg is moving from heel strike to toe off of the stance phase,

abduction Movement away from the midline of the body or from the center of the hand or foot.

adduction Movement toward the midline of the body or to the center of the hand or foot.

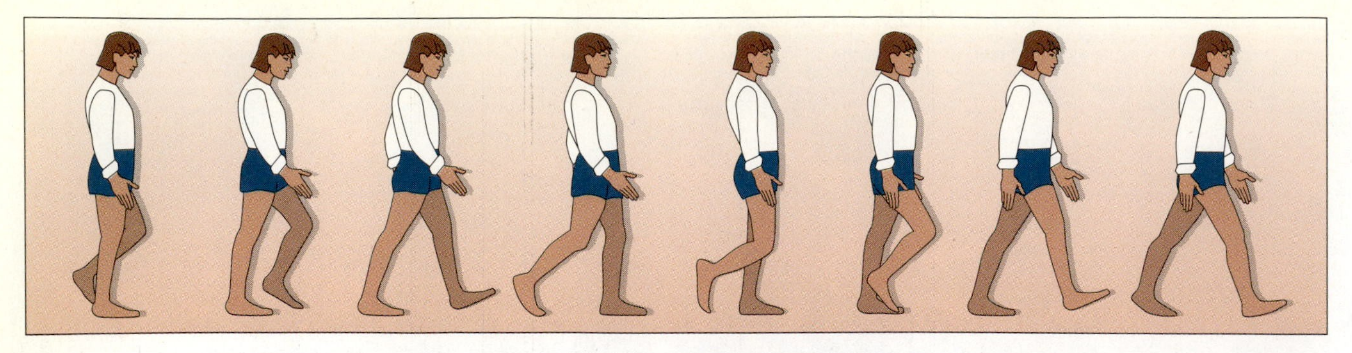

Figure 7.4 The bipedal gait in some regards is really "serial monopedalism" or locomotion one foot at a time through a series of controlled falls. Note how the body's weight shifts from one foot to the other as an individual moves through the swing phase to heel strike and toe off.

the other leg is moving forward through the swing phase of walking.

The most dramatic confirmation of our ancestors' walking ability comes from Laetoli, Tanzania, where, 3.6 mya, two (perhaps three) individuals walked across newly fallen volcanic ash. Because it was damp, the ash took the impressions of their feet, and these were sealed beneath subsequent ash falls until discovered by chemist Paul Abell in 1978. Abell was part of a team led by British paleoanthropologist Mary Leakey in search of human origins at Laetoli (see Anthropologists of Note). The shape of the footprints and the linear distance between the heel strikes and toe offs are quite human.

Once bipedalism is established in a fossil specimen, paleoanthropologists turn to other features, such as the skull or teeth, so that they can begin to establish relationships among the various fossil groups. Often scholars bring different interpretations to the fossil evidence.

Ardipithecus

Made famous through the partially complete 4.4-million-year-old skeleton specimen "Ardi," the genus *Ardipithecus* has dramatically changed what is known about the earliest bipeds. The genus is actually divided into two species, *Ardipithecus ramidus* and the older *Ardipithecus kadabba* dated to between 5.2 and 5.8 mya. The *Ardipithecus* remains show that some of the earliest bipeds inhabited a forested environment much like that of contemporary chimpanzees, bonobos, and gorillas; these remains were found in fossil-rich deposits along Ethiopia's Awash

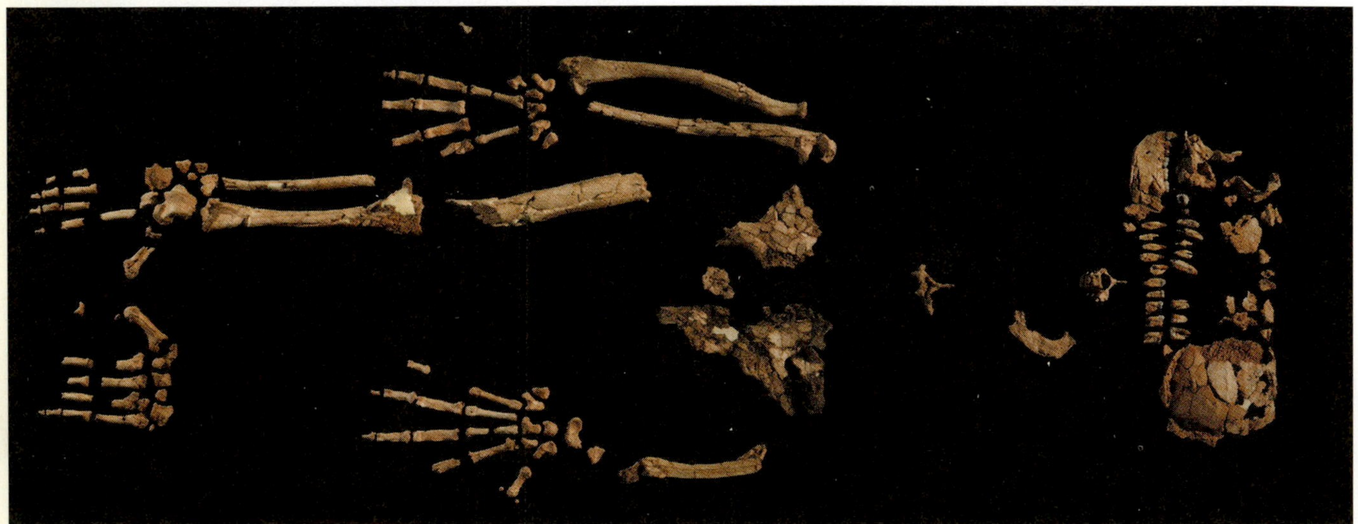

The remarkably complete remains of *Ardipithecus ramidus* have allowed paleoanthropologists to begin to reconstruct the biology and lifeways of the early forest dwelling hominins. When the first "Ardi" remains were discovered in the early 1990s she was placed on a side branch of human evolution but scientific investigation of this remarkable skeleton has lead paleoanthropologists to suggest she is a direct ancestor to the human line.

Anthropologists of Note

Louis S. B. Leakey (1903–1972) ▪ Mary Leakey (1913–1996)

© Melville Bell Grosvenor/National Geographic Collection

Few figures in the history of paleoanthropology discovered so many key fossils, received so much public acclaim, or stirred up as much controversy as **Louis Leakey** and his second wife, **Mary Leakey.** Born in Kenya of missionary parents, Louis received his early education from an English governess and subsequently was sent to England for a university education. He returned to Kenya in the 1920s to begin his career there.

It was in 1931 that Louis and his research assistant from England, Mary Nicol (whom he married in 1936), began working in their spare time at Olduvai Gorge in Tanzania, searching patiently and persistently for remains of early human ancestors. It seemed a good place to look, for there were numerous animal fossils as well as crude stone tools lying scattered on the ground and eroding out of the walls of the gorge.

Their patience and persistence were not rewarded until 1959, when Mary found the first fossil. A year later, another skull was found, and Olduvai was on its way to being recognized as one of the most important sources of fossils relevant to human evolution in all of Africa. While Louis reconstructed, described, and interpreted the fossil material, Mary made the definitive study of the Oldowan tools, a very early stone tool industry.

The Leakeys' important discoveries were not limited to those at Olduvai. In the early 1930s, they found the first fossils of Miocene apes in Africa at Rusinga Island in Lake Victoria. Also in the 1930s, Louis found a number of skulls at Kanjera, Kenya, that show a mixture of derived and more ancestral features. In 1948, at Fort Ternan, Kenya, the Leakeys found the remains of a late Miocene ape with features that seemed appropriate for an ancestor of the bipeds. After Louis's death, Paul Abell, a member of an expedition led by Mary Leakey, found the first fossilized footprints of early bipeds at Laetoli, Tanzania.

In addition to their own work, Louis Leakey promoted a good deal of important work on the part of others. He made it possible for Jane Goodall to begin her landmark field studies of chimpanzees; later he was instrumental in setting up similar studies among gorillas (by Dian Fossey) and orangutans (by Biruté Galdikas). He set into motion the fellowship program responsible for the training of numerous paleoanthropologists from Africa. The Leakey tradition has been continued by son Richard, his wife Meave, and their daughter Louise.

Louis Leakey had a flamboyant personality and a way of interpreting fossil materials that frequently did not stand up well to careful scrutiny, but this did not stop him from publicly presenting his views as if they were the gospel truth. It was this aspect of the Leakeys' work that generated controversy. Nonetheless, the Leakeys produced a great deal of work that resulted in a much fuller understanding of human origins.

River accompanied by fossils of forest animals. The name ***Ardipithecus ramidus*** is fitting for an ultimate human ancestor as *Ardi* means "floor" and *ramid* means "root" in the local Afar language.

Now that the spectacular Ardi specimen has been sufficiently analyzed by the team who discovered her, paleoanthropologists are debating her exact place on the human line. Because the other African apes share a body plan similar to one another, many paleoanthropologists expected the earliest bipeds to resemble something halfway between chimps and humans. Instead, Ardi shows that these forest creatures moved in a combination of ways: They moved across the tops of branches with the palms of their hands and feet facing downward, and they walked between the trees on the ground in an upright position. The other African apes, as we saw in previous chapters, knuckle-walk on the forest floor and hang suspended below the branches. In other words, Ardi resembles some of the early Miocene apes more than she does the living African apes.

Ardipithecus ramidus One of the earliest bipeds that lived in forested portions of eastern Africa about 4.4 million years ago.

This calls into question what the last common ancestor of humans and the other African apes looked like. Does Ardi represent the more ancestral form, with the other apes evolving independently after they split from the human line but still converging to the typical African ape body plan? Or does Ardi represent a new body plan, characteristic of the earliest bipeds that evolved away from the African ape plan shared by chimps and gorillas? And what of Ardi's relationship to the later bipeds? Until fall

branch
on the human evolutionary tree. Now, the international team has proposed that Ardi may be a direct ancestor to the later bipeds, including humans.

The famous Ardi specimen, at 120 centimeters tall and a weight of about 50 kilograms, is comparable in size to a female chimpanzee. The size and shape of this partial skeleton's brain and the enamel thickness of the specimen's teeth are similar to chimpanzees as well. Though possessing a grasping big toe, Ardi's locomotion, unlike that of a chimp, has been reconstructed as bipedal when on the ground.

The *Ardipithecus* finds, along with the *Orrorin* and Toumai specimens described in the previous chapter, have begun to provide evidence for the time period before the appearance of the ancient bipeds belonging to the genus *Australopithecus*. The first representatives of this group were discovered in the early 20th century, long before the majority of scientists were comfortable with the now-accepted notion that humans originated on the African continent.

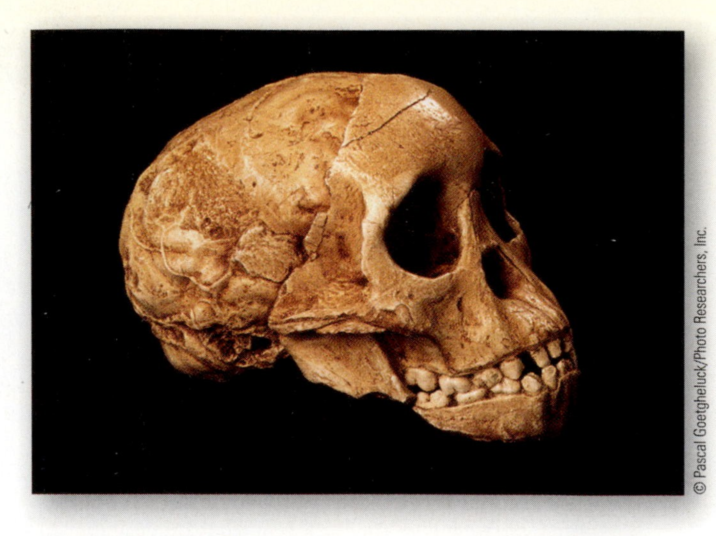

The Taung child, discovered in South Africa in 1924, was the first fossil specimen placed in the genus *Australopithecus*. Though Raymond Dart correctly diagnosed the Taung child's bipedal mode of locomotion as well as its importance in human evolution, other scientists rejected Dart's claims that this small-brained biped with a humanlike face was a direct ancestor to humans. In the early 20th century, scientists expected the ancestors to humans to possess a large brain and an apelike face and to originate from Europe or Asia rather than Africa.

Australopithecus

Most of the early bipeds from the Pliocene are members of the genus ***Australopithecus***, a genus that includes species from East, South, and Central Africa. The name for this group of fossils was coined back in 1924 when the first important fossil from Africa proposed to be a human ancestor came to light. This unusual fossil, consisting of a partial skull and natural brain cast of a young individual, was brought to the attention of anatomist Raymond Dart of the University of Witwatersrand in Johannesburg, South Africa. The "Taung child," named for the limestone quarry in the South African town of Taung (Tswana for "place of the lion") in which it was found, was unlike any creature Dart had seen before. Recognizing an intriguing mixture of ape and human characteristics in this unusual fossil, Dart proposed a new taxonomic category for his discovery—*Australopithecus africanus* or "southern ape of Africa"—suggesting that this specimen represented an extinct form that was ancestral to humans.

Although the anatomy of the base of the skull indicated that the Taung child was probably a biped, the scientific community was not ready to accept the notion of a small-brained African ancestor to humans. Dart's original paper describing the Taung child was published in the February 1925 edition of the prestigious journal *Nature*. The next month's issue was filled with venomous critiques rejecting Dart's proposal that this specimen represented an ancestor to humans. Criticisms of Dart ranged from biased to fussy to sound. Some scholars chastised Dart for incorrectly combining Latin and Greek in the genus and species name he coined. Valid critics questioned the wisdom of making inferences made about the appearance of an adult of the species based only on the fossilized remains of a young individual.

However, ethnocentric bias was the biggest obstacle to Dart's proposed human ancestor. Paleoanthropologists of the early 20th century expected that the ancestor to humans already had a large brain. Moreover, most European scientists expected to find evidence of this large-brained ancestor in Europe or, barring that, Asia.

In fact, many scientists of the 1920s even believed that the ancestor to humans had already been found in the Piltdown gravels of Sussex, England, in 1910. The Piltdown specimens consisted of a humanlike skull and an apelike jaw that seemed to fit together, though the crucial joints connecting the two were missing. They were discovered along with the bones of some other animal species known to be extinct. Charles Dawson—the British amateur archaeologist,

Australopithecus The genus including several species of early bipeds from East, South, and Central Africa living between about 1.1 and 4.3 million years ago, one of whom was directly ancestral to humans.

Discovery of the Piltdown Man in 1911, Cooke, Arthur Clark (1867–1951)/Geographical Society, London, UK/The Bridgeman Art Library

The Piltdown forgery was widely accepted as ancestral to humans, in large part because it fit with conventional expectations that the missing link would have a large brain and an apelike face. No one knows with certainty how many of the "Piltdown Gang"—scientists supporting this specimen as the missing link—were actually involved in the forgery. It is likely that Charles Dawson had help from at least one scientist. Sir Arthur Conan Doyle, the author of the Sherlock Holmes detective stories, has also been implicated.

paleontologist, and practicing lawyer who found these remains—immodestly named them *Eoanthropus dawsoni* or "Dawson's dawn man." Until the 1950s the Piltdown remains were widely accepted as representing the missing link between apes and humans; today they are known as one of the biggest hoaxes in the history of science.

There were several reasons for widespread acceptance of Dawson's "dawn man." As Darwin's theory of evolution by natural selection began to gain acceptance in the early 20th century, intense interest developed in finding traces of prehistoric human ancestors. Accordingly, predictions were made as to what those ancestors looked like. Darwin himself, on the basis of his knowledge of embryology and the comparative anatomy of living apes and humans, suggested in his 1871 book *The Descent of Man* that early humans had, among other things, a large brain and an apelike face and jaw.

Although the tools made by prehistoric peoples were commonly found in Europe, their bones were not. A few fossilized skeletons had come to light in France and Germany, but they were not at all like the predicted missing link, nor had any human fossils been discovered in England ever before. Given this state of affairs, the Piltdown finds could not have come at a better time. Here at last was the long-awaited missing link, and it was almost exactly as predicted. Even better, so far as English-speaking scientists were concerned, it was found on English soil.

In the context of the evidence available in the early 1900s, it was easy to accept the idea of an ancient human with a large brain and an apelike face. Fortunately, the self-correcting nature of science has prevailed, exposing the Piltdown specimens as a forgery. The discoveries—primarily in South Africa, China, and Java—of fossils of smaller-brained bipeds from the distant past caused scientists to question Piltdown's authenticity. Ultimately, the application of the newly developed fluorine dating method (described in Chapter 5) by British physical anthropologist Kenneth Oakley and colleagues in 1953 proved conclusively that Piltdown was a forgery. The skull, which was indeed human, was approximately 600 years old, whereas the jaw, which proved to be from an orangutan, was even more recent. Finally, Dart and the Taung child were fully vindicated.

Today, genetic and fossil evidence indicates that the human evolutionary line begins with a small-brained bipedal ape from Africa. Numerous international expeditions—including researchers from Kenya, Ethiopia, Japan, Belgium, Great Britain, Canada, France, Israel, the Netherlands, South Africa, and the United States—have scoured East, South, and Central Africa, recovering unprecedented amounts of fossil material. This wealth of evidence has allowed scientists to continually refine our understanding of early human evolution. Even though debate continues over the details, today there is widespread agreement over its broad outline. Each new discovery, such as the Ardi skeleton, confirms our African origins and the importance of bipedalism to distinguishing humans and their ancestors from the other African apes.

The Pliocene Environment and Hominin Diversity

As described in the previous chapter, the Miocene epoch was a time of tremendous geologic change. The effects of these changes continued into the Pliocene. The steady movement of geologic plates supporting the African and Eurasian continents resulted in a collision of the two landmasses at either end of what now is the Mediterranean Sea (Figure 7.5). This contact allowed for the spread of species between these continents.

A suite of geologic changes, known as the Great Rift Valley system, are associated with this collision. This system consists of a separation between geologic plates, extending from the Middle East through the Red Sea and eastern Africa into southern Africa. Part of rifting involves the steady increase in the elevation of the eastern third of the African continent, which experienced a cooler and dryer climate and a transformation of vegetation from forest to dry grassy **savannah.**

The system also contributed to the volcanic activity in the region, which provides opportunities for accurate dating of fossil specimens. Also in the Miocene, the Indian subcontinent, which had been a solitary landmass for many millions of years, came into its present position through a collision with Eurasia, contributing further to cooler, dryer conditions globally. In addition to causing global climate change, these geologic events also provided excellent opportunities for the discovery of fossil specimens as layers of the earth became exposed through the rifting process.

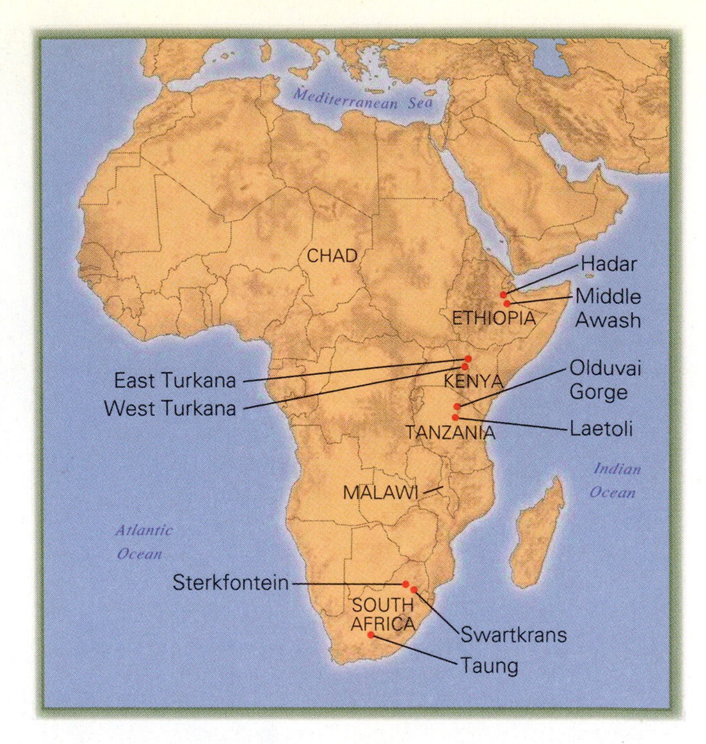

Figure 7.5 Australopithecine fossils have been found in South Africa, Malawi, Tanzania, Kenya, Ethiopia, and Chad. In the Miocene the Eurasian and African continents made contact at the eastern and western ends of what now is the Mediterranean Sea. As these landmasses met, "rifting" also occurred, gradually raising the elevation of the eastern third of Africa. The dryer climates that resulted may have played a role in human evolution in the distant past. This rifting also gives us excellent geologic conditions for finding fossils today.

Diverse Australopithecine Species

Since Dart's original find, hundreds of other fossil bipeds have been discovered, first in South Africa and later in Tanzania, Malawi, Kenya, Ethiopia, and Chad. As they were discovered, many were placed in a variety of different genera and species, but now usually all are considered to belong to the single genus *Australopithecus.* Anthropologists recognize up to eight species of the genus (Table 7.1). In addition, some other groups of fossil bipeds from the Pliocene epoch (1.6 to around 5 mya) have been discovered, including the earliest representatives of the genus *Homo.*

First we will describe the australopithecines and their contemporaries in the order in which they inhabited the earth up to the middle Pliocene (2.5 mya) when the genus *Homo* first appeared. The East African and South African evidence will be presented separately because the dating for East African sites is more reliable. Next we will examine late-appearing australopithecines, including a grade of australopithecine found in both eastern and southern Africa that coexisted with the genus *Homo.*

savannah Semi-arid plains environment as in eastern Africa.

East Africa

The oldest australopithecine species known so far consists of some jaw and limb bones from Kenya that date to between 3.9 and 4.2 mya (see *Australopithecus anamensis* in Table 7.1). Meave and Louise Leakey, daughter-in-law and granddaughter of Louis and Mary Leakey, discovered these fossils in 1995 and decided to place them in a separate species from other known australopithecines. Its name means "ape-man of the lake," and it shows particularities in the teeth such as a true *sectorial*: a lower premolar tooth shaped to hone the upper canine as seen in apes. In humans and more recent ancestors, the premolar has a characteristic bicuspid shape and does not sharpen the canine each time the jaws come together. As

Lucy, the 3.2-million-year-old fossil specimen, is on a six-year U.S. tour as part of a traveling exhibit organized and curated by the Ethiopian government and the Houston Museum of Natural History. Though Lucy has done much to popularize paleoanthropology and evolutionary studies since her discovery in 1974, some paleoanthropologists—like C. Owen Lovejoy and Richard Leakey—have said that placing her fragile ancient skeleton on public display is far too risky. The Smithsonian Institution and the Cleveland Museum of Natural History have declined to host the show for this reason. Others—like her discoverer Donald Johanson, pictured here with Lucy in the exhibition space in Times Square, New York—feel that the benefits outweigh the risks. Benefits include the study of Lucy's remains via CT scans so that future generations of scientists can study them without actually handling the fragile bones. In addition, the revenues from the tour will be used to help modernize Ethiopia's museums. Finally, the exhibit will increase public awareness of human origins and the vital role of Africa and, in particular, Ethiopia in our evolutionary history.

in other australopithecines and humans, the enamel in the molar teeth is thick. The limb bone fragments indicate bipedalism.

Moving closer to the present, the next species defined in the fossil record is *Australopithecus afarensis.* No longer the earliest australopithecine species, it still remains one of the best known due to the Laetoli footprints from Tanzania, the famous Lucy specimen, and the recent discovery of the 3.3-million-year-old remains of a young child called "Lucy's baby," both from Ethiopia.

Table 7.1 Species of *Australopithecus* and Other Pliocene Fossil Hominins*

Species	Location	Dates	Notable Features/Fossil Specimens
Ardipithecus ramidus	Ethiopia	4.4 mya†	Fossil remains of over thirty-five individuals including Ardi (another species, *Ardipithecus kadabba*, dates to 5.4–5.8 mya)
A. anamensis	Kenya	3.9–4.2 mya	Oldest australopithecine
Kenyanthropus platyops	Kenya	3.2–3.5 mya	Contemporary with australopithecines, believed by some to be a member of that genus
A. africanus	South Africa	2.3–3 mya	First discovered, gracile, well represented in fossil record (Taung)
A. aethiopicus	Kenya	2.5 mya	Oldest robust australopithecine (Black Skull)
A. bahrelghazali	Chad	3–3.5 mya	Only australopithecine from Central Africa
A. boisei	Kenya	1.2–2.3 mya	Later robust form coexisted with early *Homo* (Zinj)
A. garhi	Ethiopia	2.5 mya	Later East African australopithecine with humanlike dentition
A. robustus	South Africa	1–2 mya	Coexisted with early *Homo*

*Paleoanthropologists differ in the number of species they recognize, some suggesting separate genera.

†Million years ago.

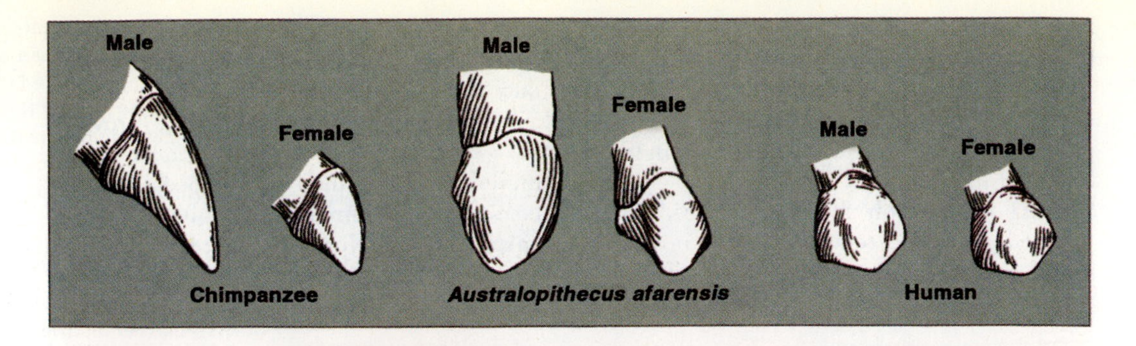

Figure 7.6 Sexual dimorphism in canine teeth.

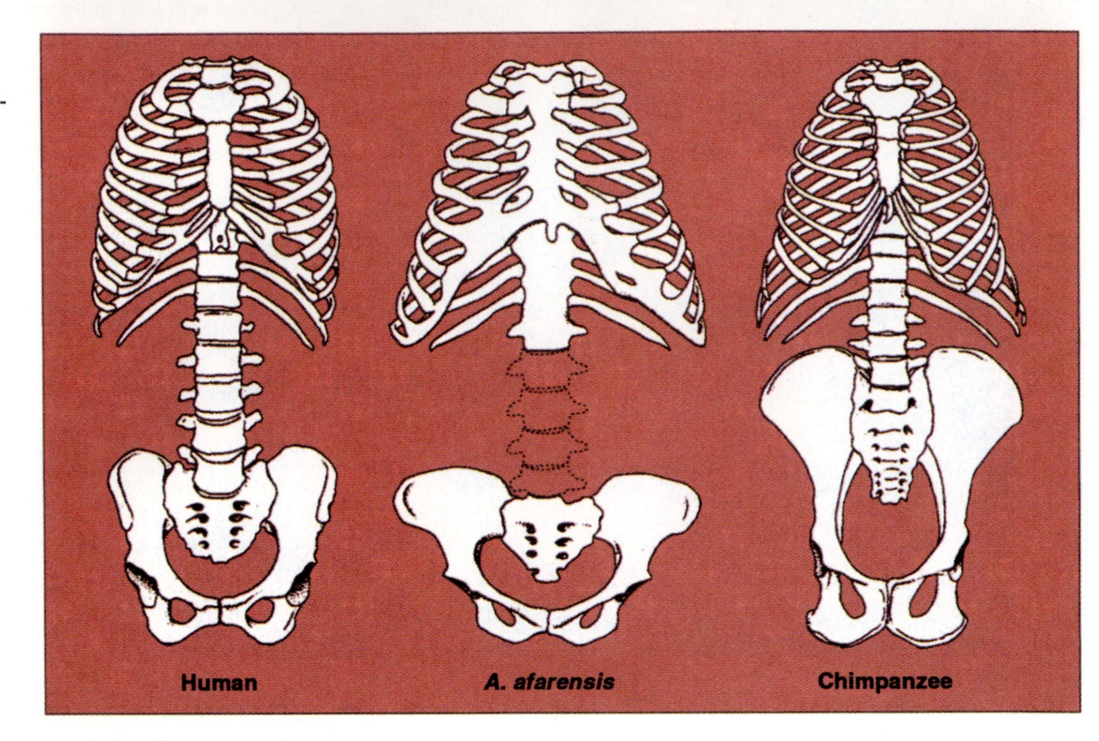

Figure 7.7 Trunk skeletons of modern human, *A. afarensis*, and chimpanzee, compared. In its pelvis, the australopithecine resembles the modern human, but its rib cage shows the pyramidal configuration of the ape.

Lucy consists of bones from almost all parts of a single 3.2-million-year-old skeleton discovered in 1974 in the Afar Triangle of Ethiopia (hence the name *afarensis*). Standing only 3½ feet tall, this adult female was named after the Beatles song "Lucy in the Sky with Diamonds," which the paleoanthropologists listened to as they celebrated her discovery. The Afar region is also famous for the "First Family," a collection of bones from at least thirteen individuals, ranging in age from infancy to adulthood, who died together as a result of some single calamity.

At least sixty individuals from *A. afarensis* (once the name of a genus has been established, it can be abbreviated with the first letter followed by the complete species name) have been removed from fossil localities in Ethiopia and Tanzania. Specimens from Ethiopia's Afar region are securely dated by potassium argon to between 2.9 and 3.9 mya. Material from Laetoli, in Tanzania, is securely dated to 3.6 mya. Altogether, *A. afarensis* appears to be a sexually dimorphic bipedal species with estimates of body size and weight ranging between 1.1 and 1.6 meters (3½–5 feet) and 29 and 45 kilograms (64–100 pounds), respectively.[2]

If paleoanthropologists are correct in assuming that larger fossil specimens were males and smaller specimens females, males were about 1½ times the size of females. In this respect, they were somewhat like the Miocene African apes, with sexual dimorphism greater than one sees in a modern chimpanzee but less than one sees in gorillas and orangutans. Male canine teeth, too, are significantly larger than canine teeth of females, though canine size is reduced compared to that of chimps (Figure 7.6).

Nearly 40 percent complete, the Lucy specimen has provided invaluable information about the shape of the pelvis and torso of early human ancestors. The physical appearance of *A. afarensis* was unusual by human standards: They may be described as looking like an ape from the waist up and like a human from the waist down (Figure 7.7). In

---

[2] McHenry, H. M. (1992). Body size and proportions in early hominids. *American Journal of Physical Anthropology 87,* 407.

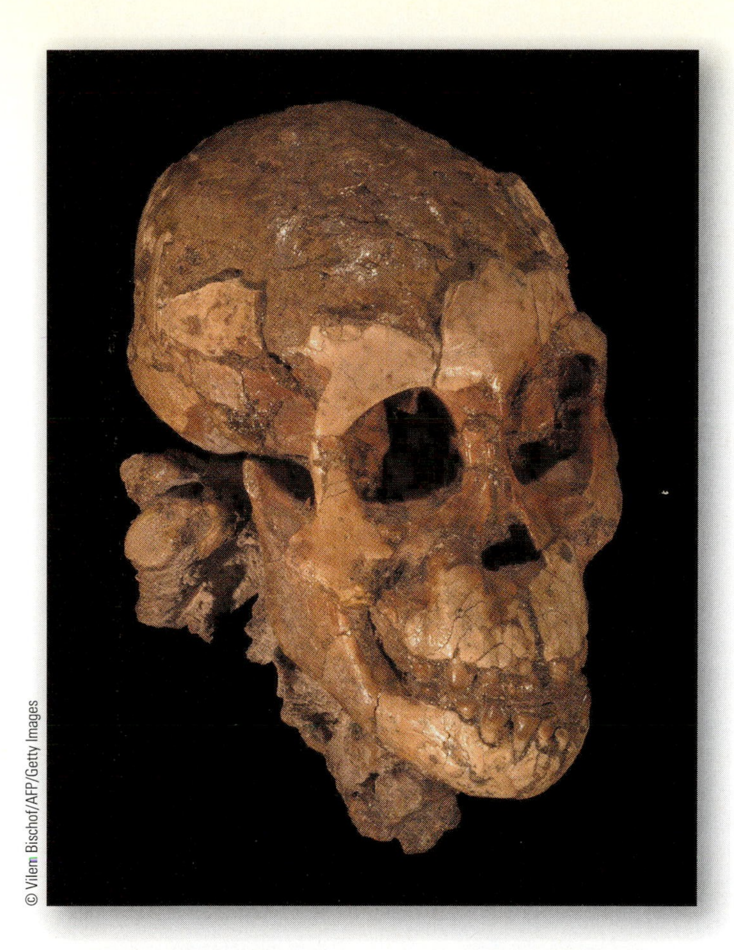
© Vilem Bischof/AFP/Getty Images

Fossil finds are rare enough, but a well-preserved juvenile specimen is especially unusual. The skull and skeleton of this young girl are actually tens of thousands of years older than Lucy, but due to her incredible preservation, she has been nicknamed "Lucy's baby." In addition to the skull pictured here, this specimen includes a torso, fingers, and a foot.

addition, a forearm bone from Lucy, which is relatively shorter than that of an ape, suggests that the upper limb was lighter and the center of gravity lower in the body than in apes. Still, the arms of Lucy and other early australopithecines are long in proportion to their legs when compared to the proportions seen in humans.

Though she lived about 150,000 years before her namesake, "Lucy's baby," the discovery from Ethiopia announced in 2006, will add considerably to our knowledge about *A. afarensis* once the analyses are complete.[3] These fossilized remains of a young child, dated to 3.3 mya, were discovered in the Dikika area of northern Ethiopia in 2000. Because the remains of this child, thought to have died in a flash flood, are particularly well preserved, scientists can investigate new aspects of this species' biology and behavior. For example, a preserved hyoid bone (located in the throat region) will allow scientists to reconstruct australopithecine patterns of vocalization. While the lower limbs clearly indicate bipedalism, the specimen's scapula and long curved finger bones are more apelike.

The curvature of the fingers and toes and the somewhat elevated position of the shoulder joint seen in adult specimens indicate that *A. afarensis* was more adapted to tree climbing compared to more recent human ancestors. In the following Original Study, paleoanthropologist John Hawks discusses the kinds of evidence used to reconstruct a behavior such as tree climbing in our ancestors.

[3] Zeresenay, A., et al. (2006). A juvenile early hominin skeleton from Dikika, Ethiopia. *Nature 443,* 296–301.

Original Study

Ankles of the Australopithecines *by John Hawks*

Recent University of Michigan Ph.D. Jeremy DeSilva gets some nice press about his work demonstrating that fossil hominins didn't climb like chimpanzees.

"Frankly, I thought I was going to find that early humans would be quite capable, but their ankle morphology was decidedly maladaptive for the kind of climbing I was seeing in chimps," DeSilva told LiveScience. "It kind of reinvented in my mind what they were doing and how they could have survived in an African savannah without the ability to go up in the trees."[a]

This is a good example of the comparative method in paleoanthropology. We can't observe the behavior of extinct species; we can only observe the behavior of their living relatives. We can observe the anatomy of fossil specimens, but testing hypotheses about their behavior requires us to understand the relationship between anatomy and behavior in living species. We've known about the anatomy of fossil hominid ankles for a long time, but it's not so obvious how the anatomical differences between them and chimpanzee ankles relates to behavior.

DeSilva studied the tibiae and ankle bones of early hominins and concludes "that if hominins included tree climbing as part of their locomotor repertoire, then they were performing this activity in a manner decidedly unlike modern chimpanzees."

DeSilva's conclusion is straightforward and easy to illustrate. Chimpanzees climb vertical tree trunks pretty much like a logger does. A logger slings a strap around the trunk and leans back on it. Friction from the strap holds him up as he moves his feet upward; spikes on his boots hold him while he moves the strap.

Of course, chimpanzees don't have spikes on their feet, and they don't use a strap. Instead, their arms are long enough to wrap around the trunk, and they can wedge a foot against the trunk by flexing their ankle upward—dorsiflexing it—or grip the trunk by bending the ankle sideways—inverting the foot—around it. The paper includes

CONTINUED

CONTINUED

a photo that shows the chimpanzee style of climbing clearly.

You might wonder, yeah so what? Isn't it obvious that chimpanzees climb this way?

Well, it wasn't so obvious which features of the ankle might adapt chimpanzees to this style of climbing. By watching the chimpanzees (and other apes) DeSilva was able to determine the average amount (and range) of dorsiflexion and inversion of the feet while climbing, and could also assess the extent to which dorsiflexion is accomplished at the ankle joint (as opposed to the midfoot). In this case, the observations were pretty obvious—chimpanzees were habitually flexing their ankles in ways that would damage a human ankle. Then, by examining the bony limits on human ankle flexibility, DeSilva showed that fossil hominins shared the same constraints on ankle movement as recent people. They couldn't have climbed like chimpanzees.

Human Climbing

I would say that the ankle-joint observations match the rest of the skeleton. It seems pretty obvious that *Australopithecus afarensis* and later hominids couldn't possibly have climbed in the chimpanzee-like manner described in DeSilva's paper, because the hominins' arms were too short. If a logger tried to climb with his arms instead of a strap, even spikes on his feet would be relatively ineffective holding him up. Dorsiflexion would be hopeless—the normal component of force against the tree trunk would be insufficient to prevent slipping.

Humans who *aren't* loggers use a different strategy to climb vertical tree trunks—they put a large fraction of the surface area of their legs directly in contact with the trunk. Wrapping legs around and pressing them together gives the necessary friction to hold the body up.

If you're like me, you'll remember this climbing strategy ruefully from gym class, where "rope climbing" is the lowest common denominator of fitness tests. The sad fact is that many otherwise-normal humans fall on the wrong side of the line between mass and muscle power. Straining my groin muscles to the max, I still could never pull my way up a rope.

There's nothing magical about getting a human to climb. Ladders, after all, are relatively easy for the large fraction of the population who can't climb a rope or tree trunk. The trick with a ladder is that friction is organized in a more effective way for our ankle mechanics and arm length. But you don't need to schlep a ladder, if you can manage a little extra arm strength and a low enough body mass.

Early Hominin Climbing

Australopithecines were light in mass, and from what we can tell, they had strong arms. So they had what it takes for humans today to climb trees effectively—not like chimpanzees, but like humans. Up to *A. afarensis*, every early hominin we know about lived in an environment that was at least partially wooded.

In his comments about the paper, DeSilva hypothesizes a trade-off between climbing ability and effective bipedality, so that early hominins could not have effectively adapted to both. I don't think a chimpanzee-like ankle would have been any use with arms as short as australopithecines'. So I don't see the necessity of a trade-off in ankle morphology. *A. afarensis*—long before any evidence of stone tool manufacture—had very non-apelike arms, hands and thumbs.

But there's one significant question that DeSilva omits discussing—the footbones of a South African australopithecine: StW 573. Clarke and Tobias[b] describe the foot of StW 573 as having a big toe that is abducted (sticks out) from the foot, intermediate between the chimpanzee and human condition. They conclude:

> [W]e now have the best available evidence that the earliest South African australopithecine, while bipedal, was equipped to include arboreal, climbing activities in its locomotor repertoire. Its foot has departed to only a small degree from that of the chimpanzee. It is becoming clear that *Australopithecus* was not an obligate terrestrial biped, but rather a facultative biped and climber. (p. 524)

DeSilva studied the talus (an ankle bone), not the toe. StW 573 has a talus, and although it is not in DeSilva's sample, it probably would place very close to the other hominins in his comparison. Even Clarke and Tobias described its talus as humanlike—their argument for an intermediate form was based mostly on the toe.

The amount of dorsiflexion in a chimpanzee's foot allows it to climb trees with the feet in a position that is impossible for humans. Comparisons like this between living species allow paleoanthropologists to reconstruct the pattern of locomotion in fossil groups.

But still, it's hard to believe that australopithecines would retain a chimpanzee-like big toe, if they couldn't use that big toe by inverting or dorsiflexing their foot in any significant way. By all other accounts, an abducted hallux (big toe) would only impede effective bipedality. It is of no use at all for a human-like pattern of climbing. The only remaining utility would be for small-branch grasping, but small branches would seem unlikely as a support for hominin arboreality.

One possibility is that Clarke and Tobias were simply mistaken. That appears to be the explanation favored by Harcourt-Smith and Aiello[c] and McHenry and Jones[d] who concluded that all known hominin feet appear to lack any "ape-like ability to oppose the big toe." They also point to the Laetoli footprint trails, most observers of which agree that the big toe was adducted, not abducted.

I tend to favor that explanation—australopithecines simply didn't have a grasping foot. But they may not have shared the medial longitudinal arch, at least not in the human configuration, and without it one might doubt that their gait featured as strong a toe-off as that of later humans. Who knows?

---

[a] DeSilva, J. M. (2009). Functional morphology of the ankle and the likelihood of climbing in early hominins. *Proceeding of the National Academy of Sciences, USA 106*, 6567–6572.

[b] Clarke, R. J., & Tobias, P. V. (1995). Sterkfontein Member 2 foot bones of the oldest South African hominid. *Science 269*, 521–524.

[c] Harcourt-Smith, W. E. H., & Aiello, L. C. (2004). Fossils, feet and the evolution of human bipedal locomotion. *Journal of Anatomy 204*, 403–416, at 412.

[d] McHenry, H. M., & Jones, A. L. (2006). Hallucial convergence in early hominids. *Journal of Human Evolution 50*, 534–539.

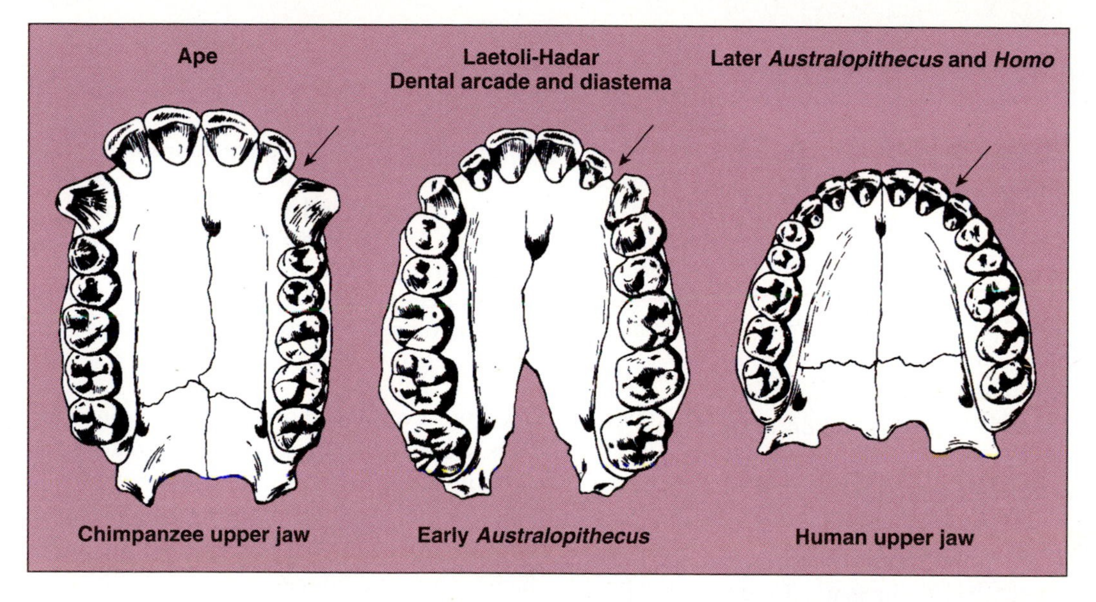

Figure 7.8 The upper jaws of an ape, *Australopithecus,* and modern human show important differences in the shape of the dental arch and the spacing between the canines and adjoining teeth. Only in the earliest australopithecines can a diastema (a large gap between the upper canine and incisor) be seen.

The skull bones are particularly important for reconstructing evolutionary relationships as well as for learning about the cognitive capacities of ancestral species. The skull of *A. afarensis* is relatively low, the forehead slopes backward, and the brow ridge that helps give apes such massive-looking foreheads is also present. The lower half of the face is chinless and accented by jaws that are quite large, relative to the size of the skull. The brain is small and apelike, and the general conformation of the skull seems nonhuman. Even the semicircular canal, a part of the ear crucial to maintenance of balance, is apelike. Cranial capacity, commonly used as an index of brain size for *A. afarensis,* averages about 420 cubic centimeters (cc), roughly equivalent to the size of a chimpanzee and about one-third the size of living humans.[4] Intelligence, however, is indicated not only by absolute brain size but also by the ratio of brain to body size. Unfortunately, with such a wide range of adult weights, it is not clear whether australopithecine brain size was larger than a modern ape's, relative to body size.

Much has been written about australopithecine teeth because they are one of the primary means for distinguishing among closely related groups. In *A. afarensis,* unlike humans, the teeth are all quite large, particularly the molars. The premolar is no longer fully sectorial as in *A. anamensis,* but most other features of the teeth represent a more ancestral rather than derived condition. For example, the rows of the teeth are more parallel (the ancestral ape condition) compared to the arch seen in the human tooth rows. The canines project slightly, and a slight space or gap known as a **diastema** remains between the upper incisors and canines as found in the apes (Figure 7.8).

---

[4] Grine, F. E. (1993). Australopithecine taxonomy and phylogeny: Historical background and recent interpretation. In R. L. Ciochon & J. G. Fleagle (Eds.), *The human evolution source book* (pp. 201–202). Englewood Cliffs, NJ: Prentice-Hall.

diastema A space between the canines and other teeth allowing the large projecting canines to fit within the jaw.

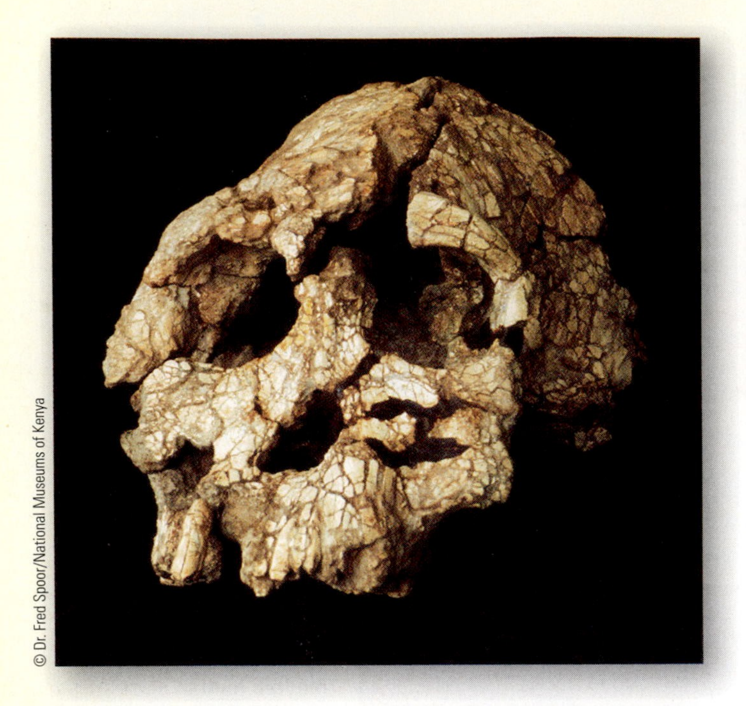

This 3- to 4-million-year-old skull could be another australopithecine or, as its discoverers suggest, a separate genus: *Kenyanthropus platyops*.

To further complicate the diversity seen in *A. afarensis*, in 2001 Meave and Louise Leakey announced the discovery of an almost complete cranium, parts of two upper jaws, and assorted teeth from a site in northern Kenya, dated to between 3.2 and 3.5 mya.[5] Contemporary with early East African *Australopithecus*, the Leakeys see this as a different genus named ***Kenyanthropus platyops*** ("flat-faced man of Kenya"). Unlike early australopithecines, *Kenyanthropus* is said to have a small braincase and small molars set in a large, humanlike, flat face. But again, there is controversy; the Leakeys see the fossils as ancestral to the genus *Homo*. Other paleoanthropologists are not convinced, suggesting that the Leakeys' interpretation rests on a questionable reconstruction of badly broken fossil specimens.[6]

Central Africa

Dated to the same time period as *Kenyanthropus platyops* is another recent discovery of an australopithecine from Chad in Central Africa. The name of the new species, *Australopithecus bahrelghazali*, is for a nearby riverbed and consists of a jaw and several teeth dated to between 3 and 3.5 mya.[7] This is the first australopithecine discovered in Central Africa. With time, perhaps more discoveries from this region will give a fuller understanding of the role of *A. bahrelghazali* in human evolution and its relationship to the possible bipeds from the Miocene.

[5] Leakey, M. G., et al. (2001). New hominin genus from eastern Africa shows diverse middle Pliocene lineages. *Nature 410*, 433–440.

[6] White, T. D. (2003). Early hominids—diversity or distortion? *Science 299*, 1994–1997.

Kenyanthropus platyops A proposed genus and species of biped contemporary with early australopithecines; may not be a separate genus.

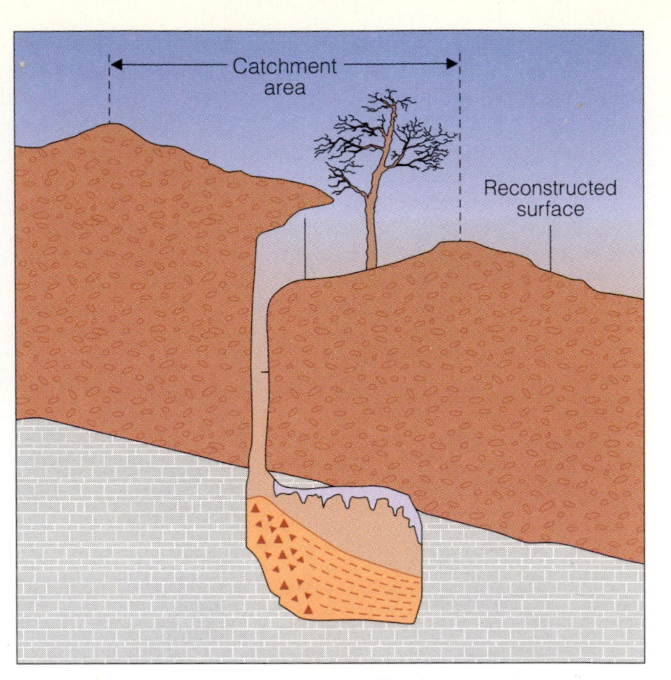

Figure 7.9 Many of the fossil sites in South Africa were limestone caverns connected to the surface by a shaft. Over time, dirt, bones, and other matter that fell down the shaft accumulated inside the cavern, becoming fossilized. In the Pliocene, the earth next to the shaft's opening provided a sheltered location for trees that, in turn, may have been used by predators for eating without being bothered by scavengers.

South Africa

Throughout the 20th century and into the present, paleoanthropologists have continued to recover australopithecine fossils from a variety of sites in South Africa. Included in this group are numerous fossils found beginning in the 1930s at Sterkfontein and Makapansgat, in addition to Dart's original find from Taung.

It is important to note, however, that South African sites, lacking the clear stratigraphy and volcanic ash of East African sites, are much more difficult to date and interpret (Figure 7.9). One unusually complete skull and skeleton has been dated by paleomagnetism to about 3.5 mya,[8]

[7] Brunet, M., et al. (1995).The first australopithecine 2,500 kilometers west of the Rift Valley (Chad). *Nature 16*, 378 (6554), 273–275.

[8] Clarke, R. J. (1998). First ever discovery of a well preserved skull and associated skeleton of Australopithecus. *South African Journal of Science 94*, 460–464.

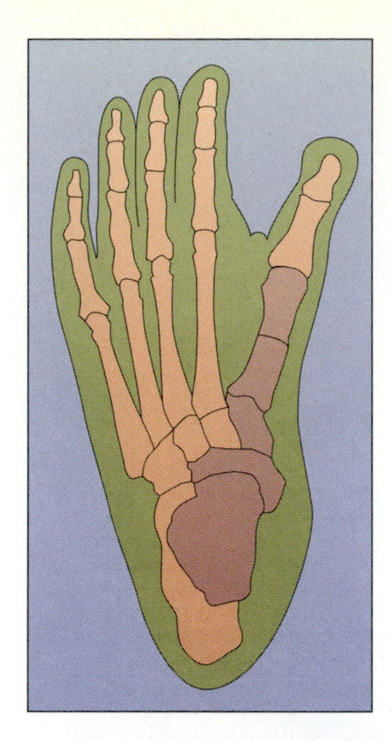

Figure 7.10 Drawing of the foot bones of a 3- to 3.5-million-year-old *Australopithecus* from Sterkfontein, South Africa, as they would have been in the complete foot. Note how long and flexible the first toe (at right) is. This is a drawing of the StW specimen referred to in this chapter's Original Study.

as was a partial foot skeleton (Figure 7.10) described in 1995.[9] The other South African remains are difficult to date. A faunal series established in East Africa places these specimens between 2.3 and 3 mya. These specimens are all classified in the australopithecine species named by Dart—*A. africanus,* also known as **gracile australopithecines.**

The reconstruction of australopithecine biology is controversial. Some researchers think they see evidence for some expansion of the brain in *A. africanus,* while others vigorously disagree. Paleoanthropologists also compare the outside appearance of the brain, as revealed by casts of the insides of skulls. Some researchers suggest that cerebral reorganization toward a human condition is present,[10] while others argue the organization of the brain is more apelike than human.[11] At the moment, the weight of the evidence favors mental capabilities for all gracile australopithecines as being comparable to those of modern great apes (chimps, bonobos, gorillas, orangutans).

Using patterns of tooth eruption in young australopithecines such as Taung, paleoanthropologist Alan Mann and colleagues suggest that the developmental pattern of australopithecines was more humanlike than apelike,[12] though some other paleoanthropologists do not agree. Evidence from the recent discovery of the young *A. afarensis* specimen (Lucy's baby) will help scientists to resolve this debate. Our current understanding of genetics and the macroevolutionary process indicates that a developmental shift is likely to have accompanied a change in body plan such as the emergence of bipedalism among the African hominoids.

Other South African sites have yielded fossils whose skulls and teeth looked quite different from the gracile australopithecines described above. These South African fossils are known as *Australopithecus robustus.* They are notable for having teeth, jaws, and chewing muscles that are massive (robust) relative to the size of the braincase. The gracile forms are slightly smaller on average and lack such robust chewing structures. Over the course of evolution, several distinct groups of **robust australopithecines** have appeared not only in South Africa, but throughout East Africa as well.

Robust Australopithecines

The remains of robust australopithecines were first found at Kromdraai and Swartkrans by South African paleoanthropologists Robert Broom and John Robinson in the 1930s in deposits that, unfortunately, cannot be securely dated. Current thinking puts them between 1 and 1.8 mya. Usually referred to as *A. robustus* (see Table 7.1), this species possessed a characteristic robust chewing apparatus including a **sagittal crest** running from front to back along the top of the skull (Figure 7.11). This feature provides sufficient area on a relatively small braincase for attachment of the huge temporal muscles required to operate powerful jaws. Present in robust australopithecines and gorillas today, the sagittal crest feature provides an example of convergent evolution.

[9] Clarke, R. J., & Tobias, P. V. (1995). Sterkfontein member 2 foot bones of the oldest South African hominid. *Science 269,* 521–524.

[10] Holloway, R. L., & de LaCoste-Lareymondie, M. C. (1982). Brain endocast asymmetry in pongids and hominids: Some preliminary findings on the paleontology of cerebral dominance. *American Journal of Physical Anthropology 58,* 101–110.

[11] Falk, D. (1989). Apelike endocast of "ape-man" Taung. *American Journal of Physical Anthropology 80,* 335–339.

[12] Mann, A., Lampl, M., & Monge, J. (1990). Patterns of ontogeny in human evolution: Evidence from dental development. *Yearbook of Physical Anthropology 33,* 111–150.

gracile australopithecines Members of the genus *Australopithecus* possessing a more lightly built chewing apparatus; likely had a diet that included more meat than that of the robust *australopithecines;* best represented by the South African species *A. africanus.*

robust australopithecines Several species within the genus *Australopithecus,* who lived from 2.5 to 1.1 million years ago in eastern and southern Africa; known for the rugged nature of their chewing apparatus (large back teeth, large chewing muscles, and a bony ridge on their skull tops for the insertion of these large muscles).

sagittal crest A crest running from front to back on the top of the skull along the midline to provide a surface of bone for the attachment of the large temporal muscles for chewing.

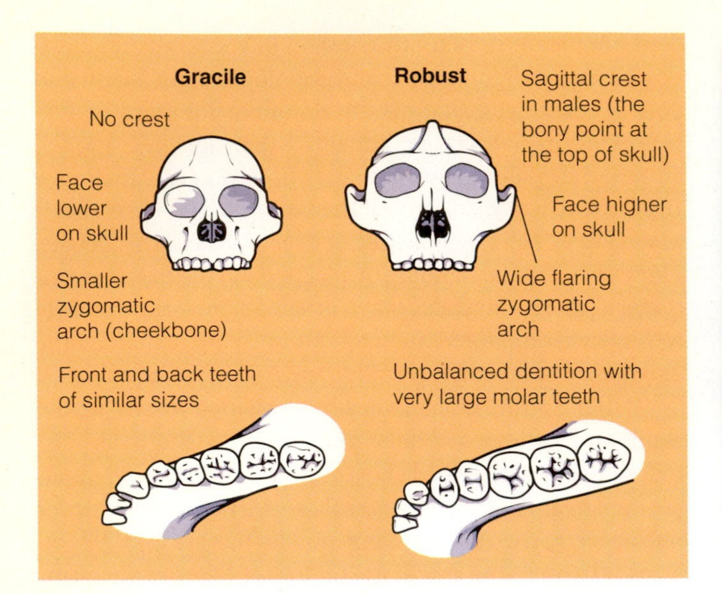

Figure 7.11 **The differences between gracile and robust australopithecines are related primarily to their chewing apparatus. Robust species have extremely large cheek teeth, large chewing muscles, and a bony ridge on the top of their skulls for the attachment of large temporal muscles for chewing. The front and back teeth of gracile species are balanced in size, and their chewing muscles (reflected in a less massive skull) are more like those seen in the later genus *Homo*. If you place your own hands on the sides of your skull above your ears while opening and closing your jaw, you can feel where your temporal muscles attach to your skull. By moving your hands toward the top of your skull you can feel where these muscles end in humans.**

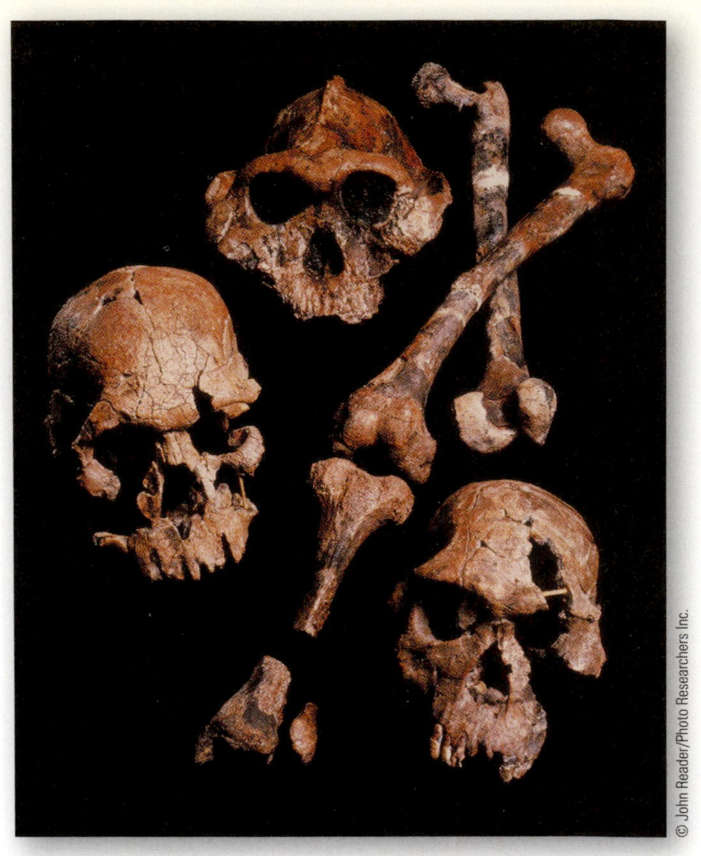

The robust australopithecines and the earliest members of genus *Homo* inhabited the earth at the same time. These skulls and leg bones were all found along the eastern shores of Lake Turkana in Kenya and are dated to between 1.7 and 1.9 mya. The two specimens with the rounded skulls are classified by many paleoanthropologists as members of the species *Homo habilis*. The robust australopithecine at the top of the photograph has the bony ridge along the top of its skull.

The first robust australopithecine to be found in East Africa was discovered by Mary Leakey in the summer of 1959, the centennial year of the publication of Darwin's *On the Origin of Species*. She found it in Olduvai Gorge, a fossil-rich area near Ngorongoro Crater, on the Serengeti Plain of Tanzania. Olduvai is a huge gash in the earth, about 40 kilometers (25 miles) long and 91 meters (300 feet) deep, which cuts through Plio-Pleistocene and recent geologic strata revealing close to 2 million years of the earth's history.

Mary Leakey's discovery was reconstructed by her husband Louis, who gave it the name *Zinjanthropus boisei* (*Zinj*, an old Arabic name for "East Africa," *boisei* after the benefactor who funded their expedition). At first, he thought this ancient fossil seemed more humanlike than *Australopithecus* and extremely close to modern humans in evolutionary development, in part due to the stone tools found in association with this specimen. Further study, however, revealed that *Zinjanthropus*, the remains of which consisted of a skull and a few limb bones, was an East African species of robust australopithecine. Although similar in many ways to *A. robustus*, Zinj is now most commonly referred to as *Australopithecus boisei* (see Table 7.1). Potassium-argon dating places this early species at about 1.75 million years old.

Since the time of Mary Leakey's original *A. boisei* find, numerous other fossils of this robust species have been found at Olduvai, as well as north and east of Lake Turkana in Kenya. Although one fossil specimen often referred to as the "Black Skull" (see *A. aethiopicus* in Table 7.1) is known to be as much as 2.5 million years old, some date to as recently as 1.1 mya.

Like robust australopithecines from South Africa, East African robust forms possessed enormous molars and premolars. Despite a large mandible and palate, the anterior teeth (canines and incisors) were often crowded, owing to the room needed for the massive molars.

The heavy skull, more massive even than seen in the robust forms from South Africa, has a sagittal crest and prominent brow ridges. Cranial capacity ranges from about 500 to 530 cubic centimeters. Body size, too, is somewhat larger; whereas the South African robust forms are estimated to have weighed between 32 and 40 kilograms, the East African robusts probably weighed from 34 to 49 kilograms.

Because the earliest robust skull from East Africa (2.5 million years old), the so-called Black Skull from Kenya, retains a number of ancestral features shared with earlier East African australopithecines, it is possible that it evolved from *A. afarensis*, giving rise to the later robust East African forms. Whether the South African robust australopithecines represent a southern offshoot of the East African line or

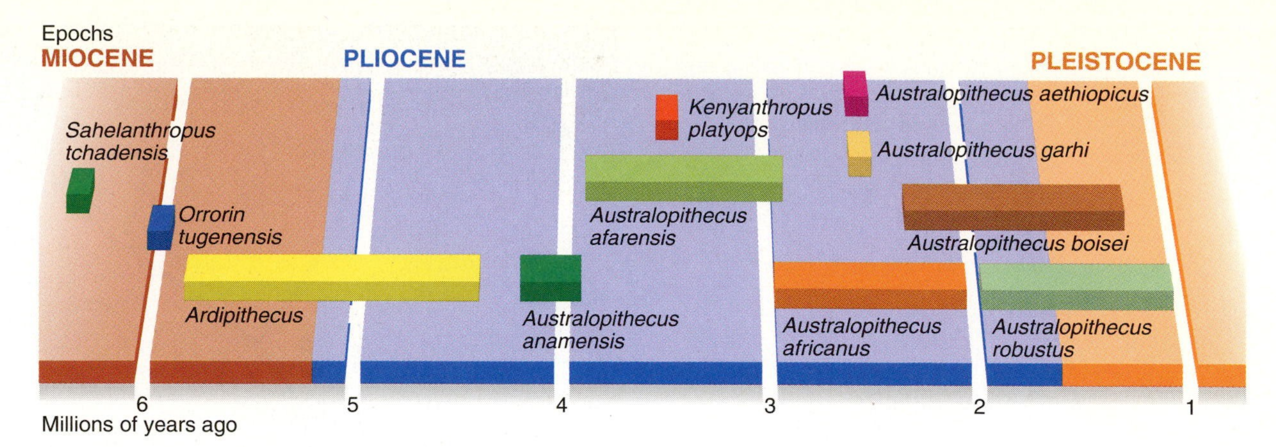

Figure 7.12 **The Pliocene fossil bipeds and the scientific names by which they have been known, arranged according to when they lived. *A. aethiopicus*, *A. boisei*, and *A. robustus* are all robust australopithecines. Whether the different species names are warranted is a matter of debate.**

convergent evolution from a South African ancestor has not been settled; arguments can be presented for both interpretations. In either case, what happened was that the later robust australopithecines developed molars and premolars that are both absolutely and relatively larger than those of earlier australopithecines who possessed front and back teeth more in proportion to those seen in the genus *Homo.*

Larger teeth require more bone to support them, hence the prominent jaws of the robust australopithecines. Larger jaws and heavy chewing activity require more jaw musculature that attaches to the skull. The marked crests seen on skulls of the late australopithecines provide for the attachment of chewing muscles on a skull that has increased very little in size. In effect, robust australopithecines had evolved into highly efficient chewing machines. Clearly, their immense cheek teeth and powerful chewing muscles bespeak the heavy chewing required for a diet of uncooked plant foods. This general level of biological organization shared by separate fossil groups as seen in the robust australopithecines is referred to as a *grade.*

Many anthropologists believe that, by becoming a specialized consumer of plant foods, the late australopithecines avoided competing for the same niche with early *Homo,* with which they were contemporaries. In the course of evolution, the **law of competitive exclusion** dictates that when two closely related species compete for the same niche, one will out-compete the other, bringing about the loser's extinction. That early *Homo* and late *Australopithecus* did not compete for the same niche is suggested by their coexistence for something like 1.5 million years from about 1 to 2.5 mya (Figure 7.12).

law of competitive exclusion When two closely related species compete for the same niche, one will out-compete the other, bringing about the latter's extinction.

Photographer David Brill, a specialist in images of fossils and paleoanthropologists at work, positions the upper jaw and the other skull fragments of *Australopithecus garhi* so that the fragments are aligned as they would be in a complete skull.

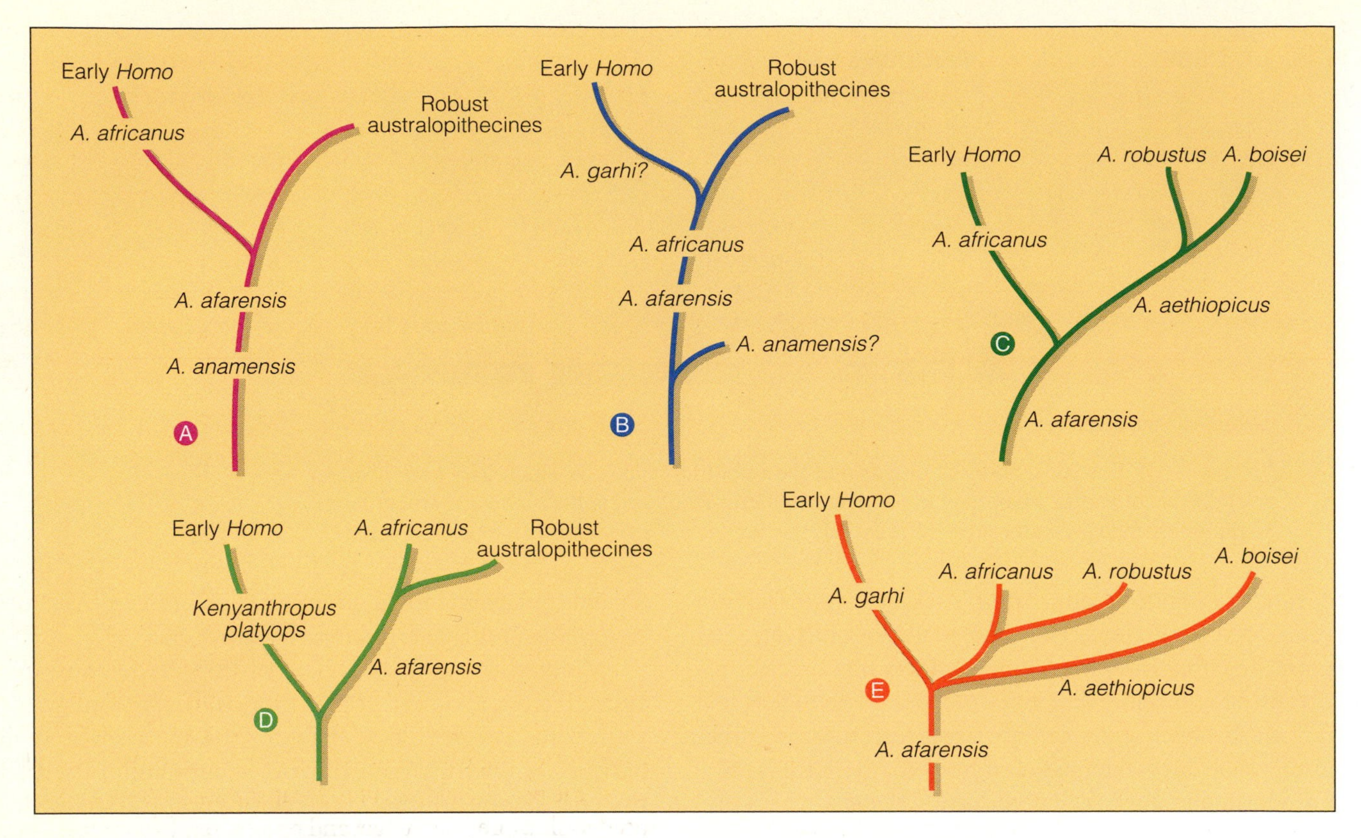

Figure 7.13 **The relationship among the various australopithecine (and other) Pliocene groups, and the question of which group is ancestral to the genus *Homo*, are debated by anthropologists. Several alternative hypotheses are presented in these diagrams. Most agree, however, that the robust australopithecines represent an evolutionary side branch. *Ardipithecus ramidus* has been proposed as ancestral to the australopithecines.**

Australopithecines and the Genus *Homo*

A variety of bipeds inhabited Africa about 2.5 mya, around the time the first evidence for the genus *Homo* begins to appear. In 1999, discoveries in East Africa added another australopithecine to the mix. Found in the Afar region of Ethiopia, these fossils were named *Australopithecus garhi* from the word for "surprise" in the local Afar language. Though the teeth were large, this australopithecine possessed an arched dental arcade and a ratio between front and back teeth more like humans and South African gracile australopithecines rather than like robust groups. For this reason, some have proposed that *A. garhi* is ancestral to the genus *Homo.* More evidence will be needed to prove whether or not this is true.

Precise relationships among all the australopithecine species (and other bipeds) that have been defined during the Pliocene are still not settled. In this mix, the question of which australopithecine was ancestral to humans remains particularly controversial. A variety of scenarios have been proposed, each one giving a different australopithecine group the starring role as the immediate human ancestor (Figure 7.13). Though paleoanthropologists debate which species is ancestral to humans, they agree that the robust australopithecines, though successful in their time, ultimately represent an evolutionary side branch.

Environment, Diet, and Origins of the Human Line

Having described the fossil material, we may now consider how evolution transformed an early ape into a hominin. Generally, such paleoanthropological reconstructions and hypotheses about the origin of bipedalism rely heavily on the evolutionary role of natural selection. The question at hand is not so much *why* bipedalism developed as much as *how* bipedalism allowed these ancestors to adapt to their environment.

Hypotheses about adaptation begin with features evident in the fossil evidence. For example, the fossil record indicates that once bipedalism appeared, over the next several million years the shape of the face and teeth shifted from a more apelike to a humanlike condition. To refine their hypotheses, paleoanthropologists add to the fossil evidence through scientific reconstructions of environmental conditions and inferences made from data gathered on living nonhuman primates and humans. In this regard, evolutionary reconstructions involve piecing together a coherent story or narrative about the past. Sometimes these narratives are tenuous. But as paleoanthropologists consider their own biases and incorporate new evidence as it is discovered, the quality of the narrative improves.

For many years, the human evolutionary narrative has been tied to the emergence of the savannah environment in eastern Africa as the global climate changes of the Miocene led to increasingly cooler and dryer conditions. While the evidence from *Ardipithecus* shows that the earliest members of the human line were forest dwellers, over time the size of tropical forests decreased or, more commonly, broke up into mosaics where patches of forest were interspersed with savannah or other types of open country. The forebears of the human line are thought to have lived in places with access to both trees and open country. With the breaking up of forests, these early ancestors found themselves spending more and more time on the ground and had to adapt to this new, more open environment.

The most obvious problem facing these ancestors in their new situation, other than getting from one patch of trees to another, was getting food. As the forest thinned or shrank, the traditional ape-type foods found in trees became less available, especially in seasons of reduced rainfall. Therefore, it became more and more necessary to forage on the ground for foods such as seeds, grasses, and roots. With reduced canine teeth, early bipeds were relatively defenseless when down on the ground and were easy targets for numerous carnivorous predators. That predators were a problem is revealed by the South African fossils, most of which are from individuals that were dropped into rock fissures by leopards or, in the case of Dart's original find, by an eagle.

Many investigators have argued that the hands of early bipeds took over the weapon functions of the reduced canine teeth. Hands enabled them to threaten predators by using wooden objects as clubs and throwing stones. This quality is shared with many of the other hominoids. Recall the male chimpanzee (Chapter 4) who wielded objects as part of his display to obtain alpha status. In australopithecines the use of clubs and throwing stones may have set the stage for the much later manufacture of more efficient weapons from bone, wood, and stone.

Although the hands of the later australopithecines were suitable for tool making, no evidence exists that any of them actually *made* stone tools. Similarly, experiments with captive bonobos have shown that they are capable of making crude chipped stone tools, but they have never been known to do so outside of captivity. Thus to be able to do something is not necessarily equivalent to doing it.

In fact, the earliest known stone tools, dating to about 2.5 mya, are about 2 million years more recent than the oldest fossils of *Australopithecus*. However, *Australopithecus* certainly had no less intelligence and dexterity than do modern great apes, all of whom make use of tools when it is to their advantage to do so. Orangutans, bonobos, chimpanzees, and even gorillas have all been observed in the wild making and using simple tools such as those described in Chapter 4. Most likely, the ability to make and use simple tools is something that goes back to the last common ancestor of the Asian and African apes, before the appearance of the first bipeds.

It is reasonable to suppose, then, that australopithecine tool use was similar to that of the other great apes. Unfortunately, few tools that they used are likely to have survived for a million and more years, and any that did would be hard to recognize as such. Although we cannot be certain about this, in addition to clubs and objects thrown for defense, sturdy sticks may have been used to dig edible roots, and convenient stones may have been used (as some chimpanzees do) to crack open nuts. In fact, some animal bones from australopithecine sites in South Africa show microscopic wear patterns suggesting their use to dig edible roots from the ground. We may also allow the possibility that, like chimpanzees, females may have used tools more often to get and process food than males, but the latter may have used tools more often as "weapons."[13] The female chimpanzees who hunted with spears as described in Chapter 4 call into question these distinct roles for the sexes.

Humans Stand on Their Own Two Feet

From the broad-shouldered, long-armed, tailless ape body plan, the human line became fully bipedal. Our late Miocene forebears seem to have been primates that combined quadrupedal tree climbing with perhaps some swinging below the branches. On the ground, they were capable of assuming an upright stance, at least on occasion (optional, versus obligatory, bipedalism).

Paleoanthropologists generally take the negative aspects of bipedal locomotion into account when considering the advantages of this pattern of locomotion. For example, paleoanthropologists have suggested that bipedalism makes an animal more visible to predators, exposes its soft underbelly or gut, and interferes with the ability to instantly change direction while running. They also

[13] Goodall, J. (1986). *The chimpanzees of Gombe: Patterns of behavior* (pp. 552, 564). Cambridge, MA: Belknap.

emphasize that bipedalism does not result in particularly fast running; quadrupedal chimpanzees and baboons, for example, are 30 to 34 percent faster than we bipeds. For 100-meter distances, our best athletes today may attain speeds of 34 to 37 kilometers per hour, while the larger African carnivores from which bipeds might need to run can attain speeds up to 60 to 70 kilometers per hour. The consequences of a leg or foot injury are more serious for a biped while a quadruped can do amazingly well on three legs. A biped with only one functional leg is seriously hindered—an easy meal for some carnivore.

Because each of these drawbacks would have placed our early ancestors at risk from predators, paleoanthropologists have asked what made bipedal locomotion worth paying such a high price. It is hard to imagine bipedalism becoming a viable adaptation in the absence of strong selective pressure in its favor; therefore, a number of theories have been proposed to account for the adaptive advantages of bipedalism.

One once-popular suggestion is that bipedal locomotion allowed males to gather food on the savannah and transport it back to females, who were restricted from doing so by the dependence of their offspring.[14] This explanation is unlikely, however, because female apes, not to mention women among food-foraging peoples, routinely combine infant care with foraging for food. Indeed, among most food foragers, it is the women who commonly supply the bulk of the food eaten by both sexes.

Moreover, the pair bonding (one male attached to one female) presumed by this model is not characteristic of terrestrial primates, nor of those displaying the degree of sexual dimorphism that was characteristic of *Australopithecus*. Nor is it really characteristic of *Homo sapiens*. In a substantial majority of recent human societies, including those in which people forage for their food, some form of polygamy—marriage to two or more individuals at the same time—is not only permitted but preferred. And even in the supposedly monogamous United States, it is relatively common for an individual to marry (and hence mate with) two or more others (the only requirement is that he or she not be married to more than one mate at the same time).

Although we may reject as culture-bound the idea of male breadwinners provisioning stay-at-home moms, it is true that bipedal locomotion does make transport of bulky foods possible. (See the Biocultural Connection for another example of the influence of socially defined roles and theories about the evolution of human childbirth.) Nevertheless, a fully erect biped on the ground—whether male or female—has the ability to gather such foods for transport back to a tree or other place of safety for consumption. The biped does not have to remain out in the open, exposed and vulnerable, to do all of its eating.

Besides making it possible to carry food, bipedalism could have facilitated the food quest in other ways. With their hands free and body upright, the animals could reach otherwise unobtainable food on thorny trees too flimsy and too spiny to climb. Furthermore, with both hands free, they could gather other small foods more quickly using both hands. And in times of scarcity, being able to see farther, with the head in an upright position, would have helped them locate food and water sources.

Food may not have been the only thing transported by early bipeds. As we saw in Chapters 3 and 4, primate infants must be able to cling to their mothers in order to be carried; because the mother is using her forelimbs in locomotion, to either walk or swing, she cannot hold her infant as well. Chimpanzee infants, for example, must cling by themselves to their mother, and even up to 4 years of age, they make long journeys on their mother's back. Injuries caused by falling from the mother are a significant cause of infant mortality among apes. Thus the ability to carry infants would have made a significant contribution to the survivorship of offspring, and the ancestors of *Australopithecus* would have been capable of doing just this.

Another suggestion—that bipedal locomotion arose as an adaptation for nonterritorial scavenging of meat[15]—is unlikely. Although it is true that a biped is able to travel long distances without tiring, and that a daily supply of dead animal carcasses would have been available to early bipeds only if they were capable of ranging over vast areas, no evidence exists to indicate that they did much in the way of scavenging prior to about 2.5 mya. Furthermore, the heavy wear seen on australopithecine teeth is indicative of a diet high in tough, fibrous plant foods. Thus scavenging was likely an unforeseen byproduct of bipedal locomotion, rather than a cause of it.

Although bipedalism appeared before our ancestors lived in the savannah, it is still possible that bipedalism served as a means to cope with heat stress out in the open as the forested environments disappeared. In addition to bipedalism, one of the most obvious differences between humans and other living hominoids is our relative nakedness. Body hair in humans is generally limited to a fine sparse layer over most of the body with a very dense cover of hair limited primarily to the head. Peter Wheeler, a British physiologist, has suggested that bipedalism and the human pattern of body hair growth are both adaptations to the heat stress of the savannah environment.[16] Building upon the earlier "radiator" theory of paleoanthropologist

[14] Lovejoy, C. O. (1981). The origin of man. *Science 211*, 341–350.

[15] Lewin, R. (1987). Four legs good, two legs bad. *Science 235*, 969–971.

[16] Quoted in Folger, T. (1993). The naked and bipedal. *Discover 14* (11), 34–35. Reprinted with permission.

Biocultural Connection

Evolution and Human Birth

Because biology and culture have always shaped human experience, it can be a challenge to separate the influences of each of these factors on human practices. For example, in the 1950s, paleoanthropologists developed the theory that human childbirth is particularly difficult compared to birth in other mammals. This theory was based in part on the observation of a "tight fit" between the human mother's birth canal and the baby's head, though several other primates also possess similarly tight fits between the newborn's head or shoulders and the birth canal. Nevertheless, changes in the birth canal associated with bipedalism coupled with the evolution of large brains were held responsible for difficult birth in humans.

At the same historical moment, American childbirth practices were changing. In one generation from the 1920s to the 1950s, birth shifted from the home to the hospital. In the process childbirth transformed from something a woman normally accomplished at home, perhaps with the help of a midwife or relatives, into the high-tech delivery of a neonate (the medical term for a newborn) with the assistance of medically trained personnel. Women in the 1950s were generally fully anesthetized during the birth process.

Paleoanthropological theories mirrored the cultural norms, providing a scientific explanation for the change in American childbirth practices.

As a scientific theory, the idea of difficult human birth stands on shaky ground. No fossil neonates have ever been recovered, and only a handful of complete pelves (the bones forming the birth canal) exist. Instead, scientists must examine the birth process in living humans and nonhuman primates to reconstruct the evolution of the human birth pattern.

Cultural beliefs and practices, however, shape every aspect of birth. Cultural factors determine where a birth occurs, the actions of the individuals present, and beliefs about the nature of the experience. When paleoanthropologists of the 1950s and 1960s asserted that human childbirth is more difficult than birth in other mammals, they may have been drawing upon their own cultural beliefs that childbirth is dangerous and belongs in a hospital.

A quick look at global neonatal mortality statistics indicates that in countries such as the Netherlands and Sweden, healthy well-nourished women give birth successfully outside of hospitals, as they did throughout human evolutionary history. In other countries, deaths related to childbirth reflect malnutrition, infectious disease, and the low social status of women, rather than an inherently faulty biology.

Tlazolteotl, the earth mother goddess of the Aztecs, is depicted here giving birth in a squatting position, which is favored by women throughout the world. For hospital births, women generally have to work against gravity to bring a child in the world, as they tend to be placed on their backs with their legs in stirrups for the benefit of attending physicians.

BIOCULTURAL QUESTION

Though well-nourished healthy women successfully birth their babies outside of hospital settings, Caesarean section (C-section) rates have been rising in industrialized societies. In the United States one in three births is by C-section. The C-section rates in many Latin American countries are greater than 50 percent of all births. What cultural factors have led to this practice? Would your personal approach to birth change with the knowledge that humans have successfully adapted to childbirth?

Dean Falk, Wheeler developed this hypothesis through comparative anatomy, experimental studies, and the observation that humans are the only apes to inhabit the savannah environment today.

Many other animals, however, inhabit the savannah, and each of them possesses some mechanism for coping with heat stress. Some animals, like many of the carnivores, are active only when the sun is low in the sky, early

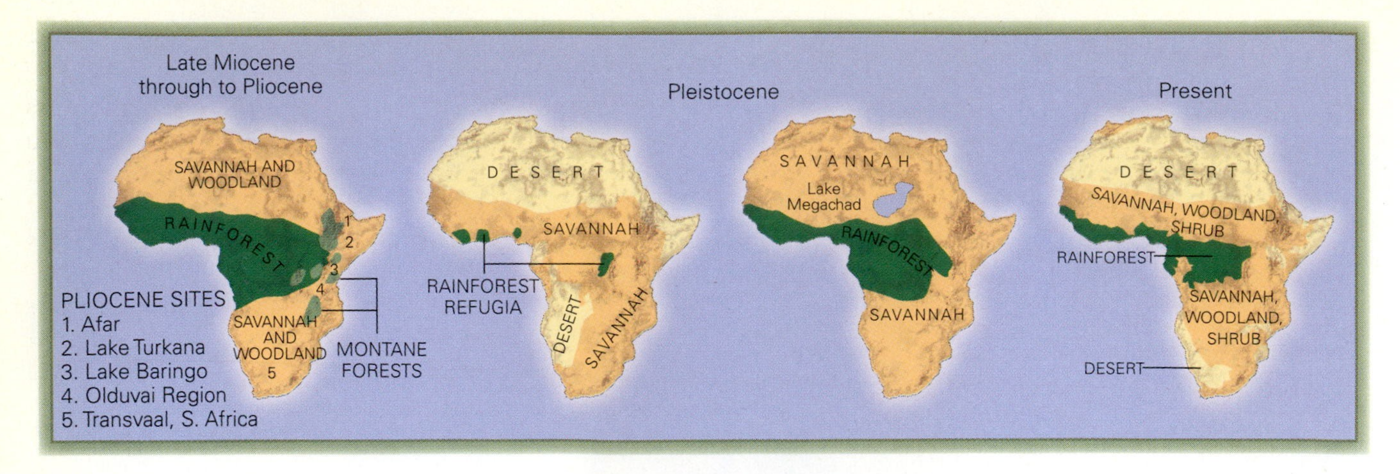

Figure 7.14 Since the late Miocene, the vegetation zones of Africa have changed considerably.

or late in the day, or when it is absent altogether at night. Some, like antelope, are evolved to tolerate high body temperatures that would kill humans due to overheating of the brain tissue. They accomplish this through cooling their blood in their muzzles through evaporation before it enters the vessels leading to the delicate tissues of the brain.

According to Wheeler, the interesting thing about humans and other primates is that

> We can't uncouple brain temperature from the rest of the body, the way an antelope does, so we've got to prevent any damaging elevations in body temperature. And of course the problem is even more acute for an ape, because in general, the larger and more complex the brain, the more easily it is damaged. So, there were incredible selective pressures on early hominids favoring adaptations that would reduce thermal stress-pressures that may have favored bipedalism.[17]

The idea that bipedal posture reduces the amount of heat to which humans are exposed is not completely new, but Wheeler has scientifically studied this phenomenon. He took a systematic series of measurements on the exposure of an early biped, like Lucy, to solar radiation in upright and quadrupedal stances. He found that the bipedal stance reduced exposure to solar radiation by 60 percent, indicating that a biped would require less water to stay cool in a savannah environment compared to a quadruped.

Wheeler further suggests that bipedalism made the human body hair pattern possible. Fur can keep out solar radiation as well as retaining heat. A biped, with reduced exposure to the sun everywhere except the head, would benefit from hair loss on the body surface to increase the efficiency of sweating to cool down. On the head, hair serves as a shield, blocking the solar radiation.

An objection to the above scenario might be that when bipedalism developed, savannah was not as extensive in Africa as it is today (Figure 7.14). In both East and South Africa, environments included closed and open bush and woodlands. Moreover, fossil flora and fauna found with *Ardipithecus* and the possible human ancestors from the Miocene are typical of a moist, closed, wooded habitat.

However, the presence of bipedalism in the fossil record without a savannah environment does not indicate that bipedalism was not adaptive to these conditions. It merely indicates that bipedalism appeared without any particular adaptive benefits at first, likely through a random macromutation. Bipedalism provided a body plan preadapted to the heat stress of the savannah environment.

In an earlier era of human evolutionary studies, larger brains were thought to have permitted the evolution of bipedalism. Around the mid-20th century, theories for the adaptability of bipedalism involved a feedback loop between tool use, brain expansion, and free hands brought about by bipedalism. We now know not only that bipedality preceded the evolution of larger brains by several million years, but we can also consider the possibility that bipedalism may have preadapted human ancestors for brain expansion. According to Wheeler,

> The brain is one of the most metabolically active tissues in the body. . . . In the case of humans it accounts for something like 20 percent of total energy consumption. So you've got an organ producing a lot of heat that you've got to dump. Once we'd become bipedal and naked and achieved this ability to dump heat, that may have allowed the expansion of the brain that took place later in human evolution. It didn't cause it, but you can't have a large brain unless you can cool it.[18]

---

[17] Ibid.

[18] Ibid.

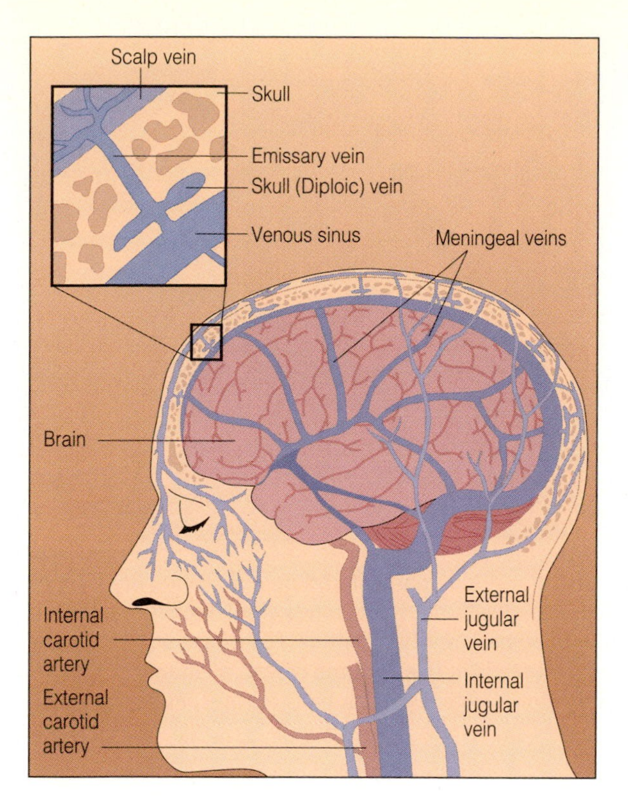

Figure 7.15 **In humans, blood from the face and scalp, instead of returning directly to the heart, may be directed instead into the braincase and then to the heart. Already cooled at the surface of the skin, blood is able to carry heat away from the brain.**

Consistent with Wheeler's hypothesis is the fact that the system for drainage of the blood from the cranium of the earlier australopithecines is significantly different from that of the genus *Homo* (Figure 7.15).

Though paleoanthropologists cannot resolve every detail of the course of human evolution from the available data, over time the narrative they have constructed has improved. Human evolution evidently took place in fits and starts, rather than at a steady pace. Today we know that bipedalism preceded brain expansion by several million years. Bipedalism likely occurred as a sudden shift in body plan, while the tempo for the evolution of brain size differed considerably. For example, fragments of an *Australopithecus* skull dated to 3.9 million years old are virtually identical to the corresponding skull fragments a million years later. Evidently, once a viable bipedal adaptation was achieved, stabilizing selection took over, and there was little change for at least a few million years.

Then, 2.5 mya, change was again in the works, resulting in the branching out of new forms, including several robust species as well as the first appearance of the genus *Homo.* But again, from about 2.3 mya until robust australopithecines became extinct around 1 mya, the robust forms underwent relatively little change.[19]

Evidently, the pattern in early human evolution has been relatively short periods of marked change with diversification, separated by prolonged periods of relative stasis or stability in the surviving species. While robust australopithecines continued this pattern, the new genus *Homo* began a steady course of brain expansion that continued over the next 2.3 million years until brain size reached its current state. With the appearance of this new larger-brained hominin, the first stone tools appear in the archaeological record.

Early Representatives of the Genus *Homo*

Just as the Leakeys thought, Olduvai Gorge with its stone tool assemblages was a good place to search for human ancestors. Part of what is now Olduvai Gorge was once a lake. Almost 2 mya, its shores were inhabited by numerous wild animals including a variety of bipeds. In 1959—when the Leakeys found the bones of the first specimen of robust *Australopithecus boisei* in association with some of these tools and the bones of birds, reptiles, antelopes, and pigs—they thought they had found the remains of one of the toolmakers. Fossils unearthed a few months later and a few feet below this first discovery led them to change their mind.

These fossil remains consisted of more than one individual, including a few cranial bones, a lower jaw, a clavicle, some finger bones (Figure 7.16), and the nearly complete left foot of an adult (Figure 7.17). Skull and jaw fragments indicated that these specimens represented a larger-brained biped without the specialized chewing apparatus of the robust australopithecines.

The Leakeys and colleagues named that contemporary *Homo habilis* (Latin for "handy man") and suggested that tool-wielding *H. habilis* may have eaten the animals and possibly had the *Australopithecus boisei* for dessert. Of course, we do not really know whether *A. boisei* from Olduvai Gorge met its end in this way, but we do know that cut marks from a stone tool are present on a 2.4-million-year-old australopithecine jaw bone from South Africa.[20] This was done, presumably, to remove the mandible, but for what purpose we do not know. In any event, it does lend credibility to the idea of *A. boisei* on occasion being dismembered by *H. habilis.*

Subsequent work at Olduvai has unearthed not only more skull fragments but other parts of the skeleton of

[19] Wood, B., Wood, C., & Konigsberg, L. (1994). *Paranthropus boisei:* An example of evolutionary stasis? *American Journal of Physical Anthropology 95,* 134.

[20] White, T. D., & Toth, N. (2000). Cutmarks on a Plio-Pleistocene hominid from Sterkfontein, South Africa. *American Journal of Physical Anthropology 111,* 579–584.

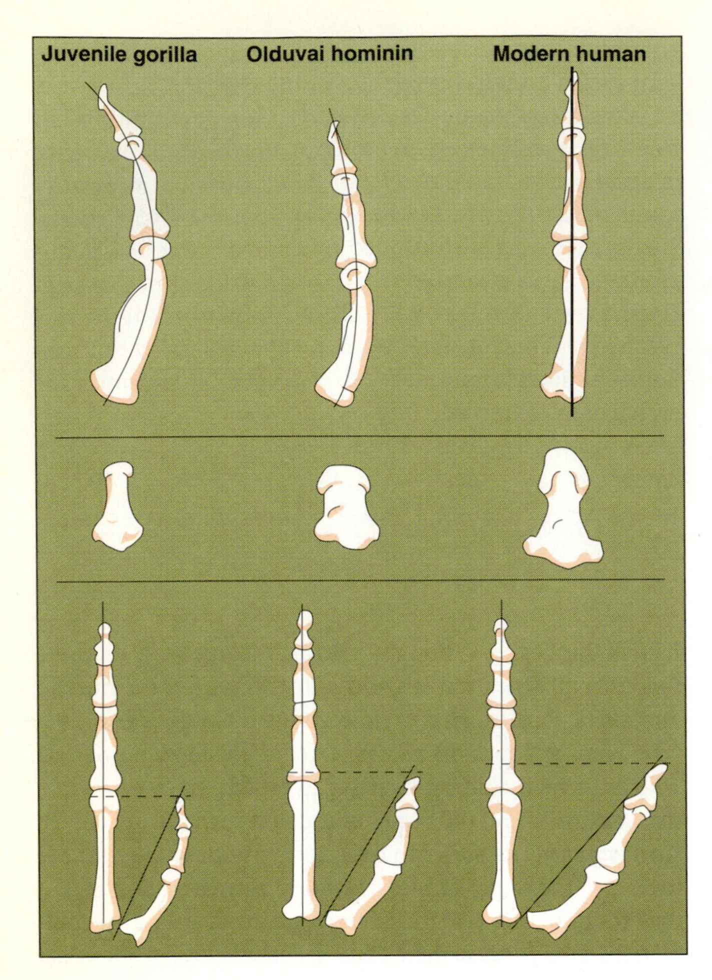

Figure 7.16 A comparison of hand bones of a juvenile gorilla, *Homo habilis* from Olduvai, and a modern human, highlights important differences in the structure of fingers and thumbs. In the top row are fingers, and in the second row are terminal (end) thumb bones. Although terminal finger bones are more human, lower finger bones are more curved and powerful. The bottom row compares thumb length and angle relative to the index finger.

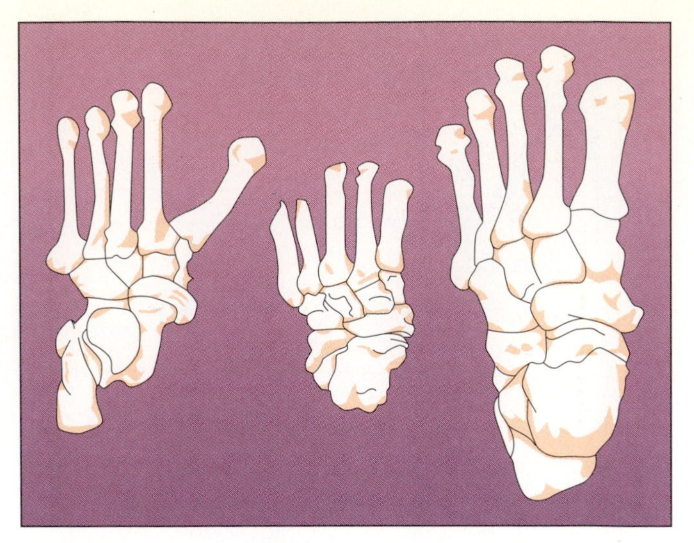

Figure 7.17 A partial foot skeleton of *Homo habilis* (center) is compared with the same bones of a chimpanzee (left) and modern human (right). Note how *H. habilis'* bone at the base of the great toe is in line with the others, as in modern humans, making for effective walking but poor grasping.

H. habilis as well. Since the late 1960s, fossils of the genus *Homo* that are essentially contemporaneous with those from Olduvai have been found elsewhere in Africa, such as South Africa, Ethiopia, and several sites in Kenya.

The eastern shores of Lake Turkana, on the border between Kenya and Ethiopia, have been particularly rich with fossils from earliest *Homo.* One of the best of these fossils, known as KNM ER 1470, was discovered by the Leakeys' son Richard at Koobi Fora. (The letters KNM stand for Kenya National Museum; the ER, for East Rudolf, the name for Lake Turkana during the colonial era in Kenya.) The deposits in which it was found are about 1.9 million years old; these deposits, like those at Olduvai, also contain crude stone tools. The KNM ER 1470 skull is more modern in appearance than any *Australopithecus* skull and has a cranial capacity of 752 cubic centimeters (cc). However, the large teeth and face of this specimen resemble the earlier australopithecines.

From this same site another well-preserved skull from the same time period (KNM ER 1813) possesses a cranial capacity of less than 600 cc but has the derived characteristics of a smaller, less projecting face and teeth (both of these specimens are shown in the photo on page 160). Though specimens attributed to *H. habilis* generally have cranial capacities greater than 600 cc, the cranial capacity of any individual is also in proportion to its body size. Therefore, many paleoanthropologists interpret KNM ER 1813 and ER 1470 as a female and male of a very sexually dimorphic species, with the smaller cranial capacity of KNM ER 1813 a reflection of her smaller body size (Figure 7.18).

Lumpers or Splitters?

Other paleoanthropologists do not agree with placing specimens as diverse as KNM ER 1813 and KNM ER 1470 in the single taxonomic group of *H. habilis.* Instead they feel that the diversity represented in these specimens warrants separating the fossils like the larger-brained KNM ER 1470 into a distinct coexisting group called *Homo*

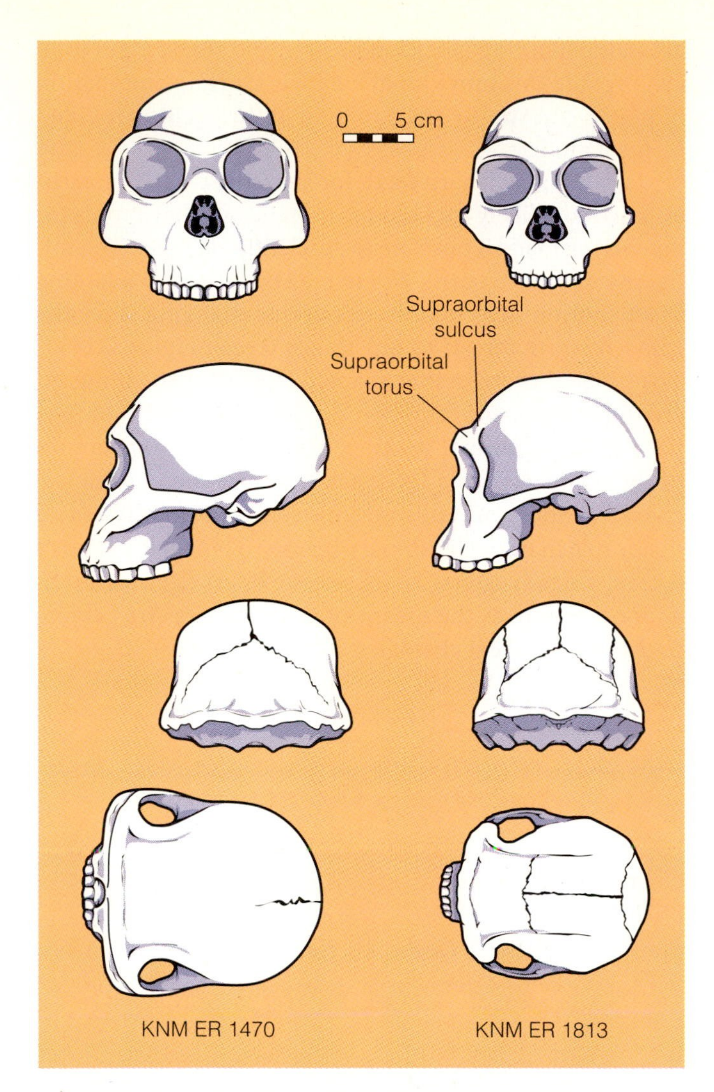

Figure 7.18 The KNM ER 1470 skull—one of the most complete skulls of *Homo habilis*—is close to 2 million years old and is probably a male; it contrasts with the considerably smaller KNM ER 1813 skull, probably a female. Some paleoanthropologists feel this variation is too great to place these specimens in the same species.

rudolphensis. Whether one chooses to call these or any other contemporary fossils *Homo rudolphensis* or *Homo habilis* is more than a name game. Fossil names indicate researchers' perspectives about evolutionary relationships among groups. When specimens are given separate species names, it signifies that they form part of a reproductively isolated group.

Some paleoanthropologists approach the fossil record with the perspective that making such detailed biological determinations is arbitrary and that variability exists within any group.[21] Arguing that it is impossible to prove whether a collection of ancient bones and teeth represents a distinct species, these paleoanthropologists tend to be "lumpers," placing similar-looking fossil specimens together in more inclusive groups. For example, gorillas show a degree of sexual dimorphism that lumpers attribute to *H. habilis.* "Splitters," by contrast, focus on the variation in the fossil record, interpreting minor differences in the shape of skeletons or skulls as evidence of distinct biological species with corresponding cultural capacities. Referring to the variable shape of the bony ridge above ancient eyes, South African paleoanthropologist Philip Tobias has quipped, "Splitters will create a new species at the drop of a brow ridge."[22] Splitting has the advantage of specificity while lumping has the advantage of simplicity. We will use a lumping approach throughout our discussion of the genus *Homo.*

Differences Between Early *Homo* and *Australopithecus*

By 2.4 mya, the evolution of the genus *Homo* was proceeding in a different direction from that of *Australopithecus.* In terms of body size, early *Homo* differs little from *Australopithecus.* Although early *Homo* had teeth that are large by modern standards—or even by those of a half-million years ago—they are smaller in relation to the size of the skull than those of any australopithecine. Early *Homo* also had undergone enlargement of the brain indicating that early *Homo*'s mental abilities probably exceeded those of *Australopithecus.* Early *Homo* likely possessed a marked increase in ability to learn and to process information compared with australopithecines.

The later robust australopithecines from East and South Africa that coexisted with early *Homo* evolved into more specialized "grinding machines" with massive jaws and back teeth for processing plant foods. Robust australopithecine brain size did not change, nor is there firm evidence that they made stone tools. Thus in the period between 1 and 2.5 mya, two kinds of bipeds were headed in very different evolutionary directions: the robust australopithecines, specializing in plant foods and ultimately becoming extinct, and the genus *Homo,* with expanding cranial capacity, a varied diet that included meat, and the earliest evidence for stone tool making.

Without stone tools early *Homo* could eat few animals (only those that could be skinned by tooth or nail); therefore, their diet was limited in terms of animal protein. On the arid savannah, it is hard for a primate with a humanlike digestive system to satisfy its protein requirements from available plant resources. Moreover,

[21] Miller, J. M. A. (2000). Craniofacial variation in *Homo habilis:* An analysis of the evidence for multiple species. *American Journal of Physical Anthropology 112,* 122.

[22] Personal communication.

failure to do so has serious consequences: stunted growth, malnutrition, starvation, and death. Leaves and legumes (nitrogen-fixing plants, familiar modern examples being beans and peas) provide the most readily accessible plant sources of protein. The problem is that these raw plants are difficult for primates to digest; substances in the leaves and legumes cause proteins to pass right through the gut without being absorbed unless cooked.[23]

Chimpanzees have a similar problem when out on the savannah. Even with canine teeth far larger and sharper than ours or those of early *Homo*, chimpanzees frequently have trouble tearing through the skin of other animals.[24] In savannah environments, chimps spend about a third of their time foraging for insects (ants and termites), eggs, and small vertebrate animals. Such animal foods not only are easily digestible, but they provide high-quality proteins that contain all the essential amino acids, the building blocks of protein. No single plant food can provide this nutritional balance. Only a combination of plants can supply the range of amino acids provided by meat alone.

Lacking long, sharp teeth for shearing meat, our earliest ancestors likely foraged for insects, but sharp tools for butchering made it possible to efficiently eat meat. The initial use of tools by early *Homo* may be related to adapting to an environment that we know was changing since the Miocene from forests to grasslands (recall Figure 7.14).[25] The physical changes that adapted bipeds for spending increasing amounts of time on the new grassy terrain may have encouraged tool making. Thus with the appearance of the genus *Homo*, a feedback loop between biological characteristics and cultural innovations began to play a major role in our evolutionary history. This set the human line on a steady course of increasing brain size and a reliance on culture as the means of adaptation, as we explore in detail in the next chapter.

[23] Stahl, A. B. (1984). Hominid dietary selection before fire. *Current Anthropology 25*, 151–168.

[24] Goodall, p. 372.

[25] Behrensmeyer, A. K., et al. (1997). Late Pliocene faunal turnover in the Turkana basin, Kenya, and Ethiopia. *Science 278*, 1589–1594.

Questions for Reflection

1. The spectacular 4.4-million-year-old Ardi specimen has captured our collective imagination. Does the fact that this specimen has a name and a face change how you respond to the scientific facts? How do these ancient bones, which we know as the individual Ardi, challenge us to think about what it means to be human? How does the splash made by Ardi challenge our understanding of the nature of human origin studies?
2. Describe the anatomy of bipedalism, providing examples from head to toe of how bipedalism can be "diagnosed" from a single bone. Do you think evidence from a single bone is enough to determine whether an organism from the past was bipedal?
3. Who were the robust australopithecines? What evidence is used to demonstrate that they are an evolutionary dead end?
4. How do paleoanthropologists decide whether a fossil specimen from the distant past is male or female? Do our cultural ideas about males and females in the present affect the interpretation of behavior in human evolutionary history?
5. Do you think that members of the genera *Ardipithecus* and *Australopithecus* were tool users? What evidence would you use to support a case for tool use in these early bipeds?

Suggested Readings

Falk, D. (2004). *Braindance: New discoveries about human origins and brain evolution—revised and updated.* Gainesville: University Press of Florida.

In this updated and expanded version of her 1994 book, Falk presents her radiator theory to account for the lag between the appearance of bipedalism and the increase in the size of the brain over the course of human evolutionary history.

Johanson, D. C., Edgar, B., & Brill, D. (1996). *From Lucy to language.* New York: Simon & Schuster.

This coffee-table-sized book includes more than 200 color pictures of major fossil discoveries along with a readable, intelligent discussion of many of the key issues in paleoanthropology.

Johanson, D. C., & Wong, K. (2009). *Lucy's legacy: The quest for human origins.* New York: Harmony.

The adventures of fossil hunters and scientific debate both shine in this accessible book. While it begins with Johanson's own discovery of Lucy, the book is notable for its balance. It presents both sides of many of paleoanthropology's recent controversies along with interesting and engaging profiles of the international scientists who are weaving together the story of our evolution.

Larsen, C. S., Matter, R. M., & Gebo, D. L. (1998). *Human origins: The fossil record.* Long Grove, IL: Waveland.

This volume covers all the major fossil discoveries relevant to the study of human origins beginning with the Miocene apes. It has detailed drawings and clear, brief descriptions of each specimen, introducing the reader to the nature of the fossil evidence.

Zimmer, C. (2005). *Smithsonian intimate guide to human origins.* New York: HarperCollins.

This book by science writer Carl Zimmer is an intelligent and engaging presentation of the evidence of human evolution that includes discoveries up to 2005. It is also beautifully illustrated.

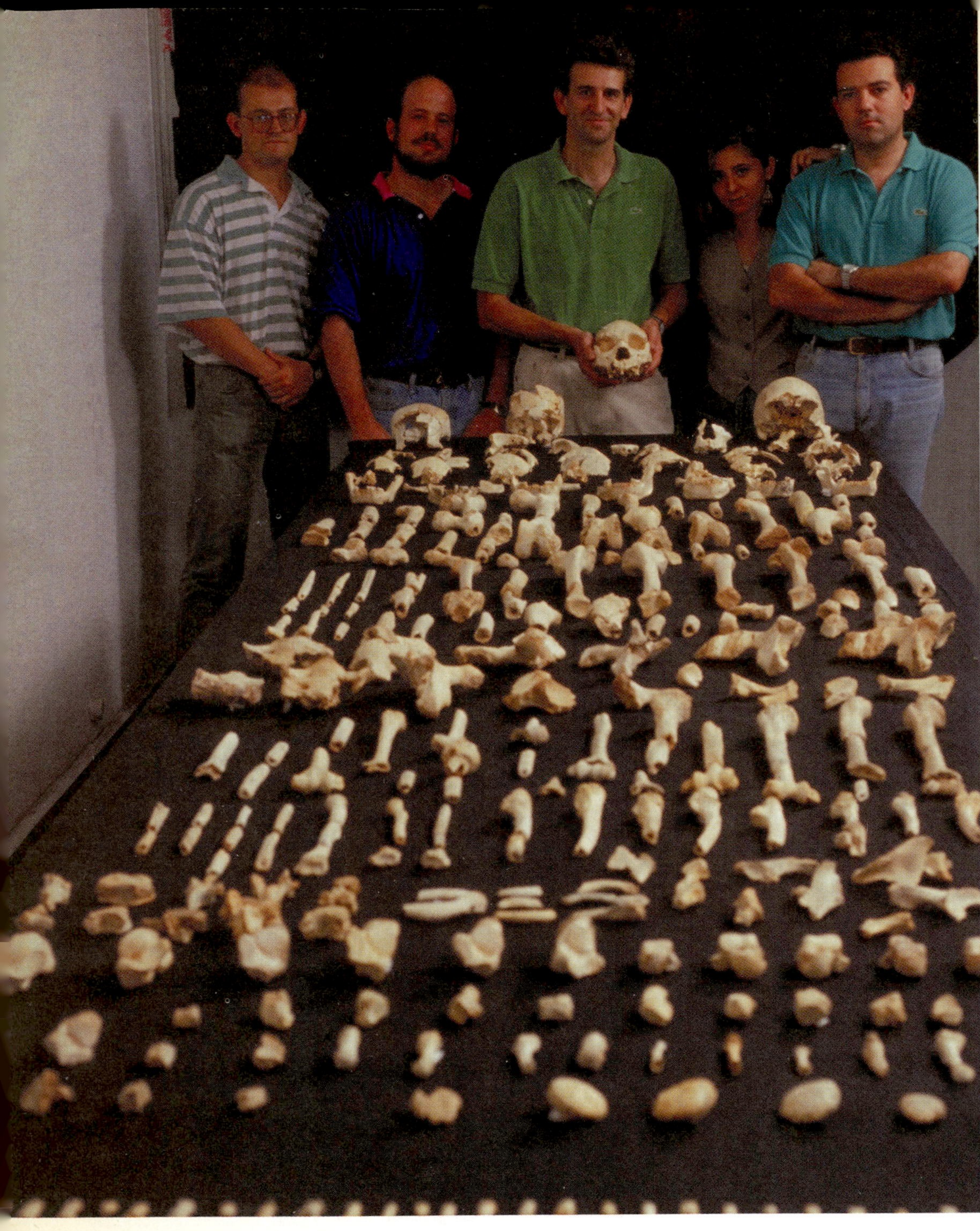

© Javier Trueba/Madrid Scientific Films

Challenge Issue With the appearance of the genus *Homo* 2.5 million years ago, our ancestors—with their increased brain size and emerging cultural repertoire—were better able to meet the challenges of survival. We know that without this brain expansion, reliance on culture could not have occurred, but we are not certain of the exact relationship between biological change and cultural capacity. Does each cultural innovation mark the appearance of a new species? Does a 20 percent increase in brain tissue do the same? And what about all the cultural changes that have occurred after brain size reached modern proportions? These fossils from Sima de los Huesos ("Pit of the Bones"), Sierra de Atapuerca, Spain, are an important part of the puzzle. They are the best collection of *Homo* fossils from a single site. Although the remains possess cranial capacities overlapping with the average size of contemporary humans, the scientists who discovered them place them in the species *Homo antecessor*. Dated to 400,000 years ago, these fossils fit into the complex period of our evolutionary history when brain size and cultural capability began to separate.

CHAPTER 8

Early *Homo* and the Origins of Culture

Chapter Preview

When, Where, and How Did the Genus *Homo* Develop?

Since the late 1960s, a number of sites in South and East Africa have produced the fossil remains of lightly built bipeds all but indistinguishable from the earlier gracile australopithecines, except that the teeth are smaller and the brain is significantly larger relative to body size. The earliest fossils to exhibit these trends appeared around 2.5 million years ago (mya), along with the earliest evidence of stone tool making. *Homo habilis* or "handy man" was the name given to the first members of the genus as a reflection of their toolmaking capacities. While paleoanthropologists debate the number of species of early *Homo* existing during this time period, most concur that the genus *Homo* developed from one of the smaller-brained bipedal australopithecines in Africa by 2.5 mya. By 1.8 mya, brain size along with cultural capabilities increased considerably, marking the appearance of the species *Homo erectus,* a fossil group that appears to have descended through variational change from *H. habilis*. Equipped with larger brains and more sophisticated tools, *H. erectus* spread from Africa into previously uninhabited regions of Eurasia and distinct regional features appear in the fossil record. Paleoanthropologists debate whether this variation constitutes separate species and the relationship of these ancestral forms to modern *Homo sapiens*. The controversy intensifies when it comes to Neandertals, the large-brained, robust, muscular members of the genus *Homo* from Southwest Asia and Europe.

What Were the Cultural Capabilities of Our Ancestors?

The archaeological record, starting with the oldest known artifacts—stone tools dated to between 2.5 and 2.6 mya from Gona, Ethiopia—provides tangible evidence of *H. habilis*' culture in the distant past. These mark the start of the Lower Paleolithic or Lower Stone Age. With the appearance of *H. erectus,* more sophisticated stone tools included the hand axe and other tools of the Acheulean industry along with innovations such as the controlled use of fire (for light, warmth, protection, and cooking), travel across bodies of water, and hunting with specialized tools. The Middle Paleolithic that followed is marked by a diversification of tool types and more sophisticated methods of fabrication. The best-known industry of this period, the Mousterian, began around 166,000 years ago and was used by *all* people—Neandertals as well as other members of the genus *Homo* said to possess more anatomically modern skulls—in Europe, North Africa, and Southwest Asia up until 40,000 years ago.

What Is the Relationship Between Biological Change and Cultural Change in the Genus *Homo*?

Paleoanthropological reconstructions of the culture and behavior of our ancestors are based on evidence about the environment; archaeological remains of tools, hearths, and shelters; and biological data about teeth, musculature, brain size and structure. Paleoanthropologists attribute the cultural change of making stone tools with the biological change of increased brain size because both appear at the same time in archaeological remains and fossil evidence. The fabrication and use of stone tools needed to crack open bones of animals for marrow or to butcher dead animals required improved eye–hand coordination and a precision grip. These behavioral abilities depended on the capacity to learn *and* communicate, which depended on larger, more complex brains. Once the brain size of genus *Homo* reached modern proportions between 200,000 and 400,000 years ago, the clear relationship between cultural capabilities and brain size uncoupled. Some fossil skulls retained a number of ancestral features, as well as some specialized features typically not seen in modern *Homo sapiens*. Archaeological evidence shows that cultures throughout the globe had become rich and varied. These ancient peoples produced tools for specific purposes and objects for purely symbolic use; they also practiced ceremonial activities and cared for the old and disabled.

Paleoanthropologists are faced with evidence that is often scant, enigmatic, or full of misleading and even contradictory clues. The quest for the origin of modern humans from more ancient bipeds confronts mysteries, none of which has been completely resolved to this day.

Some of the mystery stems from the kind of evolutionary change that was set in motion with the appearance of the genus ***Homo.*** Beginning 2.5 mya, several million years after the appearance of bipedalism separated the human evolutionary line from those of the other African apes, brain size of our ancestors began to increase. Simultaneously, these early ancestors increased their cultural manipulation of the physical world through their use of stone tools. These new bipeds were the first members of the genus *Homo.* Over time, they increasingly relied on cultural adaptation as a rapid and effective way to adjust to the environment.

While the evolution of culture became critical for human survival, it was intricately tied to underlying biological capacities, specifically the evolution of the human brain. Over the course of the next 2.2 million years, increasing brain size and specialization of function (evidence preserved in fossilized skulls) permitted the development of language, planning, new technologies, and artistic expression. With the evolution of a brain that made versatile behavior possible, members of the genus *Homo* became biocultural beings.

Biological anthropologist Misia Landau has noted that the human being can be thought of as the hero in the narrative of human evolutionary history.[1] The hero, or evolving human, is faced with a series of natural challenges that cannot be overcome from a strictly biological standpoint. Endowed with the gift of intelligence, the hero can meet these challenges and become fully human. In this narrative, cultural capabilities increasingly separate humans from other evolving animals. But biological change and cultural change are very different phenomena. Cultural equipment and techniques can develop rapidly with innovations occurring during the lifetime of individuals. By contrast, because it depends upon heritable traits, biological change requires many generations.

Paleoanthropologists consider whether an evident cultural change, such as a new type of stone tool, corresponds to a major biological change, such as the appearance of a new species. Reconciling the relation between biological and cultural change is often a source of debate within paleoanthropology.

The Discovery of the First Stone Toolmaker

The renowned paleoanthropologists Louis and Mary Leakey began their search for human origins at Olduvai Gorge, Tanzania, because of the presence of crude stone tools found there. The tools were found in deposits dating back to very early in the Pleistocene epoch, which began almost 2 mya. The oldest tools found at Olduvai Gorge defined the **Oldowan tool tradition.**

These earliest identifiable tools consist of a number of implements made using a system of manufacture called the **percussion method** (Figure 8.1). Sharp-edged flakes were obtained from a stone (often a large, waterworn cobble) either by using another stone as a hammer (a hammerstone) or by striking the cobble against a large rock (anvil) to remove the flakes. The finished flakes had

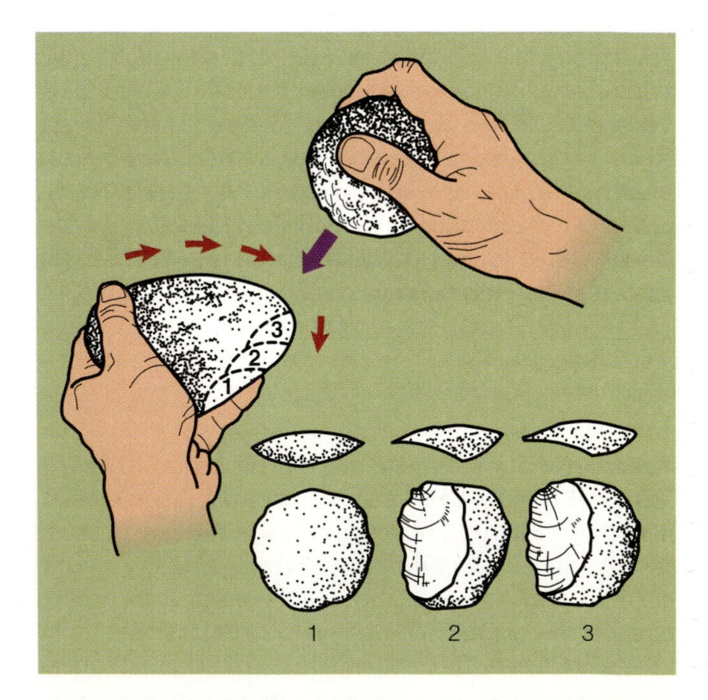

Figure 8.1 By 2.5 million years ago, early *Homo* in Africa had invented the percussion method of stone tool manufacture. This technological breakthrough, which is associated with a significant increase in brain size, made possible the butchering of meat from scavenged carcasses.

[1] Landau, M. (1991). *Narratives of human evolution.* New Haven, CT: Yale University Press.

Homo The genus of bipeds that appeared 2.5 million years ago, characterized by increased brain size compared to earlier bipeds. The genus is divided into various species based on features such as brain size, skull shape, and cultural capabilities.

Oldowan tool tradition The first stone tool industry, beginning between 2.5 and 2.6 million years ago.

percussion method A technique of stone tool manufacture performed by striking the raw material with a hammerstone or by striking raw material against a stone anvil to remove flakes.

sharp edges, effective for cutting and scraping. Microscopic wear patterns show that these flakes were used for cutting meat, reeds, sedges, and grasses and for cutting and scraping wood. Small indentations on their surfaces suggest that the leftover cores were transformed into choppers for breaking open bones, and they may also have been employed to defend the user. The appearance of these tools marks the beginning of the **Lower Paleolithic,** the first part of the Old Stone Age.

The tools from Olduvai Gorge are not the oldest stone tools known. Paleoanthropologists have dated the start of the Lower Paleolithic to between 2.5 and 2.6 mya from similar assemblages recently discovered in Gona, Ethiopia. Lower Paleolithic tools have also been found in the vicinity of Lake Turkana in northwestern Kenya, in southern Ethiopia, as well as in other sites near Gona in the Afar Triangle of Ethiopia. Before this time, tool use among early bipeds probably consisted of heavy sticks to dig up roots or ward off animals, unshaped stones to throw for defense or to crack open nuts, and perhaps simple carrying devices made of knotted plant fibers. Perishable tools are not preserved in the archaeological record.

The makers of these early tools were highly skilled, consistently and efficiently producing many well-formed sharp-edged flakes from available raw materials with the least effort.[2] To do this the toolmaker had to have in mind an abstract idea of the tool to be made, as well as a specific set of steps to transform the raw material into finished product. Furthermore, the toolmaker would have to know which kinds of stone have the flaking properties that would allow the transformation to take place, as well as where such stone could be found.

Sometimes tool fabrication required the transport of raw materials over great distances. Such planning for the future undoubtedly was associated with natural selection favoring changes in brain structure. These changes mark the beginning of the genus *Homo*. As described in the previous chapter, ***Homo habilis*** was the name given to the oldest members of the genus by the Leakeys in 1959. With larger brains and the stone tools

The oldest stone tools, dated to between 2.5 and 2.6 mya, were discovered in Gona, Ethiopia, by Ethiopian paleoanthropologist Sileshi Semaw.

preserved in the archaeological record, paleoanthropologists began to piece together a picture of the life of early *Homo*.

Sex, Gender, and the Behavior of Early *Homo*

When paleoanthropologists from the 1960s and 1970s depicted the lifeways of early *Homo,* they concentrated on "man the hunter," a tough guy with a killer instinct wielding tools on a savannah teeming with meat, while

Lower Paleolithic The first part of the Old Stone Age beginning with the earliest Oldowan tools spanning from about 200,000 or 250,000 to 2.6 million years ago.

Homo habilis "Handy man." The first fossil members of the genus *Homo* appearing 2.5 million years ago, with larger brains and smaller faces than australopithecines.

[2] Ambrose, S. H. (2001). Paleolithic technology and human evolution. *Science 291,* 1749.

In this artist's reconstruction separate roles are portrayed for males and females from early *Homo*. Do the roles depicted here derive from biological differences between the sexes or culturally established gender differences?

the female members of the species stayed at home tending their young. Similarly, until the 1960s, most cultural anthropologists doing fieldwork among foragers stressed the role of male hunters and underreported the significance of female gatherers in providing food for the community. Western notions of **gender,** the cultural elaborations and meanings assigned to the biological differentiation between the sexes, played a substantial role in creating these biases.

gender The cultural elaborations and meanings assigned to the biological differentiation between the sexes.

As anthropologists became aware of their own biases, they began to set the record straight, documenting the vital role of "woman the gatherer" in provisioning the social group in foraging cultures, past and present. (See this chapter's Biocultural Connection for the specific

Biocultural Connection

Sex, Gender, and Female Paleoanthropologists

Until the 1970s, the study of human evolution was permeated by a deep-seated bias reflecting the privileged status enjoyed by men in Western society. Beyond the obvious labeling of fossils as particular types of "men," irrespective of the sex of the individual represented, it took the form of portraying males as the active players in human evolution. Thus it was males who were seen as providers and innovators, using their wits to become ever-more effective suppliers of food and protection for passive females. The latter were seen as spending their time preparing food and caring for offspring, while the men were getting ahead by becoming ever smarter. Central to such thinking was the idea of "man the hunter," constantly honing his wits through the pursuit and killing of animals. Thus hunting by men was seen as the pivotal humanizing activity in evolution.

We now know that such ideas are culture-bound, reflecting the hopes and expectations of Euramerican culture in the late 19th and early 20th centuries. This recognition came in the 1970s and was a direct consequence of the entry of a number of highly capable women into the profession of paleoanthropology.

Up until the 1960s, there were few women in any field of physical anthropology, but with the expansion of graduate programs and changing attitudes toward the role of women in society, increasing numbers of women went on to earn doctorates. One of these was Adrienne Zihlman, who earned her doctorate at the University of California at Berkeley in 1967. Subsequently, she authored a number of important papers critical of "man the hunter" scenarios. She was not the first to do so; as early as 1971, Sally Linton had published a preliminary paper on "woman the gatherer," but it was Zihlman who from 1976 on especially elaborated on the importance of female activities for human evolution. Others have joined in the effort, including Zihlman's companion in graduate school and later colleague, Nancy Tanner, who wrote some papers with Zihlman and has produced important works of her own.

The work of Zihlman and her co-workers was crucial in forcing a reexamination of existing "man the hunter" scenarios; this produced recognition of the importance of scavenging in early human evolution as well as the value of female gathering and other activities.

Although there is still plenty to learn about human evolution, thanks to these women we now know that it was not a case of females being "uplifted" as a consequence of their association with progressively evolving males. Rather, the two sexes evolved together, with each making its own important contribution to the process.

BIOCULTURAL QUESTION

Can you think of any examples of how gender norms are influencing theories about the biological basis of male and female behavior today?

contributions of female paleoanthropologists.) The division of labor among contemporary food foragers, like all gender relations, does not conform to fixed boundaries defined through biologically based sex differences. Instead, it is influenced by cultural and environmental factors. It appears likely that the same principle applied to our human ancestors. Uncovering such biases is as important as any new discovery for interpreting the fossil record.

Evidence from chimpanzees and bonobos casts further doubt on the notion of a strict sex-based division of labor in human evolutionary history. As described in Chapter 4, female chimpanzees have been observed participating in hunting expeditions, even leading the behavior of hunting with spears. Meat gained from the successful hunt of a smaller mammal is shared within the group whether provided by a male or a female chimpanzee. Among bonobos, females hunt regularly and share meat as well as plant foods with one another. In other words, patterns of food sharing and hunting behaviors in these apes are variable, lending credit to the notion that culture plays a role in establishing these behaviors. Similarly, in our evolutionary history it is likely that culture—the shared learned behaviors of each early *Homo* group—played a role in food-sharing behaviors rather than strict biological differences between the sexes.

No evidence exists to establish definitively how procured foods may have been shared among our ancestors. When the evidence is fragmentary, as it is in all paleoanthropological reconstructions of behavior, gaps are all too easily filled in with behaviors that seem "natural" and familiar, such as the contemporary gender roles of the paleoanthropologist.

Hunters or Scavengers?

As biases in paleoanthropological interpretations were addressed, it became clear that early members of the genus *Homo* were not hunters of large game. Assemblages of Oldowan tools and broken animal bones tell us that both *H. habilis* and large carnivorous animals were active at these locations. In addition to marks on the bones made by slicing, scraping, and chopping with stone tools, there are tooth marks from gnawing. Some of the gnawing marks overlie the butcher marks, indicating that enough flesh remained on the bones after *Homo* was done with them to attract other carnivores. In other cases, though, the butcher marks overlie the tooth marks of carnivores, indicating that the animals got there first. This is what we would expect if *H. habilis* was scavenging the kills of other animals, rather than doing its own killing.

Further, areas that appear to be ancient butchering sites lack whole carcasses; apparently, only parts were transported away from the original location where they were obtained—again, the pattern that we would expect if they were "stolen" from the kill of some other animal. The stone tools, too, were made of raw material procured at distances of up to 60 kilometers from where they were used to process pieces of carcasses. Finally, the incredible density of bones at some of the sites and patterns of weathering indicate that the sites were used repeatedly for perhaps five to fifteen years.

By contrast, historically known and contemporary hunters typically bring whole carcasses back to camp or form camp around a large animal in order to fully process it. After processing, neither meat nor **marrow** (the fatty nutritious tissue inside long bones where blood cells are produced) are left. The bones themselves are broken up not just to get at the marrow (as at Oldowan sites) but to fabricate tools and other objects of bone (unlike at Oldowan sites).

The picture that emerges of our Oldowan forebears, then, is of scavengers, getting their meat from the Lower Paleolithic equivalent of modern-day roadkill, taking the spoils of their scavenging to particular places where tools, and the raw materials for making them (often procured from faraway sources), had been stockpiled in advance for the purpose of butchering. At the least, this may have required fabrication of carrying devices such as net bags and trail signs of the sort (described in Chapter 4) used by modern bonobos. Quite likely, *H. habilis* continued to sleep in trees or rocky cliffs, as do modern small-bodied terrestrial or semi-terrestrial primates, in order to be safe from predators.

Microscopic analysis of cut marks on bones has revealed that the earliest members of the genus *Homo* were actually **tertiary scavengers**—that is, third in line to get something from a carcass after a lion or leopard managed to kill some prey. After the initial kill, ferocious scavengers, such as hyenas and vultures, would swarm the rotting carcass. Next, our tool-wielding ancestors would scavenge for food, breaking open the shafts of long bones to get at the rich marrow inside. A small amount of marrow is a concentrated source of both protein and fat. Muscle alone, particularly from lean game animals, contains very little fat. Furthermore, as shown in the following Original Study, evolving humans may even have been prey themselves, and this selective pressure imposed by predators played a role in brain expansion.

marrow The tissue inside of long bones where blood cells are produced.

tertiary scavenger In a food chain, the third animal group (second to scavenge) to obtain meat from a kill made by a predator.

Original Study

Humans as Prey *by Donna Hart*

There's little doubt that humans, particularly those in Western cultures, think of themselves as the dominant form of life on earth. And we seldom question whether that view holds true for our species' distant past. . . . We swagger like the toughest kids on the block as we spread our technology over the landscape and irrevocably change it for other species.

. . . The vision of our utter superiority may even hold true for the last 500 years, but that's just the proverbial blink of an eye when compared to the 7 million years that our hominid ancestors wandered the planet.

"Where did we come from?" and "What were the first humans like?" are questions that have been asked since Darwin first proposed his theory of evolution. One commonly accepted answer is that our early ancestors were killers of other species and of their own kind, prone to violence and even cannibalism. In fact a club-swinging "Man the Hunter" is the stereotype of early humans that permeates literature, film, and even much scientific writing.

. . . Even the great paleontologist Louis S. B. Leakey endorsed it when he emphatically declared that we were not "cat food." Another legendary figure in the annals of paleontology, Raymond A. Dart, launched the killer-ape-man scenario in the mid-20th century. . . .

Dart had interpreted the finds in South African caves of fossilized bones from savannah herbivores together with damaged hominid skulls as evidence that our ancestors had been hunters. The fact that the skulls were battered in a peculiar fashion led to Dart's firm conviction that violence and cannibalism on the part of killer ape-men formed the stem from which our own species eventually flowered. In his 1953 article "The Predatory Transition from Ape to Man," Dart wrote that early hominids were "carnivorous creatures, that seized living quarries by violence, battered them to death, tore apart their broken bodies, [and] dismembered them limb from limb, . . . greedily devouring livid writhing flesh."

But what is the evidence for Man the Hunter? Could smallish, upright creatures with relatively tiny canine teeth and flat nails instead of claws, and with no tools or weapons in the earliest millennia, really have been deadly predators? Is it possible that our ancestors lacked the spirit of cooperation and desire for social harmony? We have only two reliable sources to consult for clues: the fossilized remains of the human family tree, and the behaviors and ecological relationships of our living primate relatives.

© J & B Photos/Animals, Animals

Whether hunters or hunted, early *Homo* was in competition with formidable adversaries like hyenas. Communication and cooperation helped early *Homo* avoid carnivores that saw them as prey.

When we investigate those two sources, a different view of humankind emerges. First, consider the hominid fossils that have been discovered. Dart's first and most famous find, the cranium of an *Australopithecus* child who died over 2 million years ago (called the "Taung child" after the quarry in which the fossil was unearthed), has been reassessed by Lee Berger and Ron Clarke of the University of the Witwatersrand, in light of recent research on eagle predation. The same marks that occur on the Taung cranium are found on the remains of similarly sized African monkeys eaten today by crowned hawk eagles, known to clutch the monkeys' heads with their sharp talons.

C. K. Brain, a South African paleontologist like Dart, started the process of relabeling Man the Hunter as Man the Hunted when he slid the lower fangs of a fossil leopard into perfectly matched punctures in the skull of another australopithecine, who lived between 1 million and 2 million years ago. The paradigm change initiated by Brain continues to stimulate reassessment of hominid fossils.

The idea that our direct ancestor *Homo erectus* practiced cannibalism was based on the gruesome disfigurement of faces and brain-stem areas in a cache of skulls a half-million years old, found in the Zhoukoudian cave, in China. How else to explain these strange manipulations except as relics of Man the Hunter? But studies over the past few years by Noel T. Boaz and Russell L. Ciochon—of the Ross University School of Medicine and the University of Iowa, respectively—show that extinct giant hyenas could have left the marks as they crunched their way into the brains of their hominid prey.

The list of our ancestors' fossils showing evidence of predation continues to grow. A 1.75-million-year-old hominid skull unearthed in the Republic of Georgia shows punctures from the fangs of a saber-toothed cat. Another skull, about 900,000 years old, found in Kenya, exhibits carnivore bite marks on the brow ridge. . . . Those and other fossils provide rock-hard proof that a host of large, fierce animals preyed on human ancestors.

It is equally clear that, outside the West, no small amount of predation occurs today on modern humans. Although we are not likely to see these facts in American newspaper headlines, each year 3,000 people in sub-Saharan Africa are eaten by crocodiles, and 1,500 Tibetans are killed by bears about the size of grizzlies. In one Indian state between 1988 and 1998, over 200 people were attacked by leopards; 612 people were killed by tigers in the Sundarbans delta of India and Bangladesh between 1975 and 1985. The carnivore zoologist Hans Kruuk, of the University of Aberdeen, studied death records in eastern Europe and concluded that wolf predation on humans is still a fact of life in the region, as it was until the 19th century in western European countries like France and Holland.

The fact that humans and their ancestors are and were tasty meals for a wide range of predators is further supported by research on nonhuman primate species still in existence. My study of predation found that 178 species of predatory animals included primates in their diets. The predators ranged from tiny but fierce birds to 500-pound crocodiles, with a little of almost everything in between: tigers, lions, leopards, jaguars, jackals, hyenas, genets, civets, mongooses, Komodo dragons, pythons, eagles, hawks, owls, and even toucans.

Our closest genetic relatives, chimpanzees and gorillas, are prey to humans and other species. Who would have thought that gorillas, weighing as much as 400 pounds, would end up as cat food? Yet Michael Fay, a researcher with the Wildlife Conservation Society and the National Geographic Society, has found the remnants of a gorilla in leopard feces in the Central African Republic. Despite their obvious intelligence and strength, chimpanzees often fall victim to leopards and lions. In the Tai Forest in the Ivory Coast, Christophe Boesch, of the Max Planck Institute, found that over 5 percent of the chimp population in his study was consumed by leopards annually. Takahiro Tsukahara reported, in a 1993 article, that 6 percent of the chimpanzees in the Mahale Mountains National Park of Tanzania may fall victim to lions.

The theory of Man the Hunter as our archetypal ancestor isn't supported by archaeological evidence, either. Lewis R. Binford, one of the most influential figures in archaeology during the last half of the 20th century, dissented from the hunting theory on the ground that reconstructions of early humans as hunters were based on a priori positions and not on the archaeological record. Artifacts that would verify controlled fire and weapons, in particular, are lacking until relatively recent dates. . . .

And, of course, there's also the problem of how a small hominid could subdue a large herbivore. . . . Large-scale, systematic hunting of big herbivores for meat may not have occurred any earlier than 60,000 years ago—over 6 million years after the first hominids evolved.

What I am suggesting, then, is a less powerful, more ignominious beginning for our species. Consider this alternate image: smallish beings (adult females maybe weighing 60 pounds, with males a bit heavier), not overly analytical because their brain-to-body ratio was rather small, possessing the ability to stand and move upright, who basically spent millions of years as meat walking around on two legs. Rather than Man the Hunter, we may need to visualize ourselves as more like Giant Hyena Chow, or Protein on the Go.

Our species began as just one of many that had to be careful, to depend on other group members, and to communicate danger. We were quite simply small beasts within a large and complex ecosystem.

Is Man the Hunter a cultural construction of the West? Belief in a sinful, violent ancestor does fit nicely with Christian views of original sin and the necessity to be saved from our own awful, yet natural, desires. Other religions don't necessarily emphasize the ancient savage in the human past; indeed, modern-day hunter–gatherers, who have to live as part of nature, hold animistic beliefs in which humans are a part of the web of life, not superior creatures who dominate or ravage nature and each other.

Think of Man the Hunted, and you put a different face on our past. . . . We needed to live in groups (like most other primates) and work together to avoid predators. Thus an urge to cooperate can clearly be seen as a functional tool rather than a Pollyannaish nicety, and deadly competition among individuals or nations may be highly aberrant behavior, not hard-wired survival techniques. The same is true of our destructive domination of the earth by technological toys gone mad.

Raymond Dart declared that "the loathsome cruelty of mankind to man . . . is explicable only in terms of his carnivorous, and cannibalistic origin." But if our origin was not carnivorous and cannibalistic, we have no excuse for loathsome behavior. Our earliest evolutionary history is not pushing us to be awful bullies. Instead, our millions of years as prey suggest that we should be able to take our heritage of cooperation and interdependency to make a brighter future for ourselves and our planet.

Adapted from Hart, D. (2006, April 21). Humans as prey. Chronicle of Higher Education.

Whether as hunters or as the hunted, brain expansion and tool use played a significant role in the evolution of the genus *Homo*. The advanced preparation for meat processing implied by the storing of stone tools, and the raw materials for making them, attest to considerable foresight, an ability to plan ahead, and cooperation among our ancestors.

Brain Size and Diet

From its appearance 2.5 mya until about 200,000 years ago, the genus began a course of brain expansion through variational change (see Chapter 6) that continued until about 200,000 years ago. By this point, brain size had approximately tripled, reaching the proportion of contemporary people. The cranial capacity of the largely plant-eating *Australopithecus* ranged from 310 to 530 cubic centimeters (cc); that of the earliest known meat eater, *Homo habilis* from East Africa, ranged from 580 to 752 cc; whereas *Homo erectus*, who eventually hunted as well as scavenged for meat, possessed a cranial capacity of 775 to 1,225 cc.

Larger brains, in turn, required parallel improvements in diet. The energy demands of nerve tissue, of which the brain is made, are high—higher, in fact, than the demands of other types of tissue in the human body. Although a mere 2 percent of body weight, the brain accounts for about 20 to 25 percent of energy consumed at resting metabolic rate in modern human adults.[3] One can meet

[3] Leigh, S. R., & Park, P. B. (1998). Evolution of human growth prolongation. *American Journal of Physical Anthropology 107,* 347.

the brain's energy demands on a vegetarian diet, but the overall energy content of a given amount of plant food is generally less than that of the same amount of meat. Large animals that live on plant foods, such as gorillas, spend all day munching on plants to maintain their large bodies. Meat eaters, by contrast, have no need to eat so much, or so often. Consequently, meat-eating bipeds of both sexes may have had more leisure time available to explore and manipulate their environment.

The archaeological record provides us with a tangible record of our ancestors' cultural abilities that corresponds with the simultaneous biological expansion of the brain. Tool making itself puts a premium on manual dexterity, precision, and fine manipulation (Figure 8.2). Stone tools provide evidence of handedness that bespeaks specialization and lateralization of the brain associated with language.

Beginning with the appearance of the genus *Homo* in Africa 2.5 mya, increasing brain size and increasing cultural development each presumably acted to promote the other. The behaviors made possible by larger brains conferred advantages to large-brained individuals, increasing their reproductive success. Over time, large-brained individuals contributed more to successive generations, so that the population evolved to a larger-brained form. Natural selection for increases in learning ability thus led to the evolution of larger and more complex brains over about 2 million years.

Though it preceded increases in brain size by several million years, bipedalism set the stage for the evolution of large brains and human culture. It freed the hands for activities such as tool making and carrying of resources or infants. This new body plan, bipedalism, opened new opportunities for change.

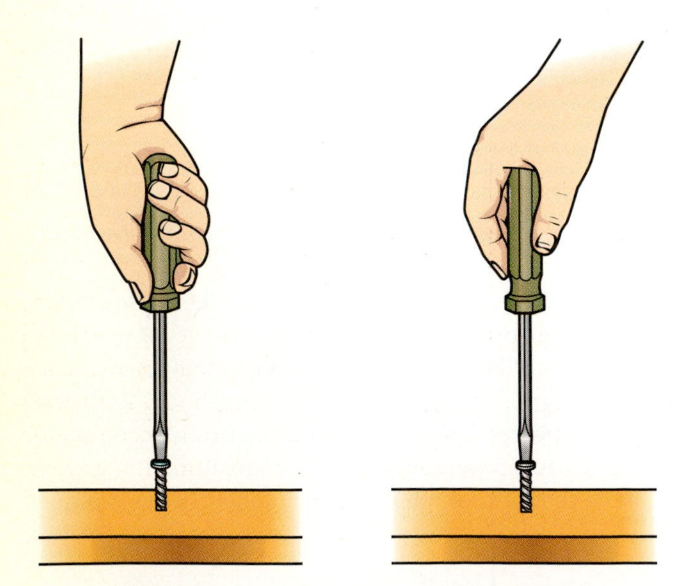

Figure 8.2 **A power grip (left) utilizes more of the hand while the precision grip (right) relies on the fingers for control, requiring corresponding organizational changes in the brain.**

Homo erectus

In 1887, long before the discovery of *Australopithecus* and early *Homo* in Africa, the Dutch physician Eugenè Dubois set out to find the missing link between humans and apes. The presence of humanlike orangutans in the Dutch East Indies (now Indonesia) led him to start his search there. He joined the colonial service as an army surgeon and set sail.

When Dubois found fossilized remains consisting of a skull cap, a few teeth, and a thighbone at Trinil, on the island of Java, the features seemed to him part ape, part human. The flat skull with its low forehead and enormous brow ridges was like that of an ape; but at about 775 cubic centimeters it possessed a cranial capacity much larger than an ape's, even though small by modern human standards. The femur, or thighbone, was clearly human in shape, and its proportions indicated the creature was a biped. Believing that his specimens represented the missing link and that the thighbone indicated this creature was bipedal, Dubois named his find *Pithecanthropus erectus* (from the Greek *pithekos* meaning "ape," *anthropus* meaning "man") or "erect ape-man." Dubois used the genus name proposed in a paper by the German zoologist Ernst Haeckel, a strong supporter of Darwin's theory of evolution.

As with the Taung child, the first australopithecine discovered in the 1920s, many in the scientific community ridiculed and criticized Dubois's claim, suggesting instead that the apelike skull and humanlike femur came from different individuals. Controversy surrounded these specimens throughout Dubois's lifetime. He eventually retreated from the controversy, keeping the fossil specimens stored safely under the floorboards of his dining room. Ultimately, the discovery of more fossils provided enough evidence to fully support his claim. In the 1950s, the Trinil skull cap and similar specimens from Indonesia and China were assigned to the species *Homo erectus* because they were more human than apelike.

Fossils of *Homo erectus*

Until about 1.8 mya, Africa was the only home to the bipedal primates. It was on this continent that the first bipeds and the genus *Homo* originated. It was also in Africa that the first stone tools were invented. But by the time of *H. erectus,* members of the genus *Homo* had begun to spread far beyond their original homeland. Fossils of this species are now known from a number of localities not just in Africa, but in China, western Europe, Georgia (in the Caucasus Mountains), and India, as well as Java (Figure 8.3).

Although remains of *H. erectus* have been found in many different places in three continents, "lumpers," as discussed in the last chapter, emphasize that they are

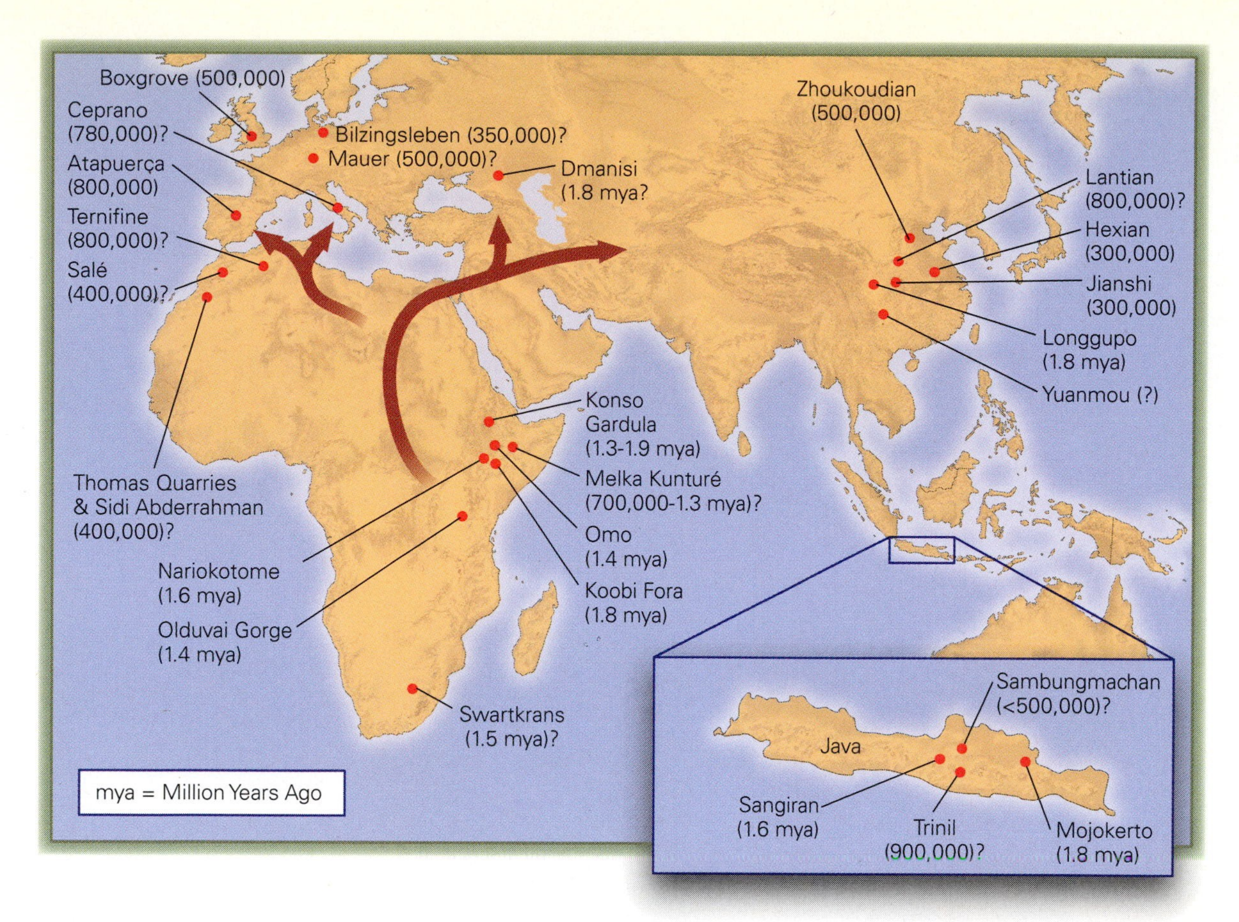

Figure 8.3 **Sites, with dates, at which *Homo erectus* remains have been found. The arrows indicate the proposed routes by which *Homo* spread from Africa to Eurasia.**

unified by a number of shared characteristics. However, because the fossil evidence also suggests some differences within and among populations of *H. erectus* inhabiting discrete regions of Africa, Asia, and Europe, "splitters" prefer to divide *H. erectus* into multiple distinct groups, limiting the species *H. erectus* only to the specimens from Asia. In this taxonomic scheme *Homo ergaster* is used for African specimens from the early Pleistocene period that others describe as early *H. erectus* (Table 8.1).

Regardless of species designation, it is clear that beginning 1.8 mya these larger-brained members of the genus *Homo* not only lived in Africa but also had spread to Eurasia. Fossil specimens dating to 1.8 million years old have been recovered from Dmanisi, Georgia, as well as from Mojokerto, Indonesia. Many additional specimens have been found at a variety of sites in Europe and Asia.

Physical Characteristics of *Homo erectus*

Characteristic features of *H. erectus* are best known from the skull. Cranial capacity in *H. erectus* ranges from 600 to 1,225 cc (average about 1,000 cc). Thus cranial capacity overlaps with the nearly 2-million-year-old KNM ER 1470 skull from

Table 8.1 **Alternate Species Designations for *Homo erectus* Fossils from Eurasia and Africa**

Name	Explanation
Homo ergaster	Some paleoanthropologists feel that the large-brained successors to *H. habilis* from Africa and Asia are too different to be placed in the same species. Therefore, they use *H. ergaster* for the African specimens, saving *H. erectus* for the Asian fossils. Some paleoanthropologists place the recent discoveries from Dmanisi into this taxon.
Homo antecessor	This name was coined by "splitters" for the earliest *Homo* fossils from western Europe discovered in Spain; *antecessor* is Latin for "explorer" or "pioneer."
Homo heidelbergensis	Originally coined for the Mauer jaw (Mauer is not far from Heidelberg, Germany), this name is now used by some as a designation for all European fossils from about 500,000 years ago until the appearance of the Neandertals.

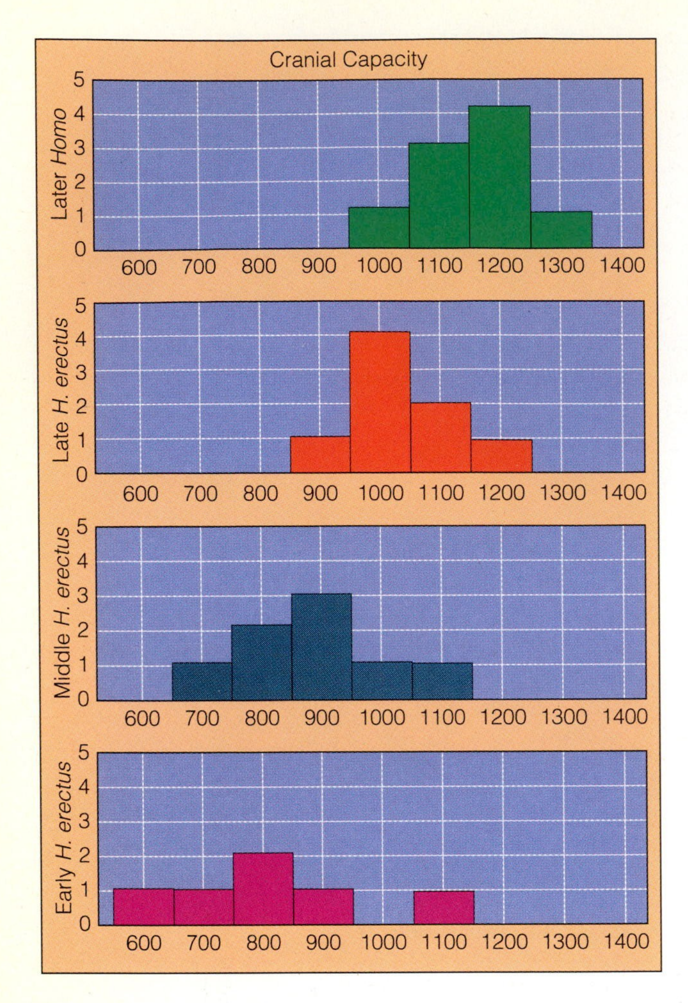

Figure 8.4 Cranial capacity in *Homo erectus* increased over time, as illustrated by these bar graphs, shown in cubic centimeters. The cranial capacity of late *Homo erectus* overlaps with the range seen in live humans.

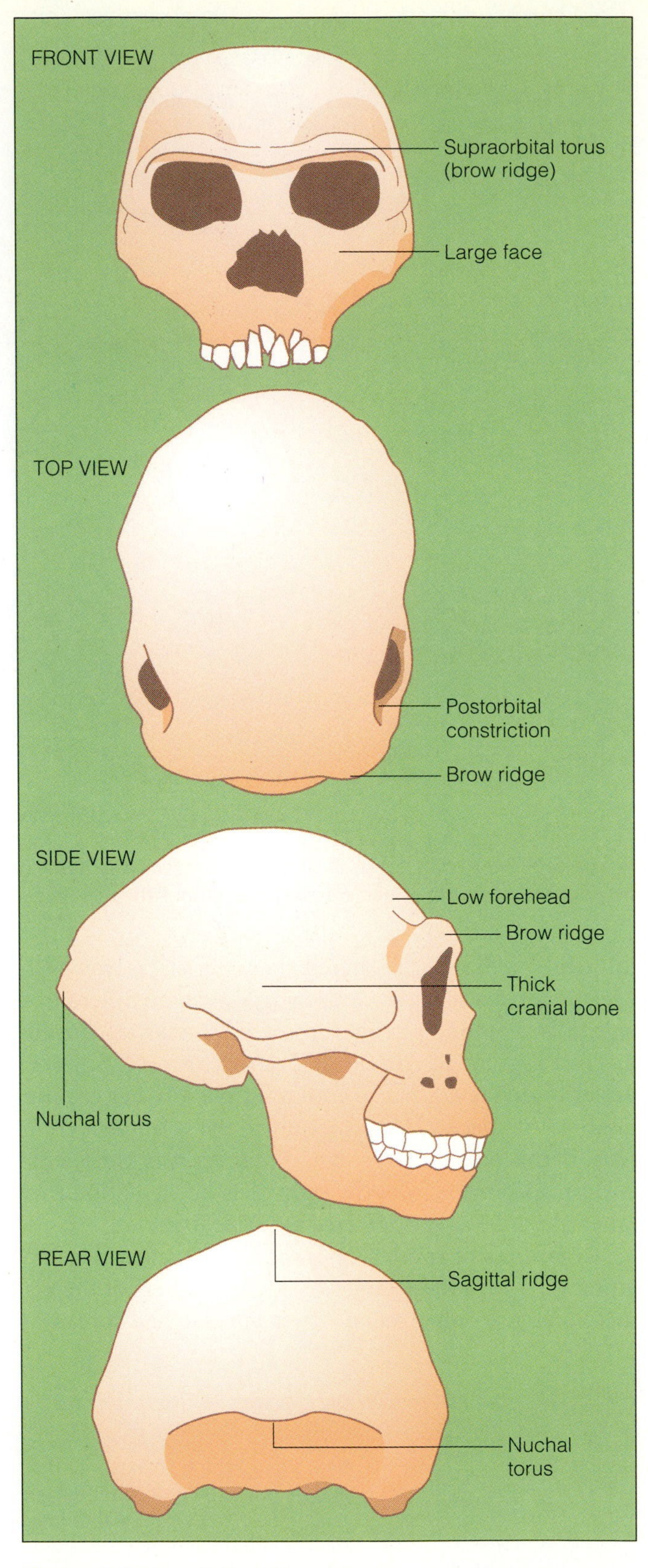

Figure 8.5 The skull of *Homo erectus*.

East Africa (752 cc) and the 1,000 to 2,000 cc range (average 1,300 cc) for modern human skulls (Figure 8.4).

The cranium itself has a low vault (height of the dome of the skull top), and the head is long and narrow. When viewed from behind, its width is greater than its height, with its greatest width at the base. The skulls of modern humans when similarly viewed are higher than they are wide, with the widest dimension in the region above the ears. The shape of the inside of *H. erectus*' braincase shows near-modern development of the brain, especially in the speech area. Although some anthropologists argue that the vocal apparatus was not adequate for speech, others claim that asymmetries of the brain suggest the same pattern of right-handedness with left cerebral dominance that, in modern peoples, is correlated with the capacity for language.[4]

H. erectus possessed massive brow ridges (Figure 8.5). When viewed from above, a marked constriction or

[4] Holloway, R. L. (1981). The Indonesian *Homo erectus* brain endocasts revisited. *American Journal of Physical Anthropology 55*, 521.

"pinching in" of the skull can be seen just behind the massive brow ridges. *H. erectus* also possessed a sloping forehead and a receding chin. Powerful jaws with large teeth, a protruding mouth, and huge neck muscles added to *H. erectus'* generally rugged appearance. Nevertheless, the face, teeth, and jaws of this species are smaller than those of *H. habilis.*

Apart from its skull, the skeleton of *H. erectus* differs only subtly from that of modern humans. Although its bodily proportions are like ours, it was more heavily muscled. Stature seems to have increased from the smaller size typical of the australopithecines and the earliest members of the genus *Homo.* The best evidence for this comes from a remarkably well-preserved skeleton of an adolescent male from Lake Turkana in Kenya. Sexual dimorphism in body size also appears to have decreased in *H. erectus* compared to earlier bipeds. A reduction in sexual dimorphism may be due to the increase in female size as an adaptation to childbirth.[5] The recent discovery of a capacious female *Homo erectus* pelvis in Gona, Ethiopia, supports this notion.[6]

Relationship among *Homo erectus, Homo habilis,* and Other Proposed Fossil Groups

The smaller teeth and larger brains of *Homo erectus* seem to mark the continuation of a trend first seen in *Homo habilis.* Increased body size, reduced sexual dimorphism, and more "human" body form of *H. erectus* are newly derived characteristics. Nonetheless, some skeletal resemblance to *H. habilis* exists, for example, in the long neck and low neck angle of the thighbone, the long low vault and marked constriction of the skull behind the eyes, and smaller brain size in the earliest *H. erectus* fossils.

Indeed, as already noted, it is very difficult to distinguish between the earliest *H. erectus* and the latest *H. habilis* fossils. Presumably the one form evolved from the other, fairly abruptly, around 1.8 to 1.9 mya. While the bones of Asian *H. erectus* are thicker and the brow ridges more pronounced compared to *H. erectus* from Africa, detailed anatomical comparisons indicate levels of variation approximating those seen in *H. sapiens.*[7] Consistent with the notion of a single species is the observation that 1.8-million-year-old specimens from Dmanisi, in the Caucasus—a region that lies along the overland route between Africa and Eurasia—show a mix of characteristics seen in African and Asian *H. erectus* populations.[8]

Throughout the globe, the most recent fossils are more derived in appearance, and the oldest fossils (up to 1.8 million years old) display features reminiscent of earlier *H. habilis.* Indeed, distinguishing early *H. erectus* from late *H. habilis* is problematic—precisely what one would expect if the one evolved from the other. We will next explore the *H. erectus* finds by region.

Homo erectus from Africa

Although our samples of *H. erectus* fossils from Asia remain among the best, several important specimens are from Africa. Fossils now assigned to this species were discovered there as long ago as 1933, but the better-known finds have been made since 1960, at Olduvai Gorge and at Lake Turkana, Kenya. Among them is the most complete *H. erectus* skeleton ever found, that of an adolescent boy who died 1.6 mya. Paleoanthropologists infer the age of this specimen from his teeth (the 12-year molars are fully erupted) and the state of maturity of the bones. With a height of about 5 feet 3 inches at adolescence, this specimen was expected to attain a stature of about 6 feet by adulthood.

A trail of *H. erectus* footprints, like those from Laetoli, were also recently discovered along Lake Turkana. These footprints support the estimates of body mass (weight) and stature made from more fragmentary remains.

Homo erectus Entering Eurasia

Evidence of the spread of *H. erectus* from Africa into Eurasia is well preserved at the interesting site of Dmanisi in the Caucasus Mountains of Georgia. Dmanisi was first excavated as an archaeological site because of its importance as a crossroads for the caravan routes of Armenia, Persia, and Byzantium in medieval times. When Oldowan stone tools were found at this site in 1984, the hunt for fossil specimens began there as well.

---

[5] Hager, L. (1989). *The evolution of sex differences in the hominid bony pelvis.* PhD dissertation, University of California, Berkeley.

[6] Simpson, S. W., et al. (2008). A female *Homo erectus* pelvis from Gona, Ethiopia. *Science 322* (5904), 1089–1092.

[7] Rightmire, G. P. (1998). Evidence from facial morphology for similarity of Asian and African representatives of *Homo erectus. American Journal of Physical Anthropology 106,* 61.

[8] Rosas, A., & Bermudez de Castro, J. M. (1998). On the taxonomic affinities of the Dmanisi mandible (Georgia). *American Journal of Physical Anthropology 107,* 159.

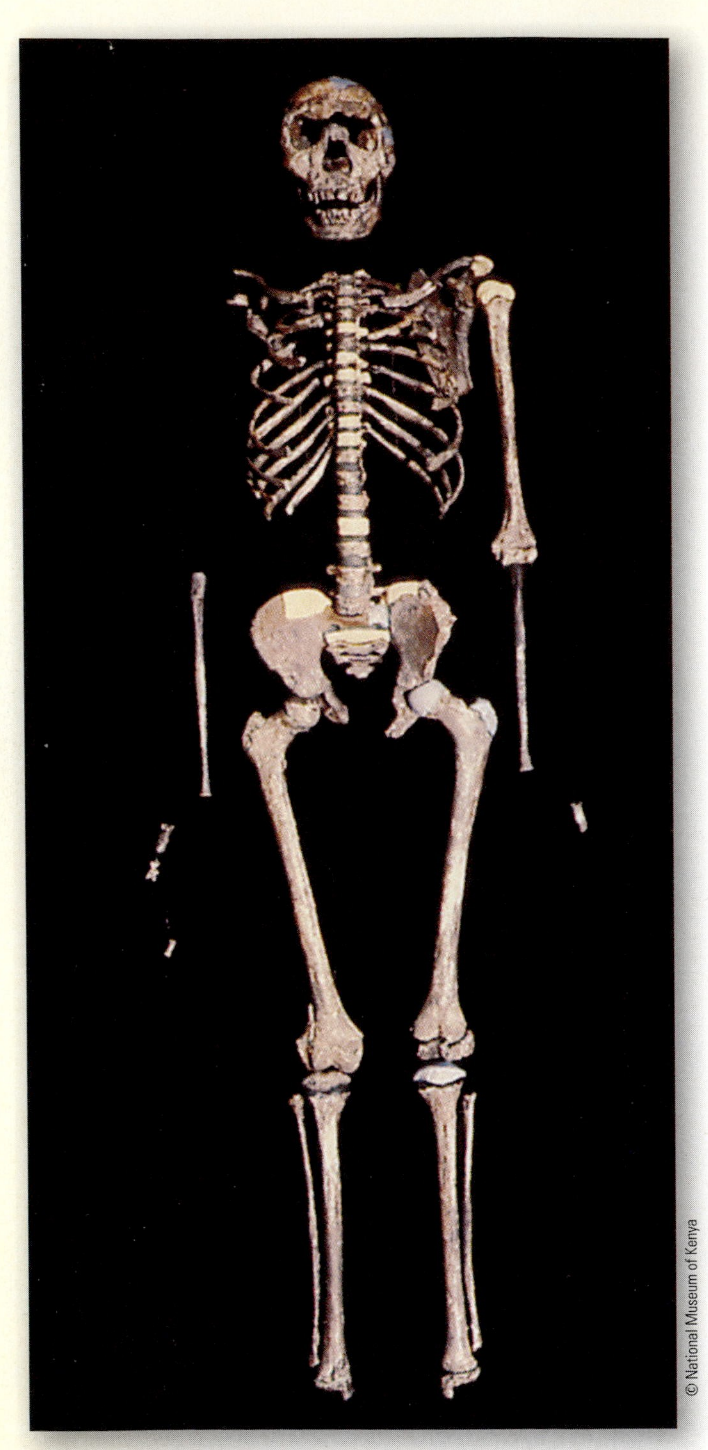

One of the oldest and certainly one of the most complete *Homo erectus* fossils is the Nariokotome Boy from Lake Turkana, Kenya. The remains are those of a tall adolescent boy.

Since then, paleoanthropologists have recovered some remarkable remains that can be accurately dated to 1.8 mya through past volcanic activity in the region. In 1999, two well-preserved skulls, one with a partial face, were discovered. Thus the early habitation of this region by members of the genus *Homo* is supported at Dmanisi with archaeological, anatomical, and geological evidence. Because rising sea levels since the Pleistocene make it impossible for paleoanthropologists to document coastal routes for the spread of *Homo* from Africa to Eurasia, the evidence from Georgia constitutes the only direct evidence of the spread of evolving humans from Africa to Europe and to Asia.

Homo erectus from Indonesia

While it took many years for the skull cap and thighbone discovered by Dubois to be accepted as part of the human line, these specimens are now considered typical Asian *H. erectus*. In the 1930s, a number of *H. erectus* fossils were discovered by German paleoanthropologist G. H. R. von Königswald at Sangiran, Java (see Figure 8.3). Von Königswald found a small skull that fluorine analysis and (later) potassium-argon dating assigned to the early Pleistocene. This indicated that these fossils were older than the Trinil skull cap found by Dubois, dating to approximately 500,000 to 700,000 years ago.

Since 1960, additional fossils have been found in Java, and we now have remains of around forty individuals. A long continuity of *H. erectus* populations in Southeast Asia is indicated, from 500,000 to 1.8 million years ago. Interestingly, the teeth and jaws of some of the earliest Javanese fossils are in many ways quite similar to those of *H. habilis*.[9] When considering the spread of *H. erectus* to Java, it is important to note that in the past, lower sea levels resulted in a continuous landmass between most of Indonesia and the Asian continent.

Homo erectus from China

In the mid-1920s another group of fossils from Asia, now known as *H. erectus,* was found by Davidson Black, a Canadian anatomist teaching at Peking Union Medical College. Black was led to this site after purchasing a few ancient humanlike teeth offered for their medicinal properties from a Beijing drugstore. He set out for the nearby

---

[9] Tobias, P. V., & von Königswald, G.H.R. (1964). A comparison between the Olduvai hominines and those of Java and some implications for hominid phylogeny. *Nature 204,* 515–518.

countryside to discover the "owner" of the teeth and perhaps a species of early human ancestor. At a place called Dragon Bone Hill in Zhoukoudian, 48 kilometers (30 miles) from Beijing, on the day before closing camp at the end of his first year of excavation, he found one molar tooth. Subsequently, Chinese paleoanthropologist W. C. Pei, who worked closely with Black, found a skull encased in limestone.

Between 1929 and 1934, the year of his death from silicosis—a lung disease caused by exposure to silica particles in the cave—Black labored along with Pei and French Jesuit paleontologist Pierre Teilhard de Chardin in the fossil-rich deposits of Zhoukoudian, uncovering fragment after fragment of ancient remains. On the basis of the anatomy of that first molar tooth, Black named these fossils *Sinanthropus pekinensis,* or "Chinese human of Peking" (Beijing), called "Peking Man" for short at the time. They are now recognized as an East Asian representative of *H. erectus.*

After Black's death, Franz Weidenreich, a German anatomist and paleoanthropologist, was sent to China by the Rockefeller Foundation to continue this work. As a Jew in Nazi Germany in the early 1930s, Weidenreich had sought refuge in the United States. By 1938, he and his colleagues recovered the remains of more than forty individuals, more than half of them women and children, from the limestone deposits of Zhoukoudian. Most fossils were fragmentary, represented by teeth, jawbones, and incomplete skulls. A spectacular composite specimen was reconstructed from the most complete remains. World War II (1939–1945) brought a halt to the digging, and the original Zhoukoudian specimens were lost during the Japanese occupation of China. The fossils had been carefully packed by Weidenreich and his team and placed with the U.S. Marines, but in the chaos of war, these precious fossils disappeared.

Fortunately, Weidenreich had made superb casts of most of the Zhoukoudian fossil specimens and sent them to the United States before the war. After the war, other specimens of *H. erectus* were discovered in China, at Zhoukoudian and a number of other localities (see Figure 8.3). The oldest skull is about 700,000 to 800,000 years old and comes from Lantian in central China. Even older is a fragment of a lower jaw from a cave in south-central China (Lunggupo) that is as old as the oldest Indonesian fossils. Like some of their Indonesian contemporaries, this Chinese fossil is reminiscent of African *H. habilis.* In contrast to these ancient remains, the original Zhoukoudian fossils appear to date between 300,000 and 600,000 years ago.

Although the two populations overlap in time, the majority of the Chinese fossils are, on the whole, not quite as old as those from Indonesia. Not surprisingly, Chinese *H. erectus* is less ancestral in appearance. Its average cranial capacity is about 1,000 cc, compared to 900 cc for Indonesian *H. erectus.* The smaller teeth and short jaw of the Chinese fossil specimens are further evidence of their more derived status.

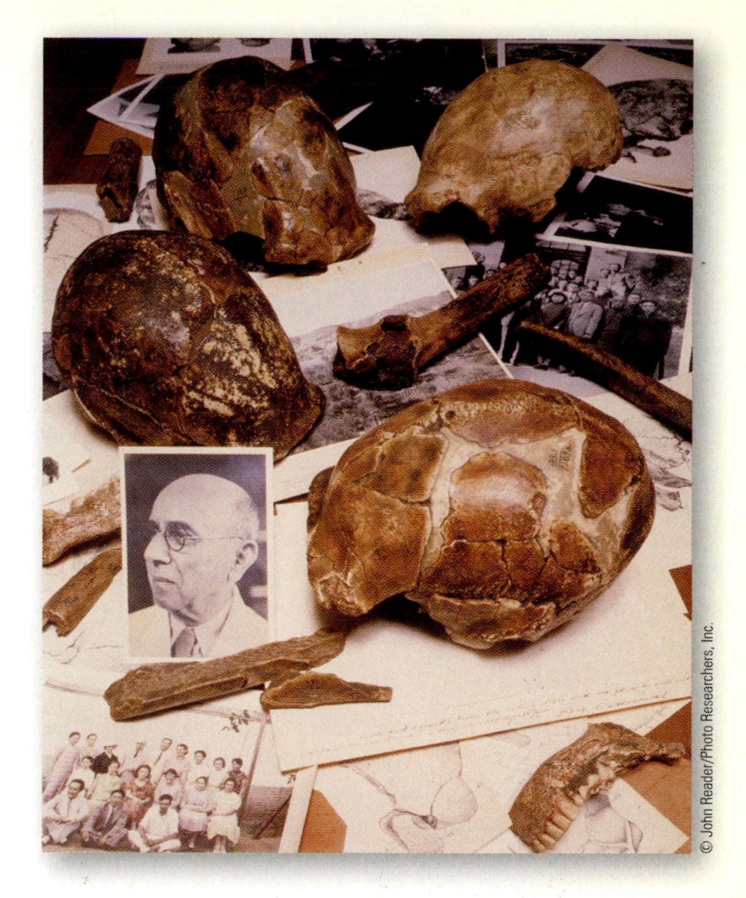

The original *Homo erectus* fossils from Zhoukoudian had been packed for shipment to the United States for safekeeping during World War II, but they mysteriously disappeared. Fortunately, excellent casts of the specimens and detailed anatomical descriptions (by Weidenreich) were made before the fossils were lost during the war.

Homo erectus from Western Europe

Although the fossil evidence indicates the presence of the genus *Homo* on the Eurasian landmass 1.8 mya (at Dmanisi, Georgia), the fossil evidence from western Europe dates to about 800,000 years ago. The evidence from the Grand Dolina site—in the Sierra de Atapuerca region of north-central Spain (see Table 8.1)—consists of fragments of four individuals dating to 800,000 years ago. A skull from Ceprano in Italy is thought to be approximately the same age if not older. Again, whether one lumps these specimens into the inclusive but varied species *H. erectus* or into several separate species differs according to the approach taken by paleoanthropologists with regard to the fossil record.

Some other fossils attributable to *H. erectus*—such as a robust shinbone from Boxgrove, England, and a large lower jaw from Mauer, Germany—are close to half a million years old. It is clear that the jaw came from a skull that was wide at the base, typical of *H. erectus.* These remains resemble *H. erectus* material from North Africa from the same time period. This observation and the fact that the earliest evidence of the genus *Homo* in western Europe comes from Spain and Italy suggest continued gene flow between this region and northern Africa.[10] At the time, a mere 6 or 7 kilometers separated Gibraltar from Morocco (compared to 13 kilometers today), and islands dotted the straits from Tunisia to Sicily. The only direct land connection between Africa and Eurasia is through the Middle East and into Turkey and the Caucasus.

The Culture of *Homo erectus*

As one might expect given its larger brain, *Homo erectus* outstripped its predecessors in cultural ability. *H. erectus* refined the technology of stone tool making and at some point began to use fire for light, protection, warmth, and cooking, though precisely when is still a matter for debate. Indirect evidence indicates that the organizational and planning abilities of *H. erectus,* or at least the later ones, were improved over those of their predecessors.

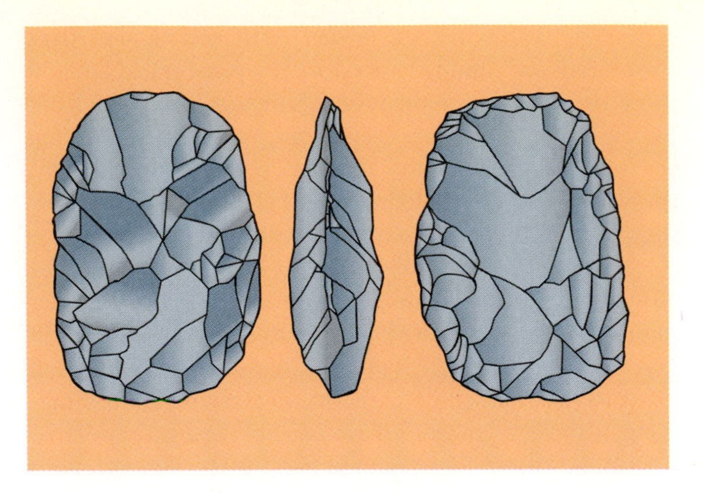

Figure 8.6 To fabricate this Acheulean hand-axe from flint, the toolmaker imposed a standardized arbitrary form on the naturally occurring raw material. The crafter made many separate strikes to create the sharp edge visible in profile.

Acheulean Tool Tradition

Tools of the **Acheulean tradition** are associated with the remains of *H. erectus* in Africa, Europe, and southwestern Asia. Named for the stone tools first identified at St. Acheul, France, the signature piece of this tradition is the hand-axe: a teardrop-shaped tool pointed at one end with a sharp cutting edge all around (Figure 8.6).

The earliest hand-axes, from East Africa, are about 1.6 million years old. Those found in Europe are no older than about 500,000 years. At the same time that hand-axes appeared, archaeological sites in Europe became dramatically more common. This suggests an influx of individuals bringing Acheulean technology with them, implying continued gene flow into Europe. Because the spread of the genus *Homo* from Africa into Asia took place before the invention of the hand-axe, it is not surprising to find that different forms of tools were developed in East Asia.

The evidence from Olduvai Gorge shows that the Acheulean grew out of the Oldowan tradition: In lower strata, chopper tools were found along with remains of *H. habilis;* above, the first crude hand-axes were found intermingled with chopper tools; and in higher strata were found more finished-looking Acheulean hand-axes with *H. erectus* remains.

Early Acheulean tools represent a significant step beyond the generalized cutting, chopping, and scraping tools of the Oldowan tradition. The shapes of Oldowan tools were largely controlled by the original form, size, and mechanical properties of raw materials. The shapes of hand-axes and some other Acheulean tools, by contrast, were more standardized, apparently reflecting arbitrary preconceived designs imposed upon a diverse range of raw materials.[11] Overall, a sharper point and a more regular and larger cutting edge were produced from the same amount of stone.

During this part of the Lower Paleolithic tool kits began to diversify. Besides hand-axes, *H. erectus* used tools that functioned as cleavers (hand-axes with a straight, sharp edge where the point would otherwise be), picks and knives (variants of the hand-axe form), and flake tools (generally smaller tools made by hitting a flint core with a hammerstone, thus knocking off flakes with sharp edges). Many flake tools were byproducts of hand-axe and cleaver manufacture. Their sharp edges made them useful "as is," but many were retouched (modified again by ancient flint knappers) to make points, scrapers, borers, and other sorts of tools. Diversification of tool kits is also indicated by the smaller numbers of hand-axes in northern and eastern Europe where people relied on simple flaked choppers, a wide variety of unstandardized flakes, and supplementary tools made of bone, antler, and wood.

In eastern Asia, by contrast, people developed a variety of choppers, scrapers, points, and burins (chisel-like tools) different from those in southwestern Asia, Europe, and Africa. Besides direct percussion, anvil (striking the raw material against a stationary stone) and bipolar percussion (holding the raw material against an anvil, but striking it at the same time with a hammerstone) methods were used in tool manufacture. Although tens of thousands of stone tools have been found with *H. erectus* remains at Zhoukoudian, stone implements are not at all common in Southeast Asia. Here, favored materials likely were ones that do not preserve

[10] Balter, M. (2001). In search of the first Europeans. *Science 291,* 1724.

Acheulean tradition The tool-making tradition of *Homo erectus* in Africa, Europe, and southwestern Asia in which hand-axes were developed from the earlier Oldowan chopper.

[11] Ambrose, p. 1750.

well, such as bamboo and other local woods, from which excellent knives, scrapers, and so on can be made.

Use of Fire

With *H. erectus* came the first evidence of ancestral populations living outside the Old World tropics. Without controlled use of fire, it is unlikely that early humans could have moved successfully into regions where winter temperatures regularly dropped to temperate climate levels—as they must have in northern China, the mountain highlands of Central Asia, and most of Europe. Members of the genus *Homo* spread to these colder regions some 780,000 years ago.

The 700,000-year-old Kao Poh Nam rock shelter in Thailand provides compelling evidence for deliberate controlled use of fire. Here, a roughly circular arrangement of fire-cracked basalt cobbles was discovered in association with artifacts and animal bones. Because basalt rocks are not native to the rock shelter and are quite heavy, they were likely carried in by *H. erectus.* Limestone rocks, more readily available in the shelter, cannot be used for hearths because, when burned, limestone produces quicklime, a caustic substance that causes itching and burning skin rashes.[12] The hearth is associated with bones, showing clear evidence of cut marks from butchering as well as burning.

H. erectus may have been using fire even earlier, based on evidence from Swartkrans in South Africa. Here, in deposits estimated to date between 1 and 1.3 mya, bones have been found that had been heated to temperatures far in excess of what one would expect as the result of natural fires. Furthermore, the burned bones at Swartkrans do not occur in older, deeper deposits. If these fires were natural, they would be distributed among all archaeological layers. Because the bones indicate heating to such high temperatures that any meat on them would have been inedible, South African paleoanthropologists Andrew Sillen and C. K. Brain suggest that the Swartkrans fires functioned as protection from predators.[13]

Fire may also have been used by *H. erectus,* as it was by subsequent members of the genus *Homo,* not just for protection from animals out in the open but to frighten away cave-dwelling predators so that the fire users might live in the caves themselves. In addition, fire could be used to provide warmth and light in these otherwise cold and dark habitations. While earlier bipeds likely used caves as part of their temperature regulation strategy as has been observed in nonhuman primates,[14] controlled use of fire expands the ability to regulate temperature considerably.

In regions where bamboo was readily available for the fabrication of effective tools, the same stone tool industries might not have developed. This contemporary scaffolding demonstrates bamboo's strength and versatility.

Not only did fire provide warmth, but it may have assisted in the quest for food. In places like central Europe and China, food would have been hard to come by in the long, cold winters when edible plants were unavailable and the large herds of animals dispersed and migrated. Our ancestors may have searched out the frozen carcasses of animals that had died naturally in the late fall and winter, using long wooden probes to locate them beneath the snow, wooden scoops to dig them out, and fire to thaw them so that they could be butchered and eaten.[15] Furthermore, such fire-assisted scavenging would have made available meat and hides of woolly mammoths, woolly rhinoceroses, and bison, which were probably beyond the ability of *H. erectus* to kill, at least until late in the species' career.

Perhaps it was the use of fire to thaw carcasses that led to the idea of cooking food. Some paleoanthropologists suggest that this behavioral change altered the forces of natural selection, which previously favored individuals

[12] Pope, G. G. (1989). Bamboo and human evolution. *Natural History 10,* 56.

[13] Sillen, A., & Brain, C. K. (1990). Old flame. *Natural History 4,* 10.

[14] Barrett, L., et al. (2004). Habitual cave use and thermoregulation in chacma baboons (*Papio hamadryas ursinus*). *Journal of Human Evolution 46* (2), 215–222.

[15] Gamble, C. (1986). *The Paleolithic settlement of Europe* (p. 387). Cambridge, England: Cambridge University Press.

with heavy jaws and large, sharp teeth (raw food is tougher and needs more chewing), favoring instead further reduction in tooth size along with supportive facial structure.

Alternatively, the reduction of tooth size and supporting structure may have occurred outside the context of adaptation. For example, the genetic changes responsible for increasing brain size may also have caused a reduction in tooth size as a secondary effect. The discovery of a genetic mutation, shared by all humans but absent in apes, that acts to prevent growth of powerful jaw muscles supports this hypothesis. Without heavy jaw muscles attached to the outside of the braincase, a significant constraint to brain growth was removed. In other words, humans may have developed large brains as an accidental byproduct of jaw-size reduction.[16]

Soft foods may have relaxed selection for massive jaws. But cooking does more than soften food. It detoxifies a number of otherwise poisonous plants; alters digestion-inhibiting substances so that important vitamins, minerals, and proteins can be absorbed while in the gut, rather than just passing through it unused; and makes high-energy complex carbohydrates like starch digestible. Cooking increased the nutritional resources available to humans and made them more secure.

The partial predigestion of food by cooking also may have allowed a reduction in the size of the digestive tract. To establish this biological change, paleoanthropologists do not have the benefit of fossilized digestive tracts. Instead they turn to comparative anatomy of the living hominoids. Despite its overall similarity of form to those of apes, the digestive tract of modern humans is substantially smaller. The advantage of this gut reduction is that it draws less energy to operate, thereby competing less with the high energy requirements of a larger brain.

Like tools, then, fire gave people more control over their environment. Fire modified the natural succession of day and night, perhaps encouraging *H. erectus* to stay up after dark to review the day's events and plan the next day's activities. Though we cannot know whether *H. erectus* enjoyed socializing and planning around campfires at night, we do have evidence at least of some planning behavior. Planning is implied by the existence of populations in temperate climates, where the ability to anticipate the needs of the winter season by advance preparation for the cold would have been crucial to survival.[17]

Although considerable variation exists, studies of modern humans indicate that most people can remain reasonably comfortable down to 50 degrees Fahrenheit (10 degrees Celsius) with minimal clothing so long as they keep active. Below that temperature, hands and feet cool to the point of pain.[18] Clothing, like many other aspects of material culture, does not fossilize, so we have no direct evidence of the kind of clothing worn by *H. erectus*. We only know that it must have been more sophisticated than was required in warmer climates. In short, when our human ancestors learned to employ fire to warm and protect themselves and to cook their food, they dramatically increased their geographic range and nutritional options.

Hunting

Sites such as 400,000-year-old Ambrona and Torralba in Spain provide evidence that *H. erectus* developed the ability to organize in order to hunt large animals. The dismembered scattered remains of several elephants, horses, red deer, wild oxen, and rhinoceroses were preserved in an ancient swamp at Torralba. This finding, which cannot be explained as a result of any natural geologic process, indicates that these animals did not accidentally get mired in a swamp where they simply died and decayed.[19] In fact, the bones are closely associated with a variety of stone tools—a few thousand of them. Furthermore, the site contains very little evidence of carnivorous animal activity and none at all for the really big carnivores. Clearly, the genus *Homo* was involved—not just in butchering the animals but evidently in killing them as well.

It appears that the animals were actually driven into the swamp so that they could be easily killed. The remains of charcoal and carbon, widely but thinly scattered in the vicinity, raise the possibility that grassfires were used to drive the animals into the swamp. This evidence indicates more than opportunistic scavenging. Not only was *H. erectus* able to hunt, but considerable organizational and communicative skills are implied as well.

Other Evidence of Complex Thought

Other evidence of *H. erectus*' capabilities comes from the small island of Flores in Indonesia. Flores lies east of a deep-water strait that throughout the Pleistocene acted as a barrier to animals to and from Southeast Asia. Even at times of lowered sea levels, getting to Flores required crossing open water: at minimum 25 kilometers from Bali to Sumbawa, with an additional 19 kilometers to Flores. The presence

[16] Stedman, H. H., et al. (2004). Myosin gene mutation correlates with anatomical changes in the human lineage. *Nature 428*, 415–418.

[17] Goodenough, W. H. (1990). Evolution of the human capacity for beliefs. *American Anthropologist 92*, 601.

[18] Whiting, J. W. M., Sodergem, J. A., & Stigler, S. M. (1982). Winter temperature as a constraint to the migration of preindustrial peoples. *American Anthropologist 84*, 289.

[19] Freeman, L. G. (1992). *Ambrona and Torralba: New evidence and interpretation.* Paper presented at the 91st Annual Meeting, American Anthropological Association, San Francisco.

of 800,000-year-old stone tools on Flores indicates that somehow our ancestors navigated across the deep, fast-moving water.[20]

Evidence for a developing symbolic life is suggested by the increased standardization and refinement of Acheulean hand-axes over time. Moreover, at several sites in Europe, deliberately marked objects of stone, bone, and ivory have been found in Acheulean contexts. These include several objects from Bilzingsleben, Germany—among them a mastodon bone with a series of regular lines that appear to have been deliberately engraved. Similarly, the world's oldest known rock carvings are associated with Acheulean tools in a cave in India.[21] Though a far cry from the later Upper Paleolithic cave art of France and Spain, these are among the earliest Paleolithic artifacts that have no obvious utility or model in the natural world. Archaeologist Alexander Marshack argues that the use of such symbolic images requires some sort of spoken language, not only to assign meaning to the images but to maintain the tradition they seem to represent.[22]

The Question of Language

Though we do not have definitive evidence of *H. erectus*' linguistic abilities, indications of a developing symbolic life, as well as the need to plan for seasonal changes and to coordinate hunting activities (and cross stretches of open water), imply improving linguistic competence. Another interesting source of evidence for evolving humans' linguistic capability is found in the fossil record. There, it is apparent that the majority of the stone tools were made by right-handed individuals, supporting the theory of the increased specialization and lateralization of the evolving brain. In other primates and most mammals, the right and left sides of the brain duplicate each other's function; these animals use the right and left sides of their bodies equally and interchangeably. In humans, the emergence of handedness seems closely linked both developmentally (at about the age of 1 year) and evolutionarily with the appearance of language. Thus evidence of handedness in Lower Paleolithic tools indicates that the kind of brain specialization required for language that is present in contemporary humans was well under way (Figure 8.7).

Broca's area (language production)
Motor cortex
Parietal lobe
Frontal lobe
Temporal lobe
Occipital lobe
Hearing
Cerebellum
Brain stem
Wernicke's area (language comprehension)

Figure 8.7 Language areas in the left side of the brain. The right side of the human brain has different specialized functions.

The vocal tract and brain of *H. erectus* are intermediate between those of *H. sapiens* and earlier *Australopithecus*. The **hypoglossal canal**—the passageway through the skull that accommodates the nerve that controls tongue movement, which is so important for spoken language—has taken on the characteristic large size seen in contemporary humans in fossil skulls dated to 500,000 years ago (Figure 8.8).[23]

Possibly, a changeover from reliance on gestural to spoken language was a driving force in these evolutionary changes. The reduction of tooth and jaw size, facilitating the ability to articulate speech sounds, may have also played a role. From an evolutionary standpoint, spoken language could be said to provide some advantages over a gestural one. Individuals do not have to stop whatever they are doing with their hands to "talk" (useful to a species increasingly dependent on tool use), and it is possible to talk in the dark, past opaque objects, or among people whose gaze is concentrated on something else (potential prey, for example).

[20] Gibbons, A. (1998). Ancient island tools suggest *Homo erectus* was a seafarer. *Science 279*, 1635.

[21] Bednarik, R. G. (1995). Concept-mediated marking in the Lower Paleolithic. *Current Anthropology 36*, 610–611.

[22] Marshack, A. (1976). Some implications of the Paleolithic symbolic evidence for the origin of language. *Current Anthropology 17*, 280.

[23] Cartmill, M. (1998). The gift of gab. *Discover 19* (11), 64.

hypoglossal canal The opening in the skull that accommodates the tongue-controlling hypoglossal nerve.

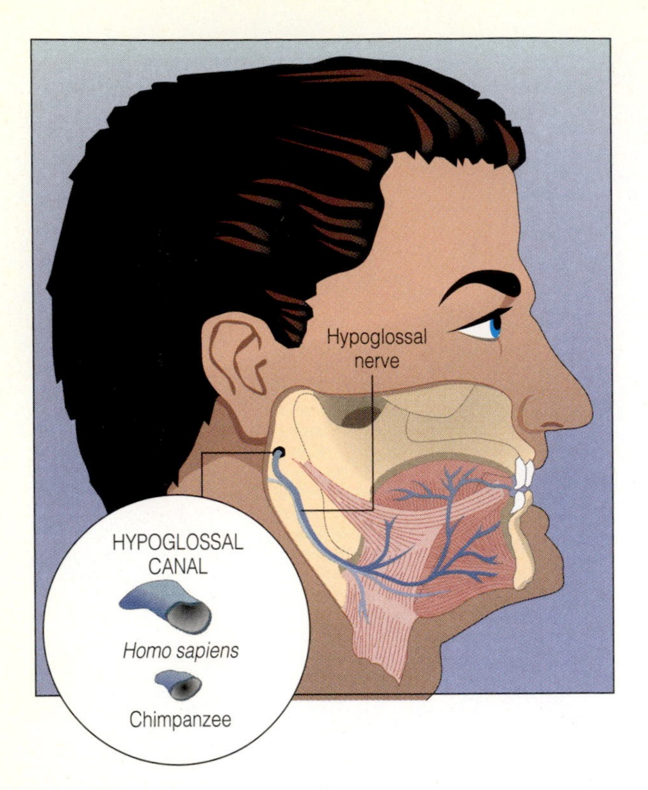

Figure 8.8 The size of the hypoglossal canal is much larger in humans than in chimpanzees. The nerve that passes through this canal controls tongue movement, and complex tongue movements are involved in spoken language. All members of the genus *Homo* after about 500,000 years ago have an enlarged hypoglossal canal.

With *H. erectus,* then, we find a clearer manifestation of the interplay among cultural, physical, and environmental factors than ever before. However slowly, social organization, technology, and communication developed in tandem with an increase in brain size and complexity. In fact, the cranial capacity of late *H. erectus* is 31 percent greater than the mean for early *H. erectus,* a rate of increase more rapid than the average fossil vertebrate rate.[24]

Archaic *Homo sapiens* and the Appearance of Modern-Sized Brains

Fossils from a number of sites in Africa, Asia, and Europe, dated to between 200,000 and 400,000 years ago, indicate that by this time cranial capacity reached modern proportions. Most fossil finds consist of parts of one or a very few individuals. The fossils from Sierra de Atapuerca in northern Spain (pictured in the chapter opener), are the only ones to exist as a population. Dated to 400,000 years ago,[25] the remains of at least twenty-eight individuals of both sexes and of various ages were deliberately dumped (after defleshing their skulls) by their contemporaries into a deep cave shaft known today as Sima de los Huesos ("Pit of the Bones"). The presence of animal bones in the same pit with humans raises the possibility that early humans simply used the site as a dump. Alternatively, the treatment of the dead at Atapuerca may have involved ritual activity that presaged burial of the dead, a practice that became common after 100,000 years ago.

As with any population, this one displays a significant degree of variation. Cranial capacity, for example, ranges from 1,125 to 1,390 cc, overlapping the upper end of the range for *H. erectus* and the average size of *H. sapiens* (1,300 cc). Overall, the bones display a mix of features, some typical of *H. erectus,* others of *H. sapiens,* including some incipient Neandertal characteristics. Despite this variation, the sample appears to show no more sexual dimorphism than displayed by modern humans.[26]

Other remains from Africa and Europe dating 200,000 to 400,000 years ago have shown a combination of *H. erectus* and *H. sapiens* features. Some—such as skulls from Ndutu in Tanzania, Swanscombe (England), and Steinheim (Germany)—have been classified as *H. sapiens*, while others—from Arago (France), Bilzingsleben (Germany), and Petralona (Greece), and several African sites—have been classified as *H. erectus.* Yet all have cranial capacities that fit within the range exhibited by the Sima de los Huesos skulls, which are classified as *H. antecessor.*

Comparisons of these skulls to those of living people or to *H. erectus* reflect their transitional nature. The Swanscombe and Steinheim skulls are large and robust, with their maximum breadth lower on the skull, more prominent brow ridges, larger faces, and bigger teeth. Similarly, the face of the Petralona skull from Greece resembles European Neandertals, while the back of the skull looks like *H. erectus.* Conversely, a skull from Salé in Morocco, which had a rather small brain for *H. sapiens* (930–960 cc), looks surprisingly modern from the back. Finally, various jaws from France and Morocco (in northern Africa) seem to combine features of *H. erectus* with those of the later European

[24] Wolpoff, M. H. (1993). Evolution in *Homo erectus:* The question of stasis. In R. L. Ciochon & J. G. Fleagle (Eds.), *The human evolution source book* (p. 396). Englewood Cliffs, NJ: Prentice-Hall.

[25] Parés, J. M., et al. (2000). On the age of hominid fossils at the Sima de los Huesos, Sierra de Atapuerca, Spain: Paleomagnetic evidence. *American Journal of Physical Anthropology 111,* 451–461.

[26] Lorenzo, C., et al. (1998). Intrapopulational body size variation and cranial capacity variation in middle Pleistocene humans: The Sima de los Huesos sample (Sierra de Atapuerca, Spain). *American Journal of Physical Anthropology 106,* 30.

Neandertals. A similar situation exists in East Asia, where skulls from several sites in China exhibit the same mix of *H. erectus* and *H. sapiens* characteristics.

"Lumpers" suggest that calling some of these early humans "late *H. erectus*" or "early *H. sapiens*" (or any of the other proposed species names within the genus *Homo*) serves no useful purpose and merely obscures their transitional status. They tend to lump these fossils into the **archaic *Homo sapiens,*** a category that reflects both their large brain size and the ancestral features on the skull. "Splitters" use a series of discrete names for specimens from this period that take into account some of the geographic and morphologic variation present in these fossils. Both approaches reflect their respective statements about evolutionary relationships among fossil groups.

Levalloisian Technique

With the appearance of large-brained members of the genus *Homo,* the pace of cultural change accelerated. A new method of flake manufacture was invented: the **Levalloisian technique,** so named after the French site where such tools were first excavated. Flake tools produced by this technique have been found widely in Africa, Europe, southwestern Asia, and even China along with Acheulean tools. In China, the technique could represent a case of independent invention, or it could indicate the spread of ideas from one part of the inhabited world to another.

The Levalloisian technique initially involves preparing a core by removing small flakes over the stone's surface. Following this, a striking platform is set up by a crosswise blow at one end of the core of stone (Figure 8.9). Striking the platform removes three or four long flakes, whose size and shape have been predetermined by the preceding preparation, leaving behind a nodule that looks like a tortoise shell. This method produces a longer edge for the same amount of flint than the previous ones used by evolving humans. Sharper edges can be produced in less time.

Other Cultural Innovations

At about the same time the Levalloisian technique was developed, our ancestors invented hafting—the fastening of small stone bifaces and flakes to handles of wood. Hafting led to the development of knives and more complex spears. Unlike the older handheld tools made simply by reduction (flaking of stone or working of wood), these new composite tools involved three components: a handle or shaft, a stone insert, and the materials to bind them. Manufacture involved planned sequences of actions that could be performed at different times and places.

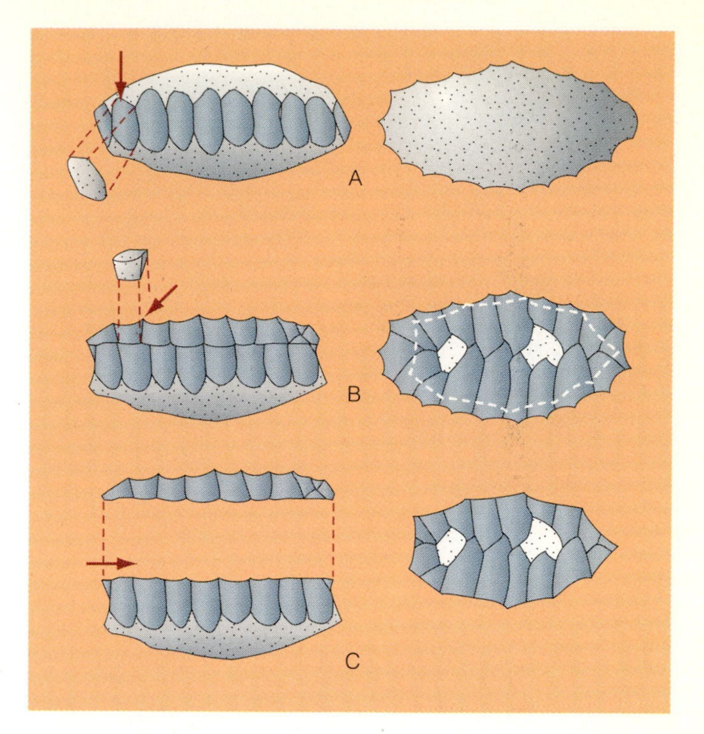

Figure 8.9 These drawings show side (left) and top (right) views of the steps in the Levalloisian technique. Drawing A shows the preparatory flaking of the stone core; B, the same on the top surface; and C, the final step of detaching a flake of a size and shape predetermined by the preceding steps.

With this new technology, regional stylistic and technological variants become more marked in the archaeological record, suggesting the emergence of distinct cultural traditions and culture areas. At the same time, the proportions of raw materials procured from faraway sources increased; whereas sources of stone for Acheulean tools were rarely more than 20 kilometers (12 miles) away, Levalloisian tools are found up to 320 kilometers (200 miles) from the sources of their stone.[27]

The use of yellow and red pigments of iron oxide, called ochre, a development first identified in Africa, became especially common by 130,000 years ago.[28] The use

---

[27] Ambrose, p. 1752.

[28] Barham, L. S. (1998). Possible early pigment use in South-Central Africa. *Current Anthropology 39,* 703–710.

archaic *Homo sapiens* A loosely defined group within the genus *Homo* that "lumpers" use for fossils with the combination of large brain size and ancestral features on the skull.

Levalloisian technique Tool-making technique by which three or four long triangular flakes were detached from a specially prepared core; developed by members of the genus *Homo* transitional from *H. erectus* to *H. sapiens.*

The practice of hafting, the fastening of small stone bifaces and flakes to handles of wood, was a major technological advance appearing in the archaeological record at about the same time as the invention of the Levalloisian technique.

of ochre may signal a rise in ritual activity, similar to the deliberate placement of the human remains in the Sima de los Huesos, Atapuerca, already noted. The use of red ochre in ancient burials may relate to its similarity to the color of blood as a powerful symbol of life.

The Neandertals

To many outside the field of anthropology, **Neandertals** are the quintessential caveman, portrayed by imaginative cartoonists as a slant-headed, stooped, dim-witted individual clad in animal skins and carrying a big club as he plods across the prehistoric landscape, perhaps dragging an unwilling female or a dead saber-toothed tiger. The stereotype has been perpetuated in novels and film. The popular image of Neandertals as brutish and incapable of spoken language, much less abstract or innovative thinking, may, in turn, have influenced the interpretation of the fossil and archaeological evidence. One of the most contentious issues in paleoanthropology today concerns whether the Neandertals represent an inferior side branch of human evolution that went extinct following the appearance of modern humans. Alternatively, descendents of the Neandertals may walk the earth today.

Neandertals A distinct group within the genus *Homo* inhabiting Europe and southwestern Asia from approximately 30,000 to 125,000 years ago.

Neandertals were an extremely muscular people living from approximately 30,000 to 125,000 years ago in Europe and southwestern Asia. While having brains larger than the modern average size, Neandertals possessed faces distinctively different from those of modern humans. Their large noses and teeth projected forward. They had prominent bony brow ridges over their eyes. On the back of their skull, there was a bunlike bony mass for attachment of powerful neck muscles. These features, not in line with classic forms of Western beauty, may have contributed to the depiction of Neandertals as brutes. Their rude reputation may also derive from the timing of their discovery.

One of the first Neandertals was found in a cave in the Neander Valley ("tal" means "valley" in German, "thal" was the old, German spelling) near Düsseldorf, Germany, in 1856—well before scientific theories to account for human evolution had gained acceptance. (Darwin published *On the Origins of Species by Means of Natural Selection* three years later in 1859.)

Initially, experts were at a loss as to what to make of this discovery. Examination of the fossil skull, a few ribs, and some limb bones revealed that the individual was a human being, but it did not look "normal." Some people believed the bones were those of a sickly and deformed contemporary. Others thought the skeleton belonged to a soldier who had succumbed to "water on the brain" during the Napoleonic Wars earlier that century. One prominent anatomist thought the remains were those of an idiot suffering from malnutrition, whose violent temper had gotten him into many fights, flattening his forehead and making his brow ridges bumpy. Similarly, an analysis of a skeleton found in 1908 near La Chapelle-aux-Saints in France mistakenly concluded that the specimen's brain was apelike and that he walked like an ape.

The evidence indicates that Neandertals were nowhere near as brutish and apelike as originally portrayed, and some scholars now see them as the archaic *H. sapiens* of Europe and Southwest Asia, ancestral to

This early 20th-century portrayal of the La Chapelle-aux-Saints Neandertal, based on the research of French paleoanthropologist Marcellin Boule, makes a powerfully negative statement about the capabilities of this group as well as their distance from living humans. In looking at this sorry specimen, it is easy to forget that this portrayal is not derived directly from the fossil remains but from the collective imagination of early 20th-century Europeans. While paleoanthropologists uniformly recognize the inaccuracies and biases present in this engraving, present-day reconstructions of Neandertals still vary tremendously and reflect the conflicting scientific theories and beliefs about their place in our evolutionary history.

the more derived, anatomically modern populations of these regions of the last 30,000 years. For example, paleoanthropologist C. Loring Brace observed that "classic" Neandertal features (Figure 8.10) are commonly present in 10,000-year-old skulls from Denmark and Norway.[29]

Nevertheless, Neandertals are somewhat distinctive when compared to more recent populations. Although they held modern-sized brains (average cranial capacity 1,400 cc versus 1,300 cc for modern *H. sapiens*), Neandertal skulls are notable for the protruding appearance of the midfacial region. The wear patterns on their large front teeth indicate that they may have been heavily used for tasks other than chewing. In many individuals, front teeth were worn down to the root stub by 35 to 40 years of age. The large noses of Neandertals probably were necessary to warm, moisten, and clean the dry, dusty frigid air of the glacial climate, preventing damage to the lungs and brain as seen in cold-adapted people of recent times. At the back of the skull, the bunlike bony mass providing attachment for the powerful neck muscles counteracted the weight of a heavy face.

All Neandertal fossils indicate that both sexes were muscular, with extremely robust and dense limb bones. Relative to body mass, the limbs were short (as they are in modern humans native to especially cold climates). Their shoulder blades indicate the importance of overarm and downward thrusting movements. Their arms

Low forehead
Large nasal aperture
Projecting midface
Low forehead
Large cranial capacity
Low, arching brow ridges
Occipital bun
Projecting midface
Lack of chin

Figure 8.10 Features of the skull seen in "classic" Neandertals.

[29] Ferrie, H. (1997). An interview with C. Loring Brace. *Current Anthropology 38,* 861.

As this face-off between paleoanthropologist Milford Wolpoff and his reconstruction of a Neandertal shows, the latter did not differ all that much from modern humans of European descent.

were exceptionally powerful, and pronounced attachments on their hand bones attest to a remarkably strong grip. Science writer James Shreeve has suggested that a healthy Neandertal could lift an average North American football player over his head and throw him through the goalposts.[30] Their massive, dense foot and leg bones suggest high levels of strength and endurance, comparable to robust individuals who live today.

Because brain size is related to overall body mass, heavy robust Neandertal bodies account for the large average size of the Neandertal brain. With *H. habilis* and *H. erectus,* increasing brain size has been linked to increasing cultural capabilities. Because Neandertal brain size falls at the high end of the human size range, paleoanthropologists shift to debating whether changes in the *shape* of the skull and skeleton are associated with changes in cultural capabilities.

Though the interpretation of Neandertal fossils has changed dramatically compared to when first discovered, they are still surrounded by controversy. Those who propose that the Neandertal line went extinct emphasize a notion of Neandertal biological difference and cultural inferiority. Those who include Neandertals in our direct ancestry emphasize the sophistication of Neandertal culture, attributing differences in skull shape and body form to regional adaptation to an extremely cold climate and the retention of ancestral traits in a somewhat isolated population.

Javanese, African, and Chinese Archaic *Homo sapiens*

While the large-brained Neandertals inhabited Europe and Southwest Asia, other parts of the world were inhabited by variants of archaic *H. sapiens;* these lacked the extreme midfacial projection and massive muscle attachments on the back of the skull characteristic of the Neandertals. Skulls found in Java, Africa, and China date from roughly the same time period.

Eleven skulls found near the Solo River in Ngandong, Java, are a prime example. These skulls indicated modern-sized brains ranging from 1,013 to 1,252 cc, while retaining features of earlier Javanese *H. erectus.* When their dating was recently revised (to between 27,000 and 53,000 years ago) some researchers concluded that this proved a late survival of *H. erectus* in Asia, contemporary with *H. sapiens* elsewhere. But the Ngandong skulls remain what they always were: representatives of archaic *H. sapiens,* with modern-sized brains in otherwise ancient-looking skulls.

Fossils from various parts of Africa show a similar combination of ancient and modern traits. Equivalent remains have been found at several localities in China. Thus the Neandertals could be said to represent an extreme form of archaic *H. sapiens.* Elsewhere, the archaics look like robust versions of the early modern populations that lived in the same regions or like somewhat more derived versions of the *H. erectus* populations that preceded them. All appear to have contained modern-sized brains, with their skulls retaining some ancestral features.

[30] Shreeve, J. (1995). *The Neandertal enigma: Solving the mystery of modern human origins* (p. 5). New York: William Morrow.

The original Neandertal cranium discovered in the Neander Valley, Germany, in 1856 (the only one without a face) is depicted here with earlier fossils and a cranium from contemporary *Homo sapiens*. The other fossils, from the left, are a gracile australopithecine; *Homo habilis* (KNM ER 1470) discovered at Koobi Fora, Kenya; *Homo erectus* also from Koobi Fora; and an African archaic *Homo sapiens* from Kabwe, Zambia. Increasing cranial capacity over time is evident from this series as is the fact Neandertal brains are in the modern human range. Even without the Neandertal face, some of the differences in the shape of the skull compared to *H. sapiens* are evident. The African archaic *H. sapiens* is also quite different from the contemporary skeleton.

Middle Paleolithic Culture

Adaptations to the environment by *Homo* from the **Middle Paleolithic,** or middle part of the Old Stone Age, were both biological and cultural, but the capacity for cultural adaptation was predictably superior to what it had been in earlier members of the genus *Homo.* Possessing brains of modern size, these members of the genus *Homo* had, as we would expect, greater cultural capabilities than their ancestors. Such a brain played a role in technological innovations, conceptual thought of considerable sophistication, and, almost surely, communication through spoken language. In addition to the Levalloisian technique already described, the Middle Paleolithic also included the development of the Mousterian tool tradition.

Mousterian Tool Tradition

The **Mousterian** and Mousterian-like tool traditions of Europe, southwestern Asia, and northern Africa, dating between about 40,000 and 125,000 years ago, are the best known of these (Figure 8.1). Comparable traditions are found in China and Japan, where they likely arose independently from local tool-making traditions.

All these traditions represent a technological advance over preceding industries. For example, the 40 centimeters (16 inches) of working edge that an Acheulean flint worker could get from a kilogram (2.2-pound) core compares with the nearly 200 centimeters (6 feet) of working edge the Mousterian could obtain from the same core. Mousterian tools were used by *all* people—Neandertals as well as other members of the genus *Homo* said to possess

Middle Paleolithic The middle part of the Old Stone Age characterized by the development of the Mousterian tradition of tool making and the earlier Levalloisian traditions.

Mousterian tradition The tool industry of the Neandertals and their contemporaries of Europe, southwestern Asia, and northern Africa from 40,000 to 125,000 years ago.

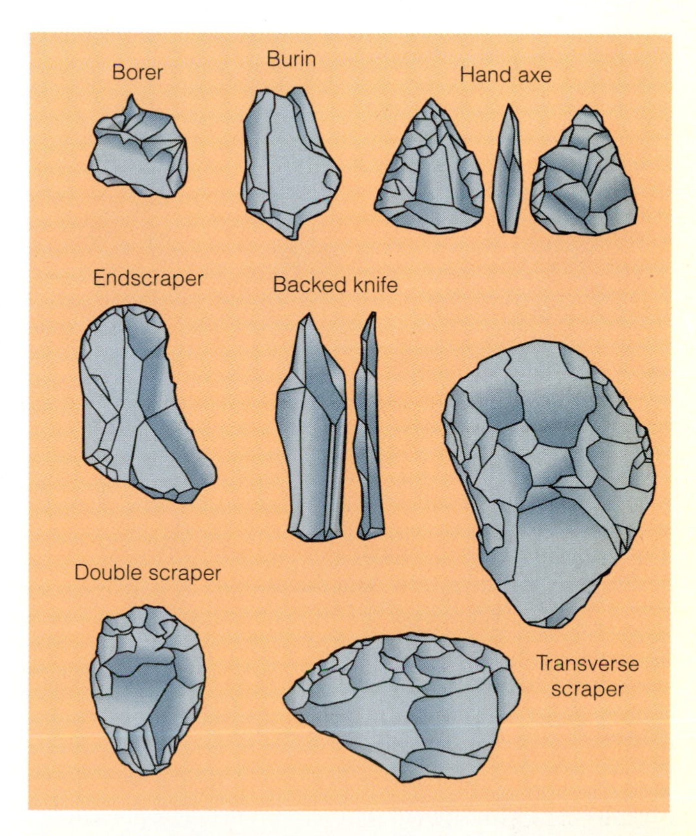

Figure 8.11 **Mousterian tool kits include a wide range of tool types with specific functions along with finer workmanship.**

Anthropology Applied

Stone Tools for Modern Surgeons

When anthropologist Irven DeVore of Harvard University was to have some minor melanomas removed from his face, he did not leave it up to the surgeon to supply his own scalpels. Instead, he had graduate student John Shea make a scalpel. Making a blade of obsidian (a naturally occurring volcanic "glass") by the same techniques used by Upper Paleolithic people to make blades, he hafted this in a wooden handle, using melted pine resin as glue and then lashing it with sinew. After the procedure, the surgeon reported that the obsidian scalpel was superior to metal ones.[a]

DeVore was not the first to undergo surgery in which stone scalpels were used. In 1975, Don Crabtree, then at Idaho State University, prepared the scalpels that his surgeon would use in Crabtree's heart surgery. In 1980, Payson Sheets at the University of Colorado prepared obsidian scalpels that were used successfully in eye surgery. And in 1986, David Pokotylo of the Museum of Anthropology at the University of British Columbia underwent reconstructive surgery on his hand with blades he himself had made (the hafting was done by his museum colleague, Len McFarlane).

The reason for these uses of scalpels modeled on ancient stone tools is that the anthropologists realized that obsidian is superior in almost every way to materials normally used to make scalpels: It is 210 to 1,050 times sharper than surgical steel, 100 to 500 times sharper than a razor blade, and three times sharper than a diamond blade (which not only costs much more but cannot be made with more than 3 mm of cutting edge).

Obsidian blades are easier to cut with and do less damage in the process (under a microscope, incisions made with the sharpest steel blades show torn ragged edges and are littered with bits of displaced flesh).[b] As a consequence, the surgeon has better control over what she or he is doing, and the incisions heal faster with less scarring and pain. Because of the superiority of obsidian scalpels, Sheets went so far as to form a corporation in partnership with Boulder, Colorado, eye surgeon Dr. Firmon Hardenbergh. Together, they developed a means of producing cores of uniform size from molten glass, as well as a machine to detach blades from the cores.

[a] Shreeve, J. (1995). *The Neandertal enigma: Solving the mystery of modern human origins* (p. 134). New York: William Morrow.

[b] Sheets, P. D. (1987). Dawn of a New Stone Age in eye surgery. In R. J. Sharer & W. Ashmore (Eds.), *Archaeology: Discovering our past* (p. 231). Palo Alto, CA: Mayfield.

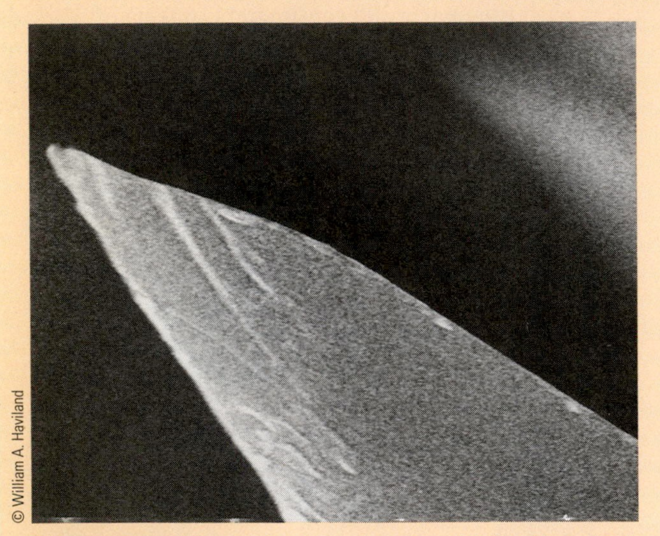

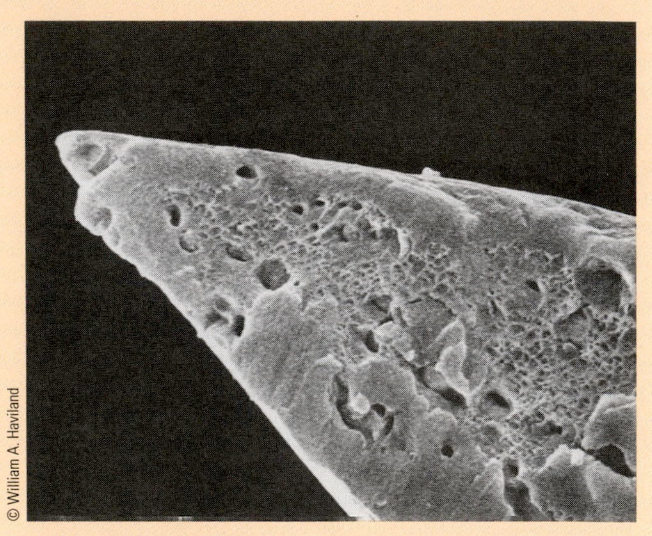

These electron micrographs of the tips of an obsidian blade (left) and a modern steel scalpel illustrate the superiority of the obsidian.

more anatomically modern skulls, in Europe, northern Africa, and southwestern Asia during this time period. At around 35,000 years ago, the Mousterian traditions were replaced by the Upper Paleolithic traditions, which are the subject of Chapter 9. However, the Anthropology Applied feature shows that stone tools continue to be important for humans today.

The Mousterian tradition is named after the Neandertal cave site of Le Moustier, in southern France. The presence of Acheulean hand-axes at Mousterian sites is one indication that this culture was ultimately rooted in the older Acheulean tradition. Mousterian tools are generally lighter and smaller than those of earlier traditions. Whereas previously only two or three flakes could be obtained from the entire core, Mousterian toolmakers obtained many smaller flakes, which they skillfully retouched and sharpened. Their tool kits also contained a greater variety of types than the earlier ones: hand-axes, flakes, scrapers, borers, notched flakes for shaving wood, and many types of points that could be attached to wooden shafts to make spears. This variety of tools facilitated more effective use of food resources and enhanced the quality of clothing and shelter.

With the Mousterian cultural traditions, members of the genus *Homo* could cope with the nearly Arctic conditions that supervened in Eurasia as the glaciers expanded about 70,000 years ago. People likely came to live in cold climates as a result of a slow but steady population increase during the Pleistocene. Once there, they had little choice but to adapt as climates turned even colder.

Population expansion into previously uninhabited colder regions was made possible through a series of cultural adaptations to cold climate. Under such cold conditions, vegetable foods are only rarely or seasonally available, and meat becomes a critical staple. In particular, animal fats, rather than carbohydrates, become the chief source of energy. Energy-rich animal fat in the diets of cold-climate meat eaters provides them with the extra energy needed for hunting, as well as for keeping the body warm.

An abundance of associated animal bones, often clearly showing cut marks, indicates the importance of meat to Mousterian toolmakers. Frequently, the remains consist almost entirely of very large game—wild cattle (including the European bison known as the aurochs), wild horses, and even mammoths and woolly rhinoceroses. At several sites evidence indicates that particular species were singled out for the hunt. For example, at one site in the French Pyrenees, well over 90 percent of the faunal assemblage (representing at least 108 animals) consists of large members of the wild cattle family. These bones accumulated at the foot of a steep riverside escarpment, over which the animals were evidently stampeded. Evidence of similar cliff-fall hunting strategy is also found at La Quina in southwestern France and at a site in the Channel Islands just off the northwest coast of France.

Clearly, the Neandertals were not merely casual or opportunistic hunters but engaged in carefully planned and organized hunting of very large and potentially dangerous game.[31] The standardization of Mousterian hunting implements compared to household tools also reflects the importance of hunting for these ancient peoples. At the same time, the complexity of the tool kit needed for survival in a cold climate may have decreased the users' mobility. Decreased mobility is suggested by the greater depth of deposits and thus longer habitation at Mousterian sites compared with those from the earlier Lower Paleolithic. Such sites contain evidence of long production sequences, resharpening and discarding of tools, and large-scale butchering and cooking of game. Pebble paving, construction of simple walls, and the digging of post holes and artificial pits show how the inhabitants worked to improve living conditions in some caves and rock shelters. This evidence suggests that Mousterian sites were not simply stopovers in people's constant quest for food.

In addition, evidence suggests that Neandertal social organization had developed to the point of providing care for physically disabled members of the group. For the first time, the remains of old people are well represented in the fossil record. Furthermore, many elderly Neandertal skeletons show evidence of treatment for trauma, with extensive healing of wounds and little or no infection.[32]

One particularly dramatic example is Shanidar Cave in Iraq, which includes the remains of a partially blind man (the eye socket indicates serious injury) with a withered upper arm indicating loss of the arm from the elbow on down. Remains of another individual found at Krapina in Croatia suggests the possibility of surgical amputation of a hand. In La Chapelle, France, fossil remains indicate prolonged survival of a man badly crippled by arthritis. The earliest example comes from a 200,000-year-old site in France, where a toothless man was able to survive probably because others in his group processed or prechewed his food so he could swallow it. Whether this evidence indicates true compassion on the part of these early people is not clear, but it is certain that cultural factors helped ensure survival, allowing individuals to provide care for others.

The Symbolic Life of Neandertals

Indications of a rich symbolic life of Neandertals exist. For example, several sites contain clear evidence for deliberate burial of the dead. This is one reason for the relative abundance of reasonably complete Neandertal skeletons. The difficulty of digging an adult-sized grave without access to metal shovels suggests how important a social activity this was. Moreover, intentional positioning of dead bodies, whatever the specific reason may have been, constitutes evidence of symbolism.[33]

To date, at least seventeen sites in Europe, South Africa, and Southwest Asia include Middle Paleolithic burials. For example, at Kebara Cave in Israel, around 60,000 years ago, a Neandertal male between 25 and 35 years of age was placed in a pit on his back, with his arms folded over his chest and abdomen (Figure 8.12). Some time later, after complete decay of attaching ligaments, the grave was reopened and the skull removed (a practice that,

[31] Mellars, P. (1989). Major issues in the emergence of modern humans. *Current Anthropology 30,* 356–357.

[32] Conroy, G. C. (1997). *Reconstructing human origins: A modern synthesis* (p. 427). New York: Norton.

[33] Schepartz, L. A. (1993). Language and modern human origins. *Yearbook of Physical Anthropology 36,* 113.

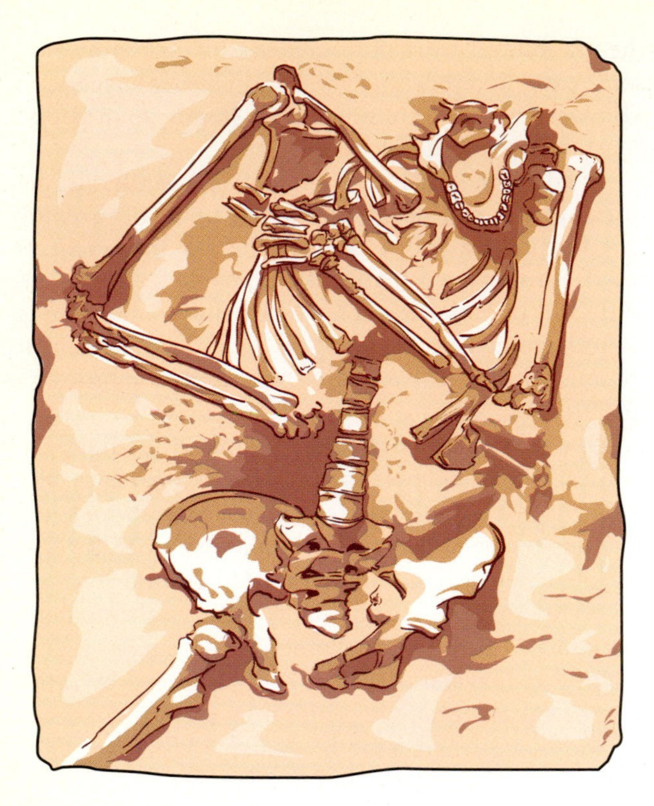

Figure 8.12 The position of the body and the careful removal of the skull indicate that the fossil from Kebara Cave in Israel was deliberately buried there about 60,000 years ago.

interestingly, is sometimes seen in burials in the same region roughly 50,000 years later).

Shanidar Cave in Iraq provides evidence of a burial accompanied by what may have been a funeral ceremony. In the back of the cave a Neandertal was buried in a pit. Pollen analysis of the soil around the skeleton indicated that flowers had been placed below the body and in a wreath about the head. Because the key pollen types came from insect-pollinated flowers, few if any of the pollen grains could have found their way into the pit via air currents. The flowers in question consist solely of varieties valued in historic times for their medicinal properties.

Other evidence for symbolic behavior in Mousterian culture comes from the naturally occurring pigments: manganese dioxide and the red and yellow forms of ochre. Recovered chunks of these pigments reveal clear evidence of scraping to produce powder, as well as facets, like those that appear on a crayon, from use. A Mousterian artist also applied color to the carved and shaped section of a mammoth tooth about 50,000 years ago. This mammoth tooth may have been made for cultural symbolic purposes. Noteworthy is its similarity to ceremonial objects made of bone and ivory dated to the later Upper Paleolithic and to the *churingas* made of wood by Australian Aborigines.

The mammoth tooth, which was once smeared with red ochre, has a highly polished face suggesting it was handled a lot. Microscopic examination reveals that it was never provided with a working edge for any utilitarian purpose. Such objects imply, as archaeologist Alexander Marshack has observed, "that the Neandertals did in fact have conceptual models and maps as well as problem-solving capacities comparable to, if not equal to, those found among anatomically modern humans."[34]

Evidence for symbolic activity on the part of Neandertals raises the possibility of the presence and use of musical instruments, such as a proposed bone flute from a Mousterian site in Slovenia in southern Europe. This object, consisting of a hollow bone with perforations, has sparked controversy. Some see it as nothing more than a cave bear bone that was chewed on by carnivores—hence the perforations. Its discoverer, French archaeologist Marcel Otte, on the other hand, sees it as a flute.

Unfortunately, the object is fragmentary; surviving are five holes, four on one side and one on the opposite side. The regular spacing of the four holes, fitting perfectly to the fingers of a human hand, and the location of the fifth hole at the base of the opposite side, at the natural location of the thumb, all lend credence to the flute hypothesis. While signs of gnawing by animals are present on this bone, they are superimposed on traces of human activity.[35] Were it found in an Upper Paleolithic context as was the flute discovered in Hohle Fels Cave in southwestern Germany, it would probably be accepted as a flute without argument. However, because its early date indicates it was made by a Neandertal, the interpretation of this object is tied to the larger controversy about Neandertals' cultural abilities and their place in human evolutionary history.

Speech and Language in the Middle Paleolithic

Among modern humans, the sharing of thoughts and ideas, as well as the transmission of culture from one generation to the next, is dependent upon language. Because the Neandertals and other Middle Paleolithic *Homo* had modern-sized brains and a sophisticated Mousterian

---

[34] Marshack, A. (1989). Evolution of the human capacity: The symbolic evidence. *Yearbook of Physical Anthropology 32,* 22.

[35] Otte, M. (2000). On the suggested bone flute from Slovenia. *Current Anthropology 41,* 271.

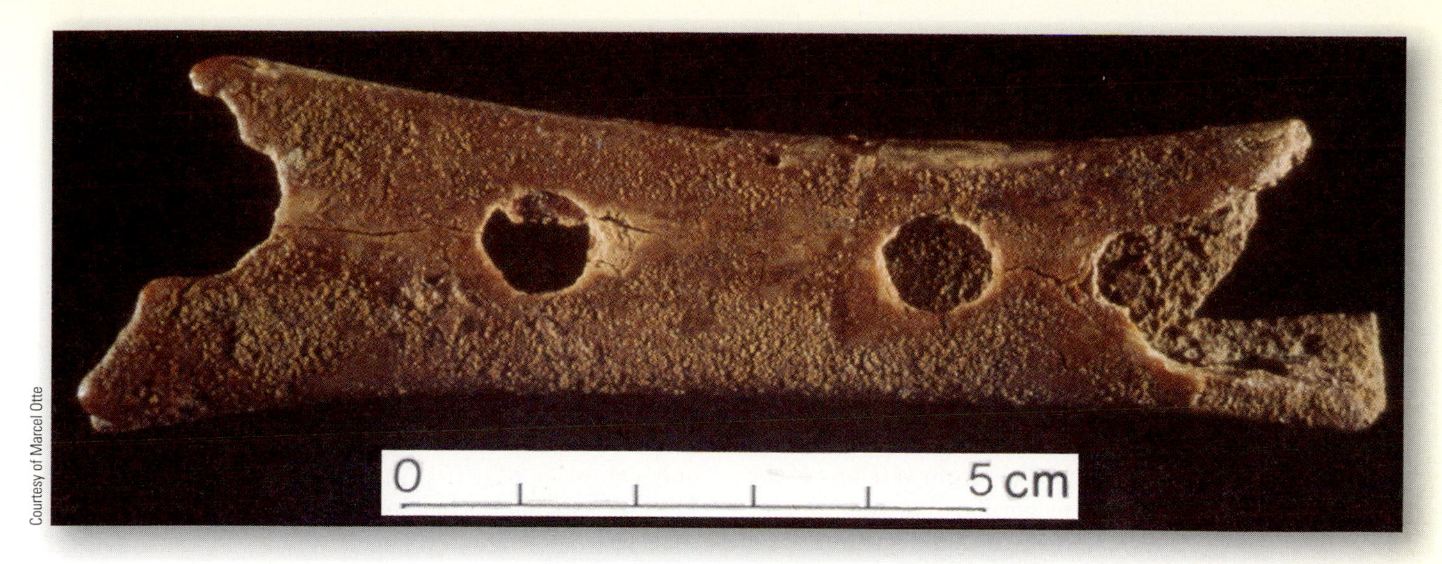

Courtesy of Marcel Otte

The first musical instrument? There is a strong possibility that this object, found in trash left by Neandertals, is the remains of a flute made of bone.

tool kit, it might be supposed that they had some form of language.

As pointed out by paleoanthropologist Stanley Ambrose, the Mousterian tool kit included composite tools involving the assembly of parts in different configurations to produce functionally different tools. He likens this ordered assembly of parts into tools to grammatical language, "because hierarchical assemblies of sounds produce meaningful phrases and sentences, and changing word order changes meaning."[36] Furthermore, "a composite tool may be analogous to a sentence, but explaining how to make one is the equivalent of a recipe or a short story."[37] In addition, the evidence for the manufacture of objects of symbolic significance supports the presence of language in Middle Paleolithic *Homo.* Objects such as the colored section of mammoth tooth already described would seem to have required some form of explanation through language.

While the archaeological evidence supports the symbolic thinking characteristic of language, specific anatomical features can be examined to determine whether this language was spoken or gestural. Some have argued that the Neandertals lacked the physical features necessary for speech. For example, an early 20th-century reconstruction of the angle at the base of the Neandertal skull was said to indicate that the larynx was higher in the throat than it is in modern humans, precluding humanlike speech. This reconstruction is now known to be faulty. Further, the hyoid bone associated with the muscles of speech in the larynx is preserved from a skeleton from the Kebara Cave burial in Israel. Its shape is identical to that of contemporary humans, indicating that the vocal tract was adequate for speech.

With respect to the brain, paleoneurologists, working from endocranial casts, are agreed that Neandertals had the neural development necessary for spoken language. Indeed, they argue that the changes associated with language began even before the appearance of archaic *Homo sapiens,*[38] as described above. Consistent, too, is an expanded thoracic vertebral canal (the thorax is the upper part of the body), a feature Neandertals share with modern humans but not with early *Homo erectus* (or any other primate). This feature suggests the increased breath control required for speech.[39] This control enables production of long phrases or single expirations of breath, punctuated with quick inhalations at meaningful linguistic breaks.

Another argument—that a relatively flat base in Neandertal skulls would have prevented speech—has no merit, as some modern adults show as much flattening, yet have no trouble talking. Clearly, when the anatomical evidence is considered in its totality, there seems no compelling reason to deny Neandertals the ability to speak.

---

[36] Ambrose, p. 1751.

[37] Ibid.

[38] Schepartz, p. 98.

[39] MacLarnon, A. M., & Hewitt, G. P. (1999). The evolution of human speech: The role of enhanced breathing control. *American Journal of Physical Anthropology 109,* 341–363.

The discovery of a "language gene" by Swedish paleogeneticist Svante Pääbo and colleagues at the Max Planck Institute for Evolutionary Anthropology in Leipzig, Germany, adds an interesting new dimension to the study of the evolution of language.[40] The gene, called FOXP2 found on chromosome 7, was identified through the analysis of a family in which members spanning several generations have severe language problems. Changes in the gene are hypothesized to control the ability to make fine movements of the mouth and larynx necessary for spoken language. The identification of this gene in humans allowed scientists to compare its structure to that found in other mammalian species.

The human FOXP2 gene differs from versions of the gene found in the chimpanzee, gorilla, orangutan, rhesus macaque, and mouse. While these differences among living species can be known, applying this knowledge to the earlier members of the genus *Homo* is far more difficult. We do not know precisely when in human evolution the human form of the FOXP2 gene appeared or whether this gene was associated with the formation of a new species of *Homo*.

In light of these genetic discoveries it is also interesting to consider the work done on language capacity in the great apes. For example, in her work with the bonobo named Kanzi, Sue Savage-Rumbaugh documented his ability to understand hundreds of spoken words and associate them with lexigrams (pictures of words) on a computer display while unable to create the sounds himself.[41] Speech and language are not identical.

[40] Lai, C. S. L., et al. (2001). A forkhead-domain gene is mutated in severe speech and language disorder. *Nature 413,* 519–523; Enard, W., et al. (2002). Molecular evolution of FOXP2, a gene involved in speech and language. *Nature 418,* 869–872.

[41] Savage-Rumbaugh, S., & Lewin, R. (1994). *Kanzi: The ape at the brink of the human mind.* New York: Wiley.

Culture, Skulls, and Modern Human Origins

For Middle Paleolithic *Homo,* cultural adaptive abilities relate to the fact that brain size was comparable to that of people living today. Archaeological evidence indicates sophisticated technology, as well as conceptual thought of considerable complexity, matching the increased cranial capacity. During this same time period, large-brained individuals with skulls with an anatomically modern shape began to appear. The earliest specimens with this skull shape—a more vertical forehead, diminished brow ridge, and a chin—appear first in Africa and later in Asia and Europe. Whether the derived features in the skull indicate the appearance of a new species with improved cultural capabilities remains a hotly debated question.

The transition from the Middle Paleolithic to the tools of the Upper Paleolithic occurred around 40,000 years ago, some 100,000 years or so after the appearance of the first anatomically modern specimens in Africa. The Upper Paleolithic is known not only for a veritable explosion of tool industries, but also for clear artistic expression preserved in representative sculptures, paintings, and engravings (see Chapter 9). But the earliest anatomically modern humans, like the Neandertals and other archaic forms, used tools of the Middle Paleolithic traditions.

The relationship between cultural developments of the Upper Paleolithic and underlying biological differences between anatomically modern humans and archaic forms remains one of the most contentious debates in paleoanthropology. Discussions concerning the fate of the Neandertals and their cultural abilities are integral to this debate. Whether or not a new kind of human—anatomically modern with correspondingly superior intellectual and creative abilities—is responsible for the cultural explosion of the Upper Paleolithic is considered in Chapter 9.

Questions for Reflection

1. Members of the genus *Homo* draw upon integrated biological and cultural capabilities to face the challenges of existence. How do these factors play into the designation of species in the fossil record?

2. Paleoanthropologists can be characterized as "lumpers" or "splitters" depending upon their approach to the identification of species in the fossil record. Which of these approaches do you prefer and why?

3. In his 1871 book *Descent of Man, and Selection in Relation to Sex,* Charles Darwin stated, "Thus man has ultimately become superior to woman. It is indeed fortunate that the law of equal transmission of characters prevails with mammals. Otherwise it is probable that man would have become as superior in mental endowment to woman as the peacock is in ornamental plumage to the peahen." How were the cultural norms of Darwin's time reflected in his statement? Can 21st-century paleoanthropologists speak about differences between the sexes in evolutionary contexts without introducing their own cultural biases?

4. Animals ranging from rabbits to plants have come to occupy new niches without the benefits of culture. Was the spread of *Homo* out of the African continent possible without the benefit of culture?

5. Though language itself does not "fossilize," the archaeological and fossil records provide some evidence of the linguistic capabilities of our ancestors. Using the evidence available, what sort of linguistic abilities do you think early *Homo* possessed?

Suggested Readings

Corballis, M. C. (2003). *From hand to mouth: The origins of human language.* Princeton, NJ: Princeton University Press.

This book, written by a psychologist, takes the position that facial and manual gestures rather than vocalization are key to the development of language. It brings data from linguistics, molecular genetics, animal behavior, psychology, and neurology to the anthropological question of when human language arose.

Delson, E., Tattersal, I., Brooks, A., & Van Couvering, J. (1999). *Encyclopedia of human evolution and prehistory.* New York: Garland.

Using an A to Z format, this user-friendly encyclopedia includes over 800 entries relating to human evolution and prehistory. It includes excellent diagrams, illustrations, and descriptions of key archaeological sites.

Potts, R. (1997). *Humanity's descent: The consequences of ecological instability.* New York: Avon.

Written by the director of the Smithsonian Institution's Human Origins Program, this book suggests that environmental instability was the unifying factor contributing to the acquisition of human language and culture.

Stanford, C. B. (2001). *The hunting apes: Meat eating and the origins of human behavior.* Princeton, NJ: Princeton University Press.

Though updated and less gender biased, this work revisits the old "man the hunter" hypothesis, suggesting that human intelligence is linked to the acquisition of meat and food sharing.

Walker, A., & Shipman, P. (1997). *The wisdom of the bones: In search of human origins.* New York: Vintage.

This book provides an engaging description of the discovery of the most complete *Homo erectus* specimen—the Nariokotome Boy from Lake Turkana, Kenya—as well as placing it within the context of the larger story of human evolution.

Zihlman, A. (2001). *The human evolution coloring book.* New York: Harper Resources.

Do not be deceived by the title or the book's visual hands-on format. This book provides an authoritative scientific approach to all aspects of the study of human evolution.

Challenge Issue Th [illegible] he size and weight of a small clus [illegible] ogically rich Hohle Fels Cave in sou [illegible] ned earliest presence of undispute [illegible] ological interpretations of the orig [illegible] earliest figurative art had included only representations of animals; female figurines did not appear until about 30,000 years ago. The exaggerated breasts and vulva and stylized markings on this carving, as on similar prehistoric statuettes known as Venus figurines, indicate the importance of female fertility to our ancestors. Did our ancestors worship the power of females to give birth? Do these figurines represent our ancestors' attempts to connect groups of people to one another across time and space? Such creations suggest that humans, as a thoughtful and self-reflecting species, have always faced the challenge of understanding where and how we fit in the larger natural system of all life forms, past and present. In turn, these figurines challenge us to weigh whether a biological change was at the root of this creative expression, which would have separated these ancestors from the archaic *Homo sapiens* that came before them.

CHAPTER 9

The Global Expansion of *Homo sapiens* and Their Technology

Chapter Preview

When Did Anatomically Modern Forms of *Homo sapiens* Appear?

Although 160,000-year-old fossils from Ethiopia have been described as anatomically modern, the answer to this question is quite complex. Anatomical modernity refers to particular characteristics in the shape of the skull. While all humans today are members of a single species, and as such are equally "modern," some contemporary populations do not meet the definition of anatomical modernity used by some paleoanthropologists. To exclude contemporary humans from the species based on the shape of their skulls is an obvious impossibility. By extension, the application of this definition of anatomical modernity to the fossil record is a source of debate. Still, it is generally agreed that by 30,000 years ago, Upper Paleolithic populations in all parts of the inhabited world showed greater resemblance to more recent human populations than earlier large-brained *Homo*.

When and How Did Humans Spread to Australia and the Americas?

Around the time of the Upper Paleolithic, humans expanded into new regions, most dramatically Australia and the Americas. Expansion into Australia and New Guinea required crossing a deep, wide ocean channel and was thus dependent upon sophisticated watercraft. Spread to the Americas involved successful adaptation to Arctic conditions and movement over land through northeastern Asia to the Americas, along with the use of watercraft over even more extended distances. Anthropologists use archaeological, linguistic, and biological evidence to reconstruct the spread of humans into these new regions.

What Is the Relationship Between Middle Paleolithic *Homo* and Modern *Homo sapiens*?

Some paleoanthropologists propose that Neandertals, like other archaic forms, evolved into anatomically modern versions of *Homo sapiens* as different features of modern anatomy arising in other regional populations were carried to them through gene flow. In this framework, human populations throughout Africa, Europe, and Asia contributed to the making of modern humans. Other paleoanthropologists propose that anatomically modern humans with superior cultural capabilities appeared first in Africa about 200,000 years ago, replacing existing archaic forms as they spread from Africa to the rest of the world.

What Was the Culture of Upper Paleolithic Peoples Like?

Between 70,000 and 40,000 years ago the global archaeological record begins to become richer, not only with varied and sophisticated tool industries but also with evidence of increased human creativity, ingenuity, and problem solving. Upper Paleolithic cultures generally include a greater diversity of tools than previously, as well as a greater frequency of blade tools. Pressure-flaking techniques and the use of burins to fashion implements of bone and antler became widespread. In Europe, success of large game hunting increased with the invention of the spear-thrower, or atlatl, and nets aided in hunting of small game. In Africa the earliest small points appropriate for arrowheads appear during this time period. There was as well an explosion of creativity, represented by impressive works of art discovered in a variety of sites in Africa, Australia, Eurasia, and Australia.

The remains of ancient people who looked more like contemporary Europeans than Neandertals were first discovered in 1868 at Les Eyzies in France, in a rock shelter together with tools of the **Upper** (late) **Paleolithic.** Consisting of eight skeletons, they are commonly referred to as **Cro-Magnons,** after the rock shelter in which they were found. The name was extended to thirteen other specimens recovered between 1872 and 1902 in the caves of southwestern France and, since then, to other Upper Paleolithic skeletons discovered in other parts of Europe.

Because Cro-Magnons were found with Upper Paleolithic tools and seemed responsible for the production of impressive works of art, they were seen as particularly clever when compared with the Neandertals. The idea that Neandertals were dimwitted comfortably supported the prevailing stereotype of their supposedly brutish appearance. Their Mousterian tools were interpreted as evidence of cultural inferiority. Hence, Cro-Magnons were regarded as an anatomically modern people with a superior culture sweeping into Europe and replacing a primitive local population. This idea mirrored the European conquest of other parts of the world during the colonial expansion that was concurrent with the discovery of these fossils.

With the invention of reliable dating techniques in the 20th century, we now know that many Neandertal specimens of Europe and the later Cro-Magnon specimens date from different time periods. The Middle Paleolithic Mousterian technology is associated with earlier fossil specimens, Upper Paleolithic technology and art with later fossil specimens. Perhaps the most Eurocentric aspect of all is that historically this discussion focused on the European fossil evidence instead of incorporating evidence from throughout the globe. Recent fossil evidence for early anatomical modernity in Africa, evidence of regional continuity from Asia, and associated genetic studies allow paleoanthropologists to develop more comprehensive theories for the origins of modern humans.

Upper Paleolithic The last part (10,000 to 40,000 years ago) of the Old Stone Age, featuring tool industries characterized by long slim blades and an explosion of creative symbolic forms.

Cro-Magnon A European of the Upper Paleolithic after about 36,000 years ago.

Upper Paleolithic Peoples: The First Modern Humans

What do we mean by modernity? Paleoanthropologists look at both skull shape of and cultural practices. But still this is a difficult designation to make. While Cro-Magnons resemble later populations of modern Europeans—in braincase shape, high broad forehead, narrow nasal openings, and common presence of chins—their faces were on average shorter and broader than those of modern

In the novel and movie *Clan of the Cave Bear*, the anatomically modern heroine is depicted as a tall blonde beauty while Neandertals are depicted as dark and sloppy. These images conform both to the stereotypes about Neandertals and aesthetic standards in the Western dominant culture.

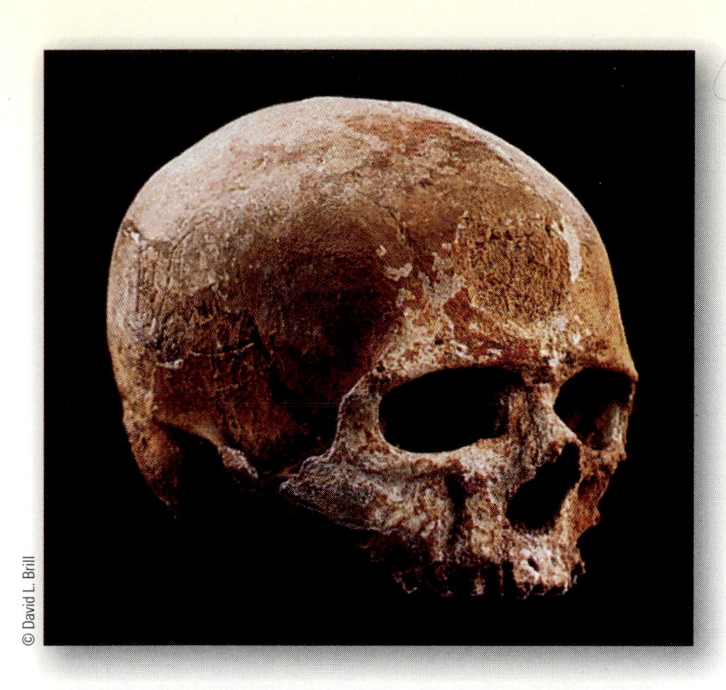

© David L. Brill

With a high forehead, the Cro-Magnon skull is more like contemporary Europeans compared to the prominent brow ridge and sloping forehead seen in the Neandertal skull. Whether these differences in skull shape account for their cultural differences rather than their relative age is hotly debated. The more recent Cro-Magnon skull even preserves evidence of cultural continuity in diet with local contemporary French people. This skull has evidence of a fungal infection, perhaps from eating tainted mushrooms. Mushrooms are a delicacy in this region of France to this day.

Europeans, their brow ridges were a bit more prominent, and their teeth and jaws were as large as those of Neandertals. Some (a skull from the original Cro-Magnon site, for instance) even display the distinctive occipital bun of the Neandertals on the back of the skull.[1] Nor were they particularly tall, as their height of 5 feet 7 or 8 inches (170–175 centimeters) does not fall outside the Neandertal range. Similarly, early Upper Paleolithic skulls from Brno, Mladec, and Predmosti, in the Czech Republic, retain heavy brow ridges and Neandertal-like muscle attachments on the back of the skull.[2]

Although the Cro-Magnons and Upper Paleolithic peoples from Africa and Asia are now routinely referred to as "anatomically modern," it is surprisingly difficult to be precise about what we mean by this. We think of people with brains the size of modern people, but this had already been achieved by archaic *H. sapiens.* Average brain size actually peaked in Neandertals at 10 percent larger than the contemporary human average. The reduction to today's average size correlates with a reduction in brawn, as bodies have become less massive overall. Modern faces and jaws are, by and large, smaller as well, but there are exceptions. For example, anthropologists Milford Wolpoff and Rachel Caspari have pointed out that any definition of modernity that excludes Neandertals also excludes substantial numbers of recent and living Aborigines in Australia, although they are, quite obviously, a contemporary people. The fact is, no multidimensional diagnosis of anatomical modernity can be both exclusive of archaic populations and inclusive of all contemporary humans.[3]

Defining modernity in terms of culture also raises some questions. The appearance of modern-sized brains in archaic *Homo* was related to increased reliance on cultural adaptation, but the Upper Paleolithic was a time of great technological innovation. The emphasis on cultural adaptation led to the development of more complex tool kits; Upper Paleolithic tool kits are known for a preponderance of blade tools, with flint flakes at least twice as long as they are wide. The earliest blade tools come from sites in Africa, but these tools do not make up the majority of the tool types until well into the Upper Paleolithic. The Upper Paleolithic archaeological record also contains a proliferation of expressive arts.

Ultimately, technological improvements may also have reduced the intensity of selective pressures that had previously favored especially massive robust bodies, jaws, and teeth. With new emphasis on elongated tools having greater mechanical advantages, more effective techniques of hafting, a switch from thrusting to throwing spears, and development of net hunting, there was a marked reduction in overall muscularity. In addition, as the environment changed to milder conditions from the extreme cold that prevailed in Eurasia during the last Ice Age, selective pressure for short stature as an adaptation to conserve body heat may have also diminished.

The Human Origins Debate

On a biological level, the great human origins debate can be distilled to a question of whether one, some, or all populations of the archaic groups played a role in the evolution of modern *Homo sapiens.* Those supporting the multiregional hypothesis argue for a simultaneous local transition from *H. erectus* to modern *H. sapiens*

[1] Brace, C. L. (1997). Cro-Magnons "R" us? *Anthropology Newsletter 38* (8), 1.

[2] Bednarik, R. G. (1995). Concept-mediated marking in the Lower Paleolithic. *Current Anthropology 36,* 627; Minugh-Purvis, N. (1992). The inhabitants of Ice Age Europe. *Expedition 34* (3), 33–34.

[3] Wolpoff, M., & Caspari, R. (1997). *Race and human evolution: A fatal attraction* (pp. 344–345, 393). New York: Simon & Schuster.

throughout the parts of the world inhabited by members of the genus *Homo*. By contrast, those supporting a theory of recent African origins argue that all contemporary peoples are derived from one single population of archaic *H. sapiens* from Africa. This model proposes that the improved cultural capabilities of anatomically modern humans allowed this group to replace other archaic forms as they began to migrate out of Africa sometime after 100,000 years ago. Both theories are explored in detail below.

The Multiregional Hypothesis

As several anthropologists have noted, African, Chinese, and southeastern Asian fossils of archaic *Homo sapiens* imply continuity within these respective populations, from *H. erectus* through to modern *H. sapiens*;[4] this lends strong support to the interpretation that there was genetic continuity in these regions. For example, in China, Pleistocene fossils from the genus *Homo* consistently have small forward-facing cheeks and flatter faces than their contemporaries elsewhere, as is still true today. In Southeast Asia and Australia, by contrast, skulls are consistently robust, with huge cheeks and forward projection of the jaws.

In this model, gene flow among populations keeps the human species unified throughout the Pleistocene. No speciation events remove ancestral populations such as *H. erectus* or Neandertals from the line leading to *H. sapiens*. Although proponents of the **multiregional hypothesis** accept the idea of continuity from the earliest European fossils through the Neandertals to living people, many other paleoanthropologists reject the idea that Neandertals were involved in the ancestry of modern Europeans.

[4] Wolpoff, M. H., Wu, X. Z., & Thorne, A. G. (1984). Modern *Homo sapiens* origins: A general theory of hominid evolution involving fossil evidence from East Asia (pp. 411–483). In F. H. Smith & F. Spencer (Eds.), *The origins of modern humans*. New York: Alan R. Liss; Wolpoff & Caspari; Pope, G. G. (1992). Craniofacial evidence for the origin of modern humans in China. *Yearbook of Physical Anthropology 35*, 291.

multiregional hypothesis The hypothesis that modern humans originated through a process of simultaneous local transition from *Homo erectus* to *Homo sapiens* throughout the inhabited world.

recent African origins or "Eve" hypothesis The hypothesis that all modern people are derived from one single population of archaic *Homo sapiens* from Africa who migrated out of Africa after 100,000 years ago, replacing all other archaic forms due to their superior cultural capabilities; also called the out of Africa hypothesis.

The Recent African Origins or "Eve" Hypothesis

The **recent African origins or "Eve" hypothesis** (also called the *out of Africa hypothesis*) states that anatomically modern humans are descended from one specific population of *Homo sapiens*, replacing not just the Neandertals but other populations of archaic *H. sapiens* as our ancestors spread out of their original homeland. This idea did not originate from fossils, but from a relatively new technique that uses mitochondrial DNA (mtDNA) to reconstruct family trees.

Unlike nuclear DNA (in the cell nucleus), mtDNA is located in the mitochondria, the cellular structures that produce the energy needed to keep cells alive. Because sperm contribute virtually no mtDNA to the fertilized egg, mtDNA is inherited essentially from one's mother and is not subject to recombination through meiosis and fertilization with each succeeding generation as is nuclear DNA. Therefore, changes in mtDNA over time occur only through mutation. By comparing the mtDNA of living individuals from diverse geographic populations, anthropologists and molecular biologists seek to determine when and where modern *H. sapiens* originated (Figure 9.1).

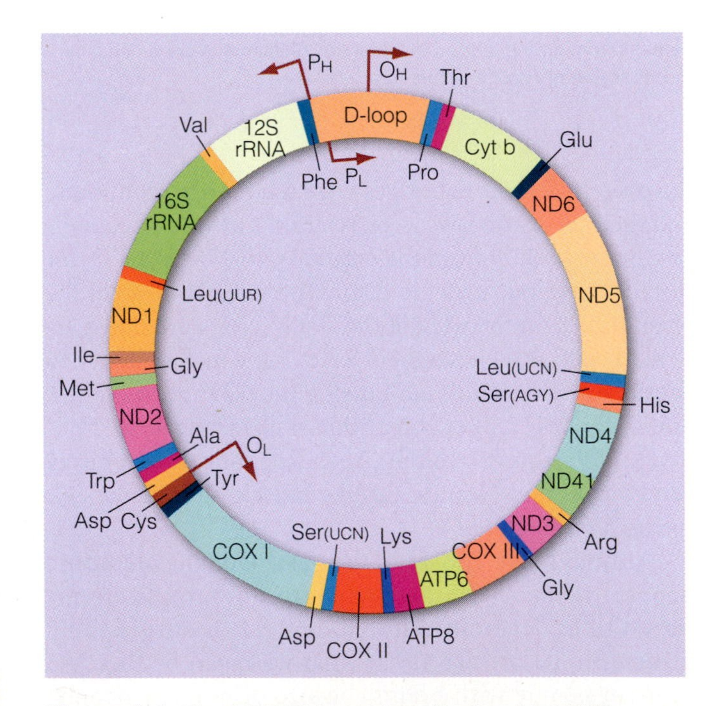

Figure 9.1 The 16,569 bases in mitochondrial DNA (mtDNA) are organized into circular chromosomes present in large numbers in every cell. The human mtDNA sequence has been entirely sequenced, with functional genes identified. Because mtDNA is maternally inherited and not subject to recombination, it can be used to establish evolutionary relationships. However, population size impacts the preservation of variation in the mtDNA genome and complicates using contemporary mtDNA variation to calibrate a molecular clock.

Visual Counterpoint

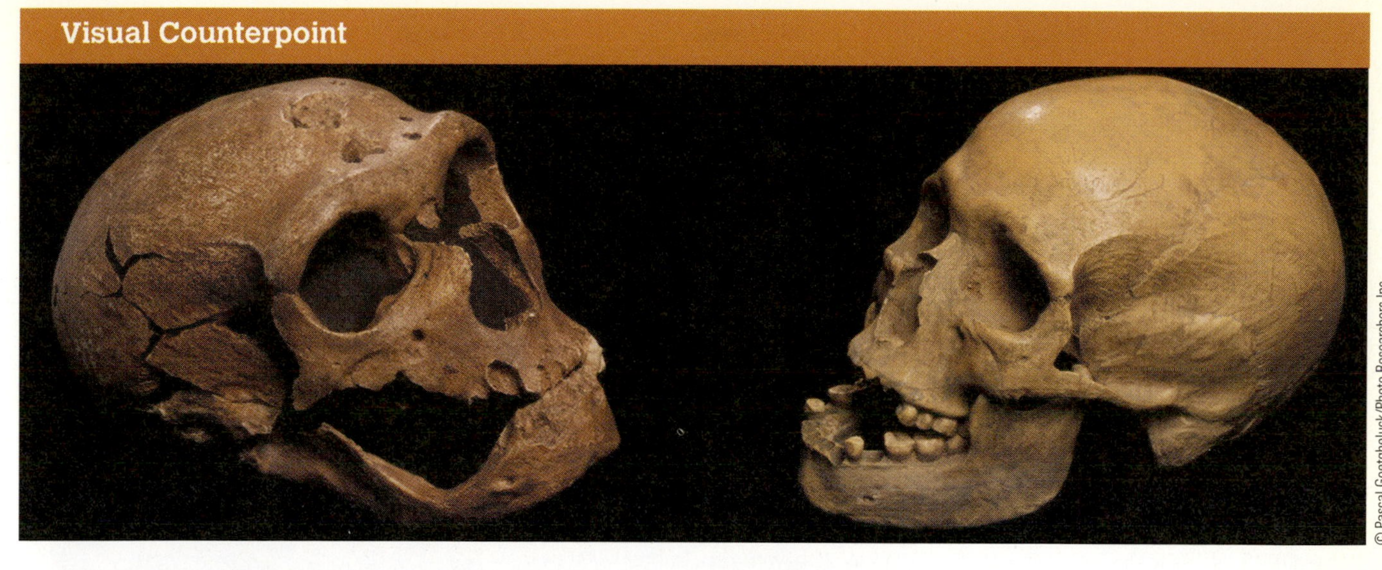

A comparison of the Neandertal (left) and the contemporary *H. sapiens* (right) shows that while both possess large brains there are distinct differences in the shape of the skull. The Neandertal has a large face, pronounced brow ridges, and a low, sloping forehead while the contemporary *H. sapiens* has a high forehead and a chin. The back of the Neandertal, though not visible from this angle, is robust (as seen in the Herto skull pictured below). In what other ways is Herto like these two specimens? How do these three skulls compare to the Cro Magnon skull pictured on page 205?

As widely reported in the popular press (including cover stories in *Newsweek* and *Time*), preliminary results suggest that the mitochondrial DNA of all living humans could be traced back to a "mitochondrial Eve" who lived in Africa some 200,000 years ago. If so, all other populations of archaic *H. sapiens,* as well as non-African *H. erectus,* would have to be ruled out of the ancestry of modern humans.

The recently discovered well-preserved specimens from Herto, Ethiopia, provide the best fossil evidence in support of the recent African origins hypothesis. Though these fossils unquestionably possess an anatomically modern appearance, they are still relatively robust. In addition, it is not clear whether the higher skull and forehead indicate superior cultural abilities.

For many years, the recent African origins theory has been weakened by the lack of good fossil evidence from Africa. In 2003, however, skulls of two adults and one child, discovered in Ethiopia in East Africa in 1997, were described as anatomically modern and were reconstructed and dated to 160,000 years ago (see Anthropologists of Note).[5] The discoverers of these fossils called them *Homo sapiens idaltu* (meaning "elder" in the local Afar language). While conceding that the skulls are robust, they believe that these skulls have conclusively proved the recent African origins hypothesis, relegating Neandertals to a side branch of human evolution.

Reconciling the Evidence

Though the recent African origins hypothesis is the majority position among Western paleoanthropologists, the theory does not prevail throughout the globe. Chinese

[5] White, T., et al. (2003). Pleistocene *Homo sapiens* from the Middle Awash, Ethiopia. *Nature 423,* 742–747.

Anthropologists of Note

Berhane Asfaw (b. 1953) ▪ Xinzhi Wu (b. 1930)

Born in Addis Ababa, Ethiopia, in 1953, **Berhane Asfaw** is a world-renowned paleoanthropologist leading major expeditions in Ethiopia. He is co-leader of the international Middle Awash Research Project, the research team responsible for the discovery of spectacular ancestral fossils dating from the entire 6-million-year course of human evolutionary history, including *Ardipithecus ramidus, Australopithecus afarensis, Australopithecus garhi, Homo erectus,* and, most recently, the *Homo sapiens idaltu* fossils from Herto, Ethiopia.

At the June 2003 press conference, organized by Teshome Toga, Ethiopia's minister of culture, Asfaw described the Herto specimens as the oldest "anatomically modern" humans, likening Ethiopia to the "Garden of Eden." This conference marked a shift in the Ethiopian government's stance toward the paleoanthropological research spanning Asfaw's career. Previous discoveries in the Middle Awash were also very important, but the government did not participate or support this research.

Asfaw entered the discipline of paleoanthropology through a program administered by the Leakey Foundation providing fellowships for Africans to pursue graduate studies in Europe and the United States. Since this program's inception in the late 1970s, the Leakey Foundation has awarded sixty-eight fellowships totaling $1.2 million to Kenyans, Ethiopians, and Tanzanians to pursue graduate education in paleoanthropology.

Asfaw, mentored by American paleoanthropologist Desmond Clark at the University of California, Berkeley, was among the earliest fellows in this program. They first met in 1979 when Asfaw was a senior studying geology in Addis Ababa. Asfaw obtained his doctorate in 1988 and returned to Ethiopia, where he had few Ethiopian anthropological colleagues, and the government had halted fossil exploration. Since that time, Asfaw has recruited and mentored many Ethiopian scholars, including Sileshi Semaw (see Chapter 8), and now has about a dozen on his team. Local scientists can protect the antiquities, keep fossils from disappearing, and mobilize government support. Asfaw's leadership in paleoanthropology has played a key role in helping the government recognize how important prehistory is for Ethiopia.

Xinzhi Wu is one of China's foremost paleoanthropological scholars, contributing to the development of the discipline for the past fifty years. As with many other paleoanthropologists, the study of human anatomy has been of vital importance to him.

He began his academic career with a degree from Shanghai Medical College followed by teaching in the Department of Human Anatomy at the Medical College in Dalian before beginning graduate studies in paleoanthropology. He is presently a professor at the Chinese Academy of Sciences Institute of Vertebrate Paleontology and Paleoanthropology in Beijing and the honorary president of the Chinese Society of Anatomical Sciences.

In addition to managing excavations in China and other parts of Asia, Wu has played a major role in the development of theories about modern human origins in cooperation with scholars internationally. He collaborated with Milford Wolpoff of the United States and Alan Thorne of Australia in the development of the theory of multiregional continuity for modern human origins. This theory fits well with the Asian fossil evidence proposing an important place for *Homo erectus* in modern human origins. Interestingly, it builds upon the model for human origins developed by Franz Weidenreich (see Chapter 8).

According to Wu, early humans from China are as old if not older than humans anyplace else. He suggests that the reason more fossils have been found in Africa recently is that Africa has been the site for more excavations.

Zhoukoudian remains a site of particular importance for Wu, as it documents continuous habitation of early humans and one of the earliest sites with evidence of controlled use of fire. Wu has predicted that more important discoveries will still be made at Zhoukoudian as a third of this site has still not been fully excavated. The Chinese government has responded to Wu's suggestions and is presently constructing a 2.4-square-kilometer "Peking Man" exhibition and paleoanthropology research area at Zhoukoudian.

Wu has welcomed many international scholars to China to study the Asian evidence. He also has led efforts to make descriptions of fossil material available in English. Collaborating with anthropologist Frank Poirier, he published the comprehensive volume *Human Evolution in China,* describing the fossil evidence and archaeological sites with great accuracy and detail.

paleoanthropologists, for example, favor the multiregional hypothesis because it fits well with the fossil discoveries from Asia and Australia. By contrast, the recent African origins hypothesis depends more upon the interpretation of fossils and cultural remains from Europe, Africa, and Southwest Asia. Three kinds of evidence are used to both support and critique each hypothesis for modern human origins: genetic, anatomical, and cultural.

The Genetic Evidence

Though genetic evidence has been the cornerstone of the recent African origins hypothesis, molecular evidence also provides grounds to challenge it. For example, upon reanalysis, the molecular evidence indicates that Africa was not the sole source of mtDNA in modern humans.[6] In addition, because both theories propose African origins for the human line, molecular data could be interpreted as evidence supporting the African origins of the genus *Homo,* rather than the more recent species *Homo sapiens.* Both models place ultimate human origins firmly in Africa.

Other assumptions made by DNA analysis are problematic. For example, it is assumed that rates of mutation are steady, when in fact they can be notoriously uneven. Another assumption is that mtDNA is not subject to selection, when in fact variants have been implicated in epilepsy and in a disease of the eye.[7] Another issue is that DNA is seen as traveling exclusively *from* Africa, when it is known that, over the past 10,000 years, there has been plenty of movement of humans *into* Africa as well. In fact, one study of DNA carried on the Y chromosome (the sex chromosome inherited exclusively in the male line) suggests that DNA on the Y chromosome of some Africans was introduced from Asia, where it originated some 200,000 years ago.[8] Nevertheless, recent work on the Y chromosome by anthropologist and geneticist Spencer Wells traces the human lineage to a single population living in Africa about 60,000 years ago.[9]

Despite the seeming conflict, all of these data indicate that gene flow has been an important aspect of human evolutionary history. The multiregional hypothesis and recent African origins hypothesis differ in terms of whether this gene flow occurred over the course of 200,000 or 2 million years.

Since 1997, studies of mitochondrial DNA have not been limited to living people. In that year, mtDNA was extracted from the original German Neandertal remains, and two other Neandertals have since been studied. Because the mtDNA of each of these differs substantially from modern Europeans, many have concluded that there can be no Neandertal ancestry in living humans and that Neandertals must constitute a separate species that went extinct.

But biological anthropologist John Relethford (a specialist in anthropological genetics) points out that these conclusions are premature.[10] For one thing, the average differences are not as great as those seen among living subspecies of the single species of chimpanzee. For another, differences between populations separated in time by tens of thousands of years tell us nothing about differences between populations contemporaneous with each other. More meaningful would be comparison of the DNA from a late Neandertal with an early anatomically modern European.

Finally, if we are to reject Neandertals in the ancestry of modern Europeans because their DNA cannot be detected in their supposed descendents, then we must also reject any connection between a 40,000- to 62,000-year-old skeleton from Australia (that everyone agrees is anatomically modern) and more recent native Australians. In this case, a mtDNA sequence present in an ancient human seems to have become extinct, in which case we must allow the same possibility for the Neandertals.[11] In short, it is definitely premature to use genetic evidence to remove from modern human ancestry all populations of archaic *H. sapiens* save those of Africa. Not even the Neandertals can be excluded.

The Anatomical Evidence

Though the recent fossil discoveries certainly provide evidence of the earliest anatomically modern specimens in Africa, they do not resolve the relationship between biological change in the shape of the skull and cultural change as preserved in the archaeological record. The changes in the archaeological record and the appearance of anatomically modern skulls are separated by some 100,000 years. The evidence from Southwest Asia is particularly interesting in this regard. Here, at a variety of sites dated to between 50,000 and 100,000 years ago, fossils described as both anatomically modern and Neandertal are present and associated with Mousterian technology.

Nevertheless, recent African origins proponents argue that anatomically modern peoples coexisted for a time with other archaic populations until the superior cultural capacities of the "moderns" resulted in extinction of the archaic peoples. Especially clear evidence of this is said to exist in Europe, where Neandertals and "moderns" are said to have coexisted in close proximity between 30,000 and 40,000 years ago. However, defining fossils as either Neandertals or "moderns" illustrates the difficulty with defining a distinct biological species, given the presence of variation found in humans.

---

[6] Templeton, A. R. (1995). The "Eve" hypothesis: A genetic critique and reanalysis. *American Anthropologist 95* (1), 51–72.

[7] Shreeve, J. (1995). *The Neandertal enigma: Solving the mystery of modern human origins* (p. 121). New York: William Morrow.

[8] Gibbons, A. (1997). Ideas on human origins evolve at anthropology gathering. *Science 276,* 535–536.

[9] Wells, S. (2002). *The journey of man: A genetic odyssey.* Princeton, NJ: Princeton University Press.

[10] Relethford, J. H. (2001). Absence of regional affinities of Neandertal DNA with living humans does not reject multiregional evolution. *American Journal of Physical Anthropology 115,* 95–98.

[11] Gibbons, A. (2001). The riddle of coexistence. *Science 291,* 1726.

If we think in terms of varied populations, as seen in living humans today,[12] we find that features reminiscent of modern humans can be discerned in some of the latest Neandertals. A specimen from Saint Césaire in France, for example, has a higher forehead and the presence of a chin. A number of other Neandertals, too, show incipient chin development as well as reduced facial protrusion and smaller brow ridges. Conversely, the earliest anatomically modern human skulls from Europe often exhibit features reminiscent of Neandertals (see Chapter 8). In addition, some typical Neandertal features such as the occipital bun are found in diverse living populations today such as Bushmen from southern Africa, Finns and Saami from Scandinavia, and Australian Aborigines. Accordingly, we might view the population of this region between 30,000 and 40,000 years ago as a varied one, with some individuals retaining a stronger Neandertal heritage than others, in whom modern characteristics are more prominent (Figure 9.2). If all these groups were members of the same species, gene flow would be expected, and individuals would express a mosaic of traits.

A mix of modern and Neandertal features is so strong in a child's skeleton recently found in Portugal as to lead several specialists to regard it as clear evidence of hybridization, or successful reproduction between the two groups.[13] This would mean that the two forms are of a single species, rather than separate ones. Others, of course, argue that features [illegible] ight ins[illegible]

[illegible] tals are [illegible] the sim[illegible] e is that [illegible] population, with [illegible] individuals showing more typical Neandertal features than others. This accords with archaeological evidence that the intellectual abilities of "late Neandertals" were no different from those of "early moderns."[15]

[12] Gould, S. J. (1996). *Full house: The spread of excellence from Plato to Darwin* (pp. 72–73). New York: Harmony.

Aurignacian tradition Tool-making tradition in Europe and western Asia at the beginning of the Upper Paleolithic.

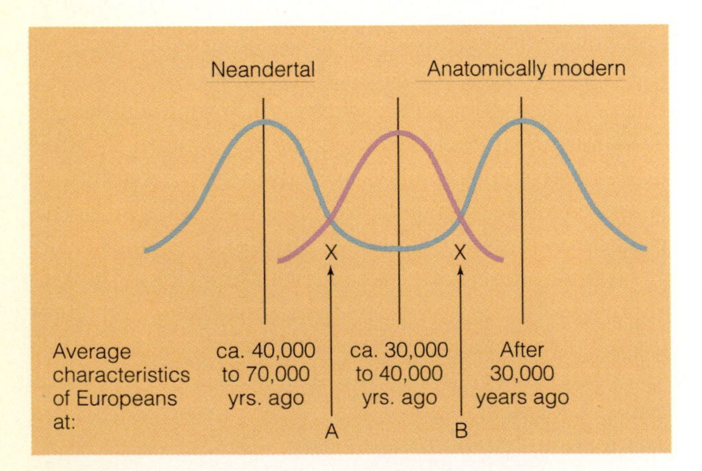

Figure 9.2 Graphically portrayed here is a shift in average characteristics of an otherwise varied population over time from Neandertal to more modern features. Between 30,000 and 40,000 years ago, we would expect to find individuals with characteristics such as those of the Saint Césaire Neandertal (A) and the almost (but not quite) modern Cro-Magnon (B).

The Cultural Evidence

Just as it is difficult to find evidence in the physical or mental makeup of Neandertals that would have prevented them from leading a typical Upper Paleolithic way of life, so too are there problems with using technology to distinguish Neandertals from their contemporaries. The Mousterian tool kits were used by Neandertals and anatomically modern humans alike during the Middle Paleolithic. At the time of the Upper Paleolithic transition, the latest Neandertals of Europe developed their own Upper Paleolithic technology (the Châtelperronian) comparable to the industries used by anatomically modern *H. sapiens.* No earlier than 36,500 years ago,[16] a new Upper Paleolithic technology, known as the **Aurignacian tradition**—named after Aurignac, France, where tools of this sort were first discovered—appeared in Europe (Figure 9.3).

Though commonly considered to have spread from southwestern Asia, a recent reanalysis failed to sustain this idea, suggesting instead that the Aurignacian is a distinctively European development.[17] Skeletal remains are rarely associated with Aurignacian tools, although anatomically modern humans are generally considered the makers of these tools. A notable exception to this notion is the central European site of Vindija, Croatia, where Neandertals are associated with an Aurignacian split-bone point.[18]

Some argue that the Upper Paleolithic technology of the Neandertals was a crude imitation of the true technological

[13] Holden, C. (1999). Ancient child burial uncovered in Portugal. *Science 283,* 169.

[14] Tattersall, I., & Schwartz, J. H. (1999). Hominids and hybrids: The place of Neanderthals in human evolution. *Proceedings of the National Academy of Science 96* (13), 7117–7119.

[15] d'Errico, F., et al. (1998). Neandertal acculturation in Western Europe? *Current Anthropology 39,* 521.

[16] Zilhão, J. (2000). Fate of the Neandertals. *Archaeology 53* (4), 30.

[17] Clark, G. A. (2002). Neandertal archaeology: Implications for our origins. *American Anthropologist 104* (1), 50–67.

[18] Karavani, I., & Smith, F. H. (2000). More on the Neanderthal problem: The Vindija case. *Current Anthropology 41,* 839.

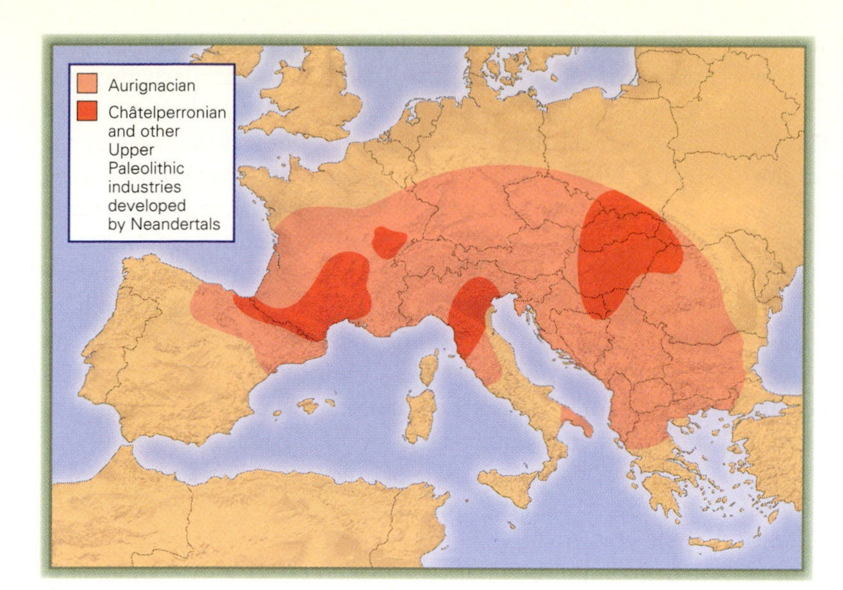

Figure 9.3 Between 30,000 and 36,500 years ago, Upper Paleolithic industries developed from the Mousterian tradition by European Neandertals coexisted with the Aurignacian industry, usually associated with anatomically modern humans.

advancements practiced by anatomically modern humans. In some respects, however, Neandertals outdid their anatomically modern contemporaries, as in the use of red ochre, a substance less frequently used by Aurignacian peoples than by their late Neandertal neighbors.[19] This cannot be a case of borrowing ideas and techniques from Aurignacians, as these developments clearly predate the Aurignacian.[20]

Coexistence and Cultural Continuity

Neandertals and anatomically modern humans also coexisted in Southwest Asia long before the cultural innovations of the Upper Paleolithic (Figure 9.4). Here neither the skeletal nor the archaeological evidence supports cultural difference between the fossil groups or absolute biological difference. Although Neandertal skeletons are clearly present at sites such as the caves of Kebara and Shanidar in Israel and Iraq, respectively, skeletons from some older sites have been described as anatomically modern.

At the cave site of Qafzeh near Nazareth in Israel, for example, 90,000-year-old skeletons are said to show none of the Neandertal hallmarks; although their faces and bodies are large and heavily built by today's standards, they are nonetheless claimed to be within the range of living peoples. Yet, a statistical study comparing a number of measurements from among Qafzeh, Upper Paleolithic, and Neandertal skulls found those from Qafzeh to fall in between the anatomically modern and

[19] Bednarik, p. 606.

[20] Zilhão, p. 40.

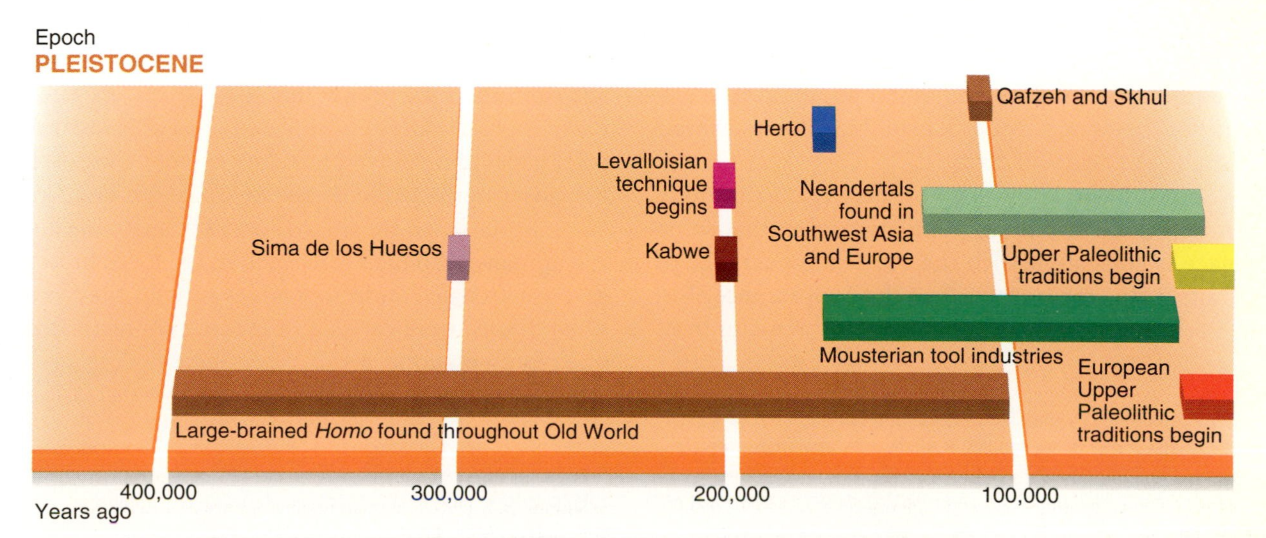

Figure 9.4 Around 400,000 years ago, large-brained members of the genus *Homo* began to be found throughout Africa and Eurasia; corresponding cultural changes are evident as well.

Neandertal norms, though slightly closer to the Neandertals.[21] Nor is the dentition functionally distinguishable when Qafzeh and Neandertal are compared.[22]

While skeletons from Skhul, a site on Mount Carmel of the same period, are similar to those from Qafzeh, they were also part of a population whose continuous range of variation included individuals with markedly Neandertal characteristics. Furthermore, the idea of two distinctly different but coexisting populations receives no support from the archaeological evidence. Individuals living at Skhul and Qafzeh were making and using the same Mousterian tools as those at Kebara and Shanidar, a fact that belies biologically distinct groups having different cultural abilities.

The examination of sites continuously inhabited throughout the Upper Pleistocene provides no significant evidence for behavioral differences between Middle Paleolithic and early Upper Paleolithic at these sites. For example, the Upper Paleolithic peoples who used Kebara Cave continued to live in exactly the same way as their Neandertal predecessors: They procured the same foods, processed them in the same way, used similar hearths, and disposed of their trash in the same way. The only evident difference is that the Neandertals did not use small stones or cobbles to bank their fires for warmth as did their Upper Paleolithic successors.[23]

Nevertheless, by 28,000 years ago, many of the extreme anatomical features seen in archaic groups like Neandertals seem to disappear from the fossil record in Europe and Southwest Asia. Instead, people with higher foreheads, smoother brow ridges, and distinct chins seemed to have Europe more or less to themselves. However, an examination of the full range of individual human variation across the globe and into the present reveals contemporary humans with skulls not meeting the anatomical definition of modernity proposed in the standard evolutionary arguments.[24] Similarly, many Neandertal features can be seen in living people today such as the occipital buns mentioned earlier. As is typical in human populations, contemporary peoples and Upper Paleolithic peoples exhibit considerable physical variability.

It is impossible to know just how much gene flow took place among ancient human populations, but that some took place is consistent with the sudden appearance of novel traits in one region later than their appearance elsewhere. For example, some Upper Paleolithic remains from North Africa exhibit the kind of midfacial flatness previously seen only in East Asian fossils; similarly, various Cro-Magnon fossils from Europe show the short upper jaws, horizontally oriented cheek bones, and rectangular eye orbits previously seen in East Asians. Conversely, the round orbits, large frontal sinuses, and thin cranial bones seen in some archaic *H. sapiens* skulls from China represent the first appearance there of traits that have greater antiquity in Europe.[25] The movement of these physical traits has a complex genetic basis that depends upon gene flow among populations.

Not only is such gene flow consistent with the remarkable tendency humans have to "swap genes" between populations, even in the face of cultural barriers, but it is also consistent with the tendency of other primates to produce hybrids when two subspecies (and sometimes even species) come into contact.[26] Moreover, without such gene flow, evolution inevitably would have resulted in the appearance of multiple species of modern humans, something that clearly has not happened. In fact, the low level of genetic differentiation among modern human populations can be explained easily as a consequence of high levels of gene flow.[27]

Race and Human Evolution

The Neandertal question can be viewed as more than simply a fascinating discussion about interpreting the fossil evidence. It raises fundamental issues about the relationship between biological and cultural variation. Can a series of biological features indicate particular cultural abilities?

As we examined the fossil record throughout this chapter and others, we made inferences about the cultural capabilities of our ancestors based on biological features in combination with archaeological features. The increased brain size of *Homo habilis* noted around 2.5 million years ago supported the notion that these ancestors were capable of more complex cultural activities than australopithecines, including the manufacture of stone tools. When we get closer to the present, can we make the same kinds of assumptions? Can we say that only the anatomically modern humans, with high foreheads and reduced brow ridges, and not archaic *Homo sapiens,* even with their modern-sized brains, were capable of making sophisticated tools and representational art?

[21] Corruccini, R. S. (1992). Metrical reconsideration of the Skhul IV and IX and Border Cave I crania in the context of modern human origins. *American Journal of Physical Anthropology 87,* 433–445.

[22] Brace, C. L. (2000). *Evolution in an anthropological view* (p. 206). Walnut Creek, CA: Altamira.

[23] Corruccini, p. 436.

[24] Wolpoff & Caspari.

[25] Pope, pp. 287–288.

[26] Simons, E. L. (1989). Human origins. *Science 245,* 1349.

[27] Relethford, J. H., & Harpending, H. C. (1994). Craniometric variation, genetic theory, and modern human origins. *American Journal of Physical Anthropology 95,* 265.

Supporters of the multiregional hypothesis argue that we cannot.[28] They suggest that using a series of biological features to represent a type of human being (Neandertals) with certain cultural capacities (inferior) is like making assumptions about cultural capabilities of living humans based on their appearance. In living peoples, such an assumption would be considered stereotyping or even racism. Supporters of the recent African origins hypothesis counter that because their theory embraces African human origins, it could hardly be considered prejudicial.

While paleoanthropologists all acknowledge African origins for the first bipeds and the genus *Homo,* considerable disagreement exists with regard to the interpretation of the relationship between biological change and cultural change as we approach the present. The fossil and archaeological evidence from the Middle Paleolithic does not indicate a simple one-to-one correspondence between cultural innovations and a biological change preserved in the shape of the skull.

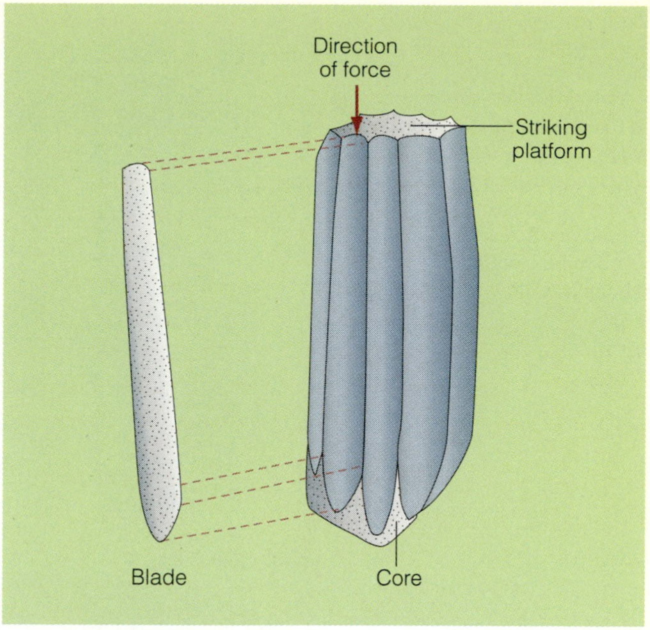

Upper Paleolithic Technology

In the Upper Paleolithic new techniques of core preparation allowed for more intensive production of highly standardized blades and permitted the proliferation of this tool type. The toolmaker formed a cylindrical core, struck the blade off near the edge of the core, and repeated this procedure, going around the core in one direction until finishing near its center (Figure 9.5). The procedure is analogous to peeling long leaves off an artichoke. With this **blade technique,** an Upper Paleolithic flint knapper could get 75 feet of working edge from a 2-pound core; a Mousterian knapper could get only 6 feet from the same sized core.

Other efficient techniques of tool manufacture also came into common use at this time. One such method was **pressure flaking,** in which a bone, antler, or wooden tool was used to press rather than strike off small flakes as the final step in stone tool manufacture (Figure 9.6). The advantage of this technique is that the toolmaker has greater control over the final shape of the tool than is possible with percussion flaking alone. The so-called Solutrean laurel leaf bifaces found in Spain and France are examples of this technique (see photo on page 214). The longest of these tools is 33 centimeters (13 inches) in length but less than a centimeter (about a quarter of an inch) thick. Through pressure flaking, tools could be worked with great precision into a variety of final forms, and worn tools could be effectively resharpened over and over until they were too small for further use.

Although invented in the Middle Paleolithic, the **burin,** a tool with a chisel-like edge, became more common in the Upper Paleolithic. Burins facilitated the working of bone, horn, antler, and ivory into such useful things as fishhooks, harpoons, and eyed needles. These implements made life easier for *Homo sapiens,* especially in colder

Direction of force

Striking platform

Blade

Core

Figure 9.5 During the Upper Paleolithic, a new technique was used to manufacture blades. The stone is worked to create a striking platform; long, almost parallel-sided flakes then are struck around the sides, providing sharp-edged blades.

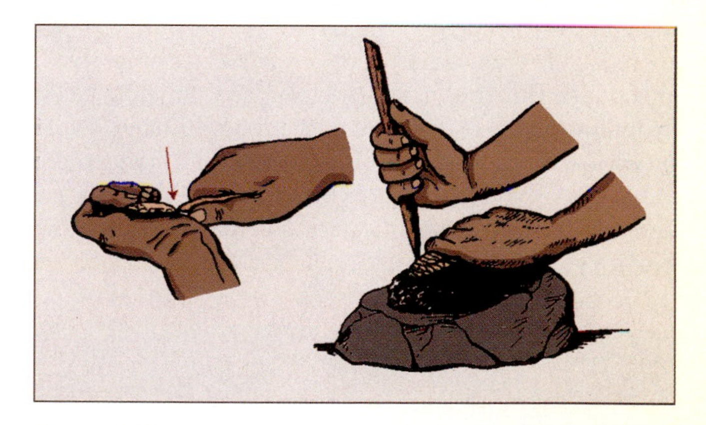

Figure 9.6 Two methods used for pressure flaking in which a bone, antler, or wooden tool is used to press rather than strike off small flakes.

blade technique A technique of stone tool manufacture in which long, parallel-sided flakes are struck off the edges of a specially prepared core.

pressure flaking A technique of stone tool manufacture in which a bone, antler, or wooden tool is used to press, rather than strike off, small flakes from a piece of flint or similar stone.

burin A stone tool with chisel-like edges used for working bone and antler.

[28] Wolpoff & Caspari.

The techniques of the Upper Paleolithic allowed for the manufacture of a wide variety of tools. The finely wrought Solutrean bifaces of Europe (shaped like the leaf of a plant) were made using the pressure-flaking technique. Tools such as eyed needles and harpoons began to be manufactured out of bone as well.

northern regions where the ability to stitch together animal hides was particularly important for warmth.

The spear-thrower, also known by its Aztec name *atlatl,* appeared at this time as well. Atlatls are wooden devices, one end of which is gripped in the hunter's hand, while the other end has a hole or hook, in or against which the end of the spear is placed. It is held so as to effectively extend the length of the hunter's arm, thereby increasing the velocity of the spear when thrown. Using a spear-thrower greatly added to the efficiency of the spear as a hunting tool (Figure 9.7).

With handheld spears, hunters had to get close to their prey to make the kill. Because many of the animals they hunted were large and fierce, this was a dangerous business. The need to get within close striking range and the improbability of an instant kill exposed the hunter to considerable risk. But with the spear-thrower, the effective killing distance was increased; experiments demonstrate

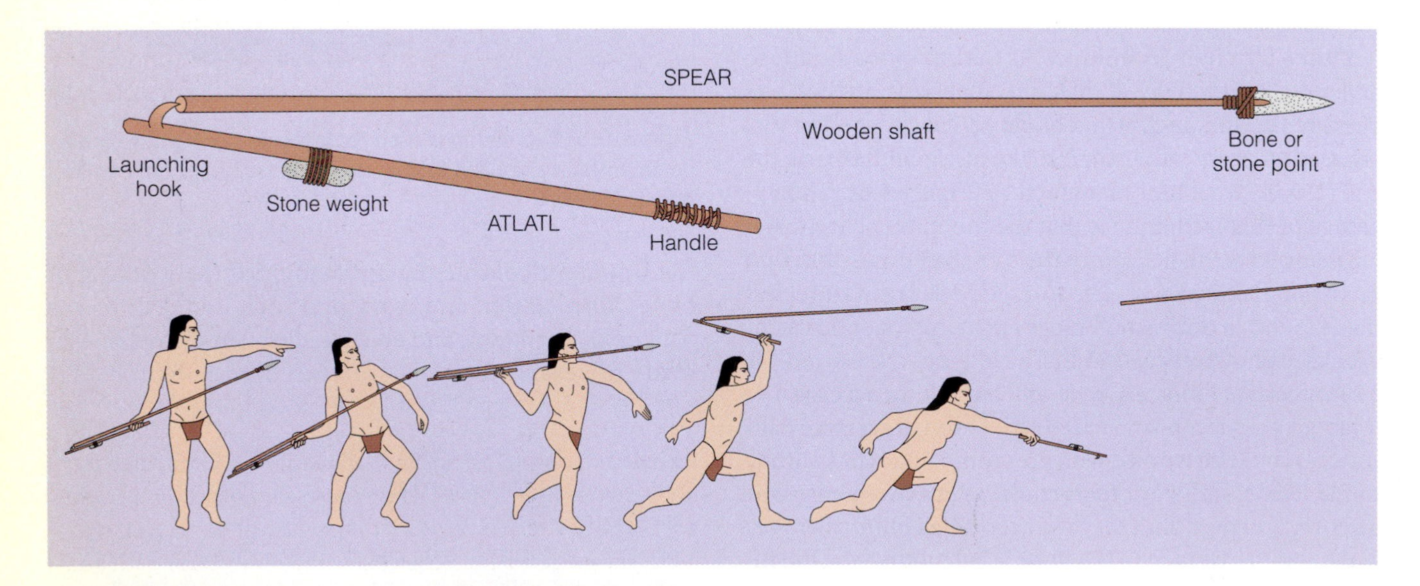

Figure 9.7 **Spear-throwers (atlatls) allowed Upper Paleolithic individuals to throw spears at animals from a safe distance while still maintaining reasonable speed and accuracy. Upper Paleolithic artists frequently combined artistic expression with practical function, ornamenting their spear-throwers with animal figures.**

that the effective killing distance of a spear when used with a spear-thrower is between 18 and 27 meters as opposed to significantly less without.[29]

Killing distance can be safely shortened when the kill is assured. The use of poison on spear tips, as employed by contemporary hunters such as the Hadza of Tanzania, will decrease the risk to a hunter at shorter range. It is not clear from the archaeological record when this innovation began, although the invention of tiny sharp stone blades for dart tips to provide a vehicle for poison delivery is clear. The earliest examples of these "microliths" began during the Upper Paleolithic in Africa, but did not become widespread until the Mesolithic or Middle Stone Age, as will be described in detail in Chapter 10.

Another important innovation, net hunting, appeared some time between 22,000 and 29,000 years ago.[30] Knotted nets, made from the fibers of wild plants such as hemp or nettle, left their impression on the clay floors of huts when people walked on them. When the huts later burned, these impressions, baked into the earth, provide evidence that nets existed. Their use accounts for the high number of hare, fox, and other small mammal and bird bones at archaeological sites. Like historically known and contemporary net hunters, such as the Mbuti of the Congo, everyone—men, women, and children—probably participated, frightening animals with loud noises to drive them to where hunters were stationed with their nets. In this way, large amounts of meat could be amassed without requiring great speed or strength on the part of the hunters.

A further improvement of hunting techniques came with the invention of the bow and arrow, which appeared first in Africa, but not until the end of the Upper Paleolithic in Europe. The greatest advantage of the bow is that it increases the distance between hunter and prey. Beyond 24 meters (79 feet), the accuracy and penetration of a spear thrown with a spear-thrower are not very good, whereas even a poor bow will shoot an arrow further, with greater accuracy and penetrating power. A good bow is effective even at nearly 91 meters (300 feet). Thus hunters were able to maintain more distance between themselves and dangerous prey, dramatically decreasing the risk to the hunter of being seriously injured by an animal fighting for survival as well as reducing the chance of startling an animal and triggering its flight.

Upper Paleolithic peoples not only had better tools but also a greater diversity of tool types than earlier peoples. The highly developed Upper Paleolithic kit included tools for use during different seasons, and regional variation in tool kits was greater than ever before. Thus it is really impossible to speak of a single Upper Paleolithic culture even in Europe, a relatively small and isolated region compared to Asia and Africa. For foot nomads, it was a formidable challenge to travel outside the region. Geologic features such as mountain ranges, oceans, and glaciers isolated groups of people from each other.

To understand the Upper Paleolithic, one must consider the many different traditions that made it possible for people to adapt ever more specifically to the various environments in which they were living. Just how proficient people had become at securing a livelihood is indicated by bone yards containing thousands of animal skeletons. At Solutré in France over a period of many years, for example, Upper Paleolithic hunters killed 10,000 horses; at Predmosti in the Czech Republic, they were responsible for the deaths of 1,000 mammoths. The favored big game of European hunters, however, was reindeer, which they killed in even greater numbers.

Upper Paleolithic Art

Although tools and weapons demonstrate the ingenuity of Upper Paleolithic peoples, artistic expression provides the best evidence of their creativity. Some have argued that artistic expression was made possible by a newly evolved biological ability to manipulate symbols and make images. However, the modern-sized brains of archaic *Homo sapiens* and increasingly compelling evidence of the presence of language or behaviors involving symbolism—such as burials—undercut this notion. Like agriculture, which came later (see Chapter 10), the artistic explosion may have been no more than a consequence of innovations made by a people who had the capacity to make them for tens of thousands of years already.

In fact, just as many of the distinctive tools that were commonly used in Upper Paleolithic times first appear in the Middle Paleolithic, so too do objects of art. In Southwest Asia, a crude figurine of volcanic tuff is some 250,000 years old.[31] While some scholars contest whether this was carved, those who believe it is state that it indicates that people had the ability to carve all sorts of things from wood, a substance easier to fashion than volcanic tuff but rarely preserved for long periods of time. Furthermore, ochre "crayons" from Middle Paleolithic contexts in various parts of the world must have been used to decorate or mark. In southern Africa, for example, regular use of yellow and red ochre goes back 130,000 years, with some

[29] Frayer, D. W. (1981). Body size, weapon use, and natural selection in the European Upper Paleolithic and Mesolithic. *American Anthropologist 83*, 58.

[30] Pringle, H. (1997). Ice Age communities may be earliest known net hunters. *Science 277*, 1203.

[31] Appenzeller, T. (1998). Art: Evolution or revolution? *Science 282*, 1452.

These 17,000-year-old images, painted on a wall in the multi-chambered Lascaux Cave in the Dordogne region of southwestern France, were discovered in 1940 by four teenage boys. In addition to the Ice Age animals depicted here—horses, wild ox, rhino, and bison—the chambers of Lascaux feature renderings of many other recognizable species. The carved and painted interiors of such caves were often deep underground and difficult to reach. Upper Paleolithic artists burned animal fat in sandstone lamps to light their way. In 1963 Lascaux Cave was closed to the public because carbon dioxide from the breath of thousands of visitors was damaging the ancient paintings. The French government built an exact replica of the cave so that visitors can still experience the wonder of these ancient works.

evidence as old as 200,000 years.[32] Perhaps pigments were used on people's bodies, as well as objects, as the 50,000-year-old mammoth-tooth *churinga* discussed in Chapter 8 might suggest. The timeline in Figure 9.8 shows some of the cultural events of the Upper Paleolithic.

Music

Evidence that music played a role in the lives of Upper Paleolithic peoples is documented through the presence of bone flutes and whistles in various sites, the most recently discovered dated to 35,000 years old. But again, such instruments may have their origin in Middle Paleolithic prototypes, such as the probable Neandertal flute discussed in Chapter 8. Although we cannot be sure just where and when it happened, some genius discovered that bows could be used not just for killing, but to make music as well. Because the bow and arrow is an Upper Paleolithic invention, the musical bow likely is as well. We do know that the musical bow is the oldest of all stringed instruments, and its invention ultimately made possible the development of all of the stringed instruments with which we are familiar today.

Cave or Rock Art

The earliest evidence of cave art comes from Australia and dates back at least 45,000 years. This consists entirely of geometric patterns and repetitive motifs. Figurative

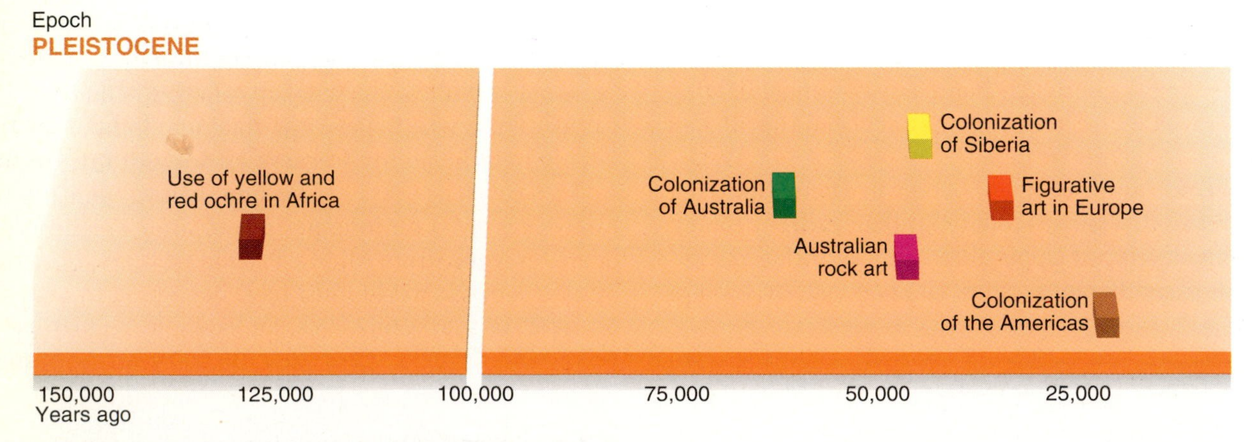

Figure 9.8 This timeline indicates the dates for some of the cultural innovations associated with the Upper Paleolithic.

© John Van Hasselt/Corbis Sygma

Rock art, like these paintings from Australia, depict things seen by dancers while in states of trance. Simple geometric designs such as zigzags, notches, dots, and spirals (as on the cave ceiling) as well as human and animal figures are common in these paintings.

pictures go back 35,000 years in Europe (the time of the Venus figurine of the chapter opener), although they do not become common until much later.

Pictorial art is probably equally old in Africa. Both engravings and paintings are known from many rock shelters and outcrops in southern Africa, where they continued to be made by Bushmen peoples until recently. Scenes feature both humans and animals, depicted with extraordinary skill, often in association with geometric and other abstract motifs. Some sites reveal that ancient peoples had the seemingly irresistible urge to add to existing rock paintings, while others used new sites for creating what we today call graffiti.

Because this rock art tradition continues unbroken into the present, it has been possible to discover what this art means. There is a close connection between the art and shamanism, and many scenes depict visions seen in states of trance. Distortions in the art, usually of human figures, represent sensations felt by individuals in a state of trance, whereas the geometric designs depict illusions that originate in the central nervous system in altered states of consciousness. These **entoptic phenomena** are luminous grids, dots, zigzags, and other designs that seem to shimmer, pulsate, rotate, and expand and are seen as one enters a state of trance. Sufferers of migraines experience similar hallucinations. Entopic phenomena are typical of the Australian cave art mentioned above.

In many recent cultures, geometric designs are used as symbolic expressions of genealogical patterns, records of origins, and the afterlife.[33] The animals depicted in this art, often with startling realism, are not the ones most often eaten. Rather, they are powerful beasts like the eland (a large African antelope), and this power is important to shamans—individuals skilled at manipulating supernatural powers and spirits for human benefit—who try to harness it for their rain-making, healing, and other rituals.

The most famous Upper Paleolithic art is that of Europe, largely because most researchers of prehistoric art are themselves of European background. Though the earliest of this art took the form of sculpture and engravings—often portraying such animals as reindeer, horses, bears, and ibexes—figurative art abounds in the spectacular paintings on the walls of 200 or so caves in southern France and northern Spain. The oldest of these date from about 32,000 years ago. Visually accurate portrayals of Ice Age mammals—including bison, aurochs, horses, mammoths, and stags—were often painted one on top of another.

Although well represented in other media, humans are not commonly portrayed in cave paintings, nor are

[32] Barham, L. S. (1998). Possible early pigment use in South-Central Africa. *Current Anthropology 39,* 709.

[33] Schuster, C., & Carpenter, E. (1996). *Patterns that connect: Social symbolism in ancient and tribal art.* New York: Abrams.

entoptic phenomena Bright pulsating forms that are generated by the central nervous system and seen in states of trance.

scenes or depictions of events at all common. Instead, the animals are often abstracted from nature and rendered two-dimensionally—no small achievement for these early artists. Sometimes the artists made use of bulges and other features of the rock to impart a more three-dimensional feeling. Frequently, the paintings are in hard-to-get-at places while suitable surfaces in more accessible places remain untouched. In some caves, the lamps by which the artists worked have been found; these are spoon-shaped objects of sandstone in which animal fat was burned. Experimentation has shown that such lamps would have provided adequate illumination over several hours.

The techniques used by Upper Paleolithic peoples to create their cave paintings were unraveled a decade ago through the experimental work of Michel Lorblanchet. Interestingly, they turn out to be the same ones used by Aboriginal rock painters in Australia. Lorblanchet's experiments are described in the following Original Study by science writer Roger Lewin.

Original Study

Paleolithic Paint Job *by Roger Lewin*

Lorblanchet's recent bid to re-create one of the most important Ice Age images in Europe was an affair of the heart as much as the head. "I tried to abandon my skin of a modern citizen, tried to experience the feeling of the artist, to enter the dialogue between the rock and the man," he explains. Every day for a week in the fall of 1990 he drove the 20 miles from his home in the medieval village of Cajarc into the hills above the river Lot. There, in a small, practically inaccessible cave, he transformed himself into an Upper Paleolithic painter.

And not just any Upper Paleolithic painter, but the one who 18,400 years ago crafted the dotted horses inside the famous cave of Pech Merle.

You can still see the original horses in Pech Merle's vast underground geologic splendor. You enter through a narrow passageway and soon find yourself gazing across a grand cavern to where the painting seems to hang in the gloom. "Outside, the landscape is very different from the one the Upper Paleolithic people saw," says Lorblanchet. "But in here, the landscape is the same as it was more than 18,000 years ago. You see what the Upper Paleolithic people experienced." No matter where you look in this cavern, the eye is drawn back to the panel of horses.

The two horses face away from each other, rumps slightly overlapping, their outlines sketched in black. The animal on the right seems to come alive as it merges with a crook in the edge of the panel, the perfect natural shape for a horse's head. But the impression of naturalism quickly fades as the eye falls on the painting's dark dots. There are more than 200 of them, deliberately distributed within and below the bodies and arcing around the right-hand horse's head and mane. More cryptic still are a smattering of red dots and half-circles and the floating outline of a fish. The surrealism is completed by six disembodied human hands stenciled above and below the animals.

Lorblanchet began thinking about recreating the horses after a research trip to Australia over a decade ago. Not only is Australia a treasure trove of rock art, but its aboriginal people are still creating it. "In Queensland I learned how people painted by spitting pigment onto the rock," he recalls. "They spat paint and used their hand, a piece of cloth, or a feather as a screen to create different lines and other effects. Elsewhere in Australia people used chewed twigs as paintbrushes, but in Queensland the spitting technique worked best." The rock surfaces there were too uneven for extensive brushwork, he adds—just as they are in Quercy.

When Lorblanchet returned home he looked at the Quercy paintings with a new eye. Sure enough, he began seeing the telltale signs of spit-painting—lines with edges that were sharply demarcated on one side and fuzzy on the other, as if they had been airbrushed—instead of the brushstrokes he and others had assumed were there. Could you produce lines that were crisp on both edges with the same technique, he wondered, and perhaps dots too? Archeologists had long recognized that hand stencils, which are common in prehistoric art,

© Jean Vertut

This spotted horse in the French cave of Pech Merle was painted by an Upper Paleolithic artist.

were produced by spitting paint around a hand held to the wall. But no one had thought that entire animal images could be created this way. Before he could test his ideas, however, Lorblanchet had to find a suitable rock face—the original horses were painted on a roughly vertical panel 13 feet across and 6 feet high. With the help of a speleologist, he eventually found a rock face in a remote cave high in the hills and set to work.

Following the aboriginal practices he had witnessed, Lorblanchet first made a light outline sketch of the horses with a charred stick. Then he prepared black pigment for the painting. "My intention had been to use manganese dioxide, as the Pech Merle painter did," says Lorblanchet, referring to one of the minerals ground up for paint by the early artists. "But I was advised that manganese is somewhat toxic, so I used wood charcoal instead." (Charcoal was used as pigment by Paleolithic painters in other caves, so Lorblanchet felt he could justify his concession to safety.) To turn the charcoal into paint, Lorblanchet ground it with a limestone block, put the powder in his mouth, and diluted it to the right consistency with saliva and water. For red pigment he used ochre from the local iron-rich clay.

He started with the dark mane of the right-hand horse. "I spat a series of dots and fused them together to represent tufts of hair," he says, unselfconsciously reproducing the spitting action as he talks. "Then I painted the horse's back by blowing the pigment below my hand held so"—he holds his hand flat against the rock with his thumb tucked in to form a straight line—"and used it like a stencil to produce a sharp upper edge and a diffused lower edge. You get an illusion of the animal's rounded flank this way."

He experimented as he went. "You see the angular rump?" he says, pointing to the original painting. "I reproduced that by holding my hand perpendicular to the rock, with my palm slightly bent, and I spat along the edge formed by my hand and the rock." He found he could produce sharp lines, such as those in the tail and in the upper hind leg, by spitting into the gap between parallel hands.

The belly demanded more ingenuity; he spat paint into a V-shape formed by his two splayed hands, rubbed it into a curved swath to shape the belly's outline, then finger-painted short protruding lines to suggest the animals' shaggy hair. Neatly outlined dots, he found, could not be made by blowing a thin jet of charcoal onto the wall. He had to spit pigment through a hole made in an animal skin. "I spent seven hours a day for a week," he says. "Puff . . . puff . . . puff. . . . It was exhausting, particularly because there was carbon monoxide in the cave. But you experience something special, painting like that. You feel you are breathing the image onto the rock—projecting your spirit from the deepest part of your body onto the rock surface."

Was that what the Paleolithic painter felt when creating this image? "Yes, I know it doesn't sound very scientific," Lorblanchet says of his highly personal style of investigation, "but the intellectual games of the structuralists haven't got us very far, have they? Studying rock art shouldn't be an intellectual game. It is about understanding humanity. That's why I believe the experimental approach is valid in this case."

Lewin, R. (1993). Paleolithic paint job. Discover 14 *(7), 67–69.*

Theories to account for the early European cave art are problematic because they often depend on conjectural and subjective interpretations. Some have argued that it is art for art's sake; but if that is so, why were animals often painted over one another, and why were they placed in inaccessible places? The latter might suggest that they were for ceremonial purposes and that the caves served as religious sanctuaries.

One suggestion is that the animals were drawn to ensure success in the hunt, another that their depiction was seen as a way to promote fertility and increase the size of the herds on which humans depended. In Altamira Cave in northern Spain, for example, the art shows a pervasive concern for the sexual reproduction of the bison.[34] In cave art generally, though, the animals painted show little relationship to those most frequently hunted. Furthermore, there are few depictions of animals being hunted or killed, nor are there depictions of animals copulating or with exaggerated sexual parts as there are in the Venus figures.[35]

Another suggestion is that initiation rites, such as those marking the transition to adulthood, took place in the painted galleries. In support of this idea, footprints, most of which are small, have been found in the clay floors of several caves, and in one they even circle a modeled clay bison. The painted animals, so this argument goes, may have had to do with knowledge being transmitted from the elders to the youths. Furthermore, the transmission of information might be implied by countless so-called signs, apparently abstract designs that accompany much Upper Paleolithic art. Some have interpreted these as tallies of animals killed, a reckoning of time according to a lunar calendar, or both.

These abstract designs, including such ones as the spots on the Pech Merle horses, suggest yet another possibility. For the most part, these are just like the entoptic designs seen by subjects in experiments dealing with altered states of consciousness and that are so consistently present in the rock art of southern Africa. Furthermore, the rock art of southern Africa shows the same painting of new

[34] Halverson, J. (1989). Review of the book *Altamira revisited and other essays on early art. American Antiquity 54,* 883.

[35] Conard, N. J. (2009). A female figurine from the basal Aurignacian deposits of Hohle Fels Cave in southwestern Germany. *Nature 459* (7244), 248.

images over older ones, as well as the same sort of fixation on large, powerful animals instead of the ones most often eaten. Thus the cave art of Europe may well represent the same depictions of trance experiences, painted after the fact. Consistent with this interpretation, the isolation of the cave and the shimmering light on the cave walls themselves are conducive to the sort of sensory distortion that can induce trance.

Ornamental Art

Artistic expression, whatever its purpose may have been, was not confined to rock surfaces and portable objects. Upper Paleolithic peoples also ornamented their bodies with necklaces of perforated animal teeth, shells, beads of bone, stone, and ivory, as well as rings, bracelets, and anklets. Clothing, too, was adorned with beads. Quite a lot of art was probably also executed in more delicate materials such as wood carving, painting on bark, and animal skins, which have not been preserved. Thus the rarity or absence of Upper Paleolithic art in some parts of the inhabited world may be due to the fact that some materials did not survive long in the archaeological record, not that they did not exist.

Gender and Art

As seen in the chapter opener, the Upper Paleolithic also includes numerous portrayals of voluptuous women with body parts often described as exaggerated. Many appear to be pregnant, and some are shown in birthing postures. These so-called Venus figures have been found at sites from southwestern France to as far as Siberia. Made of stone, ivory, antler, or baked clay, they differ little in style from place to place, testifying to the sharing of ideas over vast distances. Although some have interpreted the Venuses as objects associated with a fertility cult, others suggest that they may have been exchanged to cement alliances among groups.

Art historian LeRoy McDermott has suggested that the Venus figurines are "ordinary women's views of their own bodies" and the earliest examples of self-representation.[36] He suggests that the distortions and exaggerations of the female form visible in the Venus figurines derive from the ancient artist looking down over her own pregnant body. Paleolithic archaeologist Margaret Conkey opened the door to such interpretations through her work combining gender theory and feminist theory with the science of archaeology.

With a particular interest in the Upper Paleolithic art of Europe, Conkey has spent decades challenging the traditional notion that Paleolithic art was made by male artists as an expression of spiritual beliefs related to hunting activities. She emphasizes that many reconstructions of behavior in the past rely upon contemporary gender norms to fill in blanks left in the archaeological record. In other words, she is interested in the role of gender today in shaping the reconstruction of gender in the past. In the archaeological research she conducts, she seeks clues about gender in the deep past, evidence that is not shaped by gender stereotypes from the present.[37]

In this regard it is interesting to note that contemporary scientists describe Venus figurines largely in sexual terms rather than in terms of fertility and birth. For example, in a commentary in the prestigious journal *Nature* that accompanied the description of the the Hohle Fels Cave Venus, British archaeologist Paul Mellars states: "The figure is explicitly—and blatantly—that of a woman, with an exaggeration of sexual characteristics (large, projecting breasts, a greatly enlarged and explicit vulva, and bloated belly and thighs) that by twenty-first-century standards could be seen as bordering on the pornographic."[38]

Mellars's reaction to the Venus figurine reflects contemporary attitudes toward the nude female form rather than the intent of an ancient artist. Perhaps the artist was a female, looking at her own pregnant form or remembering the experience of giving birth. While the gender and the intention of the artist behind the Venus figurine cannot be known for sure, it is easy to imagine that pregnancy and the birth process were at least as awe-inspiring to Paleolithic peoples as were hunting experiences.

Human biology also provides us with some clues. Breasts and belly enlarge during pregnancy; the tissues around the vulva enlarge and stretch dramatically during the birth process. Breasts swell further with milk after a birth. Mellars's interpretation of the artistic depiction of these biological changes as "pornographic" derives from the gender norms of his particular culture. Many contemporary peoples with different worldviews would not react to the figurine in these terms.

Other Aspects of Upper Paleolithic Culture

Upper Paleolithic peoples lived not only in caves and rock shelters but also in structures built out in the open. In Ukraine, for example, the remains have been found of sizable settlements, in which huts were built on frameworks

[36] McDermott, L. (1996). Self-representation in Upper Paleolithic female figurines. *Current Anthropology 37*, 227–276.

[37] Gero, J. M., & Conkey, M. W. (Eds.). (1991). *Engendering archaeology: Women and prehistory.* New York: Wiley-Blackwell.

[38] Mellars, P. (2009). Archaeology: Origins of the female image. *Nature 459*, 176–177, at 176.

© Goran Burenhult

Reconstruction of an Upper Paleolithic hut with walls of interlocked mammoth mandibles.

of intricately stacked mammoth bones. Where the ground was frozen, cobblestones were heated and placed in the earth to sink in, thereby providing sturdy, dry floors. Their hearths, no longer shallow depressions or flat surfaces that radiated back little heat, were instead stone-lined pits that conserved heat for extended periods and made for more efficient cooking.

For the outdoors, they had the same sort of tailored clothing worn in historic times by Arctic and sub-Arctic peoples. And they engaged in long-distance trade, as indicated, for example, by the presence of seashells and Baltic amber at sites several hundred kilometers from the sources of these materials. Although Middle Paleolithic peoples also made use of rare and distant materials, they did not do so with the regularity seen in the Upper Paleolithic.

The Spread of Upper Paleolithic Peoples

Upper Paleolithic peoples expanded into regions previously uninhabited by their archaic forebears. Colonization of Siberia began about 42,000 years ago, although it took something like 10,000 years before humans reached the northeastern part of that region. While this spread did not involve crossing large bodies of water, this was the case for the spread to Greater Australia and the Americas.

The Sahul

Much earlier, possibly by at least 60,000 years ago, people managed to get to Australia, Tasmania, and New Guinea, then connected to one another in a single landmass called the **Sahul** (Figure 9.9).[39] To do this, they had to use some kind of watercraft because the Sahul was separated from the islands (which are geologically a part of the Asian landmass) of Java, Sumatra, Borneo, and Bali. At times of maximum glaciation and low sea levels, these islands were joined to one another in a single landmass called **Sunda,** but a deep ocean trench (called

[39] Rice, P. (2000). Paleoanthropology 2000—part 1. *General Anthropology 7* (1), 11; Zimmer, C. (1999). New date for the dawn of dream time. *Science 284,* 1243.

Sahul The greater Australian landmass including Australia, New Guinea, and Tasmania. At times of maximum glaciation and low sea levels, these areas were continuous.

Sunda The combined landmass of the contemporary islands of Java, Sumatra, Borneo, and Bali that was continuous with mainland Southeast Asia at times of low sea levels corresponding to maximum glaciation.

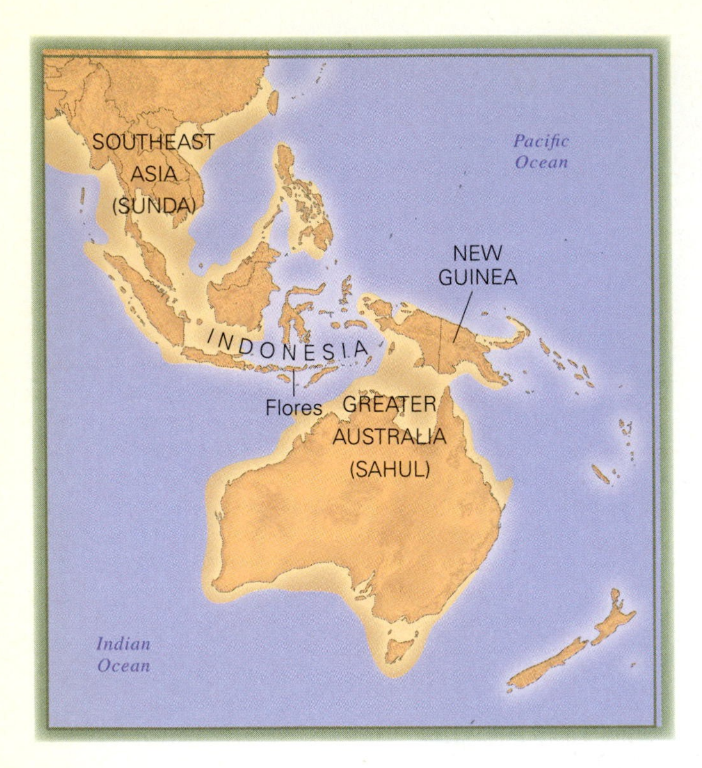

Figure 9.9 Habitation of Australia and New Guinea (joined together with Tasmania as a single landmass called Sahul) was dependent upon travel across the open ocean even at times of maximum glaciations when sea levels were low. This figure shows the coastlines of Sahul and Sunda (Southeast Asia plus the island of Java, Sumatra, Borneo, and Bali) now and in the past. As sea levels rose with melting glaciers, sites of early human habitation were submerged under water.

the Wallace Trench, after Alfred Russel Wallace, who, as described in Chapter 2, discovered natural selection at the same time as Charles Darwin) always separated Sunda and Sahul.

Anthropologist Joseph Birdsell suggested several routes of island hopping and seafaring to make the crossing between these landmasses.[40] Each of these routes still involves crossing open water without land visible on the horizon. The earliest known site in New Guinea dates to 40,000 years ago. Sites in Australia are dated to even earlier, but these dates are especially contentious because they involve the critical question of the relationship between anatomical modernity and the presence of humanlike culture. Early dates for habitation of the Sahul indicate that archaic *Homo* rather than anatomically modern forms possessed the cultural capacity for oceanic navigation. Once in Australia, these people created some of the world's earliest sophisticated rock art, perhaps some 10,000 to 15,000 years earlier than the more famous European cave paintings.

Interestingly, considerable physical variation is seen in Australian fossil specimens from this period. Some specimens have the high forehead characteristic of anatomical modernity while others possess traits providing excellent evidence of continuity between living Aborigines and the earlier *Homo erectus* and archaic *Homo sapiens* fossils from Indonesia. Willandra Lakes—the fossil lake region of southeastern Australia, far from where the earliest archaeological evidence of human habitation of the continent was found—is particularly rich with fossils. The variation present in these fossils illustrates the problems inherent with making a one-to-one correspondence between the skull of a certain shape and cultural capabilities.

Other evidence for sophisticated ritual activity in early Australia is provided by the burial of a man at least 40,000 and possibly 60,000 years ago from the Willandra Lakes region. His body was positioned with his fingers intertwined around one another in the region of his penis, and red ochre had been scattered over the body. It may be that this pigment had more than symbolic value; for example, its iron salts have antiseptic and deodorizing properties, and there are recorded instances in which red ochre is associated with prolonging life and is used medicinally to treat particular conditions or infections. One historically known Aborigine society is reported to have used ochre to heal wounds, scars, and burns. A person with internal pain was covered with the substance and placed in the sun to promote sweating. See this chapter's Globalscape to learn about the importance of Willandra Lakes to global and local heritage today.

As in many parts of the world, paleoanthropologists conducting research on human evolution in Australia are essentially constructing a view of history that conflicts with the beliefs of Aborigines. The story of human evolution is utterly dependent on Western conceptions of time, relationships established through genetics, and a definition of what it means to be human. All of these concepts are at odds with Aboriginal beliefs about human origins. Still, while conducting their research on human evolution, paleoanthropologists working in Australia have advocated and supported the Aboriginal culture.

The Americas

While scientists concur that American Indian ancestry can be traced ultimately back to Asian origins, just when people arrived in the Americas has been a matter of lively debate. This debate draws upon geographical, cultural, and biological evidence.

[40] Birdsell, J. H. (1977). The recalibration of a paradigm for the first peopling of Greater Australia. In J. Allen, J. Golson, & R. Jones (Eds.), *Sunda and Sahul: Prehistoric studies in Southeast Asia, Melanesia, and Australia* (pp. 113–167). New York: Academic.

Globalscape

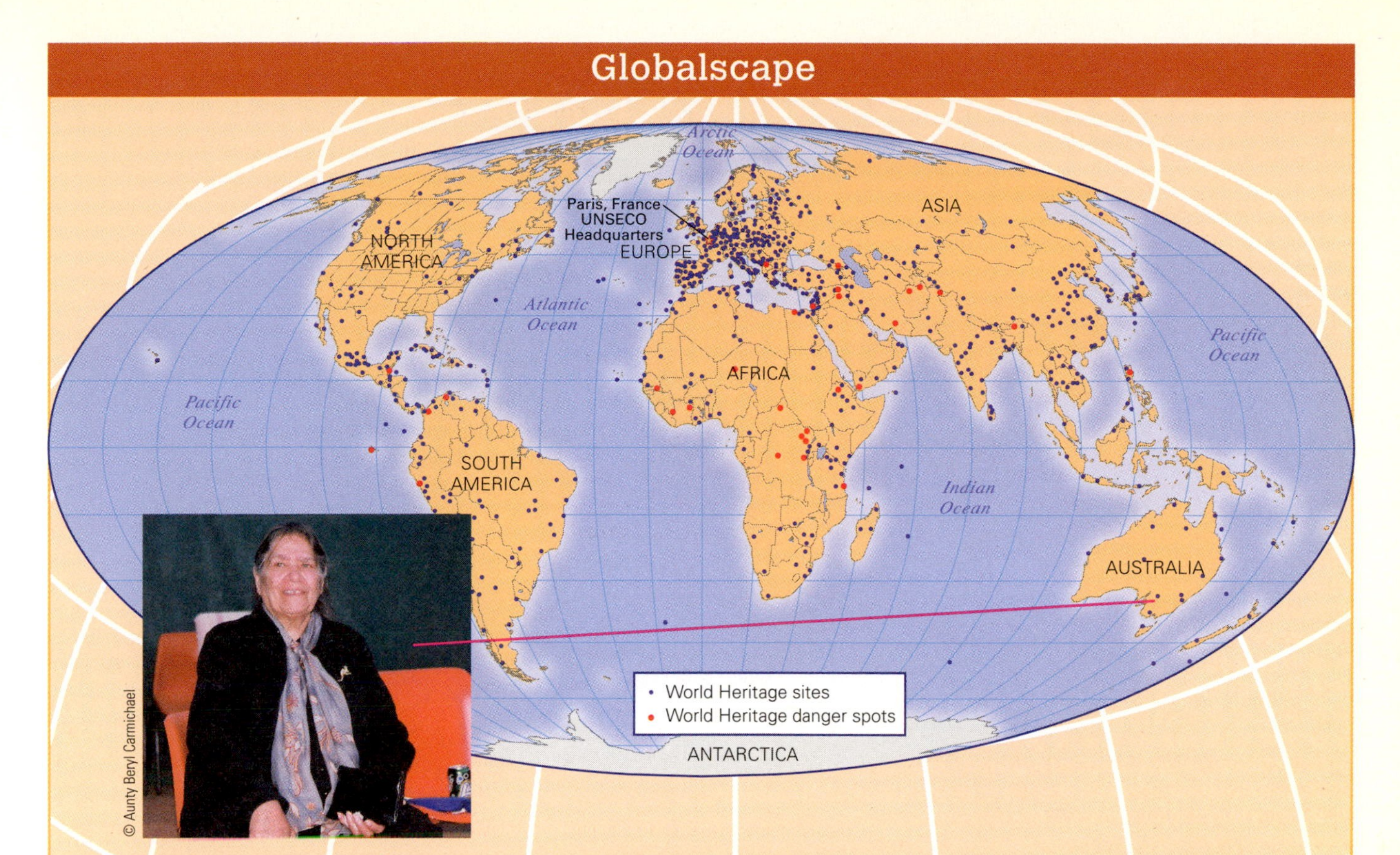

© Aunty Beryl Carmichael

Whose Lakes Are These?
Paleoanthropologists regularly travel to early fossil sites and to museums where original fossil specimens are housed. Increasingly, these same destinations are becoming popular with tourists. Making sites accessible for everyone while protecting the sites requires considerable skill and knowledge. But most importantly, long before the advent of paleoanthropology or paleotourism, these sites were and are the homelands of living people.

Aboriginal people have lived along the shores of the Willandra Lakes region of Australia for at least 50,000 years. They have passed down their stories and cultural traditions even as the lakes dried up and a spectacular crescent-shaped, wind-formed dune (called a lunette) remained. The Mungo lunette has particular cultural significance to three Aboriginal tribal groups. Several major fossil finds from the region include cremated remains as well as an ochred burial, both dated to at least 40,000 years ago. Nearly 460 fossilized footprints dated to between 19,000 and 23,000 years ago were made by people of all ages who lived in the region when the Willandra Lakes were still full of water. How can a place of local and global significance be appropriately preserved and honored?

Since 1972, UNESCO's World Heritage List has been an important part of maintaining places like Willandra Lakes, which was itself inscribed as a World Heritage Site in 1981. Individual states apply to UNESCO for site designation, and if approved they receive financial and political support for maintaining the site. When designated sites are threatened by natural disaster, war, pollution, or poorly managed tourism, they are placed on a danger list, indicated with a red dot on the map above, forcing the local governments to institute measures to protect the sites in order to continue receiving UNESCO support.

Each year approximately thirty new World Heritage sites are designated. In 2009 the list includes 890 properties: 176 natural preserves, 689 cultural sites, and 25 mixed sites. Fossil and archaeological sites are well represented on the World Heritage List. The Willandra Lakes site is recognized for both natural and cultural values.

While important to the world community, Willandra Lakes has particular meaning to the Aborigines. Aunty Beryl Carmichael, an elder of the Ngiyaampaa people, explains that this land is integrated with her culture:

> Because when the old people would tell the stories, they'd just refer to them as "marrathal warkan," which means long, long time ago, when time first began for our people, as people on this land after creation. We have various sites around in our country, we call them the birthing places of all our stories. And of course, the stories are embedded with the lore that governs this whole land. The air, the land, the environment, the universe, the stars.[a]

Not only are Aunty Beryl's stories and the land around Willandra Lakes critical for the Ngiyaampaa and other Aboriginal groups, but their survival ultimately contributes to all of us.

On the next page are listed the sites considered endangered at the June 2009 meeting of the World Heritage Committee. Committee members included representatives from countries throughout the globe including: Australia, Bahrain, Barbados, Brazil, Canada, China, Cuba, Egypt, Israel, Jordan, Kenya, South Korea, Madagascar, Mauritius, Morocco, Nigeria, Peru, Spain, Sweden, Tunisia, and the United States.

Globalscape

These Word Heritage Sites in Danger are indicated with a red dot on the preceding page.

Afghanistan
Cultural landscape and archaeological remains of the Bamiyan Valley (2003)
Minaret and archaeological remains of Jam (2002)

Belize
Belize Barrier Reef reserve system (2009)

Central African Republic
Manovo-Gounda St. Floris National Park (1997)

Chile
Humberstone and Santa Laura Saltpeter Works (2005)

Colombia
Los Katíos National Park (2009)

Côte d'Ivoire
Comoé National Park (2003)
Mount Nimba Strict Nature Reserve (1992)

Democratic Republic of the Congo
Garamba National Park (1996)
Kahuzi-Biega National Park (1997)
Okapi Wildlife Reserve (1997)
Salonga National Park (1999)
Virunga National Park (1994)

Ecuador
Galápagos Islands (2007)

Egypt
Abu Mena (2001)

Ethiopia
Simien National Park (1996)

Georgia
Historical Monuments of Mtskheta (2009)

Guinea
Mount Nimba Strict Nature Reserve (1992)

India
Manas Wildlife Sanctuary (1992)

Iran
Bam and its cultural landscape (2004)

Iraq
Ashur (Qal'at Sherqat) (2003)
Samarra archaeological city (2007)

Jerusalem (site proposed by Jordan)
Old City of Jerusalem and its walls (1982)

Niger
Air and Ténéré Natural Reserves (1992)

Pakistan
Fort and Shalamar Gardens in Lahore (2000)

Peru
Chan Chan archaeological zone (1986)

Philippines
Rice terraces of the Philippine Cordilleras (2001)

Senegal
Niokolo-Koba National Park (2007)

Serbia
Medieval monuments in Kosovo (2006)

Tanzania
Ruins of Kilwa Kisiwani and ruins of Songo Mnara (2004)

Venezuela
Coro and its port (2005)

Yemen
Historic town of Zabid (2000)

Global Twister The listing of endangered sites brings global pressure on a state to find ways to protect the natural and cultural heritage contained within its boundaries. Do you think this method of global social pressure is effective?

[a] Australian Museum Archives. http://australianmuseum.net.au/movie/Why-the-stories-are-told-Aunty-Beryl

The conventional wisdom has long been that the first people migrated into North America over dry land that connected Siberia to Alaska. This so-called land bridge was a consequence of the buildup of great continental glaciers. As these ice masses grew, there was a worldwide lowering of sea levels, causing an emergence of land in places like the Bering Strait where seas today are shallow. Thus Alaska became, in effect, an eastward extension of Siberia (Figure 9.10). Climatic patterns of the Ice Age kept this land bridge, known as Beringia or the Bering Land Bridge, relatively ice free and covered instead with lichens and mosses that could support herds of grazing animals. It is possible that Upper Paleolithic peoples could have come to the Americas simply by following herd animals. The latest genetic evidence indicates movement took place back and forth across Beringia.

According to geologists, conditions were right for ancient humans and herd animals to traverse Beringia between 11,000 and 25,000 years ago. Though this land bridge was also open between 40,000 and 75,000 years ago, there is no evidence that conclusively confirms human migration at these earlier dates. As with the Sahul, early dates open the possibility of spread to the Americas by archaic *Homo*.

Although ancient Siberians did indeed spread eastward, it is now clear that their way south was blocked by massive glaciers until 13,000 years ago at the earliest.[41] By then, people were already living further south in the Americas. Thus the question of how people first came to this hemisphere has been reopened. One possibility is that, like the first Australians, the first Americans may have come by boat or rafts, perhaps traveling between islands or ice-free pockets of coastline, from as far away as the Japanese islands and down North America's northwestern coast. Hints of such voyages are provided by a handful of North American skeletons (such as Kennewick Man) that bear a closer resemblance to the aboriginal Ainu people of northern Japan and their forebears than they do to other Asians or contemporary Native Americans. Unfortunately, because sea levels were lower than they are today, coastal sites used by early voyagers would now be under water.

Securely dated objects from Monte Verde, a site in south-central Chile, place people in southern South America by 12,500 years ago, if not earlier. Assuming the first

[41] Marshall, E. (2001). Preclovis sites fight for acceptance. *Science 291*, 1732.

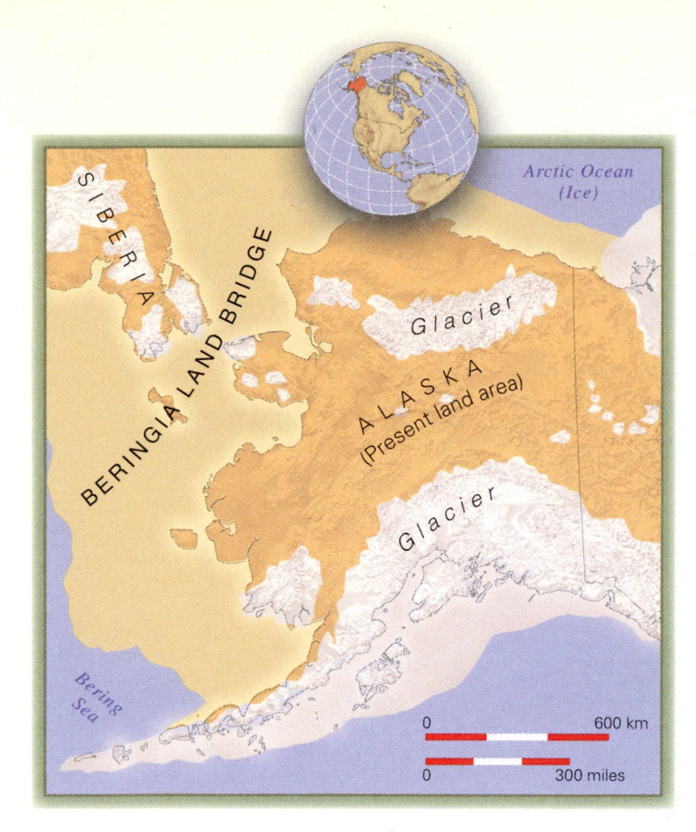

Figure 9.10 The Arctic conditions and glaciers in northeastern Asia and northwestern North America provided opportunity and challenges for ancient people spreading to the Americas. On the one hand, the Arctic conditions provided a land bridge (Beringia) between the continents, but on the other hand, these harsh environmental conditions posed considerable challenges to humans. Ancient people may have also come to the Americas by sea. Once in North America, glaciers spanning a good portion of the continent determined the areas open to habitation.

populations spread from Siberia to Alaska, linguist Johanna Nichols suggests that the first people to arrive in North America did so by 20,000 years ago. She bases this estimate on the time it took various other languages to spread from their homelands—including Eskimo languages in the Arctic and Athabaskan languages from interior western Canada to New Mexico and Arizona (Navajo). Nichols's conclusion is that it would have taken at least 7,000 years for people to reach south-central Chile.[42] Others suggest people arrived in the Americas closer to 30,000 years ago or even earlier.

A recent genetic study using mtDNA indicates that two groups of migrants crossed Beringia between 15,000 and 17,000 years ago but then took different paths. One group traveled down the Pacific Coast and the other down the center of the continent. While the dates generated in this study are as early as others have suggested, these findings support the notion that distinct language groups made separate migrations.

[42] The first Americans, ca. 20,000. (1998). *Discover 19* (6), 24.

The picture currently emerging, then, is of people, who may not have looked like modern Native Americans, arriving by boats or rafts and spreading southward and eastward over time. In fact, contact back and forth between North America and Siberia never stopped. In all probability, it became more common as the glaciers melted away. As a consequence, through gene flow as well as later arrivals of people from Asia, people living in the Americas came to have the broad faces, prominent cheekbones, and round cranial vaults that tend to characterize the skulls of many Native Americans today. Still, Native Americans, like all human populations, are physically variable. The Kennewick Man controversy described in Chapter 5 illustrates the complexities of establishing ethnic identity based on the shape of the skull. In order to trace the history of the peopling of the Americas, anthropologists must combine archaeological, linguistic, and cultural information with evidence of biological variation.

Although the earliest technologies in the Americas remain poorly known, they gave rise in North America, about 12,000 years ago, to the distinctive fluted spear points of **Paleoindian** hunters of big game, such as mammoths, mastodons, caribou, and now extinct forms of bison. Fluted points are finely made, with large channel flakes removed from one or both surfaces. This thinned section was inserted into the notched end of a spear shaft for a sturdy haft. Fluted points are found from the Atlantic seaboard to the Pacific Coast, and from Alaska down into Panama. The efficiency of the hunters who made and used these points may have hastened the extinction of the mammoth and other large Pleistocene mammals. By driving large numbers of animals over cliffs, they killed many more than they could possibly use, thus wasting huge amounts of meat.

Upper Paleolithic peoples in Australia and the Americas, like their counterparts in Africa and Eurasia, possessed sophisticated technology that was efficient and appropriate for the environments they inhabited. As in other parts of the world, when a technological innovation such as the fluted points begins, this technology is rapidly disseminated among the people inhabiting the region.

Major Paleolithic Trends

As we look at the larger picture, since the time the genus *Homo* appeared, evolving humans came to rely increasingly on cultural, as opposed to biological, adaptation. To handle environmental challenges, evolving humans developed appropriate tools, clothes, shelter, use of fire, and so forth rather than relying upon biological adaptation of the human organism. This was true whether human

Paleoindians The earliest inhabitants of North America.

Biocultural Connection

Paleolithic Prescriptions for the Diseases of Civilization

Though increased life expectancy is often hailed as one of modern civilization's greatest accomplishments, in some ways we in the developed world lead far less healthy lifestyles than our ancestors. Throughout most of our evolutionary history, humans led more physically active lives and ate a more varied low-fat diet than we do now. Our ancestors did not drink or smoke. They spent their days scavenging or hunting for animal protein while gathering vegetable foods with some insects thrown in for good measure. They stayed fit through traveling great distances each day over the savannah and beyond.

Today we may survive longer, but in old age we are beset by chronic disease. Heart disease, diabetes, high blood pressure, and cancer shape the experience of old age in wealthy industrialized nations. The prevalence of these "diseases of civilization" has increased rapidly over the past sixty years. Anthropologists Melvin Konner and Marjorie Shostak and physician Boyd Eaton have suggested that our Paleolithic ancestors have provided a prescription for a cure. They propose that as "stone-agers in a fast lane," people's health will improve by returning to the lifestyle to which their bodies are adapted.[a] Such Paleolithic prescriptions are an example of evolutionary medicine—a branch of medical anthropology that uses evolutionary principles to contribute to human health.

Evolutionary medicine bases its prescriptions on the idea that rates of cultural change exceed the rates of biological change. Our food-forager physiology was shaped over millions of years, while the cultural changes leading to contemporary lifestyles have occurred rapidly.

Anthropologists George Armelagos and Mark Nathan Cohen suggest that the downward trajectory for human health began with the earliest human village settlements some 10,000 years ago.[b] When humans began farming rather than gathering, they often switched to single-crop diets. In addition, settlement into villages led directly to the increase in infectious disease. While the cultural invention of antibiotics has cured many infectious diseases, it also led to the increase in chronic diseases.

Our evolutionary history offers clues about the diet and lifestyle to which our bodies evolved. By returning to our ancient lifeways, we can make the diseases of civilization a thing of the past.

BIOCULTURAL QUESTION

What sort of Paleolithic prescriptions would our evolutionary history contribute toward behaviors such as childrearing practices, sleeping, and work patterns? Are there any ways that your culture or personal lifestyle is well aligned with past lifeways?

---

[a] Eaton, S. B., Konner, M., & Shostak, M. (1988). Stone-agers in the fast lane: Chronic degenerative diseases in evolutionary perspective. *American Journal of Medicine 84* (4), 739–749.

[b] Cohen, M. N., & Armelagos, G. J. (Eds.). (1984). *Paleopathology at the origins of agriculture*. Orlando: Academic.

populations lived in hot or cold, wet or dry, forest or grassland areas. Though culture is ultimately based on what might loosely be called brain power or, more formally, **cognitive capacity,** it is learned and not carried by genes. Therefore, cultural innovations may occur rapidly and can easily be transferred among individuals and groups.

Scientists have recently documented key differences in the proteins involved in brain metabolism in humans compared to other species that may account for some of this brain power. Unfortunately these metabolic changes are also associated with schizophrenia, indicating that there may have been some costs in the process. This study suggests that the cultural practice of cooking freed the body to devote more energy to brain metabolism.

While cooking was certainly an innovation of ancient *Homo,* the varied low-fat diet and high exercise of our ancestors were in general healthier than the dietary patterns prevailing in many parts of the world today. See this chapter's Biocultural Connection for a discussion of how a return to the diets of our forebears may improve human health.

cognitive capacity A broad concept including intelligence, educability, concept formation, self-awareness, self-evaluation, attention span, sensitivity in discrimination, and creativity.

Certain trends stand out from the information anthropologists have gathered about the Old Stone Age in most parts of the world. One was toward increasingly more sophisticated, varied, and specialized tool kits. Tools became progressively lighter and smaller, resulting in the conservation of raw materials and a better ratio between length of cutting edge and weight of stone. Tools became specialized according to region and function. Instead of crude all-purpose tools, more effective particularized devices were made to deal with the differing conditions of savannah, forest, and shore.

As humans came to rely increasingly on culture as a means to meet the challenges of existence, they were able to inhabit new environments. With more efficient tool technology, human population size could increase, allowing humans to spill over into more diverse environments. Improved cultural abilities may also have played a role in the reduction of heavy physical features, favoring instead decreased size and weight of face and teeth, the development of larger and more complex brains, and ultimately a reduction in body size and robustness. This dependence on intelligence rather than bulk provided the key for humans' increased reliance on cultural rather than physical adaptation. The development of conceptual thought can be seen in symbolic artifacts and signs of ritual activity throughout the world.

Through Paleolithic times, at least in the colder parts of the world, hunting became more important, and people became more proficient at it. Humans' intelligence enabled them to develop composite tools as well as the social organization and cooperation so important for survival and population growth. As discussed in the next chapter, this trend was reversed during the Mesolithic, when hunting lost its preeminence, and the gathering of wild plants and seafood became increasingly important.

As human populations grew and spread, cultural differences between regions also became more marked. While some indications of cultural contact and intercommunication are evident in the development of long-distance trade networks, tool assemblages developed in response to the specific challenges and resources of specific environments.

As Paleolithic peoples eventually spread over all the continents of the world, including Australia and the Americas, changes in climate and environment called for new kinds of adaptations. In forest environments, people needed tools for working wood; on the open savannah and plains, they came to use the bow and arrow to hunt the game they could not stalk closely; the people in settlements that grew up around lakes and along rivers and coasts developed harpoons and hooks; in the sub-Arctic regions, they needed tools to work the heavy skins of seals and caribou. The fact that culture is first and foremost a mechanism by which humans adapt means that as humans faced new challenges in the Paleolithic throughout the globe, their cultures differentiated regionally.

Questions for Reflection

1. Upper Paleolithic art suggests that humans have always been challenged to understand where we fit in the larger system of life forms, past and present. What are your thoughts about how the impulse to create art relates to human efforts to make sense of our place in nature? What is your conception of the artist who might have made the Venus figurine in the chapter opening?
2. What does it mean to be "modern," biologically or culturally? How should we define "human"?
3. How do you feel personally about the possibility of having Neandertals as part of your ancestry? How might you relate the Neandertal debates to stereotyping or racism in contemporary society?
4. Why do you think that most of the studies of prehistoric art have tended to focus on Europe? Do you think this focus reflects ethnocentrism or bias about the definition of art in Western cultures?
5. Do you think that gender has played a role in anthropological interpretations of the behavior of our ancestors and the way that paleoanthropologists and archaeologists conduct their research? Do you believe that feminism has a role to play in the interpretation of the past?

Suggested Readings

Clottes, J., & Bennett, G. (2002). *World rock art* (conservation and cultural heritage series). San Francisco: Getty Trust Publication.

Written by Jean Clottes, a leading authority on rock art (and discoverer of the Upper Paleolithic cave art site Grotte de Chauvet), this book provides excellent descriptions and beautiful images of rock art throughout the world, beginning with the earliest examples from Australia to rock art from the 20th century.

Dillehay, T. D. (2001). *The settlement of the Americas.* New York: Basic.

In an engaging, clear style, Dillehay provides a detailed account of the evidence from South America that has recently challenged theories about the peopling of the Americas, with particular emphasis on the author's work in Chile.

Klein, R. (2002). *The dawn of human culture.* New York: Wiley.

While this book covers the entire history of human evolution, it provides a particular focus on the theory of recent African origins of the species *Homo sapiens* and associated cultural abilities.

White, R. (2003). *Prehistoric art: The symbolic journey of humankind.* New York: Abrams.

This sumptuously illustrated volume demonstrates the power of prehistoric imagery as well as providing a comprehensive overview of the theoretical approaches to studying prehistoric art. White presents a global survey of prehistoric art and demonstrates that Western notions of art have interfered with interpretations of prehistoric art.

Wolpoff, M., & Caspari, R. (1997). *Race and human evolution: A fatal attraction.* New York: Simon & Schuster.

This book is a detailed but readable presentation of the multiregional hypothesis of modern human origins. Among its strengths is a discussion of the problem of defining what "anatomically modern" means.

Challenge Issue This embroidery by Hmong artist Pangxiong Sirathasuk depicts not only her culture's story of the origins of farming—a way of life that first began as early as 10,000 years ago—but also some of the consequences of this shift from food foraging to food production. According to Hmong folklore, the vegetables started out walking into villages. But they became disgusted with human greed and walked back to the fields, stating that humans in the future would have to work very hard to receive the earth's bounty. Farming and the domestication of animals, along with settlement, mark the start of the Neolithic period. These cultural innovations solved some of the challenges of existence, but they also created new ones. Diets limited by reliance on single crops sometimes led to malnutrition and even famine when these crops failed. Crowded living conditions and close contact with animals in Neolithic villages promoted the spread of infectious disease. And as this embroidery shows, food production involves considerable labor. This artwork also demonstrates that the innovations from one part of the world disseminated globally. While the traditional Hmong homeland is in Southeast Asia, the pumpkins and corn depicted here are crops that were originally domesticated in the Americas. The development of permanent settlements and the domestication of animals and plants introduced new beliefs, daily routines, social relationships, and political structures that together continue to challenge humans globally.

CHAPTER 10

The Neolithic Revolution: The Domestication of Plants and Animals

Chapter Preview

When and Where Did the Change from Food Foraging to Food Production Begin?

Independent centers of early plant and animal domestication exist in Africa, China, Mesoamerica, North and South America, as well as Southwest and Southeast Asia. From these places, food production spread to most other parts of the world. Food production began independently at more or less the same time around 10,000 years ago in these different places—perhaps a bit earlier in Southwest Asia than elsewhere. Due to the breadth of changes induced by this transition, it is commonly referred to as the Neolithic revolution. Though farming has changed dramatically over the millennia, crops people rely on today, such as rice, wheat, and maize, originated with those earliest farmers.

Why Did the Change Take Place?

Though the Neolithic revolution can appear to be a cultural advancement because later cities and states developed from Neolithic villages, food production is not necessarily a more secure means of subsistence than food foraging. In the Neolithic, farming often limited the diversity of the human diet and required more work than hunting, gathering, and fishing. In addition, being sedentary created new vulnerability to disease. It may be that people did not become food producers due to clear-cut advantages of this way of life. Of various theories that have been proposed, the most likely is that food production came about as a consequence of a chance convergence of separate natural events and cultural developments.

What Were the Consequences of the Neolithic Revolution?

Although food production generally leaves less leisure time than food foraging, it does permit reallocation of the workload. Some people can produce enough food to support those who undertake other tasks, and so a number of technological developments, such as weaving and pottery making, generally accompany food production. In addition, a sedentary lifestyle in villages allows for the construction of more substantial housing. Finally, the new modes of work and resource allocation require new ways of organizing people, generally into lineages, clans, and common-interest associations.

Throughout the Paleolithic, people depended exclusively on wild sources of food for their survival. They hunted and trapped wild animals, fished, and gathered shellfish, eggs, berries, nuts, roots, and other plant foods, relying on their wits and muscles to acquire what nature provided. Whenever favored sources of food became scarce, people adjusted by increasing the variety of foods eaten and incorporating less desirable foods into their diets.

Over time, the subsistence practices of some people began to change in ways that radically transformed their way of life as they became food producers rather than food foragers.[1] For some human groups, food production was accompanied by a more sedentary existence, which in turn permitted a reorganization of the workload in society: Some individuals could be freed from the food quest to devote their energies to other tasks. Over the course of thousands of years, these changes brought about an unforeseen way of life. With good reason, the **Neolithic** (literally, the "New Stone" Age), when this change took place, has been characterized as revolutionary.

The Mesolithic Roots of Farming and Pastoralism

As seen in the previous chapter, by the end of the Paleolithic humans had spread throughout the globe. During this period much of the northern hemisphere was covered with glaciers. By 12,000 years ago, warmer climates prevailed, and these glaciers receded, causing changes in human habitats globally. As sea levels rose throughout the world, many areas that had been dry land during periods of glaciation—such as the Bering Strait, parts of the North Sea, and an extensive land area that had joined the eastern islands of Indonesia to mainland Asia—flooded.

In some northern regions, warmer climates brought about particularly marked changes, allowing the replacement of barren tundra with forests. In the process, the herd animals—upon which northern Paleolithic peoples had depended for much of their food, clothing, and shelter—disappeared from many areas. Some, like the caribou and musk ox, moved to colder climates; others, like the mammoths, died out completely. In the new forests, animals were often more solitary in their habits. As a result, large cooperative hunts were less productive than before. Diets shifted to abundant plant foods as well as fish and other foods around lakeshores, bays, and rivers. In Europe, Asia, and Africa, this transitional period between the Paleolithic and the Neolithic is called the **Mesolithic,** or Middle Stone Age. In the Americas, comparable cultures are referred to as **Archaic cultures.**

New technologies accompanied the changed postglacial environment. Manufacture began of ground stone tools, shaped and sharpened by grinding the tool against sandstone, often using sand as an additional abrasive. These shaped, sharpened stones were set into wooden or sometimes antler handles to make effective axes and adzes, cutting tools with a sharp blade set at right angles to a handle. Though such implements take longer to make, they are less prone to breakage under heavy-duty usage than those made of chipped stone. Thus they were helpful in clearing forest areas and in the woodwork needed for the creation of dugout canoes and skin-covered boats. Evidence of seaworthy watercraft at Mesolithic sites indicates that human foraging for food took place on the open water as well as on land. Thus it was possible to make use of deep-water resources as well as those of coastal areas, rivers, and lakes.

The **microlith**—a small but hard, sharp blade—was the characteristic tool of the Mesolithic. Although a microlithic ("small stone") tool tradition existed in Central Africa by about 40,000 years ago,[2] such tools did not become common elsewhere until the Mesolithic. Microliths could be mass produced because they were small, easy to make, and could be fashioned from sections of blades. This small tool could be attached to an arrow or other tool shaft by using melted resin (from pine trees) as a binder.

Microliths provided Mesolithic people with an important advantage over their Upper Paleolithic forebears: The small size of the microlith enabled them to devise a wider array of composite tools made out of stone and wood or bone. Thus they could make sickles, harpoons, arrows, knives, and daggers by fitting microliths into slots in

Neolithic The New Stone Age; prehistoric period beginning about 10,000 years ago in which peoples possessed stone-based technologies and depended on domesticated plants and/or animals.

Mesolithic The Middle Stone Age period between the end of the Paleolithic and the start of the Neolithic; referred to as Archaic cultures in the Americas.

Archaic cultures Term used to refer to Mesolithic cultures in the Americas.

microlith A small blade of flint or similar stone, which were hafted together in handles or shafts made of wood, bone, or antler to make tools; widespread in the Mesolithic.

[1] Rindos, D. (1984). *The origins of agriculture: An evolutionary perspective* (p. 99). Orlando: Academic.

[2] Bednarik, R. G. (1995). Concept-mediated marking in the Lower Paleolithic. *Current Anthropology 36,* 606.

wood, bone, or antler handles. Later experimentation with these forms led to more sophisticated tools and weapons such as bows to propel arrows.

Dwellings from the Mesolithic provide some evidence of a more sedentary lifestyle during this period. By contrast, most hunting peoples, and especially those depending on herd animals, are highly mobile. To be successful, hunters must follow migratory game. People subsisting on a diet of seafood and plants in the milder northern forested environments of this time period did not need to move regularly over large geographic areas.

In the warmer parts of the world, wild plant foods were more readily available, and so their collection complemented hunting in the Upper Paleolithic more than had been the case in the colder northern regions. Hence, in areas like Southwest Asia, the Mesolithic represents less of a changed way of life than was true in Europe. Here, the important **Natufian culture** flourished.

The Natufians lived between 10,200 and 12,500 years ago at the eastern end of the Mediterranean Sea in caves, rock shelters, and small villages with stone- and mud-walled houses. They are named after Wadi en-Natuf, a ravine near Jerusalem, Israel, where the remains of this culture were first found. They buried their dead in communal cemeteries, usually in shallow pits without any other objects or decorations. A small shrine is known from one of their villages—a 10,500-year-old settlement at Jericho in the Jordan River Valley. Basin-shaped depressions in the rocks found outside homes and plastered storage pits beneath the floors of the houses indicate that the Natufians were the earliest Mesolithic people known to have stored plant foods. Certain tools found among Natufian remains bear evidence of their use to cut grain. These Mesolithic sickles consisted of small stone blades set in straight handles of wood or bone.

The new way of life of the various Mesolithic and Archaic cultures generally provided supplies of food sufficiently abundant to permit people in some parts of the world to live in larger and more sedentary groups. They became village dwellers, and some of these settlements went on to expand into the first farming villages, towns, and ultimately cities.

The Neolithic Revolution

The Neolithic, or New Stone Age, derives its name from the polished stone tools that are characteristic of this period. But more important than the presence of these tools is the cultural transition from a foraging economy based on hunting, gathering, and fishing to one based on food production, representing a major change in the subsistence practices of early peoples. While many of the early food producers became village dwellers, other groups used Neolithic tools and settled in villages while still maintaining a foraging lifestyle as some groups do into the present. The **Neolithic revolution** was by no means smooth or instantaneous; in fact, the switch to food production spread over many centuries—even millennia—and was a direct outgrowth of the preceding Mesolithic. Where to draw the line between the two periods is not always clear.

The ultimate source of all cultural change is **innovation**: any new idea, method, or device that gains widespread acceptance in society. **Primary innovation** is the creation, invention, or discovery by chance of a completely new idea, method, or device. A chance discovery, such as the observation that clay permanently hardens when exposed to high temperatures, is the kind of primary innovation that likely took place around numerous ancient campfires. This perception allowed our ancestors to begin to make figurines of fired clay some 35,000 years ago.

A **secondary innovation** is a deliberate application or modification of an existing idea, method, or device. For example, ancient people applied the knowledge about fired clay to make pottery containers and cooking vessels. Recent evidence from Yuchanyan Cave, located in the southwest of China's Hunan Province, indicates the presence of the earliest pottery vessels; these are radio-carbon dated to between 15,430 and 18,300 years ago.

The transition to relatively complete reliance on domesticated plants and animals took several thousand years. While this transition has been particularly well studied in Southwest Asia, archaeological evidence for food production also

Natufian culture A Mesolithic culture living in the lands that are now Israel, Lebanon, and western Syria, between about 10,200 and 12,500 years ago.

Neolithic revolution The profound cultural change beginning about 10,000 years ago and associated with the early domestication of plants and animals and settlement in permanent villages. Sometimes referred to as the Neolithic transition.

innovation Any new idea, method, or device that gains widespread acceptance in society.

primary innovation The creation, invention, or discovery by chance of a completely new idea, method, or device.

secondary innovation The deliberate application or modification of an existing idea, method, or device.

© Tian chao-Imaginechina/AP Images

Pottery shards were recently discovered along with rice grains and stone tools at Yuchanyan Cave, located in China's Hunan Province, by a team of American, Israeli, and Chinese archaeologists. Bone fragments and charcoal found in association with the pottery allowed scientists to accurately date the pottery to between 17,500 and 18,300 years ago by measuring the fraction of carbon isotopes in these organic materials. The careful excavation at this site has provided important evidence that connects pottery making hunter-gatherers, who inhabited this cave, to the rice farmers that came to inhabit the nearby Yangzte River basin several thousand years later.

exists from other parts of the world such as China and Central America and the Andes at similar or somewhat younger dates. The critical point is not which region invented farming first, but rather the independent but more or less simultaneous invention of food production throughout the globe.

Domestication: What Is It?

Domestication is a process whereby humans modify, either intentionally or unintentionally, the genetic makeup of a population of plants or animals, sometimes to the extent that members of the population are unable to survive and/or reproduce without human assistance. Domestication is essentially a special case of interdependence between different species frequently seen in the natural world, where one species depends on another (that feeds upon it) for its protection and reproductive success.

domestication An evolutionary process whereby humans modify, either intentionally or unintentionally, the genetic makeup of a population of plants or animals, sometimes to the extent that members of the population are unable to survive and/or reproduce without human assistance.

According to evolutionary biologist, geographer, and all-around theorist Jared Diamond, humans are not the only species known to domesticate another. Certain ants native to the American tropics grow fungi in their nests, and these fungi provide the ants with most of their nutrition. Like human farmers, the ants add manure to stimulate fungal growth and eliminate competing weeds, both mechanically and through use of antibiotic herbicides.[3] The fungi are protected and ensured reproductive success while providing the ants with a steady food supply.

In plant–human interactions, domestication ensures the plants' reproductive success while providing humans with food. Selective breeding eliminates thorns, toxins, and bad-tasting chemical compounds, which in the wild had served to ensure a plant species' survival, at the same time producing larger, tastier edible parts attractive to humans. Environmentalist Michael Pollan suggests that domesticated plant species successfully exploit human desires to out-compete other plant species and considers "agriculture as something grasses did to people to conquer trees."[4]

Evidence of Early Plant Domestication

Domesticated plants generally differ from their wild ancestors in ways favored by humans, including increased size, at least of edible parts; reduction or loss of natural means of seed dispersal; reduction or loss of protective devices such as husks or distasteful chemical compounds; loss of delayed seed germination (important to wild plants for survival in times of drought or other temporarily adverse conditions); and development of simultaneous ripening of the seed or fruit.

For example, wild cereals have a very fragile stem, whereas domesticated ones have a tough stem. Under natural conditions, plants with fragile stems scatter their seed for themselves, whereas those with tough stems do not. When the grain stalks were harvested, their soft stems would shatter at the touch of sickle or flail, and many of their seeds would be lost. Inevitably, though unintentionally, most of the seeds that people harvested would have been taken from the tough plants. Early domesticators probably also tended to select seed from plants having few husks or none at all—eventually breeding them out—because husking prior to pounding the grains into meal or flour required extra labor.

Many of the distinguishing characteristics of domesticated plants can be seen in remains from archaeological

[3] Diamond, J. (1998). Ants, crops, and history. *Science 281,* 1974–1975.

[4] Pollan, M. (2001). *The botany of desire: A plant's-eye view of the world.* New York: Random House.

Figure 10.1 **Teosinte (A), compared to 5,500-year-old maize (B) and modern maize (C). Teosinte, the wild grass from highland Mexico from which maize originated, is far less productive and does not taste very good. Like most plants that were domesticated, it was not a favored food for foraging people. Domestication transformed it into something highly desirable.**

sites. Paleobotanists can often tell the fossil of a wild plant species from a domesticated one, for example, by studying the shape and size of various plant structures (Figure 10.1).[5]

Evidence of Early Animal Domestication

Domestication also produced changes in the skeletal structure of some animals. For example, the horns of wild goats and sheep differ from those of their domesticated counterparts. Some types of domesticated sheep have no horns altogether. Similarly, the size of an animal or its parts can vary with domestication as seen in the smaller size of certain teeth of domesticated pigs compared to those of wild ones.

A study of age and sex ratios of butchered animals at an archaeological site may indicate whether animal domestication was practiced. Investigators have determined that if the age and/or sex ratios at the site differ from those in wild herds, the imbalances are due to domestication. Archaeologists documented a sharp rise in the number of young male goats killed at 10,000-year-old sites in the Zagros Mountains of Iran. Evidently people were slaughtering the young males for food and saving the females for breeding. Although such herd management does not prove that the goats were fully domesticated, it does indicate a step in that direction.[6] Similarly, archaeological sites in the Andean highlands, dating to around 6,300 years ago, contain evidence that these animals were penned up, indicating the beginning of domestication.

Why Humans Became Food Producers

Although it is tempting to think that a sudden flash of insight about the human ability to control plants and animals might have led ancient peoples to domestication, the evidence points us in different directions. As the following discussion illustrates, there are several false ideas about the motivation to becoming food producers.

Contemporary foragers show us that food production did not come about from discoveries, such as that seeds, if planted, grow into plants. These food foragers are perfectly aware of the role of seeds in plant growth, that plants grow better under certain conditions than others, and so forth. Jared Diamond aptly describes contemporary food foragers as "walking encyclopedias of natural history with individual names for as many as a thousand or more plant and animal species, and with detailed knowledge of those species' biological characteristics, distribution, and potential uses."[7] In addition, food foragers frequently apply their knowledge to actively manage the resources on which they depend. For example, indigenous people living in northern Australia deliberately alter the runoff channels of creeks to flood extensive tracts of land, converting them into fields of wild grain. Australian Aborigines choose to continue to forage while also managing the land.

Second, the switch from food foraging to food production does not free people from hard work. In fact, available ethnographic data indicate just the opposite—that

[5] Gould, S. J. (1991). *The flamingo's smile: Reflections in natural history* (p. 368). New York: Norton.

[6] Zeder, M. A., & Hesse, B. (2000). The initial domestication of goats (*Capra hircus*) in the Zagros Mountains 10,000 years ago. *Science 287*, 2254–2257.

[7] Diamond, J. (1997). *Guns, germs, and steel* (p. 143). New York: Norton.

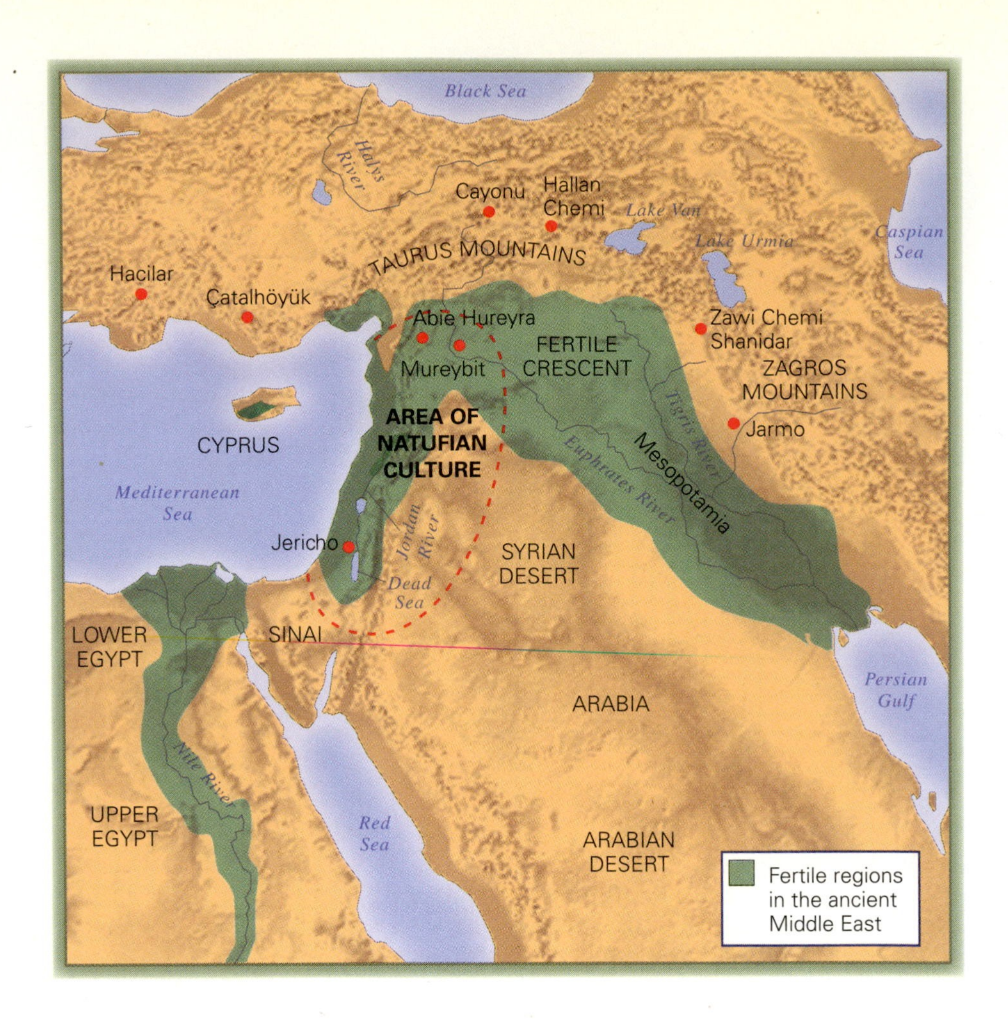

Figure 10.2 **The Fertile Crescent of Southwest Asia and the area of Natufian culture.**

farmers, by and large, work far longer hours compared to most food foragers.

Finally, food production is not necessarily a more secure means of subsistence than food foraging. Seed crops in particular—of the sort originally domesticated in Southwest Asia, Central America, and the Andean highlands—are highly productive but not stable from an ecological perspective because of low species diversity. Without constant human attention, their productivity suffers.

For these reasons, it is little wonder that food foragers do not necessarily regard farming and animal husbandry as superior to hunting, gathering, or fishing. Thus some peoples in the world have continued as food foragers into the present. However, it has become increasingly difficult for them, because food-producing peoples (including postindustrial societies) have deprived them of more and more of the land base necessary for their way of life. As long as existing practices work well, there is no need for food foragers to abandon them, especially if they provide an eminently satisfactory way of life. Noting that food foragers have more time for play and relaxation than food producers, anthropologist Marshall Sahlins has labeled hunter-gatherers "the original affluent society."[8] Farming brings with it a whole new system of relationships that disturbs an age-old balance between humans and nature.

In view of what has been said so far, it is puzzling why any human beings abandoned food foraging in favor of food production. Several theories have been proposed to account for this change in human subsistence practices.

One older theory, championed by Australian archaeologist V. Gordon Childe, is the desiccation (from the Latin "to dry completely"), or oasis, theory, which is based on environmental determinism. Its proponents advanced the idea that the glacial cover over Europe and Asia caused a shift in rain patterns from Europe to northern Africa and southwestern Asia. When the glaciers retreated northward, so did the rain patterns. As a result, formerly lush regions of northern Africa and southwestern Asia became dryer, and people were forced to congregate at oases for water.

Because of the relative food scarcity in such an environment, necessity drove people to collect the wild grasses and seeds growing around the oases, congregating in a part of Southwest Asia known as the Fertile Crescent (Figure 10.2).

[8] Sahlins, M. (1972). *Stone age economics.* Chicago: Aldine.

Eventually they began to cultivate various plants to provide enough food for the community. According to this theory, animal domestication began because the oases attracted hungry animals, such as wild goats, sheep, and also cattle, which came to graze on the stubble of the grain fields and to drink. Finding that these animals were often too thin to kill for food, people began to fatten them up.

Although Childe's oasis theory can be critiqued on a number of grounds and many other theories have been proposed to account for the shift to domestication, it remains historically significant as the first scientifically testable explanation for the origins of food production. Childe's theory set the stage for the development of archaeology as a science. Later theories developed by archaeologists built on Childe's ideas and took into account the role of chance environmental circumstances of the specific region along with other specific cultural factors that may have driven change.

The Fertile Crescent

Present evidence indicates that the earliest plant domestication took place gradually in the Fertile Crescent, the long arc-shaped sweep of river valleys and coastal plains extending from the Upper Nile (Sudan) to the Lower Tigris (Iraq). Archaeological data suggest the domestication of rye as early as 13,000 years ago by people living at a site (Abu Hureyra) east of Aleppo, Syria, although wild plants and animals continued to be their major food sources. Over the next several millennia they became full-fledged farmers, cultivating rye and wheat.[9] By 10,300 years ago, others in the region were also growing crops.

This domestication process may have been the consequence of a chance convergence of independent natural events and other cultural developments.[10] The Natufians, whose culture we looked at earlier in this chapter, illustrate this process. These people lived at a time of dramatically changing climates in Southwest Asia. With the end of the last glaciation, temperatures became not only significantly warmer but markedly seasonal as well. Between 6,000 and 12,000 years ago, the region experienced the most extreme seasonality in its history, with dry summers significantly longer and hotter than today. As a consequence of increased evaporation, many shallow lakes dried up, leaving just three in the Jordan River Valley.

At the same time, the region's plant cover changed dramatically. Those plants best adapted to environmental instability and seasonal dryness were annuals, including wild cereal grains and legumes (such as peas, lentils, and chickpeas). Because they complete their life cycle in a single year, annuals can evolve very quickly under unstable conditions. Moreover, they store their reproductive abilities for the next wet season in abundant seeds, which can remain dormant for prolonged periods.

The Natufians, who lived where these conditions were especially severe, adapted by modifying their subsistence practices in two ways. First, they probably burned the landscape regularly to promote browsing by red deer and grazing by gazelles, the main focus of their hunting activities. Second, they placed greater emphasis on the collection of wild seeds from the annual plants that could be effectively stored to see people through the dry season. The importance of stored foods, coupled with the scarcity of reliable water sources, promoted more sedentary living patterns, reflected in the substantial villages of late Natufian times. The reliance upon seeds in Natufian subsistence was made possible by the fact that they already possessed sickles (originally used to cut reeds and sedges for baskets) for harvesting grain and grinding stones for processing a variety of wild foods.[11]

The use of sickles to harvest grain turned out to have important consequences, again unexpected, for the Natufians. In the course of harvesting, it was inevitable that many easily dispersed seeds would be lost at the harvest site, whereas those from plants that did not readily scatter their seeds would be mostly carried back to where people processed and stored them.[12]

The periodic burning of vegetation carried out to promote the deer and gazelle herds may have also affected the development of new genetic variation. Heat is known to affect mutation rates. Also, fire removes individuals from a population, which changes the genetic structure of a population drastically and quickly. With seeds for nondispersing variants being carried back to settlements, it was inevitable that some lost seeds would germinate and grow there on dump heaps and other disturbed sites (latrines, areas cleared of trees, or burned-over terrain).

Many of the plants that became domesticated were "colonizers," variants that do particularly well in disturbed habitats. Moreover, with people becoming increasingly sedentary, disturbed habitats became more extensive as resources closer to settlements were depleted over time. Thus, variants of plants particularly susceptible to human manipulation had more opportunities to

---

[9] Pringle, H. (1998). The slow birth of agriculture. *Science 282,* 1449.

[10] McCorriston, J., & Hole, F. (1991). The ecology of seasonal stress and the origins of agriculture in the Near East. *American Anthropologist 93,* 46–69.

[11] Olszewki, D. I. (1991). Comment. *Current Anthropology 32,* 43.

[12] Blumer, M. A., & Byrne, R. (1991). The ecological genetics and domestication and the origins of agriculture. *Current Anthropology 32,* 30.

flourish where people were living. Under such circumstances, it was inevitable that eventually people would begin to actively promote their growth, even by deliberately sowing them. Ultimately, people realized that they could play a more active role in the process by trying to breed the strains they preferred. With this, domestication shifted from an unintentional to an intentional process.

The development of animal domestication in Southwest Asia seems to have proceeded along somewhat similar lines in the hilly country of southeastern Turkey, northern Iraq, and the Zagros Mountains of Iran. Large herds of wild sheep and goats, as well as much environmental diversity, characterized these regions. From the flood plains of the valley of the Tigris and Euphrates Rivers, for example, travel to the north or east takes one into high country through three other zones: first steppe, then oak and pistachio woodlands, and finally high plateau country with grass, scrub, or desert vegetation. Valleys that run at right angles to the mountain ranges afford relatively easy access across these zones. Today, a number of peoples in the region still graze their herds of sheep and goats on the low steppe in the winter and move to high pastures on the plateaus in the summer.

Moving back in time prior to the domestication of plants and animals, we find the region inhabited by peoples whose subsistence pattern, like that of the Natufians, was one of food foraging. Different plants were found in different ecological zones, and because of the difference in altitude, plant foods matured at different times in different zones. Many animal species were hunted for meat and hides by these people, most notably the hoofed animals: deer, gazelles, wild goats, and wild sheep. Their bones are far more common in human refuse piles than those of other animals. This is significant, for most of these animals naturally move back and forth from low winter pastures to high summer pastures. People followed these animals in their seasonal migrations, making use along the way of other wild foods in the zones through which they passed: palm dates in the lowlands; acorns, almonds, and pistachios higher up; apples and pears higher still; wild grains maturing at different times in different zones; woodland animals in the forested zone between summer and winter grazing lands. All in all, it was a rich, varied fare.

The archaeological record indicates that, at first, animals of all ages and sexes were hunted by the people of the Southwest Asian highlands. But, beginning about 11,000 years ago, the percentage of immature sheep eaten increased to about 50 percent of the total. At the same time, the percentage of females among animals eaten decreased. (Feasting on male lambs increases yields by sparing the females for breeding.)

This marks the beginning of human management of sheep. As this management of flocks became more efficient, sheep were increasingly shielded from the effects of natural selection, allowing variants preferred by humans to have increased reproductive success. Variants attractive to humans did not arise out of need but at random, as mutations do. But then humans selectively bred the varieties they favored. In such a way, those features characteristic of domestic sheep—such as greater fat and meat production, excess wool, and so on—began to develop.

By 9,000 years ago, the shape and size of the bones of domestic sheep had become distinguishable from those of wild sheep (Figure 10.3). At about the same

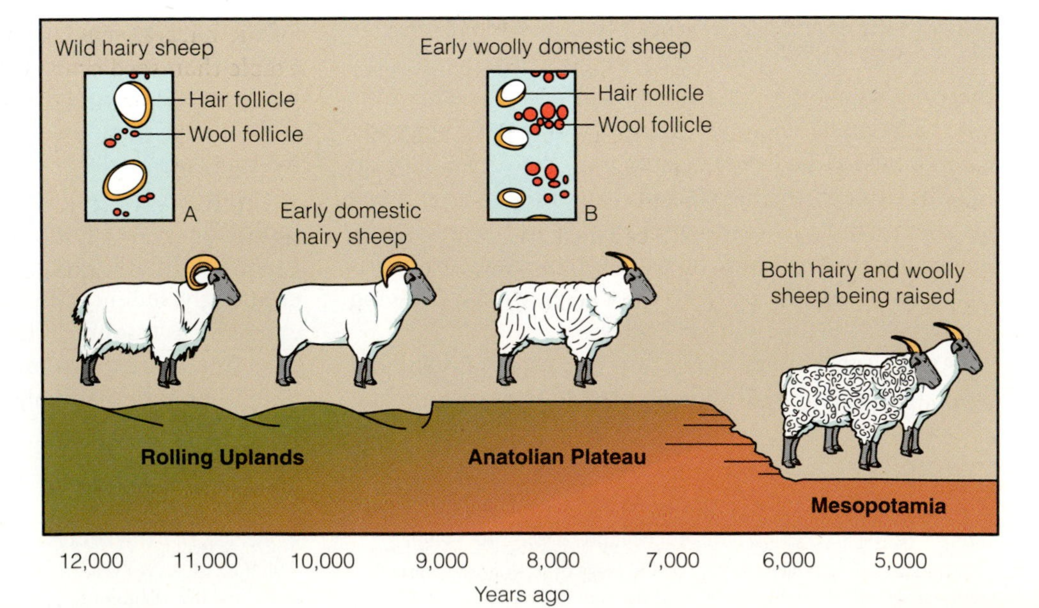

Figure 10.3 Domestication of sheep resulted in evolutionary changes that created more wool. Inset A shows a section, as seen through a microscope, of skin of wild sheep, showing the arrangement of primary (hair) and secondary (wool) follicles. Inset B shows a section of similarly enlarged skin of domestic sheep, showing the changed relationship and the change in size of follicles that accompanied the development of wool.

Today, deliberate attempts to create new varieties of plants take place in many greenhouses, experiment stations, and labs. But when first begun, the creation of domestic plants was not deliberate; rather, it was the unforeseen outcome of traditional food-foraging activities. Today, genetically engineered crops are being created to survive massive applications of herbicides and pesticides. They are also engineered to *not* produce viable seeds, which solidifies corporate control of the food industry.

time, similar developments were taking place in southeastern Turkey and the lower Jordan River Valley, where pigs were the focus of attention.[13] The recent analysis of pottery vessels from the Near East and southeastern Europe indicates that people were using milk from domesticated cattle in a part of the Fertile Crescent by this time as well.[14]

Some researchers have recently linked animal domestication to the development of fixed territories and settlements. Without a notion of resource ownership, they suggest that hunters would not be likely to postpone the short-term gain of killing prey for the long-term gain of continued access to animals in the future.[15] Eventually, animal species domesticated in one area were introduced into areas outside their natural habitat.

To sum up, the domesticators of plants and animals sought only to maximize the food sources available to them. They were not aware of the long-term and revolutionary cultural consequences of their actions. But as the process continued, the productivity of the domestic species increased relative to wild species. Thus these domesticated species became increasingly important to subsistence, resulting in further domestication and further increases in productivity.

Other Centers of Domestication

In addition to Southwest Asia, the domestication of plants and, in some cases, animals took place independently in Southeast Asia, parts of the Americas (Central America, the Andean highlands, the tropical forests of South America, and eastern North America), northern China, and Africa (Figure 10.4). In China, domestication of rice was under way along the middle Yangtze River by about 11,000 years ago.[16] It was not until 4,000 years later, however, that domestic rice dominated wild rice to become the dietary staple.

In Southeast Asia, decorations on pottery depicting rice dated to between 5,000 and 8,800 years ago document it as the earliest species to be domesticated there. Nevertheless, the region is primarily known for the domestication of root crops, most notably yams and taro. Root crop farming, or **vegeculture,** typically involves the growing of many different species together in a single field. Because this approximates the complexity of the natural vegetation, vegeculture tends to be more stable than seed crop cultivation. Propagation or breeding of new plants typically occurs through vegetative means—the planting of cuttings—rather than the planting of seeds.

In the Americas, the domestication of plants began about as early as it did in these other regions. One species of domestic squash may have been grown as early as

[13] Pringle, p. 1448.

[14] Evershed, R. P., et al. (2008). Earliest date for milk use in the Near East and southeastern Europe linked to cattle herding. *Nature.* doi:10.1038/nature07180.

[15] Alvard, M. S., & Kuznar, L. (2001). Deferred harvest: The transition from hunting to animal husbandry. *American Anthropologist 103* (2), 295–311.

[16] Pringle, p. 1449.

vegeculture The cultivation of domesticated root crops, such as yams and taro.

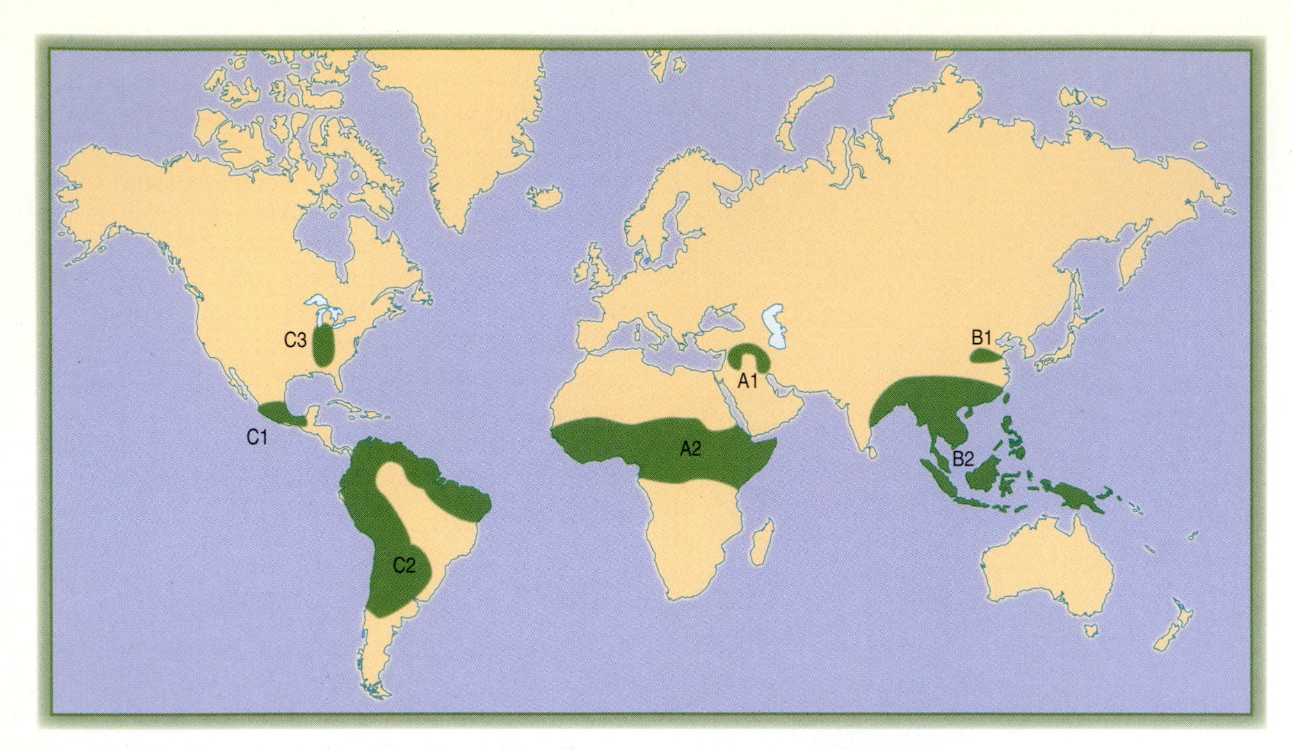

Figure 10.4 Early plant and animal domestication took place in such widely scattered areas as Southwest Asia (A1), Central Africa (A2), China (B1), Southeast Asia (B2), Central America (C1), South America (C2), and North America (C3).

The Dani people of New Guinea specialize in growing sweet potatoes, a crop introduced in the 17th century into a region with a long history of vegeculture. Today villagers grow more than seventy species of sweet potato and have incorporated this root crop into many important rituals. Here Dani women are roasting sweet potatoes on a fire as part of a ceremonial pig feast.

CULTIGENS		Hunting (percentage)	Horticulture (percentage)	Wild plant use (percentage)
Squash, Chili, Amaranth, Avocado	Cotton, Maize, Beans, Gourd, Sapote	29%		31%
Squash, Chili, Amaranth, Avocado	Maize, Beans, Gourd, Sapote	25%		50%
Squash, Chili, Amaranth, Avocado	Maize, Beans, Gourd, Sapote	34%		52%
Squash, Chili, Amaranth, Avocado		54%		40%

Years ago: 3,000; 3,500; 4,000; 4,500; 5,000; 5,500; 6,000; 6,500; 7,000; 7,500; 8,000; 8,500

Figure 10.5 **Subsistence trends in Mexico's Tehuacan Valley show that here, as elsewhere, dependence of horticulture came about gradually, over a prolonged period of time.**

10,000 years ago in the coastal forests of Ecuador; at the same time another species was being grown in an arid region of highland Mexico.[17] Evidently, these developments were independent of each other. The ecological diversity of the highland valleys of Mexico, like the hill country of Southwest Asia, provided an excellent environment for domestication (Figure 10.5). Movement of people through a variety of ecological zones as they changed altitude brought plant and animal species into new habitats, providing opportunities for "colonizing" to domesticated species and humans alike.

Domestication in the Andean highlands of Peru, another highly diverse region, emphasized root crops, the best known being potatoes (of which about 3,000 varieties were grown, versus the mere 250 grown today in North America). South Americans also domesticated guinea pigs, llamas, alpacas, and ducks, whereas people in the Mexican highlands never did much with domestic livestock. They limited themselves to dogs, turkeys, and bees.

[17] Ibid., p. 1447.

In coastal Peru, the earliest domesticates were the inedible bottle gourd (like the one shown here) and cotton. They were used to make nets and floats to catch fish, which was an important source of food.

American Indians living north of Mexico developed some of their own indigenous domesticates. These included local varieties of squash and sunflower.

Ultimately, American Indians domesticated over 300 food crops, including two of the four most important ones in the world today: potatoes and maize (the other two are wheat and rice). In fact, America's indigenous peoples first cultivated over 60 percent of the crops grown in the world today. They remain not only the developers of the world's largest array of nutritious foods but also the primary contributors to the world's varied cuisines.[18] After all, where would Italian cuisine be without tomatoes? Thai cooking without peanuts? Northern European cooking without potatoes? Small wonder American Indians have been called the world's greatest farmers.[19]

As plant species became domesticated, **horticultural** societies came into being. These are small communities of gardeners working with simple hand tools and using neither irrigation nor the plow. Horticulturists typically cultivate a variety of crops in small gardens they have

[18] Weatherford, J. (1988). *Indian givers: How the Indians of the Americas transformed the world* (pp. 71, 115). New York: Fawcett Columbine.

[19] Ibid., p. 95.

horticulture Cultivation of crops carried out with simple hand tools such as digging sticks or hoes.

Anthropology Applied

The Real Dirt on Rainforest Fertility *by Charles C. Mann*

IRANDUBA, AMAZÔNAS STATE, BRAZIL—Above a pit dug by a team of archaeologists here is a papaya orchard filled with unusually vigorous trees bearing great clusters of plump green fruit. Below the surface lies a different sort of bounty: hundreds, perhaps thousands, of burial urns and millions of pieces of broken ceramics, all from an almost unknown people who flourished here before the conquistadors. But surprisingly, what might be most important about this central Amazonian site is not the vibrant orchard or the extraordinary outpouring of ceramics but the dirt under the trees and around the ceramics. A rich, black soil known locally as *terra preta do Indio* (Indian dark earth), it sustained large settlements on these lands for 2 millennia, according to the Brazilian-American archaeological team working here.

Throughout Amazonia, farmers prize *terra preta* for its great productivity—some farmers have worked it for years with minimal fertilization. Such long-lasting fertility is an anomaly in the tropics. Despite the exuberant growth of rainforests, their red and yellow soils are notoriously poor: weathered, highly acidic, and low in organic matter and essential nutrients. In these oxisols, as they are known, most carbon and nutrients are stored not in the soil, as in temperate regions, but in the vegetation that covers it. When loggers, ranchers, or farmers clear the vegetation, the intense sun and rain quickly decompose the remaining organic matter in the soil, making the land almost incapable of sustaining life—one reason ecologists frequently refer to the tropical forest as a "wet desert."

Because *terra preta* is subject to the same punishing conditions as the surrounding oxisols, "its existence is very surprising," says Bruno Glaser, a chemist at the Institute of Soil Science and Soil Geography at the University of Bayreuth, Germany. "If you read the textbooks, it shouldn't be there." Yet according to William I. Woods, a geographer at Southern Illinois University, Edwardsville, *terra preta* might cover as much as 10 percent of Amazonia, an area the size of France. More remarkable still, *terra preta* appears to be the product of intensive habitation by precontact Amerindian populations. "They practiced agriculture here for centuries," Glaser says. "But instead of destroying the soil, they improved it—and that is something we don't know how to do today."

In the past few years, a small but growing group of researchers—geographers, archaeologists, soil scientists, ecologists, and anthropologists—has been investigating this "gift from the past," as *terra preta* is called by one member of the Iranduba team, James B. Petersen of the University of Vermont, Burlington. By understanding how indigenous groups created Amazonian dark earths, these researchers hope, today's scientists might be able to transform some of the region's oxisols into new *terra preta*. Indeed, experimental programs to produce *"terra preta nova"* have already begun. Population pressure and government policies are causing rapid deforestation in the tropics, and poor tropical soils make much of the clearing as economically nonviable in the long run as it is ecologically damaging.

The Good Earth

Terra preta is scattered throughout Amazonia, but it is most frequently found on low hills overlooking rivers—the kind of terrain on which indigenous groups preferred to live. According to Eduardo Neves, an archaeologist at the University of São Paulo who is part of the Iranduba team, the oldest deposits date back more than 2,000 years and occur in the lower and central Amazon; *terra preta* then appeared to spread to cultures upriver. By AD 500 to 1000, he says, "it appeared in almost every part of the Amazon Basin."

Typically, black-soil regions cover 1 to 5 hectares, but some encompass 300 hectares or more. The black soils are generally 40 to 60 centimeters deep but can reach more than 2 meters. Almost always they are full of broken ceramics. Although they were created centuries ago—probably for agriculture, researchers such as Woods believe—patches of *terra preta* are still among the most desirable land in the Amazon. Indeed, *terra preta* is valuable enough that locals sell it as potting soil. To the consternation of archaeologists, long planters full of *terra preta*, complete with pieces of pre-Columbian pottery, greet visitors to the airport in the lower Amazon town of Santarém.

As a rule, *terra preta* has more "plant-available" phosphorus, calcium, sulfur, and nitrogen than surrounding oxisols; it also has much more organic matter, retains moisture and nutrients better, and is not rapidly exhausted by agricultural use when managed well.

The key to *terra preta*'s long-term fertility, Glaser says, is charcoal: *Terra preta* contains up to 70 times as much as adjacent oxisols. "The charcoal prevents organic matter from being rapidly mineralized," Glaser says. "Over time,

cleared by hand. The sophistication of the ancient farming methods as used by Indians in the Amazon rainforest is evident in the research conducted by an international team of archaeologists and other scientists. These ancient methods, which left behind rich dark soils, have important applications for humans today, as explained in this chapter's Anthropology Applied feature. By reviving these ancient soil-enrichment techniques, we can better manage the rainforests as well as mitigate the damage of climate change.

Considering the separate innovations of plant domestication, it is interesting to note that in all cases people

Pits dug to the same depth where *terra preta* is and is not show immediately the difference in the color and quality of the soil.

it partly oxidizes, which keeps providing sites for nutrients to bind to." But simply mixing charcoal into the ground is not enough to create *terra preta*. Because charcoal contains few nutrients, Glaser says, "high nutrient inputs via excrement and waste such as turtle, fish, and animal bones were necessary." Special soil microorganisms are also likely to play a role in its persistent fertility, in the view of Janice Thies, a soil ecologist who is part of a Cornell University team studying *terra preta*. "There are indications that microbial biomass is higher in terra preta," she says, which raises the possibility that scientists might be able to create a "package" of charcoal, nutrients, and microfauna that could be used to transform oxisols into *terra preta*.

Slash-and-Char

Surprisingly, *terra preta* seems not to have been created by the "slash-and-burn" agriculture famously practiced in the tropics. In slash-and-burn, farmers clear and then burn their fields, using the ash to flush enough nutrients into the soil to support crops for a few years; when productivity declines, they move on to the next patch of forest. Glaser, Woods, and other researchers believe that the long-ago Amazonians created *terra preta* by a process that Christoph Steiner, a University of Bayreuth soil scientist, has dubbed "slash-and-char." Instead of completely burning organic matter to ash, in this view, ancient farmers burned it only incompletely, creating charcoal, then stirred the charcoal directly into the soil. Later they added nutrients and, in a process analogous to adding sourdough starter to bread, possibly soil previously enriched with microorganisms. In addition to its potential benefits to the soil, slash-and-char releases less carbon into the air than slash-and-burn, which has potential implications for climate change.

Adapted from Mann, C. C. (2002). The real dirt on rainforest fertility. Science *297, 920–923. Reprinted by permission of the AAAS.*

developed the same categories of foods. Everywhere, starchy grains (or root crops) are accompanied by one or more legumes: wheat and barley with peas, chickpeas, and lentils in Southwest Asia; maize with various kinds of beans in Mexico, for example. Together the amino acids (building blocks of proteins) in these starch and legume combinations provide humans with sufficient protein. The starchy grains are the core of the diet and are eaten at every meal in the form of bread, some sort of food wrapper (like a tortilla), or a gruel or thickening agent in a stew along with one or more legumes. Being rather bland, these sources of carbohydrates and proteins are invariably combined with flavor-giving substances that help the food go down.

In Mexico, for example, the flavor enhancer par excellence is the chili pepper; in other cuisines it may be a bit of meat, a dairy product, or mushrooms. Anthropologist Sidney Mintz refers to this as the "core-fringe-legume pattern" (CFLP), noting that only recently has it been upset by the worldwide spread of processed sugars and high-fat foods.[20]

Food Production and Population Size

Since the Neolithic, the global population of humans has grown steadily. The exact relationship between population growth and food production resembles the old chicken-and-egg question. Some assert that population growth creates pressure that results in innovations such as food production while others suggest that population growth is a consequence of food production. As already noted, domestication inevitably leads to higher yields, and higher yields make it possible to feed more people, albeit at the cost of more work.

While increased dependence on farming is associated with increased fertility across human populations,[21] the reasons behind this illustrate the complex interplay between human biology and culture in all human activity. Some researchers have suggested that the availability of soft foods for infants brought about by farming promoted population growth. In humans, frequent breastfeeding has a dampening effect on the mother's ovulation, inhibiting pregnancy in a nursing mother who breastfeeds exclusively. Because breastfeeding frequency declines when soft foods are introduced, fertility tends to increase.

However, it would be overly simplistic to limit the explanation for changes in fertility to the introduction of soft foods. Many other pathways can also lead to fertility changes. For example, among farmers, numerous children are frequently seen as assets to help out with the many household chores. Further, it is now known that sedentary lifestyles and diets emphasizing a narrow range of resources characteristic of the Neolithic led to growing rates of infectious disease and higher mortality. High infant mortality may well have led to a cultural value placed on increased fertility. In other words, the relationship between farming and fertility is far from simple, as explored in this chapter's Biocultural Connection.

[20] Mintz, S. (1996). A taste of history. In W. A. Haviland & R. J. Gordon (Eds.), *Talking about people* (2nd ed., pp. 81–82). Mountain View, CA: Mayfield.

[21] Sellen, D. W., & Mace, R. (1997). Fertility and mode of subsistence: A phylogenetic analysis. *Current Anthropology 38,* 886.

In Mexico, chili peppers have been a part of the diet for millennia. Chili peppers enhance the flavor of foods and aid digestion by helping with the breakdown of cellulose in diets heavy in plant foods. They had other uses as well: This illustration from a 16th-century Aztec manuscript shows a woman threatening her child with punishment by being exposed to smoke from chili peppers. Chili smoke was also used as a kind of chemical weapon in warfare.

Biocultural Connection

Breastfeeding, Fertility, and Beliefs

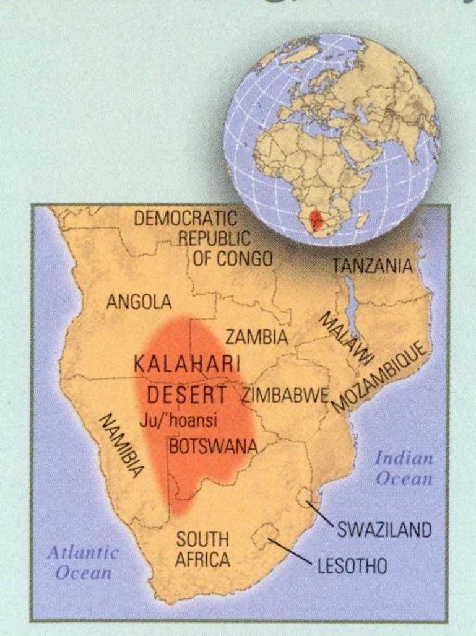

Cross-cultural studies indicate that farming populations tend to have higher rates of fertility than hunter-gatherers. These differences in fertility were calculated in terms of the average number of children born per woman and through the average number of years between pregnancies or birth spacing. Hunter-gatherer mothers have their children about four to five years apart while some contemporary farming populations not practicing any form of birth control have another baby every year and a half.

For many years this difference was interpreted as a consequence of nutritional stress among the hunter-gatherers. This theory was based in part on the observation that humans and many other mammals require a certain percentage of body fat in order to reproduce successfully. The theory was also grounded in the mistaken cultural belief that the hunter-gatherer lifestyle, supposedly inferior to that of "civilized" people, could not provide adequate nutrition for closer birth spacing.

Detailed studies by anthropologists Melvin Konner and Carol Worthman, among the !Kung or Ju/'hoansi people (also, "Bushmen") of the Kalahari Desert in southern Africa, disproved this theory, revealing instead a remarkable interplay between cultural and biological processes in human infant feeding.

Konner and Worthman combined detailed observations of Ju/'hoansi infant feeding practices with studies of hormonal levels in nursing Ju/'hoansi mothers. Ju/'hoansi mothers do not believe that babies should be fed on a schedule, as recommended by some North American child-care experts, nor do they believe that crying is "good" for babies. Instead, they respond rapidly to their infants and breastfeed them whenever the infant shows any signs of fussing during both the day and night. The resulting pattern is breastfeeding in short, very frequent bouts.

As Konner and Worthman document,[a] this pattern of breastfeeding stimulates the body to suppress ovulation, or the release of a new egg into the womb for fertilization. They documented that hormonal signals from nipple stimulation through breastfeeding controls the process of ovulation. Thus the average number of years between children among the Ju/'hoansi is not a consequence of nutritional stress. Instead, Ju/'hoansi infant feeding practices and beliefs directly affect the biology of fertility.

BIOCULTURAL QUESTION

From both evolutionary and child development perspectives, what might be the advantages of breastfeeding babies for the first few years of life? What cultural processes work against this in your culture?

---

[a] Konner, M., & Worthman, C. (1980). Nursing frequency, gonadal function, and birth spacing among !Kung hunter-gatherers. *Science 207*, 788–791.

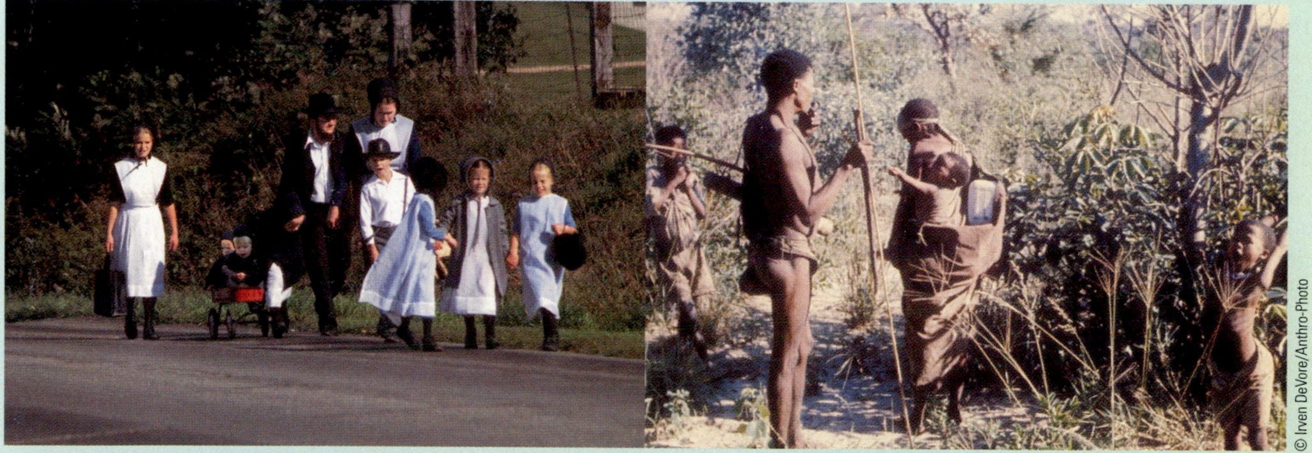

© Dennis MacDonald/PhotoEdit © Irven DeVore/Anthro-Photo

The higher fertility of the Amish, a religious farming culture in North America, compared to that of the Ju/'hoansi hunter-gatherers from the Kalahari Desert, was originally attributed to differences in nutrition. It is now known to be related to differences in childrearing beliefs and practices.

The Spread of Food Production

Paradoxically, although domestication increases productivity, it also increases instability. This is so because those varieties with the highest yields become the focus of human attention, while other varieties are less valued and ultimately ignored. As a result, farmers become dependent on a rather narrow range of resources, compared to the wide range utilized by food foragers. Today, this range is even narrower. Modern agriculturists rely on a mere dozen species for about 80 percent of the world's annual tonnage of all crops.[22]

This dependence upon fewer varieties means that when a crop fails, for whatever reason, farmers have less to fall back on than do food foragers. Furthermore, the likelihood of failure is increased by the common practice of planting crops together in one locality, so that a disease contracted by one plant can easily spread to others. Moreover, by relying on seeds from the most productive plants of a species to establish next year's crop, farmers favor genetic uniformity over diversity. The result is that if some virus, bacterium, or fungus is able to destroy one plant, it will likely destroy them all. This is what happened in the Irish potato famine of 1845 to 1850, which caused the deaths of about a million people due to hunger and disease and forced another 2 million to abandon their homes and emigrate. The population of Ireland dropped from 8 million before the famine to 5 million afterward.

This concentration of domesticates and the consequent vulnerability to disease intensify with contemporary agribusiness and factory farming. This chapter's Globalscape examines the role of pig farming in the current swine flu pandemic that began to sweep the world early in 2009.

The Irish potato famine illustrates how the combination of increased productivity and vulnerability may contribute to the geographic spread of farming. Time and time again in the past, population growth, followed by crop failure, has triggered movements of people from one place to another, where they have reestablished their familiar subsistence practices. Once farming came into existence, its spread to neighboring regions through such migrations was more or less guaranteed. From Southwest Asia, for instance, farming spread northwestward eventually to all of Europe, westward to North Africa, and eastward to India. Domesticated variants also spread from China and Southeast Asia westward. Those who brought crops to new locations brought other things as well, including languages, beliefs, and new alleles for human gene pools.

A similar spread occurred from West Africa to the southeast, creating the modern far-reaching distribution of speakers of Bantu languages. Crops including sorghum (so valuable today it is grown in hot, dry areas on all continents), pearl millet, watermelon, black-eyed peas, African yams, oil palms, and kola nuts (source of modern cola drinks) were first domesticated in West Africa but began spreading eastward by 5,000 years ago. Between 2,000 and 3,000 years ago, Bantu speakers with their crops reached the continent's east coast and a few centuries later reached deep into what is now the country of South Africa. Being well adapted to summer rains, African crops spread no further, for the Cape of South Africa has a Mediterranean climate with winter rains.

The Culture of Neolithic Settlements

A number of Neolithic settlements have been excavated, particularly in Southwest Asia. The structures, artifacts, and food debris found at these sites have revealed much about the daily activities of their former inhabitants as they pursued the business of making a living. Perhaps the best known of these sites is Jericho, an early farming community in the Jordan River Valley.

Jericho: An Early Farming Community

Excavations at the Neolithic settlement that later grew to become the biblical city of Jericho revealed the remains of a sizable farming community inhabited as early as 10,350 years ago. Here, in the Jordan River Valley, crops could be grown almost continuously, due to the presence of a bounteous spring and the rich soils of an Ice Age lake that had dried up some 3,000 years earlier. In addition, flood-borne deposits originating in the Judean highlands to the west regularly renewed the fertility of the soil.

To protect against these floods and associated mudflows, as well as invaders, the people of Jericho built massive walls of stone surrounding their settlement.[23] Within these walls, which were 2 meters (6½ feet) wide and almost 4 meters (12 feet) high, and behind a large rock-cut ditch, which was 8 meters (27 feet) wide and 2¾ meters (9 feet) deep, an estimated 400 to 900 people lived in houses of mud brick with plastered floors arranged around

[22]Diamond, *Guns, germs, and steel*, p. 132.

[23] Bar-Yosef, O. (1986). The walls of Jericho: An alternative interpretation. *Current Anthropology 27*, 160.

Globalscape

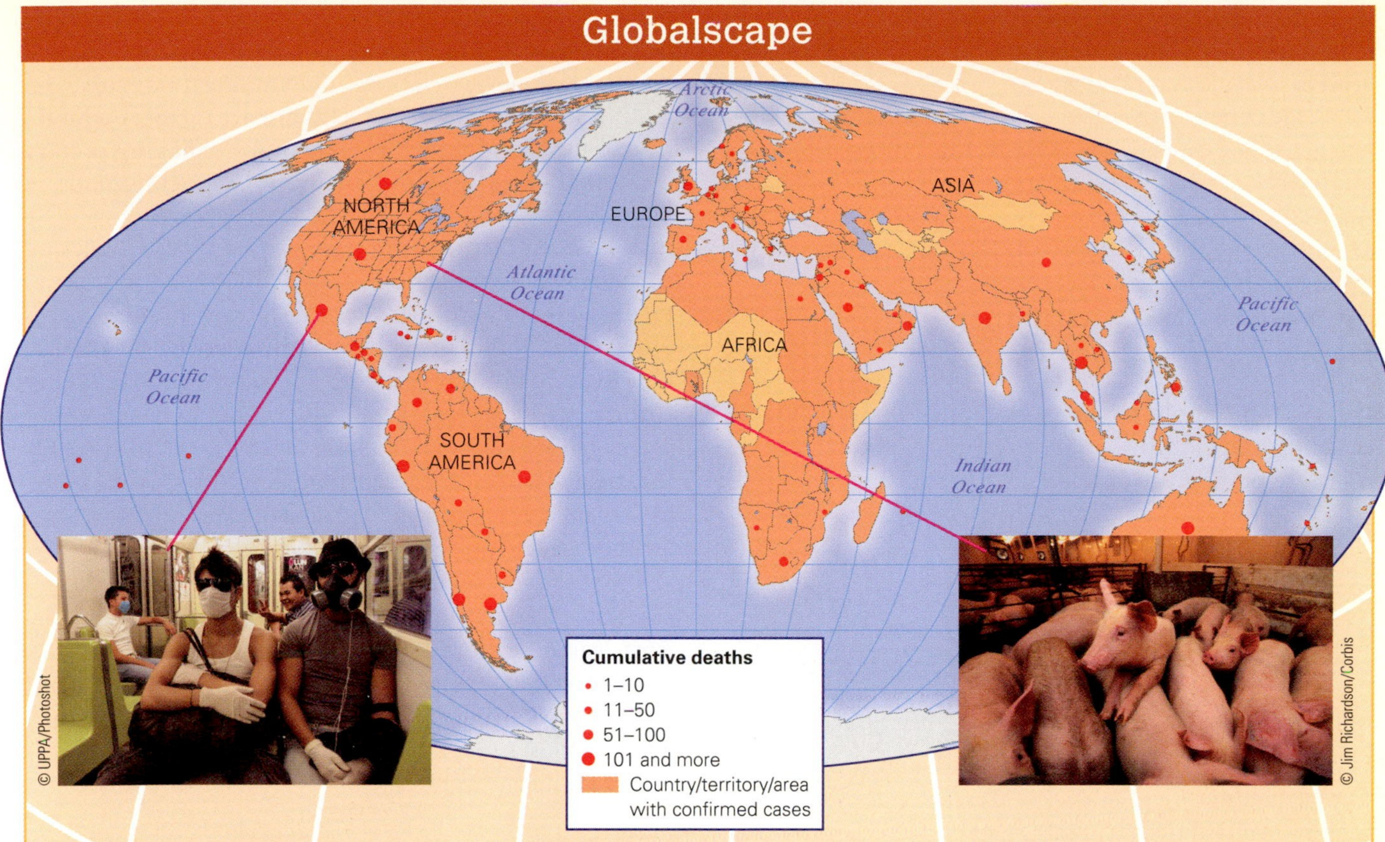

© UPPA/Photoshot

© Jim Richardson/Corbis

Factory Farming Fiasco?

In April 2009 protective masks and gloves were a common sight in Mexico City as the news of the first cases of swine flu pandemic appeared in the United States and Mexico. On June 11, 2009, the World Health Organization (WHO) made the pandemic official, and by July cases had been reported in three quarters of the states and territories the WHO monitors. Scientists across the world are examining the genetic makeup of the virus to determine its origins.

From the outset of the pandemic, many signs have pointed to a pig farming operation in Veracruz, Mexico, called Granjas Caroll, which is a subsidiary of Smithfield Foods, the world's largest pork producer. However, Ruben Donis, an expert virologist from the U.S. Centers for Disease Control and Prevention in Atlanta, Georgia, has come to a different conclusion based on genetic analysis. According to an article in the journal *Science*, Donis "suggests that the virus may have originated in a U.S. pig that traveled to Asia as part of the hog trade. The virus may have infected a human there, who then traveled back to North America, where the virus perfected human-to-human spread, maybe even moving from the United States to Mexico."[a] Another report has linked the current strain of swine flu to a strain that ran through factory farms in North Carolina in 1998 and to the avian flu that killed over 50 million people in 1918.[b]

While scientists examine the genetic evidence for swine flu, a look at factory farming shows how these practices facilitate the proliferation of disease. For example, the pig population of North Carolina numbers about 10 million, and most of these pigs are crowded onto farms of over 5,000 animals. These pigs travel across the country as part of farming operations. A pig may be born in North Carolina, then travel to the heartland of the United States to fatten up before a final trip to the slaughterhouses in California.

The crowded conditions in pig farms mean that if the virus enters a farm it quickly can infect many pigs, which are then shipped to other places spreading the virus further, with many opportunities for the virus to pass between species. Health risks of global food distribution have long been a concern, and the swine flu outbreak elevates these concerns to a new level.

Global Twister Do you think the swine flu pandemic should lead to changes in meat production and distribution globally?

[a] Cohen, J. (2009). Out of Mexico? Scientists ponder swine flu's origin. *Science 324* (5928), 700–702.

[b] Trifonov, V., et al. (2009). The origin of the recent swine influenza A (H1N1) virus infecting humans. *Eurosurveillance 14* (17). http://www.eurosurveillance.org/ViewArticle.aspx?ArticleId=19193.

courtyards. In addition to these houses, a stone tower that would have taken a hundred people over a hundred days to build was located inside one corner of the wall, near the spring. A staircase inside it probably led to a mud-brick building on top. This massive wall—near mud-brick storage facilities as well as peculiar structures of possible ceremonial significance—provides evidence of social changes in these early farming communities. A village cemetery also reflects the sedentary life of these early people; nomadic groups, with few exceptions, rarely buried their dead in a single central location.

Close contact between the farmers of Jericho and other villages is indicated by common features in art, ritual, use of prestige goods, and burial practices. Other evidence of trade consists of obsidian and turquoise from Sinai as well as marine shells from the coast, all discovered inside the walls of Jericho.

Neolithic Material Culture

Various innovations in the realms of tool making, pottery, housing, and clothing characterized life in Neolithic villages. All of these are examples of material culture.

TOOL MAKING

Early harvesting tools were made of wood or bone into which razor-sharp flint blades were inserted. Later tools continued to be made by chipping and flaking stone, but during the Neolithic period stone that was too hard to be chipped was ground and polished for tools. People developed sickles, scythes, forks, hoes, and simple plows to replace their digging sticks. Mortars and pestles were used to grind and crush grain. Later, when domesticated animals became available for use as draft animals, plows were redesigned. Along with the development of diverse technologies, individuals acquired specialized skills for creating a variety of implements, including leatherworks, weavings, and pottery.

POTTERY

Hard work on the part of those producing the food would also support other members of the society who could then apply their skills and energy to various craft specialties such as pottery. In the Neolithic, different forms of pottery were created for transporting and storing food, water, and various material possessions.

Because pottery vessels are impervious to damage by insects, rodents, and dampness, they could be used for storing small grain, seeds, and other materials. Moreover, food can be boiled in pottery vessels directly over the fire rather than by such ancient techniques as dropping stones heated directly in the fire into the food being cooked. Pottery was also used for pipes, ladles, lamps, and other objects, and some cultures used large vessels for disposal of the dead. Significantly, pottery containers remain important for much of humanity today.

Widespread use of pottery, which is made of clay and fired in very hot ovens, is a good, though not foolproof, indication of a sedentary community. It is found in abundance in all but a few of the earliest Neolithic settlements. Its fragility and weight make it less practical for use by nomads and hunters, who more commonly use woven bags, baskets, and animal-hide containers. Nevertheless, there are some modern nomads who make and use pottery, just as there are farmers who do not. In fact, food foragers in Japan were making pottery by 13,000 years ago, long before it was being made in Southwest Asia.

The manufacture of pottery requires artful skill and considerable technological sophistication. To make a useful vessel requires knowledge of clay: how to remove impurities from it, how to shape it into desired forms, and how to dry it in a way that does not cause cracking. Proper firing is tricky as well; it must be heated to over 600 degrees Fahrenheit so that the clay will harden and resist future disintegration from moisture, but care must be taken to prevent the object from cracking or even exploding as it heats and later cools down.

Pottery is decorated in various ways. For example, designs can be engraved on the vessel before firing, or special rims, legs, bases, and other details may be made separately and fastened to the finished pot. Painting is the most common form of pottery decoration, and there are literally thousands of painted designs found among the pottery remains of ancient cultures.

HOUSING

Food production and the new sedentary lifestyle emphasized another technological development—permanent house building. Because they move frequently, most food foragers show little interest in permanent housing. Cave shelters, pits dug in the earth, and simple lean-tos made of hides and tree limbs serve the purpose of keeping the weather out. In the Neolithic, however, dwellings became more complex in design and more diverse in type. Some Neolithic peoples constructed houses of wood, while others built more elaborate shelters made of stone, sun-dried brick, or poles plastered together with mud or clay.

Although permanent housing frequently goes along with food production, there is evidence of substantial housing without domestication. For example, on the northwestern coast of North America, people lived in extensive houses made of heavy planks split from cedar logs, yet their food consisted entirely of wild plants and animals, especially salmon and sea mammals.

CLOTHING

During the Neolithic, for the first time in human history, clothing was made of woven textiles. The raw materials and technology necessary for the production of clothing came from several sources: flax and cotton from farming; wool from domesticated sheep, llamas, or goats; silk from silk worms. Human invention contributed the spindle for spinning and the loom for weaving.

Sometimes Neolithic villagers organized to carry out impressive communal works. Shown here is Stonehenge, the famous ceremonial and astronomical center in England, which dates back about 4,500 years. Used as a burial ground long before the massive stone circle was constructed, Stonehenge reflects the builders' understanding of the forces of nature and their impact on food production. For instance, the opening of the stone circles aligns precisely so that the sunlight passes through with the sunrise of the summer solstice and with the sunset of the winter solstice. This careful alignment indicates that the people of the Neolithic were paying close attention to the movements of the sun and the growing cycle of the seasons.

Neolithic Social Structure

Evidence of the economic and technological developments listed thus far has enabled archaeologists to make some inferences about the organization of Neolithic societies. For example, archaeological evidence reveals little in the way of a centrally organized and directed religious life, and burial sites exhibit no social differentiation. Early Neolithic graves tend not to be covered by stone slabs and rarely included elaborate objects. Burial practices tend to apply equally to all members of a community.

The small size of most villages and the absence of elaborate buildings suggest that the inhabitants knew one another very well and were even related; most of their relationships were probably highly personal ones, with equal emotional significance. Still, Neolithic people sometimes organized to carry out impressive communal works preserved in the archaeological record, such as the site of Stonehenge in England.

From all the evidence, it seems that Neolithic societies were relatively egalitarian with minimal division of labor, but they did develop some new and more specialized social roles. Villages appear to have been made up of several households, each providing for most of its own needs. The organizational needs of society beyond the household level were probably met by kinship groups.

Neolithic Culture in the Americas

In the Americas the shape and timing of the Neolithic revolution differed compared to other parts of the world. For example, Neolithic agricultural villages were common in Southwest Asia between 8,000 and 9,000 years ago, but similar villages did not appear in the Americas until about 4,500 years ago, in **Mesoamerica** (the region encompassing central and southern Mexico and northern Central America) and the Andean highlands. Moreover, pottery, which developed in Southwest Asia shortly after plant and animal domestication, did not emerge in the Americas until much later. The potter's wheel was

Mesoamerica The region encompassing central and southern Mexico and northern Central America.

not used by early Neolithic people in the Americas. Instead, elaborate pottery was manufactured by hand. Looms and the hand spindle appeared in the Americas about 3,000 years ago.

None of these absences indicate any backwardness on the part of Native American peoples, many of whom, as we have already seen, were highly sophisticated farmers and plant breeders. Rather, the effectiveness of existing practices was such that they continued to be satisfactory. When food production developed in Mesoamerica and the Andean highlands, it did so wholly independently of Europe and Asia, with different crops, animals, and technologies.

Outside Mesoamerica and the Andean highlands, hunting, fishing, and the gathering of wild plant foods remained important elements in the economy of Neolithic peoples in the Americas. Apparently, most American Indians chose not to entirely switch from a food-foraging to a food-producing mode of life, even though maize and other domestic crops came to be cultivated just about everywhere that climate permitted. The Indian lifeways were so effective, so well integrated into a complete cultural system, and so environmentally stable that for many of these groups the change to food production was unnecessary. The stable American Indian cultures were only disrupted by the arrival of European explorers who brought disease and devastation with them.

The Neolithic and Human Biology

Although we tend to think of the invention of food production in terms of its cultural impact, it obviously had a biological impact as well. From studies of human skeletons from Neolithic burials, physical anthropologists have found evidence for somewhat less mechanical stress on peoples' bodies and teeth. Although there are exceptions, the teeth of Neolithic peoples show less wear, their bones are less robust, and osteoarthritis (the result of stressed joint surfaces) is not as marked as in the skeletons of Paleolithic and Mesolithic peoples.

Though Neolithic teeth show less wear, recent discoveries from Pakistan provide the earliest evidence of human dentistry: tiny holes made in the molar teeth of ancient live humans, with fine flint drills.[24] Whether dentistry accompanied an increase in dental decay brought about by the dietary shift of this period remains to be seen. This would parallel the clear evidence for a marked overall deterioration in health and mortality during the Neolithic. Anthropologist Anna Roosevelt sums up our knowledge of this in the following Original Study.

[24] Coppa, A., et al. (2006). Early Neolithic tradition of dentistry. *Nature 440*, 755–756.

Original Study

History of Mortality and Physiological Stress *by Anna Roosevelt*

Although there is a relative lack of evidence for the Paleolithic stage, enough skeletons have been studied that it seems clear that seasonal and periodic physiological stress regularly affected most prehistoric hunting-gathering populations, as evidenced by the presence of enamel hypoplasias [horizontal linear defects in tooth enamel] and Harris lines [horizontal lines near the ends of long bones].

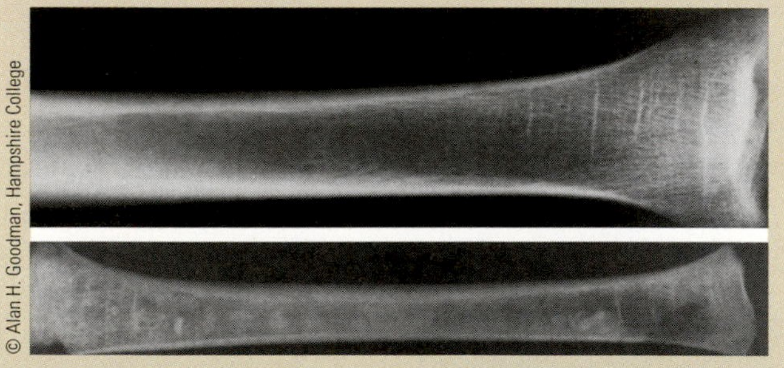

Harris lines near the ends of these youthful thigh bones, found in a prehistoric farming community in Arizona, are indicative of recovery after growth arrest, caused by famine or disease.

What also seems clear is that severe and chronic stress, with high frequency of hypoplasias, infectious disease lesions, pathologies related to iron-deficiency anemia, and high mortality rates, is not characteristic of these early populations. There is no evidence of frequent, severe malnutrition, and so the diet must have been adequate in calories and other nutrients most of the time.

During the Mesolithic, the proportion of starch in the diet rose, to judge from the increased occurrence of certain dental diseases, but not enough to create an impoverished diet. At this time, diets seem to have been made up of a rather large number of foods, so that the failure of one food source would not be catastrophic. There is a possible slight tendency for Paleolithic people to be healthier and taller than Mesolithic people, but there is no apparent trend toward increasing physiological stress during the Mesolithic. Thus, it seems that both hunter-gatherers and incipient agriculturalists regularly underwent population pressure, but only to a moderate degree.

During the periods when effective agriculture first comes into use, there seems to be a temporary upturn in health and survival rates in a few regions: Europe, North America, and the eastern Mediterranean. At this stage, wild foods are still consumed periodically, and a variety of plants are cultivated, suggesting the availability of adequate amounts of different nutrients. Based on the increasing frequency of tooth disease related to high carbohydrate consumption, it seems that cultivated plants probably increased the storable calorie supply, removing for a time any seasonal or periodic problems in food supply. In most regions, however, the development of agriculture seems not to have had this effect, and there seems to have been a slight increase in physiological stress.

Stress, however, does not seem to have become common and widespread until after the development of high degrees of sedentism, population density, and reliance on intensive agriculture. At this stage in all regions the incidence of physiological stress increases greatly, and average mortality rates increase appreciably.

Most of these agricultural populations have high frequencies of porotic hyperostosis and cribra orbitalia [bone deformities indicative of chronic iron-deficiency anemia], and there is a substantial increase in the number and severity of enamel hypoplasias and pathologies associated with infectious disease. Stature in many populations appears to have been considerably lower than would be expected if genetically determined height maxima had been reached, which suggests that the growth arrests associated with pathologies were causing stunting.

Accompanying these indicators of poor health and nourishment, there is a universal drop in the occurrence of Harris lines, suggesting a poor rate of full recovery from the stress. Incidence of carbohydrate-related tooth disease increases, apparently because subsistence by this time is characterized by a heavy emphasis on a few starchy food crops. Populations seem to have grown beyond the point at which wild food resources could be a meaningful dietary supplement, and even domestic animal resources were commonly reserved for farm labor and transport rather than for diet supplementation.

It seems that a large proportion of most sedentary prehistoric populations under intensive agriculture underwent chronic and life-threatening malnutrition and disease, especially during infancy and childhood. The causes of the nutritional stress are likely to have been the poverty of the staple crops in most nutrients except calories, periodic famines caused by the instability of the agricultural system, and chronic lack of food due to both population growth and economic expropriation by elites. The increases in infectious disease probably reflect both a poorer diet and increased interpersonal contact in crowded settlements, and it is, in turn, likely to have aggravated nutritional problems.

Adapted from Roosevelt, A. C. (1984). Population, health, and the evolution of subsistence: Conclusions from the conference. In M. N. Cohen & G. J. Armelagos (Eds.), Paleopathology at the origins of agriculture *(pp. 572–574). Orlando: Academic Press.*

Enamel hypoplasias, such as those shown on these teeth, are indicative of arrested growth caused by famine or disease. These teeth are from an adult who lived in an ancient farming community in Arizona.

For the most part, the crops on which Neolithic peoples came to depend were selected for their higher productivity and storability rather than their nutritional value. Moreover, as already noted, their nutritional shortcomings would have been exacerbated by their susceptibility to periodic failure, particularly as populations grew in size. Thus the worsened health and mortality of Neolithic peoples are not surprising. Some have gone so far as to assert that the switch from food foraging to food production was the worst mistake that humans ever made.

Another key contributor to the increased incidence of disease and mortality was probably the new mode of life in Neolithic communities. Sedentary life in fixed villages brings with it sanitation problems as garbage and human waste accumulate. These are not a problem for small groups of people who move about from one campsite to another. Moreover, airborne diseases are more easily transmitted where people are gathered into villages. As discussed in Chapter 2, farming practices also created the ideal environment for the species of mosquito that spreads malaria.

Another factor, too, was the close association between humans and their domestic animals, a situation conducive to the transmission of diseases. A host of life-threatening diseases—including smallpox, chicken pox, swine flu, and many of those infectious diseases of childhood that were not overcome by medical science until the latter half of the 20th century—were transmitted to humans through their close association with domestic animals (Table 10.1). Higher mortality rates in Neolithic villages were offset by increased fertility, for population growth accelerated dramatically at precisely the moment that health and mortality worsened.

Table 10.1 Diseases Acquired from Domesticated Animals

Human Disease	Animal with Most Closely Related Pathogen	Deaths Globally According to WHO (Year)	Prevention Strategies
Measles	Cattle (rinderpest)	197,000 (2007)	Immunization
Tuberculosis	Cattle	1.6 million (2005)	Treatment of infected individuals to prevent spread
Smallpox	Cattle (cowpox) or other livestock with related pox viruses	Eradicated as of December 1979; between 1900 and eradication, smallpox killed 300–500 million people	Immunization
Influenza	Pigs, ducks	Several different types; all are seasonal and variable, with 250,000 to 500,000 deaths estimated annually	Immunization
Pertussis (whooping cough)	Pigs, dogs	297,000 (2000)	Immunization

Source: Diamond, J. (1997). *Guns, germs, and steel* (p. 207). New York: Norton; World Health Organization Fact Sheets.

The Neolithic and the Idea of Progress

Although the overall health of Neolithic peoples suffered as a consequence of this cultural shift, many view the transition from food foraging to food production as a great step upward on a ladder of progress. In part this interpretation is due to one of the more widely held beliefs of Western culture—that human history is basically a record of steady progress over time. To be sure, farming allowed people to increase the size of their populations, to live together in substantial sedentary communities, and to reorganize the workload in ways that permitted craft specialization. However, this idea of progress is the product of a set of cultural beliefs, not a universal truth. Each culture defines progress (if it does so at all) in its own terms.

Whatever the benefits of food production, however, a substantial price was paid.[25] As anthropologists Mark Cohen and George Armelagos put it, "Taken as a whole, indicators fairly clearly suggest an overall decline in the quality—and probably in the length—of human life associated with the adoption of agriculture."[26]

Rather than imposing ethnocentric notions of progress on the archaeological record, it is best to view the advent of food production as but one more factor contributing to the diversification of cultures, something that had begun in the Paleolithic. Although some societies continued to practice various forms of hunting, gathering, and fishing, others became horticultural, and some of those developed **agriculture.** Technologically more complex than horticultural societies, agriculturalists practice intensive crop cultivation, employing plows, fertilizers, and possibly irrigation. They may use a wooden or metal plow pulled by one or more harnessed draft animals, such as horses, oxen, or water buffaloes, to produce food on larger plots of land. The distinction between horticulturalist and intensive agriculturalist is not always an easy one to make. For example, the Hopi Indians of the North American Southwest traditionally employed irrigation in their farming while at the same time using basic hand tools.

Pastoralism arose in environments that were too dry, too grassy, too steep, too cold, or too hot for effective horticulture or intensive agriculture. Pastoralists breed and manage migratory herds of domesticated grazing animals, such as goats, sheep, cattle, llamas, or camels. For example, the Russian steppes, with their heavy grass cover, were not suitable to farming without a plow, but they were ideal for herding. Thus a number of peoples living in the arid grasslands and deserts that stretch from northwestern Africa into Central Asia kept large herds of domestic animals, relying on their neighbors for plant foods. Finally, some societies went on to develop civilizations—the subject of the next chapter.

[25] Cohen, M. N., & Armelagos, G. J. (1984). *Paleopathology at the origins of agriculture.* Orlando: Academic; Goodman, A., & Armelagos, G. J. (1985). Death and disease at Dr. Dickson's mounds. *Natural History 94* (9), 12–18.

[26] Cohen, M. N., & Armelagos, G. J. (1984). Paleopathology at the origins of agriculture: Editors' summation. In M. N. Cohen & G. J. Armelagos, *Paleopathology at the origins of agriculture* (p. 594). Orlando: Academic.

agriculture The cultivation of food plants in soil prepared and maintained for crop production. Involves using technologies other than hand tools, such as irrigation, fertilizers, and the wooden or metal plow pulled by harnessed draft animals.

pastoralism Breeding and managing large herds of domesticated grazing and browsing animals, such as goats, sheep, cattle, horses, llamas, or camels.

Questions for Reflection

1. The changed lifeways of the Neolithic included the domestication of plants and animals as well as settlement into villages. How did these cultural transformations solve the challenges of existence while at the same time create new problems? Did the Neolithic set into motion problems that are still with us today?

2. Why do you think some people of the past did not make the change from food foragers to food producers? What problems existing in today's world have their origins in the lifeways of the Neolithic?

3. Though human biology and culture are always interacting, the rates of biological change and cultural change uncoupled at some point in the history of our development. Think of examples of how the differences in these rates had consequences for humans in the Neolithic and in the present.

4. Why are the changes of the Neolithic sometimes mistakenly associated with progress? Why have the social forms that originated in the Neolithic come to dominate the earth?

5. Although the archaeological record indicates some differences in the timing of domestication of plants and animals in different parts of the world, why is it incorrect to say that one region was more advanced than another?

Suggested Readings

Childe, V. G. (1951). *Man makes himself.* New York: New American Library.

In this classic, originally published in 1936, Childe presented his concept of the Neolithic revolution. He places special emphasis on the technological inventions that helped transform humans from food gatherers to food producers.

Coe, S. D. (1994). *America's first cuisines.* Austin: University of Texas Press.

Writing in an accessible style, Coe discusses some of the more important crops grown by Native Americans and explores their early history and domestication. Following this she describes how these foods were prepared, served, and preserved by the Aztec, Maya, and Inca.

Diamond, J. (1997). *Guns, germs, and steel.* New York: Norton.

This Pulitzer Prize–winning bestseller addresses the question of the distribution of wealth and power in the world today. For Diamond, this answer requires an understanding of events associated with the origin and spread of food production. Although Diamond falls into various ethnocentric traps, he provides a great deal of solid information on the domestication and spread of crops and the biological consequences for humans.

Mann, C. C. (2005). *1491: New revelations of the Americas before Columbus.* New York: Knopf.

Mann dispels the myth of the Americas as an uninhabited wasteland before the arrival of Columbus and the European colonizers who followed him. He shows not only the richness of various Native American cultures but also the devastating effects of colonization.

Rindos, D. (1984). *The origins of agriculture: An evolutionary perspective.* Orlando: Academic.

This is one of the most important books on agricultural origins. After identifying the weaknesses of existing theories, Rindos presents his own evolutionary theory of agricultural origins.

Challenge Issue With the emergence of cities and states, human societies began to develop organized central governments and a concentration of power that made it possible to build monumental structures, such as the great pyramids of Egypt. But cities and states also ushered in a series of challenges, many of which city dwellers still face. For example, social stratification, in which a ruling elite controls the means of subsistence and many other aspects of daily life, exploits many city dwellers and poor people in outlying areas. While the people of stratified societies are interdependent, the elite classes have disproportionate access to and control of all resources, including human labor. In Cairo, as in other big cities, housing, for example, is dramatically different for different social classes. While the elite live in luxurious homes, 5 million urban poor live illegally in tomb rooms of cemeteries known as the City of the Dead.

CHAPTER 11

The Emergence of Cities and States

Chapter Preview

When and Where Did the World's First Cities Develop?

Cities are urban settlements with well-defined centers and populations that are large, dense, and diversified both economically and socially. They are characteristic of civilizations that developed independently in Eurasia, Africa, and the Americas. Between 4,500 and 6,000 years ago, cities began to develop in China, the Indus and Nile Valleys, Mesopotamia, Mesoamerica, and the central Andes. The world's oldest cities were those of Mesopotamia, but one of the largest was located in Mesoamerica.

What Changes in Culture Accompanied the Rise of Cities?

Four basic cultural changes mark the transition from Neolithic village existence to life in urban centers: agricultural innovation, as new farming methods were developed; diversification of labor, as more people were freed from food production to pursue a variety of full-time craft specialties; the development of centralized governments to deal with the new problems of urban life; and the emergence of social classes, as people were ranked according to the work they did or the position of the families into which they were born.

Why Did Cities Develop into Civilizations?

Ancient cities developed into what anthropologists call civilizations: societies in which large numbers of people live in cities, are socially stratified, and are governed by centrally organized political systems called states. A number of theories have been proposed to explain why civilizations developed. For example, population growth led to competition for space and scarce resources. This competition favored the development of centralized authority to control resources and, incidentally, organized warfare. Some civilizations, though, appear to have developed as a result of unifying beliefs and values. In some cases, the self-promoting actions of powerful individuals may have played a role. Thus it may be that civilizations arose in different places for different reasons.

A walk down a busy street of a city such as New York or San Francisco brings us into contact with numerous activities essential to life in North American society. Sidewalks are crowded with people going to and from offices and stores. Heavy traffic of cars, buses, and trucks periodically comes to a standstill. A brief two-block stretch may contain a grocery store; sidewalk vendors; shops selling clothing, appliances, or books; a restaurant; a newsstand; a gas station; and a movie theater. Other features such as a museum, a police station, a school, a hospital, or a church distinguish some neighborhoods.

Each of these services or places of business is dependent on others from outside this two-block radius. A butcher shop, for instance, depends on slaughterhouses and beef ranches. A clothing store could not exist without designers, farmers who produce cotton and wool, and workers who manufacture synthetic fibers. Restaurants rely on refrigerated trucking and vegetable and dairy farmers. Hospitals need insurance companies, pharmaceutical companies, and medical equipment industries. All institutions, finally, depend on the public utilities—the telephone, gas, water, and electric companies. Although interdependence is not immediately apparent to the passerby, it is an important aspect of modern cities.

The interdependence of goods and services in a big city makes a variety of products readily available. But interdependence also creates vulnerability. If strikes, bad weather, or acts of violence cause one service to stop functioning, other services can deteriorate.

At the same time, cities are resilient in their response to stresses. When one service breaks down, others take over its functions. During a long newspaper strike in New York City in the 1960s, for example, several new magazines were launched, and television networks expanded their coverage of news and events. This phenomenon resembles the flourishing of reality television programs in the United States that took place during the 2007–2008 Hollywood writers' strike.

In many parts of the world the violence of war has caused extensive damage to basic infrastructure, leading to the development of alternative systems to cope with everything from procuring food to communicating within global political systems. The same is true for people coping with the aftermath of a natural disaster such as Hurricane Katrina in 2005 or the massive tsunami that hit the Pacific in 2004. With the interconnectedness of modern life due to the Internet and globalization, the interdependence of goods and services transcends far beyond city limits.

On the surface, city life seems so orderly that we take it for granted; but a moment's reflection reminds us that the intricate fabric of city life did not always exist, and the concentrated availability of diverse goods is a very recent development in human history.

civilization In anthropology, a type of society marked by the presence of cities, social classes, and the state.

Since the American invasion in 2003, bombing and pillaging have damaged the infrastructure of Baghdad. Four days of heavy rain led to a collapse of the city's sewage system, which flooded the streets with contaminated water. Makeshift bridges were constructed and alternate routes were created to help people avoid waterborne disease.

Defining Civilization

The word *civilization* comes from the Latin *civis*, which refers to one who is an inhabitant of a city, and *civitas*, which refers to the urban community in which one dwells. In everyday North American and European usage, the word *civilization* connotes refinement and progress and may imply ethnocentric judgments about cultures. In anthropology, by contrast, the term has a more precise meaning that avoids culture-bound notions. As used by anthropologists, **civilization** refers to societies in which large numbers of people live in cities, are socially stratified, and are

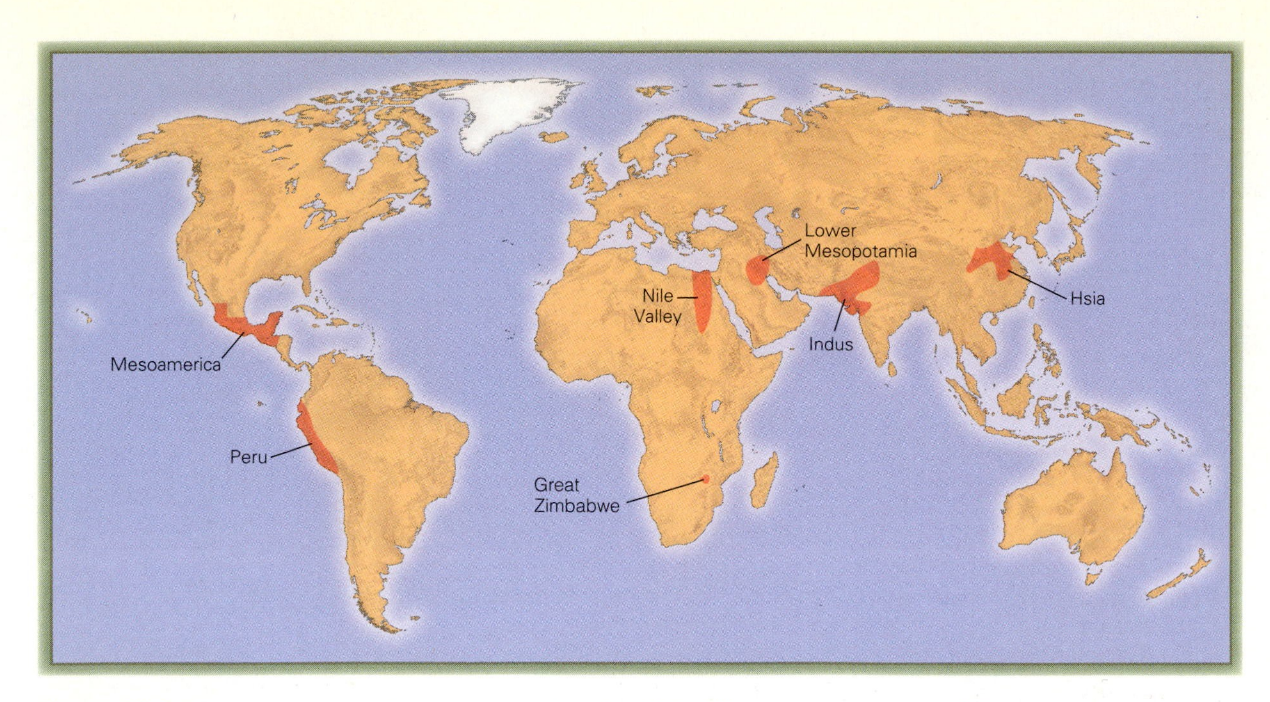

Figure 11.1 The major early civilizations sprang from Neolithic villages in various parts of the world. Those of the Americas developed wholly independently of those in Africa and Eurasia. Chinese civilization seems to have developed independently of Southwest Asia civilization, including the Nile and Indus civilizations.

governed by a ruling elite working through centrally organized political systems called states. We shall elaborate on all of these points in this chapter.

As Neolithic villages grew into towns, the world's first cities developed. This happened between 4,500 and 6,000 years ago—first in Mesopotamia (modern-day Iraq), then in Egypt's Nile Valley and India and Pakistan's Indus Valley. In China, civilization was under way by 5,000 years ago. Independent of these developments in Eurasia and Africa, the first American Indian cities appeared in Peru around 4,000 years ago and in Mesoamerica about 2,000 years ago (Figure 11.1).

What characterized these first cities? Why are they called the birthplaces of civilization? The first feature of cities—and of civilization—is their large size and population.

But cities are more than overgrown towns. Consider the case of Çatalhöyük, a compact 9,500-year-old settlement in south-central Turkey.[1] The tightly packed houses for its more than 5,000 inhabitants left no room for streets. People traversed the roofs of neighboring houses and dropped through a hole in the roof to get into their own home. While house walls were covered with paintings and bas-reliefs, the houses were structurally similar to one another, and no known public architecture existed. People grew some crops and tended livestock but also collected significant amounts of food from wild plants and animals, never intensifying their agricultural practices. Evidence of a division of labor or of a centralized authority is minimal or nonexistent. It was as if several Neolithic villages were crammed together in one place at Çatalhöyük.

Archaeological evidence from early urban centers, by contrast, demonstrates organized planning by a central authority, technological intensification, and social stratification. For example, flood control and protection were vital components of the great ancient cities of the Indus River Valley, located in today's India and Pakistan. Mohenjo-Daro—an urban center at its peak some 4,500 years ago with a population of at least 20,000—was built on an artificial mound, safe from floodwaters. Further, the streets of this densely populated city were laid out in a grid pattern and included individual homes with sophisticated drainage systems.

[1] Material on Çatalhöyük is drawn from Balter, M. (1998). Why settle down? The mystery of communities. *Science 282,* 1442–1444; Balter, M. (1999). A long season puts Çatalhöyük in context. *Science 286,* 890–891; Balter, M. (2001). Did plaster hold Neolithic society together? *Science 294,* 2278–2281; Kunzig, R. (1999). A tale of two obsessed archaeologists, one ancient city and nagging doubts about whether science can ever hope to reveal the past. *Discover 20* (5), 84–92.

Visual Counterpoint

The view looking south down Teotihuacan's principal avenue, the Street of the Dead. This urban axis was unequaled in its scale until the construction of such modern-day avenues as the Champs-Élysées in Paris.

Ancient peoples incorporated their spiritual beliefs and social order into the cities they built. For example, the layout of the great Mesoamerican city Teotihuacan, founded 2,200 years ago, translated the solar calendar into a unified spatial pattern. The Street of the Dead—a grand north-south axis running from the Pyramid of the Moon and bordered by the Pyramid of the Sun and the royal palace compound—was deliberately oriented to an astronomical marker, east of true north. Ancient city planners even channeled the San Juan River to run through the city in conformity with the grid (Figure 11.2). Surrounding this core were thousands of apartment compounds, separated

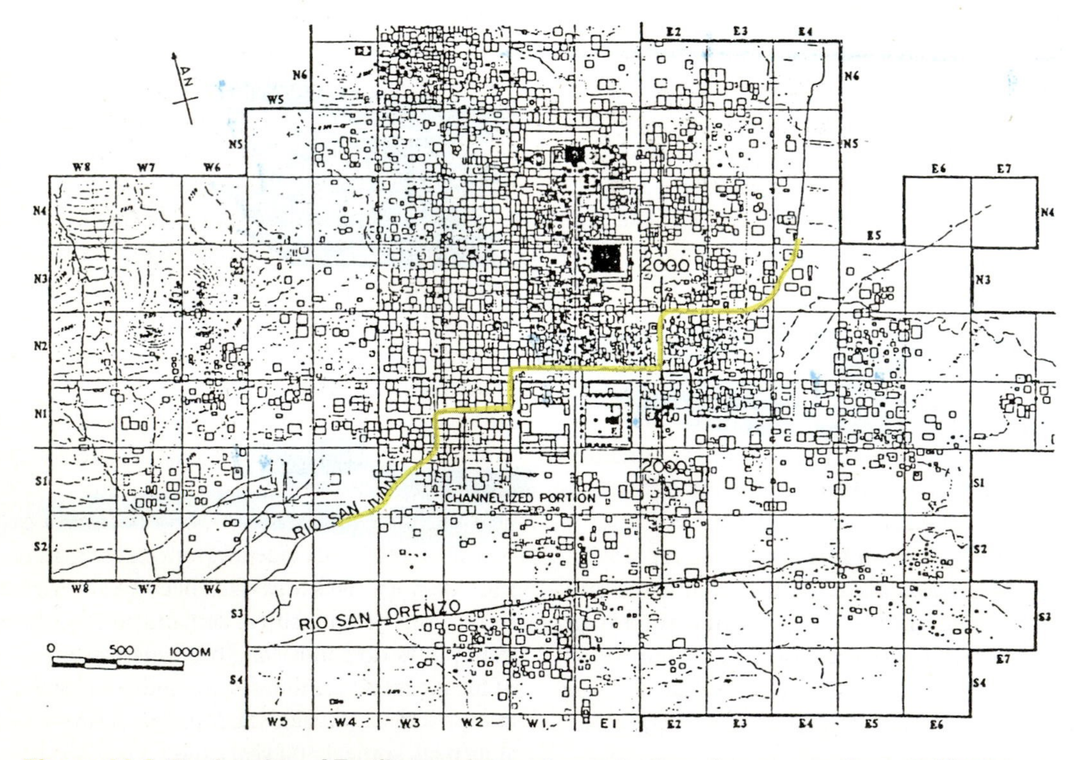

Figure 11.2 **The founders of Teotihuacan imposed an audacious plan on several square kilometers of landscape in central Mexico. At the center is the Street of the Dead, running from the Pyramid of the Moon (near top), past the Pyramid of the Sun, and, south of the San Juan River (Rio), the palace compound. Note the gridded layout of surrounding apartment compounds and the channeled San Juan River.**

from one another by a grid of narrow streets, maintaining the east-of-north orientation throughout the city. It is estimated that over 100,000 people inhabited this great city until its sudden collapse possibly in the 7th century.

Finally, clear evidence for both social and economic diversity exists in Teotihuacan. Some six levels of society can be discerned through the varying size and quality of apartment rooms. Those at and near the top of the social scale lived on or near the Street of the Dead. The Pyramid of the Sun along this avenue was built above a cave, which was seen as a portal to the underworld and as the home of deities associated with death. Teotihuacan artisans worked on exotic goods and raw materials imported from afar, and at least two neighborhoods housed people with foreign affiliations—one with Oaxaca, the other (the "merchant's quarter") with the Gulf and Maya lowlands. Farmers, whose labor in fields (some of them irrigated) supplied the food to fellow city dwellers, also resided in the city.[2]

Mohenjo-Daro and Teotihuacan, like other early cities throughout the globe, were far more than expanded Neolithic villages. The changes that took place in the transition from village to city were so great that many consider the emergence of urban living to be one of the great developments in human culture. The following case study gives us a glimpse of another of the world's ancient cities, including how archaeologists have studied it and how it may have grown from a smaller farming community.

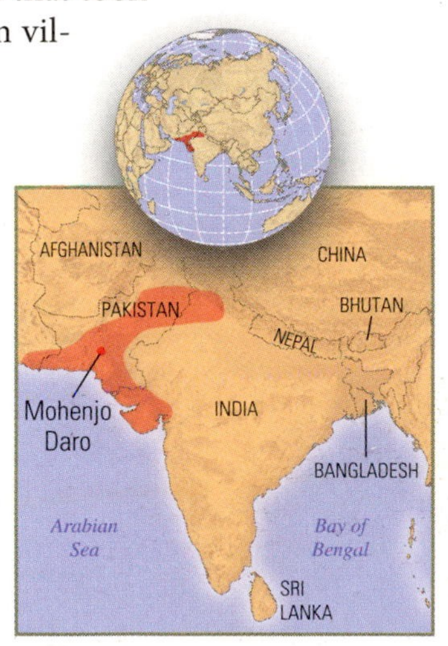

Tikal: A Case Study

The ancient city of Tikal, one of the largest lowland Maya centers in existence, is situated in Central America about 300 kilometers north of Guatemala City. Tikal was built on a broad limestone terrace in a rainforest. Here the Maya settled 3,000 years ago. Because the Maya calendar can be precisely correlated with our own, it is known that their civilization flourished until 1,100 years ago.

At its height, Tikal covered about 120 square kilometers (km^2), and its center or nucleus was the Great Plaza, a large, paved area surrounded by about 300 major structures and thousands of houses (Figure 11.3). Starting from a small, dispersed population, Tikal swelled to at least 45,000 people. By 1,550 years ago, its population density had reached 600 to 700 people per square kilometer, which was three times that of the surrounding region.

Tikal and the surrounding region were intensively explored under the joint auspices of the University of Pennsylvania Museum and the Guatemalan government from 1956 through the 1960s. At the time, it was the most ambitious archaeological project undertaken in the western hemisphere.

In the first few years of the Tikal Project, archaeologists investigated only major temple and palace structures found in the vicinity of the Great Plaza, at the site's epicenter. But in 1959, aiming to gain a balanced view of Tikal's development and composition, they turned their attention to the hundreds of small mounds that surround larger buildings and were thought to be the remains of dwellings. In a sense, this represented a shift in the practice of archaeology toward studying the complexities of everyday life. Imagine how difficult it would be to get a realistic view of life in a major city such as Washington, DC, or Beijing by looking only at their monumental public buildings. Similarly, a realistic view of Tikal cannot be reconstructed without examining the full range of ruins in the area.

The excavation of small structures, most of which were probably houses, permitted the estimation of Tikal's population size and density. This information allowed archaeologists to test the conventional assumption that the Maya inhabitants' subsistence practices were inadequate to sustain large population concentrations.

Extensive excavation also provided a sound basis for a reconstruction of the everyday life and social organization of the Maya, a people who had been known almost entirely through the study of ceremonial remains. For example, differences in architecture, house construction, and associated artifacts and burials suggest differences in social class. Features of house distribution might reflect the existence of extended families or other types of kin groups. The excavation of both large and small structures revealed the social structure of the total population of Tikal.[3]

[2] Cowgill, G. L. (1997). State and society at Teotihuacan, Mexico. *Annual Review of Anthropology 26,* 129–161.

[3] Haviland, W. A. (2002). Settlement, society and demography at Tikal. In J. Sabloff (Ed.), *Tikal.* Santa Fe: School of American Research.

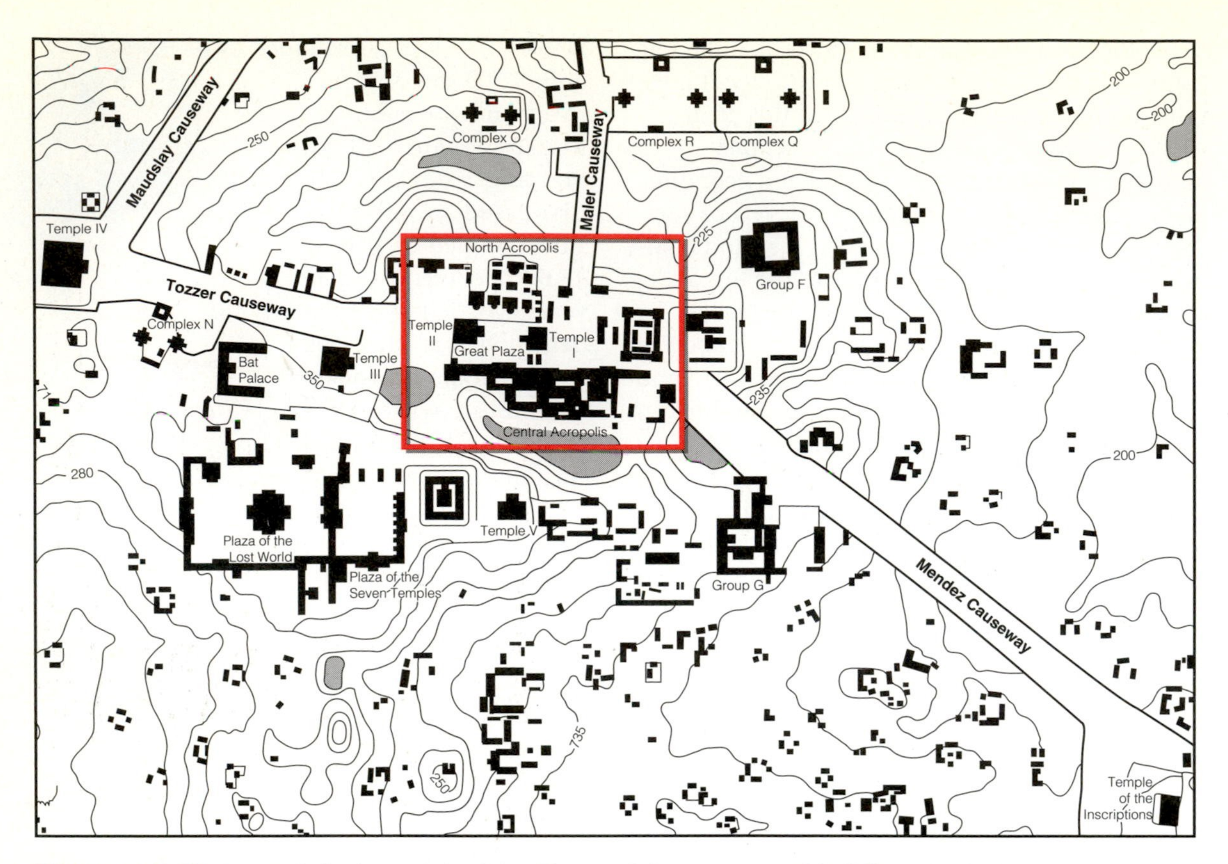

Figure 11.3 Tikal spreads far beyond the Great Plaza and the monumental buildings that have been excavated and are mapped here. Archaeologists used surveying techniques, test pits, and other strategies to fully define the city's boundaries and to understand the full spectrum of lifeways that took place there. The red outline in the center of the map delineates the royal court, royal burial ground, and central marketplace. In addition to what is pictured here, Tikal extends several kilometers outward in every direction. Those familiar with the original *Star Wars* movie will be interested to know that the aerial views of the rebel camp were filmed at Tikal, where monumental structures depicted in this map rise high above the forest canopy.

Surveying and Excavating the Site

Mapping crews surveyed 16 square kilometers of forested land surrounding the Great Plaza, providing a preliminary map to guide the small-structure excavation process.[4] Aerial photography could not be used for this mapping, because the tree canopy in this area is often 30 meters (about 100 feet) above the ground, obscuring all but the tallest temples. Many of the small ruins are practically invisible even to observers on the ground. Four years of mapping revealed that ancient Tikal was far larger than the original 16 km^2 surveyed. More time and money allowed continued surveying of the area to fully define the city's boundaries and calculate its overall size.[5]

The initial excavation of six structures, two plazas, and a platform revealed new structures not visible before excavation, the architectural complexity of the structures, and an enormous quantity of artifacts that had to be washed and catalogued. Some structures were partially excavated, and some remained uninvestigated. Following this initial work, the archaeological team excavated over a hundred additional small structures in different parts of the site in order to ensure investigation of a representative sample. The team also sank numerous test pits in various other small-structure groups to supplement the information gained from more extensive excavations.

[4] Haviland, W. A., et al. (1985). *Excavations in small residential groups of Tikal: Groups 4F-1 and 4F-2.* Philadelphia: University Museum.

[5] Puleston, D. E. (1983). *The settlement survey of Tikal.* Philadelphia: University Museum.

Evidence from the Excavation

Excavation at Tikal produced considerable information about the social organization, technology, and diversity in this ancient city, as well as the relationship between people in Tikal and other regions. For example, the site provided evidence of trade in nonperishable items. Granite, quartzite, hematite, pyrite, jade, slate, and obsidian all were imported, as either raw materials or finished products. Marine materials from Caribbean and Pacific coastal areas were found as well. Because Tikal is located on top of an abundant source of chert (a flintlike stone used to manufacture tools), this may have been exported in the form of raw material and finished objects. In addition, Tikal's location between two river systems may have facilitated an overland trade route. Evidence of trade in perishable goods—such as textiles, feathers, salt, and cacao—indicated that there were full-time traders among the Tikal Maya.

Technologically, specialized woodworking, pottery, obsidian, and shell workshops have been found. The skillful stone carving displayed on stone monuments suggests that occupational specialists did this work. The same is true of the fine artwork exhibited on ceramic vessels. Ancient artists had to envision what their work would look like after their pale, relatively colorless ceramics had been fired.

To control the large population, Tikal must have had some form of bureaucratic organization. From Maya written records (glyphs), we know that the government was headed by a hereditary ruling dynasty with sufficient power to organize massive construction and maintenance. This included a system of defensive ditches and embankments on the northern and southern edges of the city. The longest of these ran for a distance of perhaps 19 to 28 kilometers. Although we do not have direct evidence, there are clues to the existence of textile workers, dental workers, makers of bark cloth "paper," scribes, masons, astronomers, and other occupational specialists.

The religion of the Tikal Maya may have developed initially as a means to cope with the uncertainties of agriculture. Tikal soil is thin, and the only available water comes from rain that has been collected in reservoirs. Rain is abundant in season, but its onset tends to be unreliable. Conversely, the elevation of Tikal, high relative to surrounding terrain, may have caused it to be perceived as a "power place," especially suited for making contact with supernatural forces and beings.

The Maya priests tried not only to win over and please the deities in times of drought but also to honor them in times of plenty. Priests—experts on the Maya calendar—determined the most favorable time to plant crops and were involved with other agricultural matters. This tended to keep people in or near the city so that they could receive guidance on their crops. The population in and around Tikal depended upon their priests to influence supernatural beings and forces on their behalf.

Archaeologists have proposed that Tikal may have emerged as an important site due to its relative altitude in the region. Today it is still an important religious center for local Maya, who gather in front of the acropolis for a traditional ceremony.

As the population increased, land for agriculture became scarce, forcing the Maya to find new methods of food production that could sustain the dense population concentrated at Tikal. They added the planting and tending of fruit trees and other crops that could be grown around their houses in soils enriched by human waste. (Unlike houses at Teotihuacan, those at Tikal were not built close to one another.) Along with increased reliance on household gardening, the Maya constructed artificially raised fields in areas that were flooded each rainy season. In these fields, crops could be intensively cultivated year after year, as long as they were carefully maintained. Measures were taken to maximize collection of water for the dry season—by converting low areas into reservoirs and constructing channels to carry runoff from plazas and other architecture into these reservoirs.

Carved monuments like this were commissioned by Tikal's rulers to commemorate important events in their regions. Portrayed on this one is a king who ruled about 1,220 years ago. Such skilled stone carving could only have been accomplished by a specialist. (For a translation of the inscription on the monument's left side, see Figure 11.7.)

As these changes were taking place, a class of artisans, craftspeople, and other occupational specialists emerged to serve the needs of an elite consisting of the priesthood and a ruling dynasty. The Maya built numerous temples, public buildings, and various kinds of houses appropriate to the distinct social classes of their society.

For several hundred years, Tikal was able to sustain its ever-growing population. When the pressure for food and land reached a critical point, population growth stopped. At the same time, warfare with other cities became increasingly destructive. These events are marked archaeologically by the abandonment of houses on prime land in rural areas, by the advent of nutritional problems visible in skeletons recovered from burials, and by the construction of the previously mentioned defensive ditches and embankments. In other words, a period of readjustment set in, which must have been directed by an already strong central authority. Activities then continued as before, but without further population growth for another 250 years or so.

As this case study shows, excavations at Tikal demonstrated the splendor, the social organization, the belief system, and the agricultural practices of the ancient Maya civilization, among other things. This chapter's Original Study illustrates a very different Maya site, just a day's walk from Tikal.

Original Study

Action Archaeology and the Community at El Pilar *by Anabel Ford*

Resource management and conservation are palpable themes of the 21st century. Nowhere is this more keenly felt than in the tropics, seemingly our last terrestrial frontier. The Maya forest, one of the world's most biodiverse areas, is experiencing change at a rapid rate. Over the next two decades this area's population will double, threatening the integrity of the tropical ecosystems with contemporary development strategies that are at odds with the rich biodiversity of the region.

Curiously, in the past the Maya forest was home to a major civilization with at least three to nine times the current population of the region. The prosperity of the Classic Maya civilization has been touted for the remarkable quality of their unique hieroglyphic writing; the beauty of their art expressed in stone, ceramics, and plaster; and the precision of their mathematics and astronomy. What was the secret of Maya conservation and prosperity? How can archaeology shed light on the conservation possibilities for the future? These are the questions I address in my research at El Pilar.

I began my work as an archaeologist in the Maya forest in 1972. Eschewing the monumental civic centers that draw tourist and scholar alike, I was interested in the everyday life of the Maya through the study of their cultural ecology—the multifaceted relationships of humans and their environment. Certainly, the glamorous archaeological centers intrigued me; they were testaments to the wealth of the Maya civilization. Yet, it seemed to me that an understanding of the ancient Maya landscape would tell us more about the relationship of the Maya and their forest than yet another major temple. After all, the Maya were an agrarian civilization.

The ancient Maya agricultural system must be the key to their growth and accomplishments. With more than a century of exploration of the temple centers, we know that the civic centers were made for the ceremonial use of the ruling elite, that the temples would hold tombs of the royals and would include dedications of some of the most astounding artworks of the ancient world. Centers, too, would present stone stele erected in commemoration of regal accomplishments with hieroglyphic writing that is increasingly understood as codification of the Mayan language. These facts about the Maya point to successful development founded in their land use strategies that supported the increasing populations, underwrote the affluent elite glamor, and allowed for the construction of major civic centers over 2 millennia. The Maya farmers were at the bottom of this astounding expansion, and that is where I thought there could be a real discovery.

Since agriculture figures so importantly in preindustrial agrarian societies, such as the Maya, we would expect that the majority of the settlements would be farming ones. But how can we understand the farming techniques and strategies? Our appreciation of the traditional land use methods has been subverted with technology and a European ecological imperialism that inhibits a full understanding of other land use systems.

During the conquest of the Maya area, Spaniards felt there was nothing to eat in the forest; presented with a staggering cornucopia of fruits and vegetables that could fill pages, they asserted they were starving, as there was no grain or cattle. Today, we use European terms to describe agricultural lands around the world that are in many ways inappropriate to describe traditional systems. The words *arable* specifically means "plowable" and is derived from the Egyptian word *Ard*, or "plow." *Arable* is equated with *cultivable* by the United Nations Food and Agriculture Organization, and by doing so eliminates realms of land use and management that have a subtler impact on the environment. *Fallow* is loosely used to indicate abandoned fields, but really *fallow* means "unseeded plowed field." For European eyes, plowing was equivalent to cultivating, but in the New World cultivating embraced a much broader meaning that included fields of crops, selective succession, diverse orchards, and managed forests. In fact, it meant the entire landscape mosaic.

It is important to remember that the Maya, like all Native Americans prior to the tumultuous conquest 500 years ago, lived in the Stone Age without metal tools and largely without domesticated animals. This was not a hindrance, as it would seem today, but a fact that focused land use and intensification in other realms. Farmers were called upon to use their local skill and knowledge to provide for daily needs. And, as with all Native Americans, this skill would involve the landscape and most particularly the plants.

Reports of yields of grain from the Mesoamerican maize fields, or *milpas*, suggest that they were more than two to three times as productive as the fertile fields of the Seine River near Paris of the 16th century, the time of the conquest. The Maya farmed in cooperation with the natural environment. Like the Japanese rice farmer Masanubu Fukuoka describes in his book *One Straw Revolution*, Maya farmers today use their knowledge of the insects to insure pollination, their understanding of animals to promote propagation, their appreciation of water to determine planting, and their observations of change and nuance to increase their yields. This is not at all like the current agricultural development models that rely on increasingly complex techniques to raise production, disregarding nature in the process.

My focus on the patterns of the ancient Maya settlements has guided me along a path that I believe can provide important answers to questions of how the Maya achieved their success. The answers lie in finding where the everyday Maya lived, when they lived there, and what they did there. While popular notions would have you think that the Maya were a seething sea of humanity displacing the forest for their cities, I have discovered patterns on the landscape indicating that at their height in the Late Classic from 600 to 900 CE, the Maya occupied less that two thirds of the landscape. More than 80 percent of the settlements were concentrated into less than 40 percent of the area, while another 40 percent of the region was largely unoccupied.

This diversity of land use intensity created a patchwork of stages of what traditional farmers see as a cycle from forest to field and from field to orchard and back to forest again. The result in the Maya forest garden was an economic landscape that supported the ancient Maya, fueled wealth in the colonial and independence eras with lumber, and underwrote capitalism with the natural gum chicle. Today more than 90 percent of the dominant trees of the forest are of economic value. The Maya constructed this valuable forest over the millennia.

Despite my interest in daily life in the forest, monumental buildings became a part of my work. While conducting a settlement survey in the forest, I uncovered and mapped El Pilar, a major ancient Maya urban center with enormous temples towering more than 22 meters high and plaza expanses greater than soccer fields. The whole center of civic buildings covers more than 50 hectares. El Pilar is the largest center in the Belize River area and is located only 50 km from Tikal. This center was bound to become a tourist destination, presenting an opportunity to explore new ways to tell the Maya story. My observation that the ancient Maya evolved a sustainable economy in the tropics of Mesoamerica led my approach to developing El Pilar.

Astride the contemporary border separating Belize from Guatemala, El Pilar has been the focus of a bold conservation design for an international peace park on a long-troubled border. The vision for El Pilar is founded on the preservation of cultural heritage in the context of the natural environment. With a collaborative and interdisciplinary team of local villagers, government administrators, and scientists, we have established the El Pilar Archaeological Reserve for Maya Flora and Fauna. Since 1993, the innovations of the El Pilar program have forged new ground in testing novel strategies for community participation in the conservation development of the El Pilar Archaeological Reserve.

This program touches major administrative themes of global importance: tourism, natural resources, foreign

CONTINUED

CONTINUED

affairs, agriculture, rural development, and education. Yet the program's impact goes further. Working with traditional forest gardeners affects agriculture, rural enterprise, and capacity building. There are few areas untouched by the program's inclusive sweep, and more arenas can contribute to its evolution.

At El Pilar, I practice what I call "action archaeology," a pioneering conservation model that draws on lessons learned from the recent and distant past to benefit contemporary populations. For example, the co-evolution of Maya society and the environment provide clues about sustainability in this region today. At El Pilar we have advanced programs that will simulate Maya forest gardens as an alternative to resource-diminishing plow-and-pasture farming methods. Working with the traditional farmers, school models are being established. These models will help to transfer knowledge to the younger generation and carry on important conservation strategies. The forest survives and demonstrates resilience to impacts brought on by human expansion. The ancient Maya lived with this forest for millennia, and the El Pilar program argues there are lessons to be learned from that past.

The El Pilar program recognizes the privilege it has enjoyed in forging an innovative community participatory process, in creating a unique management planning design, and in developing a new tourism destination. The success of local outreach at El Pilar can best be seen in the growth of the community organizations such as the El Pilar Forest Garden Network and Amigos de El Pilar (Friends of El Pilar). With groups based in both Belize and Guatemala working together, the El Pilar program can help build an inclusive relationship between the community and the reserve that is mutually beneficial. The development of this dynamic relationship lies at the heart of the El Pilar philosophy—resilient and with the potential to educate communities, reform local-level resource management, and inform conservation designs for the Maya forest.

© Rolox Awards for Excellence, Susan Gray

Anabel Ford is the Director of the Mesoamerican Research Center, University of California-Santa Barbara, and President of the nonprofit Exploring Solutions Past: The Maya Forest Alliance. http://www.marc.ucsb.edu/elpilar/

Cities and Cultural Change

If a person who grew up in a rural North American village today moved to Chicago, Montreal, or Los Angeles, she or he would experience a very different way of life. The same would be true for a Neolithic village dweller who moved into one of the world's first cities in Mesopotamia 5,500 years ago. Four basic changes mark the transition from Neolithic village life to life in the first urban centers: agricultural innovation, diversification of labor, central government, and social stratification.

Agricultural Innovation

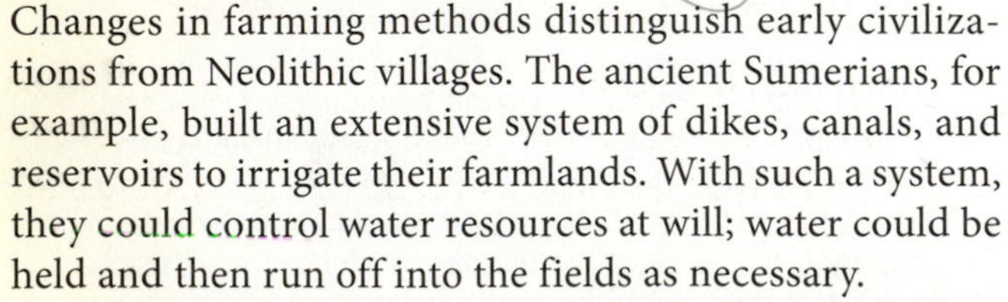

Changes in farming methods distinguish early civilizations from Neolithic villages. The ancient Sumerians, for example, built an extensive system of dikes, canals, and reservoirs to irrigate their farmlands. With such a system, they could control water resources at will; water could be held and then run off into the fields as necessary.

Irrigation was important for crop yield, because not having to depend on the seasonal rain cycles allowed farmers to harvest more crops in one year. Increased crop yield, resulting from agricultural innovations, contributed to the high population densities of ancient civilizations.

Diversification of Labor

Diversified labor activity was also characteristic of early civilizations. In a Neolithic village without irrigation or plow farming, every family member participated in the raising of crops. But the high crop yields made possible by new farming methods and the increased population of cities permitted a sizable number of people to pursue nonagricultural activities on a full-time basis.

Ancient public records document a variety of specialized workers. For example, an early Mesopotamian document from the old Babylonian city of Lagash (modern Tell Al-Hiba, Iraq) lists the artisans, craftspeople, and others paid from crop surpluses stored in the temple granaries. These lists included coppersmiths, silversmiths, sculptors, merchants, potters, tanners, engravers, butchers, carpenters, spinners, barbers, cabinetmakers, bakers, clerks, and brewers.

With specialization came the expertise that led to the invention of new ways of making and doing things. In Eurasia and Africa, civilization ushered in what

Courtesy Andrew Snavely of Dobra Teas

While there is archaeological evidence suggestive of tea drinking by *Homo erectus* in China, according to legend, the mythical emperor Shen Nung (c. 3000 BCE) was the first to drink a cup after tea leaves fell into his pot of boiling water. What is certain is that this crop contributed to the development of early civilizations and trade networks across Asia. Today, tea is farmed by a combination of these ancient methods along with all the tools of modern science. Here, a delightful tea lady in the Gao Shan, high mountains of Nantou, Taiwan, hand picks leaves from plants cloned from original oolong plants in Fujian, China. Fresh oolong leaves are plucked during the spring and are processed by a variety of methods (from machine to foot rolling) to semi-oxidize the tea leaves. Taiwanese oolongs are best grown in altitudes of 1,500 to 2,800 meters (5,000–9,000 feet) where the air is thin and the sun is close, giving the teas a very vegetal, creamy tropical flavor.

archaeologists often refer to as the **Bronze Age,** a period marked by the production of tools and ornaments made of this metal alloy. Metals were in great demand for the manufacture of farmers' and artisans' tools, as well as for weapons. Copper and tin (the raw materials from which bronze is made) were smelted, or separated from their ores, then purified, and cast to make plows, swords, axes, and shields. Later, such tools were made from smelted iron. In violent disputes over borders or territory, stone knives, spears, and slings could not stand up against metal spears, arrowheads, swords, helmets, or other armor.

Bronze also allowed for a proliferation of ornamental objects that are found in museums around the world today (Figure 11.4). See this chapter's Globalscape for the story of the recovery of one artifact that was stolen from the Iraqi National Museum in Baghdad.

The indigenous civilizations of the Americas also used metals. In South America, copper, silver, and gold were used primarily for ceremonial and ornamental objects. The Aztec and Maya used the same soft metals for ceremonial and ornamental objects while continuing to rely on stone for their everyday tools. To those who assume that metal is inherently superior, this seems puzzling. However, the ready availability of obsidian (a glass formed by volcanic activity), its extreme sharpness (many times sharper than the finest steel), and the ease with which it could be worked made it perfectly suited to their needs. Moreover, unlike bronze—and especially iron—copper, silver, and gold are soft metals and have limited practical use. Obsidian tools provide some of the sharpest cutting edges ever made (recall the Anthropology Applied feature "Stone Tools for Modern Surgeons" in Chapter 8).

Early civilizations developed extensive trade systems to procure the raw materials needed for their technologies. In many parts of the world, boats provided greater access to trade centers, transporting large loads of imports and exports between cities at lower cost than if they had been carried overland. A one-way trip from the ancient Egyptian cities along the Nile River to the Mediterranean port city of Byblos in Phoenicia (not far from the present city of Beirut, Lebanon) took far less time by rowboat compared to the overland route. With a sailboat, it took even less time.

Egyptian kings, or pharaohs, sent expeditions south to Nubia (northern Sudan) for gold; east to the Sinai Peninsula for copper; to Arabia for spices and perfumes; to Asia for lapis lazuli (a blue semiprecious stone) and other jewels; north to Lebanon for cedar, wine, and funerary oils; and southwest to Central Africa for ivory, ebony, ostrich feathers, leopard skins, cattle, as well as for the people they enslaved. Evidence of trading from Great Zimbabwe in southern Africa indicates that by the 11th century these trading networks had extended throughout the Old World. Increased contact with foreign peoples through trade brought new information to trading economies, furthering the spread of innovations and bodies of knowledge such as geometry and astronomy.

Central Government

The emergence of a governing elite also characterized early civilizations. Because of their size and complexity, new cities required a strong central authority. The governing elite

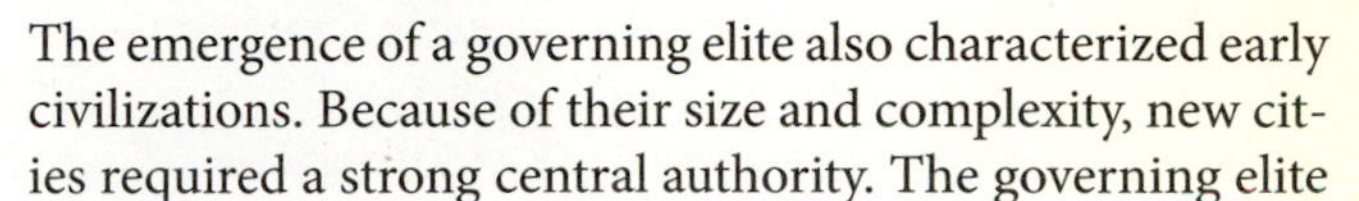

Bronze Age In the Old World, the period marked by the production of tools and ornaments of bronze; began about 5,000 years ago in China and Southwest Asia and about 500 years earlier in Southeast Asia.

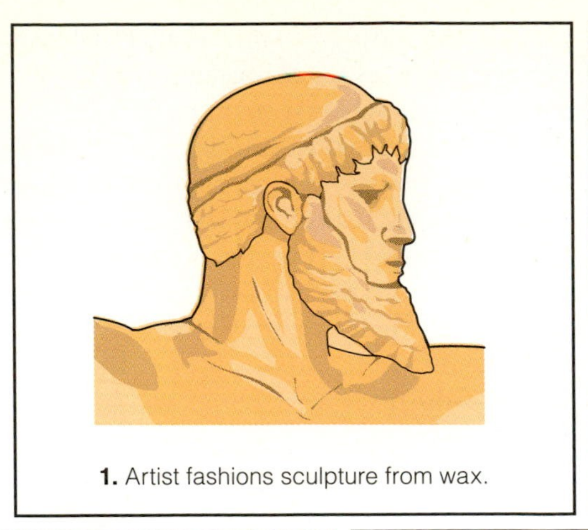

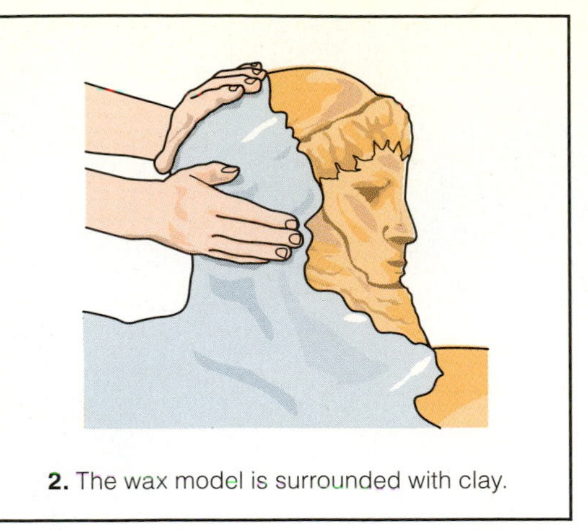

1. Artist fashions sculpture from wax.

2. The wax model is surrounded with clay.

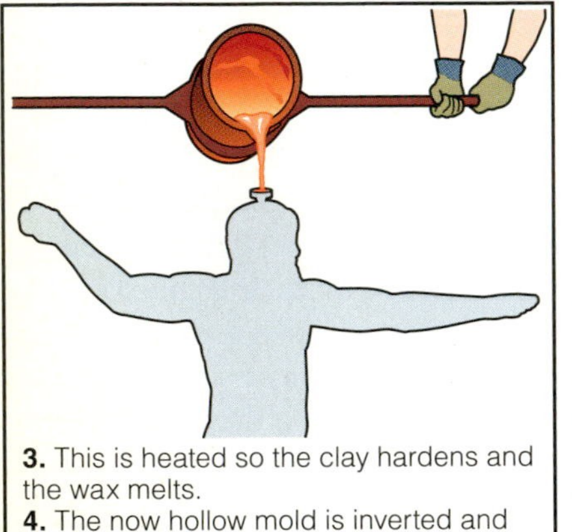

3. This is heated so the clay hardens and the wax melts.
4. The now hollow mold is inverted and molten bronze metal is poured into it.

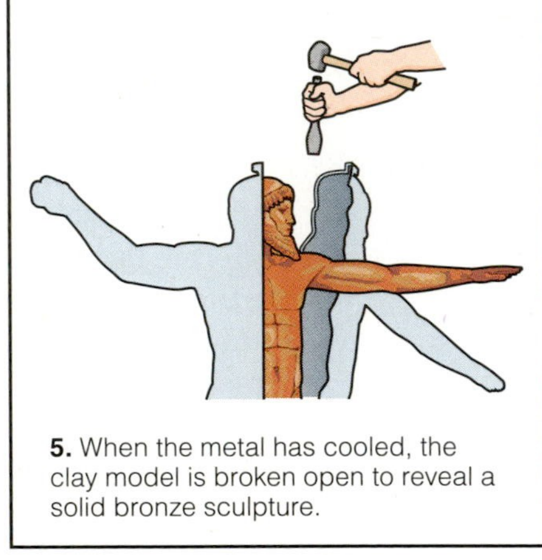

5. When the metal has cooled, the clay model is broken open to reveal a solid bronze sculpture.

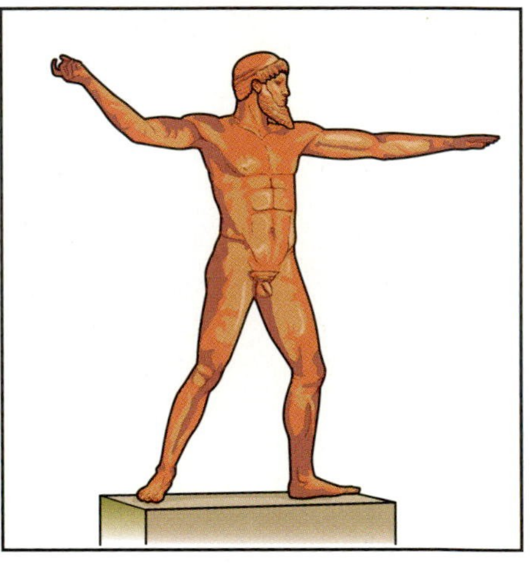

Figure 11.4 The same lost wax casting method used to create sculptures—such as the 3,000-year-old bronze Zeus, from the National Museum of Archaeology in Athens, Greece—is still used by artists today.

These elliptical granite walls held together without any mortar at Great Zimbabwe in southern Zimbabwe, Africa, attest to the skill of the builders. When European explorers unwilling to accept the notion of civilization in sub-Saharan Africa discovered these magnificent ruins, they wrongly attributed them to white non-Africans. This false notion persisted until archaeologists demonstrated that these structures were part of a city with 12,000 to 20,000 inhabitants that served as the center of the Bantu state.

Globalscape

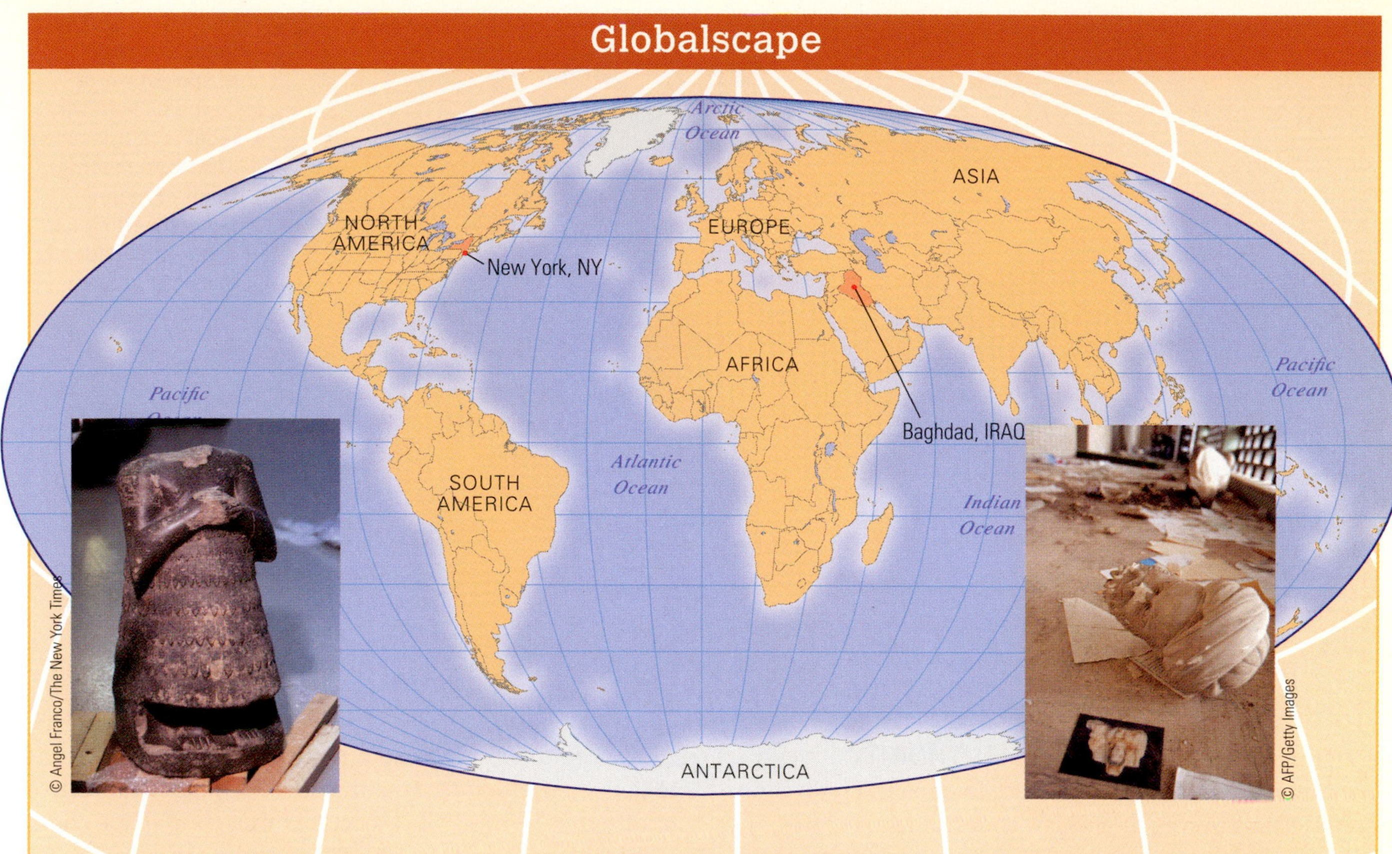

Iraqi Artifacts in New York City? A clandestine operation carried out by the U.S. government led to the recovery in New York City of a priceless (though headless) 4,400-year-old stone statue of the Sumerian King Entemena of Lagash. The statue will be returned to its rightful place in the center of the Sumerian Hall of the Iraqi National Museum in Baghdad.

The modern-day state of Iraq, located in an area known as the cradle of civilization, is home to 10,000 archaeological sites preserving evidence of the earliest cities, laws, and civilizations. Though many Mesopotamian artifacts were brought to museums in Europe and the United States in the 19th and early 20th centuries, the Iraqi National Museum in Baghdad still housed an extraordinary collection of priceless artifacts. That was the case until the weeks following the U.S. invasion in 2003, when several waves of looters removed tens of thousands of artifacts. According to Matthew Bogdanos, the Marine colonel who led the task force to track down and recover these artifacts, "The list of missing objects read like a 'who's who' of Near Eastern archaeology." Ironically, looting during the first Gulf War had led local archaeologists to move artifacts from regional museums to the National Museum of Baghdad for safekeeping.

This statue, like many other stolen artifacts, was first taken across the border into Syria and then made its way into the international black market in antiquities. Many artifacts have been returned to the museum through a no-questions-asked amnesty program. Others have required a combination of international cooperation and investigation, along with raids and seizures once artifacts have been tracked down.

Global Twister If artifacts from ancient civilizations from throughout the world represent our shared global heritage, how can such treasures be kept safe from the chaos and desperation that result from war?

saw to it that different interest groups, such as farmers or craft specialists, provided their respective services and did not infringe on one another.

Just as they do today, governments of the past ensured that cities were safe from their enemies by constructing fortifications and raising an army. They levied taxes and appointed tax collectors so that construction workers, the army, and other public expenses could be paid. They saw to it that merchants, carpenters, or farmers who made legal claims received justice according to standards of the legal system. They guaranteed safety for the lives and property of ordinary people and assured them that any harm done to one person by another would be justly handled. In addition, surplus food had to be stored for times of scarcity, and public works such as extensive irrigation systems or fortifications had to be supervised by competent, fair individuals. The mechanisms of government served all these functions.

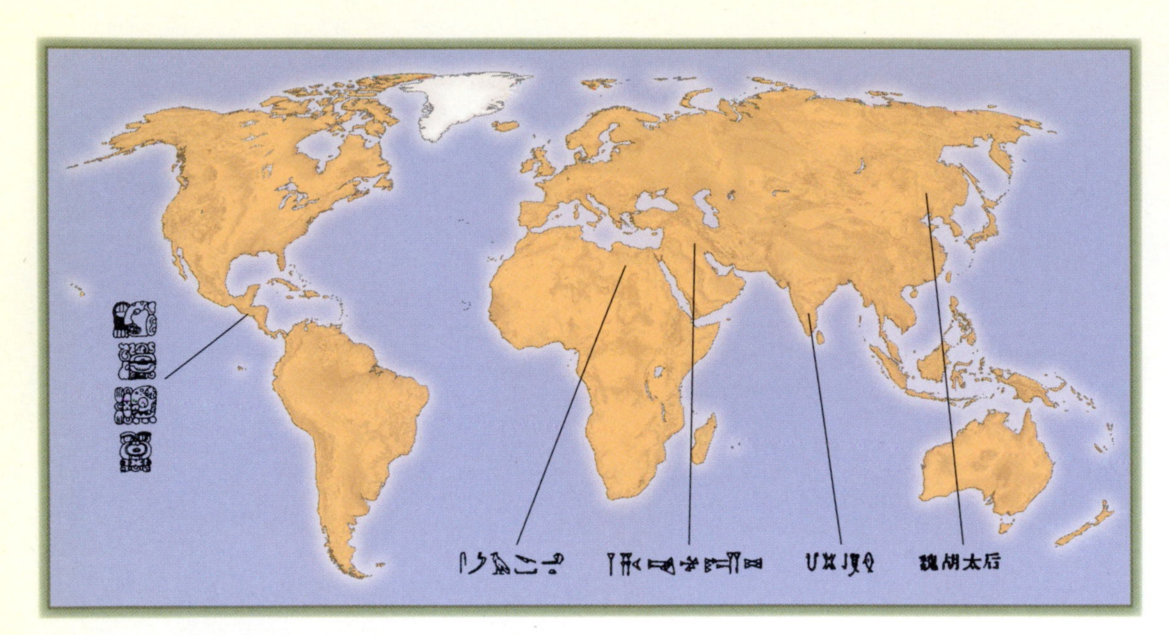

Figure 11.5 The impermanence of spoken words contrasts with the relative permanence of written records. In all of human history, writing has been independently invented at least five times.

EVIDENCE OF CENTRALIZED AUTHORITY

Evidence of centralized authority in ancient civilizations comes from sources such as law codes, temple records, and royal chronicles. Excavation of the city structures themselves provides additional evidence because they can show definite signs of city planning. The precise astronomical layout of the Mesoamerican city Teotihuacan, described earlier, attests to strong, centralized control.

Monumental buildings and temples, palaces, and large sculptures are usually found in ancient civilizations. For example, the Great Pyramid for the tomb of Khufu, the Egyptian pharaoh, is 755 feet long (236 meters) and 481 feet high (147 meters); it contains about 2.3 million stone blocks, each with an average weight of 2.5 tons. The Greek historian Herodotus reports that it took 100,000 men twenty years to build this tomb. Such gigantic structures required a powerful central authority to harness the considerable labor force, engineering skills, and raw materials necessary for their construction.

Another indicator of the existence of centralized authority is writing, or some form of recorded information (Figure 11.5). With writing, central authorities could disseminate information and store, systematize, and deploy memory for political, religious, and economic purposes.

Scholars attribute the initial motive for the development of writing in Mesopotamia to record keeping of state affairs. Writing allowed early governments to track accounts of their food surplus, tribute records, and other business receipts. Some of the earliest documents appear to be just such records—accountings of bought and sold vegetables and animals, taxes, and storehouse inventories.

Before 5,500 years ago, records were comprised of tokens—ceramic pieces with different shapes indicative of different commercial objects. Thus a cone shape could represent a measure of grain, or a cylinder could be an animal. As the system developed, tokens became more sophisticated, representing different animals; processed foods such as oil, trussed ducks, or bread; and manufactured or imported goods such as textiles and metal.[6] Ultimately, clay tablets with impressed marks representing objects replaced these tokens.

By 5,000 years ago in the Mesopotamian city of Uruk in Iraq (which likely derives its modern name from this ancient place), a new writing technique emerged. Writers would use a reed stylus to make wedge-shaped markings on a tablet of damp clay. Originally, each marking stood for a word. Because most words in this language were monosyllabic, over time the markings came to stand for syllables (Figure 11.6).

Controversy surrounds the question of the earliest evidence of writing. Traditionally, the earliest writing was linked to Mesopotamia. However, in 2003 archaeologists working in the Henan Province of central China discovered signs carved into 8,600-year-old tortoise shells; these markings resemble later-written characters and predate the Mesopotamian evidence by about 2,000 years.[7]

[6] Lawler, A. (2001). Writing gets a rewrite. *Science 292,* 2419.

[7] Li, X., et al. (2003). The earliest writing? Sign use in the seventh millennium BC at Jiahu, Henan Province, China. *Antiquity 77,* 31–44.

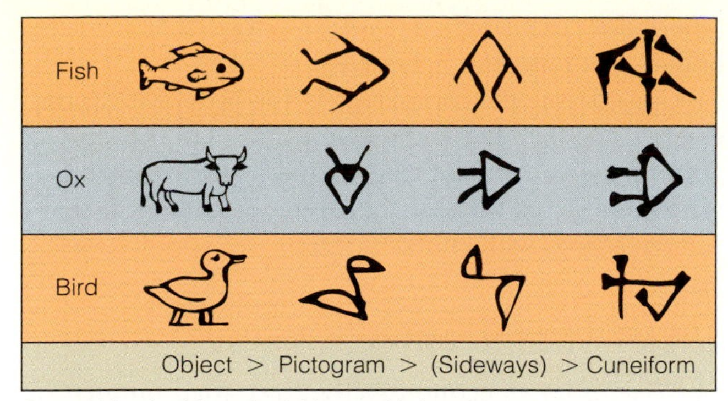
Fish
Ox
Bird
Object > Pictogram > (Sideways) > Cuneiform

Source: University of Pennsylvania Museum of Anthropology

Figure 11.6 **Cuneiform writing developed from representational drawings of objects. Over time the drawings became simplified and more abstract, as well as being wedge-shaped so that they could be cut into a clay tablet with a stylus.**

In the Americas, writing systems came into use among various Mesoamerican peoples, but the Maya system was particularly sophisticated. The Maya writing system, like other aspects of that culture, appears to have roots in the Olmec civilization,[8] though discoveries announced in 2006 of a stone tablet with a different writing system indicate that the Olmec had another form of writing distinct from Maya glyphs.[9]

The Maya hieroglyphic system had less to do with keeping track of state property than with extravagant celebrations of the accomplishments of their rulers. Maya lords glorified themselves by recording their dynastic genealogies, important conquests, and royal marriages; by using grandiose titles to refer to themselves; and by associating their actions with important astronomical events (Figure 11.7). Different though this may be from the recordkeeping of ancient Mesopotamia, all writing systems share a concern with political power and its maintenance.

THE EARLIEST GOVERNMENTS

A king and his advisors typically headed the earliest city governments. Of the many ancient kings known, one stands out as truly remarkable for the efficient government organization and highly developed legal system characterizing his reign. This is Hammurabi, the Babylonian king who lived in Mesopotamia (modern Iraq) sometime between 3,700 and 3,950 years ago. From Babylon, the

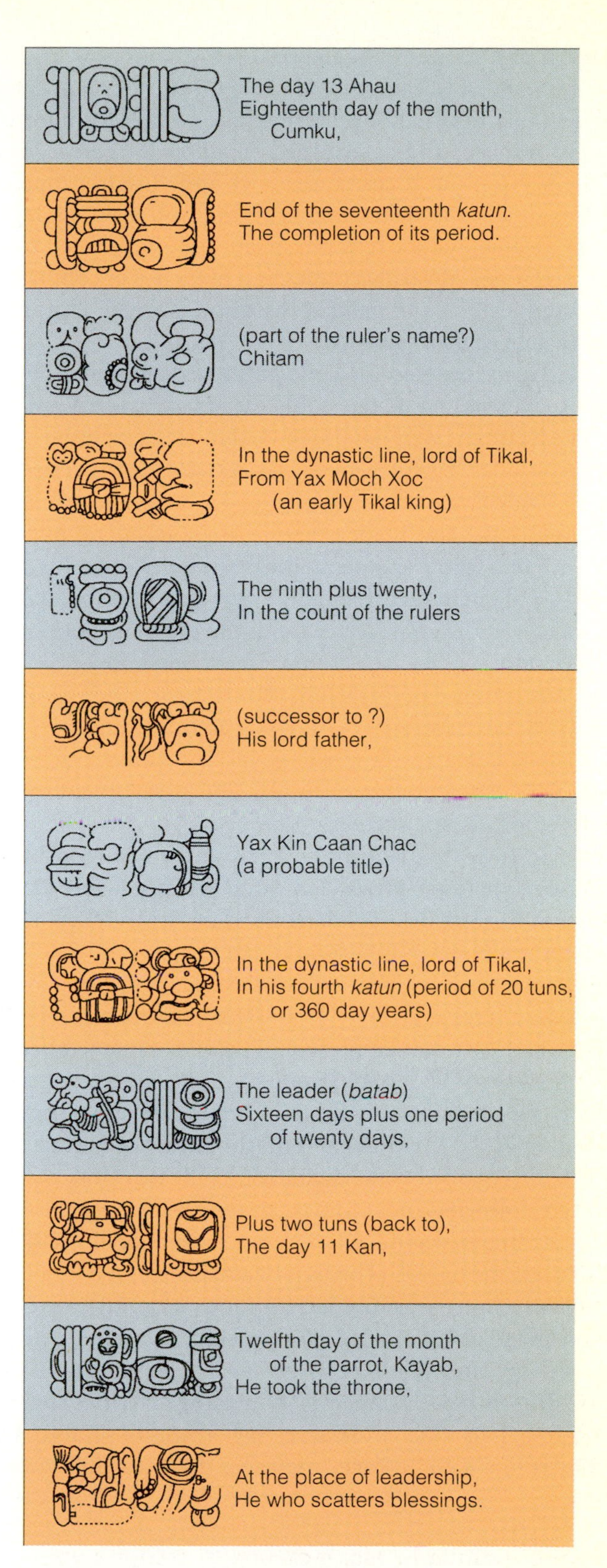
The day 13 Ahau
Eighteenth day of the month, Cumku,
End of the seventeenth *katun*.
The completion of its period.
(part of the ruler's name?)
Chitam
In the dynastic line, lord of Tikal,
From Yax Moch Xoc (an early Tikal king)
The ninth plus twenty,
In the count of the rulers
(successor to ?)
His lord father,
Yax Kin Caan Chac
(a probable title)
In the dynastic line, lord of Tikal,
In his fourth *katun* (period of 20 tuns, or 360 day years)
The leader (*batab*)
Sixteen days plus one period of twenty days,
Plus two tuns (back to),
The day 11 Kan,
Twelfth day of the month of the parrot, Kayab,
He took the throne,
At the place of leadership,
He who scatters blessings.

Figure 11.7 **The translation of the text on the monument shown on page 260 gives some indication of the importance of dynastic genealogy to Maya rulers. The "scattering" mentioned may refer to bloodletting as part of the ceremonies associated with the end of one twenty-year period, or *katun*, and the beginning of the next.**

[8] Pohl, M.E.D., Pope, K. O., & von Nagy, C. (2002). Olmec origins of Mesoamerican writing, *Science 298,* 1984–1987.

[9] del Carmen Rodríguez Martínez, M. (2006). Oldest writing in the New World. *Science 313,* 1610–1614.

capital of his empire, he issued a set of laws now known as the Code of Hammurabi, notable for its thorough detail and standardization. It prescribed the correct form for legal procedures and determined penalties for perjury and false accusation. It contained laws applying to property rights, loans and debts, family rights, and even damages paid for malpractice by a physician. It defined fixed rates to be charged in various trades and branches of commerce and mechanisms to protect the poor, women, children, and slaves against injustice.

Officials ordered the code publicly displayed on huge stone slabs so that no one could plead ignorance. Even the poorest citizens were supposed to know their rights and responsibilities. Distinct social classes were clearly reflected in the code ("rule of law" does not necessarily mean "equality before the law"). For example, if an aristocrat put out the eye of a fellow aristocrat, the law required that his own eye be put out in turn; hence, the saying "an eye for an eye." However, if the aristocrat put out the eye of a commoner, the punishment was simply a payment of silver.[10]

While some civilizations flourished under a single ruler with extraordinary governing abilities, other civilizations possessed a widespread governing bureaucracy that was very efficient at every level. The government of the Inca empire is one such example.

The Inca civilization of Peru and its surrounding territories reached its peak 500 years ago, just before the arrival of the Spanish invaders. By 1525, it stretched 4,000 kilometers (2,500 miles) from north to south and 800 kilometers (500 miles) from east to west, making it one of the largest empires at the time. Its population, which numbered in the millions, was composed of people of many different ethnic groups. In the achievements of its government and political system, Inca civilization surpassed every other civilization of the Americas and most of those of Eurasia. An emperor, regarded as the divine son of the Sun God, headed the government. Under him came the royal family, the aristocracy, imperial administrators, and lower nobility, and below them the masses of artisans, craftspeople, and farmers.

The empire was divided into four administrative regions, further subdivided into provinces, and so on down to villages and families. Government agricultural and tax officials closely supervised farming activities such as planting, irrigation, and harvesting. Teams of professional relay runners could carry messages up to 400 kilometers (250 miles) in a single day over a network of roads and bridges that remains impressive even today.

Considering the complexity of the Inca civilization, it is surprising that they had no known form of conventional writing. Instead, public records and historical chronicles were maintained through an ingenious coding system of colored strings with knots.

Social Stratification

The rise of large, economically diversified populations presided over by centralized governing authorities brought with it the fourth cultural change characteristic of civilization: social stratification, or the emergence of social classes. For example, symbols of special status and privilege appeared in the ancient cities of Mesopotamia, where people were ranked according to the kind of work they did or the family into which they were born.

People who stood at or near the head of government were the earliest holders of high status. Although specialists of one sort or another—metalworkers, tanners, traders, or the like—generally outranked farmers, such specialization did not necessarily bring with it high status. Rather, people engaged in these kinds of economic activities were either members of the lower classes or outcasts.[11] Merchants in these societies could sometimes buy their way into a higher class. With time, the possession of wealth and the influence it could buy became in itself a requisite for high status, as it is in some contemporary cultures.

Archaeologists know that different social classes existed in ancient civilizations through evidence of laws and other written documents, as well as archaeological features including dwelling size and location. Social stratification is also revealed by burial customs. Graves excavated at early Neolithic sites are mostly simple pits dug in the ground, containing few, if any, grave goods. **Grave goods** consist of objects such as utensils, figurines, and personal possessions, symbolically placed in the grave for the deceased person's use in the afterlife. Early Neolithic grave sites reveal little variation, indicating essentially classless societies. Graves excavated in civilizations, by contrast, vary widely in size, mode of burial, and the number and variety of grave goods. This reflects a stratified society, divided into social classes. The graves of important people contain not only various artifacts made from precious materials, but sometimes, as in some early Egyptian burials, the remains of servants who were evidently killed to serve their master in the afterlife.

Skeletons from the burials may also provide evidence of stratification. Age at death as well as presence of certain

[10] Moscati, S. (1962). *The face of the ancient orient* (p. 90). New York: Doubleday.

[11] Sjoberg, G. (1960). *The preindustrial city* (p. 325). New York: Free Press.

grave goods Items such as utensils, figurines, and personal possessions, symbolically placed in the grave for the deceased person's use in the afterlife.

© Tavid Rankin Bingham

Grave goods frequently indicate the status of deceased individuals in stratified societies. For example, China's first emperor was buried with 7,000 life-size terra cotta figures of warriors.

diseases can be determined from skeletal remains. In stratified societies of the past, the dominant groups usually lived longer, ate better, and enjoyed an easier life than lower-ranking members of society, just as they do today.

The Making of States

From Africa to China to the South American Andes, ancient civilizations are almost always associated with magnificent palaces built high aboveground—with sculptures beautifully rendered using techniques that continue into the present and with vast, awe-inspiring engineering projects. These impressive accomplishments could indicate that civilization is better than other cultural forms, particularly when these societies came to dominate peoples with other social systems. But domination is more a reflection of aggression, size, and power than it is cultural superiority. In other words, the emergence of centralized governments, characteristic of civilizations, has allowed some cultures to dominate others and for civilizations to flourish. Anthropologists have proposed several theories to account for the transition from small, egalitarian farming villages to large urban centers in which population density, social inequality, and diversity of labor required a centralized government.

Ecological Theories

Ecological approaches emphasize the role of the environment in the development of states. Among these, the irrigation or **hydraulic theory** holds that civilizations developed when Neolithic peoples realized that the best farming occurred in the fertile soils of river valleys, provided that they could control the periodic flooding.[12] The centralized effort to control the irrigation process blossomed into the first governing body, elite social class, and civilization.

Another theory suggests that in regions of ecological diversity, trade is necessary to procure scarce resources. In Mexico, for example, trade networks distributed chilies grown in the highlands, cotton and beans from intermediate elevations, and salt from the coasts to people throughout the region. Some form of centralized authority developed to organize trade for the procurement of these commodities and to redistribute them.

A third theory developed by anthropologist Robert Carneiro suggests that states develop where populations are hemmed in by such environmental barriers as mountains, deserts, seas, or other human populations as an outcome of warfare and conflict in these circumscribed regions.[13] As these populations grow, they have no space

[12] Wittfogel, K. A. (1957). *Oriental despotism, a comparative study of total power.* New Haven, CT: Yale University Press.

[13] Carneiro, R. L. (1970). A theory of the origin of the state. *Science 169,* 733–738.

hydraulic theory The theory that explains civilization's emergence as the result of the construction of elaborate irrigation systems, the functioning of which required full-time managers whose control blossomed into the first governing body and elite social class.

Anthropology Applied

Tell It to the Marines: Teaching Troops about Cultural Heritage

by Jane C. Waldbaum

The need to protect ancient sites, museums, and antiquities in war-torn Iraq and Afghanistan has led the Archaeological Institute of America (AIA) to begin an innovative program to help educate troops soon to be sent to those countries. Conceived by AIA vice president C. Brian Rose, the program sends experienced lecturers to military bases to teach the basics of Middle Eastern archaeology and the importance of protecting the evidence of past cultures. The class, taken by both officers and enlisted men and women, is mandatory.

The effort is a supplement to the AIA's longstanding, nationwide lecture program in which scholars in archaeology and related fields present the latest research and developments to more than 102 local societies in the United States and Canada. The lectures for the troops focus specifically on the areas where military personnel will be deployed and on the specific sites, monuments, museums, and artifacts that they might be called upon to protect.

The current lectures, funded in part by the Packard Humanities Institute, emphasize Mesopotamia's role in the development of writing, schools, libraries, law codes, calendars, and astronomy, as well as connections with familiar biblical figures such as Abraham and Daniel and ancient sites such as Ur and Babylon. Afghanistan's position as a crossroads of ancient civilizations and the route of Alexander the Great through the region is discussed. Troops also learn about basic archaeological techniques, the importance of preserving context, the necessity of working with archaeologists and conservators, and the most effective ways to protect sites against looters.

The first series of lectures was given at the Marine Corps base at Camp Lejeune, North Carolina, and there are plans to expand the program to other bases and services in the near future. "Many of the officers have M.A. degrees; some are reservists and high-school history teachers," says Rose, who delivered the inaugural lectures last spring. "They care a great deal about the history of the areas in which they serve; some of them have actually lived in or near Babylon on earlier tours of duty. All of us have been struck by their thirst for knowledge during and after our lectures."

Many have helped get this program up and running, including U.S. Marine Colonel Matthew Bogdanos, who was instrumental in securing the return of many antiquities stolen from the Iraq Museum. "When it comes to clearing a building, neutralizing a land mine, or making a neighborhood safe for children, we know what to do," says Bogdanos. "When it comes to protecting a country's cultural heritage, we are just as eager to do the right thing—we just don't always know the best way to do it. This is where Brian Rose's groundbreaking program will pay dividends for generations."

in which to expand, and so they begin to compete for increasingly scarce resources. Internally, this may result in the development of social stratification, in which an elite controls important resources to which lower classes have limited access. Externally, this leads to warfare and even conquest, which, to be successful, require elaborate organization under a centralized authority. As this chapter's Anthropology Applied feature shows, in times of war centralized authorities such as the U.S. military are drawing upon archaeological expertise to protect cultural resources.

Problems exist with each of these ecological theories. Across the globe and through time, cultures can be found that do not fit these models. For example, some of the earliest large-scale irrigation systems developed in highland New Guinea, where strong centralized governments never emerged. North American Indians possessed trade networks that extended from Labrador in northeastern Canada to the Gulf of Mexico and the Yellowstone region of the Rocky Mountains and even to the Pacific—all without centralized control.[14] And in many of the cultures that do not fit the theories of ecological determinism, neighboring cultures learned to coexist rather than pursuing warfare to the point of complete conquest.

Although few anthropologists would deny the importance of the human–environment relationship, many are dissatisfied with approaches that do not take into account human beliefs and values.[15] For example, as described in the case study of Tikal—while religion was tied to the earth in that the priests determined the most favorable time for planting crops—the beliefs and power relations that developed within Maya culture were not environmentally determined. Human societies past and present bring their beliefs and values into their interactions with the environment.

Action Theory

One criticism of the above theories is that they fail to recognize the capacity of aggressive, charismatic leaders to shape the course of human history. Accordingly, anthropologists Joyce Marcus and Kent Flannery have

[14] Haviland, W. A., & Power, M. W. (1994). *The original Vermonters* (2nd ed., chs. 3 & 4). Hanover, NH: University Press of New England.

[15] Adams, R. M. (2001). Scale and complexity in archaic states. *Latin American Antiquity 11,* 188.

The relative dearth of ancient monumental structures in North America has led some to assume the superiority of European civilization, rather than to acknowledge the successful nomadic cultural pattern of many North American Indian groups. Cities were present in precontact North America. Take for example Cahokia, located in Southern Illinois, a city with an estimated population of 40,000 people dating from 650 to 1400 CE. Cahokia's pyramid-shaped ceremonial mounds spanned an area larger than the great pyramids of Egypt. Until 1800, when Philadelphia surpassed it, Cahokia was the largest city in the land that is now the United States.

developed what they call **action theory.**[16] This theory acknowledges the relationship of society to the environment in shaping social and cultural behavior, but it also recognizes that forceful leaders strive to advance their positions through self-serving actions. In so doing, they may create change.

In the case of Maya history, for example, local leaders, who once relied on personal charisma for the economic and political support needed to sustain them in their positions, may have seized upon religion to solidify their power. Through religion they developed an ideology that endowed them and their descendants with supernatural ancestry and gave them privileged access to the gods, on which their followers depended. In this case, certain individuals could monopolize power and emerge as divine kings, using their power to subjugate any rivals.

As the above example makes clear, the context in which a forceful leader operates is critical. In the case of the Maya, the combination of existing cultural and ecological factors opened the way to the emergence of political dynasties. Thus explanations of civilization's emergence are likely to involve multiple causes, rather than just one. Furthermore, we may also have the cultural equivalent of what biologists call *convergence,* where similar societies come about in different ways. Consequently, a theory that accounts for the rise of civilization in one place may not account for its rise in another.

Civilization and Its Discontents

Living in the context of civilization ourselves, we are inclined to view its development as a great step up on a so-called ladder of progress. Whatever benefits civilization has brought, the cultural changes it represents have produced new problems. Among them is the problem of waste disposal. In fact, waste disposal probably began to be a problem in settled, farming communities even before civilizations emerged. But as villages grew into towns and towns grew into cities, the problem became far more serious, as crowded conditions and the buildup of garbage and sewage created optimal environments for infectious diseases such as bubonic plague, typhoid, and cholera. Early cities therefore tended to be disease-ridden places, with relatively high death rates.

Genetically based adaptation to diseases may also have influenced the course of civilization. In northern Europeans, for example, the mutation of a gene on chromosome 7

[16] Marcus, J., & Flannery, K. V. (1996). Zapotec civilization: How urban society evolved in Mexico's Oaxaca Valley. New York: Thames & Hudson.

action theory The theory that self-serving actions by forceful leaders play a role in civilization's emergence.

East of Naples, Italy, dumping of toxic waste and the sheer volume of normal garbage have become serious environmental threats. Organized crime syndicates provide illegal, less expensive ways to dispose of toxic waste, which has led to a contamination of the environment and the foods produced there. Dioxin, asbestos, and other toxins may have made their way into the food supply, including into water buffalo milk that is used to make the gourmet food buffalo mozzarella. In 2008, when the crime syndicate–run landfill reached capacity, garbage collectors went on strike leaving uncollected trash to pile up in the city.

makes carriers resistant to cholera, typhoid, and other bacterial diarrheas.[17] Because of the mortality caused by these diseases, selection favored spread of this allele among the population. But, as with sickle-cell anemia, protection comes at a price. That price is cystic fibrosis—a usually fatal disease present in people who are homozygous for the altered gene.

The rise of towns and cities brought with it other acute, infectious diseases. In a small population, diseases such as chicken pox, influenza, measles, mumps, pertussis, polio, rubella, and smallpox will kill or immunize so high a proportion of the population that the virus cannot continue to propagate. Measles, for example, is likely to die out in any human population with fewer than half a million people.[18] Hence, such diseases, when introduced into small communities, spread immediately to the whole population and then die out. For these diseases to continue, they require a large population, such as is found in cities. Survivors possessed immunity to these deadly diseases.

The disease tuberculosis (TB) would not have become widespread without the development of cities. The bacteria that cause TB cannot survive in the presence of sunlight and fresh air. Before humans lived in dark, crowded urban centers, if an infected individual coughed and released the TB bacteria into the air, sunlight would prevent the spread of infection. Therefore, TB, like many other sicknesses, can be called a disease of civilization.

Social Stratification and Disease

Civilization affects disease in another powerful way. Social stratification is as much a determinant of disease as any bacterium, past and present. For example, Ashkenazi Jews of eastern Europe were forced into urban ghettos over several centuries, becoming especially vulnerable to the TB thriving in crowded, dark, confined neighborhoods. As we have seen with the genetic response to malaria (sickle cell and other abnormal hemoglobins) and bacterial diarrheas (the cystic fibrosis gene), TB triggered a genetic response in the form of the Tay-Sachs allele. Individuals heterozygous for the Tay-Sachs allele were protected from this disease.[19]

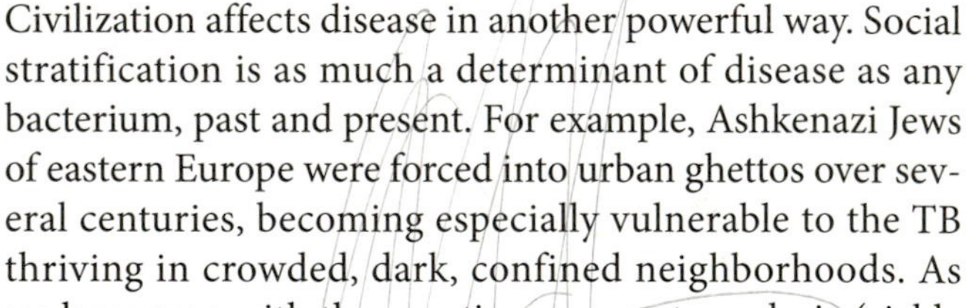

Unfortunately, homozygotes for the Tay-Sachs allele develop a lethal, degenerative condition that remains common in Ashkenazi Jews. Without the selective pressure of TB, the frequency of the Tay-Sachs allele would never have increased. Similarly, without the strict social

---

[17] Ridley, M. (1999). *Genome, the autobiography of a species in 23 chapters* (p. 142). New York: HarperCollins.

[18] Diamond, J. (1997). *Guns, germs, and steel* (p. 203). New York: Norton.

[19] Ridley, p. 191.

rules confining poor Jews to the ghettos (compounded by social and religious rules about marriage), the frequency of the Tay-Sachs allele would never have increased. In recent times, cultural mechanisms such as prenatal and premarital genetic testing have resulted in a decrease in the frequency of the Tay-Sachs allele.

Before the discovery of antibiotics in the early 20th century, individuals infected with the bacteria causing TB would invariably waste away and die. While antibiotics have reduced deaths from TB, resistant forms of the bacteria require an expensive regime of multiple drugs. Not only are poor individuals more likely to become infected with TB, they are also less likely to be able to afford expensive medicines required to treat this disease. For people in poor countries and for disadvantaged people in wealthier countries, TB—like AIDS—can be an incurable, fatal, infectious disease. As Holger Sawert from the World Health Organization has said, "Both TB and HIV thrive on poverty."[20] Before the social stratification accompanying the emergence of cities and states, as far as infectious microbes were concerned, all humans were the same.

Colonialism and Disease

Infectious disease played a major role in European colonization of the Americas. When Europeans with immunity to so-called Old World diseases came to the Americas for the first time, they brought these devastating diseases with them. Millions of Native Americans—who had never been exposed to influenza, smallpox, typhus, and measles—died as a result. The microbes causing these diseases and the human populations upon which they depend developed in tandem over thousands of years of urban life in Eurasia, and before that in village life with a variety of domesticated animal species. Thus anyone who survived acquired immunity in the process. See this chapter's Biocultural Connection for more on the death and disease Europeans brought with them when they colonized the Americas.

Very few diseases traveled back to Europe from the Americas. Instead, these colonizers brought back riches that they had pillaged and papers that gave them ownership of lands they had claimed. One rare exception is that Charles Darwin seems to have returned from his famous journey on the *H.M.S. Beagle* with Chagas disease, a parasitic infection caused by a bug bite.[21] Traditionally it was a disease of the rural poor, but today the large influx of poor farmers into urban centers in Mexico, Central America, and South America means that Chagas disease has become a problem in urban areas as well.

Anthropology and Cities of the Future

Not until relatively recent times did public health measures reduce the risk of living in cities, and had it not been for a constant influx of rural peoples, areas of high population density might not have persisted. Europe's urban population, for example, did not become self-sustaining until early in the 20th century.[22]

What led people to live in such unhealthy places? Most likely, people were attracted by the same things that lure people to cities today: They are vibrant, exciting places that provide people with new opportunities and protection in times of warfare. Of course, people's experience in the cities did not always live up to advance expectations, particularly for the poor.

In addition to health problems, many early cities faced social problems strikingly similar to those found in cities all over the world today. Dense population, inequalities of class systems, and oppressive centralized governments created internal stress. The poor saw that the wealthy had all the things that they themselves lacked. It was not just a question of luxury items; the poor did not have enough food or space in which to live with comfort, dignity, and health.

Evidence of warfare in early civilizations is common. Cities were fortified. Ancient documents list battles, raids, and wars between groups. Cylinder seals, paintings, and sculptures depict battle scenes, victorious kings, and captured prisoners of war. Increasing population and the accompanying scarcity of fertile farming land often led to boundary disputes and quarrels over land between civilized states or between so-called tribal peoples and a state. When war broke out, people crowded into walled cities for protection and for access to irrigation systems.

What we would call development today—the transformation of rural open spaces into densely populated and built-up environments—posed similar problems in the past. At the Maya city of Copan, in the present-day country of Honduras, much of the fertile bottom lands along the Copan River were paved over as the city grew, making the people more and more dependent on food grown in the fragile soils of the valley slopes. This ultimately led to catastrophic soil loss through erosion and a breakdown of food production. Similarly, in ancient Mesopotamia, evaporation of water from extensive irrigation works resulted in a buildup of salt in the soil, ruining it for agricultural use.

---

[20] Sawert, H. (2002). *TB and poverty in the context of global TB control.* World Health Organization. http://www.healthinitiative.org/html/Conf/satsymp/index.htm#2

[21] Adler, S. (1959). Darwin's illness. *Nature*, 1102–1103; Bernstein, R. E., et al. (1984). Darwin's illness: Chagas' disease resurgens. *Journal of the Royal Society of Medicine 77,* 608–609.

[22] Diamond, p. 203.

Biocultural Connection

Perilous Pigs: The Introduction of Swine-Borne Disease to the Americas *by Charles C. Mann*

On May 30, 1539, Hernando de Soto landed his private army near Tampa Bay, in Florida. . . . Half warrior, half venture capitalist, Soto had grown very rich very young by becoming a market leader in the nascent trade for Indian slaves. The profits had helped to fund Pizarro's seizure of the Incan empire, which had made Soto wealthier still. Looking quite literally for new worlds to conquer, he persuaded the Spanish Crown to let him loose in North America. . . . He came to Florida with 200 horses, 600 soldiers, and 300 pigs.

From today's perspective, it is difficult to imagine the ethical system that would justify Soto's actions. For four years his force, looking for gold, wandered through what is now Florida, Georgia, North and South Carolina, Tennessee, Alabama, Mississippi, Arkansas, and Texas, wrecking almost everything it touched. The inhabitants often fought back vigorously, but they had never before encountered an army with horses and guns. . . . Soto's men managed to rape, torture, enslave, and kill countless Indians. But the worst thing the Spaniards did, some researchers say, was entirely without malice—bring the pigs.

According to Charles Hudson, an anthropologist at the University of Georgia, . . . Soto crossed the Mississippi a few miles downstream from the present site of Memphis. . . . [T]he Spaniards were watched by several thousand Indian warriors. Utterly without fear, Soto brushed past the Indian force into what is now eastern Arkansas, through thickly settled land—"very well peopled with large towns," one of his men later recalled. . . . Eventually the Spaniards approached a cluster of small cities, each protected by earthen walls, sizeable moats, and deadeye archers. In his usual fashion, Soto brazenly marched in, stole food, and marched out.

After Soto left, no Europeans visited this part of the Mississippi Valley for more than a century. Early in 1682 whites appeared again, this time Frenchmen in canoes. . . . area[s] where Soto had found cities cheek by jowl . . . [were] deserted [without an] Indian village for 200 miles. About fifty settlements existed in this strip of the Mississippi when Soto showed up, according to Anne Ramenofsky, an anthropologist at the University of New Mexico. . . . Soto "had a privileged glimpse" of an Indian world, Hudson says. "The window opened and slammed shut. When the French came in and the record opened up again, it was a transformed reality. A civilization crumbled. The question is, how did this happen?"

The question is even more complex than it may seem. Disaster of this magnitude suggests epidemic disease. In the view of Ramenofsky and Patricia Galloway, an anthropologist at the University of Texas, the source of the contagion was very likely not Soto's army but its ambulatory meat locker: his 300 pigs. Soto's force itself was too small to be an effective biological weapon. Sicknesses like measles and smallpox would have burned through his 600 soldiers long before they reached the Mississippi. But the same would not have held true for the pigs, which multiplied rapidly and were able to transmit their diseases to wildlife in the surrounding forest. When human beings and domesticated animals live close together, they trade microbes with abandon. Over time mutation spawns new diseases: Avian influenza becomes human influenza, bovine rinderpest becomes measles. Unlike Europeans, Indians did not live in close quarters with animals—they domesticated only the dog, the llama, the alpaca, the guinea pig, and, here and there, the turkey and the Muscovy duck. . . . [W]hat scientists call zoonotic disease was little known in the Americas. Swine alone can disseminate anthrax, brucellosis, leptospirosis, taeniasis, trichinosis, and tuberculosis. Pigs breed exuberantly and can transmit diseases to deer and turkeys. Only a few of Soto's pigs would have had to wander off to infect the forest.

Indeed, the calamity wrought by Soto apparently extended across the whole Southeast. The Coosa city-states, in western Georgia, and the Caddoan-speaking civilization, centered on the Texas-Arkansas border, disintegrated soon after Soto appeared. The Caddo had had a taste for monumental architecture: public plazas, ceremonial platforms, mausoleums. After Soto's army left, notes Timothy K. Perttula, an archaeological consultant in Austin, Texas, the Caddo stopped building community centers and began digging community cemeteries. . . . [After] Soto's . . . visit, Perttula believes, the Caddoan population fell from about 200,000 to about 8,500—a drop of nearly 96 percent. . . . "That's one reason whites think of Indians as nomadic hunters," says Russell Thornton, an anthropologist at the University of California at Los Angeles. "Everything else—all the heavily populated urbanized societies—was wiped out."

How could a few pigs truly wreak this much destruction? . . . One reason is that Indians were fresh territory for many plagues, not just one. Smallpox, typhoid, bubonic plague, influenza, mumps, measles, whooping cough—all rained down on the Americas in the century after Columbus. (Cholera, malaria, and scarlet fever came later.) Having little experience with epidemic diseases, Indians had no knowledge of how to combat them. In contrast, Europeans were well versed in the brutal logic of quarantine. They boarded up houses in which plague appeared and fled to the countryside. In Indian New England, Neal Salisbury, a historian at Smith College, wrote . . . [that] family and friends gathered with the shaman at the sufferer's bedside to wait out the illness—a practice that "could only have served to spread the disease more rapidly."

To Elizabeth Fenn, the smallpox historian, the squabble over numbers obscures a central fact. Whether one million or 10 million or 100 million died, . . . the pall of sorrow that engulfed the hemisphere was immeasurable. Languages, prayers, hopes, habits, and dreams—entire ways of life hissed away like steam. . . . In the long run, Fenn says, the consequential finding is not that many people died but that many people once lived. The Americas were filled with a stunningly diverse assortment of peoples who had knocked about the continents for millennia. "You have to wonder," Fenn says. "What were all those people *up* to in all that time?"

BIOCULTURAL QUESTION

Does the history of the decimation of American Indians through infectious disease have any parallels in the contemporary globalized world? Do infectious diseases impact all peoples equally?

Adapted from Mann, C. C. (2005). 1491: New revelations of the Americas before Columbus. *New York: Knopf.*

It is discouraging to note that many of the problems associated with the first civilizations are still with us. Waste disposal, pollution-related health problems, crowding, social inequities, and warfare continue to be serious problems. Through the study of past civilizations and through comparison of contemporary societies, we now stand a chance of understanding such problems. Such understanding represents a central part of the anthropologist's mission and can contribute to the ability of our species to transcend human-made problems.

Questions for Reflection

1. In large-scale societies of the past and present, people face the challenge of social stratification. Elite classes have disproportionate access to and control of all resources. Is social stratification an inevitable consequence of the emergence of cities and states? How can the study of social stratification in the past contribute to the resolution of contemporary issues of social justice?
2. In previous chapters it was emphasized that human evolutionary history should not be thought of as progress. Why is it similarly incorrect to think of the shift from village to city to state as progress?
3. What are some of the ways that differences in social stratification are expressed in your community? Does your community have any traditions surrounding death that serve to restate the social differentiation of individuals?
4. With today's global communication and economic networks, will it be possible to shift away from social systems involving centralized governments, or will a centralized authority have to control and protect resources for the entire world?
5. With many archaeological discoveries there is a value placed on "firsts," such as the earliest writing, the first city, or the earliest government. Given the history of the independent emergence of cities and states throughout the world, do you think that scientists should place more value on some of these events just because they are older?

Suggested Readings

Diamond, J. (1997). *Guns, germs, and steel.* New York: Norton.

Also recommended in Chapter 10, this book has an excellent discussion of the relation among diseases, social complexity, and social change.

Fagan, B. (2001). *The seventy great mysteries of the ancient world.* New York: Thames & Hudson.

Archaeologist Brian Fagan edited contributions from twenty-eight other archaeologists and historians about some of the great controversies in the field in this readable book.

Mann, C. C. (2005). *1491: New revelations of the Americas before Columbus.* New York: Knopf.

Also recommended in Chapter 10, this book demonstrates the devastation European colonizers brought to the Americas.

Marcus, J., & Flannery, K. V. (1996). *Zapotec civilization: How urban society evolved in Mexico's Oaxaca Valley.* New York: Thames & Hudson.

With its lavish illustrations, this looks like a coffee table book, but it is a thoughtful and serious work on the rise of a pristine civilization and a presentation of the authors' action theory.

McNeill W. (1992). *Plagues and people.* New York: Anchor.

This book offers an interpretation of world history through the impact of infectious disease. It documents the role disease played in the colonization of the Americas as well as continuing the investigation into the present with a social history of AIDS.

Sabloff, J. A. (1997). *The cities of ancient Mexico* (rev. ed.). New York: Thames & Hudson.

This well-written and lavishly illustrated book describes the major cities of the Olmecs, Zapotecs, Maya, Teotihuacans, Toltecs, and Aztecs. Following the descriptions, Sabloff discusses the question of origins, the problems of archaeological reconstruction, and the basis on which he provides vignettes of life in the ancient cities. The book concludes with a gazetteer of fifty sites in Mesoamerica.

Challenge Issue The people of the United States of America took a significant step toward redressing a history of slavery and racism with the election of Barack Hussein Obama as their forty-fourth president in 2008. This moment of extraordinary social and political significance challenges us to look at race and racism both in the past and in the present. It challenges us to recognize our common origins and to avoid oversimplification, discrimination, bigotry, and even bloodshed fueled by superficial differences. It requires us to recognize that racism feeds on folk beliefs that so-called racial groups are natural and separate divisions within our species based on visible physical differences. Biological evidence demonstrates that separate races do not exist. Broadly defined, geographic "racial" groupings differ from one another in only 7 percent of their genes. Having exchanged genes throughout evolutionary history, human populations continue to do so today. Instead of leading to the development of distinctive subspecies (biologically defined races), this genetic exchange has maintained all of humankind as a single species. Although race functions as a social and political category that promotes inequality in some societies, it is a cultural construct without an objective scientific basis.

CHAPTER 12

Modern Human Diversity: Race and Racism

Chapter Preview

What Is the History of Human Classification?

European scholars of the 18th through early 20th centuries classified humans into a series of subspecies based on geographic location and phenotypic features such as skin color, body size, head shape, and hair texture. Some scholars went a step farther and placed these types into a hierarchical framework in which the "white" race was considered to be superior to other races. With time, these efforts to classify humans into higher and lower forms were discredited for being racist and unscientific.

Is the Biological Concept of Race Useful for Studying Physical Variation in the Human Species?

No. Biologically defined, "race" refers to subspecies, and no subspecies exist within modern *Homo sapiens.* The vast majority of biological variation within our species occurs *within* populations rather than among them. Furthermore, the differences that do exist among populations occur in gradations from one neighboring population to another without sharp breaks. For these and other reasons, anthropologists have actively worked to expose the fallacy of race as a biological concept while at the same time acknowledging the existence of race as a cultural construct.

Is Studying Differences in Intelligence among Populations Valid?

These studies are flawed in many ways. First, studies attempting to document biological differences generally involve comparisons among races—a category that for humans is biologically false. Second, intelligence is a multifaceted phenomenon, and cultures vary in terms of which aspects of intelligence they value. Third, most instruments (tests) used to measure intelligence are biased toward the dominant culture of the people who created the test. Finally, as a complex set of traits, intelligence cannot be linked to discrete evolutionary forces acting in a particular environment.

What Are the Causes of Physical Variability?

Physical variability is a product of underlying genetic variation as it is expressed in a particular environment. Some physical traits are controlled by single genes, with variation present in alternate forms of the gene (alleles). Many physical characteristics like height, weight, or skin color are controlled by multiple genes and are thus expressed continuously, meaning this variation cannot be divided into discrete categories. Because evolutionary forces such as natural selection and random drift act on each physical trait independently, human biological variation can be studied only "one trait at a time."

From male to female, short to tall, light to dark, biological variation can be categorized in a number of ways, but in the end we are all members of the same species. Minute variations of our DNA give each of us a unique genetic fingerprint, yet this variation remains within the bounds of being genetically human. Visible differences are expressed within the framework of biological features shared throughout the species, and as a species, humans vary.

Human genetic variation generally is distributed across the globe in a continuous fashion. From a biological perspective, this variation sometimes follows a pattern imposed by interaction with the environment through the evolutionary process of natural selection. At other times, the variation results from random genetic drift. The significance we give our biological variation, however, is always patterned because the way we perceive variation—in fact, whether we perceive it at all—is determined by culture.

For example, in many Polynesian cultures, where skin color is not a determinant of social status, people pay little attention to this physical characteristic. By contrast, in countries such as the United States, Brazil, and South Africa, where skin color is a significant social and political category, it is one of the first things people notice. Furthermore, our brains appear to be hardwired for categorical thinking that, once learned, predisposes us to use these kinds of distinctions. We use different parts of our brain to think about people we consider to be like ourselves compared to the parts of the brain used when we are thinking about others. Biological diversity, therefore, cannot be studied without an awareness of the cultural dimensions that shape the questions asked about diversity as well as the history of how this knowledge has been used.

When European scholars first began their systematic study of worldwide human variation in the 18th century, they were concerned with documenting differences among human groups. Soon afterward, some began to divide these groups hierarchically into progressively "better types" of humans. Today, this hierarchical approach has been appropriately abandoned. Before exploring how contemporary biological variation is studied, we will examine the effects of social ideas about race and racial hierarchy on the interpretation of biological variation, past and present.

The History of Human Classification

Early European scholars tried to systematically classify *Homo sapiens* into subspecies, or races, based on geographic location and phenotypic features such as skin color, body size, head shape, and hair texture. The 18th-century Swedish naturalist Carolus Linnaeus originally divided humans into subspecies based on geographic location and classified all Europeans as "white," Africans as "black," American Indians as "red," and Asians as "yellow."

The German physician Johann Blumenbach (1752–1840) introduced some significant changes to this four-race scheme with the 1795 edition of his book *On the Natural Variety of Mankind*. Most notably, this book formally extended the notion of a hierarchy of human types. Based on a comparative examination of his human skull collection, Blumenbach judged as most beautiful the skull of a woman from the Caucasus Mountain range (located between the Black Sea and the Caspian Sea of southeastern Europe and southwestern Asia). The skull was more symmetrical than the others, and he saw it as a reflection of nature's ideal form: the circle. Surely, Blumenbach reasoned, this "perfect" specimen resembled God's original creation. Moreover, he thought that the living inhabitants of the Caucasus region were the most beautiful in the world. Based on these criteria, he concluded that this high mountain range, not far from the lands mentioned in the Bible, was the place of human origins.

Blumenbach concluded that all light-skinned peoples in Europe and adjacent parts of western Asia and northern Africa belonged to the same race. On this basis, he dropped the "European" race label and replaced it with "Caucasian." Although he continued to distinguish American Indians as a separate race, he regrouped dark-skinned Africans as "Ethiopian" and split those Asians not considered Caucasian into two separate races: "Mongolian" (referring to most inhabitants of Asia, including China and Japan) and "Malay" (indigenous Australians, Pacific Islanders, and others).

Convinced that Caucasians were closest to the original ideal humans supposedly created in God's image, Blumenbach ranked them as superior. The other races, he argued, were the result of "degeneration"; by moving away from their place of origin and adapting to different environments and climates, they had degenerated physically and morally into what many Europeans came to think of as inferior races.[1]

We now clearly recognize the factual errors and ethnocentric prejudices embedded in Blumenbach's work, as well as others, with respect to the concept of race. Especially disastrous is the notion of superior and inferior races, as this has been used to justify brutalities ranging from repression to slavery to mass murder to genocide.

[1] Gould, S. J. (1994). The geometer of race. *Discover 15* (11), 65–69.

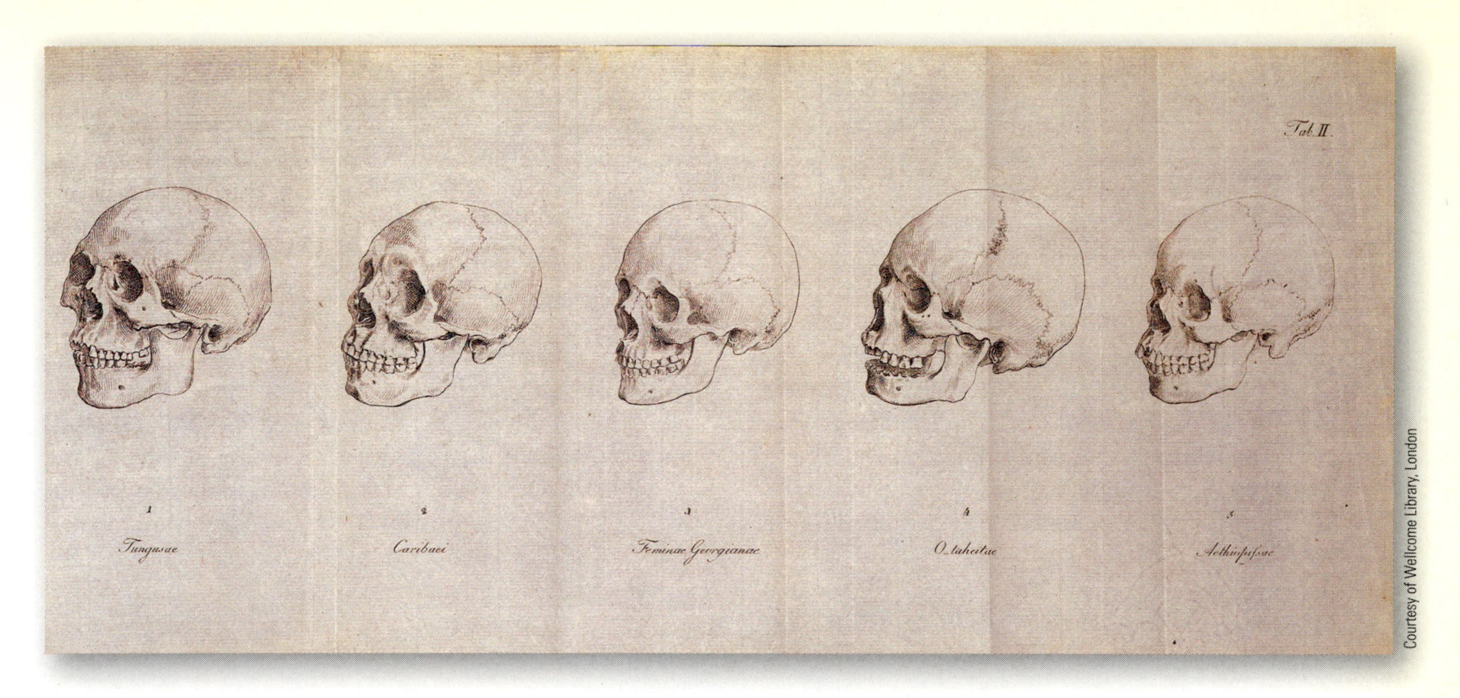

Courtesy of Wellcome Library, London

Johann Blumenbach ordered humans into a hierarchical series with Caucasians (his own group) ranked the highest and created in God's image. He suggested that the variation seen in other races was a result of "degeneration" or movement away from this ideal type. (The five types he identified from left to right are: Mongolian, American Indian, Caucasian, Malay, and Ethiopian.) This view is both racist and an oversimplification of the way that human variation is expressed in the skeleton. While people from one part of the world might be more likely to possess a particular nuance of skull shape, within every population there is significant variation. Humans do not exist as discrete types.

It has also been employed to rationalize cruel mockery, as painfully illustrated in the tragic story of Ota Benga, an African Pygmy man who in the early 1900s was caged in a New York zoo with an orangutan.

Captured in a raid in Congo, Ota Benga came into the possession of a North American businessman, Samuel Verner, looking for exotic "savages" for exhibition in the United States. In 1904, Ota and a group of fellow Pygmies were shipped across the Atlantic and exhibited at the World's Fair in Saint Louis, Missouri. About 23 years old at the time, Ota was 4 feet 11 inches (150 centimeters) in height and weighed 103 pounds (47 kilograms). Throngs of visitors came to see displays of dozens of indigenous peoples from around the globe, shown in their traditional dress and living in replica villages doing their customary activities. The fair was a success for the organizers, and all the Pygmies survived to be shipped back to their homeland. Verner also returned to Congo and with Ota's help collected artifacts to be sold to the American Museum of Natural History in New York City.

In the summer of 1906, Ota came back to the United States with Verner, who soon went bankrupt and lost his entire collection. Left stranded in the big city, Ota was placed in the care of the museum and then taken to the Bronx Zoo and exhibited in the monkey house, with an orangutan as company. Ota's sharpened teeth (a cultural practice among his own people) were seen as evidence of

Missouri History Museum, St. Louis

The placement of Ota Benga on display in the Bronx Zoo illustrates the depths of the racism in the early 20th century. Here's Ota Benga posing for the camera when he was part of the "African Exhibit" at the St. Louis World's Fair.

his supposedly cannibal nature. After intensive protest, zoo officials released Ota from his cage and during the day let him roam free in the park, where he was often harassed by teasing visitors. Ota (usually referred to as a "boy") was then turned over to an orphanage for African American children. In 1916, upon hearing that he would never return to his homeland, he took a revolver and shot himself through the heart.[2]

The racist display at the Bronx Zoo a century ago was by no means unique. Just the tip of the ethnocentric iceberg, it was the manifestation of a powerful ideology in which one small part of humanity sought to demonstrate and justify its claims of biological and cultural superiority. This had particular resonance in North America, where people of European descent colonized lands originally inhabited by Native Americans and then went on to exploit African slaves and Asians imported as a source of cheap labor. Indeed, such claims, based on false notions of race, have resulted in the oppression and genocide of millions of humans because of the color of their skin or the shape of their skull.

Fortunately, by the early 20th century, some scholars began to challenge the concept of racial hierarchies. Among the strongest critics was Franz Boas (1858–1942), a Jewish scientist who immigrated to the United States because of rising anti-Semitism in his German homeland and who became a founder of North America's four-field anthropology. As president of the American Association for the Advancement of Science, Boas criticized false claims of racial superiority in an important speech titled "Race and Progress," published in the prestigious journal *Science* in 1909. Boas's scholarship in both cultural and biological anthropology contributed to the depth of his critique.

Ashley Montagu (1905–1999), a student of Boas and one of the best-known anthropologists of his time, devoted much of his career to combating scientific racism. Born Israel Ehrenberg to a working-class Jewish family in England, he also felt the sting of anti-Semitism. After changing his name in the 1920s, he immigrated to the United States, where he went on to fight racism in his writing and in academic and public lectures. Of all his works, none is more important than his book *Man's Most Dangerous Myth: The Fallacy of Race*. Published in 1942, it debunked the concept of clearly bounded races as a "social myth." The book has since gone through many editions, the last in 2008. Montagu's once controversial ideas have now become mainstream, and his text remains one of the most comprehensive treatments of its subject. (For a contemporary approach to human biological variation, see this chapter's Anthropologist of Note.)

Generalized references to human types such as "Asiatic" or "Mongoloid," "European" or "Caucasoid," and "African"

[2] Bradford, P. V., & Blume, H. (1992). *Ota Benga: The Pygmy in the zoo*. New York: St. Martin's.

Anthropologist of Note

Fatimah Jackson

While at first glance Fatimah Jackson's research areas seem quite diverse, they are unified by consistent representation of African American perspectives in biological anthropological research.

With a keen awareness of how culture determines the content of scientific questions, Jackson chooses hers carefully. One of her earliest areas of research concerned the use of common African plants as foods and medicines. She has examined the co-evolution of plants and humans and the ways plant compounds serve to attract and repel humans at various stages of ripeness. Through laboratory and field research, she has documented that cassava, a New World root crop providing the major source of dietary energy for over 500 million people, also guards against malaria. This crop has become a major food throughout Africa in areas where malaria is common.

© Courtesy of Robert T. Jackson

Jackson, who received her PhD from Cornell in 1981, is also the genetics group leader for the African Burial Ground Project (mentioned in Chapter 1). In a small area uncovered during a New York City construction project, scientists found the remains of thousands of Africans and people of African descent. Jackson is recovering DNA from skeletal remains and attempting to match the dead with specific regions of Africa through the analysis of genetic markers in living African people.

Jackson, one of the early advocates for appropriate ethical treatment of minorities in the human genome project, is concerned with ensuring that the genetic work for the African Burial Ground Project is conducted with sensitivity to African people. She is therefore working to establish genetic laboratories and repositories in Africa. For Jackson, these laboratories are symbolic of the fact of human commonality and that all humans today have roots in Africa. As Director of the Institute of African American Research at the University of North Carolina, Chapel Hill, Jackson continues with her own research while connecting and advancing scholars from diverse academic disciplines.

or "Negroid" were at best mere statistical abstractions about populations in which certain physical features appeared in higher frequencies than in other populations; no example of "pure" racial types could be found. These categories turned out to be neither definitive nor particularly helpful. The visible traits were generally found to occur not in abrupt shifts from population to population but in a continuum that changed gradually, with few sharp breaks. To compound the problem, one trait might change gradually over a north-south gradient, whereas another might show a similar change from east to west. Human skin color, for instance, becomes progressively darker as one moves from northern Europe to Central Africa, whereas blood type B becomes progressively more common as one moves from western to eastern Europe.

Finally, there are many variations within each group, and those within groups are often greater than those between groups. In Africa, the light-brown skin color of someone from the Kalahari Desert might more closely resemble that of a person from Southeast Asia than the darkly pigmented person from southern Sudan who is supposed to be of the same race.

Race as a Biological Concept

To understand why the "racial" approach to human variation has been so unproductive and even damaging, we must first understand the race concept in strictly biological terms. In biology, a **race** is defined as a subspecies, or a population of a species differing geographically, morphologically, or genetically from other populations of the same species.

As straightforward as such a definition may seem, it has three very serious flaws. First, it is arbitrary; there is no agreement on how many differences it takes to make a race. For example, if one researcher emphasizes skin color while another emphasizes blood group differences, they will not classify people in the same way. Ultimately, it is impossible to reach agreement on the number of genes and precisely which ones are the most important for defining races.

The second weakness in the biological definition of race is that no one race has exclusive possession of any particular variant of any gene or genes. In human terms, the frequency of a trait like the type O blood group, for example, may be high in one population and low in another, but it is present in both. In other words, populations are genetically "open," meaning that genes flow between them. Because populations are genetically open, no fixed racial groups can exist. The only reproductive barriers that exist for humans are the cultural rules some societies impose regarding appropriate mates. As President Obama's family illustrates (Kenyan father and Euramerican mother, who, incidentally, was an anthropologist), these social barriers are changing.

Third, the biological definition of race does not apply to humans because the differences among individuals and within a so-called racial population are greater than the differences among populations. Evolutionary biologist Richard Lewontin demonstrated this through genetic analyses in the 1970s. He compared the amount of genetic variation within populations and among so-called racial types, finding a mere 7 percent of human variation existing among groups.[3] Instead, the vast majority of genetic variation exists *within* groups. As the science writer James Shreeve puts it, "most of what separates me genetically from a typical African or Eskimo also separates me from another average American of European ancestry."[4] This follows from the fact of genetic openness of races; no one race has an exclusive claim to any particular form of a gene or trait.

Considering the above, it is small wonder that most anthropologists have abandoned the race concept as being of utility in understanding human biological variation. Instead, they have found it more productive to study *clines*—the distribution and significance of single, specific, genetically based characteristics and continuous traits related to adaptation (see Chapter 2). They examine human variation within small breeding populations, the smallest units in which evolutionary change occurs.

Fingerprint patterns of loops, whorls, and arches are genetically determined. Grouping people on this basis would place most Europeans, sub-Saharan Africans, and East Asians together as "loops." Australian Aborigines and the people of Mongolia would be together as "whorls." The Bushmen of southern African would be grouped as "arches."

[3] Lewontin, R. C. (1972). The apportionment of human diversity. In T. Dobzhansky, et al. (Eds.), *Evolutionary biology* (pp. 381–398). New York: Plenum.

[4] Shreeve, J. (1994). Terms of estrangement. *Discover 15* (11), 60.

race In biology, a subspecies or a population of a species differing geographically, morphologically, or genetically from other populations of the same species; not applicable to people because the division of humans into discrete types does not represent the true nature of human biological variation. In some societies, race is an important social category.

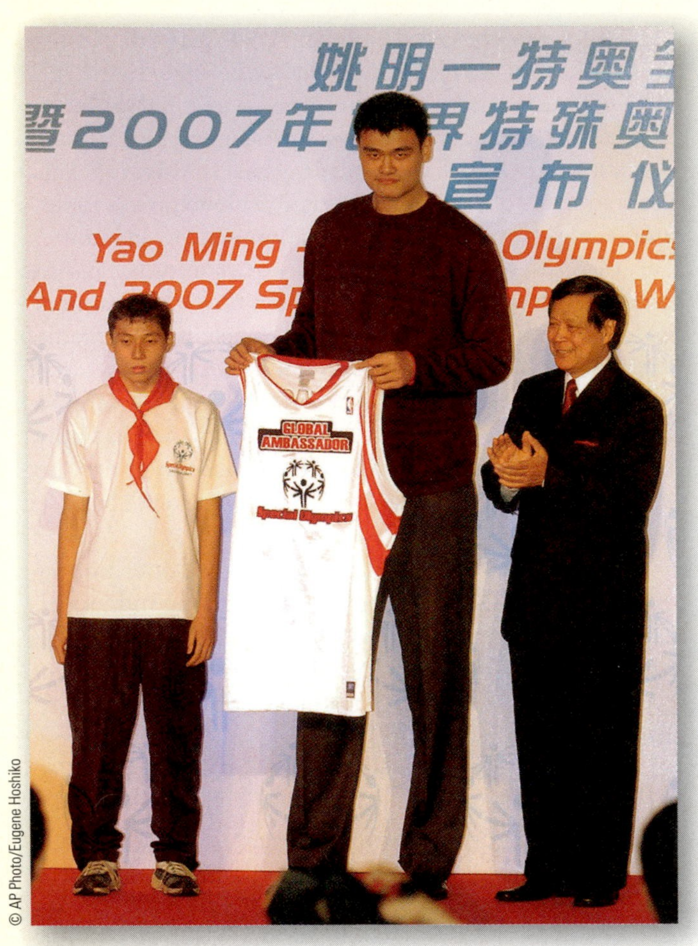

© AP Photo/Eugene Hoshiko

Yao Ming, center for the Houston Rockets, receives his Special Olympics Global Ambassador jersey from athlete Xu Chuang (left) and Special Olympics East Asia President Dicken Yung. Standing side by side, these three individuals illustrate the wide range of variation seen within a single so-called racial category.

Conflation of the Biological into the Cultural Category of Race

While the biological race concept is not applicable to human variation, nevertheless race exists as a significant cultural category. Human groups frequently insert a false notion of biological difference into the cultural category of race to make it appear more factual and objective. In various ways, cultures define religious, linguistic, and ethnic groups as "races," thereby confusing linguistic and cultural traits with physical traits.

For example, in many Latin American countries, people are commonly classified as Indio (Indian), Mestizo (mixed), or Ladino (of Spanish descent). But despite the biological connotations of these terms, the criteria used for assigning individuals to these categories involve things such as whether they wear shoes, sandals, or go barefoot; speak Spanish or an Indian language; live in a thatched hut or a European-style house; and so forth. Thus an Indio—by speaking Spanish, wearing Western-style clothes, and living in a house in a non-Indio neighborhood—ceases to be an Indio, no matter how many "Indio genes" he or she may possess.

This sort of confusion of nonbiological characteristics with the biological notion of heredity is by no means limited to Latin American societies. To various extents, such confusion is found in most societies of Europe and North America. Take, for example, the fact that the racial categories used by the U.S. Census Bureau change with every census. Large catch-all categories (white, black, American Indian or Alaskan Native, Asian and Pacific Islander or native Hawaiian) include diverse peoples. Asian, for example, includes such different peoples as Chinese and East Indians, whereas native

© Schalkwijk/Art Resource, NY

In colonial Mexico, sixteen different *castas* ("castes") were named, giving specific labels to individuals who were various combinations of Spanish, Indian, and African ancestry. These paintings of *castas* are traditionally arranged from light to dark as a series and reflect an effort to impose hierarchy despite the fluid social system in place. In the United States the hierarchy was more rigid; the "one drop rule," also known as *hypodescent*, would ascribe the "lower" position to individuals if they had even one drop of blood from a grouping within the hierarchy.

Hawaiian and Alaskan are far more restrictive. The Census Bureau also asks people to identify Hispanic ethnicity, a category that includes people who, in their countries of origin, might be classified as Indio, Mestizo, or Ladino. The addition of categories for native Hawaiians, Middle Easterners, and people who consider themselves multiracial does nothing to improve the situation.

To compound the confusion, inclusion in one or another of these categories is usually based on self-identification, which means that these are not biological categories at all. The observation that the purported race of an individual can vary over the course of his or her lifetime speaks to the fact that cultural forces shape the designation of membership in a particular racial category.

Similarly, genetics research in medicine is regularly oversimplified according to the racial types defined in the 18th and 19th centuries. It remains to be seen whether this genetics research will avoid creating false genetic types that do not reflect the true nature of human variation. Recent claims of race-specific drugs and vaccines that are based on limited scientific data indicate that the social category of race may again be interfering with our understanding of the true nature of human genetic diversity.

To make matters worse, the confusion of social with biological factors is frequently combined with prejudices that then serve to exclude whole categories of people from certain roles or positions in society. For example, in colonial North America, a "racial" worldview, rooted in the unequal power relations between the English or Saxon "race" and the Irish or Celtic "race" in Europe, assigned American Indians and Africans imported as slaves to perpetual low status. A supposed biological inferiority

These skulls, from the genocide war memorial in Rwanda, record some of the horror that took place in this Central African country in 1994. Over the course of only about a hundred days, a militia of the ruling Hutu majority brutally murdered close to 1 million ethnic Tutsis. With clear genocidal intent, systematic organization, and intense speed, Hutu actions, resembling those of the Nazi regime, remind us that genocide is far from a thing of the past. The global effects of the Rwandan genocide have been massive. Millions of Rwandans, both refugees and killers, now live in neighboring regions, disrupting the stability of these states. Through the United Nations and individual governments, the international community has recognized that it failed to act to prevent this genocide and collectively has taken steps toward maintaining peace in the region. The parallels between Rwanda and current conflicts in Congo, Burundi, and Sudan are chilling.

was used to justify this low status, whereas access to privilege, power, and wealth was reserved for favored groups of European descent.[5]

Because of the colonial association of lighter skin with greater power and higher social status, people whose history includes domination by lighter-skinned Europeans have sometimes valued this phenotype. In Haiti, for example, the "color question" has been the dominant force in social and political life. Skin texture, facial features, hair color, and socioeconomic class collectively play a role in the ranking. According to Haitian anthropologist Michel-Rolph Trouillot, "a rich black becomes a mulatto, a poor mulatto becomes black."[6]

The Nazis in Germany elevated a racialized worldview to state policy, with particularly evil consequences. The Nuremberg race laws of 1935 declared the superiority of the Aryan "race" and the inferiority of the Gypsy and Jewish "races." The Nazi doctrine justified, on supposed biological grounds, political repression and extermination. In all, 11 million people (Jews, Gypsies, homosexuals, and other so-called inferior people, as well as political opponents of the Nazi regime) were deliberately put to death.

Tragically, the Nazi Holocaust (from the Greek word for "wholly burnt" or "sacrificed by fire") is not unique in human history. Such genocides, programs of extermination of one group by another, have a long history that predates World War II and continues today. Recent and ongoing genocide in parts of South America, Africa, Europe, and Asia, like previous genocides, are accompanied by a rhetoric of dehumanization and a depiction of the people being exterminated as a lesser type of human.

The Social Significance of Race: Racism

Scientific facts, unfortunately, have been slow to change what people think about race. **Racism,** a doctrine of superiority by which one group justifies the dehumanization of others based on their distinctive physical characteristics, is not just about discriminatory ideas, values, or attitudes but is also a political problem. Indeed, politicians have often exploited this concept as a means of mobilizing support, demonizing opponents, and eliminating rivals. Racial conflicts result from social stereotypes, not scientific facts.

Race and Behavior

The assumption that behavioral differences exist among so-called human races remains an issue to which many people still cling tenaciously. Throughout history, certain characteristics have been attributed to groups of people under a variety of names—national character, spirit, temperament—all of them vague and standing for a number of concepts unrelated to any biological phenomena. Common myths involve the "coldness" of Scandinavians or the "rudeness" of Americans or the "fierceness" of the Yanomami Indians. Such unjust characterizations rely upon a false notion of biological difference.

To date, no inborn behavioral characteristic can be attributed to any group of people (which the nonscientist might term a "race") that cannot be explained in terms of cultural practices. If the Chinese happen to exhibit exceptional visual-spatial skills, it is probably because reading Chinese characters requires a visual-spatial kind of learning, one that is not as necessary in mastering Western alphabets.[7] Similarly, the relative exclusion of "non-whites" from honors in the sport of golf (until Tiger Woods) had more to do with the social rules of country clubs and the sport's expense.[8] All such differences or characteristics can be explained in terms of culture.

In the same vein, high crime rates, alcoholism, and drug use among certain groups can be explained with reference to culture rather than biology. Individuals alienated and demoralized by poverty, injustice, and unequal opportunity tend to abandon the traditional paths to success of the dominant culture because these paths are blocked. In a racialized society, poverty and all its ill consequences affect some groups of people much more severely than others.

Race and Intelligence

A question frequently asked by those unfamiliar with the fallacy of biological race in humans is whether some "races" are inherently more intelligent than others. First we must ask, what do we mean by the term *intelligence*?

[5] American Anthropological Association. (1998). Statement on "race." Available: www.ameranthassn.org.

[6] Trouillot, M. R. (1996). Culture, color, and politics in Haiti. In S. Gregory & R. Sanjek (Eds.), *Race*. New Brunswick, NJ: Rutgers University Press.

[7] Chan, J.W.C., & Vernon, P. E. (1988). Individual differences among the peoples of China. In J. W. Berry (Ed.), *Human abilities in cultural context* (pp. 340–357). Cambridge, England: Cambridge University Press.

[8] Before Tiger Woods came Charles Sifford (b. 1922), the first African American to win honors in golf. Sifford did so at a time when desegregating the sport meant being subjected to threats and racial abuse. In 2004, the World Golf Hall of Fame inducted him as their first African American member.

racism A doctrine of superiority by which one group justifies the dehumanization of others based on their distinctive physical characteristics.

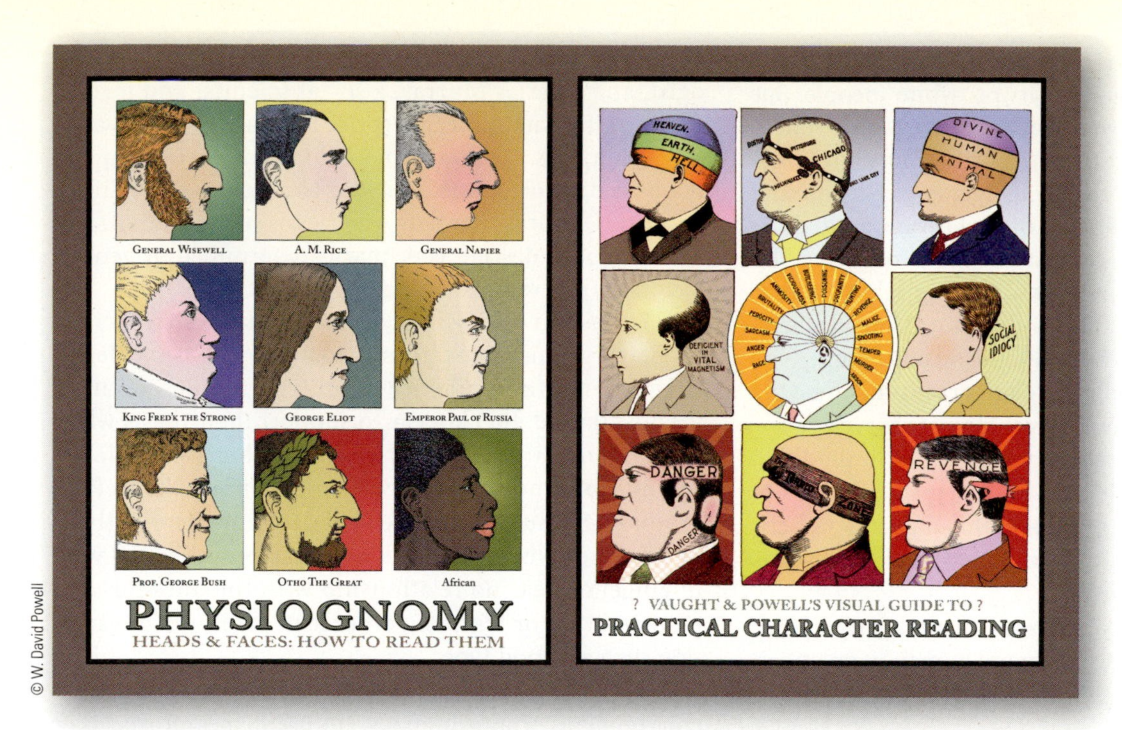

In the late 19th and early 20th centuries, "physiognomists" practiced a pseudo-science in which they associated particular facial or skull features with criminal behavior or insanity. Though these ideas may seem humorous and far-fetched to us today, they were only a step away from the racism embedded in the science of the time. Academic texts regularly use the terms "degraded" and "animalized" when describing the skulls and skeletons of non-whites. To challenge contemporary people to think about the boundary between science and pseudo-science, graphic artist W. David Powell has taken a series of these historical images as the subject of his artwork. The images and words he presents are taken directly from two books from that time: *Heads and Faces and How to Study Them: A Manual of Phrenology and Physiognomy for the People* (1885) by Nelson Sizer and H. S. Drayton; and *Vaught's Practical Character Reader* (1902) by Louis Allen Vaught. What signs of racism and stereotyping do you see in these images?

Unfortunately, there is no general agreement as to what abilities or talents actually make up what we call intelligence, even though some psychologists insist that it is a single quantifiable thing measured by IQ tests. Many more psychologists consider intelligence to be the product of the interaction of different sorts of cognitive abilities: verbal, mathematical-logical, spatial, linguistic, musical, bodily kinesthetic, social, and personal.[9] Each may be thought of as a particular kind of intelligence, unrelated to the others. This being so, these types of intelligence must be independently inherited (to the degree they are inherited), just as height, blood type, skin color, and so forth are independently inherited. Thus the various abilities that constitute intelligence are independently distributed like other phenotypic traits such as skin color and blood type.

But IQ tests themselves are not a fully valid measure of inborn intelligence. An IQ test measures performance (something that the individual does) rather than genetic disposition (something that the individual was born with). Performance reflects past experience and present motivational state, as well as innate ability.

Though IQ tests are not a reliable measure of inborn intelligence, using them to prove the existence of significant differences in intelligence among human populations has been going on for at least a century. In the United States systematic comparisons of intelligence between "whites" and "blacks" began in the early 20th century and were frequently combined with data gathered by physical anthropologists about skull shape and size.

During World War I, for example, a series of IQ tests, known as Alpha and Beta, were regularly given to draftees. The results showed that the average score attained by Euramericans was higher than that obtained by African Americans. Even though African Americans from the urban northern states scored higher than Euramericans from the rural South, and some African Americans scored

[9] Jacoby, R., & Glauberman, N. (Eds.). (1995). *The Bell Curve debate* (pp. 7, 55–56, 59). New York: Random House.

higher than most Euramericans, many people took this as proof of the intellectual superiority of "white" people. But all the tests really showed was that, on the average, "whites" outperformed "blacks" in the social situation of IQ testing. The tests did not measure intelligence per se, but the ability, conditioned by culture, of certain individuals to respond appropriately to certain questions conceived by Americans of European descent for comparable middle-class "whites." These tests frequently require knowledge of "white" middle-class values and linguistic behavior.

For such reasons, intelligence tests continue to be the subject of controversy. Many psychologists as well as anthropologists are convinced that they are of limited use, because they are applicable only to particular cultural settings. When researchers controlled for cultural and environmental factors, African and European Americans tended to score equally well.[10]

Nevertheless some researchers still insist that significant differences in intelligence exist among human populations. Proponents of this view are Richard Herrnstein, a psychologist, and Charles Murray, a social scientist and former fellow of the American Enterprise Institute, a conservative U.S. think tank. Their argument, in a lengthy (and highly publicized) book entitled *The Bell Curve*, is that the difference in IQ scores between Americans of African, Asian, and European descent is primarily determined by genetic factors and therefore immutable.

Herrnstein and Murray's book has been criticized on many grounds, including violation of basic rules of statistics and their practice of utilizing studies, no matter how flawed, that appear to support their thesis while ignoring or barely mentioning those that contradict it. In addition, they are also wrong on purely theoretical grounds. Because genes are inherited independently of one another, whatever alleles that may be associated with intelligence bear no relationship with the ones for skin pigmentation or with any other aspect of human variation such as blood type.

Further, the expression of genes always occurs in an environment. Among humans, culture shapes all aspects of the environment. In the following Original Study, physical anthropologist Jonathan Marks extends the discussion of race and intelligence to stereotypes about athletic abilities of different so-called races.

[10] Sanday, P. R. (1975). On the causes of IQ differences between groups and implications for social policy. In M. F. A. Montagu (Ed.), *Race and IQ* (pp. 232–238). New York: Oxford.

Original Study

A Feckless Quest for the Basketball Gene *by Jonathan Marks*

You know what they say about a little knowledge. Here's some: The greatest sprinters and basketball players are predominantly black. Here's some more: Nobel laureates in science are predominantly white.

What do we conclude? That blacks have natural running ability, and whites have natural science ability? Or perhaps that blacks have natural running ability, but whites don't have natural science ability, because that would be politically incorrect?

Or perhaps that we can draw no valid conclusions about the racial distribution of abilities on the basis of data like these.

That is what modern anthropology would say.

But it's not what a new book, *Taboo: Why Black Athletes Dominate Sports and Why We're Afraid to Talk about It,* says. It says that blacks dominate sports because of their genes and that we're afraid to talk about it on account of a cabal of high-ranking politically correct postmodern professors—myself, I am flattered to observe, among them.

The book is a piece of good old-fashioned American anti-intellectualism (those dang perfessers!) that plays to vulgar beliefs about group differences of the sort we recall from *The Bell Curve* six years ago. These are not, however, issues that anthropologists are "afraid to talk about"; we talk about them a lot. The author, journalist, and former television producer Jon Entine, simply doesn't like what we're saying. But to approach the subject with any degree of rigor, as anthropologists have been trying to do for nearly a century, requires recognizing that it consists of several related questions.

First, how can we infer a genetic basis for differences among people? The answer: Collect genetic data. There's no substitute. We could document consistent differences in physical features, acts, and accomplishments until the Second Coming and be entirely wrong in thinking they're genetically based. A thousand Nigerian Ibos and a thousand Danes will consistently be found to differ in complexion, language, and head shape. The first is genetic, the second isn't, and the third we simply don't understand.

What's clear is that, developmentally, the body is sufficiently plastic that subtle differences in the conditions of growth and life can affect it profoundly. Simple observation of difference is thus not a genetic argument.

Which brings us to the second question: How can we accept a genetic basis for athletic ability and reject it for intelligence? The answer: We can't. Both conclusions are based on the same standard of evidence. If we accept that blacks are genetically endowed jumpers because "they" jump so well, we are obliged to accept that they are genetically unendowed at schoolwork because "they" do so poorly.

In either case, we are faced with the scientifically impossible task of drawing conclusions from a mass of poorly controlled data. Controls are crucial in science. If every black schoolboy in America knows he's supposed to be good at basketball and bad at algebra, and we have no way to measure schoolboys outside the boundaries of such an expectation, how can we gauge their "natural" endowments? Lots of things go into the observation of excellence or failure, only one of which is genetic endowment.

But obviously humans differ. Thus, the last question: What's the relationship between patterns of human genetic variation and groups of people? The answer: It's complex.

All populations are heterogeneous and are built in some sense in opposition to other groups. Jew or Muslim, Hutu or Tutsi, Serb or Bosnian, Irish or English, Harvard or Yale—one thing we're certain of is that the groups of most significance to us don't correspond to much in nature.

Consider, then, the category "black athlete"—and let's limit ourselves to men here. It's broad enough to encompass Arthur Ashe, Mike Tyson, and Kobe Bryant.

When you read about the body of the black male athlete, whose body do you imagine? Whatever physical gift these men share is not immediately apparent from looking at them.

Black men of highly diverse builds enter athletics and excel.

Far more don't excel. In other words, there is a lot more to being black and to being a prominent athlete than mere biology. If professional excellence or overrepresentation could be regarded as evidence for genetic superiority, there would be strong implications for Jewish comedy genes and Irish policeman genes.

Inferring a group's excellence from the achievements of some members hangs on a crucial asymmetry: To accomplish something means that you had the ability to do it, but the failure to do it doesn't mean you didn't have the ability. And the existing genetic data testify that known DNA variations do not respect the boundaries of human groups.

To be an elite athlete, or elite anybody, presumably does require some kind of genetic gift. But those gifts must be immensely diverse, distributed broadly across the people of the world—at least to judge from the way that the erosion of social barriers consistently permits talent to manifest itself in different groups of people.

In an interview with *The Philadelphia Daily News* in February, Mr. Entine observed that Jews are overrepresented among critics of the views he espouses. But is that a significantly Jewish thing? Or is it simply a consequence of the fact that among any group of American intellectuals you'll find Jews overrepresented because they are a well-educated minority? There's certainly no shortage of non-Jews who find the ideas in *Taboo* to be demagogic quackery.

Of course, Jewish academics may sometimes be speaking as academics, not as Jews. Likewise black athletes may perform as athletes, not just as embodied blackness.

How easy it is to subvert Michael Jordan, the exceptional and extraordinary man, into merely the representative of the black athlete.

The problem with talking about the innate superiority of the black athlete is that it is make-believe genetics applied to naïvely conceptualized groups of people. It places a spotlight on imaginary natural differences that properly belongs on real social differences.

More important, it undermines the achievements of individuals as individuals. Whatever gifts we each have are far more likely, from what we know of genetics, to be unique individual constellations of genes than to be expressions of group endowments.

From Marks, J. (2000, April 8). A feckless quest for the basketball gene. New York Times. *Copyright © 2000 by the New York Times Co. Reprinted by permission.*

Separating genetic components of intelligence (or any other continuous trait) from environmental contributors poses enormous problems.[11] Most studies of intelligence rely on comparisons between identical twins: genetically identical individuals raised in the same or different environments. Twin studies are plagued by a host of problems: inadequate sample sizes, biased subjective judgments, failure to make sure that "separated twins" really were raised separately, unrepresentative samples of adoptees to serve as controls, untested assumptions about similarity of environments. In fact, children reared by the same mother resemble her in IQ to the same degree, whether or not they share her genes.[12] Clearly, the degree to which intelligence is inherited through genes is far from understood.[13]

Undoubtedly, the effects of social environment are important for intelligence. This should not surprise us, as other genetically determined traits are influenced by environmental factors. Height in humans, for example, has a genetic basis while also being dependent upon both nutrition and health status. (Severe illness in childhood arrests growth, and renewed growth never makes up for this loss.) While it is possible to see the effects of the environment on growth, the exact relative contributions of genetic and environmental factors on either the height or the intelligence of an individual are unknown.

Nevertheless, documentation of the importance of the environment in the expression of intelligence exposes further the problems with generalizations about IQ and "race." For example, IQ scores of all groups in the United States, as in most industrial and postindustrial countries, have risen some 15 points since World War II. In addition, the gap between Americans of African and European descent, for example, is narrower today than in the past. Other studies show impressive IQ scores for African American children born into socially deprived and economically disadvantaged backgrounds who have been adopted into highly educated and prosperous homes. It is now known that underprivileged children adopted into such privileged families can boost their IQs by 20 points.

[11] Andrews, L. B., & Nelkin, D. (1996). The Bell Curve: A statement. *Science 271,* 13.

[12] Lewontin, R. C., Rose, S., & Kamin, L. J. (1984). *Not in our genes* (pp. 100, 113, 116). New York: Pantheon.

[13] Ibid., pp. 9, 121.

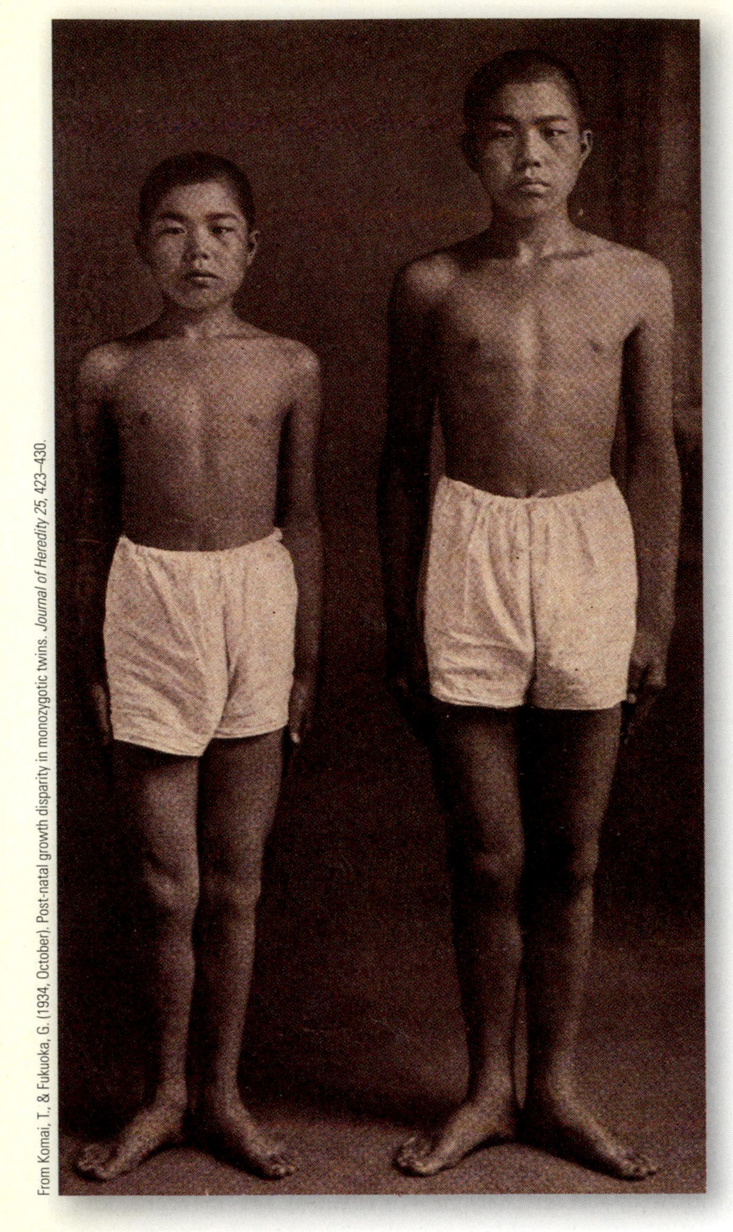

From Komai, T., & Fukuoka, G. (1934, October). Post-natal growth disparity in monozygotic twins. *Journal of Heredity 25*, 423–430.

Differences in the growth process can lead to very different outcomes in terms of size as seen in these twins, who are genetically identical. Even starting from inside their mother's womb, twins may experience environmental differences in terms of blood and nutrient supply. This can impact not only size but cognitive development.

It is also well known that IQ scores rise in proportion to the test-takers' amount of schooling.

More such cases could be cited, but these three observations suffice to make the point. First, there is a bias in IQ testing based on social class. Second, the assertion that IQ is biologically fixed and immutable is clearly false. Third, ranking human beings with respect to their intelligence scores in terms of "racial" difference is doubly false.

Over the past 2.5 million years, all populations of the genus *Homo* have adapted primarily through culture—actively inventing solutions to the problems of survival, rather than relying only on biological adaptation. Thus we would expect a comparable degree of intelligence in all present-day human populations. The only way for individual human beings to develop their innate abilities and skills to the fullest is to ensure that they have access to the necessary resources and the opportunity to do so.

polymorphic Describing species with alternative forms (alleles) of particular genes.

Studying Human Biological Diversity

A [illegible] valid w[illegible]o say t[illegible] skin c[illegible]xcel-le[illegible]ping human variation.

The physical characteristics of both populations and individuals are a product of the interaction between genes and environments. For example, genes predispose people to a particular skin color, but an individual's skin color is also influenced by cultural and environmental factors. The skin of sailors, for example, is darkened or burned after many hours of exposure to the sun, depending on not only genetic predisposition but cultural practices regarding exposure to the sun. In other cases, such as A-B-O blood type, phenotypic expression closely reflects genotype.

For characteristics controlled by a single gene, different versions of that gene, known as alleles (see Chapter 2), also mediate variation. Such traits are called **polymorphic** (meaning "many shapes"). Our blood types—determined by the alleles for types A, B, and O blood—are an example of a polymorphism and may appear in any of four distinct phenotypic forms (A, B, O, and AB).

A species can also be considered polymorphic, meaning that there is wide variation among individuals (beyond differences between males and females). Here "polymorphic" refers to continuous phenotypic variation that may be genetically controlled by interactions among multiple different genes, in addition to the allelic variation described above. When a polymorphic species faces changing environmental conditions, the variation it has within its gene pool fosters survival of the species, since some of those individuals may possess traits that prove adaptive in the altered environment. Individuals whose physical characteristics enable them to do well in the new environment will usually reproduce more successfully, so that their

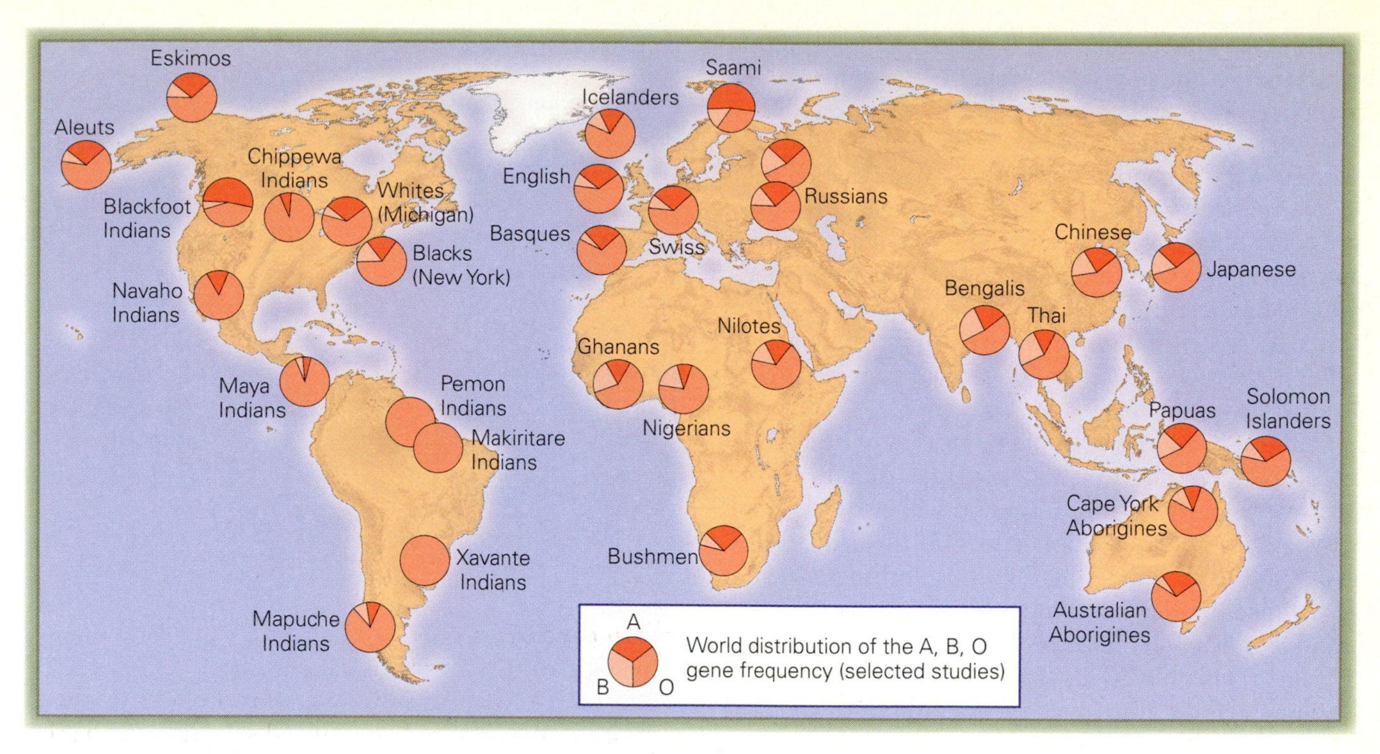

Figure 12.1 **Frequencies of the three alleles for the A, B, and O blood groups for selected populations around the world illustrate the polytypic nature of *Homo sapiens*. The frequency of the alleles differs among populations.**

genes become more common in subsequent generations. Similarly, the polymorphism of the human species has allowed us to thrive in a wide variety of environments.

When polymorphisms of a species are distributed into geographically dispersed populations, biologists describe this species as **polytypic** ("many types"); that is, genetic variability is unevenly distributed among populations. For example, in the distribution of the polymorphism for blood type (four distinct phenotypic groups: A, B, O, or AB), the human species is polytypic. The frequency of the O allele is highest in American Indians, especially among some populations native to South America; the highest frequencies of the allele for type A blood tend to be found among certain European populations (although the highest frequency is found among the Blackfoot Indians of the northern Plains in North America); the highest frequencies of the B allele are found in some Asian populations (Figure 12.1). Even though single traits may be grouped within specific geographic regions, when a greater number of traits are considered, specific human "types" cannot be identified. Instead each of these traits is independently subject to evolutionary forces.

As mentioned above, today anthropologists study biological diversity in terms of *clines*, or the continuous gradation over space in the form or frequency of a trait. As mentioned in Chapter 2, the spatial distribution or cline for the sickle-cell allele allowed anthropologists to identify the adaptive function of this gene in a malarial environment. Clinal analysis of a continuous trait such as body shape, which is controlled by a series of genes, allows anthropologists to interpret human global variation in body build as an adaptation to climate.

Generally, people long native to regions with cold climates tend to have greater body bulk (not to be equated with fat) relative to their extremities (arms and legs) than do people native to regions with hot climates, who tend to be relatively long and slender. Interestingly, these differences show up as early as the time of *Homo erectus,* as described in Chapter 8. A person with larger body bulk and relatively shorter extremities may suffer more from summer heat than someone whose extremities are relatively long and whose body is slender. But they do conserve needed body heat under cold conditions. A bulky body tends to conserve more heat than a less bulky one, because it has less surface area relative to volume. In hot, open country, by contrast, people benefit from a long slender body that can get rid of excess heat quickly. A small slender body can also promote heat loss due to a high surface area-to-volume ratio.

In addition to very long-term effects that climate may have imposed on human variation, climate can also

polytypic Describing the expression of genetic variants in different frequencies in different populations of a species.

contribute to human variation through its impact on the process of growth and development (developmental adaptation). For example, some of the physiological mechanisms for withstanding cold or dissipating heat have been shown to vary depending upon the climate that an individual experiences as a child. Individuals who grow up in very cold climates develop circulatory system modifications that allow them to remain comfortable at temperatures that people from warmer climates cannot tolerate. Similarly, hot climate promotes the development of a higher density of sweat glands, creating a more efficient system for sweating to keep the body cool.

Cultural processes complicate studies of body build and climatic adaptation. For example, dietary differences particularly during childhood will cause variation in body shape through their effect on the growth process. Another complicating factor is clothing. Much of the way people adapt to cold is cultural rather than biological. For example, Inuit peoples of Arctic Canada live where it is very cold much of the year. To cope with this, they long ago developed efficient clothing to keep the body warm. Inside their clothing, the Inuit are provided with what amounts to an artificial tropical environment. Such cultural adaptations allow humans to inhabit the entire globe.

Some anthropologists have also suggested that variation in features such as face and eye shape relate to climate. For example, biological anthropologist Carleton Coon and his colleagues once proposed that the "Mongoloid face," common in populations native to East and Central Asia, as well as Arctic North America, exhibits features adapted to life in very cold environments.[14] The **epicanthic eye fold** (which minimizes the eye's exposure to the cold), a flat facial profile, and extensive fatty deposits may help to protect the face against frostbite.

Although experimental studies have failed to sustain the frostbite hypothesis, it is true that a flat facial profile generally goes with a round head. A significant percentage of body heat may be lost from the head. A round head, having less surface area relative to volume, loses less heat than a longer, more elliptical head. As one would predict from this, populations with more elliptical-shaped heads are generally found in hotter climates; those with rounder-shaped heads are more common in cold climates. However, these same features also could be present in populations due to genetic drift.

[14] Coon, C. S. (1962). *The origins of races.* New York: Knopf.

epicanthic eye fold A fold of skin at the inner corner of the eye that covers the true corner of the eye; common in Asiatic populations.

© Steve Elmore

The epicanthic eye fold is common among people of East Asia. While some anthropologists have suggested that this feature might be an adaptation to cold, genetic drift could also be responsible for the frequency of this trait.

Culture and Biological Diversity

Although cultural adaptation has reduced the importance of biological adaptation and physical variation, at the same time cultural forces impose their own selective pressures. For example, take the reproductive fitness of individuals with diabetes—a disease with a known genetic predisposition. In North America and Europe today, where medication is relatively available, people with diabetes are as biologically fit as anyone else. However, if people with diabetes do not have access to the necessary medication, as is true in many parts of the world, their biological fitness is lost and they die out. Because financial status affects access to medical resources, one's biological fitness may be determined by this cultural factor.

Culture can also contribute directly to the development of disease. For example, one type of diabetes is very common among overweight individuals who get little exercise—a combination that describes 61 percent of people in the United States today. As peoples from traditional

© Terrol Dew Johnson

Loss of traditional cultural practices brought about by forced reservation life has resulted in high rates of diabetes among American Indians. The Pima Indians of Arizona have the highest rates of diabetes in the world today. Diabetes was not a problem for the Pima before the plentiful high-carbohydrate diet and low activity patterns typical of U.S. culture replaced their traditional lifeways. Despite the sociopolitical roots of this disease in their community, the Pima have participated in government-funded research aimed at both understanding the genetic origins of diabetes and finding effective treatment for it. Here a Pima woman prepares to give herself an insulin injection.

cultures throughout the world adopt a Western high-sugar diet and low activity pattern, their incidence rates will rise for diabetes and obesity as well.

Another example of culture acting as an agent of biological selection is lactose tolerance: the ability to digest **lactose,** the primary constituent of fresh milk. To digest milk, the body has to make a particular enzyme—**lactase.** Most mammals as well as most human populations—especially Asian, Native Australian, Native American, and many (but not all) African populations—do not continue to produce lactase into adulthood. Adults with lactose intolerance suffer from gas pains and diarrhea when they consume milk or milk products. Only 10 to 30 percent of Americans of African descent and 0 to 30 percent of adult Asians are lactose tolerant.[15] By contrast, lactase retention and lactose tolerance are normal for over 80 percent of adults of northern European descent. Eastern Europeans, Arabs, and some East Africans are closer to northern Europeans in lactase retention than they are to Asians and other Africans.

Generally speaking, a high retention of lactase is found in populations with a long tradition of dairying. For them, fresh milk is an important dietary item. In such populations, selection in the past favored those individuals with the allele that confers the ability to assimilate lactose, selecting out those without this allele.

Because milk is associated with health in North American and European countries, powdered milk has long been a staple of economic aid to other countries. In fact, such practices work against the members of populations in which lactase is not commonly retained into adulthood. Those individuals who are not lactose tolerant are unable to utilize the many nutrients in milk. Frequently they also suffer diarrhea, abdominal cramping, and even bone degeneration, with serious results. In fact, the shipping of powdered milk to victims of South American earthquakes in the 1960s caused many deaths.

Among Europeans, lactose tolerance is linked with the evolution of a non-thrifty genotype as opposed to the thrifty genotype that characterized humans until about 6,000 years ago.[16] The **thrifty genotype** permits efficient storage of fat to draw on in times of food shortage. In times of scarcity, individuals with the thrifty genotype conserve glucose (a simple sugar) for use in brain and red blood cells (as opposed to other tissues such as muscle), as well as nitrogen (vital for growth and health).

Regular access to glucose through the lactose in milk led to selection for the non-thrifty genotype as protection against adult-onset diabetes, or at least its onset relatively late in life (at a nonreproductive age). Populations that are lactose intolerant retain the thrifty genotype. As a

[15] Harrison, G. G. (1975). Primary adult lactase deficiency: A problem in anthropological genetics. *American Anthropologist 77,* 815–819.

[16] Allen, J. S., & Cheer, S. M. (1996). The non-thrifty genotype. *Current Anthropology 37,* 831–842.

lactose A sugar that is the primary constituent of fresh milk.

lactase An enzyme in the small intestine that enables humans to assimilate lactose.

thrifty genotype Human genotype that permits efficient storage of fat to draw on in times of food shortage and conservation of glucose and nitrogen.

Biocultural Connection

Beans, Enzymes, and Adaptation to Malaria

Some human adaptations to the deadly malarial parasite are biological while others are strictly tied to cultural practices such as local cuisine. The phenotype of the sickle-cell allele, for example, manifests specifically in red blood cells. Biological and dietary adaptations to malaria converge with the interaction between one form of the glucose-6-phosphate-dehydrogenase (G-6-PD) enzyme and fava bean consumption.

The fava bean is a broad flat bean (*Vivia faba*) that is a dietary staple in malaria-endemic areas along the Mediterranean coast. G-6-PD is an enzyme that serves to reduce one sugar, glucose-6-phosphate, to another sugar—in the process releasing an energy-rich molecule. The malaria parasite lives in red blood cells off of energy produced via G-6-PD. Individuals with a mutation in the G-6-PD gene, so-called G-6-PD-deficiency, produce energy by an alternate pathway not involving this enzyme that the parasite cannot use. Furthermore, G-6-PD-deficient red blood cells seem to turn over more quickly, thus allowing less time for the parasite to grow and multiply. While a different form of G-6-PD deficiency is also found in some sub-Saharan African populations, the form found in Mediterranean populations is at odds with an adaptation embedded in the cuisine of the region.

© Charles O. Cecil/Alamy

Fava beans, a dietary staple in the countries around the Mediterranean Sea, also provide some protection against malaria. However, in individuals with G-6-PD deficiency, the protective aspects of fava beans turn deadly. This dual role has led to a rich folklore surrounding fava beans.

Enzymes naturally occurring in fava beans also contain substances that interfere with the development of the malarial parasite. In cultures around the Mediterranean Sea, where malaria is common, fava beans are incorporated into the diet through foods eaten at the height of the malaria season. However, if an individual with G-6-PD deficiency eats fava beans, the result is that the substances toxic to the parasite become toxic to humans. With G-6-PD deficiency, fava bean consumption leads to *hemolytic crisis* (Latin for "breaking of red blood cells") and a series of chemical reactions that release free radicals and hydrogen peroxide into the blood stream. This condition is known as *favism.*

The toxic effect of fava bean consumption in G-6-PD individuals has prompted a rich folklore around this simple food, including the ancient Greek belief that fava beans contain the souls of the dead. The link between favism and G-6-PD deficiency has led parents of children with this condition to limit consumption of this favorite dietary staple.

Unfortunately, this has sometimes become a generalized elimination of many excellent sources of protein such as peanuts, lentils, chickpeas, soy beans, and nuts. Another biocultural connection is again at the root of this unnecessary deprivation. The Arabic name for fava beans is *foul* (pronounced "fool"), while the soy beans are called *foul-al-Soya,* and peanuts are *foul-al-Soudani*; in other words, the plants are linked linguistically even though they are unrelated biologically.[a]

An environmental stressor as potent as malaria has led to a number of human adaptations. In the case of fava beans and G-6-PD deficiency, these adaptations can work at cross purposes. Cultural knowledge of the biochemistry of these interactions will allow humans to adapt, regardless of their genotype.

BIOCULTURAL QUESTION

How does what you have learned from this chapter about the falsehood of the biological category of race relate to the way the varied adaptations to malaria described here work against one another?

[a]Babiker, M. A., et al. (1996). Unnecessary deprivation of common food items in glucose-6-phosphate dehydrogenase deficiency. *Annals of Saudi Arabia* *16* (4), 462–463.

consequence, when they are introduced to Western-style diets (characterized by abundance, particularly of foods high in sugar content), the incidence of obesity and diabetes skyrockets. This chapter's Biocultural Connection describes another example of genetic and cultural adaptations working at cross purposes.

melanin The chemical responsible for dark skin pigmentation that helps protect against damage from ultraviolet radiation.

Skin Color: A Case Study in Adaptation

Generally, the notion of race is most commonly equated with skin color. Skin color is subject to great variation and is attributed to several key factors: the transparency or thickness of the skin; a copper-colored pigment called carotene; reflected color from the blood vessels (responsible for the rosy color of lightly pigmented people); and, most significantly, the amount of **melanin** (from *melas,* a Greek word meaning "black")—a dark pigment in the skin's outer layer. People with dark skin have more melanin-producing

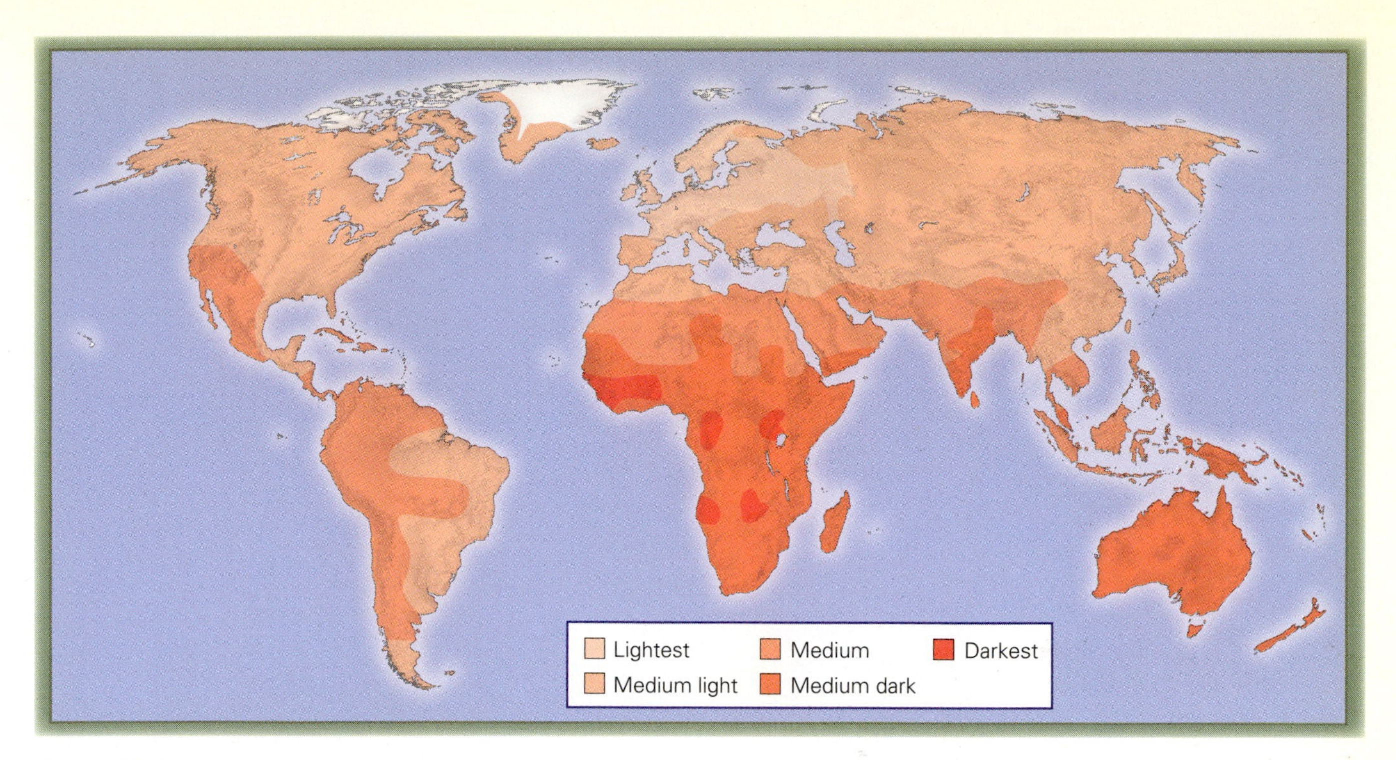

Figure 12.2 This map illustrates the distribution of dark and light human skin pigmentation before 1492. Medium-light skin color in Southeast Asia reflects the spread into that region of people from southern China, whereas the medium darkness of people native to southern Australia is a consequence of their tropical Southeast Asian ancestry. Lack of dark skin pigmentation among tropical populations of Native Americans reflects their more recent ancestry in northeastern Asia a mere 20,000 or so years ago.

cells than those with light skin, but everyone (except those with a condition called albinism) has a measure of melanin. Exposure to sunlight increases melanin production, causing skin color to deepen.

Melanin is known to protect skin against damaging ultraviolet solar radiation;[17] consequently, dark-skinned people are less susceptible to skin cancer and sunburn than are those with less melanin. They also seem to be less susceptible to destruction of certain vitamins under intense exposure to sunlight. Because the highest concentrations of dark-skinned people tend to be found in the tropical regions of the world, it appears that natural selection has favored heavily pigmented skin as a protection against exposure where ultraviolet radiation is most constant.

The inheritance of skin color involves several genes (rather than variants of a single gene), each with several alleles, thus creating a continuous range of phenotypic expression for this trait. In addition, the geographic distribution or cline of skin color, with few exceptions, tends to be continuous (Figures 12.2 and 12.3). The exceptions have to do with the historic movement of certain populations from their original homelands to other regions, or the practice of selective mating, or both.

Because skin cancer generally does not develop until later in life, it is less likely to have interfered with the reproductive success of lightly pigmented individuals in the tropics and so is probably not the agent of selection. On the other hand, severe sunburn, which is especially dangerous to infants, causes the body to overheat and interferes with its ability to sweat and rid itself of excess heat. Furthermore, it makes one susceptible to other kinds of infection. In addition to all this, decomposition of folate, an essential vitamin sensitive to heavy doses of ultraviolet radiation, can cause anemia, spontaneous abortion, and infertility.[18]

In northern latitudes, light skin has an adaptive advantage related to the skin's important biological function as the manufacturer of vitamin D through a chemical reaction dependent upon sunlight. Vitamin D is vital for maintaining the balance of calcium in the body. In northern climates with little sunshine, light skin allows enough sunlight to penetrate the skin so as to stimulate the

[17] Neer, R. M. (1975). The evolutionary significance of vitamin D, skin pigment, and ultraviolet light. *American Journal of Physical Anthropology 43,* 409–416.

[18] Branda, R. F., & Eatoil, J. W. (1978). Skin color and photolysis: An evolutionary hypothesis. *Science 201,* 625–626.

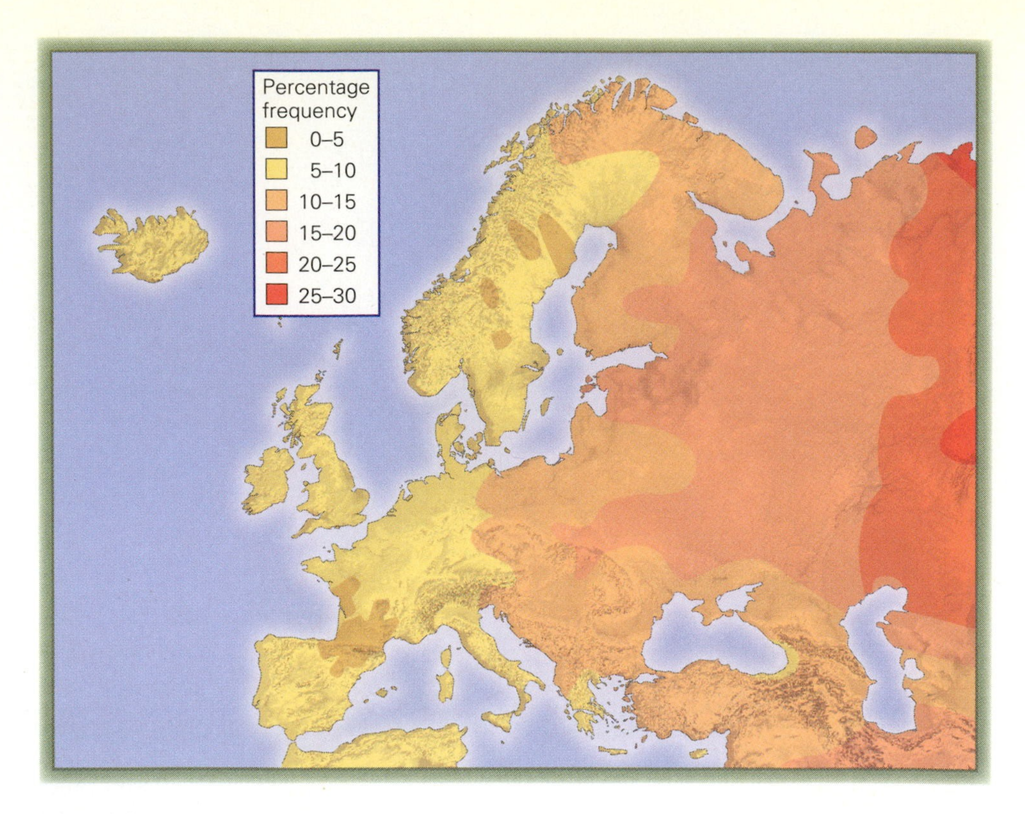

Figure 12.3 The east-west gradient in the frequency of type B blood in Europe contrasts with the north-south gradient in skin color shown in Figure 12.2. Just as the clines for skin color and blood type must be considered independently, so too must be whatever genes are involved in the complex of abilities known as "intelligence."

production of vitamin D, which is essential for healthy bones and for balance within the central nervous system. Without sufficient vitamin D, bone growth in children is impaired, resulting in misshapen, fragile bones, a condition known as rickets (Figure 12.4). There is an adult form of bone disease resulting from vitamin D deficiency as well. Dark pigmentation can interfere with vitamin D synthesis and with calcium balance when there is limited natural light.

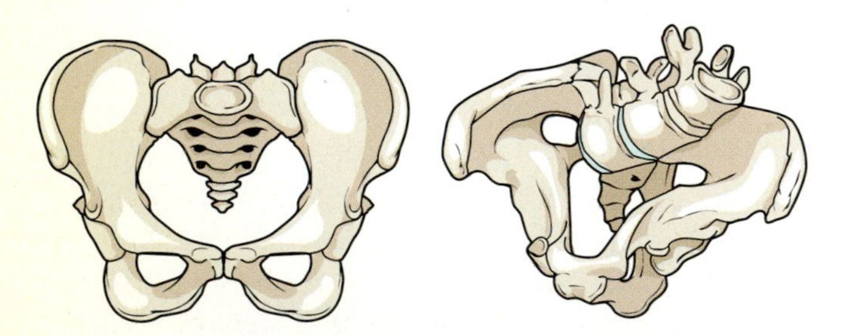

Figure 12.4 Bone diseases such as osteomalacia and rickets caused by vitamin D deficiency can deform the birth canal of the pelvis to the degree that it can interfere with successful childbirth. Because sunshine is vital to the body's production of vitamin D, this disease was very common in the past among the poor in northern industrial cities because they had limited exposure to sunlight. Dietary supplements have reduced the impact of bone diseases, such as rickets, although they continue to be a problem in cultures that require women and girls to dress so that they are completely veiled from the sun.

The severe consequences of vitamin D deficiency can be avoided through cultural practices. Until recently, children in northern Europe and northern North America were regularly fed a spoonful of cod liver oil during the dark winter months. Today, pasteurized milk is often fortified with vitamin D.

Race and Human Evolution

Throughout this chapter we have explored the fallacy of the biological category of race when applied to the human species. Generalizations cannot be made about "types" of humans because no discrete types of humans exist. By contrast, the paleoanthropological analysis of the fossil record explored in previous chapters includes defining specific types of ancestors based on biological and cultural capacities that go hand in hand.

The increased brain size of *Homo habilis* noted around 2.5 million years ago supports the notion that these ancestors were capable of more complex cultural activities than australopithecines, including the manufacture of stone tools. Closer to the present, the same assumptions do not hold. At some point in our evolutionary history we became a single, unified global species. Bearing this in mind, we can frame the modern human origins debate in the terms of the content of this chapter.

Living people today such as this Aborigine do not meet the definition of anatomical modernity proposed in the recent African origins model. Some paleoanthropologists suggest that this proves that the definition is problematic because all living people are clearly full-fledged members of the species *Homo sapiens*.

The modern human origins debate hinges on the question of whether cultural abilities and intelligence can be inferred from details of skull and skeletal shape and size. Supporters of the multiregional hypothesis argue that they cannot.[19] They suggest that using a series of biological features to represent a type of human being (Neandertals) with certain cultural capacities (inferior) is like making assumptions about the cultural capabilities of living humans based on their appearance. In living people, such assumptions are considered stereotypes or racism. By arguing that ancient groups like Neandertals represent a distinct species, supporters of the recent African origins hypothesis bypass the potential prejudice inherent in these assumptions. Both theories embrace African human origins, and in doing so they confront the issue of skin color—the physical feature that has extreme political significance today.

At present, we clearly cannot make any assumptions about intelligence or behavior based on a single phenotypic trait such as skin color. Given what we know about the adaptive significance of human skin color and the fact that, until 800,000 years ago, the genus *Homo* exclusively inhabited the tropics, it is likely that lightly pigmented skins are a recent development in human history. Darkly pigmented skins are probably quite ancient. Consistent with humanity's African origins, the enzyme tyrosinase, which converts the amino acid tyrosine into the compound that forms melanin, is present in lightly pigmented peoples in sufficient quantity to make them very "black." The reason it does not is that they have genes that inactivate or inhibit it.[20]

Human skin, more liberally endowed with sweat glands and lacking heavy body hair compared to other primates, effectively eliminates excess body heat in a

[19] Ibid.

[20] Wills, C. (1994). The skin we're in. *Discover 15* (11), 79.

hot climate as described in Chapter 7. This would have been especially advantageous to our ancestors on the savannah, who could have avoided confrontations with carnivorous animals by carrying out most of their activities in the heat of the day. For the most part, large carnivores such as lions rest during this period, being active from dusk until early morning. Without much hair to cover their bodies, selection would have favored dark skins in our ancestors. All humans appear to have had a "black" ancestry, no matter how "white" some of them may appear to be today.

An interesting question is how long it took for light pigmentation to develop in populations living outside the tropics. Whether one subscribes to the multiregional continuity model or the recent African origins hypothesis, the settling of Greater Australia can be used to examine this question, as we know that the first people to reach Australia did so sometime between 40,000 and 60,000 years ago. These people came there from tropical Southeast Asia, spreading throughout Australia eventually to what is now the island of Tasmania, with a latitude and levels of ultraviolet radiation similar to New York City, Rome, or Beijing.

As Aboriginal Australians originally came from the tropics, we would expect them to have had darkly pigmented skin. In Australia, those populations that spread south of the tropics (where, as in northern latitudes, ultraviolet radiation is less intense) underwent some reduction of pigmentation. But for all that, their skin color is still far darker than that of Europeans or East Asians. Most of today's Southeast Asian population spread there from southern China following the invention of farming. This expansion of lighter-skinned populations effectively "swamped" the original populations of this region, except in a few out-of-the-way places like the Andaman Islands, in the Bay of Bengal between India and Thailand.[21] The obvious conclusion is that 40,000 to 60,000 years is not enough to produce significant depigmentation.[22] These observations also suggest that Europeans and East Asians may have lived outside the tropics for far longer than the people of Tasmania or that settlement in latitudes even more distant from the equator were required for depigmentation to occur.

One should not conclude that, because it is newer, lightly pigmented skin is better or more highly evolved than heavily pigmented skin. The latter is clearly better adapted to the conditions of life in the tropics, although with cultural adaptations like protective clothing, hats, and sunscreen lotions, very lightly pigmented peoples can survive there. Conversely, supplementary sources of vitamin D allow heavily pigmented peoples to do quite well away from the tropics. In both cases, culture has rendered skin color differences largely irrelevant from a biological perspective. With time, skin color may lose its social significance as well.

---

[21] Diamond, J. (1996). Empire of uniformity. *Discover 17* (3), 83–84.

[22] Ferrie, H. (1997). An interview with C. Loring Brace. *Current Anthropology 38,* 864.

Questions for Reflection

1. Humans are challenged to find ways to embrace and comprehend the range of biological diversity without succumbing to oversimplification, discrimination, and even bloodshed fueled by superficial differences. How do anthropological approaches to race contribute to meeting this challenge?

2. From an evolutionary perspective, why is human biological diversity a key component of our collective identity as a species?

3. Why do biological anthropologists and evolutionary biologists use clines to study human variation rather than the biological concept of subspecies? Can you imagine another species of animal, plant, or microorganism for which the subspecies concept makes sense?

4. How do you define the concept of intelligence? Do you think scientists will ever be able to discover the genetic basis of intelligence?

5. Globally, health statistics are gathered by country. In addition, some countries such as the United States gather health statistics by race. How are these two endeavors different and similar? Should health statistics be gathered by group?

Suggested Readings

Cohen, M. N. (1998). *Culture of intolerance: Chauvinism, class, and racism in the United States.* New Haven, CT: Yale University Press.

This very readable book summarizes what scientific data really say about biological differences among humans and exposes questionable assumptions in U.S. culture that promote intolerance and generate problems where none need exist.

Gould, S. J. (1996). *The mismeasure of man* (2nd ed.). New York: Norton.

This is an update of a classic critique of supposedly scientific studies that attempt to rank all people on a linear scale of intrinsic and unalterable mental worth. The revision was prompted by what Gould refers to as the "latest cyclic episode of biodeterminism" represented by the publication of the widely discussed book, *The Bell Curve.*

Graves, J. L. (2001). *The emperor's new clothes: Biological theories of race at the millennium.* New Brunswick, NJ: Rutgers University Press.

Graves, a laboratory geneticist, aims to show that there is no biological basis for separation of human beings into races and that the idea of race is a relatively recent social and political construction. His grasp of science is solid and up-to-date.

Jacoby, R., & Glauberman, N. (Eds.). (1995). *The Bell Curve debate.* New York: Random House.

This collection of articles by a wide variety of authors (biologists, anthropologists, psychologists, mathematicians, essayists) critically examines the claims raised in *The Bell Curve.* For anyone who hopes to understand the race and intelligence debate, this book is a must.

Marks, J. (1995). *Human biodiversity: Genes, race, and history.* Hawthorne, NY: Aldine.

In this book, Marks shows how genetics has undermined the fundamental assumptions of racial taxonomy. In addition to its presentation of the nature of human biodiversity, the book also deals with the history of cultural attitudes toward race and diversity.

Smedley, A. (1998). *Race in North America: Origin and evolution of a worldview.* Boulder, CO: Westview.

Audrey Smedley traces the cultural invention of the idea of race and how this false biological category has been used to rationalize inequality in North America.

Wolpoff, M., & Caspari, R. (1997). *Race and human evolution: A fatal attraction.* New York: Simon & Schuster.

Along with providing an excellent history of the pseudoscience of racial difference, this book is a detailed but readable presentation of the multiregional hypothesis of modern human origins. Among its strengths is a discussion of the problem of defining what "anatomically modern" means.

Challenge Issue Among the primate species, humans are the only ones capable of inhabiting the entire globe. Over the course of human evolutionary history, both our cultural and biological capabilities have contributed to our adaptability as a species. But today it seems that we are approaching the limits of our biological and cultural adaptability. The actions of human societies have changed the world on such a massive scale and at such a rapid pace that we, as a species, are facing novel challenges. If birth and death rates continue at current rates, global population size of 6.8 billion will double in less than fifty years, placing untenable pressures on the world's natural resources. As water, food, and fuel become impossibly scarce, how will humans adapt? Will this lead to warfare and to an impossible distance between the have-nots and the have-lots? Here, women in Mehdiganj, India, hold water urns called *gharas* with the words "Water Is Life" written on them to protest the nearby Coca-Cola bottling plant. As the plant uses up the local water, nearby farmers lose their livelihood and way of life. In a competition for resources such as this, global corporations like Coca-Cola have advantages over local inhabitants. But ultimately, for all of us to win, strategies must be implemented to ensure a planet in balance.

Lok Samiti (translation: People's Committee) of Mehdiganj, India. Photograph by Nandial Master.

CHAPTER 13

Human Adaptation to a Changing World

Chapter Preview

How Have Humans Adapted Biologically to Naturally Occurring Environmental Stressors?

When faced with an environmental stressor, the human species has responded biologically at three distinct levels: genetic, developmental, and physiological. Some genetic adaptations are expressed in terms of phenotypic variation of continuous traits. Even when the genetic bases to these adaptations are not precisely known, scientists can study them through comparative measurement of the associated phenotypic variation. In addition, the long period of human growth and development allows the environment to interact with genes and shape the human body. Short-term changes or physiological adaptations occur in response to a particular environmental stimulus. Today, the rapid rates at which cultural processes change human environments pose new biological challenges with important consequences for our species.

How Are Humans Adapting in the Face of Globalization?

The interconnectedness of humans to one another and to the environment is critical for understanding human adaptation and disease. Today, because local human environments are shaped by global political and economic systems, these features directly impact the distribution of health and disease. Simply describing disease in terms of biological processes, such as those associated with infection or malnutrition, leaves out the ultimate reasons that some individuals are likelier than others to become sick. Examination of the impact of political processes on disease can reveal its social causes, bringing us closer to finding long-lasting cures.

What Is Evolutionary Medicine?

Evolutionary medicine, a branch of medical anthropology, uses the principles of evolutionary theory to contribute to human health. Basic to this approach is framing health issues in terms of the relationship between biological change and cultural change. Biological evolution shaped humans slowly over millions of years while cultural change occurs relatively quickly. The resulting dissociation between human biology and current cultural practices may lead to disease. Also, because culture shapes even scientific interpretations of the human body, evolutionary medicine acknowledges that some physiological phenomena regarded as symptoms of disease can also be understood as naturally evolving defense mechanisms.

Throughout millions of years of human evolutionary history, biology and culture interacted to make humans the species we are today. The archaeological record and contemporary human variation reveal that biology and culture continue to shape all areas of human experience, including health and disease. Indeed, an inside joke among anthropologists is that if you do not know the answer to an exam question about biology and culture, the answer is either "both" or "malaria." Our current understanding of malaria, as explained in previous chapters, illustrates how answering "malaria" is just like answering "both." Farming practices (culture) of the past created the perfect environment for the malarial parasite. The genetic response (biology) to this environmental change was increased frequencies of the sickle-cell allele.

To add a few more biocultural layers closer to the present, think about how contemporary global inequalities contribute to the continued devastating effects of malaria in poorer countries today. For example, if malaria were a problem plaguing North America or Europe today, would most citizens of the countries with rampant malaria still be without adequate treatment or cure? Similarly, public health initiatives for genetic counseling to reduce frequencies of sickle-cell anemia in the United States have been met with distrust by African Americans who have experienced racism rooted in a false message of biological difference.[1] Would the average Euramerican feel comfortable with genetic testing to eliminate a disease gene if he or she had experienced some of the wrongs underprivileged ethnic minorities have experienced in the name of science?

Consider, for example, the Tuskegee Syphilis Study, carried out by the U.S. Public Health Service in Macon County, Alabama, from 1932 to 1972. This study involved withholding syphilis medication from a group of poor African American men without their knowledge, so that the scientists could learn more about the biology of syphilis in the "Negro." These methods are now widely recognized as a moral breach that caused unnecessary pain and suffering to the men and their families. As a result of these unethical practices, the U.S. government changed its research policies involving the biological study of human subjects. In short, when examining a seemingly biological phenomenon such as disease, cultural factors must be considered at every level—from how that phenomenon is represented in each social group (reflected in this case in the false notion that the biology of syphilis would differ between people of different skin colors) to how biological research is conducted.

An integrated biocultural approach is one of the hallmarks of anthropology. In examples ranging from infant feeding and sleeping practices to the relationship between poverty and tuberculosis, biocultural connections have been emphasized throughout this book. In this chapter, we take a deeper look at this connection and examine some of the theoretical approaches biological and medical anthropologists use to examine the interaction of biology and culture.

[1] Tapper, M. (1999). *In the blood: Sickle-cell anemia and the politics of race*. Philadelphia: University of Pennsylvania Press.

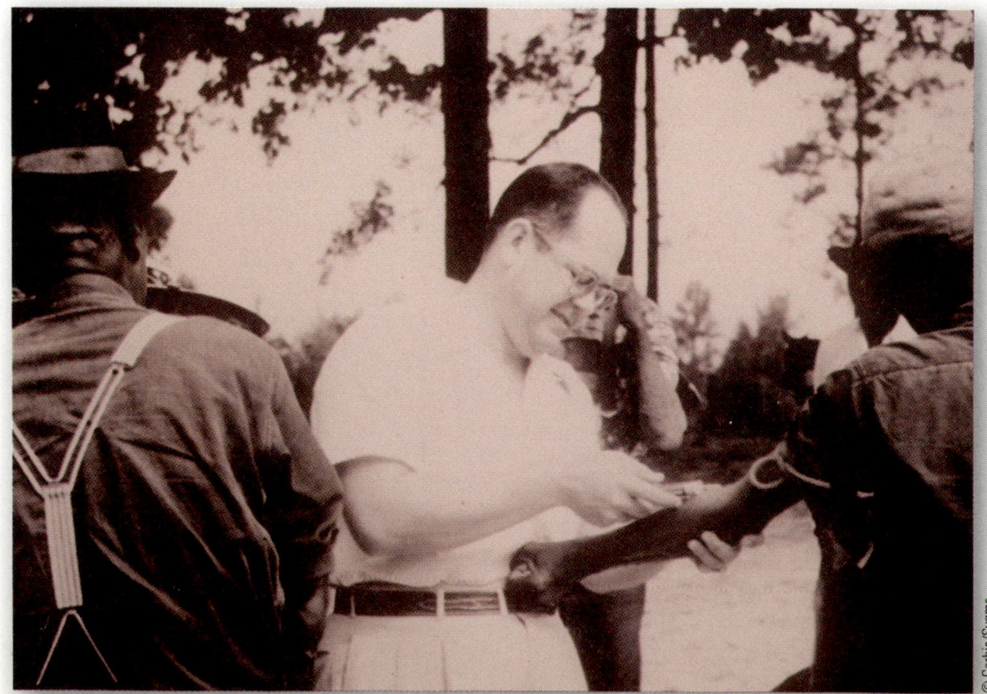

The Tuskegee Syphilis Study denied appropriate medical treatment to African American men in order to study the supposed differences in the biology of the disease in the "Negro." This human experimentation was not only false from a biological perspective but represents a moral breach in research conduct. Public outcry about this experiment led to regulations that protect all human subjects in biomedical research.

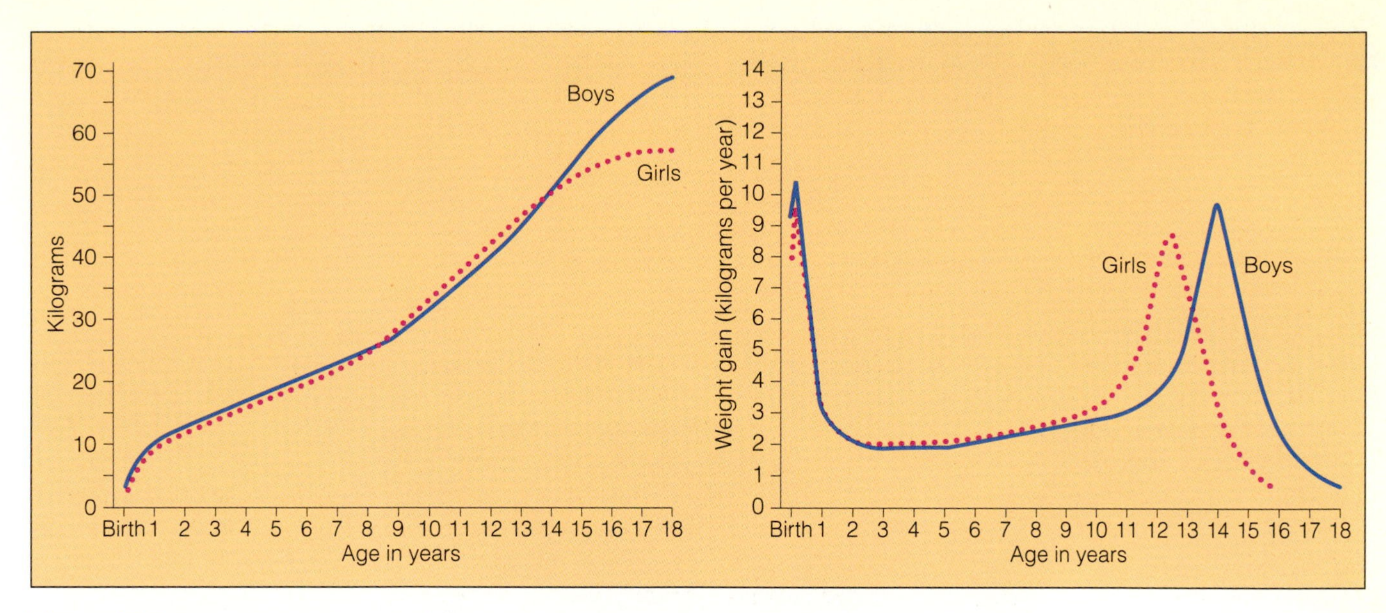

Figure 13.1 Franz Boas defined the features of the human growth curve. The graph on the left depicts distance, or the amount of growth attained over time, while the graph on the right shows the velocity, or rate of growth over time. These charts are widely used throughout the globe to determine the health status of children.

While humans possess a number of exquisite biological mechanisms through which they have adapted to the natural environment, these mechanisms can fall terribly short in today's globalizing world. Before turning to the challenges we face from the dramatic changes we have made in our environment today, we will explore the biological mechanisms humans have used over millennia to adapt to three naturally occurring environmental extremes: high altitude, cold, and heat.

Human Adaptation to Natural Environmental Stressors

Studies of human adaptation traditionally focus on the capacity of humans to adapt or adjust to their environment through biological and/or cultural mechanisms. Darwin's theory of natural selection accounts for discrete genetic changes built into the allele frequencies of populations, such as the various adaptations to malaria that we have examined. It also provides the mechanism for understanding that adaptations, evident in population variation of continuous phenotypic traits, depend upon multiple interacting genes. Even when the genetic bases to these adaptations (such as skin color or body build) are not precisely known, scientists can study them through comparative measurement of the associated phenotypic variation.

Humans possess two additional biological mechanisms through which they can adapt. The first of these, **developmental adaptation,** also produces permanent phenotypic variation as the environment shapes the expression of the genes each individual possesses. The extended period of growth and development characteristic of humans allows for a prolonged time period during which the environment can exert its effects on the developing organism.

The anthropological focus on growth and development has a long history dating back to the work of Franz Boas, the founder of American four-field anthropology. Boas is credited with discovering the features of the human growth curve (Figure 13.1). He demonstrated that the rate of human growth varies in typical patterns until adulthood, when physical growth ceases. Humans experience a period of very rapid growth after birth through infancy, followed by a gradually slower rate of growth during childhood. At adolescence, the rate of growth increases again during the adolescent growth spurt.

In addition to describing the long-term pattern of human growth, anthropologists have also demonstrated that within periods of growth, the actual growth process proceeds as a series of alternating bursts and relative quiet.[2]

[2] Lampl, M., Velhuis, J. D., & Johnson, M. L. (1992). Saltation and stasis: A model of human growth. *Science 258* (5083), 801–803.

developmental adaptation A permanent phenotypic variation derived from interaction between genes and the environment during the period of growth and development.

Anthropologist of Note

Peter Ellison

Reproductive biology and human health across cultures have been the focus of the work of biological anthropologist **Peter Ellison.** In the 1970s, Ellison first read Darwin's *Origin of Species* as a college student at St. John's College in Annapolis, Maryland. He found Darwin's text transformative and went to the University of Vermont to study biology; later he earned a doctorate in biological anthropology from Harvard, where he now runs a comprehensive program in reproductive ecology.

Ellison has pioneered techniques for hormonal analysis from saliva, and he uses this technique to monitor individuals' hormonal response to a variety of environmental stressors. This noninvasive technique has allowed Ellison to conduct hormonal studies throughout the world and to correlate hormonal levels with social events. People from long-term field sites in Congo, Poland, Japan, Nepal, and Paraguay have participated in this research, allowing Ellison to document the hormonal variation around biological events, such as egg implantation and breast-feeding, as well as cultural factors such as farm work or foraging.

He is especially interested in how behavior and social stimuli affect reproductive physiology. In Western societies, he has explored hormonal levels of males and females in response to stimuli, such as winning a championship or taking a stressful exam. He has also studied the relationship cancer development has to exercise and stress. In his recent book *On Fertile Ground,* Ellison illustrates how evolutionary forces have shaped human reproductive physiology into a system capable of precise responses to environmental stimuli.

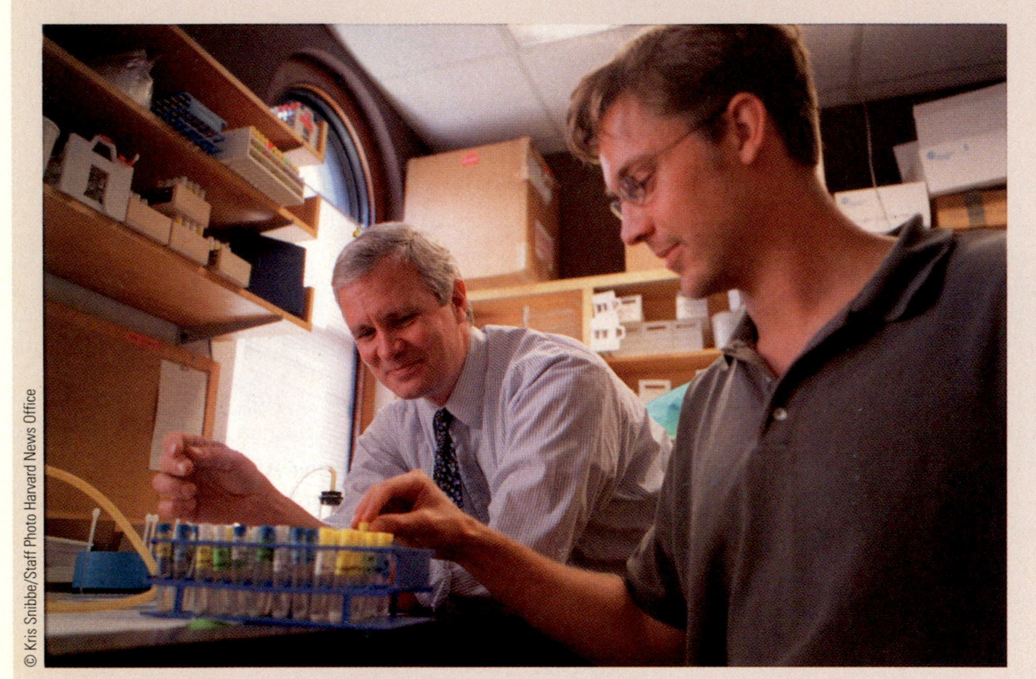

Peter Ellison (left) and Peter Gray discuss how male testosterone levels differ between married and single men and among men of different cultures.

When challenged by malnutrition, physical growth slows to permit immediate survival at the expense of height in adulthood. This adaptive mechanism may have negative consequences for subsequent generations as individuals who were malnourished as children have been shown to experience reduced reproductive success as adults.[3]

Boas also demonstrated differences in the growth of immigrant children in the United States compared to their parents. This work was the earliest documentation of the variable effects of different environments on the growth process. Presumably, immigrant children resemble their parents genetically; therefore, size differences between immigrant children and their parents could be attributed to the environment alone. This kind of difference, known as a **secular trend,** allows anthropologists to make inferences about environmental effects on growth and development.

For example, across the globe tremendous variation is seen in the age at menarche (first menstruation). Some of this variation can be attributed to genetically based population differences, while the remainder is due to environmental effects. The Bundi of New Guinea have the oldest average age (18) at menarche. An important theory accounting for the timing of sexual maturation ties age at menarche to the percentage of body fat possessed by growing individuals as a regulator of hormonal production. Hormones impact fertility into adulthood, but teasing apart the role of biology and culture with respect to hormones has proven to be complex. Take, for example, the case of androgen hormone levels, waist-to-hip ratio,

[3] Martorell, R. (1988). Body size, adaptation, and function. *GDP*, 335–347.

secular trend A physical difference among related people from distinct generations that allows anthropologists to make inferences about environmental effects on growth and development.

and fertility levels of women in high-powered careers. These women tend to have a more cylindrical shape, which could be because their bodies produce relatively more androgen than hourglass-shaped women. A higher androgen level, however, may be the reason for lower fertility among these women. High androgen levels may also represent a biological response to a specific work environment that ultimately impedes the fertility of women in high-powered careers.[4] The bottom line is that human hormonal systems are highly sensitive to a variety of environmental stimuli.

Over the past fifty years a secular trend of lower age at menarche has become evident in North America. Whether this secular trend is attributable to healthy or problematic environmental stimuli (such as childhood obesity or hormones in the environment) has yet to be determined. Biological anthropologist Peter Ellison works extensively on the connections between hormones and the environment—a subspecialty defined as reproductive ecology (see Anthropologist of Note).

While genetic and developmental adaptations are permanent parts of an adult's phenotype, **physiological adaptations,** short-term changes in response to a specific environmental stimulus, come and go. Along with cultural adaptations, these various biological mechanisms allow humans to be the only primate species to inhabit the entire globe. Over the course of our evolutionary history, most environmental stressors were climatic and geographic. Today, humans face a series of new environmental stressors of their own making.

Adaptation to High Altitude

High altitude differs from other natural environmental stressors because it is the least amenable to cultural adaptation. The major challenge of high altitude is the reduced availability of oxygen. Before the invention of oxygen masks and pressurized cabins in airplanes, there was no way to modify this environmental stressor.

When people speak of the air being "thinner" at high altitude, they are referring to the concentration (partial pressure) of oxygen available to the lungs, and so to the circulatory system. At high altitudes, the partial pressure of oxygen is sufficiently reduced so that most lowlanders experience severe oxygen deprivation (Figure 13.2).

Populations that have lived at high altitudes for generations, such as the Quechua Indians of the highlands of Peru and the Sherpa native to the Himalaya Mountains, possess a remarkable ability to tolerate oxygen deprivation, living and working at altitudes as high as 17,000 to 20,000 feet above sea level. Physiological adaptation to the lower partial pressure of oxygen in the environment has rendered their body tissues resistant to oxygen deprivation.

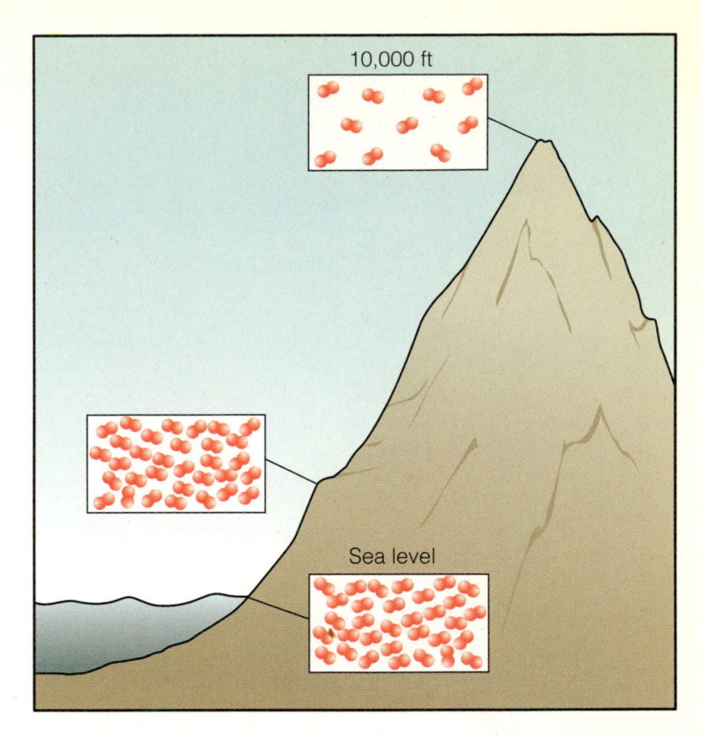

Figure 13.2 The amount of atmosphere above us determines the amount of pressure being exerted on oxygen molecules in the air. At sea level, the pressure of the atmosphere packs oxygen molecules more tightly together compared to the density of oxygen molecules at higher altitudes. This in turn impacts the ease at which oxygen can enter the lungs when we breathe.

Typical lowlanders can make both short- and long-term physiological adjustments to high altitude. In general, short-term changes help an individual avoid an immediate crisis, but the poor efficiency of these changes makes them difficult to sustain. Instead, long-term responses take over as the individual's physiological responses attain equilibrium with the environment. This process is known as **acclimatization.** Most lowlanders stepping off an airplane in Lima, Peru, will experience increased respiratory rate, cardiac output, and pulse rate. Their arteries will expand as blood pressure increases in order to get oxygen to the tissues. This kind of response cannot be maintained indefinitely. Instead, lowlanders acclimatize as their bodies begin to produce more red blood cells and hemoglobin in

physiological adaptation A short-term physiological change in response to a specific environmental stimulus. An immediate short-term response is not very efficient and is gradually replaced by a longer term response (see *acclimatization*).

acclimatization Long-term physiological adjustments made in order to attain an equilibrium with a specific environmental stimulus.

[4] Cashdan, E. (2008). Waist-to-hip ratio across cultures: Trade-offs between androgen- and estrogen-dependent traits. *Current Anthropology 49* (6).

© Reuters/Mike Segar/Landov

Observing that Kenyan runners, like Rita Jeptoo pictured here, have won most of the major marathon competitions over the past several decades, coaches have emulated the Kenyan approach. Adaptation to the hot, dry yet mountainous region leads to a long lean build (a product of the heat adaptation) and increased oxygen-carrying capacity. Although runners worldwide tend to be tall and lean, many athletes now train at high altitude so that when race day comes, their red blood cell count and hemoglobin levels allow them to carry more oxygen.

order to carry more oxygen. Because of differences in genetic makeup, individuals' physiological responses begin at varying altitudes.

Developmental adaptations are seen in individuals who spend their childhood period of growth and development at high altitude. Among the highland Quechua, for example, both the chest cavity and the right ventricle of the heart (which pushes blood to the lungs) are enlarged compared to lowland Quechua. This may have genetic underpinnings in that all Quechua experience a long period of growth and development compared to the average person in the United States.

Bergmann's rule The tendency for the bodies of mammals living in cold climates to be shorter and rounder than members of the same species living in warm climates.

Allen's rule The tendency for the bodies of mammals living in cold climates to have shorter appendages (arms and legs) than members of the same species living in warm climates.

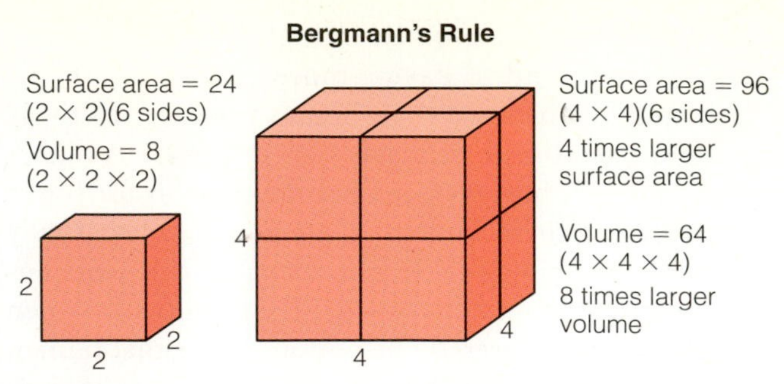

Figure 13.3 **Bergmann's rule refers to the observation that as overall body size increases, the amount of surface area increases less rapidly than the amount of volume. This accounts for the tendency for mammals living in cold climates to be more massive than members of the same species living in warmer climates. This allows for the conservation of heat in cold climates and its dissipation in warm climates.**

The process of growth and development begins with reproduction, and high altitude exerts considerable effects on this process. For populations who have not adapted to high altitude, successful reproduction is not possible without some cultural interventions. For example, take the case of fertility among Spanish colonialists in the city of Potosi high in the Andes founded in order to mine the "mountain of silver" that towers above the community. For the first fifty-four years of this city's existence no Spanish child was born who survived childhood. Indigenous populations did not have these problems. To ensure reproductive success, Spanish women began the cultural practice of retreating to lower altitude for their pregnancies and the first year of their children's lives.[5]

At high altitudes cold stress is also a problem. As described in the previous chapter, a stocky body and short limbs help individuals conserve heat while the opposite facilitates heat loss. These phenomena have been formalized into two rules named after the naturalists who made such observations in mammals. **Bergmann's rule** refers to the tendency for the bodies of mammals living in cold climates to be more massive than members of the same species living in warm climates (Figure 13.3). **Allen's rule** refers to the tendency of mammals living in cold climates to have shorter appendages (arms and legs) than members of the same species living in warm climates (Figure 13.4).

Adaptation to Cold

Cold stress can exist without high altitude, as it does in the Arctic. In addition to the previously mentioned patterns of body and limb shape and size, other cold responses are also evident in Arctic populations.

[5] Wiley, A. S. (2004). *An ecology of high-altitude infancy: A biocultural perspective.* Cambridge, England: Cambridge University Press.

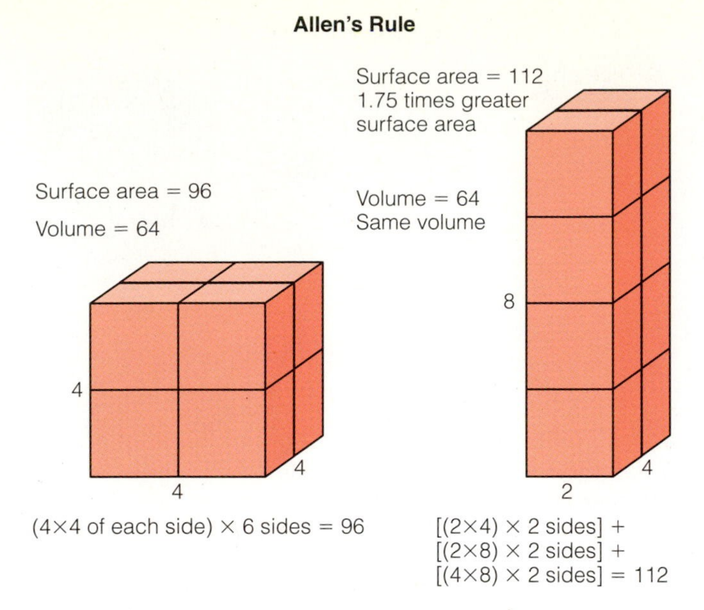

Figure 13.4 Allen's rule refers to the observation that in two bodies that have the same volume, the one that is long and lean rather than short and squat will have a greater surface area. This accounts for the tendency for mammals living in cold climates to have shorter appendages (arms and legs) than the same species living in warmer climates. Heat can be dissipated through long limbs or conserved through short ones.

In extreme cold, the limbs need enough heat to prevent frostbite, but giving up heat to the periphery takes it away from the body core. Humans balance this through a cyclic expansion and contraction of the blood vessels of their limbs called the **hunting response**. Blood vessels oscillate between closing down to prevent heat loss and opening up to warm the hands and feet. When first exposed to cold as gloves are taken off, blood vessels immediately constrict. Initial alternations between open (warm) and shut (cold) and the corresponding temperature of the skin range dramatically. But the oscillations become smaller and more rapid, allowing a hunter to maintain the warmth-derived manual dexterity required for tying knots or positioning arrows.

Eskimos (including the Inuit) also deal with cold through a high metabolic rate: the rate at which their bodies burn energy. This may result from a diet high in protein and fat (whale blubber is the common food). In addition, genetic factors likely also contribute to Eskimos' high metabolic rate.

One short-term physiological response to cold is shivering. Shivering generates heat for the body quickly but cannot be maintained for long periods of time. Instead, as an individual acclimatizes to the cold, adjustments to diet, activity pattern, metabolic rate, and the circulatory system must occur.

Adaptation to Heat

The human body's primary physiological mechanism for coping with extreme heat is sweating or perspiring. Sweating is a process through which water released from sweat glands gives up body heat as the sweat evaporates. Therefore, water availability is a crucial aspect of adaptation to heat. Without drinking enough water to replace that which is lost through sweating, exposure to heat can be fatal.

Though there is some individual and population variation, each human has roughly 2 million sweat glands. These glands are spread out over a greater surface area on tall, thin bodies, facilitating water evaporation and heat loss. Thus Bergmann's and Allen's rules also apply to heat adaptation. The more surface area a body has, the more surface for the sweat glands. In addition, because heat is produced by unit of volume, having a high surface area-to-volume ratio is beneficial for heat loss. A long, slender body is best for dissipating heat. In a hot and humid environment such as a rainforest, water evaporation is a major challenge. In this environment, human populations have adapted to minimize heat production through a reduction in overall size while keeping a slender, lean build.

Human-Made Stressors of a Changing World

Traditionally, culture has played an important role in modifying natural stressors such as heat and cold. Housing, diet, and clothing traditions can alter such stressors considerably. But in today's globalizing world, the effects of culture are much more complex. Rather than alleviating physical stressors through simple cultural adaptations such as housing, diet, and clothing, cultural processes are *adding* stressors such as pollution, global warming, and exhaustion of the world's natural resources.

People cannot biologically adapt to these human-made stressors because biological change simply cannot keep pace with the rapid rate at which humans are changing the earth. Until human cultures cooperate to collectively address these global challenges, unnatural stressors will inevitably lead to sickness and suffering. An integrated, holistic anthropological perspective has much to contribute to alleviating if not eliminating these human-made stressors.

hunting response A cyclic expansion and contraction of the blood vessels of the limbs that balances releasing enough heat to prevent frostbite while maintaining heat in the body core.

Visual Counterpoint

© Topham/The Image Works

© Ronnie Kaufman/Corbis

Shamans and biomedical doctors both rely upon manipulation of symbols to heal their patients. The physician's white coat is a powerful symbol of medical knowledge and authority that communicates to patients just as clearly as does the shaman's drum. Interestingly, medical schools in the United States are increasingly incorporating a "white coat" ceremony into medical education, conferring the power of the white coat onto new doctors.

The anthropological perspective holds that, beyond biology, cultural factors must be taken into account in any examination of human sickness and suffering. Human-made environments are shaped not only by local culture but by global political and economic systems. In short, anthropological perspectives are vital for successful adaptation to today's changing world.

The Development of Medical Anthropology

Medical anthropology, a specialization that cuts across all four fields of anthropology, contributes significantly to the understanding of sickness and suffering in the 21st century. Some of the earliest medical anthropologists were individuals trained as physicians and ethnographers who investigated the health beliefs and practices of peoples in "exotic" places while also providing them with Western medicine. Medical anthropologists during this early period translated local experiences of sickness into the scientific language of Western biomedicine. Following a reevaluation of this ethnocentric approach in the 1970s, medical anthropology emerged as a specialization that brings theoretical and applied approaches from cultural and biological anthropology to the study of human health and sickness.

Medical anthropologists study **medical systems,** or patterned sets of ideas and practices relating to illness. Medical systems are cultural systems, similar to any other social institution. Medical anthropologists examine healing traditions and practices cross-culturally and the qualities all medical systems have in common. For example, the terms used by French cultural anthropologist Claude Lévi-Strauss to describe the healing powers of *shamans* (the name for indigenous healers, originally from Siberia, and now applied to many traditional healers) also apply to medical practices in Europe and North America.[6] In both situations, the healer has access to a world of restricted

medical system A patterned set of ideas and practices relating to illness.

[6] Lévi-Strauss, C. (1963). The sorcerer and his magic. In *Structural anthropology.* New York: Basic.

knowledge (spiritual or scientific) from which the average community member is excluded.

Medical anthropologists also use scientific models drawn from biological anthropology, such as evolutionary theory, to understand and improve human health. Moreover, they have turned their attention to the connections between human health and political and economic forces, both globally and locally. Because global flows of people, germs, cures, guns, and pollution underlie the distribution of sickness and health in the world today, a broad anthropological understanding of the origins of sickness is vital for alleviating human suffering.

Science, Illness, and Disease

During the course of medical anthropology's development as a distinct specialty within anthropology, the theoretical relationship between biological and cultural knowledge was transformed. The earliest research on medical systems was carried out by physician-anthropologists—individuals trained as medical doctors and as anthropologists who participated in the international public health movement emerging early in the 20th century. While delivering the medical care developed in Europe and North America, these physician-anthropologists simultaneously studied the health beliefs and practices of the cultures they were sent to help. Local cultural categories about sickness were translated into Western biomedical terms.

Initially, these Western approaches were thought to be culture-free depictions of human biology and were therefore used as an interpretive framework for examining the medical beliefs and practices of other cultures. Implicit in this work was the notion that the Western approach, with its supposed objectivity, was superior. Fieldwork conducted by cultural anthropologists, however, has shown that medical categories, like other aspects of a people's unique worldview, reflect the value system of their particular culture. For example, the Subinam people of Mindinao, one of the large islands of the Philippines, give different names to fungal infections of the skin depending on whether the infection is openly visible or hidden under clothes.[7] The biomedical and scientific categorization of fungal infections refers only to genus and species of the fungus.

In the 1970s the place of biological and cultural knowledge in medical anthropology was dramatically reorganized. The admission of mainland China to the United Nations in 1971, and the subsequent improvement of diplomatic and other relationships between that communist country and Western powers, played a role in this theoretical shift.[8] Cultural exchanges revealed a professional medical system in the East rivaling that of Western biomedicine in its scientific basis and technical feats. For example, the practice of open heart surgery in China, using only acupuncture needles as an anesthetic, challenged the assumption of biomedical superiority within anthropological thought. At this time scholars proposed that biomedicine is a cultural system, just like the medical systems in other cultures, and that it, too, is worthy of anthropological study.[9]

To effectively compare medical systems and health cross-culturally, medical anthropologists have made a theoretical distinction between the terms *disease* and *illness*. **Disease** refers to a specific pathology: a physical or biological abnormality. **Illness** refers to the meanings and elaborations given to particular physical states. Disease and illness do not necessarily overlap. An individual may experience illness without having a disease, or a disease may occur in the absence of illness.

In cultures with scientific medical systems, a key component of the social process of illness involves delineating human suffering in terms of biology. At times this extends to labeling an illness as a disease even though the biology is poorly understood. Think about alcoholism in the United States, for example. A person who is thought of as a drunk, partier, barfly, or boozer tends not to get sympathy from the rest of society. By contrast, a person struggling with the disease alcoholism receives cultural help from physicians, support from groups such as Alcoholics Anonymous, and financial aid from health insurance covering medical treatment. It matters little that the biology of this disease is still poorly understood and that alcoholism is treated through social support rather than expert manipulation of biology. By calling alcoholism a disease, it becomes a socially sanctioned and recognized illness within the dominant medical system of the United States. See this chapter's Globalscape for an innovative method of reducing the stigma and improving the health education of ordinary people in daily life.

---

[7] Frake, C. (1961). The diagnosis of disease among the Subinam of Mindinao. *American Anthropologist 63,* 113–132.

[8] Young, A. (1981). The creation of medical knowledge: Some problems in interpretation. *Social Science and Medicine 17,* 1205–1211.

[9] Kleinman, A. (1976). Concepts and a model for the comparison of medical systems as cultural systems. *Social Science and Medicine 12* (2B), 85–95.

disease A specific pathology; a physical or biological abnormality.

illness The meanings and elaborations given to a particular physical state.

Globalscape

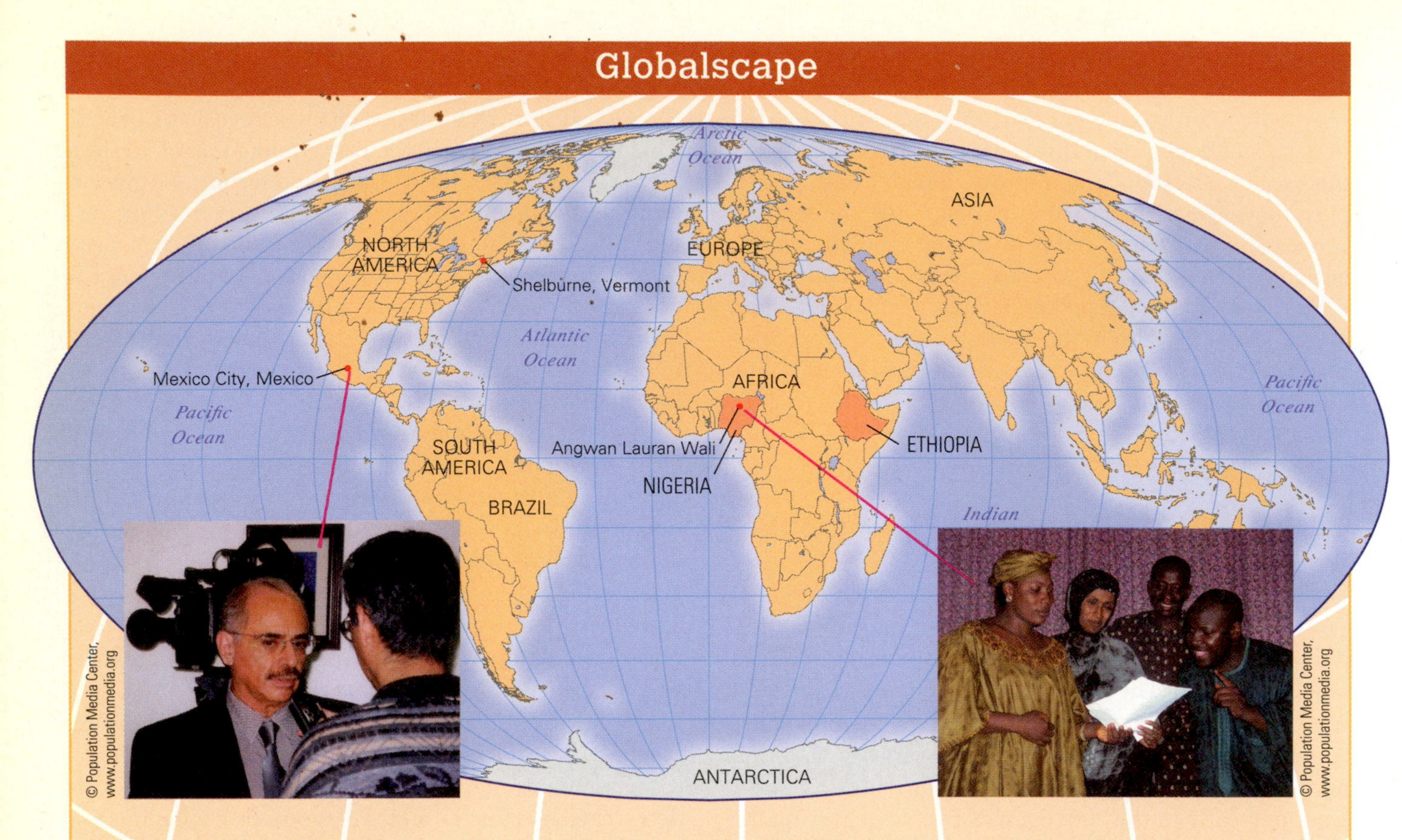

From Soap Opera to Clinic?
When Hajara Nasiru in Angwan Lauran Wali, Nigeria, listened to the radio soap opera *Gugar Goge* (*Tell It to Me Straight*), she learned something that changed her life. Created in Nigeria using a methodology developed originally in Mexico, the radio drama tells the story of 12-year-old Kande who is forced to marry a man more than twice her age. She soon becomes pregnant. After a prolonged labor, her baby dies, and Kande develops an obstetric fistula (a hole between either the rectum and vagina or the bladder and vagina) leading to incontinence, infection, and nerve damage. Kande's husband abandons her, but a neighbor brings her to the hospital in the nearby city of Zaira. After the fistula is repaired, Kande is able to return to her father's home in full health.

Like Kande, Hajara married young (at 15), and by the age of 25 she had experienced eight labors, lost five children, and developed a fistula with her last labor. After living with the debilitating discomfort for nine weeks, she invited her husband to listen to the soap opera too. *Gugar Goge* gave Hajara and her husband the information they needed. From the show, they learned that the fistula could be repaired and that Hajara need not suffer.

This radio drama is one of many created by the local branches of the Population Media Center (PMC), a U.S.-based international nongovernmental organization, headquartered in Shelburne, Vermont, that uses "entertainment-education for social change." PMC's methodology was developed by Mexican television producer Miguel Sabido, pictured above, whose *telenovelas* created dramatic social change across Mexico during the 1970s. For example, one program resulted in an eightfold increase in adult education and another led to a 50 percent increase in contraceptive use.

Population Media Center is bringing the Sabido methodology to the world, through work with local radio and television broadcasters, appropriate government ministries, and nongovernmental organizations. Their goal is to design and implement a comprehensive media strategy for addressing family and reproductive health issues. This collaborative process takes place locally with local constituents, identifying and addressing various health issues. These issues, once transformed into a radio drama such as *Gugar Goge,* are performed by professional local radio actors.

In addition to the individual success stories like Hajara's, success can be measured quantitatively at the country-wide level. For example, radio programs broadcast in Ethiopia in two different languages between 2002 and 2004 changed the reproductive health behavior in that region. The percentage of married women using contraception increased from 23 percent to 79 percent, and the birth rates for Ethiopia decreased by one whole child. Reduction in fertility is a vital part of the transition each society must make to achieve better overall health. In exit interviews at family planning clinics, a fourth of the 14,000 people surveyed cited the radio drama as their reason for coming.

Global Twister Would the Sabido method work in your community? Is it already at work? What health issues would you like to see embedded in soap operas?

© Reza; Webistan/Corbis

Building the Aswan Dam was a vital part of Egypt's modernization. Unfortunately, the dam has also caused problems. It increased the rates of schistosomiasis in the Nile River by creating a massive artificial lake upstream from the dam, thus providing the ideal environment for water snails. Downstream, the reduced flow of Nile waters caused a loss of silt and fertile soil previously brought into the Mediterranean Sea. The silt and soil had built up the Egyptian coastline. Thus, an unintended consequence of the dam has been soil erosion along the coast, allowing the sea to encroach upon people's homes.

Disease can also exist without illness. Schistosomiasis, infection with a kind of parasitic flatworm called a blood fluke, is an excellent example. Scientists have fully documented the life cycle of this parasite that alternates between water snail and human hosts. The adult worms live for many years inside human intestine or urinary tract. Human waste then spreads the mobile phase of the parasite to freshwater snails. Inside the snails, the parasite develops further to a second mobile phase of the flatworm life cycle, releasing thousands of tiny creatures into freshwater. If humans swim, wade, or do household chores such as laundry in this infested water, the parasite can bore its way through the skin, traveling to the intestine or bladder where the life cycle continues.

The idea of parasites boring through the skin and living permanently inside the bladder or intestine may well be revolting; ingesting poisons to rid the body of these parasites is an acceptable alternative for people at certain social and economic levels. But to people living where schistosomiasis is **endemic** (the public health term for a disease that is widespread in the population), this disease state is regarded as normal, and no treatment is sought. In other words schistosomiasis is not an illness. Individuals may know about expensive effective biomedical treatments, but given the likelihood of reinfection and the inaccessibility of the drugs, treatment with pharmaceutical agents is not the social norm. Over time, the forces of evolution generally lead to a tolerance between parasite and host so that infected individuals can live normal lives. So accustomed are some societies to this parasitic infection that the appearance of bloody

endemic The public health term for a disease that is widespread in a population.

urine at the time of adolescence (due to a high enough parasite load to cause this symptom) is regarded as a male version of menstruation.[10]

[10] Desowitz, R. S. (1987). *New Guinea tapeworms and Jewish grandmothers.* New York: Norton.

Cultural perspectives can thus be at odds with international public health goals that are based on a strictly Western biomedical understanding of disease. In the following Original Study, biological anthropologist Katherine Dettwyler shows that each perspective brings with it particular challenges and benefits.

Original Study

Dancing Skeletons: Life and Death in West Africa *by Katherine Dettwyler*

I stood in the doorway, gasping for air, propping my arms against the door frame on either side to hold me up. I sucked in great breaths of cool, clean air and rested my gaze on the distant hills, trying to compose myself. Ominous black thunderclouds were massed on the horizon and moved rapidly toward the schoolhouse. . . .

The morning had begun pleasantly enough, with villagers waiting patiently under the huge mango tree in the center of the village. But before long, the approaching storm made it clear that we would have to move inside. The only building large enough to hold the crowd was the one-room schoolhouse, located on the outskirts of the village. . . .

Inside the schoolhouse, chaos reigned. It was 20 degrees hotter, ten times as noisy, and as dark as gloom. What little light there was from outside entered through the open doorway and two small windows. The entire population of the village crowded onto the rows of benches, or stood three deep around the periphery of the room. Babies cried until their mothers pulled them around front where they could nurse, children chattered, and adults seized the opportunity to converse with friends and neighbors. It was one big party, a day off from working in the fields, with a cooling rain thrown in for good measure. I had to shout the measurements out to Heather, to make myself heard over the cacophony of noise. . . .

A middle-aged man dressed in a threadbare pair of Levis shoved a crying child forward. I knelt down to encourage the little boy to step up onto the scales and saw that his leg was wrapped in dirty bandages. He hesitated before lifting his foot and whimpered as he put his weight onto it. . . .

"What's the matter with his leg?" I asked his father.

"He hurt it in a bicycle accident," he said.

I rolled my eyes at Heather. "Let me guess. He was riding on the back fender, without wearing long pants, or shoes, and he got his leg tangled in the spokes." Moussa translated this aside into Bambara, and the man acknowledged that that was exactly what had happened. . . .

The festering wound encompassed the boy's ankle and part of his foot, deep enough to see bone at the bottom. His entire lower leg and foot were swollen and putrid; it was obvious that gangrene had a firm hold. . . .

"You have to take him to the hospital in Sikasso immediately," I explained.

"But we can't afford to," he balked.

"You can't afford not to," I cried in exasperation, turning to Moussa. "He doesn't understand," I said to Moussa. "Please explain to him that the boy is certain to die of gangrene poisoning if he doesn't get to a doctor right away. It may be too late already, but I don't think so. He may just lose his leg." Moussa's eyes widened with alarm. Even he hadn't realized how serious the boy's wounds were. As the father took in what Moussa was saying, his face crumpled. . . . Father and son were last seen leaving Merediela, the boy perched precariously on the back of a worn-out donkey hastily borrowed from a neighbor, while the father trotted alongside, shoulders drooping, urging the donkey to greater speed. . . .

Lunch back at the animatrice's compound provided another opportunity for learning about infant feeding beliefs in rural Mali, through criticism of my own child feeding practices. This time it was a chicken that had given its life for our culinary benefit. As we ate, without even thinking, I reached into the center pile of chicken meat and pulled pieces of meat off the bone. Then I placed them over in Miranda's section of the communal food bowl and encouraged her to eat.

"Why are you giving her chicken?" Bakary asked.

"I want to make sure she gets enough to eat," I replied. "She didn't eat very much porridge for breakfast, because she doesn't like millet."

"But she's just a child. She doesn't need good food. You've been working hard all morning, and she's just been lying around. Besides, if she wanted to eat, she would," he argued.

"It's true that I've been working hard," I admitted, "but she's still growing. Growing children need much more food, proportionately, than adults. And if I didn't encourage her to eat, she might not eat until we get back to Bamako."

Bakary shook his head. "In Dogo," he explained, "people believe that good food is wasted on children. They don't appreciate its good taste or the way it makes you feel. Also, they haven't worked hard to produce the food. They have their whole lives to work for good food for themselves, when they get older. Old people deserve the best food, because they're going to die soon." . . .

. . . In rural southern Mali, "good food" (which included all the high protein/high calorie foods) was reserved for elders and other adults. Children subsisted almost entirely on the carbohydrate staples, flavored with a little sauce. My actions in giving Miranda my share of the chicken were viewed as bizarre and misguided. I was wasting good food on a mere child, and depriving myself. . . .

In N'tenkoni the next morning, we were given use of the men's sacred meeting hut for our measuring session. A round hut about 20 feet in diameter, it had a huge center pole made from the trunk of a tree that held up the thatched roof. Because it had two large doorways, it was light and airy and would provide protection in the event of another thunder storm. . . .

There was some initial confusion caused by the fact that people outside couldn't really see what we were doing, and everyone tried to crowd in at once. That was straightened out by the chief, however, and measuring proceeded apace, men, women, children, men, women, children. One family at a time filed into the hut through one door, had their measurements taken, and departed through the other door. It was cool and pleasant inside the hut, in contrast to the hot sun and glare outside. Miranda sat off to one side, reading a book, glancing up from time to time, but generally bored by the whole thing.

"Mommy, look!" she exclaimed in mid-morning. "Isn't that an *angel*?" she asked, using our family's code word for a child with Down syndrome. Down syndrome children are often (though not always!) sweet, happy, and affectionate kids, and many families of children with Down syndrome consider them to be special gifts from God, and refer to them as angels. I turned and followed the direction of Miranda's gaze. A little girl had just entered the hut, part of a large family with many children. She had a small round head, and all the facial characteristics of a child with Down syndrome—Oriental-shaped eyes with epicanthic folds, a small flat nose, and small ears. There was no mistaking the diagnosis. Her name was Abi, and she was about 4 years old, the same age as Peter.

I knelt in front of the little girl. "Hi there, sweetie," I said in English. "Can I have a hug?" I held out my arms, and she willingly stepped forward and gave me a big hug.

I looked up at her mother. "Do you know that there's something 'different' about this child?" I asked, choosing my words carefully.

"Well, she doesn't talk," said her mother, hesitantly, looking at her husband for confirmation. "That's right," he said. "She's never said a word."

"But she's been healthy?" I asked.

"Yes," the father replied. "She's like the other kids, except she doesn't talk. She's always happy. She never cries. We know she can hear, because she does what we tell her to. Why are you so interested in her?"

"Because I know what's the matter with her. I have a son like this." Excitedly, I pulled a picture of Peter out of my bag and showed it to them. They couldn't see any resemblance, though. The difference in skin color swamped the similarities in facial features. But then, Malians think all white people look alike. And it's not true that all kids with Down syndrome look the same. They're "different in the same way," but they look most like their parents and siblings.

"Have you ever met any other children like this?" I inquired, bursting with curiosity about how rural Malian culture dealt with a condition as infrequent as Down syndrome. Children with Down syndrome are rare to begin with, occurring about once in every 700 births. In a community where thirty or forty children are born each year at the most, a child with Down syndrome might be born only once in twenty years. And many of them would not survive long enough for anyone to be able to tell that they were different. Physical defects along the midline of the body (heart, trachea, intestines) are common among kids with Down syndrome; without immediate surgery and neonatal intensive care, many would not survive. Such surgery is routine in American children's hospitals, but nonexistent in rural Mali. For the child without any major physical defects, there are still the perils of rural Malian life to survive: malaria, measles, diarrhea, diphtheria, and polio. Some, like Peter, have poor immune systems, making them even more susceptible to childhood diseases. The odds against finding a child with Down syndrome, surviving and healthy in a rural Malian village, are overwhelming.

Not surprisingly, the parents knew of no other children like Abi. They asked if I knew of any medicine that could cure her. "No," I explained, "this condition can't be cured. But she will learn to talk, just give her time. Talk to her a lot. Try to get her to repeat things you say. And give her lots of love and attention. It may take her longer to learn some things, but keep trying. In my country, some people say these children are special gifts from God." There was no way I could explain cells and chromosomes and nondisjunction to them, even with Moussa's help. And how, I thought to myself, would that have helped them anyway? They just accepted her as she was.

We chatted for a few more minutes, and I measured the whole family, including Abi, who was, of course, short for her age. I gave her one last hug and a balloon and sent her out the door after her siblings. . . .

I walked out of the hut, . . . trying to get my emotions under control. Finally I gave in, hugged my knees close to my chest, and sobbed. I cried for Abi—what a courageous heart she must have; just think what she might have achieved given all the modern infant stimulation programs available in the West. I cried for Peter—another courageous heart; just think of what he might achieve given the chance to live in a culture that simply accepted him, rather than stereotyping and pigeonholing him, constraining him because people didn't think he was capable of more. I cried for myself—not very courageous at all; my heart felt as though it would burst with longing for Peter, my own sweet angel.

There was clearly some truth to the old adage that ignorance is bliss. Maybe pregnant women in Mali had to worry about evil spirits lurking in the latrine at night, but they didn't spend their pregnancies worrying about chromosomal abnormalities, the moral implications of amniocentesis, or the heart-wrenching exercise of trying to evaluate handicaps, deciding which ones made life not worth living. Women in the United States might have the freedom to choose not to give birth to children with handicaps, but women in Mali had freedom from worrying about it. Children in the United States had the freedom to attend special programs to help them overcome their handicaps, but children in Mali had freedom from the biggest handicap of all—other people's prejudice.

I had cried myself dry. I splashed my face with cool water from the bucket inside the kitchen and returned to the task at hand.

Adapted from Dettwyler, K. A. (1994). Dancing skeletons: Life and death in West Africa *(Ch. 8). Prospect Heights, IL: Waveland.*

While diseases are generally described in biological terms as understood through scientific investigation, the medical anthropological framework admits that notions of disease are not universal. Each culture's medical system provides individuals with a "map" of how to think about themselves in sickness and health. All cultures define specific terms and mechanisms for thinking about, preventing, and managing illness. In this way, Western medical systems define whether a particular biological state such as malnutrition, Down syndrome, or schistosomiasis is recognized as an illness. Each cultural system delineates the choices and constraints available to individuals afflicted by particular disease states.

Evolutionary Medicine

Evolutionary medicine—an approach to human sickness and health combining principles of evolutionary theory and human evolutionary history—draws from both scientific medicine and anthropology. While it may seem at first to concentrate on human biological mechanisms, evolutionary medicine's emphasis is true to the biocultural integration that figures so prominently in anthropological approaches. In this approach, biological processes are given cultural meanings, and cultural practices are understood to affect human biology.

As with evolutionary theory in general, it is difficult to prove conclusively that specific ideas and theories from evolutionary medicine are indeed beneficial to human health. Instead, scientists work to amass a sufficient body of knowledge that supports their theories. Where appropriate, the theories can lead to hypotheses that can be tested experimentally. Frequently treatments derived from evolutionary medicine lead to alterations in cultural practices and to a return to a more natural state in terms of human biology. As described in the Biocultural Connection in Chapter 9, evolutionary medicine has contributed to current attitudes about the diseases of civilization.

The work of biological anthropologist James McKenna is an excellent example of evolutionary medicine. McKenna has suggested that the human infant, immature compared to some other mammals, has evolved to co-sleep with adults who provide breathing cues to the sleeping infant, protecting the child from sudden infant death syndrome (SIDS).[11] He uses cross-cultural data of sleeping patterns and rates of SIDS to support his claim.

[11] McKenna, J. (1999). Co-sleeping and SIDS. In W. Trevathan, E. O. Smith, & J. J. McKenna (Eds.), *Evolutionary medicine.* London: Oxford University Press.

evolutionary medicine An approach to human sickness and health combining principles of evolutionary theory and human evolutionary history.

McKenna conducted a series of experiments documenting differences between the brainwave patterns of mother–infant pairs who co-sleep compared to mother–infant pairs who sleep in separate rooms. These data fit McKenna's theory, challenging North America's predominant cultural practice of solitary sleeping. Further, McKenna shows how the cultural pattern of sleeping directly impacts infant feeding practices, demonstrating that co-sleeping and breastfeeding are mutually reinforcing behaviors.

Evolutionary medicine suggests that cultural practices in industrial and postindustrial societies are responsible for a variety of other biomedically defined diseases, ranging from psychological disorders to hepatitis (inflammation of the liver).

Symptoms as Defense Mechanisms

Scientists have documented that when faced with infection from a bacterium or virus, the human body mounts a series of physiological responses. For example, as a young individual learns his or her culture's medical system, the person might learn to recognize an illness as a cold or flu by responses of the body, such as fever, aches, runny nose, sore throat, vomiting, or diarrhea.

Think of how you may have learned about sickness as a young child. A caregiver or parent might have touched your forehead or neck with the back of the hand or lips to gauge your temperature. Maybe you had a thermometer placed under your arm or in your mouth to see if you had an elevated temperature or fever. (In the past, young children's temperatures were usually taken rectally in North America.) If any of these methods revealed a temperature above the value defined as normal, a medicine might have been given to lower the fever.

Evolutionary medicine proposes that many of the symptoms that biomedicine treats are themselves nature's treatments developed over millennia. Some of these symptoms, such as fever, perhaps should be tolerated rather than suppressed, so the body can heal itself. An elevated temperature is part of the human body's response to infectious particles, whereas eliminating the fever provides favorable temperatures for bacteria or viruses. Similarly within some physiological limits, vomiting, coughing, and diarrhea may be adaptive as they remove harmful substances and organisms from the body. In other words, the cultural prescription to lower a fever or suppress a cough might actually prolong the disease.

Evolutionary biologist Margie Profet proposes a particular benefit for the symptoms of nausea and vomiting during early pregnancy.[12] She suggests that many plants,

[12] Profet, M. (1991). The function of allergy: Immunological defense against toxins. *Quarterly Review of Biology 66* (1), 23–62; Profet, M. (1995). *Protecting your baby to be.* New York: Addison Wesley.

particularly those in the broccoli and cabbage family, naturally contain toxins developed through the plants' evolutionary process to prevent them from being eaten by animals. Profet suggests that eating these plants during the first weeks of pregnancy, when the developing embryo is rapidly creating new cells through mitosis and differentiating into specific body parts, makes the embryo vulnerable to mutation. Therefore, a heightened sense of smell and lowered nausea threshold serve as natural defenses for the body. Pregnant women tend to avoid these foods, thus protecting the developing embryo.

Evolution and Infectious Disease

Understanding infectious disease is all the more important in a globalizing world where people, viruses, and bacteria cross national boundaries freely. Evolutionary medicine provides key insights with regard to infectious disease.

First, if infectious disease is viewed as competition between microorganisms and humans—as it is in biomedicine where patients and doctors "fight" infectious disease—microorganisms possess one very clear advantage. Viruses, bacteria, fungi, and parasites all have very short life cycles compared to humans. Therefore, when competing on an evolutionary level, they will continue to pose new threats to health, because any new genetic variants appearing through a random mutation will quickly become incorporated in the population's genome. This notion is of particular importance with regard to the use of antibiotics to fight infectious disease.

While antibiotics do kill many bacteria, increasingly resistant strains are becoming more common. "Resistant strains" refers to genetic variants of a specific bacterium that are not killed by antibiotics. If a resistant strain appears in an infected individual who is being treated with antibiotics, the removal of all the nonresistant strains essentially opens up an entire ecological niche for that resistant strain inside the infected human. Here, without competition from the original form of the bacterium wiped out by the antibiotic, this mutant can proliferate easily and then spread to other individuals. The practice of taking antibiotics artificially alters the environment inside the human body.

In order to avoid the development of resistant strains, complex lengthy treatment regimes, often of multiple drugs, must be followed exactly. These expensive treatments are cost-prohibitive in many parts of the world. The unfortunate result is not only increased human suffering but also the possibility of creating environments for the development of resistant strains as individuals receive partial treatments.

Another problem is that although individuals seek treatment within their own country's health care system, infectious microbes do not observe these same national boundaries. To eradicate or control any infectious process, the world has to be considered in its entirety.

Medical anthropologist Emily Martin has shown that scientific depictions of infectious disease draw upon military imagery common to the culture of the United States. Biomedical treatments involve taking antibiotics to kill "invading" organisms. An evolutionary perspective suggests that the quick life cycle of microorganisms makes this "battle" a losing proposition for humans.

On a positive note, treatments can also be allowed to flow freely. For example, Brazil's HIV/AIDS program is internationally recognized as a model for prevention, education, and treatment for several reasons. Through a national policy of developing generic alternative antiretroviral agents and negotiating for reduced prices on patented agents, in 1996 Brazil became the first country to guarantee free antiretroviral access to all its citizens. At the same time, Brazilian public health officials developed counseling and prevention programs in collaboration with community groups and religious organizations. Their AIDS program's success is in part due to the candid public education on disease transmission targeted at heterosexual women and young people, who are now the fastest-growing groups affected by HIV.

In 2004, Brazil continued its innovations with the South to South Initiative providing assistance to the HIV and AIDS programs in the Portuguese-speaking African countries of Mozambique and Angola. The Brazilian approach of providing free antiretroviral agents and collaborating with civil and religious groups to develop appropriate counseling, education, and prevention programs has been replicated directly in these African countries.[13]

---

[13] D'Adesky, A.-C. (2004). *Moving mountains: The race to treat global AIDS.* New York: Verso.

Another method for fighting infectious disease is the development of vaccines. These stimulate the body to mount its own immune response from the vaccine that will protect the individual from the real infectious agent if the individual is exposed at a later date. Vaccinations have been responsible for major global reduction of disease, as in the case of smallpox. Historical records show that people in India, China, Europe, and the colonizers of North America practiced a form of vaccination for this deadly disease through what were known as "pox parties."

Recently this tradition has been revived by parents who choose to deliberately expose their children to chicken pox rather than opt for the vaccine. Despite numerous medical reports to the contrary, some parents believe that vaccinations may lead to other health problems. Although the vaccine to eradicate smallpox—a disease that killed 300 million people in the 20th century alone—is clearly beneficial, it is harder to convince parents of the need for vaccines for less fatal, although still serious, childhood diseases.

The vaccine for chicken pox provides an interesting case in point. Before this vaccination became standard care in the United States, most American children experienced chicken pox as a rite of childhood. Parents watched their children become covered with ugly poxes that then disappeared. This experience modeled a pattern of intense sickness followed by full recovery, which, in and of itself, can provide some comfort. Only very rarely is chicken pox fatal.

Infectious disease and the human efforts to stop it always occur in the context of the human-made environment. Humans have been altering their external environments with increasing impact since the Neolithic revolution, resulting in an increase in a variety of infectious diseases. In this regard, evolutionary medicine shares much with political ecology—a discipline closely related to medical anthropology and described below.

The Political Ecology of Disease

An ecological perspective considers organisms in the context of their environment. Because human environments are shaped not only by local culture but by global political and economic systems, these features must all be included in a comprehensive examination of human disease. Simply describing disease in terms of biological processes leaves out the deeper, ultimate reasons that some individuals are likelier than others to become sick. A strictly biological approach also leaves out differences in the resources available to individuals, communities, and states to cope with disease and illness. Prion diseases provide excellent illustrations of the impact of local and global factors on the social distribution of disease.

prion An infectious protein lacking any genetic material but capable of causing the reorganization and destruction of other proteins.

Prion Diseases

In 1997 physician-scientist Stanley Prusiner won the Nobel Prize in medicine for his discovery of an entirely new disease agent called a **prion**—a protein lacking any genetic material that behaves as an infectious particle. Prions are a kind of protein that can cause the reorganization and destruction of other proteins, which may result in neurodegenerative disease as brain tissue and the nervous system are destroyed.

This discovery provided a mechanism for understanding mad cow disease, a serious problem in postindustrial societies. But knowing the biological mechanism alone is not enough to truly grasp how this disease spreads. The beef supply of several countries in Europe and North America became tainted by prions introduced through the cultural practice of grinding up sheep carcasses and adding them to the commercial feed of beef cattle. This practice began before prions were discovered, but postindustrial farmers were aware that these sheep had a condition known as *scrapie;* they just did not know that this condition was infectious. Through the wide distribution of tainted feed, prion disease spread from sheep to cows and then to humans who consumed tainted beef. Today countries without confirmed mad cow disease ban the importation of beef from neighboring countries with documented prion disease. Such bans have a tremendous negative impact on the local economies.

Mad cow disease is not new. This type of disease was a major concern for the Fore (pronounced "foray") people of Papua New Guinea during the middle of the 20th century. Kuru is the name given in the local language to the prion disease that claimed the lives of great numbers of women and children in Fore communities. To deal with the devastation, the Fore welcomed assistance provided by an international team of health workers led by a physician from the United States, Carleton Gajdusek. As with mad cow disease, local and global cultural processes affected both the transmission of kuru and the measures taken to prevent its spread long before prion biology was understood.

Kuru did not fit neatly into any known biomedical categories. Because the disease seemed to be limited to families of related individuals, cultural anthropologists Shirley Lindenbaum from Australia and Robert Glasse from the United States, who were doing fieldwork in the region, were recruited to contribute documentation of Fore kinship relationships. It was hoped this knowledge would reveal an underlying genetic mechanism for the disease.[14]

When kinship records did not reveal a pattern of genetic transmission, the medical team turned instead to the notion of infectious disease, even though the slow progression of kuru seemed to weigh against an infectious cause. Material derived from infected individuals was injected into chimpanzees (see Chapter 3 for a discussion of the ethics of this practice) to see whether they developed the disease. After 18 months, injected chimpanzees succumbed to the classic symptoms of kuru, and their autopsied brains indicated the same pathologies as seen in humans with kuru. At this point, the disease was defined as infectious (garnering Gajdusek a Nobel Prize). Because prions had not yet been discovered, scientists defined this infectious agent as an unidentified "slow virus."

Scientists knew that kuru is infectious, but they still did not understand why some individuals were infected but not others. For the explanation, a wider anthropological perspective is required, as Lindenbaum explains in her book *Kuru Sorcery.* Lindenbaum demonstrates that kuru is related to cultural practices regarding the bodies of individuals who have died from kuru and the way global factors impacted local practices.

Culturally, Fore women are responsible for preparing the bodies of their loved ones for the afterlife. This practice alone put women at a greater risk for exposure to kuru. Lindenbaum also discovered that women and children were at risk due to a combination of these local practices with global economic forces. In Fore society, men were responsible for raising pigs and slaughtering and distributing meat. The middle of the 20th century was a time of hardship and transition for the Fore people. Colonial rule by Australia had changed the fabric of society, threatening traditional subsistence patterns and resulting in a shortage of protein in the form of pigs. The limited amount of pig meat available was distributed by men preferentially to other men.

Fore women told Lindenbaum that, as a practical solution to their hunger, they consumed their own dead. Fore women preferred eating their loved ones who had died in a relatively "meaty" state from kuru compared to eating individuals wasted away from malnutrition. This temporary practice was abandoned as the Fore subsistence pattern recovered, and the Fore learned of the biological mechanisms of kuru transmission.

[14] Lindenbaum, S. (1978). *Kuru sorcery: Disease and danger in the New Guinea highlands.* New York: McGraw-Hill.

Medical Pluralism

The Fore medical system had its own explanations for the causes of kuru, primarily involving sorcery, that were compatible with biomedical explanations for the mechanisms of disease. Such blending of medical systems is common throughout the globe today.

Medical pluralism refers to the presence of multiple medical systems, each with its own practices and beliefs in a society. As illustrated with the Fore, individuals generally can reconcile conflicting medical systems and incorporate diverse elements from a variety of systems to ease their suffering. While Western biomedicine has contributed some spectacular treatments and cures for a variety of diseases, many of its practices and values are singularly associated with the Euramerican societies in which they developed. The international public health movement attempts to bring many of the successes of biomedicine based on the scientific understanding of human biology to the rest of the world. But to do so successfully, local cultural practices and beliefs must be taken into account.

Both mad cow disease and kuru illustrate that no sickness in the 21st century can be considered in isolation; an understanding of these diseases must take into account political and economic influences as well as how these forces affect the ability to treat or cure.

Globalization, Health, and Structural Violence

One global generalization that can be made with regard to most diseases is that wealth means health. The World Health Organization defines health as "a complete state of physical, psychological, and social well-being, not the mere absence of disease or infirmity."[15] While the international public health community works to improve health throughout the globe, heavily armed states,

[15] World Health Organization. http://www.who.int/about/definition/en.

medical pluralism The presence of multiple medical systems, each with its own practices and beliefs in a society.

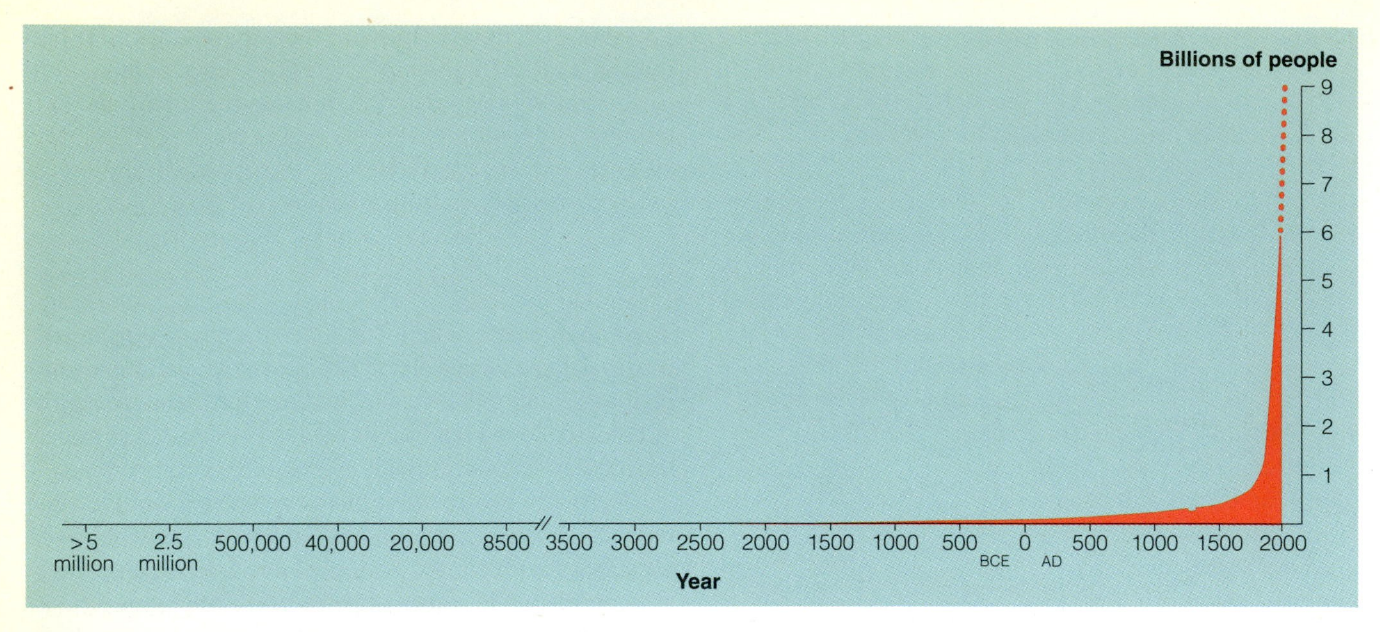

Figure 13.5 Human population size grew at a relatively steady pace until the industrial revolution, when a geometric pattern of growth began. Since that time, human population size has been doubling at an alarming rate. The earth's natural resources will not be able to accommodate ever-increasing human population if the rates of consumption seen in Western industrialized nations, particularly in the United States, persist.

megacorporations, and very wealthy elites are using their powers to rearrange the emerging world system to their own competitive advantage. When such power relationships undermine the well-being of others, we may speak of **structural violence**—physical and/or psychological harm (including repression, environmental destruction, poverty, hunger, illness, and premature death) caused by exploitative and unjust social, political, and economic systems.

As we saw in Chapter 11, **health disparities,** or differences in the health status between the wealthy elite and the poor in stratified societies, are nothing new. Globalization has expanded and intensified structural violence, leading to enormous health disparities among individuals, communities, and even states. Medical anthropologists have examined how structural violence leads not only to unequal access to treatment but also to the likelihood of contracting disease through exposure to malnutrition, crowded conditions, and toxins.

Population Size and Health

At the time of the speciation events of early human evolutionary history, population size was relatively small compared to what it is today. With human population size at over 6.8 billion and still climbing, we are reaching the carrying capacity of the earth (Figure 13.5). India and China alone have well over 1 billion inhabitants each. And population growth is still rapid in South Asia, which is expected to become even more densely populated in the early 21st century. Population growth threatens to increase the scale of hunger, poverty, and pollution—and the many problems associated with these issues.

While human population growth must be curtailed, government-sponsored programs to do so have posed new health and ethical problems. For example, China's much-publicized "one child" policy, introduced in 1979 to control its soaring population growth, led to sharp upward trends in sex-selective abortions, female infanticide, and female infant mortality due to abandonment and neglect. The resulting imbalance in China's male and female populations is referred to as the "missing girl gap." One study reports that China's male-to-female sex ratio has become so distorted that 111 million men will not be able to find a wife. Government regulations softened slightly in the 1990s, when it became legal for rural couples to have a second child if their first was a girl—and if they paid a fee. Millions of rural couples have circumvented regulations by not registering births—resulting in millions of young people who do not "officially" exist.[16]

structural violence Physical and/or psychological harm (including repression, environmental destruction, poverty, hunger, illness, and premature death) caused by exploitative and unjust social, political, and economic systems.

health disparity A difference in the health status between the wealthy elite and the poor in stratified societies.

[16] Bongaarts, J. (1998). Demographic consequences of declining fertility. *Science 282,* 419.

Poverty and Health

With an ever-expanding population, a shocking number of people worldwide face hunger on a regular basis, leading to a variety of health problems including premature death. It is no accident that poor countries and poorer citizens of wealthier countries are disproportionately malnourished. All told, about 1 billion people in the world are undernourished. Some 6 million children age 5 and under die every year due to hunger, and those who survive often suffer from physical and mental impairment.[17]

In wealthy industrialized countries a particular version of malnourishment—obesity—is becoming increasingly common. Obesity primarily affects poor working-class people who are no longer physically active at their work (because of increasing automation) and who cannot afford more expensive, healthy foods to stay fit. High sugar and fat content of mass-marketed foods and "super size" portions underlie this dramatic change. The risk of diabetes, heart disease, and stroke is also greatly increased in the presence of obesity. High rates of obesity among U.S. youth have led public health officials to project that the current generation of adults may be the first generation to outlive their children due to a cause other than war.

Environmental Impact and Health

Just as the disenfranchised experience a disproportionate share of famine and associated death, this same population also must contend with the lion's share of contaminants and pollution. The industries of wealthier communities and states create the majority of the pollutants that are changing the earth today. Yet the impact of these pollutants is often felt most keenly by those who do not have the resources to consume, and thus pollute, at high rates.

For example, increasing emissions of greenhouse gases, as a consequence of deforestation and human industrial activity, have resulted in global warming. As the carbon emissions from the combustion of petroleum in wealthy nations warm the climate globally, the impact will be most severe for individuals in the tropics because these populations must contend with increases in deadly infectious diseases such as malaria. Annually it is estimated that 1.5 million to 2.7 million deaths worldwide are caused by malaria, making it the fifth largest infectious killer in the world. Children account for about 1 million of these deaths, and more than 80 percent of these cases are in tropical Africa. It is possible that over the next century, an average temperature increase of 3 degrees Celsius could result in 50 million to 80 million new malaria cases per year.[18]

Experts predict that global warming will lead to an expansion of the geographic ranges of tropical diseases and to an increase the incidence of respiratory diseases due to additional smog caused by warmer temperatures. As witnessed in the 15,000 deaths attributed to the 2003 heat wave in France, global warming may also increase the number of fatalities.[19] To solve the problem of global

[17] Hunger Project 2003; Swaminathan, M. S. (2000). Science in response to basic human needs. *Science 287,* 425; *Historical atlas of the twentieth century.* http://users.erols.com/mwhite28/20centry.htm.

[18] Stone, R. (1995). If the mercury soars, so may health hazards. *Science 267,* 958.

[19] World Meteorological Organization, quoted in "Increasing heat waves and other health hazards." greenpeaceusa.org/climate/index.fpl/7096/article/907.html.

Visual Counterpoint

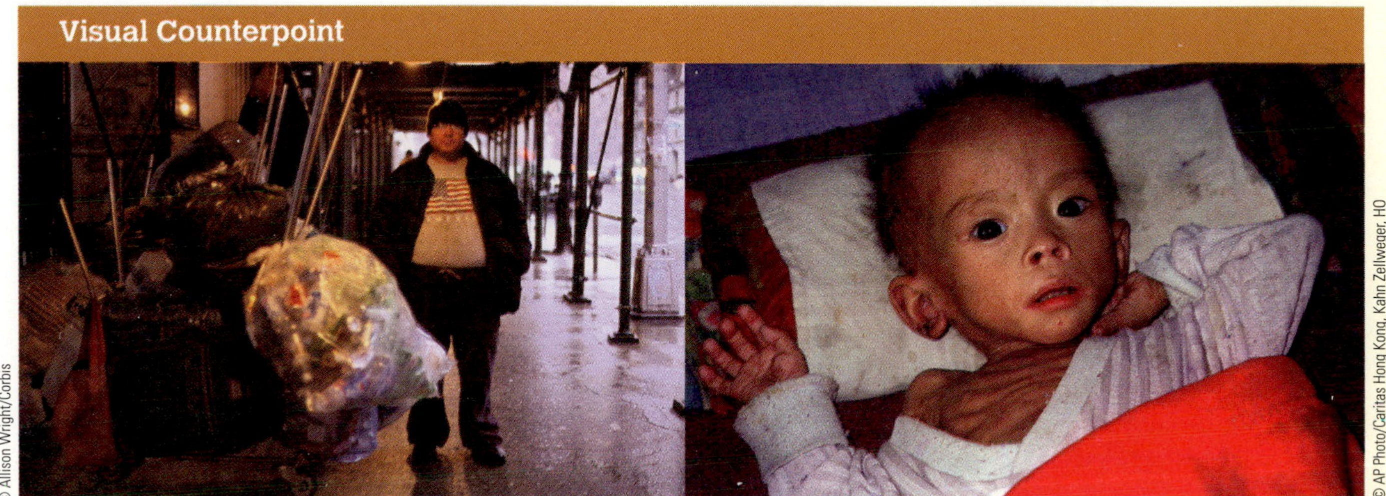

The scientific definition of malnutrition includes undernutrition as well as excess consumption of foods, healthy or otherwise. Malnutrition leading to obesity is increasingly common among poor working-class people in industrialized countries. Starvation is more common in poor countries or in those that have been beset by years of political turmoil, as is evident in this emaciated North Korean child.

warming, our species needs to evolve new cultural tools in order to anticipate environmental consequences that eventuate over decades. Regulating human population size globally and using the earth's resources more conservatively are necessary to ensure our survival.

Global warming is merely one of a host of problems today that will ultimately have an impact on human gene pools. In view of the consequences for human biology of such seemingly benign innovations as dairying or farming (as discussed in Chapter 10), we may wonder about many recent practices—for example, the effects of increased exposure to radiation from use of x-rays, nuclear accidents, production of radioactive waste, ozone depletion (which increases human exposure to solar radiation), and the like.

Again the impact is often most severe for those who have not generated the pollutants in the first place. Take, for example, the flow of industrial and agricultural chemicals via air and water currents to Arctic regions. Icy temperatures allow these toxins to enter the food chain. As a result toxins generated in temperate climates end up in the bodies (and breast milk) of Arctic peoples who do not produce the toxins but who eat primarily foods that they hunt and fish.

In addition to exposure to radiation, humans also face increased exposure to other known mutagenic agents, including a wide variety of chemicals, such as pesticides. Despite repeated assurances about their safety, there have been tens of thousands of cases of poisonings in the United States alone and thousands of cases of cancer related to the manufacture and use of pesticides. The impact may be greater in so-called underdeveloped countries, where substances banned in the United States are routinely used.

Pesticides are responsible for millions of birds being killed each year (many of which would otherwise be happily gobbling down bugs and other pests), serious fish kills, and decimation of honey bees (bees are needed for the efficient pollination of many crops). In all, pesticides alone (not including other agricultural chemicals) are responsible for billions of dollars of environmental and public health damage in the United States each year.[20] Anthropologists are documenting the effects on individuals, as described in the Biocultural Connection feature.

The shipping of pollutant waste between countries represents an example of structural violence. Individuals in the government or business sector of either nation may profit from these arrangements, creating another obstacle to addressing the problem. Similar issues may arise within countries, when authorities attempt to coerce ethnic minorities to accept disposal of toxic waste on their lands.

Hormone-disrupting chemicals are of particular concern because they interfere with the reproductive process. For example, in 1938 a synthetic estrogen known as DES (diethylstilbestrol) was developed and subsequently prescribed for a variety of ailments ranging from acne to prostate cancer. Moreover, DES was routinely added to animal feed. It was not until 1971, however, that researchers realized that DES causes vaginal cancer in young women. Subsequent studies have shown that DES causes problems with the male reproductive system and can produce deformities of the female reproductive tract of individuals exposed to DES in utero. DES mimics the natural hormone, binding with appropriate receptors in and on cells, and thereby turns on biological activity associated with the hormone.[21]

DES is not alone in its effects: At least fifty-one chemicals—many of them in common use—are now known to disrupt hormones, and even this could be the tip of the iceberg. Some of these chemicals mimic hormones in the manner of DES, whereas others interfere with other parts of the endocrine system, such as thyroid and testosterone metabolism. Included are such supposedly benign and inert substances as plastics widely used in laboratories and chemicals added to polystyrene and polyvinyl chloride (PVCs) to make them more stable and less breakable. These plastics are widely used in plumbing, food processing, and food packaging.

Hormone-disrupting chemicals are also found in many detergents and personal care products, contraceptive creams, the giant jugs used to bottle drinking water, and plastic linings in cans. About 85 percent of food cans in the United States are so lined. Similarly, the harmful health consequences of the release of compounds from plastic wrap and plastic containers during microwaving are now known, though for many years using plastic in the microwave was an acceptable cultural practice. Similarly, bisphenol-A (BPA)—a chemical widely used in water bottles and baby bottles (hard plastics)—has recently been associated with higher rates of chronic diseases such as heart disease and diabetes, and it has been shown to disrupt a variety of other reproductive and metabolic processes. Infants and fetuses are at the greatest risk from exposure to BPA.

While there is consensus in the scientific community and governments are starting to take action (the Canadian government declared BPA a toxic compound), removing this compound from the food industry may be easier that ridding the environment of this contaminant. For decades billions of pounds of BPA have been produced each year, and in turn it has been dumped into landfills and bodies of water. As with the Neolithic revolution and the development of civilization, each invention creates new challenges for humans.

The implications of all these developments are sobering. We know that pathologies result from extremely low levels of exposure to harmful chemicals. Yet, besides those used domestically, the United States exports millions of pounds of these chemicals to the rest of the world.[22]

---

[20] Pimentel, D. (1991). Response. *Science 252*, 358.

[21] Colburn, T., Dumanoski, D., & Myers, J. P. (1996). Hormonal sabotage. *Natural History 3*, 45–46.

[22] Ibid., 45–46.

Biocultural Connection

Picturing Pesticides

The toxic effects of pesticides have long been known. After all, these compounds are designed to kill bugs. However, documenting the toxic effects of pesticides on humans has been more difficult, as they are subtle—sometimes taking years to become apparent.

Anthropologist Elizabeth Guillette, working in a Yaqui Indian community in Mexico, combined ethnographic observation, biological monitoring of pesticide levels in the blood, and neurobehavioral testing to document the impairment of child development by pesticides.[a] Working with colleagues from the Technological Institute of Sonora in Obregón, Mexico, Guillette compared children and families from two Yaqui communities: one living in farm valleys who were exposed to large doses of pesticides and one living in ranching villages in the foothills nearby.

Guillette documented the frequency of pesticide use among the farming Yaqui to be forty-five times per crop cycle with two crop cycles per year. In the farming valleys she also noted that families tended to use household bug sprays on a daily basis, thus increasing their exposure to toxic pesticides. In the foothill ranches, she found that the only pesticides that the Yaqui were exposed to consisted of DDT sprayed by the government to control malaria. In these communities, indoor bugs were swatted or tolerated.

Pesticide exposure was linked to child health and development through two sets of measures. First, levels of pesticides in the blood of valley children at birth and throughout their childhood were examined and found to be far higher than in the children from the foothills. Further, the presence of pesticides in breast milk of nursing mothers from the valley farms was also documented. Second, children from the two communities were asked to perform a variety of normal childhood activities, such as jumping, memory games, playing catch, and drawing pictures.

The children exposed to high doses of pesticides had significantly less stamina, eye–hand coordination, large motor coordination, and drawing ability compared to the Yaqui children from the foothills. These children exhibited no overt symptoms of pesticide poisoning—instead exhibiting delays and impairment in their neurobehavioral abilities that may be irreversible.

Though Guillette's study was thoroughly embedded in one ethnographic community, she emphasizes that the exposure to pesticides among the Yaqui farmers is typical of agricultural communities globally and has significance for changing human practices regarding the use of pesticides everywhere.

BIOCULTURAL QUESTION

Given the documented developmental damage these pesticides have inflicted on children, should their sale and use be regulated globally? Are there potentially damaging toxins in use in your community?

---

[a] Guillette, E. A., et al. (1998, June). An anthropological approach to the evaluation of preschool children exposed to pesticides in Mexico. *Environmental Health Perspectives 106,* 347.

Foothills | **Valley**

60-month-old female | 71-month-old male | 71-month-old female | 71-month-old male

Compare the drawings typically done by Yaqui children heavily exposed to pesticides (valley) to those made by Yaqui children living in nearby areas who were relatively unexposed (foothills).

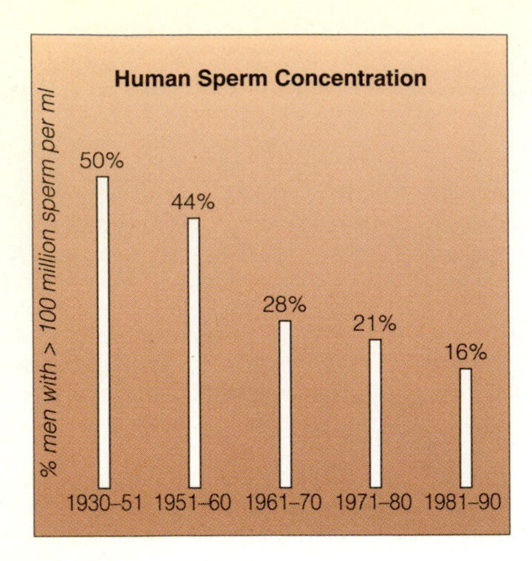

Figure 13.6 A documented decline in human sperm counts worldwide may be related to widespread exposure to hormone-disrupting chemicals.

Hormone disruptions may be at least partially responsible for certain trends that have recently concerned scientists. These range from increasingly early onset of puberty in human females to dramatic declines in human sperm counts. With respect to the latter, some sixty-one separate studies confirm that sperm counts have dropped almost 50 percent from 1938 to 1990 (Figure 13.6). Most of these studies were carried out in the United States and Europe, but some from Africa, Asia, and South America show that this is a worldwide phenomenon.

The Future of *Homo sapiens*

One of the difficulties with managing environmental and toxic health risks is that serious consequences of new cultural practices are often not apparent until years or even decades later. By then, of course, these practices are fully embedded in the cultural system, and huge financial interests are at stake. Today, cultural practices, probably as never before, are having an impact on human gene pools. It remains to be seen just what the long-term effects on the human species as a whole will be, but it is undeniable that poor people and people of color bear a disproportionate burden for these practices.

In addition to the problems human cultures are creating through changing the environment, new challenges have blossomed from cultural advances. The values of wealthy consumers living in industrialized countries have spread to the inhabitants of poorer and developing countries, influencing their expectations and dreams. Of course, the resources necessary to maintain a luxurious standard of living are limited. Instead of globalizing a standard of living that the world's natural resources cannot meet, it is time for all of humanity to use today's global connections to learn how to live within the carrying capacity of the earth.

We are a social species with origins on the African continent over 5 million years ago. Over the course of our evolutionary history, we came to inhabit the entire globe. From cities, to deserts, to mountain tops, to grassy

In Gangzhou, a sprawling city of nearly 10 million people on the southeastern coast of China, modern and older methods of transportation coexist. Here a cyclist transports live fish and eels from the harbor to downtown markets and restaurants in Styrofoam containers. The small quantities carried guarantee freshness. In addition, the low carbon footprint of bicycle transportation is more sustainable for the planet's future. A return to older transportation methods and an emphasis on local, small-scale food production represents a growing global trend. Ironically, the use of Styrofoam boxes rather than traditional baskets to carry items is at odds with the carbon footprint created by the bicycle transport. The high-energy process used to manufacture polystyrene not only consumes considerable energy but it also generates vast amounts of hazardous waste.

plains, to rich tropical forests, human cultures in these varied places became distinct from one another. In each environment, human groups devised their own specific beliefs and practices to meet the challenges of survival. In the future, dramatic changes in cultural values will be required if our species is to thrive. "New, improved" values might, for example, include a worldview that sees humanity as *part of* the world, rather than as *master over* it, as it is in many of the world's cultures today. Included, too, might be a sense of social responsibility that recognizes and affirms re
as well as our collective stev
inhabit.

Our continued survival wi
cultivate positive social conne
people and to recognize the wa
in a world interconnected by th ... ization. Together, we can use the adaptive faculty of culture, the hallmark of our species, to ensure our continued survival.

Questions for Reflection

1. Considering that population size has been expanding throughout our evolutionary history, why is this continuing trend a challenge of critical proportions for humans today?
2. The anthropological distinction between illness and disease provides a way to separate biological states from cultural elaborations given to those biological states. Can you think of some examples of illness without disease and disease without illness?
3. What do you think of the notion of letting a fever run its course instead of taking a medicine to lower it? Do these Paleolithic prescriptions suggested by evolutionary medicine run counter to your own medical beliefs and practices?
4. Are there any examples in your experience of how the growth process or human reproductive physiology helped you adapt to environmental stressors? Does this ability help humans from an evolutionary perspective?
5. Do you see examples of structural violence in your community that make some individuals more vulnerable to disease than others?

Suggested Readings

Ehrlich, P. R., & Ehrlich, A. H. (2008). *The dominant animal: Human evolution and the environment.* Washington, DC: Island.

From the scientists leading global efforts to contain human population size, this book traces the ways humans have modified the environment and themselves over the course of our evolutionary history in order to ensure our future.

Ellison, P. T. (2003). *On fertile ground: A natural history of human reproduction.* Cambridge, MA: Harvard University Press.

A leader in the field of reproductive ecology, Ellison demonstrates the extreme responsiveness of human reproductive hormones to a variety of environmental stimuli including the changing human-made environments of today.

Farmer, P. (2001). *Infections and inequalities: The modern plagues.* Berkeley: University of California Press.

Paul Farmer, continuing the tradition of the physician-anthropologist, traces the relationship between structural violence and infectious disease, demonstrating that the world's poor bear a disproportionate burden of disease.

Helman, C. B. (2003). *Culture, health, and illness: An introduction for health professionals.* New York: Butterworth Heinemann Medical.

This well-referenced book provides a good overview and introduction to medical anthropology. Though written with health professionals in mind, it is very accessible for North American students who have firsthand experience with biomedicine, the dominant medical system of North America.

McElroy, A., & Townsend, P. K. (2003). *Medical anthropology in ecological perspective.* Boulder, CO: Westview.

Now in its fourth edition, this text lays out ecological approaches in medical anthropology, including biocultural, environmental, and evolutionary perspectives. In addition to providing a clear theoretical perspective, it offers excellent examples of applied work by medical anthropologists to improve health globally.

Trevathan, W., Smith, E. O., & McKenna, J. J. (Eds.). (1999). *Evolutionary medicine.* London: Oxford University Press.

This comprehensive edited volume collects primary research conducted by leaders in the field of evolutionary medicine. Examples from throughout the human life cycle range from sexually transmitted diseases to cancer.

Glossary

abduction Movement away from midline of the body or from the center of the hand or foot.
absolute or chronometric dating In archaeology and paleoanthropology, dates for recovered material based on solar years, centuries, or other units of absolute time.
acclimatization Long-term physiological adjustments made in order to attain an equilibrium with a specific environmental stimulus.
Acheulean tradition The tool-making tradition of *Homo erectus* in Africa, Europe, and southwestern Asia in which hand-axes were developed from the earlier Oldowan chopper.
action theory The theory that self-serving actions by forceful leaders play a role in civilization's emergence.
adaptation A series of beneficial adjustments to the environment.
adaptive radiation Rapid diversification of an evolving population as it adapts to a variety of available niches.
adduction Movement toward the midline of the body or to the center of the hand or foot.
affiliative Tending to promote social cohesion.
agriculture The cultivation of food plants in soil prepared and maintained for crop production. Involves using technologies other than hand tools, such as irrigation, fertilizers, and the wooden or metal plow pulled by harnessed draft animals.
alleles Alternate forms of a single gene.
Allen's rule The tendency for the bodies of mammals living in cold climates to have shorter appendages (arms and legs) than members of the same species living in warm climates.
altruism Concern for the welfare of others expressed as increased risk undertaken by individuals for the good of the group.
anagenesis A sustained directional shift in a population's average characteristics.
analogies In biology, structures possessed by different organisms that are superficially similar due to similar function; without sharing a common developmental pathway or structure.
ancestral Characteristics that define a group of organisms that are due to shared ancestry.
Anthropoidea A suborder of the primates that includes New World monkeys, Old World monkeys, and apes (including humans).
anthropology The study of humankind in all times and places.
applied anthropology The use of anthropological knowledge and methods to solve practical problems, often for a specific client.
arboreal Living in the trees.
arboreal hypothesis A theory for primate evolution that proposes that life in the trees was responsible for enhanced visual acuity and manual dexterity in primates.
archaeology The study of human cultures through the recovery and analysis of material remains and environmental data.
Archaic cultures Term used to refer to Mesolithic cultures in the Americas.
archaic *Homo sapiens* A loosely defined group within the genus *Homo* that "lumpers" use for fossils with the combination of large brain size and ancestral features on the skull.
Ardipithecus ramidus One of the earliest bipeds that lived in eastern Africa about 4.4 million years ago.
artifact Any object fashioned or altered by humans.
Aurignacian tradition Tool-making tradition in Europe and western Asia at the beginning of the Upper Paleolithic.
Australopithecus The genus including several species of early bipeds from East, South, and Central Africa living between about 1.1 and 4.3 million years ago, one of whom was directly ancestral to humans.

Bergmann's rule The tendency for the bodies of mammals living in cold climates to be shorter and rounder than members of the same species living in warm climates.
binocular vision Vision with increased depth perception from two eyes set next to each other allowing their visual fields to overlap.
bioarchaeology The archaeological study of human remains emphasizing the preservation of cultural and social processes in the skeleton.
biocultural Focusing on the interaction of biology and culture.
bipedalism The mode of locomotion in which an organism walks upright on its two hind legs characteristic of humans and their ancestors; also called bipedality.
blade technique A technique of stone tool manufacture by which long, parallel-sided flakes are struck off the edges of a specially prepared core.
brachiation Using the arms to move from branch to branch, with the body hanging suspended beneath the arms.
Bronze Age In the Old World, the period marked by the production of tools and ornaments of bronze; began about 5,000 years ago in China and Southwest Asia and about 500 years earlier in Southeast Asia.
burin A stone tool with chisel-like edges used for working bone and antler.

Catarrhini An anthropoid infraorder that includes Old World monkeys, apes, and humans.
chromatid One half of the "X" shape of chromosomes visible once replication is complete. Sister chromatids are exact copies of each other.
chromosomes In the cell nucleus, the structures visible during cellular division containing long strands of DNA combined with a protein.
civilization In anthropology, a type of society marked by the presence of cities, social classes, and the state.
clade A taxonomic grouping that contains a single common ancestor and all of its descendants.
cladogenesis Speciation through a branching mechanism whereby an ancestral population gives rise to two or more descendant populations.
clavicle The collarbone connecting the sternum (breastbone) with the scapula (shoulder blade).
clines Gradual changes in the frequency of an allele or trait over space.
codon Three-base sequence of a gene that specifies a particular amino acid for inclusion in a protein.
cognitive capacity A broad concept including intelligence, educability, concept formation, self-awareness, self-evaluation, attention span, sensitivity in discrimination, and creativity.
community A unit of primate social organization composed of fifty or more individuals who inhabit a large geographic area together.
continental drift According to the theory of plate tectonics, the movement of continents embedded in underlying plates on the earth's surface in relation to one another over the history of life on earth.
convergent evolution In biological evolution, a process by which unrelated populations develop similarities to one another due to similar function rather than shared ancestry.
coprolites Preserved fecal material providing evidence of the diet and health of past organisms.
cranium The braincase of the skull.

Cro-Magnon A European of the Upper Paleolithic after about 36,000 years ago.
cultural anthropology The study of customary patterns in human behavior, thought, and feelings. It focuses on humans as culture-producing and culture-reproducing creatures. Also known as social or sociocultural anthropology.
cultural resource management A branch of archaeology tied to government policies for the protection of cultural resources and involving surveying and/or excavating archaeological and historical remains threatened by construction or development.
culture A society's shared and socially transmitted ideas, values, and perceptions, which are used to make sense of experience and generate behavior and are reflected in that behavior.
culture-bound Describing theories about the world and reality based on the assumptions and values of one's own culture.

datum point The starting point, or reference, for a grid system.
demographics Population characteristics such as the number of individuals of each age and sex.
dendrochronology In archaeology and paleoanthropology, a technique of chronometric dating based on the number of rings of growth found in a tree trunk.
dental formula The number of each tooth type (incisors, canines, premolars, and molars) on one half of each jaw. Unlike other mammals, primates possess equal numbers on their upper and lower jaws so the dental formula for the species is a single series of numbers.
derived Characteristics that define a group of organisms and that did not exist in ancestral populations.
developmental adaptation A permanent phenotypic variation derived from interaction between genes and the environment during the period of growth and development.
diastema A space between the canines and other teeth allowing the large projecting canines to fit within the jaw.
discourse An extended communication on a particular subject.
disease Refers to a specific pathology; a physical or biological abnormality.
diurnal Active during the day and at rest at night.
DNA Deoxyribonucleic acid. The genetic material consisting of a complex molecule whose base structure directs the synthesis of proteins.
doctrine An assertion of opinion or belief formally handed down by an authority as true and indisputable.
domestication An evolutionary process whereby humans modify, either intentionally or unintentionally, the genetic makeup of a population of plants or animals, sometimes to the extent that members of the population are unable to survive and/or reproduce without human assistance.
dominance The ability of one allele for a trait to mask the presence of another allele.
dominance hierarchies Observed ranking systems in primate societies ordering individuals from high (alpha) to low standing corresponding to predictable behavioral interactions including domination.

ecofact The natural remains of plants and animals found in the archaeological record.
ecological niche A species' way of life considered in the full context of its environment, including factors such as diet, activity, terrain, vegetation, predators, prey, and climate.
empirical Based on observations of the world rather than on intuition or faith.
endemic The public health term for a disease that is widespread in a population.
endocast A cast of the inside of a skull; used to help determine the size and shape of the brain.
entoptic phenomena Bright pulsating forms that are generated by the central nervous system and seen in states of trance.
enzyme Protein that initiates and directs chemical reactions.
estrus In some primate females, the time of sexual receptivity during which ovulation is visibly displayed.
ethnocentrism The belief that the ways of one's own culture are the only proper ones.
ethnography A detailed description of a particular culture primarily based on fieldwork.
ethnology The study and analysis of different cultures from a comparative or historical point of view, utilizing ethnographic accounts and developing anthropological theories that help explain why certain important differences or similarities occur among groups.
evolution Changes in allele frequencies in populations; also known as microevolution.
evolutionary medicine An approach to human sickness and health combining principles of evolutionary theory and human evolutionary history.

feature A non-portable element such as a hearth or an architectural element such as a wall that is preserved in the archaeological record.
fieldwork The term anthropologists use for on-location research.
flotation An archaeological technique employed to recover very tiny objects by immersion of soil samples in water to separate heavy from light particles.
fluorine dating In archaeology or paleoanthropology, a technique for relative dating based on the fact that the amount of fluorine in bones is proportional to their age.
foramen magnum A large opening in the skull through which the spinal cord passes and connects to the brain.
forensic anthropology Applied subfield of physical anthropology that specializes in the identification of human skeletal remains for legal purposes.
fossil Any mineralized trace or impression of an organism that has been preserved in the earth's crust from past geologic time.
founder effects A particular form of genetic drift deriving from a small founding population not possessing all the alleles present in the original population.
fovea centralis A shallow pit in the retina of the eye that enables an animal to focus on an object while maintaining visual contact with its surroundings.

gender The cultural elaborations and meanings assigned to the biological differentiation between the sexes.
gene A portion of the DNA molecule containing a sequence of base pairs that is the fundamental physical and functional unit of heredity.
gene flow The introduction of alleles from the gene pool of one population into that of another.
gene pool All the genetic variants possessed by members of a population.
genetic code The sequence of three bases (a codon) that specifies the sequence of amino acids in protein synthesis.
genetic drift Chance fluctuations of allele frequencies in the gene pool of a population.
genome The complete structure sequence of DNA for a species.
genotype The alleles possessed for a particular gene.
genus (genera, pl.) In the system of plant and animal classification, a group of like species.
globalization Worldwide interconnectedness, evidenced in global movements of natural resources, trade goods, human labor, finance capital, information, and infectious diseases.
gracile australopithecines Members of the genus *Australopithecus* possessing a more lightly built chewing apparatus; likely had a diet that included more meat than that of the robust australopithecines; best represented by the South African species *A. africanus*.
grade A general level of biological organization seen among a group of species; useful for constructing evolutionary relationships.
grave goods Items such as utensils, figurines, and personal possessions, symbolically placed in the grave for the deceased person's use in the afterlife.
grid system A system for recording data in three dimensions for an archaeological excavation.
grooming The ritual cleaning of another animal's coat to remove parasites and other matter.

Haplorhini In the alternate primate taxonomy, the suborder that includes tarsiers, monkeys, apes, and humans.
Hardy-Weinberg principle Demonstrates algebraically that the percentage of individuals that are homozygous for the dominant allele, homozygous for the recessive allele, and heterozygous should remain constant from one generation to the next, provided that certain specified conditions are met.
health disparity A difference in the health status between the wealthy elite and the poor in stratified societies.
hemoglobin The protein that carries oxygen in red blood cells.
heterochrony Change in the timing of developmental events that is often responsible for changes in the shape or size of a body part.
heterozygous Refers to a chromosome pair that bears different alleles for a single gene.

holistic perspective A fundamental principle of anthropology: that the various parts of human culture and biology must be viewed in the broadest possible context in order to understand their interconnections and interdependence.

home range The geographic area within which a group of primates usually moves.

homeobox gene A gene responsible for large-scale effects on growth and development that are frequently responsible for major reorganization of body plans in organisms.

homeotherm An animal that maintains a relatively constant body temperature despite environmental fluctuations.

hominid African hominoid family that includes humans and their ancestors. Some scientists, recognizing the close relationship of humans, chimps, bonobos, and gorillas, use the term *hominid* to refer to all African hominoids. They then divide the hominid family into two subfamilies: the Paninae (chimps, bonobos, and gorillas) and the Homininae (humans and their ancestors).

hominin The taxonomic subfamily or tribe within the primates that includes humans and our ancestors.

hominoid The taxonomic division superfamily within the Old World primates that includes gibbons, siamangs, orangutans, gorillas, chimpanzees, bonobos, and humans.

Homo The genus of bipeds that appeared 2.5 million years ago characterized by increasing brain size compared to earlier bipeds. The genus is divided into various species based on features such as brain size, skull shape, and cultural capabilities.

Homo habilis "Handy man." The first fossil members of the genus *Homo* appearing 2.5 million years ago, with larger brains and smaller faces than australopithecines.

homologies In biology, structures possessed by two different organisms that arise in similar fashion and pass through similar stages during embryonic development though they may possess different functions.

homozygous Refers to a chromosome pair that bears identical alleles for a single gene.

horticulture Cultivation of crops carried out with simple hand tools such as digging sticks or hoes.

hunting response A cyclic expansion and contraction of the blood vessels of the limbs that balances releasing enough heat to prevent frostbite with maintaining heat in the body core.

hydraulic theory The theory that explains civilization's emergence as the result of the construction of elaborate irrigation systems, the functioning of which required full-time managers whose control blossomed into the first governing body and elite social class.

hypoglossal canal The opening in the skull that accommodates the tongue-controlling hypoglossal nerve.

hypothesis A tentative explanation of the relation between certain phenomena.

illness The meanings and elaborations given to a particular physical state.

informed consent Formal recorded agreement to participate in research; federally mandated for all research in the United States and Europe.

innovation Any new idea, method, or device that gains widespread acceptance in society.

ischial callosities Hardened, nerveless pads on the buttocks that allow baboons and other primates to sit for long periods of time.

isolating mechanism A factor that separates breeding populations, thereby preventing gene flow, creating divergent subspecies, and ultimately (if maintained) divergent species.

isotherm An animal whose body temperature rises or falls according to the temperature of the surrounding environment.

Kenyanthropus platyops A proposed genus and species of biped contemporary with early australopithecines; may not be a separate genus.

k-selected Reproduction involving the production of relatively few offspring with high parental investment in each.

lactase An enzyme in the small intestine that enables humans to assimilate lactose.

lactose A sugar that is the primary constituent of fresh milk.

law of competitive exclusion When two closely related species compete for the same niche, one will out-compete the other, bringing about the latter's extinction.

law of independent assortment The Mendelian principle that genes controlling different traits are inherited independently of one another.

law of segregation The Mendelian principle that variants of genes for a particular trait retain their separate identities through the generations.

Levalloisian technique Tool-making technique by which three or four long triangular flakes were detached from a specially prepared core; developed by members of the genus *Homo* transitional from *H. erectus* to *H. sapiens*.

linguistic anthropology The study of human languages—looking at their structure, history, and relation to social and cultural contexts.

Lower Paleolithic The first part of the Old Stone Age beginning with the earliest Oldowan tools spanning from about 200,000 or 250,000 to 2.6 million years ago.

macroevolution Evolution above the species level.

mammal The class of vertebrate animals distinguished by bodies covered with fur, self-regulating temperature, and, in females, milk-producing mammary glands.

marrow The tissue inside of long bones where blood cells are produced.

material culture The durable aspects of culture such as tools, structures, and art.

medical anthropology A specialization in anthropology that combines theoretical and applied approaches from cultural and biological anthropology with the study of human health and disease.

medical pluralism The presence of multiple medical systems, each with its own practices and beliefs in a society.

medical system A patterned set of ideas and practices relating to illness.

meiosis A kind of cell division that produces the sex cells, each of which has half the number of chromosomes found in other cells of the organism.

melanin The chemical responsible for dark skin pigmentation that helps protect against damage from ultraviolet radiation.

Mesoamerica The region encompassing central and southern Mexico and northern Central America.

Mesolithic The Middle Stone Age period between the end of the Paleolithic and the start of the Neolithic; referred to as Archaic cultures in the Americas.

microlith A small blade of flint or similar stone, several of which were hafted together in wooden handles to make tools; widespread in the Mesolithic.

middens A refuse or garbage disposal area in an archaeological site.

Middle Paleolithic The middle part of the Old Stone Age characterized by the development of the Mousterian tradition of tool making and the earlier Levalloisian traditions.

mitosis A kind of cell division that produces new cells having exactly the same number of chromosome pairs, and hence copies of genes, as the parent cell.

molecular anthropology A branch of biological anthropology that uses genetic and biochemical techniques to test hypotheses about human evolution, adaptation, and variation.

molecular clock The hypothesis that dates of divergences among related species can be calculated through an examination of the genetic mutations that have accrued since the divergence.

monogamous Mating for life with a single individual of the opposite sex.

Mousterian tradition The tool industry of the Neandertals and their contemporaries of Europe, southwestern Asia, and northern Africa from 40,000 to 125,000 years ago.

multiregional hypothesis The hypothesis that modern humans originated through a process of simultaneous local transition from *Homo erectus* to *Homo sapiens* throughout the inhabited world.

mutation Chance alteration of genetic material that produces new variation.

natal group The group or the community an animal has inhabited since birth.

Natufian culture A Mesolithic culture living in the lands that are now Israel, Lebanon, and western Syria, between about 10,200 and 12,500 years ago.

natural selection The evolutionary process through which factors in the environment exert pressure, favoring some individuals over others to produce the next generation.

Neandertals A distinct group within the genus *Homo* inhabiting Europe and southwestern Asia from approximately 30,000 to 125,000 years ago.

Neolithic The New Stone Age; prehistoric period beginning about 10,000 years ago in which peoples possessed stone-based technologies and depended on domesticated plants and/or animals.

Neolithic revolution The profound cultural change beginning about 10,000 years ago and associated with the early domestication of plants and animals and settlement in permanent villages. Sometimes referred to as the Neolithic transition.

nocturnal Active at night and at rest during the day.
notochord A rodlike structure of cartilage that, in vertebrates, is replaced by the vertebral column.

Oldowan tool tradition The first stone tool industry, beginning between 2.5 and 2.6 million years ago.
opposable Able to bring the thumb or big toe in contact with the tips of the other digits on the same hand or foot in order to grasp objects.

paleoanthropology The study of the origins and predecessors of the present human species; the study of human evolution.
Paleoindians The earliest inhabitants of North America.
palynology In archaeology and paleoanthropology, a technique of relative dating based on changes in fossil pollen over time.
participant observation In ethnography, the technique of learning a people's culture through social participation and personal observation within the community being studied, as well as interviews and discussion with individual members of the group over an extended period of time.
pastoralism Breeding and managing large herds of domesticated grazing and browsing animals, such as goats, sheep, cattle, horses, llamas, or camels.
percussion method A technique of stone tool manufacture performed by striking the raw material with a hammerstone or by striking raw material against a stone anvil to remove flakes.
phenotype The observable characteristic of an organism that may or may not reflect a particular genotype due to the variable expression of dominant and recessive alleles.
physical anthropology The systematic study of humans as biological organisms; also known as biological anthropology.
physiological adaptation A short-term physiological change in response to a specific environmental stimulus. An immediate short-term response is not very efficient and is gradually replaced by a longer term response (see *acclimatization*).
Platyrrhini An anthropoid infraorder that includes New World monkeys.
polygenetic inheritance When two or more genes contribute to the phenotypic expression of a single characteristic.
polymerase chain reaction (PCR) A technique for amplifying or creating multiple copies of fragments of DNA so that it can be studied in the laboratory.
polymorphic Describing species with alternative forms (alleles) of particular genes.
polytypic Describing the expression of genetic variants in different frequencies in different populations of a species.
population In biology, a group of similar individuals that can and do interbreed.
potassium-argon dating In archaeology and paleoanthropology, a technique of chronometric dating that measures the ratio of radioactive potassium to argon in volcanic debris associated with human remains.
preadapted Possessing characteristics that, by chance, are advantageous in future environmental conditions.
prehensile Having the ability to grasp.
prehistory A conventional term used to refer to the period of time before the appearance of written records; does not deny the existence of history, merely of *written* history.
pressure flaking A technique of stone tool manufacture in which a bone, antler, or wooden tool is used to press, rather than strike off, small flakes from a piece of flint or similar stone.
primary innovation The creation, invention, or discovery by chance of a completely new idea, method, or device.
primate The group of mammals that includes lemurs, lorises, tarsiers, monkeys, apes, and humans.
primatology The study of living and fossil primates.
prion An infectious protein lacking any genetic material but capable of causing the reorganization and destruction of other proteins.
Prosimii A suborder of the primates that includes lemurs, lorises, and tarsiers.
punctuated equilibria A model of macroevolutionary change that suggests evolution occurs via long periods of stability or stasis punctuated by periods of rapid change.

race In biology, a subspecies or a population of a species differing geographically, morphologically, or genetically from other populations of the same species; not applicable to people because the division of humans into discrete types does not represent the true nature of human biological variation. In some societies, race is an important social category.
racism A doctrine of superiority by which one group justifies the dehumanization of others based on their distinctive physical characteristics.
radiocarbon dating In archaeology and paleoanthropology, a technique of chronometric dating based on measuring the amount of radioactive carbon (^{14}C) left in organic materials found in archaeological sites.
recent African origins or "Eve" hypothesis The hypothesis that all modern people are derived from one single population of archaic *Homo sapiens* from Africa who migrated out of Africa after 100,000 years ago, replacing all other archaic forms due to their superior cultural capabilities; also called the out of Africa hypothesis.
recessive An allele for a trait whose expression is masked by the presence of a dominant allele.
relative dating In archaeology and paleoanthropology, designating an event, object, or fossil as being older or younger than another.
reproductive success The relative production of fertile offspring by a genotype. In practical terms, the number of offspring produced by individual members of a population is tallied and compared to that of others.
ribosomes Structures in the cell where translation occurs.
RNA Ribonucleic acid; similar to DNA but with uracil substituted for the base thymine. Transcribes and carries instructions from DNA from the nucleus to the ribosomes where it directs protein synthesis. Some simple life forms contain RNA only.
robust australopithecines Several species within the genus *Australopithecus,* who lived from 2.5 to 1.1 million years ago in eastern and southern Africa; known for the rugged nature of their chewing apparatus (large back teeth, large chewing muscles, and a bony ridge on their skull tops for the insertion of these large muscles).
r-selected Reproduction involving the production of large numbers of offspring with relatively low parental investment in each.

sagittal crest A crest running from front to back on the top of the skull along the midline to provide a surface of bone for the attachment of the large temporal muscles for chewing.
Sahul The greater Australian landmass including Australia, New Guinea, and Tasmania. At times of maximum glaciation and low sea levels, these areas were continuous.
savannah Semi-arid plains environment as in eastern Africa.
scapula The shoulder blade.
secondary innovation The deliberate application or modification of an existing idea, method, or device.
secular trend A physical difference among related people from distinct generations that allows anthropologists to make inferences about environmental effects on growth and development.
seriation In archaeology and paleoanthropology, a technique for relative dating based on putting groups of objects into a sequence in relation to one another.
sexual dimorphism Within a single species, differences in the shape or size of a feature for males and females in body features not directly related to reproduction such as body size or canine tooth shape and size.
sickle-cell anemia An inherited form of anemia caused by a mutation in the hemoglobin protein that causes the red blood cells to assume a sickle shape.
soil mark A stain that shows up on the surface of recently plowed fields that reveals an archaeological site.
speciation The process of forming new species.
species The smallest working unit in the system of classification. Among living organisms, species are populations or groups of populations capable of interbreeding and producing fertile viable offspring.
stabilizing selection Natural selection acting to promote stability rather than change in a population's gene pool.
stereoscopic vision Complete three-dimensional vision (or depth perception) from binocular vision and nerve connections that run from each eye to both sides of the brain, allowing nerve cells to integrate the images derived from each eye.
stratified Layered; term used to describe archaeological sites where the remains lie in layers, one upon another.
stratigraphy In archaeology and paleoanthropology, the most reliable method of relative dating by means of strata.
Strepsirhini In the alternate primate taxonomy, the suborder that includes the lemurs and lorises without the tarsiers.
structural violence Physical and/or psychological harm (including repression, environmental destruction, poverty, hunger, illness, and premature death) caused by exploitative and unjust social, political, and economic systems.

Sunda The combined landmass of the contemporary islands of Java, Sumatra, Borneo, and Bali that was continuous with mainland Southeast Asia at times of low sea levels corresponding to maximum glaciation.

suspensory hanging apparatus The broad powerful shoulder joints and muscles found in all the hominoids, allowing these large-bodied primates to hang suspended below the tree branches.

taphonomy The study of how bones and other materials come to be preserved in the earth as fossils.

taxonomy The science of classification.

tertiary scavenger In a food chain, the third animal group (second to scavenge) to obtain meat from a kill made by a predator.

theory In science, an explanation of natural phenomena, supported by a reliable body of data.

thrifty genotype Human genotype that permits efficient storage of fat to draw on in times of food shortage and conservation of glucose and nitrogen.

tool An object used to facilitate some task or activity. Although tool making involves intentional modification of the material of which it is made, tool use may involve objects either modified for some particular purpose or completely unmodified.

transcription Process of conversion of instructions from DNA into RNA.

translation Process of conversion of RNA instructions into proteins.

Upper Paleolithic The last part (10,000 to 40,000 years ago) of the Old Stone Age, featuring tool industries characterized by long slim blades and an explosion of creative symbolic forms.

vegeculture The cultivation of domesticated root crops, such as yams and taro.

vertebrate An animal with a backbone, including fish, amphibians, reptiles, birds, and mammals.

visual predation hypothesis A theory for primate evolution that proposes that hunting behavior in tree-dwelling primates was responsible for their enhanced visual acuity and manual dexterity.

Bibliography

Abbot, E. (2001). *A history of celibacy.* Cambridge, MA: Da Capo.

Aberle, D. F., Bronfenbrenner, U., Hess, E. H., Miller, D. R., Schneider, D. H., & Spuhler, J. N. (1963). The incest taboo and the mating patterns of animals. *American Anthropologist 65,* 253–265.

Abu-Lughod, L. (1986). *Veiled sentiments: Honor and poetry in a Bedouin society.* Berkeley: University of California Press.

Abzhanov, A., Kuo, W. P., Hartmann, C., Grant, B. R., Grant, P. R., & Tabin, C. J. (2006). The calmodulin pathway and evolution of elongated beak morphology in Darwin's finches. *Nature 442,* 563–567.

Abzhanov, A., Protas, M., Grant, B. R., Grant, P. R., & Tabin, C. J. (2004). *Bmp4* and morphological variation of beaks in Darwin's finches. *Science 305* (5689), 1462.

Adams, R.E.W. (1977). *Prehistoric Mesoamerica.* Boston: Little, Brown.

Adams, R. M. (1966). *The evolution of urban society.* Chicago: Aldine.

Adams, R. M. (2001). Scale and complexity in archaic states. *Latin American Antiquity 11,* 188.

Adbusters. www.adbusters.org

Adherents. www.adherents.com

Adler, S. (1959). Darwin's illness. *Nature,* 1102–1103.

African Wildlife Foundation, Facebook blog. http://www.facebook.com/pages/African-Wildlife-Foundation/11918108948 (accessed June 13, 2009)

AIDS Epidemic Update. (2007), p. 7. Geneva: Joint United Nations Program on HIV/AIDS (USAID) and World Health Organization. www.unaids.org

Alemseged, Z., et al. (2006, September 21). *Nature 443,* 296–301.

Alland, A., Jr. (1970). *Adaptation in cultural evolution: An approach to medical anthropology.* New York: Columbia University Press.

Alland, A., Jr. (1971). *Human diversity.* New York: Columbia University Press.

Allen, J. L., & Shalinsky, A. C. (2004). *Student atlas of anthropology.* New York: McGraw-Hill.

Allen, J. S., & Cheer, S. M. (1996). The non-thrifty genotype. *Current Anthropology 37,* 831–842.

Alper, J. S., Ard, C., Asch, A., Beckwith, J., Conrad, P., & Geller, L. N. (Eds.). (2002). *The double-edged helix: Social implications of genetics in a diverse society.* Baltimore: Johns Hopkins University Press.

Alvard, M. S., & Kuznar, L. (2001). Deferred harvest: The transition from hunting to animal husbandry. *American Anthropologist 103* (2), 295–311.

Amábile-Cuevas, C. F., & Chicurel, M. E. (1993). Horizontal gene transfer. *American Scientist 81,* 332–341.

Ambrose, S. H. (2001). Paleolithic technology and human evolution. *Science 291,* 1748–1753.

American Anthropological Association. (1998). Statement on "race." www.ameranthassn.org

American Anthropological Association. (2007). Executive board statement on the Human Terrain System Project. http://www.aaanet.org/pdf/EB_Resolution_110807.pdf

Amiran, R. (1965). The beginnings of pottery-making in the Near East. In F. R. Matson (Ed.), *Ceramics and man* (pp. 240–247). Viking Fund Publications in Anthropology, 41.

Anderson, A. (2002). Faunal collapse, landscape change, and settlement history in Remote Oceania. *World Archaeology 33* (3), 375–390.

Andrews, L. B., & Nelkin, D. (1996). The Bell Curve: A statement. *Science 271,* 13.

Angrosino, M. V. (2004). *Projects in ethnographic research.* Long Grove, IL: Waveland.

Ankel-Simons, F., Fleagle, J. G., & Chatrath, P. S. (1998). Femoral anatomy of *Aegyptopithecus zeuxis,* an early Oligocene anthropoid. *American Journal of Physical Anthropology 106,* 421–422.

"A pocket guide to social media and kids." (2009, November 2). blog.nielsen.com.

Appadurai, A. (1990). Disjuncture and difference in the global cultural economy. *Public Culture 2,* 1–24.

Appadurai, A. (1996). *Modernity at large: Cultural dimensions of globalization.* Minneapolis: University of Minnesota Press.

Appenzeller, T. (1998). Art: Evolution or revolution? *Science 282,* 1451–1454.

Arctic Monitoring Assessment Project (AMAP). (2003). *AMAP assessment 2002: Human health in the Arctic.* Oslo: Author.

Armstrong, D. F., Stokoe, W. C., & Wilcox, S. E. (1993). Signs of the origin of syntax. *Current Anthropology 34,* 349–368.

Ashmore, W. (Ed.). (1981). *Lowland Maya settlement patterns.* Albuquerque: University of New Mexico Press.

Aureli, F., & de Waal, F.B.M. (2000). *Natural conflict resolution.* Berkeley: University of California Press.

Australian Museum Archives. http://australianmuseum.net.au/movie/Why-the-stories-are-told-Aunty-Beryl

Avedon, J. F. (1997). *In exile from the land of snows: The definitive account of the Dalai Lama and Tibet since the Chinese conquest.* New York: Harper.

"Average TV viewing for 2008–09 TV season at all-time high." (2009, November 10). blog.nielsen.com.

Babiker, M. A., Alumran, K., Alshahri, A., Almadan, M., & Islam, F. (1996). Unnecessary deprivation of common food items in glucose-6-phosphate dehydrogenase deficiency. *Annals of Saudi Arabia 16* (4), 462–463.

Bailey, R. C., & Aunger, R. (1989). Net hunters vs. archers: Variation in women's subsistence strategies in the Ituri forest. *Human Ecology 17,* 273–297.

Baker, P. (Ed.). (1978). *The biology of high altitude peoples.* London: Cambridge University Press.

Balikci, A. (1970). *The Netsilik Eskimo.* Garden City, NY: Natural History.

Balter, M. (1998). On world AIDS day, a shadow looms over southern Africa. *Science 282,* 1790.

Balter, M. (1998). Why settle down? The mystery of communities. *Science 282,* 1442–1444.

Balter, M. (1999). A long season puts Çatalhöyük in context. *Science 286,* 890–891.

Balter, M. (2001). Did plaster hold Neolithic society together? *Science 294,* 2278–2281.

Balter, M. (2001). In search of the first Europeans. *Science 291,* 1724.

Banton, M. (1968). Voluntary association: Anthropological aspects. In *International encyclopedia of the social sciences* (Vol. 16, pp. 357–362). New York: Macmillan.

Barham, L. S. (1998). Possible early pigment use in South-Central Africa. *Current Anthropology 39,* 703–710.

Barnard, A. (1995). Monboddo's *Orang Outang* and the definition of man. In R. Corbey & B. Theunissen (Eds.), *Ape, man, apeman: Changing views since 1600* (pp. 71–85). Leiden: Department of Prehistory, Leiden University.

Barnouw, V. (1985). *Culture and personality* (4th ed.). Homewood, IL: Dorsey.

Barr, R. G. (1997, October). The crying game. *Natural History,* 47.

Barrett, L., Gaynor, D., Rendall, D., Mitchell, D., & Henzi, S. P. (2004). Habitual cave use and thermoregulation in chacma baboons (*Papio hamadryas ursinus*). *Journal of Human Evolution 46* (2), 215–222.

Barth, F. (1961). *Nomads of South Persia: The Basseri tribe of the Khamseh confederacy.* Boston: Little, Brown.

Barth, F. (1962). Nomadism in the mountain and plateau areas of Southwest Asia. *The problems of the arid zone* (pp. 341–355). Paris: UNESCO.

Bar-Yosef, O. (1986). The walls of Jericho: An alternative interpretation. *Current Anthropology 27,* 160.

Bar-Yosef, O., Vandermeesch, B., Arensburg, B., Belfer-Cohen, A., Goldberg, P., Laville, H., Meignen, L., Rak, Y., Speth, J. D., Tchernov, E., Tillier, A-M., & Weiner, S. (1992). The excavations in Kebara Cave, Mt. Carmel. *Current Anthropology 33,* 497–550.

Bascom, W. (1969). *The Yoruba of southwestern Nigeria.* New York: Holt, Rinehart & Winston.

Bates, D. G. (2001). *Human adaptive strategies: Ecology, culture, and politics* (2nd ed.). Boston: Allyn & Bacon.

Bates, D. G., & Plog, F. (1991). *Human adaptive strategies.* New York: McGraw-Hill.

Bayer, R. (1987). *Homosexuality and American psychiatry: The politics of diagnosis.* Princeton, NJ: Princeton University Press.

Becker, J. (2004, March). *National Geographic, 90.*

Bednarik, R. G. (1995). Concept-mediated marking in the Lower Paleolithic. *Current Anthropology 36,* 606.

Beeman, W. O. (2000). Introduction: Margaret Mead, cultural studies, and international understanding. In M. Mead & R. Métraux (Eds.), *The study of culture at a distance* (pp. xiv–xxxi). New York and Oxford: Berghahn.

Behrend, H., & Luig, U. (Eds.). (2000). *Spirit possession, modernity, and power in Africa.* Madison: University of Wisconsin Press.

Behrensmeyer, A. K., Todd, N. E., Potts, R., & McBrinn, G. E. (1997). Late Pliocene faunal turnover in the Turkana basin, Kenya, and Ethiopia. *Science 278,* 1589–1594.

Bekoff, M., et al. (Eds.). (2002). *The cognitive animal: Empirical and theoretical perspectives on animal cognition.* Cambridge, MA: MIT Press.

Belshaw, C. S. (1958). The significance of modern cults in Melanesian development. In W. Lessa & E. Z. Vogt (Eds.), *Reader in comparative religion: An anthropological approach.* New York: Harper & Row.

Benedict, R. (1934). *Patterns of culture.* Boston: Houghton Mifflin.

Bennett, M. R., Harris, J.W.K., Richmond, B. G., Braun, D. R., Mbua, E., Kiura, P., Olago, D., Kibunjia, M., Omuombo, C., Behrensmeyer, A. K., Huddart, D., & Gonzalez, S. (2009). Early hominim foot morphology based on 1.5-million-year-old footprints from Ileret, Kenya. *Science 323* (5918), 1197–1201.

Bennett, R. L., et al. (2002, April). Genetic counseling and screening of consanguineous couples and their offspring: Recommendations of the National Society of Genetic Counselors. *Journal of Genetic Counseling 11* (2), 97–119.

Bergendorff, S. (2009). *Simple lives, cultural complexity: Rethinking culture in terms of complexity theory.* Lanham, MD: Rowman & Littlefield.

Bermúdez de Castro, J. M., Arsuaga, J. L., Cabonell, E., Rosas, A., Martinez, I., & Mosquera, M. (1997). A hominid from the lower Pleistocene of Atapuerca, Spain: Possible ancestor to Neandertals and modern humans. *Science 276,* 1392–1395.

Bernard, H. R. (2002). *Research methods in anthropology: Qualitative and quantitative approaches* (3rd ed.). Walnut Creek, CA: Altamira.

Bernardi, B. (1985). *Age class systems: Social institutions and policies based on age.* New York: Cambridge University Press.

Berndt, R. M., & Berndt, C. H. (1989). *The speaking land: Myth and story in Aboriginal Australia.* New York: Penguin.

Bernstein, R. E., Child, P., Famous, P., & South, A. (1984). Darwin's illness: Chagas' disease resurgens. *Journal of the Royal Society of Medicine 77,* 608–609.

Berra, T. M. (1990). *Evolution and the myth of creationism.* Stanford, CA: Stanford University Press.

Betzig, L. (1989). Causes of conjugal dissolution: A cross-cultural study. *Current Anthropology 30,* 654–676.

Bicchieri, M. G. (Ed.). (1972). *Hunters and gatherers today: A socioeconomic study of eleven such cultures in the twentieth century.* New York: Holt, Rinehart & Winston.

Binford, L. R. (1972). *An archaeological perspective.* New York: Seminar.

Binford, L. R., & Chuan, K. H. (1985). Taphonomy at a distance: Zhoukoudian, the cave home of Beijing man? *Current Anthropology 26,* 413–442.

Birdsell, J. H. (1977). The recalibration of a paradigm for the first peopling of Greater Australia. In J. Allen, J. Golson, & R. Jones (Eds.), *Sunda and Sahul: Prehistoric studies in Southeast Asia, Melanesia, and Australia* (pp. 113–167). New York: Academic.

Bjorn, G. (2008). Fearful of vaccines, some parents find cause for celebration. *Nature Medicine 14,* 699.

Blackless, M., et al. (2000). How sexually dimorphic are we? Review and synthesis. *American Journal of Human Biology 12,* 151–166.

Blakey, M. (2003). *African Burial Ground Project.* Department of Anthropology, College of William & Mary.

Blok, A. (1974). *The mafia of a Sicilian village 1860–1960.* New York: Harper & Row.

Blok, A. (1981). Rams and billy-goats: A key to the Mediterranean code of honour. *Man, New Series 16* (3), 427–440.

Blok, A. (1992). Beyond the bounds of anthropology. In J. Abbink & H. Vermeulen (Eds.), *History and culture: Essays on the work of Eric R. Wolf* (pp. 5–20). Amsterdam: Het Spinhuis.

Blom, A., et al. (2001). A survey of the apes in the Dzanga-Ndoki National Park, Central African Republic. *African Journal of Ecology 39,* 98–105.

Blumberg, R. L. (1991). *Gender, family, and the economy: The triple overlap.* Newbury Park, CA: Sage.

Blumer, M. A., & Byrne, R. (1991). The ecological genetics and domestication and the origins of agriculture. *Current Anthropology 32,* 30.

Boaretto, E., Wu, X., Yuan, J., Bar-Yosef, O., Chu, V., Pan, Y., Liu, K., Cohen, D., Jiao, T., Li, S., Gu, H., Goldberg, P., & Weiner, S. (2009). Radiocarbon dating of charcoal and bone collagen associated with early pottery at Yuchanyan Cave, Hunan Province, China. *Proceedings of the National Academy of Sciences, USA 106* (24), 9595–9600.

Boas, F. (1962). *Primitive art.* Gloucester, MA: Peter Smith.

Boas, F. (1966). *Race, language and culture.* New York: Free Press.

Bodley, J. H. (2007). *Anthropology and contemporary human problems* (5th ed.). Lanham, MD: Alta Mira.

Bodley, J. H. (2008). *Victims of progress* (5th ed.). Lanham, MD: Alta Mira.

Boehm, C. (1984). *Blood revenge.* Lawrence: University of Kansas Press.

Boehm, C. (2000). The evolution of moral communities. *School of American Research, 2000 Annual Report,* 7.

Bogucki, P. (1999). *The origins of human society.* Oxford, England: Blackwell.

Bohannan, P. (Ed.). (1967). *Law and warfare: Studies in the anthropology of conflict.* Garden City, NY: Natural History.

Bohannan, P., & Middleton, J. (Eds.). (1968). *Kinship and social organization.* Garden City, NY: Natural History.

Bohannan, P., & Middleton, J. (Eds.). (1968). *Marriage, family, and residence.* Garden City, NY: Natural History.

Bolinger, D. (1968). *Aspects of language.* New York: Harcourt.

Bongaarts, J. (1998). Demographic consequences of declining fertility. *Science 182,* 419.

Bonn-Muller, E. (2009). Oldest oil paintings: Bamiyan, Afghanistan. *Archaeology 62* (1).

Bonvillain, N. (2007). *Language, culture, and communication: The meaning of messages* (5th ed.). Upper Saddle River, NJ: Prentice-Hall.

Bordes, F. (1972). *A tale of two caves.* New York: Harper & Row.

Bornstein, M. H. (1975). The influence of visual perception on culture. *American Anthropologist 77* (4), 774–798.

Boshara, R. (2003, January/February). Wealth inequality: The $6,000 solution. *Atlantic Monthly.*

Boškovic, A. (Ed.). (2009). *Other people's anthropologies: Ethnographic practice on the margins.* Oxford, England: Berghahn.

Bowen, J. R. (2004). *Religions in practice: An approach to the anthropology of religion* (3rd ed.). Boston: Allyn & Bacon.

Bowie, F. (2006). *The anthropology of religion: An introduction* (2nd ed.). Malden, MA: Blackwell.

Brace, C. L. (1981). Tales of the phylogenetic woods: The evolution and significance of phylogenetic trees. *American Journal of Physical Anthropology 56,* 411–429.

Brace, C. L. (1997). Cro-Magnons "R" us? *Anthropology Newsletter 38* (8), 1, 4.

Brace, C. L. (2000). *Evolution in an anthropological view.* Walnut Creek, CA: Altamira.

Brace, C. L., Nelson, H., & Korn, N. (1979). *Atlas of human evolution* (2nd ed.). New York: Holt, Rinehart & Winston.

Bradfield, R. M. (1998). *A natural history of associations* (2nd ed.). New York: International Universities Press.

Bradford, P. V., & Blume, H. (1992). *Ota Benga: The Pygmy in the zoo.* New York: St. Martin's.

Braidwood, R. J. (1960). The agricultural revolution. *Scientific American 203,* 130–141.

Braidwood, R. J. (1975). *Prehistoric men* (8th ed.). Glenview, IL: Scott, Foresman.

Brain, C. K. (1968). Who killed the Swartkrans ape-men? *South African Museums Association Bulletin 9,* 127–139.

Brain, C. K. (1969). The contribution of Namib Desert Hottentots to an understanding of australopithecine bone accumulations. *Scientific Papers of the Namib Desert Research Station,* 13.

Branda, R. F., & Eatoil, J. W. (1978). Skin color and photolysis: An evolutionary hypothesis. *Science 201,* 625–626.

Braudel, F. (1979). *The structures of everyday life: Civilization and capitalism 15th–18th century* (vol. 1, pp. 163–167). New York: Harper & Row.

Brettell, C. B., & Sargent, C. F. (Eds.). (2000). *Gender in cross-cultural perspective* (3rd ed.). Upper Saddle River, NJ: Prentice-Hall.

Brew, J. O. (1968). *One hundred years of anthropology.* Cambridge, MA: Harvard University Press.

Brody, H. (1981). *Maps and dreams.* New York: Pantheon.

Broecker, W. S. (1992, April). Global warming on trial. *Natural History,* 14.

Brown, B., Walker, A., Ward, C. V., & Leakey, R. E. (1993). New *Australopithecus boisei* calvaria from East Lake Turkana, Kenya. *American Journal of Physical Anthropology 91,* 137–159.

Brown, D. E. (1991). *Human universals.* New York: McGraw-Hill.

Brown, P., et al. (2004). A new small-bodied hominin from the Late Pleistocene of Flores, Indonesia. *Nature 431,* 1055–1061.

Brues, A. M. (1977). *People and races.* New York: Macmillan.

Brunet, M., Beauvilain, A., Coppens, Y., Heintz, E., Moutaye, A. H., & Pilbeam, D. (1995). The first australopithecine 2,500 kilometers west of the Rift Valley (Chad). *Nature 16,* 378 (6554), 273–275.

Brunet, M., et al. (2002). A new hominid from the Upper Miocene of Chad, Central Africa. *Nature 418,* 145–151.

Buchan, J. C., Alberts, S. C., Silk, J. B., & Altmann, J. (2003). *Nature 425,* 179–181.

Buck, P. H. (1938). *Vikings of the Pacific.* Chicago: University Press of Chicago.

Buckland, T. J. (Ed.). (2007). *Dancing from past to present: Nation, culture, identities.* Madison: University of Wisconsin Press.

Burling, R. (1969). Linguistics and ethnographic description. *American Anthropologist 71,* 817–827.

Burling, R. (1970). *Man's many voices: Language in its cultural context.* New York: Holt, Rinehart & Winston.

Burling, R. (1993). Primate calls, human language, and nonverbal communication. *Current Anthropology 34,* 25–53.

Burling, R. (2005). *The talking ape: How language evolved.* Oxford: Oxford University Press.

Butanayev, V. (n.d.). *Xooray attari* [Xakas names]. Cited by Harrison, K. D. (2002). Naming practices and ethnic identity in Tuva. *Proceedings of the Chicago Linguistics Society 35* (2).

Butynski, T. M. (2001). Africa's great apes. In B. Beck et al. (Eds.), *Great apes and humans: The ethics of co-existence* (pp. 3–56). Washington, DC: Smithsonian Institution.

Butzer, K. (1971). *Environment and anthropology: An ecological approach to prehistory* (2nd ed.). Chicago: Aldine.

Byers, D. S. (Ed.). (1967). *The prehistory of the Tehuacan Valley: Vol. 1. Environment and subsistence.* Austin: University of Texas Press.

Cachel, S. (1997). Dietary shifts and the European Upper Paleolithic transition. *Current Anthropology 38,* 590.

Calloway, C. (1997). Introduction: Surviving the dark ages. In C. G. Calloway (Ed.), *After King Philip's war: Presence and persistence in Indian New England* (pp. 1–28). Hanover, NH: University Press of New England.

Cardarelli, F. (2003). *Encyclopaedia of scientific units, weights, and measures: Their SI equivalences and origins.* London: Springer.

Carneiro, R. L. (1970). A theory of the origin of the state. *Science 169,* 733–738.

Carneiro, R. L. (2003). *Evolutionism in cultural anthropology: A critical history.* Boulder, CO: Westview.

Caroulis, J. (1996). Food for thought. *Pennsylvania Gazette 95* (3),16.

Carroll, J. B. (Ed.). (1956). *Language, thought and reality: Selected writings of Benjamin Lee Whorf* (p. 148). Cambridge, MA: MIT Press.

Carroll, S. B. (2005). *Endless forms most beautiful: The new science of evo devo.* New York: Norton.

Carson, R. C., Butcher, J. N., & Coleman, J. C. (1990). *Abnormal psychology and modern life* (8th ed.). Glenview, IL: Scott Foresman.

Carsten, J. (Ed.). (2008). *Cultures of relatedness: New approaches to the study of kinship.* Cambridge, England: Cambridge University Press.

Cartmill, M. (1998). The gift of gab. *Discover 19* (11), 64.

Cashdan, E. (1989). Hunters and gatherers: Economic behavior in bands. In S. Plattner (Ed.), *Economic anthropology* (pp. 21–48). Stanford, CA: Stanford University Press.

Cashdan, E. (2008). Waist-to-hip ratio across cultures: Trade-offs between androgen- and estrogen-dependent traits. *Current Anthropology 49* (6).

Catford, J. C. (1988). *A practical introduction to phonetics.* Oxford, England: Clarendon.

Caton, S. C. (1999). *Lawrence of Arabia: A film's anthropology.* Berkeley: University of California Press.

Cavalieri, P., & Singer, P. (1994). *The Great Ape Project: Equality beyond humanity.* New York: St. Martin's.

Cavalli-Sforza, L. L. (1977). *Elements of human genetics.* Menlo Park, CA: Benjamin.

Centers for Disease Control and Prevention. (2009). Differences in prevalence of obesity among black, white, and Hispanic adults—United States, 2006–2008. *Morbidity and Mortality Weekly Report 58* (27), 740–744.

Chagnon, N. A. (1988). Life histories, blood revenge, and warfare in a tribal population. *Science 239,* 935–992.

Chagnon, N. A. (1988). *Yanomamo: The fierce people* (3rd ed.). New York: Holt, Rinehart & Winston.

Chambers, R. (1983). *Rural development: Putting the last first.* New York: Longman.

Chan, J.W.C., & Vernon, P. E. (1988). Individual differences among the peoples of China. In J. W. Berry (Ed.), *Human abilities in cultural context* (pp. 340–357). Cambridge, England: Cambridge University Press.

Chance, N. A. (1990). *The Iñupiat and Arctic Alaska: An ethnography of development.* New York: Harcourt.

Chang, K. C. (Ed.). (1968). *Settlement archaeology.* Palo Alto, CA: National.

Chang, L. (2005, June 9). A migrant worker sees rural home in new light. *Wall Street Journal.*

Charpentier, M.J.E., Van Horn, R. C., Altmann, J., & Alberts, S. C. (2008). *Proceeding of the National Academy of Sciences, USA.* doi: 10.1073/pnas.0711219105.

Chase, C. (1998). Hermaphrodites with attitude. *Gay and Lesbian Quarterly 4* (2), 189–211.

Chasin, B. H., & Franke, R. W. (1983). US farming: A world model? *Global Reporter 1* (2), 10.

Chatty, D. (1996). *Mobile pastoralists: Development planning and social change in Oman.* New York: Columbia University Press.

Cheater, A. (2005). *The anthropology of power.* London: Routledge.

Cheney, D. L., & Seyfarth, R. M. (2007). *Baboon metaphysics: The evolution of a social mind.* Chicago: University of Chicago Press.

Chicurel, M. (2001). Can organisms speed their own evolution? *Science 292,* 1824–1827.

Childe, V. G. (1951). *Man makes himself.* New York: New American Library. (orig. 1936)

Ciochon, R. L., & Fleagle, J. G. (Eds.). (1987). *Primate evolution and human origins.* Hawthorne, NY: Aldine.

Ciochon, R. L., & Fleagle, J. G. (1993). *The human evolution source book.* Englewood Cliffs, NJ: Prentice-Hall.

Clark, E. E. (1966). *Indian legends of the Pacific Northwest.* Berkeley: University of California Press.

Clark, G. (1967). *The stone age hunters.* New York: McGraw-Hill.

Clark, G. A. (1997). Neandertal genetics. *Science 277,* 1024.

Clark, G. A. (2002). Neandertal archaeology: Implications for our origins. *American Anthropologist 104* (1), 50–67.

Clark, W.E.L. (1960). *The antecedents of man.* Chicago: Quadrangle.

Clark, W.E.L. (1966). *History of the primates* (5th ed.). Chicago: University of Chicago Press.

Clark, W.E.L. (1967). *Man-apes or ape-men? The story of discoveries in Africa.* New York: Holt, Rinehart & Winston.

Clarke, R. J. (1998). First ever discovery of a well preserved skull and associated skeleton of *Australopithecus. South African Journal of Science 94,* 460–464.

Clarke, R. J., & Tobias, P. V. (1995). Sterkfontein member 2 foot bones of the oldest South African hominid. *Science 269,* 521–524.

Clay, J. W. (1996). What's a nation? In W. A. Haviland & R. J. Gordon (Eds.), *Talking about people* (2nd ed., p. 188). Mountain View, CA: Mayfield

Clottes, J., & Bennett, G. (2002). *World rock art* (conservation and cultural heritage series). San Francisco: Getty Trust Publication.

Coe, S. D. (1994). *America's first cuisines.* Austin: University of Texas Press.

Coe, S. D., & Coe, M. D. (1996). *The true history of chocolate.* New York: Thames and Hudson.

Coe, W. R. (1967). *Tikal: A handbook of the ancient Maya ruins.* Philadelphia: University of Pennsylvania Museum.

Coe, W. R., & Haviland, W. A. (1982). *Introduction to the archaeology of Tikal.* Philadelphia: University Museum.

Cohen, J. (1997). Is an old virus up to new tricks? *Science 277,* 312–313.

Cohen, J. (2009). Out of Mexico? Scientists ponder swine flu's origin. *Science 324* (5928), 700–702.

Cohen, M. N. (1977). *The food crisis in prehistory.* New Haven, CT: Yale University Press.

Cohen, M. N. (1995). Anthropology and race: The Bell Curve phenomenon. *General Anthropology 2* (1), 1–4.

Cohen, M. N. (1998). *Culture of intolerance: Chauvinism, class, and racism in the United States.* New Haven, CT: Yale University Press.

Cohen, M. N., & Armelagos, G. J. (1984). *Paleopathology at the origins of agriculture.* Orlando: Academic.

Colborn, T., et al. (1997). *Our stolen future.* New York: Plume/Penguin.

Colburn, T., Dumanoski, D., & Myers, J. P. (1996). Hormonal sabotage. *Natural History 3,* 45–46.

Cole, J. W., & Wolf, E. R. (1999). *The hidden frontier: Ecology and ethnicity in an alpine valley* (with a new introduction). Berkeley: University of California Press.

Cole, S. (1975). *Leakey's luck: The life of Louis Seymour Bazett Leakey. 1903–1972.* New York: Harcourt Brace Jovanovich.

Collier, J., & Collier, M. (1986). *Visual anthropology: Photography as a research method.* Albuquerque: University of New Mexico Press.

Collier, J., Rosaldo, M. Z., & Yanagisako, S. (1982). Is there a family? New anthropological views. In B. Thorne & M. Yalom (Eds.), *Rethinking the family: Some feminist questions* (pp. 25–39). New York: Longman.

Collier, J. F., & Yanagisako, S. J. (Eds.). (1987). *Gender and kinship: Essays toward a unified analysis.* Stanford, CA: Stanford University Press.

Committee on the Elimination of Racial Discrimination, India. (2007, March). Consideration of reports submitted by states parties under Article 9 of the International Convention on the Elimination of All Forms of Racial Discrimination, 70th Session. www2.ohchr.org/english/bodies/cerd/cerds70.htm

Conard., N. J. (2009). A female figurine from the basal Aurignacian deposits of Hohle Fels Cave in southwestern Germany. *Nature 459* (7244), 248.

Conard, N. J., Malina, M., & Münzel, S. C. (2009). New flutes document the earliest musical tradition in southwestern Germany. *Nature.* doi:10.1038/nature08169.

Cone, M. (2005) *Silent snow: The slow poisoning of the Arctic.* New York: Grove.

Connelly, J. C. (1979). Hopi social organization. In A. Ortiz (Ed.), *Handbook of North American Indians, Vol. 9, Southwest* (pp. 539–553). Washington, DC: Smithsonian Institution.

Conroy, G. C. (1997). *Reconstructing human origins: A modern synthesis.* New York: Norton.

Coon, C. S. (1954). *The story of man.* New York: Knopf.

Coon, C. S. (1958). *Caravan: The story of the Middle East* (2nd ed.). New York: Holt, Rinehart & Winston.

Coon, C. S. (1962). *The origins of races.* New York: Knopf.

Coontz, S. (2005). *Marriage, a history: From obedience to intimacy, or how love conquered marriage.* New York: Viking Adult.

Cooper, A., Poinar, H. N., Pääbo, S., Radovci, C. J., Debénath, A., Caparros, M., Barroso-Ruiz, C., Bertranpetit, J., Nielsen-March, C., Hedges, R.E.M., & Sykes, B. (1997). Neanderthal genetics. *Science 277,* 1021–1024.

Coppa, A., et al. (2006). Early Neolithic tradition of dentistry. *Nature 440,* 755–756.

Coppens, Y., Howell, F. C., Isaac, G. L., & Leakey, R.E.F. (Eds.). (1976). *Earliest man and environments in the Lake Rudolf Basin: Stratigraphy, paleoecology, and evolution.* Chicago: University of Chicago Press.

Corballis, M. C. (2003). *From hand to mouth: The origins of human language.* Princeton, NJ: Princeton University Press.

Corbey, R. (1995). Introduction: Missing links, or the ape's place in nature. In R. Corbey & B. Theunissen (Eds.), *Ape, man, apeman: Changing views since 1600* (p.1). Leiden: Department of Prehistory, Leiden University.

Cornwell, T. (1995, November 10). Skeleton staff. *Times Higher Education,* 20. http://www.timeshighereducation.co.uk/story.asp?storyCode=96035§ioncode=26

Corruccini, R. S. (1992). Metrical reconsideration of the Skhul IV and IX and Border Cave I crania in the context of modern human origins. *American Journal of Physical Anthropology 87,* 433–445.

Cotte, M. (2008). *Journal of Analytical Atomic Spectrometry.* doi: 10.1039/b801358f.

Cowgill, G. L. (1980). Letter. *Science 210,* 1305.

Cowgill, G. L. (1997). State and society at Teotihuacan, Mexico. *Annual Review of Anthropology 26,* 129–161.

Crane, H. (2001). *Men in spirit: The masculinization of Taiwanese Buddhist nuns.* Doctoral dissertation, Brown University.

Crane, L. B., Yeager, E., & Whitman, R. L. (1981). *An introduction to linguistics.* Boston: Little, Brown.

Cretney, S. (2003). *Family law in the twentieth century: A history.* New York: Oxford University Press.

Crocker, W. H., & Crocker, J. G. (1994). *The Canela, bonding through kinship, ritual, and sex.* Fort Worth: Harcourt Brace.

Crocker, W. H., & Crocker, J. G. (2004). *The Canela: Kinship, ritual, and sex in an Amazonian tribe.* Belmont, CA: Wadsworth.

Culbert, T. P. (Ed.). (1973). *The Classic Maya collapse.* Albuquerque: University of New Mexico Press.

Culotta, E. (1995). Asian hominids grow older. *Science 270,* 1116–1117.

Culotta, E. (1995). New finds rekindle debate over anthropoid origins. *Science 268,* 1851.

Culotta, E., & Koshland, D. E., Jr. (1994). DNA repair works its way to the top. *Science 266,* 1926.

Cultural Survival Quarterly. (1991). *15* (4).

D'Adesky, A.-C. (2004). *Moving mountains: The race to treat global AIDS.* New York: Verso.

Dalton, G. (Ed.). (1967). *Tribal and peasant economics: Readings in economic anthropology.* Garden City, NY: Natural History.

Dalton, G. (1971). *Traditional tribal and peasant economies: An introductory survey of economic anthropology.* Reading, MA: Addison-Wesley.

Daniel, G. (1970). *The first civilizations: The archaeology of their origins.* New York: Apollo Editions.

Dalton, G. (1971). *Traditional tribal and peasant economics: An introductory survey of economic anthropology.* Reading, MA: Addison-Wesley.

Darwin, C. (1887). *Autobiography.* Reprinted in F. Darwin (Ed.), (1902), *The life and letters of Charles Darwin.* London: John Murray.

Darwin, C. (1936). *The descent of man and selection in relation to sex.* New York: Random House (Modern Library). (orig. 1871)

Darwin, C. (2007). *On the origin of species by means of natural selection, or the preservation of favoured races in the struggle for life.* New York: Cosimo. (orig. 1859)

Davenport, W. (1959). Linear descent and descent groups. *American Anthropologist 61,* 557–573.

Davies, G. (2005). *A history of money from the earliest times to present day* (3rd ed.). Cardiff: University of Wales Press.

Davies, J. B., et al. (2007). *The world distribution of household wealth.* University of California, Santa Cruz, Mapping Global Inequalities, Center for Global, International, and Regional Studies.

Davis, S. H. (1982). *Victims of the miracle.* Cambridge, England: Cambridge University Press.

Deetz, J. (1977). *In small things forgotten: The archaeology of early American life.* Garden City, NY: Anchor/Doubleday.

de la Torre, S., & Snowden, C. T. (2009). Dialects in pygmy marmosets? Population variation in call structure. *American Journal of Primatology 71* (4), 333–342.

del Carmen Rodríguez Martínez, M., et al. (2006). Oldest writing in the New World. *Science 313* (5793), 1610–1614.

del Castillo, B. D. (1963). *The conquest of New Spain* (translation and introduction by J. M. Cohen). New York: Penguin.

Delson, E., Tattersal, I., Brooks, A., & Van Couvering, J. (1999). *Encyclopedia of human evolution and prehistory.* New York: Garland.

DeMello, M. (2000). *Bodies of inscription: A cultural history of the modern tattoo community.* Durham: Duke University Press.

De Mott, B. (1990). *The imperial middle: Why Americans can't think straight about class.* New York: Morrow.

d'Errico, F., Zilhão, J., Julien, M., Baffier, D., & Pelegrin, J. (1998). Neandertal acculturation in western Europe? *Current Anthropology 39,* 521.

DeSilva, J. M. (2009). Functional morphology of the ankle and the likelihood of climbing in early hominins. *Proceedings of the National Academy of Sciences, USA 106,* 6567–6572.

Desowitz, R. S. (1987). *New Guinea tapeworms and Jewish grandmothers.* New York: Norton.

Dettwyler, K. A. (1994). *Dancing skeletons: Life and death in West Africa.* Prospect Heights, IL: Waveland.

Dettwyler, K. A. (1997, October). When to wean. *Natural History,* 49.

DeVore, I. (Ed.). (1965). *Primate behavior: Field studies of monkeys and apes.* New York: Holt, Rinehart & Winston.

de Waal, F.B.M. (1998). Comment. *Current Anthropology 39,* 407.

de Waal, F.B.M. (2000). Primates—A natural heritage of conflict resolution. *Science 28,* 586–590.

de Waal, F.B.M. (2001). *The ape and the sushi master.* New York: Basic.

de Waal, F.B.M. (2001). Sing the song of evolution. *Natural History 110* (8), 77.

de Waal, F.B.M. (2003). *My family album: Thirty years of primate photography.* Berkeley: University of California Press.

de Waal, F.B.M., & Johanowicz, D. L. (1993). Modification of reconciliation behavior through social experience: An experiment with two macaque species. *Child Development 64,* 897–908.

de Waal, F.B.M., Kano, T., & Parish, A. R. (1998). Comments. *Current Anthropology 39,* 408, 410, 413.

de Waal, F.B.M., & Lanting F. (1998). *Bonobo: The forgotten ape.* Berkeley: University of California Press.

Diamond, J. (1996). Empire of uniformity. *Discover 17* (3), 83–84.

Diamond, J. (1997). *Guns, germs, and steel.* New York: Norton.

Diamond, J. (1998). Ants, crops, and history. *Science 281,* 1974–1975.

Diamond, J. (2005). *Collapse: How societies choose to fail or succeed.* New York: Penguin.

Dicks, B., et al. (2005). *Qualitative research and hypermedia: Ethnography for the digital age (New technologies for social research).* Thousand Oaks, CA: Sage.

Dillehay, T. D. (2001). *The settlement of the Americas.* New York: Basic.

Dirie, W., & Miller, C. (1998). *Desert flower: The extraordinary journey of a desert nomad.* New York: Morrow.

Dissanayake, E. (2000). Birth of the arts. *Natural History 109* (10), 89.

Dixon, J. E., Cann, J. R., & Renfrew, C. (1968). Obsidian and the origins of trade. *Scientific American 218,* 38–46.

Dobyns, H. F., Doughty, P. L., & Lasswell, H. D. (Eds.). (1971). *Peasants, power, and applied social change.* London: Sage.

Dobzhansky, T. (1962). *Mankind evolving.* New Haven, CT: Yale University Press.

Dorit, R. (1997). Molecular evolution and scientific inquiry, misperceived. *American Scientist 85,* 474–475.

Douglas, M. (1966). *Purity and danger: An analysis of concepts of pollution and taboo.* London: Routledge & Kegan Paul.

Dozier, E. (1970). *The Pueblo Indians of North America.* New York: Holt, Rinehart & Winston.

Draper, P. (1975). !Kung women: Contrasts in sexual egalitarianism in foraging and sedentary contexts. In R. Reiter (Ed.), *Toward an anthropology of women* (pp. 77–109). New York: Monthly Review.

Drewnowski, A., & Specter, S. E. (2004). Poverty and obesity: the role of energy density and energy costs. *American Journal of Clinical Nutrition 79* (1), 6–16.

Driver, H. (1964). *Indians of North America.* Chicago: University of Chicago Press.

Dubos, R. (1968). *So human an animal.* New York: Scribner.

Dumurat-Dreger, A. (1998, May/June). "Ambiguous sex" or ambivalent medicine? *Hastings Center Report 28* (3), 2435 (posted on the website for Intersex Society of North America: www.isna.org)

Dunbar, P. (2008, January 19). The pink vigilantes. www.dailymail.co.uk

Duncan, A. S., Kappelman, J., & Shapiro, L. J. (1994). Metasophalangeal joint function and positional behavior in *Australopithecus afarensis. American Journal of Physical Anthropology 93,* 67–81.

Dundes, A. (1980). *Interpreting folklore.* Bloomington: Indiana University Press.

Durant, J. C. (2000, April 23). Everybody into the gene pool. *New York Times Book Review,* 11.

Duranti, A. (2001). Linguistic anthropology: History, ideas, and issues. In A. Duranti (Ed.), *Linguistic anthropology: A reader* (pp. 1–38). Oxford: Blackwell.
Durkheim, E. (1964). *The division of labor in society.* New York: Free Press. (orig. 1893)
Durkheim, E. (1965). *The elementary forms of the religious life.* New York: Free Press. (orig. 1912)
Durkheim, E., & Mauss, M. (1963). *Primitive classification.* Chicago: University of Chicago Press. (orig. 1902)
duToit, B. M. (1991). *Human sexuality: Cross cultural readings.* New York: McGraw-Hill.
Eastman, C. M. (1990). *Aspects of language and culture* (2nd ed.). Novato, CA: Chandler & Sharp.
Eaton, S. B., Konner, M., & Shostak, M. (1988). Stone-agers in the fast lane: Chronic degenerative diseases in evolutionary perspective. *American Journal of Medicine 84* (4), 739–749.
Edwards, J. (Ed.). (1999). *Technologies of procreation: Kinship in the age of assisted conception.* New York: Routledge.
Edwards, S. W. (1978). Nonutilitarian activities on the Lower Paleolithic: A look at the two kinds of evidence. *Current Anthropology 19* (l), 135–137.
Egan, T. (1999, February 28). The persistence of polygamy. *New York Times Magazine,* 52.
Ehrlich, P. R., & Ehrlich, A. H. (2008). *The dominant animal: Human evolution and the environment.* Washington, DC: Island.
Eiseley, L. (1958). *Darwin's century: Evolution and the men who discovered it.* New York: Doubleday.
Eisenstadt, S. N. (1956). *From generation to generation: Age groups and social structure.* New York: Free Press.
El Guindi, F. (2004). *Visual anthropology: Essential method and theory.* Walnut Creek, CA: Altamira.
Elkin, A. P. (1964). *The Australian Aborigines.* Garden City, NY: Doubleday/Anchor.
Ellis, C. (2006). *A dancing people: Powwow culture on the southern plains.* Lawrence: University Press of Kansas.
Ellison, P. T. (1990). Human ovarian function and reproductive ecology: New hypotheses. *American Anthropologist 92,* 933–952.
Ellison, P. T. (2003). *On fertile ground: A natural history of human reproduction.* Cambridge, MA: Harvard University Press.
Ember, C. R., & Ember, M. (1996). What have we learned from cross-cultural research? *General Anthropology 2* (2), 5.
Enard, W., et al. (2002). Molecular evolution of FOXP2, a gene involved in speech and language. *Nature 418,* 869–872.
Erickson, P. A., & Murphy, L. D. (2003). *A history of anthropological theory* (2nd ed.). Peterborough, Ontario: Broadview.
Errington, F. K., & Gewertz, D. B. (2001). *Cultural alternatives and a feminist anthropology: An analysis of culturally constructed gender interests in Papua New Guinea.* Cambridge, England, and New York: Cambridge University Press.
Ervin-Tripp, S. (1973). *Language acquisition and communicative choice.* Stanford, CA: Stanford University Press.
Esber, G. S. (1987). Designing Apache houses with Apaches. In R. M. Wulff & S. J. Fiske (Eds.), *Anthropological praxis: Translating knowledge into action* (pp. 187–196). Boulder, CO: Westview.
Eugenides, J. (2002). *Middlesex: A novel.* New York: Farrar, Straus and Giroux.
Evans-Pritchard, E. E. (1937). *Witchcraft, oracles and magic among the Azande.* London: Oxford University Press.
Evans-Pritchard, E. E. (1951). *Kinship and marriage among the Nuer.* New York: Oxford University Press.
Evans-Pritchard, E. E. (1968). *The Nuer: A description of the modes of livelihood and political institutions of a Nilotic people.* London: Oxford University Press.
Evershed, R. P., et al. (2008). Earliest date for milk use in the Near East and southeastern Europe linked to cattle herding. *Nature.* doi:10.1038/nature07180.
Fagan, B. M. (1995). *People of the earth* (8th ed.). New York: HarperCollins.
Fagan, B. M. (2000). *Ancient lives: An introduction to archaeology.* Englewood Cliffs, NJ: Prentice-Hall.
Fagan, B. (2001). *The seventy great mysteries of the ancient world.* New York: Thames & Hudson.
Fagan, B. M. (2005). *Archaeology: A brief introduction* (9th ed.). New York: Longman.
Fagan, B. M., Beck, C., & Silberman, N. A. (1998). *The Oxford companion to archaeology.* New York: Oxford University Press.
Falk, D. (1975). Comparative anatomy of the larynx in man and the chimpanzee: Implications for language in Neanderthal. *American Journal of Physical Anthropology 43* (1), 123–132.
Falk, D. (1989). Apelike endocast of "ape-man" Taung. *American Journal of Physical Anthropology 80,* 335–339.
Falk, D. (1993). A good brain is hard to cool. *Natural History 102* (8), 65.
Falk, D. (1993). Hominid paleoneurology. In R. L. Ciochon & J. G. Fleagle (Eds.), *The human evolution source book.* Englewood Cliffs, NJ: Prentice-Hall.
Falk, D. (2004). *Braindance: New discoveries about human origins and brain evolution—revised and updated.* Gainesville: University Press of Florida.
Falk, D., et al. (2005). The brain of LB1, *Homo floresiensis. Science 308,* 242–245.
Farmer, P. (1992). *AIDS and accusation: Haiti and the geography of blame.* Berkeley: University of California Press.
Farmer, P. (1996). On suffering and structural violence: A view from below. *Daedelus 125* (1), 261–283.
Farmer, P. (2001). *Infections and inequalities: The modern plagues.* Berkeley: University of California Press.
Farmer, P. (2003). *Pathologies of power: Health, human rights, and the new war on the poor.* Berkeley: University of California Press.
Farmer, P. (2004, June). An anthropology of structural violence. *Current Anthropology 45,* 3.
Farnell, B. (1995). *Do you see what I mean? Plains Indian sign talk and the embodiment of action.* Austin: University of Texas Press.
Fausto-Sterling, A. (1993, March/April). The five sexes: Why male and female are not enough. *The Sciences 33* (2), 20–24.
Fausto-Sterling, A. (2000, July/August). The five sexes revisited. *The Sciences 40* (4), 19–24.
Fausto-Sterling, A. (2003, August 2). Personal e-mail communication.
Feder, K. L. (2008). *Frauds, myths, and mysteries: Science and pseudoscience in archaeology* (6th ed.). New York: McGraw-Hill.
Fedigan, L. M. (1986). The changing role of women in models of human evolution. *Annual Review of Anthropology 15,* 25–56.
Fedigan, L. M. (1992). *Primate paradigms: Sex roles and social bonds.* Chicago: University of Chicago Press.
"Female genital mutilation." (2000). Fact sheet no. 241. World Health Organization.
Fernandez-Carriba, S., & Loeches, A. (2001). Fruit smearing by captive chimpanzees: A newly observed food-processing behavior. *Current Anthropology 42,* 143–147.
Ferrie, H. (1997). An interview with C. Loring Brace. *Current Anthropology 38,* 851–869.
Field, L. W. (2004). Beyond "applied" anthropology. In T. Biolsi (Ed.), *A companion to the anthropology of American Indians* (pp. 472–489). Oxford: Blackwell.
Finkler, K. (2000). *Experiencing the new genetics: Family and kinship on the medical frontier.* Philadelphia: University of Pennsylvania Press.
"The first Americans, ca. 20,000 B.C." (1998). *Discover 19* (6), 24.
Firth, R. (1946). *Malay fishermen: Their peasant economy.* London: Kegan Paul.
Firth, R. (1952). *Elements of social organization.* London: Watts.
Firth, R. (1957). *Man and culture: An evaluation of Bronislaw Malinowski.* London: Routledge.
Firth, R. (Ed.). (1967). *Themes in economic anthropology.* London: Tavistock.
Fisher, R., & Ury, W. L. (1991). *Getting to yes: Negotiating agreement without giving in* (2nd ed.). Boston: Houghton Mifflin.
Flannery, K. V. (1973). The origins of agriculture. In B. J. Siegel, A. R. Beals, & S. A. Tyler (Eds.), *Annual Review of Anthropology* (Vol. 2, pp. 271–310). Palo Alto, CA: Annual Reviews.
Flannery, K. V. (Ed.). (1976). *The Mesoamerican village.* New York: Seminar.
Fleagle, J. (1998). *Primate adaptation and evolution.* New York: Academic.
Fogel, R, & Riquelme, M. A. (2005). *Enclave sorjero. Merma de soberania y pobreza.* Ascuncion: Centro de Estudios Rurales Interdisciplinarias.
Folger, T. (1993). The naked and the bipedal. *Discover 14* (11), 34–35.
Food and Agriculture Organization (FAO), United Nations. (2009). *1.02 billion people hungry: One sixth of humanity undernourished—more than ever before.* http://www.fao.org/news/story/en/item/20568/icode/
Forbes, J. D. (1964). *The Indian in America's past.* Englewood Cliffs, NJ: Prentice-Hall.
Forbes International 500 List. (2008).
Forde, C. D. (1955). The Nupe. In D. Forde (Ed.), *Peoples of the Niger-Benue confluence.* London: International African Institute (Ethnographic Survey of Africa. Western Africa, part 10).
Forde, C. D. (1968). Double descent among the Yakö. In P. Bohannan & J. Middleton (Eds.), *Kinship and social organization* (pp. 179–191). Garden City, NY: Natural History.
Forste, R. (2008). *Prelude to marriage, or alternative to marriage? A social demographic look at cohabitation in the U.S.* Working paper. Social Science Electronic Publishing, Inc. http://papers.ssrn.com/sol3/papers.cfm?abstract_id=269172.
Fortes, M. (1950). Kinship and marriage among the Ashanti. In A. R. Radcliffe-Brown & C. D. Forde (Eds.), *African systems of kinship and marriage.* London: Oxford University Press.
Fortes, M. (1969). *Kinship and the social order: The legacy of Lewis Henry Morgan.* Chicago: Aldine.
Fortes, M., & Evans-Prichard, E. E. (Eds.). (1962). *African political systems.* London: Oxford University Press. (orig. 1940)
Fossey, D. (1983). *Gorillas in the mist.* Burlington, MA: Houghton Mifflin.
Foster, G. M. (1955). Peasant society and the image of the limited good. *American Anthropologist 67,* 293–315.
Fountain, H. (2000, January 30). Now the ancient ways are less mysterious. *New York Times,* 5.

"4.1 billion mobile phone subscribers worldwide." (2009, March 27). www.mocom2020.com/2009/03/41-billion-mobile-phone-subscribers-worldwide/

Fouts, R. S., & Waters, G. (2001). Chimpanzee sign language and Darwinian continuity: Evidence for a neurology continuity of language. *Neurological Research 23*, 787–794.

Fox, R. (1968). *Encounter with anthropology*. New York: Dell.

Fox, R. (1968). *Kinship and marriage in an anthropological perspective*. Baltimore: Penguin.

Fox, R. (1981, December 3). [Interview]. Coast Telecourses, Inc., Los Angeles.

Frake, C. (1961). The diagnosis of disease among the Subinam of Mindinao. *American Anthropologist 63*,113–132.

Frake, C. O. (1992). Lessons of the Mayan sky. In A. F. Aveni (Ed.), *The sky in Mayan literature* (pp. 274–291). New York: Oxford University Press.

Franzen, J. L., Gingerich, P. D., Habersetzer, J., Hurum, J. H., von Koenigswald, W., et al. (2009). Complete primate skeleton from the middle Eocene of Messel in Germany: Morphology and paleobiology. *PLoS ONE 4* (5), e5723.

Fraser, D. (Ed.). (1966). *The many faces of primitive art: A critical anthology*. Englewood Cliffs, NJ: Prentice-Hall.

Frayer, D. W. (1981). Body size, weapon use, and natural selection in the European Upper Paleolithic and Mesolithic. *American Anthropologist 83*, 57–73.

Frazer, Sir J. G. (1961 reissue). *The new golden bough*. New York: Doubleday, Anchor.

Freeman, J. D. (1960). The Iban of western Borneo. In G. P. Murdock (Ed.), *Social structure in Southeast Asia*. Chicago: Quadrangle.

Freeman, L. G. (1992). *Ambrona and Torralba: New evidence and interpretation*. Paper presented at the 91st Annual Meeting, American Anthropological Association.

Fried, M. (1967). *The evolution of political society: An essay in political anthropology*. New York: Random House.

Fried, M., Harris, M., & Murphy, R. (1968). *War: The anthropology of armed conflict and aggression*. Garden City, NY: Natural History.

Friedl, E. (1975). *Women and men: An anthropologist's view*. New York: Holt, Rinehart & Winston.

Friedman, J. (Ed.). (2003). *Globalization, the state, and violence*. Walnut Creek, CA: Altamira.

Friedman, T. (2007, April). *New York Times*.

Frisch, R. (2002). *Female fertility and the body fat connection*. Chicago: University of Chicago Press.

Frye, D. P. (2000). Conflict management in cross-cultural perspective. In F. Aureli & F.B.M. de Waal (Eds.), *Natural conflict resolution* (pp. 334–351). Berkeley: University of California Press.

Furst, P. T. (1976). *Hallucinogens and culture* (p. 7). Novato, CA: Chandler & Sharp.

Galdikas, B. (1995). *Reflections on Eden: My years with the orangutans of Borneo*. New York: Little, Brown.

Gamble, C. (1986). *The Paleolithic settlement of Europe*. Cambridge, England: Cambridge University Press.

Gardner, R. A., Gardner, B. T., & Van Cantfort, T. E. (Eds.). (1989). *Teaching sign language to chimpanzees*. Albany: State University of New York Press.

Garn, S. M. (1970). *Human races* (3rd ed.). Springfield, IL: Thomas.

Gates, H. (1996). Buying brides in China—again. *Anthropology Today 12* (4), 10.

Gebo, D. L., Dagosto, D., Beard, K. C., & Tao, Q. (2001). Middle Eocene primate tarsals from China: Implications for haplorhine evolution. *American Journal of Physical Anthropology 116*, 83–107.

Geertz, C. (1965). The impact of the concept of culture on the concept of man. In J. R. Platt (Ed.), *New views of man*. Chicago: University of Chicago Press.

Geertz, C. (1973). *The interpretation of culture*. London: Hutchinson.

Geertz, C. (1984). Distinguished lecture: Anti anti-relativism. *American Anthropologist 86*, 263–278.

Geertz, C. (2004). Religion as a cultural system. In M. Banton (Ed.), *Anthropological approaches to the study of religion* (pp. 1–46). London: Routledge. (orig. 1966)

Gell, A. (1988). Technology and magic. *Anthropology Today 4* (2), 6–9.

"Gene study suggests Polynesians came from Taiwan." (2005, July 4). Reuters.

Gero, J. M., & Conkey, M. W. (Eds.). (1991). *Engendering archaeology: Women and prehistory*. New York: Wiley-Blackwell.

Gibbons, A. (1993). Where are new diseases born? *Science 261*, 680–681.

Gibbons, A. (1997). Ideas on human origins evolve at anthropology gathering. *Science 276*, 535–536.

Gibbons, A. (1998). Ancient island tools suggest *Homo erectus* was a seafarer. *Science 279*, 1635.

Gibbons, A. (2001). The riddle of coexistence. *Science 291*, 1726.

Gibbons, A. (2001). Studying humans—and their cousins and parasites. *Science 292*, 627.

Gibbs, J. L., Jr. (1965). The Kpelle of Liberia. In J. L. Gibbs, Jr. (Ed.), *Peoples of Africa* (pp. 216–218). New York: Holt, Rinehart & Winston.

Gibbs, J. L., Jr. (1983). [Interview]. *Faces of culture: Program 18*. Fountain Valley, CA: Coast Telecourses.

Giddens, A. (1990). *The consequences of modernity*. Stanford, CA: Stanford University Press.

Ginsburg, F. D., Abu-Lughod, L., & Larkin, B. (Eds.). (2009). *Media worlds: Anthropology on new terrain*. Berkeley: University of California Press.

Gladdol, D. (2006). *English next*. London: British Council.

Gledhill, J. (2000). *Power and its disguises: Anthropological perspectives on politics* (2nd ed.). Boulder, CO: Pluto.

Godfrey, T. (2000, December 27). Biotech threatening biodiversity. *Burlington Free Press*, 10A.

Godlier, M. (1971). Salt currency and the circulation of commodities among the Baruya of New Guinea. In G. Dalton (Ed.), *Studies in economic anthropology*. Washington, DC: American Anthropological Association (Anthropological Studies No. 7).

González, R. J. (2009). *American counterinsurgency: Human science and the human terrain*. Chicago: University of Chicago Press.

Goodall, J. (1986). *The chimpanzees of Gombe: Patterns of behavior*. Cambridge, MA: Belknap.

Goodall, J. (1990). *Through a window: My thirty years with the chimpanzees of Gombe*. Boston: Houghton Mifflin.

Goodall, J. (2000). *Reason for hope: A spiritual journey*. New York: Warner.

Goodenough, W. (Ed.). (1964). *Explorations in cultural anthropology: Essays in honor of George Murdock*. New York: McGraw-Hill.

Goodenough, W. (1965). Rethinking status and role: Toward a general model of the cultural organization of social relationships. In M. Benton (Ed.), *The relevance of models for social anthropology*. New York: Praeger.

Goodenough, W. H. (1970). *Description and comparison in cultural anthropology*. Chicago: Aldine.

Goodenough, W. H. (1990). Evolution of the human capacity for beliefs. *American Anthropologist 92*, 601.

Goodman, A., & Armelagos, G. J. (1985). Death and disease at Dr. Dickson's mounds. *Natural History 94* (9), 12–18.

Goodman, M., Bailey, W. J., Hayasaka, K., Stanhope, M. J., Slightom J., & Czelusniak, J. (1994). Molecular evidence on primate phylogeny from DNA sequences. *American Journal of Physical Anthropology 94*, 7.

Goodwin, R. (1999). *Personal relationships across cultures*. New York: Routledge.

Goody, J. (1969). *Comparative studies in kinship*. Stanford, CA: Stanford University Press.

Goody, J. (1976). *Production and reproduction: A comparative study of the domestic domain*. Cambridge, MA: Cambridge University Press.

Goody, J. (1983). *The development of the family and marriage in Europe*. Cambridge, MA: Cambridge University Press.

Gordon, R. (2000). *Eating disorders: Anatomy of a social epidemic* (2nd ed.). New York: Wiley-Blackwell.

Gordon, R., Lyons, H., & Lyons, A. (Eds.). (2010). *Fifty key anthropologists*. New York: Routledge.

Gordon, R. J. (1992). *The Bushman myth: The making of a Namibian underclass*. Boulder, CO: Westview.

Gordon, R. J., & Megitt, M. J. (1985). *Law and order in the New Guinea highlands*. Hanover, NH: University Press of New England.

Gough, K. (1959). The Nayars and the definition of marriage. *Journal of the Royal Anthropological Institute of Great Britain and Ireland 89*, 23–34.

Gould, S. J. (1983). *Hen's teeth and horses' toes*. New York: Norton.

Gould, S. J. (1985). *The flamingo's smile: Reflections in natural history*. New York: Norton.

Gould, S. J. (1989). *Wonderful life*. New York: Norton.

Gould, S. J. (1991). *Bully for brontosaurus*. New York: Norton.

Gould, S. J. (1994). The geometer of race. *Discover 15* (11), 65–69.

Gould, S. J. (1996). *Full house: The spread of excellence from Plato to Darwin*. New York: Harmony.

Gould, S. J. (1996). *The mismeasure of man* (2nd ed.). New York: Norton.

Gould, S. J. (2000). The narthex of San Marco and the pangenetic paradigm. *Natural History 109* (6), 29.

Gould, S. J. (2000). What does the dreaded "E" word mean anyway? *Natural History 109* (1), 34–36.

Graburn, N.H.H. (1969). *Eskimos without igloos: Social and economic development in Sugluk*. Boston: Little, Brown.

Graburn, N. H. (1971). *Readings in kinship and social structure*. New York: Harper & Row.

Graves, J. L. (2001). *The emperor's new clothes: Biological theories of race at the millennium*. New Brunswick, NJ: Rutgers University Press.

Graves, P. (1991). New models and metaphors for the Neanderthal debate. *Current Anthropology 32*(5), 513–543.

Gray, P. B. (2004, May). HIV and Islam: Is HIV prevalence lower among Muslims? *Social Science & Medicine 58* (9), 1751–1756.

Gray, P. M., Krause, B., Atema, J., Payne, R., Krumhansl, C., & Baptista, L. (2001). The music of nature and the nature of music. *Science 291*, 52.

Green, E. C. (1987). The planning of health education strategies in Swaziland, and the integration of modern and traditional health sectors in Swaziland. In R. M. Wulff & S. J. Fiske (Eds.), *Anthropological praxis: Translating knowledge into action* (pp. 15–25, 87–97). Boulder, CO: Westview.

Greenberg, J. H. (1968). *Anthropological linguistics: An introduction.* New York: Random House.

Greymorning, S. N. (2001). Reflections on the Arapaho Language Project or, when Bambi spoke Arapaho and other tales of Arapaho language revitalization efforts. In K. Hale & L. Hinton (Eds.), *The green book of language revitalization in practice* (pp. 287–297). New York: Academic.

Grine, F. E. (1993). Australopithecine taxonomy and phylogeny: Historical background and recent interpretation. In R. L. Ciochon & J. G. Fleagle (Eds.), *The human evolution source book.* Englewood Cliffs, NJ: Prentice-Hall.

Grivetti, L. E. (2005). From aphrodisiac to health food: A cultural history of chocolate. *Karger Gazette,* 68.

Grossman, J. (2002). Should the law be kinder to kissin' cousins? A genetic report should cause a rethinking of incest laws. *Find Law.* (accessed October 16, 2009)

Grün, R., & Thorne, A. (1997). Dating the Ngandong humans. *Science 276,* 1575.

Guillette, E. A., et al. (1998, June). An anthropological approach to the evaluation of preschool children exposed to pesticides in Mexico. *Environmental Health Perspectives 106,* 347.

Guthrie, S. (1993). *Faces in the clouds: A new theory of religions.* New York: Oxford University Press.

Gutin, J. A. (1995). Do Kenya tools root birth of modern thought in Africa? *Science 270,* 1118–1119.

Haeri, N. (1997). The reproduction of symbolic capital: Language, state and class in Egypt. *Current Anthropology 38,* 795–816.

Hafkin, N., & Bay, E. (Eds.). (1976). *Women in Africa.* Stanford, CA: Stanford University Press.

Hager, L. (1989). *The evolution of sex differences in the hominid bony pelvis.* Ph.D. dissertation, University of California, Berkeley.

Haglund, W. D., Conner, M., & Scott, D. D. (2001). The archaeology of contemporary mass graves. *Historical Archaeology 35* (1), 57–69.

Hahn, R. A. (1992). The state of federal health statistics on racial and ethnic groups. *Journal of the American Medica Association 267* (2), 268–271.

Hall, E. T. (1959). *The silent language.* Garden City, NY: Anchor/Doubleday.

Hall, E. T., & Hall, M. R. (1986). The sounds of silence. In E. Angeloni (Ed.), *Anthropology 86/87* (pp. 65–70). Guilford, CT: Dushkin.

Hall, K.R.L., & DeVore, I. (1965). Baboon social behavior. In I. DeVore (Ed.), *Primate behavior.* New York: Holt, Rinehart & Winston.

Hallowell, A. I. (1955). *Culture and experience.* Philadelphia: University of Pennsylvania Press.

Halperin, R. H. (1994). *Cultural economies: Past and present.* Austin: University of Texas Press.

Halverson, J. (1989). Review of the book *Altamira Revisited and other essays on early art. American Antiquity 54,* 883.

Handwerk, B. (2005, March 8). King Tut not murdered violently, CT scans show. *National Geographic News,* 2.

Hannah, J. L. (1988). *Dance, sex and gender.* Chicago: University of Chicago Press.

Hanson, A. (1989). The making of the Maori: Culture invention and its logic. *American Anthropologist 91* (4), 890–902.

Harcourt-Smith, W.E.H., & Aiello, L. C. (2004). Fossils, feet and the evolution of human bipedal locomotion. *Journal of Anatomy 204,* 403–416.

Harlow, H. F. (1962). Social deprivation in monkeys. *Scientific America 206,* 1–10.

Harner, M. (1980). *The way of the shaman: A guide to power and healing.* San Francisco: Harper & Row.

Harpending, H., & Cochran, G. (2002). In our genes. *Proceedings of the National Academy of Sciences, USA 99* (1), 10–12.

Harpending, J. H., & Harpending, H. C. (1995). Ancient differences in population can mimic a recent African origin of modern humans. *Current Anthropology 36,* 667–674.

Harris, M. (1965). The cultural ecology of India's sacred cattle. *Current Anthropology 7,* 51–66.

Harris, M. (1968). *The rise of anthropological theory: A history of theories of culture.* New York: Crowell.

Harris, M. (1979). *Cultural materialism: The struggle for a science of culture.* New York: Random House.

Harris, M. (1989). *Cows, pigs, wars, and witches: The riddles of culture.* New York: Vintage/Random House.

Harrison, G. G. (1975). Primary adult lactase deficiency: A problem in anthropological genetics. *American Anthropologist 77,* 815–819.

Harrison, K. D. (2008). *When languages die: The extinction of the world's languages and the erosion of human knowledge.* New York: Oxford University Press.

Harrison, K. D. *Pop!Tech 2008: Scarcity and abundance: Global and local trends in language extinction.* www.poptech.org/popcasts/k_david_harrison__poptech_2008

Hart, C. W., Pilling, A. R., & Goodale, J. (1988). *Tiwi of North Australia* (3rd ed.). New York: Holt, Rinehart & Winston.

Hart, D. (2006, April 21). Humans as prey. *Chronicle of Higher Education.*

Hart, D., & Sussman, R. W. (2005). *Man the hunted: Primates, predators, and human evolution.* Boulder, CO: Westview.

Hartwig, W. C. (2002). *The primate fossil record.* New York: Cambridge University Press.

Hartwig, W. C., & Doneski, K. (1998). Evolution of the hominid hand and toolmaking behavior. *American Journal of Physical Anthropology 106,* 401–402.

Hatch, E. (1983). *Culture and morality: The relativity of values in anthropology.* New York: Columbia University Press.

Hatcher, E. P. (1985). *Art as culture, an introduction to the anthropology of art.* New York: University Press of America.

Haviland, W. A. (1967). Stature at Tikal, Guatemala: Implications for ancient Maya, demography, and social organization. *American Antiquity 32,* 316–325.

Haviland, W. A. (1970). Tikal, Guatemala and Mesoamerican urbanism. *World Archaeology 2,* 186–198.

Haviland, W. A. (1972). A new look at Classic Maya social organization at Tikal. *Ceramica de Cultura Maya 8,* 1–16.

Haviland, W. A. (1974). Farming, seafaring and bilocal residence on the coast of Maine. *Man in the Northeast 6,* 31–44.

Haviland, W. A. (1997). Cleansing young minds, or what should we be doing in introductory anthropology? In C. P. Kottak, J. J. White, R. H. Furlow, & P. C. Rice (Eds.), *The teaching of anthropology: Problems, issues, and decisions* (p. 35). Mountain View, CA: Mayfield.

Haviland, W. A. (1997). The rise and fall of sexual inequality: Death and gender at Tikal, Guatemala. *Ancient Mesoamerica 8,* 1–12.

Haviland, W. A. (2002). Settlement, society and demography at Tikal. In J. Sabloff (Ed.), *Tikal.* Santa Fe: School of American Research.

Haviland, W. A. (2003). *Tikal, Guatemala: A Maya way to urbanism.* Paper prepared for 3rd INAH/Penn State Conference on Mesoamerican Urbanism.

Haviland, W. A., & Gordon, R. J. (Eds.). (1993). *Talking about people.* Mountain View, CA: Mayfield.

Haviland, W. A., et al. (1985). *Excavations in small residential groups of Tikal: Groups 4F-1 and 4F-2.* Philadelphia: University Museum.

Haviland, W. A., & Moholy-Nagy, H. (1992). Distinguishing the high and mighty from the hoi polloi at Tikal, Guatemala. In A. F. Chase & D. Z. Chase (Eds.), *Mesoamerican elites: An archaeological assessment.* Norman: Oklahoma University Press.

Haviland, W. A., & Power, M. W. (1994). *The original Vermonters: Native inhabitants, past and present* (2nd ed.). Hanover, NH: University Press of New England.

Hawkes, K., O'Connell, J. F., & Blurton Jones, N. G. (1997). Hadza women's time allocation, offspring, provisioning, and the evolution of long postmenopausal life spans. *Current Anthropology 38,* 551–577.

Hawks, J. (2006, July 21). Neandertal Genome Project. http://johnhawks.net/weblog.

"Hazardous waste trafficking." www.Choike.org

Heilbroner, R. L., & Thurow, L. C. (1981). *The economic problem* (6th ed.). Englewood Cliffs, NJ: Prentice-Hall.

Heita, K. (1999). Imanishi's world view. *Journal of Japanese Trade and Industry 18* (2), 15.

Heitzman, J., & Wordem, R. L. (Eds.). (2006). *India: A country study* (sect. 2, 5th ed.). Washington, DC: Federal Research Division, Library of Congress.

Helm, J. (1962). The ecological approach in anthropology. *American Journal of Sociology 67,* 630–649.

Helman, C. B. (2003). *Culture, health, and illness: An introduction for health professionals.* New York: Butterworth Heinemann Medical.

Henry, D. O., et al. (2004). Human behavioral organization in the Middle Paleolithic: Were Neandertals different? *American Anthropologist 107* (1), 17–31.

Henry, J. (1974). A theory for an anthropological analysis of American culture. In J. G. Jorgensen & M. Truzzi (Eds.), *Anthropology and American life.* Englewood Cliffs, NJ: Prentice-Hall.

Herdt, G. (Ed.). (1996). *Third sex, third gender: Beyond sexual dimorphism in culture and history.* New York: Zone.

Herdt, G. H. (1993). Semen transactions in Sambia culture. In D. N. Suggs & A. W. Mirade (Eds.), *Culture and human sexuality* (pp. 298–327). Pacific Grove, CA: Brooks/Cole.

Herskovits, M. J. (1952). *Economic anthropology: A study in comparative economics* (2nd ed.). New York: Knopf.

Hertz, N. (2001). *The silent takeover: Global capitalism and the death of democracy.* New York: Arrow.

Hewes, G. W. (1973). Primate communication and the gestural origin of language. *Current Anthropology 14,* 5–24.

"Hidden apartheid: Caste discrimination against India's Untouchables." (2007). Human Rights Watch and the Center for Human Rights and Global Justice.

Himmelfarb, E. J. (2000, January/February). First alphabet found in Egypt. Newsbrief. *Archaeology 53* (1).

Hirsch, J. S., & Wardlow, H. (Eds.). (2006). *Modern loves: The anthropology of romantic*

courtship and companionate marriage. Ann Arbor: University of Michigan Press.
Historical atlas of the twentieth century. http://users.erols.com/mwhite28/20centry.htm
Hitchcock, R. K., & Enghoff, M. (2004). *Capacity-building of first people of the Kalahari, Botswana: An evaluation.* Copenhagen: International Work Group for Indigenous Affairs.
Hodgen, M. (1964). *Early anthropology in the sixteenth and seventeenth centuries.* Philadelphia: University of Pennsylvania Press.
Hoebel, E. A. (1954). *The law of primitive man: A study in comparative legal dynamics.* Cambridge, MA: Harvard University Press.
Hoebel, E. A. (1958). *Man in the primitive world: An introduction to anthropology.* New York: McGraw-Hill.
Hoebel, E. A. (1960). *The Cheyennes: Indians of the Great Plains.* New York: Holt, Rinehart & Winston.
Holden, C. (1996). Missing link for Miocene apes. *Science 271,* 151.
Holden, C. (1999). Ancient child burial uncovered in Portugal. *Science 283,* 169.
Hole, F. (1966). Investigating the origins of Mesopotamian civilization. *Science 153,* 605–611.
Hole, F., & Heizer, R. F. (1969). *An introduction to prehistoric archeology.* New York: Holt, Rinehart & Winston.
Holloway, R. L. (1980). The O. H. 7 (Olduvai Gorge, Tanzania) hominid partial brain endocast revisited. *American Journal of Physical Anthropology 53,* 267–274.
Holloway, R. L. (1981). The Indonesian *Homo erectus* brain endocast revisited. *American Journal of Physical Anthropology 55,* 503–521.
Holloway, R. L. (1981). Volumetric and asymmetry determinations on recent hominid endocasts: Spy I and II, Djebel Jhroud 1, and the Salb *Homo erectus* specimens, with some notes on Neanderthal brain size. *American Journal of Physical Anthropology 55,* 385–393.
Holloway, R. L., & de LaCoste-Lareymondie, M. C. (1982). Brain endocast asymmetry in pongids and hominids: Some preliminary findings on the paleontology of cerebral dominance. *American Journal of Physical Anthropology 58,* 101–110.
Holmes, L. D. (2000). *Paradise bent* (film review). *American Anthropologist 102* (3), 604–605.
Holy, L. (1996). *Anthropological perspectives on kinship.* London: Pluto.
Horst, H. A., & Miller, D. (Eds.). (2006). *The cell phone: An anthropology of communication.* New York: Berg.
Hostetler, J., & Huntington, G. (1971). *Children in Amish society.* New York: Holt, Rinehart & Winston.
Houle, A. (1999). The origin of platyrrhines: An evaluation of the Antarctic scenario and the floating island model. *American Journal of Physical Anthropology 109,* 554–556.
Howell, F. C. (1970). *Early man.* New York: Time-Life.
Hrdy, S. B. (1999). Body fat and birth control. *Natural History 108* (8), 88.
Hsiaotung, F. (1939). *Peasant life in China.* London: Kegan, Paul.
Hsu, F. L. (1961). *Psychological anthropology: Approaches to culture and personality.* Homewood, IL: Dorsey.
Hsu, F.L.K. (1979). The cultural problems of the cultural anthropologist. *American Anthropologist 81,* 517–532.
Hubert, H., & Mauss, M. (1964). *Sacrifice.* Chicago: University of Chicago Press.
Human development report. (2002). *Deepening democracy in a fragmented world.* United Nations Development Program.
Hunger Project. (2003). www.thp.org
Hunt, R. C. (Ed.). (1967). *Personalities and cultures: Readings in psychological anthropology.* Garden City, NY: Natural History.
Hutter, M. (Ed.). (2003). *The family experience: A reader in cultural diversity* (4th ed.). Boston: Allyn & Bacon.
Hymes, D. (1964). *Language in culture and society: A reader in linguistics and anthropology.* New York: Harper & Row.
Hymes, D. (Ed.). (1972). *Reinventing anthropology.* New York: Pantheon. icasualties.org.
Hymes, D. (1974). *Foundations in sociolinguistics: An ethnographic approach.* Philadelphia: University of Pennsylvania Press.
Imanishi, K., & Asquith, P. (2002). *Japanese view of nature: The world of living things.* New York: Routledge/Curzon.
Inda, J. X., & Rosaldo, R. (Eds.). (2001). *The anthropology of globalization: A reader.* Malden, MA, and Oxford: Blackwell.
Ingmanson, E. J. (1998). Comment. *Current Anthropology 39,* 409.
Inkeles, A., & Levinson, D. J. (1954). National character: The study of modal personality and socio-cultural systems. In G. Lindzey (Ed.), *Handbook of social psychology.* Reading, MA: Addison-Wesley.
International Lesbian, Gay, Bisexual, Trans and Intersex Association (ILGA). (2009). The *2009 report on state-sponsored homophobia.*
Internet World Stats. (2009). www.internetworldstats.com
"Interview with Laura Nader." (2000, November). *California Monthly.*
Inuit Tapiirit Katami. http://www.taprisat.ca/english- text/itk/departments/enviro/ncp
Irvine, M. (1999, November 24). Mom-and-pop houses grow rare. *Burlington Free Press.*
"Italy-Germany verbal war hots up." (2003, July 9). *Deccan Herald* (Bangalore, India).
"It's the law: Child labor protection." (1997, November/December). *Peace and Justice News,* 11.
Jacobs, S. E. (1994). Native American two-spirits. *Anthropology Newsletter 35* (8), 7.
Jacoby, R., & Glauberman, N. (Eds.). (1995). *The Bell Curve debate.* New York: Random House.
Jane Goodall Institute. http://www.janegoodall.org/jane/study-corner/Jane/bio.asp (accessed June 16, 2009)
Jenkins, A. C., Macrae, C. N., & Mitchell, J. P. (2008). Repetition suppression of ventromedial prefrontal activity during judgments of self and others. *Proceedings of the National Academy of Sciences, 105* (11), 4507–4512.
Jennings, F. (1976). *The invasion of America.* New York: Norton.
Jennings, J. D. (1974). *Prehistory of North America* (2nd ed.). New York: McGraw-Hill.
Johansen, B. E. (2002). The Inuit's struggle with dioxins and other organic pollutants. *American Indian Quarterly 26* (3), 479–490.
Johanson, D., & Shreeve, J. (1989). *Lucy's child: The discovery of a human ancestor.* New York: Avon.
Johanson, D. C., & Edey, M. (1981). *Lucy, the beginnings of humankind.* New York: Simon & Schuster.
Johanson, D. C, Edgar, B., & Brill, D. (1996). *From Lucy to language.* New York: Simon & Schuster.
Johanson, D. C., & White, T. D. (1979). A systematic assessment of early African hominids. *Science 203,* 321–330.
Johanson, D. C., & Wong, K. (2009). *Lucy's legacy: The quest for human origins.* New York: Harmony.
John, V. (1971). Whose is the failure? In C. L. Brace, G. R. Gamble, & J. T. Bond (Eds.), *Race and intelligence.* Washington, DC: American Anthropological Association.
Johnson, A. (1989). Horticulturalists: Economic behavior in tribes. In S. Plattner (Ed.), *Economic anthropology* (pp. 49–77). Stanford, CA: Stanford University Press.
Johnson, A. W., & Earle, T. (1987). *The evolution of human societies, from foraging group to agrarian state.* Stanford, CA: Stanford University Press.
Johnson, D. (1996). Polygamists emerge from secrecy, seeking not just peace but respect. In W. A. Haviland & R. J. Gordon (Eds.), *Talking about people* (2nd ed., pp. 129–131). Mountain View, CA: Mayfield.
Johnson, N. B. (1984). Sex, color, and rites of passage in ethnographic research. *Human Organization 43* (2), 108–120.
Jolly, A. (1985). *The evolution of primate behavior* (2nd ed.). New York: Macmillan.
Jolly, A. (1991). Thinking like a vervet. *Science 251,* 574.
Jolly, C. J. (1970). The seed eaters: A new model of hominid differentiation based on a baboon analogy. *Man 5,* 5–26.
Jones, S. (2005). Transhumance re-examined. *Journal of the Royal Anthropological Institute 11* (4), 841–842.
Jones, S., Martin, R., & Pilbeam, D. (Eds.). (1994). *The Cambridge encyclopedia of human evolution.* New York: Cambridge University Press.
Jorgensen, J. (1972). *The sun dance religion.* Chicago: University of Chicago Press.
Joukowsky, M. A. (1980). *A complete field manual of archaeology: Tools and techniques of field work for archaeologists.* Englewood Cliffs, NJ: Prentice-Hall.
Kaiser, J. (1994). A new theory of insect wing origins takes off. *Science 266,* 363.
Kalwet, H. (1988). *Dreamtime and inner space: The world of the shaman.* New York: Random House.
Kaplan, D. (1972). *Culture theory.* Englewood Cliffs, NJ: Prentice-Hall (Foundations of Modern Anthropology).
Kaplan, D. (2000). The darker side of the original affluent society. *Journal of Anthropological Research 53*(3), 301–324.
Kaplan, M. (2008, August 5). Almost half of primate species face extinction. doi: 10.1038/news.2008.1013.
Karavani, I., & Smith, F. H. (2000). More on the Neanderthal problem: The Vindija case. *Current Anthropology 41,* 839.
Kawamura S. (1959). The process of sub-culture propagation among Japanese macaques. *Primates 2,* 43–60.
Kay, R. F., Fleagle, J. G., & Simons, E. L. (1981). A revision of the Oligocene apes of the Fayum Province, Egypt. *American Journal of Physical Anthropology 55,* 293–322.
Kay, R. F., Ross, C., & Williams, B. A. (1997). Anthropoid origins. *Science 275,* 797–804.
Kay, R. F., Theweissen, J.G.M., & Yoder, A. D. (1992). Cranial anatomy of *Ignacius graybullianus* and the affinities of the plesiadapiformes. *American Journal of Physical Anthropology 89* (4), 477–498.
Kedia, S., & Van Willigen, J. (2005). *Applied anthropology: Domains of application.* New York: Praeger.
Keen, B. (1971). *The Aztec image in western thought.* New Brunswick, NJ: Rutgers University Press.
Kehoe, A. (1989). *The ghost dance: Ethno-history and revitalization.* Fort Worth: Holt, Rinehart & Winston.
Kehoe, A. (2000). *Shamans and religion: An anthropological exploration in critical thinking.* Prospect Heights, IL: Waveland.

Keiser, L. (1991). *Friend by day, enemy by night: Organized vengeance in a Kohistani community.* Fort Worth: Holt, Rinehart & Winston.
Kelly, T. L. (2006). *Sadhus, the great renouncers.* Photography exhibit, Indigo Gallery, Naxal, Kathmandu, Nepal. www.asianart.com/exhibitions/sadhus/index.html
Kendall, L. (1990, October). In the company of witches. *Natural History,* 92.
Kennickell, A. B. (2003, November). *A rolling tide: Changes in the distribution of wealth in the U.S. 1989–2001.* Levy Economics Institute.
Kertzer, D. I. (1989). *Ritual, politics, and power.* New Haven, CT: Yale University Press.
Key, M. R. (1975). *Paralanguage and kinesics: Nonverbal communication.* Metuchen, NJ: Scarecrow.
Khaitovich, P., Lockstone, H. E., Wayland, M. T., Tsang, T. M., Jayatilaka, S. D., Guo, A. J., Zhou, J., Somel, M., Harris, L. W., Holmes, E., Pääbo, S., & Bahn, S. (2008). Metabolic changes in schizophrenia and human brain evolution. *Genome Biology* 9 (8), R124.
Kidder, T. (2003). *Mountains beyond mountains: The quest of Dr. Paul Farmer, a man who would cure the world.* New York: Random House.
Kirkpatrick, R. C. (2000). The evolution of human homosexual behavior. *Current Anthropology 41,* 384.
Klass, M. (1995). *Ordered universes: Approaches to the anthropology of religion.* Boulder, CO: Westview.
Klass, M., & Weisgrau, M. (Eds.). (1999). *Across the boundaries of belief: Contemporary issues in the anthropology of religion.* Boulder, CO: Westview.
Klein, R. (2002). *The dawn of human culture.* New York: Wiley.
Klein, R. G., & Edgar, B. (2002). *The dawn of human culture.* New York: Wiley.
Kleinman, A. (1976). Concepts and a model for the comparison of medical systems as cultural systems. *Social Science and Medicine 12* (2B), 85–95.
Kluckhohn, C. (1970). *Mirror for man.* Greenwich, CT: Fawcett.
Kluckhohn, C. (1994). Navajo witchcraft. *Papers of the Peabody Museum of American Archaeology and Ethnology 22* (2).
Knauft, B. M. (1991). Violence and sociality in human evolution. *Current Anthropology 32,* 391–409.
Koch, G. (1997). Songs, land rights, and archives in Australia. *Cultural Survival Quarterly 20* (4).
Komai, T., & Fukuoka, G. (1934, October). Postnatal growth disparity in monozygotic twins. *Journal of Heredity 25,* 423–430.
Konner, M., & Worthman, C. (1980). Nursing frequency, gonadal function, and birth spacing among !Kung hunter-gatherers. *Science 207,* 788–791.
Koufos, G. (1993). Mandible of *Ouranopithecus macedoniensis* (hominidae: primates) from a new late Miocene locality in Macedonia (Greece). *American Journal of Physical Anthropology 91,* 225–234.
Krader, L. (1968). *Formation of the state.* Englewood Cliffs, NJ: Prentice-Hall.
Krajick, K. (1998). Greenfarming by the Incas? *Science 281,* 323.
Kramer, P. A. (1998). The costs of human locomotion: Maternal investment in child transport. *American Journal of Physical Anthropology 107,* 71–85.
Kraybill, D. B. (2001). *The riddle of Amish culture.* Baltimore: Johns Hopkins University Press.
Kroeber, A. (1958). Totem and taboo: An ethnologic psycho-analysis. In W. Lessa & E. Z. Vogt (Eds.), *Reader in comparative religion: An anthropological approach.* New York: Harper & Row.
Kroeber, A. L. (1939). Cultural and natural areas of native North America. *American Archaeology and Ethnology* (Vol. 38). Berkeley: University of California Press.
Kroeber, A. L. (1963). *Anthropology: Cultural processes and patterns.* New York: Harcourt.
Kroeber, A. L., & Kluckhohn, C. (1952). *Culture: A critical review of concepts and definitions.* Cambridge, MA: Harvard University Press (*Papers of the Peabody Museum of American Archaeology and Ethnology, 47*).
Kruger, J., et al. (2005, December). Egocentrism over e-mail: Can people communicate as well as they think? *Journal of Personality and Social Psychology 89* (6), 925–936.
Kummer, H. (1971). *Primate societies: Group techniques of ecological adaptation.* Chicago: Aldine.
Kunnie, J. (2003). Africa's fast growing indigenous churches. http://coh.arizona.edu/newandnotable/kunnie/kunnie.html
Kunnie, J. (2007). *Umoya: The spirit in Africa.* Self-produced DVD, available at www.coh.arizona.edu/aas/aas.htm
Kunzig, R. (1999). A tale of two obsessed archaeologists, one ancient city and nagging doubts about whether science can ever hope to reveal the past. *Discover 20* (5), 84–92.
Kuper, H. (1965). The Swazi of Swaziland. In J. L. Gibbs (Ed.), *Peoples of Africa* (pp. 479–511). New York: Holt, Rinehart & Winston.
Kurth, P. (1998, October 14). Capital crimes. *Seven Days,* 7.
Kurtz, D. V. (2001). *Political anthropology: Paradigms and power.* Boulder, CO: Westview.
Kushner, G. (1969). *Anthropology of complex societies.* Stanford, CA: Stanford University Press.
LaFont, S. (Ed.). (2003). *Constructing sexualities: Readings in sexuality, gender, and culture.* Upper Saddle River, NJ: Prentice-Hall.
Lai, C.S.L., et al. (2001). A forkhead-domain gene is mutated in severe speech and language disorder. *Nature 413,* 519–523.
Lakoff, R. T. (2004). *Language and woman's place.* M. Bucholtz (Ed.). New York: Oxford University Press.
Lambek, M. (2002). *A reader in the anthropology of religion.* London: Blackwell.
Lampl, M., Velhuis, J. D., & Johnson, M. L. (1992). Saltation and stasis: A model of human growth. *Science 258* (5083), 801–803.
Lancaster, J. B. (1975). *Primate behavior and the emergence of human culture.* New York: Holt, Rinehart & Winston.
Landau, M. (1991). *Narratives of human evolution.* New Haven, CT: Yale University Press.
Lang, I. A., et al. (2008). Association of urinary bisphenol A concentration with medical disorders and laboratory abnormalities in adults. *Journal of the American Medical Association 300* (11), 1303–1310.
Langan, P., & Harlow, C. (1994). *Child rape victims, 1992.* Washington, DC: Bureau of Justice Statistics, U.S. Department of Justice.
Lanning, E. P. (1967). *Peru before the Incas.* Englewood Cliffs, NJ: Prentice-Hall.
Larsen, C. S., Matter, R. M., & Gebo, D. L. (1998). *Human origins: The fossil record.* Long Grove, IL: Waveland.
Larsen, J. (2006, July 28). *Setting the record straight.* Earth Policy Institute, Eco-economy updates.
Latimer, B., Ohman, J. C., & Lovejoy, C. O. (1987). Talocrural joint in African hominoids: Implications for *Australopithecus afarensis. American Journal of Physical Anthropology 74,* 155–175.
Lawler, A. (2001). Writing gets a rewrite. *Science 292,* 2419.
Layton, R. (1991). *The anthropology of art* (2nd ed.). Cambridge, MA: Cambridge University Press.
Leach, E. (1961). *Rethinking anthropology.* London: Athione.
Leach, E. (1962). The determinants of differential cross-cousin marriage. *Man 62,* 238.
Leach, E. (1962). On certain unconsidered aspects of double descent systems. *Man 214,* 13–34.
Leach, E. (1964). Anthropological aspects of language: Animal categories and verbal abuse. In W. Lessa & E. Vogt (Eds.), *Reader in comparative religion* (4th ed.). New York: Harper & Row.
Leach, E. (1982). *Social anthropology.* Glasgow: Fontana.
Leacock, E. (1981). *Myths of male dominance: Collected articles on women cross culturally.* New York: Monthly Review.
Leacock, E. (1981). Women's status in egalitarian society: Implications for social evolution. In *Myths of male dominance: Collected articles on women cross culturally.* New York: Monthly Review.
Leakey, L.S.B. (1965). *Olduvai Gorge, 1951–1961* (Vol. 1). London: Cambridge University Press.
Leakey, L.S.B., Tobias, P. B., & Napier, J. R. (1964). A new species of the genus *Homo* from Olduvai Gorge. *Nature 202,* 7–9.
Leakey, M. D. (1971). *Olduvai Gorge: Excavations in Beds I and II. 1960–1963.* London and New York: Cambridge University Press.
Leakey, M. G., Spoor, F., Brown, F. H., Gathogo, P. N., Kiare, C., Leakey, L. N., & McDougal, I. (2001). New hominin genus from eastern Africa shows diverse middle Pliocene lineages. *Nature 410,* 433–440.
Leap, W. L. (1987). Tribally controlled culture change: The Northern Ute language revival project. In R. M. Wulff & S. J. Fiske (Eds.), *Anthropological praxis: Translating knowledge into action* (pp. 197–211). Boulder, CO: Westview.
Leavitt, G. C. (1990). Sociobiological explanations of incest avoidance: A critical review of evidential claims. *American Anthropologist 92,* 982.
Leclerc-Madlala, S. (2002). Bodies and politics: Healing rituals in the democratic South Africa. In V. Faure (Ed.), *Les cahiers de 'l'IFAS,* No. 2. Johannesburg: French Institute.
Lee, R. B. (1993). *The Dobe Ju/'hoansi.* Ft. Worth: Harcourt Brace.
Lee, R. B., & Daly, R. H. (1999). *The Cambridge encyclopedia of hunters and gatherers.* New York: Cambridge University Press.
Lee, R. B., & DeVore, I. (Eds.). (1968). *Man the hunter.* Chicago: Aldine.
Lees, R. (1953). The basis of glottochronology. *Language 29,* 113–127.
Lehman, E. C., Jr. (2002, Fall). Women's path into the ministry. *Pulpit & Pew Research Reports 1,* 4.
Lehmann, A. C., & Myers, J. E. (Eds.). (2000). *Magic, witchcraft, and religion: An anthropological study of the supernatural* (5th ed.). Mountain View, CA: Mayfield.
Lehmann, J., & Joseph, S. (2009). *Biochar for environmental management: Science and technology.* London: Earthscan.
Leigh, S. R., & Park, P. B. (1998). Evolution of human growth prolongation. *American Journal of Physical Anthropology 107,* 331–350.

Leinhardt, G. (1964). *Social anthropology.* London: Oxford University Press.

LeMay, M. (1975). The language capability of Neanderthal man. *American Journal of Physical Anthropology 43* (1), 9–14.

Lenski, G. (1966). *Power and privilege: A theory of social stratification.* New York: McGraw-Hill.

Leroi-Gourhan, A. (1968). The evolution of Paleolithic art. *Scientific American 218, 58ff.*

Lestel, D. (1998). How chimpanzees have domesticated humans. *Anthropology Today 12* (3).

Leth, P. M. (2007).The use of CT scanning in forensic autopsy. *Forensic Science, Medicine, and Pathology 3* (1), 65–69.

Levine, N. E., & Silk, J. B. (1997). Why polyandry fails. *Current Anthropology 38,* 375–398.

Levine, R. A. (2007). Ethnographic studies of childhood: A historical overview. *American Anthropologist 109* (2), 247–260.

Lévi-Strauss, C. (1963). The sorcerer and his magic. In *Structural anthropology.* New York: Basic.

Lévi-Strauss, C. (1969). *The raw and the cooked.* New York: Harper & Row.

Lewellen, T. C. (2002). *The anthropology of globalization: Cultural anthropology enters the 21st century.* Westport, CT: Greenwood.

Lewin, R. (1987). Four legs bad, two legs good. *Science 235,* 969.

Lewin, R. (1993). Paleolithic paint job. *Discover 14* (7), 64–70.

Lewis, I. M. (1976). *Social anthropology in perspective.* Harmondsworth, England: Penguin.

Lewis-Williams, J. D. (1990). *Discovering southern African rock art.* Cape Town and Johannesburg: David Philip.

Lewis-Williams, J. D. (1997). Agency, art, and altered consciousness: A motif in French (Quercy) Upper Paleolithic parietal art. *Antiquity 71,* 810–830.

Lewis-Williams, J. D., & Dowson, T. A. (1988). Signs of all times: Entoptic phenomena in Upper Paleolithic art. *Current Anthropology 29,* 201–245.

Lewis-Williams, J. D., & Dowson, T. A. (1993). On vision and power in the Neolithic: Evidence from the decorated monuments. *Current Anthropology 34,* 55–65.

Lewis-Williams, J. D., Dowson, T. A., & Deacon, J. (1993). Rock art and changing perceptions of Southern Africa's past: Ezeljagdspoort reviewed. *Antiquity 67,* 273–291.

Lewontin, R. C. (1972). The apportionment of human diversity. In T. Dobzhansky et al. (Eds.), *Evolutionary biology* (pp. 381–398). New York: Plenum.

Lewontin, R. C., Rose, S., & Kamin, L. J. (1984). *Not in our genes.* New York: Pantheon.

Li, X., Harbottle, G., Zhang, J., & Wang, C. (2003).The earliest writing? Sign use in the seventh millennium bc at Jiahu, Henan Province, China. *Antiquity 77,* 31–44.

Lieberman, P. (2006). *Toward an evolutionary biology of language.* Cambridge, MA: Belknap.

Lindenbaum, S. (1978). *Kuru sorcery: Disease and danger in the New Guinea highlands.* New York: McGraw-Hill.

Lindstrom, L. (1993). *Cargo cult: Strange stories of desire from Melanesia and beyond.* Honolulu: University of Hawaii Press.

Little, K. L. (1973). *African women in towns: An aspect of Africa's social revolution.* New York: Cambridge University Press.

Littlewood, R. (2004). Commentary: Globalization, culture, body image, and eating disorders. *Culture, Medicine, and Psychiatry 28* (4), 597–602.

Livingstone, F. B. (1973). The distribution of abnormal hemoglobin genes and their significance for human evolution. In C. Loring Brace & J. Metress (Eds.), *Man in evolutionary perspective.* New York: Wiley.

Living Tongues. www.livingtongues.org/background.html

Lloyd, C. B. (Ed.). (2005). *Growing up global: The changing transitions to adulthood in developing countries* (pp. 450–453). Washington, DC: National Academies Press, Committee on Population, National Research Council, and Institute of Medicine of the National Academies.

Lock, M. (2001). *Twice dead: Organ transplants and the reinvention of death.* Berkeley: University of California Press.

Lorenzo, C., Carretero, J. M., Arsuaga, J. L., Gracia, A., & Martinez, I. (1998). Intrapopulational body size variation and cranial capacity variation in middle Pleistocene humans: The Sima de los Huesos sample (Sierra de Atapuerca, Spain). *American Journal of Physical Anthropology 106,* 19–33.

Loubser, J.H.N. (2003). *Archaeology: The comic.* Lanham, MD: Altamira.

Louckey, J., & Carlsen, R. (1991). Massacre in Santiago Atitlán. *Cultural Survival Quarterly 15* (3), 70.

Louie, A. (2004). *Chineseness across borders: Renegotiating Chinese identities in China and the United States.* Durham and London: Duke University Press.

Lounsbury, F. (1964). The structural analysis of kinship semantics. In H. G. Lunt (Ed.), *Proceedings of the Ninth International Congress of Linguists.* The Hague: Mouton.

Lovejoy, C. O. (1981). Origin of man. *Science 211,* 341–350.

Lowie, R. H. (1948). *Social organization.* New York: Holt, Rinehart & Winston.

Lowie, R. H. (1956). *Crow Indians.* New York: Holt, Rinehart & Winston. (orig. 1935)

Lucy, J. A. (1997). Linguistic relativity. *Annual Review of Anthropology 26,* 291–312.

Luhrmann, T. M. (2001). *Of two minds: An anthropologist looks at American psychiatry.* New York: Vintage.

Lurie, N. O. (1973). Action anthropology and the American Indian. In *Anthropology and the American Indian: A symposium.* San Francisco: Indian Historical.

MacCormack, C. P. (1977). Biological events and cultural control. *Signs 3,* 93–100.

MacLarnon, A. M., & Hewitt, G. P. (1999). The evolution of human speech: The role of enhanced breathing control. *American Journal of Physical Anthropology 109,* 341–363.

MacNeish, R. S. (1992). *The origins of agriculture and settled life.* Norman: University of Oklahoma Press.

"Madison Avenue relevance." (1999). *Anthropology Newsletter 40* (4), 32.

Maggioncalda, A. N., & Sapolsky, R. M. (2002). Disturbing behaviors of the orangutan. *Scientific American 286* (6), 60–65.

Mair, L. (1957). *An introduction to social anthropology.* London: Oxford University Press.

Mair, L. (1969). *Witchcraft.* New York: McGraw-Hill.

Mair, L. (1971). *Marriage.* Baltimore: Penguin.

Malefijt, A. de W. (1969). *Religion and culture: An introduction to anthropology of religion.* London: Macmillan.

Malinowski, B. (1945). *The dynamics of culture change: An inquiry into race relations in Africa.* New Haven, CT: Yale University Press.

Malinowski, B. (1951). *Crime and custom in savage society.* London: Routledge.

Malinowski, B. (1954). *Magic, science, and religion.* Garden City, NY: Doubleday.

Malinowski, B. (1961). *Argonauts of the western Pacific.* New York: Dutton. (orig. 1922)

Mann, A., Lampl, M., & Monge, J. (1990). Patterns of ontogeny in human evolution: Evidence from dental development. *Yearbook of Physical Anthropology 33,* 111–150.

Mann, C. C. (2000). Misconduct alleged in Yanomamo studies. *Science 289* (2), 253.

Mann, C. C. (2002).The real dirt on rainforest fertility. *Science 297,* 920–923.

Mann, C. C. (2005). *1491: New revelations of the Americas before Columbus.* New York: Knopf.

Marcus, G. (1995). Ethnography in/of the world system: The emergence of multi-sited ethnography. *Annual Review of Anthropology 24,* 95–117.

Marcus, J., & Flannery, K. V. (1996). *Zapotec civilization: How urban society evolved in Mexico's Oaxaca Valley.* New York: Thames & Hudson.

Marks, J. (1995). *Human biodiversity: Genes, race and history.* Hawthorne, NY: Aldine.

Marks, J. (2000, April 8). A feckless quest for the basketball gene. *New York Times.*

Marks, J. (2000, May 12). 98% alike (what our similarity to apes tells us about our understanding of genetics). *Chronicle of Higher Education,* B7.

Marks, J. (2002). *What it means to be 98 percent chimpanzee: Apes, people, and their genes.* Berkeley: University of California Press.

Marks, J. (2009). *Why I am not a scientist: Anthropology and modern knowledge.* Berkeley: University of California Press.

Marsella, A. J. (1982). Pulling it together: Discussion and comments. In S. Pastner & W. A. Haviland (Eds.), *Confronting the creationists* (pp. 79–80). *Northeastern Anthropological Association, Occasional Proceedings 1.*

Marsella, A. J., & White, G. (1982). *Cultural conceptions of mental health and therapy.* New York: Springer.

Marshack, A. (1976). Some implications of the Paleolithic symbolic evidence for the origin of language. *Current Anthropology 17* (2), 274–282.

Marshack, A. (1989). Evolution of the human capacity: The symbolic evidence. *Yearbook of Physical Anthropology 32,*1–34.

Marshall, E. (2001). Preclovis sites fight for acceptance. *Science 291,* 1732.

Marshall, L. (1961). Sharing, talking and giving: Relief of social tensions among !Kung bushmen. *Africa 31,* 231–249.

Marshall, M. (1990). Two tales from the Trukese taproom. In P. R. DeVita (Ed.), *The humbled anthropologist* (pp. 12–17). Belmont, CA: Wadsworth.

Martin, E. (1994). *Flexible bodies: Tracking immunity in American culture—from the days of polio to the age of AIDS.* Boston: Beacon.

Martin, E. (1999). Flexible survivors. *Anthropology News 40* (6), 5–7.

Martorell, R. (1988). Body size, adaptation, and function. *GDP,* 335–347.

Mascia-Lees, F. E., & Black, N. J. (2000). *Gender and anthropology.* Prospect Heights, IL: Waveland.

Mason, J. A. (1957). *The ancient civilizations of Peru.* Baltimore: Penguin.

Mathieu, C. (2003). *A history and anthropological study of the ancient kingdoms of the Sino-Tibetan borderland—Naxi and Mosuo.* New York: Mellen.

Matthews, G. (2006). Happiness and the pursuit of a life worth living: An anthropological approach. In Y.-K. Ng & L. S. Ho (Eds.), *Happiness and public policy* (pp. 147–168). Hampshire, England: Palgrave Macmillan.

Mauss, M. (2000). *The gift: The form and reason for exchange in archaic societies* (translation by W. D. Halls and foreword by M. Douglas). New York: Norton.

May, R. (2000). Melding heart and head. *Beyond 2000.* New York: United Nations Environment Programme. http://www.unep.org/ourplanet/imgversn/111/may.html

Maybury-Lewis, D. (1960). Parallel descent and the Apinaye anomaly. *Southwestern Journal of Anthropology 16,* 191–216.

Maybury-Lewis, D. (1984). The prospects for plural societies. *1982 Proceedings of the American Ethnological Society.*

Maybury-Lewis, D. (1993, fall). A new world dilemma: The Indian question in the Americas. *Symbols,* 17–23.

Maybury-Lewis, D. (2001). *Indigenous peoples, ethnic groups, and the state* (2nd ed.). Boston: Allyn & Bacon.

Maybury-Lewis, D.H.P. (1993). A special sort of pleading. In W. A. Haviland & R. J. Gordon (Eds.), *Talking about people* (2nd ed., p. 17). Mountain View, CA: Mayfield.

Mayo Clinic. http://www.mayoclinic.com/

Mayr, E., & Diamond, J. (2002). *What evolution is.* New York: Basic.

McBride, B. (1980). *Eric. R. Wolf interview. Between subjectivity and objectivity.* Unpublished masters thesis, anthropology department, Columbia University.

McCorriston, J., & Hole, F. (1991). The ecology of seasonal stress and the origins of agriculture in the Near East. *American Anthropologist 93,* 46–69.

McDermott, L. (1996). Self-representation in Upper Paleolithic female figurines. *Current Anthropology 37,* 227–276.

McElroy, A., & Townsend, P. K. (2003). *Medical anthropology in ecological perspective.* Boulder, CO: Westview.

McFate, M. (2007). *Role and effectiveness of sociocultural knowledge for counterinsurgency.* Alexandria, VA: Institute for Defense Analysis.

McFee, M. (1972). *Modern Blackfeet: Montanans on a reservation.* New York: Holt, Rinehart & Winston.

McGrew, W. C. (2000). Dental care in chimps. *Science 288,* 1747.

McHenry, H. (1975). Fossils and the mosaic nature of human evolution. *Science 190,* 524–431.

McHenry, H. M. (1992). Body size and proportions in early hominids. *American Journal of Physical Anthropology 87,* 407–431.

McHenry, H. M., & Jones, A. L. (2006). Hallucial convergence in early hominids. *Journal of Human Evolution 50,* 534–539.

McKenna, J. J. (1999). Co-sleeping and SIDS. In W. Trevathan, E. O. Smith, & J. J. McKenna (Eds.), *Evolutionary medicine.* London: Oxford University Press.

McKenna, J. J. (2002, September–October). Breastfeeding and bedsharing. *Mothering,* 28–37.

McKenna, J. J., & McDade, T. (2005, June). Why babies should never sleep alone: A review of the co-sleeping controversy in relation to SIDS, bedsharing, and breast feeding. *Pediatric Respiratory Reviews 6* (2), 134–152.

McNeill, W. (1992). *Plagues and people.* New York: Anchor.

Mead, A.T.P. (1996). Genealogy, sacredness, and the commodities market. *Cultural Survival Quarterly 20* (2).

Mead, M. (1928). *Coming of age in Samoa: A psychological study of primitive youth for western civilization.* New York: Morrow.

Mead, M. (1960). Anthropology among the sciences. *American Anthropologist 63,* 475–482.

Mead, M. (1963). *Sex and temperament in three primitive societies* (3rd ed.). New York: Morrow. (orig. 1935)

Mead, M., & Metraux, R. (Eds.). (1953). *The study of culture at a distance.* Chicago: University of Chicago Press.

Medicine, B. (1994). Gender. In M. B. Davis (Ed.), *Native America in the twentieth century.* New York: Garland.

Melaart, J. (1967). *Catal Hüyük: A Neolithic town in Anatolia.* London: Thames & Hudson.

Mellars, P. (1989). Major issues in the emergence of modern humans. *Current Anthropology 30,* 356–357.

Mellars, P. (2009). Archaeology: Origins of the female image. *Nature 459,* 176–177.

Meltzer, D., Fowler, D., & Sabloff, J. (Eds.). (1986). *American archaeology: Past & future.* Washington, DC: Smithsonian Institution.

Merin, Y. (2002). *Equality for same-sex couples: The legal recognition of gay partnerships in Europe and the United States.* Chicago: University of Chicago Press.

Merriam, A. P. (1964). *The anthropology of music.* Chicago: Northwestern University Press.

Mesghinua, H. M. (1966). Salt mining in Enderta. *Journal of Ethiopian Studies 4* (2).

Métraux, A. (1953). Applied anthropology in government: United Nations. In A. A. Kroeber (Ed.), *Anthropology today: An encyclopedic inventory* (pp. 880–894).Chicago: University of Chicago Press.

Meyer, J. (2008). Typology and acoustic strategies of whistled languages: Phonetic comparison and perceptual cues of whistled vowels. *Journal of the International Phonetic Association 38,* 69–94.

Meyer J., & Gautheron, B. (2006). Whistled speech and whistled languages. In K. Brown (Ed.), *Encyclopedia of language & linguistics* (2nd ed., vol. 13, pp. 573–576). Oxford, England: Elsevier.

Meyer, J., Meunier, F., & Dentel, L. (2007). Identification of natural whistled vowels by non-whistlers. *Proceedings of Interspeech 2007* (pp. 1593–1596). Antwerpen, Belgium.

Miles, H.L.W. (1993). Language and the orangutan: The "old person" of the forest. In P. Cavalieri & P. Singer (Eds.), *The Great Ape Project* (pp. 45–50). New York: St. Martin's.

Miller, J.M.A. (2000). Craniofacial variation in *Homo habilis:* An analysis of the evidence for multiple species. *American Journal of Physical Anthropology 112,* 122.

Millon, R. (1973). *Urbanization of Teotihuacán, Mexico: Vol. 1, Part 1. The Teotihuacán map.* Austin: University of Texas Press.

Mintz, S. (1996). A taste of history. In W. A. Haviland & R. J. Gordon (Eds.), *Talking about people* (2nd ed., pp. 81–82). Mountain View, CA: Mayfield.

Minugh-Purvis, N. (1992). The inhabitants of Ice Age Europe. *Expedition 34* (3), 23–36.

Mitchell, W. E. (1973, December). A new weapon stirs up old ghosts. *Natural History,* 77–84.

Modell, J. (1994). *Kinship with strangers: Adoption and interpretations of kinship in American culture.* Berkeley: University of California Press.

Molnar, S. (1992). *Human variation: Races, types and ethnic groups* (3rd ed.). Englewood Cliffs, NJ: Prentice-Hall.

Monaghan, L., Hinton, L., & Kephart, R. (1997). Can't teach a dog to be a cat? The dialogue on ebonics. *Anthropology Newsletter 38* (3), 1, 8, 9.

Montagu, A. (1964). *The concept of race.* London: Macmillan.

Montagu, A. (1964). *Man's most dangerous myth: The fallacy of race* (4th ed.) New York: World Publishing.

Montagu, A. (1975). *Race and IQ.* New York: Oxford University Press.

Moore, J. (1998). Comment. *Current Anthropology 39,* 412.

Morgan, L. H. (1877). *Ancient society.* New York: World Publishing.

Morphy, H., & Perkins, M. (Eds.). (2006). *Anthropology of art: A reader.* Boston: Blackwell.

Morse, D., et al. (1979). *Gestures: Their origins and distribution.* New York: Stein & Day.

Moscati, S. (1962). *The face of the ancient orient.* New York: Doubleday.

Murdock, G. P. (1960). Cognatic forms of social organization. In G. P. Murdock (Ed.), *Social structure in Southeast Asia* (pp. 1–14). Chicago: Quadrangle Books.

Murdock, G. P. (1965). *Social structure.* New York: Free Press.

Murphy, R. (1971). *The dialectics of social life: Alarms and excursions in anthropological theory.* New York: Basic.

Murphy, R., & Kasdan, L. (1959). The structure of parallel cousin marriage. *American Anthropologist 61,* 17–29.

Mydens, S. (2001, August 12). He's not hairy, he's my brother. *New York Times,* sec. 4, 5.

Myrdal, G. (1974). Challenge to affluence: The emergence of an "under-class." In J. G. Jorgensen & M. Truzzi (Eds.), *Anthropology and American life.* Englewood Cliffs, NJ: Prentice-Hall.

Nader, L. (Ed.). (1965). The ethnography of law, part II. *American Anthropologist 67* (6).

Nader, L. (Ed.). (1969). *Law in culture and society.* Chicago: Aldine.

Nader, L. (Ed) (1981). *No access to law: Alternatives to the American judicial system.* New York: Academic.

Nader, L. (Ed.). (1996). *Naked science: Anthropological inquiry into boundaries, power, and knowledge.* New York: Routledge.

Nader, L. (1997). Controlling processes: Tracing the dynamics of power. *Current Anthropology 38,* 715–717.

Nader, L. (Ed.). (1997). *Law in culture and society.* Berkeley: University of California Press.

Nader, L. (2002). *The life of the law: Anthropological projects.* Berkeley: University of California Press.

Nader, L., & Todd, Jr., H. F. (1978). *The disputing process: Law in ten societies.* New York: Columbia University Press.

Nanda, S. (1990). *Neither man nor woman: The hijras of India.* Belmont, CA: Wadsworth.

Nanda, S. (1992). Arranging a marriage in India. In P. R. De Vita (Ed.), *The naked anthropologist* (pp. 139–143). Belmont, CA: Wadsworth.

Nash, J. (1976). Ethnology in a revolutionary setting. In M. A. Rynkiewich & J. P. Spradley (Eds.), *Ethics and anthropology: Dilemmas in fieldwork* (pp. 148–166). New York: Wiley.

Natadecha-Sponsal, P. (1993). The young, the rich and the famous: Individualism as an American cultural value. In P. R. DeVita & J. D. Armstrong (Eds.), *Distant mirrors: America as a foreign culture* (pp. 46–53). Belmont, CA: Wadsworth.

NationMaster.com. http://www.nationmaster.com/graph/mor_eat_dis-mortality-eating-disorders

Natural Resources Defense Council. (2005, March 25). Healthy milk, healthy baby: Chemical pollution and mother's milk. www.NRDC.org

Needham, R. (Ed.). (1971). *Rethinking kinship and marriage.* London: Tavistock.

Needham, R. (1972). *Belief, language and experience.* Chicago: University of Chicago Press.

Neer, R. M. (1975). The evolutionary significance of vitamin D, skin pigment, and ultraviolet

light. *American Journal of Physical Anthropology 43,* 409–416.
Nesbitt, L. M. (1935). *Hell-hole of creation.* New York: Knopf.
Nesse, R. M., & Williams, G. C. (1996). *Why we get sick.* New York: Vintage.
Netting, R. M., Wilk, R. R., & Arnould, E. J. (Eds.). (1984). *Households: Comparative and historical studies of the domestic group.* Berkeley: University of California Press.
Nettl, B. (2005). *The study of ethnomusicology: Thirty-one issues and concepts.* Chicago: University of Illinois Press.
Nieftagodien, N. (2008, June 18). Incoherent response to crisis. *The Star,* Johannesburg. http://web.wits.ac.za/NewsRoom/NewsItems/Noor+Nieftagodien+xenophobia+opinion.htm
Nietschmann, B. (1987). The third world war. *Cultural Survival Quarterly 11* (3), 1–16.
Nishinda T. (1987). Local traditions and cultural transmission (pp. 462–474). In B. B. Smuts et al. (Eds.), *Primate society.* Chicago: University of Chicago Press.
Noack, T. (2001). Cohabitation in Norway: An accepted and gradually more regulated way of living. *International Journal of Law, Policy, and the Family 15* (1), 102–117.
Normile, D. (1998). Habitat seen as playing larger role in shaping behavior. *Science 279,* 1454.
Norris, R. S., & Kristensen, H. M. (2006, July/August). Global nuclear stockpiles, 1945–2006. *Bulletin of the Atomic Scientists 62* (4), 64–66.
Nunney, L. (1998). Are we selfish, are we nice, or are we nice because we are selfish? *Science 281,* 1619.
Nye, J. (2002). *The paradox of American power: Why the world's only superpower can't go it alone.* New York: Oxford University Press.
Oakley, K. P. (1964). *Man the tool-maker.* Chicago: University of Chicago Press.
O'Barr, W. M., & Conley, J. M. (1993). When a juror watches a lawyer. In W. A. Haviland & R. J. Gordon (Eds.), *Talking about people* (2nd ed., pp. 42– 45). Mountain View, CA: Mayfield.
Obler, R. S. (1982). Is the female husband a man? Woman/woman marriage among the Nandi of Kenya. *Ethnology 19,* 69–88.
O'Carroll, E. (2008, June 27). Spain to grant some human rights to apes. *Christian Science Monitor.*
Offiong, D. (1985). Witchcraft among the Ibibio of Nigeria. In A. C. Lehmann & J. E. Myers (Eds.), *Magic, witchcraft, and religion* (pp. 152–165). Palo Alto, CA: Mayfield.
Okonjo, K. (1976). The dual-sex political system in operation: Igbo women and community politics in midwestern Nigeria. In N. Hafkin & E. Bay (Eds.), *Women in Africa.* Stanford, CA: Stanford University Press.
Olszewki, D. I. (1991). Comment. *Current Anthropology 32,* 43.
O'Mahoney, K. (1970). The salt trade. *Journal of Ethiopian Studies 8* (2).
Ong, A. (1999). *Flexible citizenship: The cultural logics of transnationality.* Durham, NC: Duke University Press.
Orlando, L., et al. (6 June 2006). Correspondence: Revisiting Neandertal diversity with a 100,000 year old mtDNA sequence. *Current Biology 16,* 400–402.
Oswalt, W. H. (1972). *Habitat and technology.* New York: Holt, Rinehart & Winston.
Otte, M. (2000). On the suggested bone flute from Slovenia. *Current Anthropology 41,* 271.
Otten, C. M. (1971). *Anthropology and art: Readings in cross-cultural aesthetics.* Garden City, NY: Natural History.
Ottenberg, P. (1965). The Afikpo Ibo of eastern Nigeria. In J. L. Gibbs (Ed.), *Peoples of Africa.* New York: Holt, Rinehart & Winston.
Ottenheimer, M. (1996). *Forbidden relatives: The American myth of cousin marriage.* Chicago: University of Illinois Press.
Otterbein, K. F. (1971). *The evolution of war.* New Haven, CT: HRAF Press.
Pandian, J. (1998). *Culture, religion, and the sacred self: A critical introduction to the anthropological study of religion.* Englewood Cliffs, NJ: Prentice-Hall.
Paredes, J. A., & Purdum, E. D. (1990). "Bye, bye Ted . . ." *Anthropology Today 6* (2), 9.
Parés, J. M., Perez-Gonzalez, A., Weil, A. B., & Arsuaga, J. L. (2000). On the age of hominid fossils at the Sima de los Huesos, Sierra de Atapuerca, Spain: Paleomagnetic evidence. *American Journal of Physical Anthropology 111,* 451–461.
Parish, A. R. (1998). Comment. *Current Anthropology 39,* 414.
Parker, R. G. (1991). *Bodies, pleasures, and passions: Sexual culture in contemporary Brazil.* Boston: Beacon.
Parkin, R. (1997). *Kinship: An introduction to basic concepts.* Cambridge, MA: Blackwell.
Parnell, R. (1999). Gorilla exposé. *Natural History 108* (8), 43.
Partridge, W. (Ed.). (1984). *Training manual in development anthropology.* Washington, DC: American Anthropological Association.
Patterson, F.G.P., & Gordon, W. (2002). Twenty-seven years of Project Koko and Michael. In B. Galdikas et al. (Eds.), *All apes great and small* (vol. 1): *Chimpanzees, bonobos, and gorillas* (pp. 165–176). New York: Kluwer Academic.
Patterson, F., & Linden, E. (1981). *The education of Koko.* New York: Holt, Rinehart & Winston.
Peacock, J. L. (2002). *The anthropological lens: Harsh light, soft focus* (2nd ed.). New York: Cambridge University Press.
Pease, T. (2000, Spring). Taking the third side. *Andover Bulletin.*
Pelto, G. H., Goodman, A. H., & Dufour, D. L. (Eds.). (2000). *Nutritional anthropology: Biocultural perspectives on food and nutrition.* Mountain View, CA: Mayfield.
Pelto, P. J. (1973). *The snowmobile revolution: Technology and social change in the Arctic.* Menlo Park, CA: Cummings.
Pennisi, E. (1999). Genetic study shakes up out of Africa theory. *Science 283,* 1828.
Perego, U. A., Achilli, A., Angerhofer, N., Accetturo, M., Pala, M., Olivieri, A., Kashani, B. H., Ritchie, K. H., Scozzari, R., Kong, P., Myres, N. M., Salas, A., Semino, O., Bandelt, H-J., Woodward, S. R., & Torroni, A. (2009). Distinctive Paleo-Indian migration routes from Beringia marked by two rare mtDNA haplogroups. *Current Biology 19* (1), 1–8, 13.
Peters, C. R. (1979). Toward an ecological model of African Plio-Pleistocene hominid adaptations. *American Anthropologist 81*(2), 261–278.
Petersen J. B., Neuves, E., & Heckenberger, M. J. (2001). Gift from the past: *Terra preta* and prehistoric American occupation in Amazonia. In C. McEwan and C. Barreo (Eds.), *Unknown Amazon* (pp. 86–105). London: British Museum.
Pew Research Center. (2007). *Global attitudes survey.*
Pew Research Center. (2009). Mapping the global Muslim population: A report on the size and distribution of the world's Muslim population. http://pewforum.org/newassets/images/reports/Muslimpopulation/Muslimpopulation.pdf
Pfeiffer, J. E. (1978). *The emergence of man.* New York: Harper & Row.
Pfeiffer, J. E. (1985). *The creative explosion.* Ithaca, NY: Cornell University Press.
Piddocke, S. (1965). The potlatch system of the southern Kwakiutl: A new perspective. *Southwestern Journal of Anthropology 21,* 244–264.
Piggott, S. (1965). *Ancient Europe.* Chicago: Aldine.
Pilbeam, D. R. (1987). Rethinking human origins. In R. L. Ciochon & J. G. Fleagle (Eds.), *Primate evolution and human origins* (p. 217). Hawthorne, NY: Aldine.
Pimentel, D. (1991). Response. *Science 252,* 358.
Pimentel, D., Hurd, L. E., Bellotti, A. C., Forster, M. J., Oka, I. N., Sholes, O. D., & Whitman, R. J. (1973). Food production and the energy crisis. *Science,* 182.
Pink, S. (2001). *Doing visual ethnography: Images, media and representation in research.* Thousand Oaks, CA: Sage.
Pinker, S. (1994). *The language instinct: How the mind creates language.* New York: Morrow.
Piperno, D. R., & Fritz, G. J. (1994). On the emergence of agriculture in the new world. *Current Anthropology 35,* 637–643.
Pitts, V. (2003). *In the flesh: The cultural politics of body modification.* New York: Palgrave Macmillan.
Plane, A. M. (1996). Putting a face on colonization: Factionalism and gender politics in the life history of Awashunkes, the "Squaw Sachem" of Saconnet. In R. S. Grumet (Ed.), *Northeastern Indian lives, 1632–1816* (pp.140–175). Amherst: University of Massachusetts Press.
Plattner, S. (Ed.). (1989). *Economic anthropology.* Stanford, CA: Stanford University Press.
Plattner, S. (1989). Markets and marketplaces. In S. Plattner (Ed.), *Economic anthropology.* Stanford, CA: Stanford University Press.
Pluralism Project, Harvard University. pluralism.org
Pohl, M.E.D., Pope, K. O., & von Nagy, C. (2002). Olmec origins of Mesoamerican writing. *Science 298,* 1984–1987.
Polanyi, K. (1968). The economy as instituted process. In E. E. LeClair, Jr., & H. K. Schneider (Eds.), *Economic anthropology: Readings in theory and analysis* (pp. 127–138). New York: Holt, Rinehart & Winston.
Pollan, M. (2001). *The botany of desire: A plant's-eye view of the world.* New York: Random House.
Pollan, M. (2008). *In defense of food: An eater's manifesto.* New York: Penguin.
Pollock, N. J. (1995). Social fattening patterns in the Pacific—the positive side of obesity. A Nauru case study. In I. DeGarine & N. J. Pollock (Eds.), *Social aspects of obesity* (pp. 87–109). London: Routledge.
Pope, G. G. (1989, October). Bamboo and human evolution. *Natural History 98,* 48–57.
Pope, G. G. (1992). Craniofacial evidence for the origin of modern humans in China. *Yearbook of Physical Anthropology 35,* 243–298.
Pope Pius XII. (1954). *Sacra Virginitas. Encyclical on consecrated virginity.* The Catholic Encyclopedia Online: www.newadvent.org
Pospisil, L. (1963). *The Kapauku Papuans of west New Guinea.* New York: Holt, Rinehart & Winston.
Pospisil, L. (1971). *Anthropology of law: A comparative theory.* New York: Harper & Row.
Potts, R. (1997). *Humanity's descent: The consequences of ecological instability.* New York: Avon.
Powdermaker, H. (1939). *After freedom: A cultural study in the Deep South.* New York: Viking.
Powdermaker, H. (1976). *Stranger and friend: The way of an anthropologist.* London: Secker and Warburg.

Power, M. G. (1995). Gombe revisited: Are chimpanzees violent and hierarchical in the free state? *General Anthropology 2* (1), 5–9.
Premack, A. J., & Premack, D. (1972). Teaching language to an ape. *Scientific American 277*(4), 92–99.
Price, T. D., & Feinman, G. M. (Eds.). (1995). *Foundations of social inequality.* New York: Plenum.
Pringle, H. (1997). Ice Age communities may be earliest known net hunters. *Science 277,* 1203–1204.
Pringle, H. (1998). The slow birth of agriculture. *Science 282,* 1449.
Prins, A.H.J. (1953). *East African class systems.* Groningen, the Netherlands: J. B. Wolters.
Prins, H.E.L. (1996). *The Mi'kmaq: Resistance, accommodation, and cultural survival* (p. 106). Orlando: Harcourt Brace.
Prins, H.E.L. (1998). Book review of Schuster, C., & Carpenter, E. *American Anthropologist 100* (3), 841.
Prins, H.E.L. (2002). Visual media and the primitivist perplex: Colonial fantasies, indigenous imagination, and advocacy in North America. In F. D. Ginsburg et al. (Eds.), *Media worlds: Anthropology on new terrain* (pp. 58–74). Berkeley: University of California Press.
Prins, H.E.L., & Carter, K. (1986). *Our lives in our hands.* Video and 16mm. Color. 50 min. Distributed by Watertown, MA: Documentary Educational Resources and Bucksport, ME: Northeast Historic Film
Prins, H.E.L., & Krebs, E. (2006). Toward a land without evil: Alfred Métraux a UNESCO anthropologist 1948–1962. In *60 years of UNESCO history. Proceedings of the international symposium in Paris, 16–18 November 2005.* Paris: UNESCO.
Profet, M. (1991). The function of allergy: Immunological defense against toxins. *Quarterly Review of Biology 66* (1), 23–62.
Profet, M. (1995). *Protecting your baby to be.* New York: Addison Wesley.
Pruetz, J. D., & Bertolani, P. (2007, March 6).Savanna chimpanzees, *Pan troglodytes verus,* hunt with tools. *Current Biology 17,* 412–417.
Puleston, D. E. (1983). *The settlement survey of Tikal.* Philadelphia: University Museum.
Quinn, N. (2005). Universals of child rearing. *Anthropological Theory 5,* 475–514.
Radcliffe-Brown, A. R. (1931). Social organization of Australian tribes. *Oceana Monographs 1,* 29.
Radcliffe-Brown, A. R., & Forde, C. D. (Eds.). (1950). *African systems of kinship and marriage.* London: Oxford University Press.
Radin, P. (1923). The Winnebago tribe. In *37th annual report of the Bureau of American Ethnology, 1915–1916* (pp. 33–550). Washington, DC: Government Printing Office.
Rapp, R. (1999). *Testing women, testing the fetus: The social impact of amniocentesis in America.* New York: Routledge.
Rappaport, R. A. (1969). Ritual regulation of environmental relations among a New Guinea people. In A. P. Vayda (Ed.), *Environment and cultural behavior* (pp. 181–201). Garden City, NY. Natural History.
Rappaport, R. A. (1984). *Pigs for the ancestors* (Enl. ed.). New Haven, CT: Yale University Press.
Rappaport, R. A. (1999). *Holiness and humanity: Ritual in the making of religious life.* New York: Cambridge University Press.
Rathje, W. L. (1974). The garbage project: A new way of looking at the problems of archaeology. *Archaeology 27,* 236–241.
Rathje, W. L. (1993). Rubbish! In W. A. Haviland & R. J. Gordon (Eds.), *Talking about people: Readings in contemporary cultural anthropology.* Mountain View, CA: Mayfield.
Rathke, L. (1989). To Maine for apples. *Salt Magazine 9* (4), *24–47.*
Read-Martin, C. E., & Read, D. W. (1975). Australopithecine scavenging and human evolution: An approach from faunal analysis. *Current Anthropology 16* (3), 359–368.
Recent demographic developments in Europe—2000. Council of Europe.
Recer, P. (1998, February 16). Apes shown to communicate in the wild. *Burlington Free Press,* 12A.
Redfield, R. (1953). *The primitive world and its transformations.* Ithaca, NY: Cornell University Press.
Redman, C. L. (1978). *The rise of civilization: From early farmers to urban society in the ancient Near East.* San Francisco: Freeman.
Reid, J. J., Schiffer, M. B., & Rathje, W. L. (1975). Behavioral archaeology: Four strategies. *American Anthropologist 77,* 864–869.
Reina, R. E. (1966). *The law of the saints.* Indianapolis: Bobbs-Merrill.
Relethford, J. H. (2001). Absence of regional affinities of Neandertal DNA with living humans does not reject multiregional evolution. *American Journal of Physical Anthropology 115,* 95–98.
Relethford, J. H., & Harpending, H. C. (1994). Craniometric variation, genetic theory, and modern human origins. *American Journal of Physical Anthropology 95,* 249–270.
Renfrew, C. (1973). *Before civilization: The radiocarbon revolution and prehistoric Europe.* London: Jonathan Cape.
"Return to the African Burial Ground: An interview with physical anthropologist Michael L. Blakey." (2003, November 20). *Archaeology.* http://www.archaeology.org/online/interviews/blakey/
Reynolds, V. (1994). Primates in the field, primates in the lab. *Anthropology Today 10* (2), 4.
Ribeiro, G. L. (2009). Non-hegemonic globalizations: Alternative transnational processes and agents. *Anthropological Theory 9* (3), 297–329.
Rice, P. (2000). Paleoanthropology 2000—part 1. *General Anthropology 7* (1), 11.
Richmond, B. G., Fleagle, J. K., & Swisher III, C. C. (1998). First Hominoid elbow from the Miocene of Ethiopia and the evolution of the Catarrhine elbow. *American Journal of Physical Anthropology 105,* 257–277.
Richter, C. A., et al. (2007). In vivo effects of bisphenol A in laboratory rodent studies. *Reproductive Toxicology 24* (2), 199–224.
Ridley, M. (1999). *Genome: The autobiography of a species in 23 chapters.* New York: HarperCollins.
Rightmire, G. P. (1990). *The evolution of Homo erectus: Comparative anatomical studies of an extinct human species.* Cambridge, MA: Cambridge University Press.
Rightmire, G. P. (1998). Evidence from facial morphology for similarity of Asian and African representatives of *Homo erectus. American Journal of Physical Anthropology 106,* 61–85.
Rindos, D. (1984). *The origins of agriculture: An evolutionary perspective.* Orlando: Academic.
Ritzer, G. (1983). The McDonaldization of society, *Journal of American Culture 6* (1), 100–107.
Ritzer, G. (2007). *The coming of post-industrial society* (2nd ed.). New York: McGraw-Hill.
Robben, A.C.G.M. (2007). Fieldwork identity: Introduction. In A.C.G.M. Robben & J. A. Sluka (Eds.), *Ethnographic fieldwork: An anthropological reader* (pp. 59–63). Malden, MA: Blackwell.
Robben, A.C.G.M. (2007). Reflexive ethnography: Introduction. In A.C.G.M. Robben & J. A. Sluka (Eds.), *Ethnographic fieldwork: An anthropological reader* (pp. 443–446). Malden, MA: Blackwell.
Robben, A.C.G.M., & Sluka, J. A. (Eds.). (2007). *Ethnographic fieldwork: An anthropological reader.* Malden, MA: Blackwell.
Rogers, J. (1994). Levels of the genealogical hierarchy and the problem of hominid phylogeny. *American Journal of Physical Anthropology 94,* 81–88.
Romer, A. S. (1945). *Vertebrate paleontology.* Chicago: University of Chicago Press.
Roosevelt, A. C. (1984). Population, health, and the evolution of subsistence: Conclusions from the conference. In M. N. Cohen & G. J. Armelagos (Eds.), *Paleopathology at the origins of agriculture* (pp. 572–574). Orlando: Academic.
Rosas, A., & Bermdez de Castro, J. M. (1998). On the taxonomic affinities of the Dmanisi mandible (Georgia). *American Journal of Physical Anthropology 107,* 145–162.
Roscoe, P. B. (1995). The perils of "positivism" in cultural anthropology. *American Anthropologist 97,* 497.
Roscoe, W. (1991). *Zuni man-woman.* Albuquerque: University of New Mexico Press.
Rowe, N., & Mittermeier, R. A. (1996). *The pictorial guide to the living primates.* East Hampton, NY: Pogonias.
Ruhlen, M. (1994). *The origin of language: Tracing the evolution of the mother tongue.* New York: Wiley.
Rupert, J. L., & Hochachka, P. W. (2001). The evidence for hereditary factors contributing to high altitude adaptation in Andean natives: A review. *High Altitude Medicine & Biology 2* (2), 235–256.
Ruvdo, M. (1994). Molecular evolutionary processes and conflicting gene trees: The hominoid case. *American Journal of Physical Anthropology 94,* 89–113.
Sabloff, J. A. (1997). *The cities of ancient Mexico* (rev. ed.). New York: Thames & Hudson.
Sabloff, J. A., & Lambert-Karlovsky, C. C. (Eds.). (1974). *The rise and fall of civilizations, modern archaeological approaches to ancient cultures.* Menlo Park, CA: Cummings.
Sacks, O. (1998). *Island of the colorblind.* New York: Knopf.
Sahlins, M. (1961). The segmentary lineage: An organization of predatory expansion. *American Anthropologist 63,* 322–343.
Sahlins, M. (1968). *Tribesmen.* Englewood Cliffs, NJ: Prentice-Hall (Foundations of Modern Anthropology).
Sahlins, M. (1972). *Stone age economics.* Chicago: Aldine.
Salzman, P. C. (1967). Political organization among nomadic peoples. *Proceedings of the American Philosophical Society 111,* 115–131.
Sanday, P. R. (1975). On the causes of IQ differences between groups and implications for social policy. In M.F.A. Montagu (Ed.), *Race and IQ* (pp. 232–238). New York: Oxford.
Sanday, P. R. (1981). *Female power and male dominance: On the origins of sexual inequality.* Cambridge, England: Cambridge University Press.
Sanday, P. R. (2002). *Women at the center: Life in a modern matriarchy.* Ithaca: Cornell University Press.
Sangree, W. H. (1965). The Bantu Tiriki of western Kenya. In J. L. Gibbs, Jr. (Ed.), *Peoples of Africa* (pp. 69–72). New York: Holt, Rinehart & Winston.
Sanjek, R. (1990). On ethnographic validity. In R. Sanjek (Ed.), *Field notes.* Ithaca, NY: Cornell University Press.

Sapir, E. (1921). *Language.* New York: Harcourt.

Sapolsky, R. (2002). *A primate's memoir: Love, death, and baboons in East Africa.* New York: Vintage.

Savage-Rumbaugh, S., & Lewin, R. (1994). *Kanzi: The ape at the brink of the human mind.* New York: Wiley.

Sawert, H. (2002). *TB and poverty in the context of global TB control.* World Health Organization. http://www.healthinitiative.org/html/Conf/satsymp/index.htm#2

Scaglion, R. (1987). Contemporary law development in Papua New Guinea. In R. M. Wulff & S. J. Fiske (Eds.), *Anthropological praxis: Translating knowledge into action.* Boulder, CO: Westview.

Schaeffer, S. B., & Furst, P. T. (Eds.). (1996). *People of the peyote: Huichol Indian history, religion, and survival.* Albuquerque: University of New Mexico Press.

Scheflen, A. E. (1972). *Body language and the social order.* Englewood Cliffs, NJ: Prentice-Hall.

Schepartz, L.A. (1993). Language and human origins. *Yearbook of Physical Anthropology 36,* 91–126.

Scheper-Hughes, N., & Waquant, L. (2002). *Commodifying bodies.* London: Sage (Theory, Culture, and Society series).

Schlegel, A. (1977). Male and female in Hopi thought and action. In A. Schlegel (Ed.), *Sexual stratification* (pp. 245–269). New York: Columbia University Press.

Schoepfle, M. (2001). Ethnographic resource inventory and the National Park Service. *Cultural Resource Management 5,* 1–7.

Schrire, C. (Ed.). (1984). *Past and present in hunter-gatherer studies.* Orlando: Academic.

Schusky, E. L. (1983). *Manual for kinship analysis* (2nd ed.). Lanham, MD: University Press of America.

Schuster, C., & Carpenter, E. (1996). *Patterns that connect: Social symbolism in ancient and tribal art.* New York: Abrams.

Schuster, G., Smits, W., & Ullal, J. (2008). *Thinkers of the jungle: The orangutan report.* H. F. Uhlmann.

Schwartz, J. H. (1984). Hominoid evolution: A review and a reassessment. *Current Anthropology 25* (5), 655–672.

Schwartz, M. (1997). *A history of dogs in the early Americas.* New Haven: Yale University Press.

Scully, T. (2008). Online anthropology draws protest from aboriginal group. *Nature 453,* 1155.

Scupin, R. (Ed.). (2000). *Religion and culture: An anthropological focus.* Upper Saddle River, NJ: Prentice-Hall.

Seeger, A. (2004). *Why Suyá sing: A musical anthropology.* Champaign: University of Illinois Press.

Sellen, D. W., & Mace, R. (1997). Fertility and mode of subsistence: A phylogenetic analysis. *Current Anthropology 38,* 886.

Semenov, S. A. (1964). *Prehistoric technology.* New York: Barnes & Noble.

Senut, B., Pickford, M., Gommery, D., Mein, P., Cheboi, K., & Coppens, Y. (2001). First hominid from the Miocene (Lukeino Formation, Kenya). *Comptes Rendus de l'Académie de Sciences 332,* 137–144.

Seyfarth, R. M., Cheney, D. L., & Marler, P. (1980). Vervet monkey alarm calls: Semantic communication in a free-ranging primate. *Animal Behavior 28* (4),1070–1094.

Seyfarth, R. M., et al. (1980). Monkey responses to three different alarm calls: Evidence for predator classification and semantic communication. *Science 210,* 801–803.

Seymour, D. Z. (1986). Black children, black speech. In P. Escholz, A. Rosa, & V. Clark (Eds.), *Language awareness* (4th ed.). New York: St. Martin's.

Shane, L., III. (2005). Happy couple both no-show wedding: Deployed troops make use of double-proxy ceremony. *Stars & Stripes 3* (17), 6.

Shapiro, H. (Ed.). (1971). *Man, culture and society* (2nd ed.). New York: Oxford University Press.

Sharer, R. J., & Ashmore, W. (2007). *Archaeology: Discovering our past* (4th ed.). New York: McGraw-Hill.

Shaw, D. G. (1984). A light at the end of the tunnel: Anthropological contributions toward global competence. *Anthropology Newsletter 25,* 16.

Shearer, R. R., & Gould, S. J. (1999). Of two minds and one nature. *Science 286,* 1093.

Sheets, P. D. (1993). Dawn of a new Stone Age in eye surgery. In R. J. Sharer & W. Ashmore (Eds.), *Archaeology: Discovering our past* (2nd ed.). Palo Alto, CA: Mayfield.

Shipman, P. (1993). *Life history of a fossil: An introduction to taphonomy and paleoecology.* Cambridge, MA: Harvard University Press.

Shook, J. R., et al. (Eds.). (2004). *Dictionary of modern American philosophers, 1860–1960.* Bristol, England: Thoemmes.

Shore, B. (1996). *Culture in mind: Meaning, construction, and cultural cognition.* New York: Oxford University Press.

Shostak, M. (1983). *Nisa: The life and words of a !Kung woman.* New York: Vintage.

Shreeve, J. (1994). Terms of estrangement. *Discover 15* (11), 60.

Shreeve, J. (1995). *The Neandertal enigma: Solving the mystery of modern human origins.* New York: William Morrow.

Shuey, A. M. (1966). *The testing of Negro intelligence.* New York: Social Science.

Sillen, A., & Brain, C. K. (1990). Old flame. *Natural History 4,* 6–10.

Simons, E. L. (1972). *Primate evolution.* New York: Macmillan.

Simons, E. L. (1989) Human origins. *Science 245,* 1349.

Simons, E. L. (1995). Skulls and anterior teeth of *Catopithecus* (Primates: Anthropoidea) from the Eocene and anthropoid origins. *Science 268,* 1885–1888.

Simons, E. L., Rasmussen, D. T., & Gebo, D. L. (1987). A new species of *Propliopithecus* from the Fayum, Egypt. *American Journal of Physical Anthropology 73,* 139–147.

Simons, R. C., & Hughes, C. C. (Eds.). (1985). *The culture-bound syndromes: Folk illnesses of psychiatric and anthropological interest.* Dordrecht, Netherlands: Reidel.

Simpson, G. G. (1949). *The meaning of evolution.* New Haven, CT: Yale University Press.

Simpson, S. (1995, April). Whispers from the ice. *Alaska,* 23–28.

Simpson, S. W., Quade, J., Levin, N. E., Butler, R., Dupont-Nivet, G., Everett, M., & Semaw, S. (2008). A female *Homo erectus* pelvis from Gona, Ethiopia. *Science 322* (5904), 1089–1092.

Sjoberg, G. (1960). *The preindustrial city.* New York: Free Press.

Sluka, J. A. (2007). Fieldwork relations and rapport: Introduction. In A.C.G.M. Robben & J. A. Sluka (Eds.), *Ethnographic fieldwork: An anthropological reader.* Malden, MA: Blackwell.

Small, M. F. (1997). Making connections. *American Scientist 85,* 503.

Small, M. F. (2000). Kinship envy. *Natural History 109* (2), 88.

Small, M. F. (2008, August 15). Why red is such a potent color. *Live Science.* http://www.livescience.com/culture/080815-hn-color-red.html

Small, M. F. (2009, May 15). Why "Ida" inspires navel-gazing at our ancestry. *Live Science.* http://www.livescience.com/history/090520-hn-ida.html

Smedley, A. (2007). *Race in North America: Origin and evolution of a worldview.* Boulder, CO: Westview.

Smith, B. H. (1994). Patterns of dental development in *Homo, Australopithecus, Pan,* and gorilla. *American Journal of Physical Anthropology 94,* 307–325.

Smith, F. H., & Raynard, G. C. (1980). Evolution of the supraorbital region in Upper Pleistocene fossil hominids from South-Central Europe. *American Journal of Physical Anthropology 53,* 589–610.

Smith, P.E.L. (1976). *Food production and its consequences* (2nd ed.). Menlo Park, CA: Cummings.

Snowden, C. T. (1990). Language capabilities of nonhuman animals. *Yearbook of Physical Anthropology 33,* 215–243.

Speck, F. G. (1920). Penobscot shamanism. *Memoirs of the American Anthropological Association 6,* 239–288.

Speck, F. G. (1970). *Penobscot man: The life history of a forest tribe in Maine.* New York: Octagon.

Spencer, F., & Smith, F. H. (1981). The significance of Ales Hrdlicka's "Neanderthal phase of man": A historical and current assessment. *American Journal of Physical Anthropology 56,* 435–459.

Spencer, H. (1896). *Principles of sociology.* New York: Appleton.

Spencer, R. F. (1984). North Alaska Coast Eskimo. In D. Damas (Ed.), *Arctic: Handbook of North American Indians* (Vol. 5, pp. 320–337). Washington, DC: Smithsonian Institution.

Spindler, G., & Stockard, J. E. (Eds.). (2006). *Globalization and change in fifteen cultures.* Belmont, CA: Wadsworth.

Spradley, J. P. (1979). *The ethnographic interview.* New York: Holt, Rinehart & Winston.

Spradley, J. P. (1980). *Participant observation.* New York: Holt, Rinehart & Winston.

Springen, K. (2008, September 15). What it means to be a woman: How women around the world cope with infertility. *Newsweek* Web Exclusive. http://www.newsweek.com/id/158625

Stacey, J. (1990). *Brave new families.* New York: Basic.

Stahl, A. B. (1984). Hominid dietary selection before fire. *Current Anthropology 25,* 151–168.

Standing Bear, L. (1975). *My people the Sioux.* Lincoln: University of Nebraska Press.

Stanford, C. B. (2001). *Chimpanzee and red colobus: The ecology of predator and prey.* Cambridge, MA: Harvard University Press.

Stanford, C. B. (2001). *The hunting apes: Meat eating and the origins of human behavior.* Princeton, NJ: Princeton University Press.

Stannard, D. E. (1992). *American holocaust.* Oxford, England: Oxford University Press.

Starn, O. (2005). *Ishi's brain: In search of America's last "wild" Indian.* New York: Norton.

Steady, F. C. (2001). *Women and the Amistad connection, Sierra Leone Krio Society.* Rochester, VT: Schenkman.

Steady, F. C. (2005). *Women and collective action in Africa.* New York: Palgrave Macmillan.

Stedman, H. H., et al. (2004). Myosin gene mutation correlates with anatomical changes in the human lineage. *Nature 428,* 415–418.

Stein, R., & St. George, D. (2009, May 13). Babies increasingly born to unwed mothers. *Washington Post.*

Stein, R. L., & Stein, P. L. (2004). *Anthropology of religion, magic, and witchcraft.* Boston: Allyn & Bacon.
Steward, J. H. (1972). *Theory of culture change: The methodology of multilinear evolution.* Urbana: University of Illinois Press.
Stiglitz, J. E. (2003). *Globalization and its discontents.* New York: Norton.
Stiles, D. (1979). Early Acheulean and developed Oldowan. *Current Anthropology 20* (l), 126–129.
Stockard, J. E. (2002). *Marriage in culture: Practice and meaning across diverse societies.* Ft. Worth: Harcourt College.
Stocking, G. W., Jr. (1968). *Race, culture and evolution: Essays in the history of anthropology.* New York: Free Press.
Stone, L. (2005). *Kinship and gender: An introduction* (3rd ed.). Boulder, CO: Westview.
Stone, R. (1995). If the mercury soars, so may health hazards. *Science 267,* 958.
Straus, W. L., & Cave, A.J.E. (1957). Pathology and the posture of Neanderthal man. *Quarterly Review of Biology,* 32.
Strier, K. (1993, March). Menu for a monkey. *Natural History,* 42.
Stringer, C. B., & McKie, R. (1996). *African exodus: The origins of modern humanity.* London: Jonathan Cape.
Strum, S., & Mitchell, W. (1987). Baboon models and muddles. In W. Kinsey (Ed.), *The evolution of human behavior: Primate models.* Albany: State University of New York Press.
Stuart-MacAdam, P., & Dettwyler, K. A. (Eds.). (1995). *Breastfeeding: Biocultural perspectives.* New York: Aldine.
"Study estimates 250,000 active child soldiers."(2006, July 26). Associated Press.
Suarez-Orozoco, M. M., Spindler, G., & Spindler, L. (1994). *The making of psychological anthropology, II.* Fort Worth: Harcourt Brace.
Susman, R. L. (1988). Hand of *Paranthropus robustus* from Member 1, Swartkrans: Fossil evidence for tool behavior. *Science 240,* 781–784.
Suwa, G., et al. (2007, August 23). A new species of great ape from the late Miocene epoch in Ethiopia. *Nature 448,* 921–924.
Swadesh, M. (1959). Linguistics as an instrument of prehistory. *Southwestern Journal of Anthropology 15,* 20–35.
Swaminathan, M. S. (2000). Science in response to basic human needs. *Science 287,* 425.
Swisher III, C. C., Curtis, G. H., Jacob, T., Getty, A. G., Suprijo, A., & Widiasmoro. (1994). Age of the earliest known hominids in Java, Indonesia. *Science 263,* 1118–1121.
Tapper, M. (1999). *In the blood: Sickle-cell anemia and the politics of race.* Philadelphia: University of Pennsylvania Press.
Tattersal, I. (1998). *Becoming human: Evolution and human uniqueness.* New York: Harcourt Brace.
Tattersall, I., & Schwartz, J. H. (1999). Hominids and hybrids: The place of Neanderthals in human evolution. *Proceedings of the National Academy of Science 96* (13), 7117–7119.
Tax, S. (1953). *Penny capitalism: A Guatemalan Indian economy.* Washington, DC: Smithsonian Institution, Institute of Social Anthropology, Pub. No. 16.
Taylor, G. (2000). *Castration: Abbreviated history of western manhood.* New York: Routledge.
Tedlock, B. (2005). *The woman in the shaman's body: Reclaiming the feminine in religion and medicine.* New York: Random House.
Templeton, A. R. (1994). Eve: Hypothesis compatibility versus hypothesis testing. *American Anthropologist 96* (1), 141–147.
Templeton, A. R. (1995). The "Eve" hypothesis: A genetic critique and re-analysis. *American Anthropologist 95* (1), 51–72.
Terashima, H. (1983). Mota and other hunting activities of the Mbuti archers: A socio-ecological study of subsistence technology. *African Studies Monograph* (Kyoto), 71–85.
Thin, N. (2007). "Realising the substance of their happiness": How anthropology forgot about *Homo gauisus.* In A. C. Jimenez (Ed.), *Culture and the politics of freedom: The anthropology of well-being.* London: Pluto
Thomas, E. M. (1994). *The tribe of the tiger: Cats and their culture* (pp. 109–186). New York: Simon & Schuster.
Thompson, P. (2009, March 6). Sign of the times: Jobless pitch "tent city" in Sacramento. *Mail Online* (London). http://obrag.org/?p=5008
Thomson, K. S. (1997). Natural selection and evolution's smoking gun. *American Scientist 85,* 516–518.
Thorne, A. G., & Wolpoff, M.D.H. (1981). Regional continuity in Australasian Pleistocene hominid evolution. *American Journal of Physical Anthropology 55,* 337–349.
Thornhill, N. (1993). Quoted in W. A. Haviland & R. J. Gordon (Eds.), *Talking about people* (p. 127). Mountain View, CA: Mayfield.
Timmons, H., & Kumar, H. (2009, July 3). Indian court overturns gay sex ban. *New York Times.*
Tobias, P. V., & von Konigswald, G.H.R. (1964). A comparison between the Olduvai hominines and those of Java and some implications for hominid phylogeny. *Nature 204,* 515–518.
Toth, N., Schick, K. D., Savage-Rumbaugh, E. S., Sevcik, R. A., & Rumbaugh, D. M. (1993–2001). Pan the tool-maker: Investigations into the stone tool-making and tool-using capabilities of a bonobo (*Pan panisicus*). *Journal of Archaeological Science 20* (1), 81–91.
Tracy, J. L., & Matsumoto, D. (2008). The spontaneous expression of pride and shame: Evidence for biologically innate nonverbal displays. *Proceedings of the National Academy of Sciences 105* (33), 11655–11660.
Trevathan, W., Smith, E. O., & McKenna, J. J. (Eds.). (1999). *Evolutionary medicine.* London: Oxford University Press.
Trifonov, V., et al. (2009). The origin of the recent swine influenza A (H1N1) virus infecting humans. *Eurosurveillance 14* (17). http://www.eurosurveillance.org/ViewArticle.aspx?ArticleId=19193
Trinkaus, E. (1986). The Neanderthals and modern human origins. *Annual Review of Anthropology 15,* 197.
Trinkaus, E., & Shipman, P. (1992). *The Neandertals: Changing the image of mankind.* New York: Knopf.
Trouillot, M. R. (1996). Culture, color, and politics in Haiti. In S. Gregory & R. Sanjek (Eds.), *Race.* New Brunswick, NJ: Rutgers University Press.
Trouillot, M. R. (2003). *Global transformations: Anthropology and the modern world.* New York: Palgrave Macmillan.
Tumin, M. M. (1967). *Social stratification: The forms and functions of inequality.* Englewood Cliffs, NJ: Prentice-Hall (Foundations of Modern Sociology).
Turnbull, C. M. (1961). *The forest people.* New York: Simon & Schuster.
Turnbull, C. M. (1983). *The human cycle.* New York: Simon & Schuster.
Turnbull, C. M. (1983). *Mbuti Pygmies: Change and adaptation.* New York: Holt, Rinehart & Winston.
Turner, T. (1991). Major shift in Brazilian Yanomami policy. *Anthropology Newsletter 32* (5), 1, 46.
Turner, V. W. (1957). *Schism and continuity in an African society.* Manchester, England: University Press.
Turner, V. W. (1969). *The ritual process.* Chicago: Aldine.
Tylor, E. B. (1871). *Primitive culture: Researches into the development of mythology, philosophy, religion, language, art and customs.* London: Murray.
Tylor, Sir E. B. (1931). Animism. In V. F. Calverton (Ed.), *The making of man: An outline of anthropology.* New York: Modern Library.
Unah, I., & Boger, C. (2001, April). *Race and the death penalty in North Carolina.* www.commonsense.org/pdfs/NCDeathPenaltyReport2001.pdf
UNESCO. www.unesco.org/webworld/babel
UNESCO. www.unesco.org/education/litdecade
UNESCO Institute for Statistics. (2007). http://stats.uis.unesco.org
"UN food agency warns G8 ministers of unparalleled hunger crisis as funding falls." (2009, June 12). http://www.un.org/apps/news/story.asp?NewsID=31116&Cr=WFP&Cr1=hunger
United Nations, World Tourism Organization. www.unwto.org
Universal Declaration of Human Rights. www.ccnmtl.columbia.edu/projects/mmt/udhr
Urban, G. (2001). *Metaculture: How cultures move through the modern world.* Westport, CT: Greenwood.
Ury, W. L. (1993). *Getting past no: Negotiating your way from confrontation.* New York: Bantam.
Ury, W. L. (1999). *Getting to peace: Transforming conflict at home, at work, and in the world.* New York: Viking.
Ury, W. (2002, Winter). A global immune system. *Andover Bulletin.*
Ury, W. (Ed.). (2002). *Must we fight? From the battlefield to the schoolyard—A new perspective on violent conflict and its prevention.* Hoboken, NJ: Jossey-Bass.
U.S. Census Bureau. (2002). *Current population survey.*
U.S. Census Bureau. (2008). *American Community Survey, 2006–2008.*
U.S. Census Bureau News. (2004, March 18).
U.S. Department of Health and Human Services, Administration on Children, Youth, and Families. (2005). *Child maltreatment 2003.* Washington, DC: U.S. Government Printing Office.
Van Allen, J. (1997). Sitting on a man: Colonialism and the lost political institutions of Igbo women. In R. Grinker & C. Steiner (Eds.), *Perspectives on Africa* (p. 450). Boston: Blackwell.
van den Berghe, P. (1992). The modern state: Nation builder or nation killer? *International Journal of Group Tensions 22* (3), 191–207.
Van Eck, C. (2003). *Purified by blood: Honour killings amongst Turks in the Netherlands.* Amsterdam: Amsterdam University Press.
Van Gennep, A. (1960). *The rites of passage.* Chicago: University of Chicago Press. (orig. [1909]. *Les rites de passage.* Paris: Émile Nourry)
Van Tilburg, J. A. (1994). *Easter Island: Archaeology, ecology, and culture.* London: British Museum.
Van Willigen, J. (1986). *Applied anthropology.* South Hadley, MA: Bergin & Garvey.
Veenhoven, R. (1993). *Happiness in nations: Subjective appreciation of life in 56 nations 1946–1992.* Rotterdam: RISBO.
Venbrux, E., Rosi, P. S., & Welsch, R. L. (Eds.). (2006). *Exploring world art.* Longrove, IL: Waveland.
Vincent, J. (2002). *The anthropology of politics: A reader in ethnography, theory, and critique.* Boston: Blackwell.

Vogt, E. Z. (1990). *The Zinacantecos of Mexico: A modern Maya way of life* (2nd ed.). Fort Worth: Holt, Rinehart & Winston.
vom Saal, F. S., & Myers, J. P. (2008). Bisphenol A and risk of metabolic disorders. *Journal of the American Medical Association, 300* (11), 1353–1355.
Waldbaum, J. C. (2005, November/December). Tell it to the Marines: Teaching troops about cultural heritage. *Archaeology 58* (6).
Walker, A., & Shipman, P. (1997). *The wisdom of the bones: In search of human origins.* New York: Vintage.
Wallace, A.F.C. (1956). Revitalization movements. *American Anthropologist 58,* 264–281.
Wallace, A.F.C. (1966). *Religion: An anthropological view.* New York: Random House.
Wallace, A.F.C. (1970). *Culture and personality* (2nd ed.). New York: Random House.
Wallace, E., & Hoebel, E. A. (1952). *The Comanches.* Norman: University of Oklahoma Press.
Walrath, D. (2002). Decoding the discourses: Feminism and science, review essay. *American Anthropologist 104* (1), 327–330.
Walrath, D. (2003). Rethinking pelvic typologies and the human birth mechanism. *Current Anthropology 44* (1), 5–31.
Walrath, D. (2006). Gender, genes, and the evolution of human birth. In P. L. Geller & M. K. Stockett (Eds.), *Feminist anthropology: Past, present, and future.* Philadelphia: University of Pennsylvania Press.
Ward, C. V., Walker, A., Teaford, M. F., & Odhiambo, I. (1993). Partial skeleton of Proconsul nyanzae from Mfangano Island, Kenya. *American Journal of Physical Anthropology 90,* 77–111.
Washburn, S. L., & Moore, R. (1980). *Ape into human: A study of human evolution* (2nd ed.). Boston: Little, Brown.
Wattenberg, B. J. (1997, November 23). The population explosion is over. *New York Times Magazine,* 60.
Weatherford, J. (1988). *Indian givers: How the Indians of the Americas transformed the world.* New York: Ballantine.
Weiner, A. B. (1977). Review of Trobriand cricket: An ingenious response to colonialism. *American Anthropologist 79,* 506.
Weiner, A. B. (1988). *The Trobrianders of Papua New Guinea.* New York: Holt, Rinehart & Winston.
Weiner, J. S. (1955). *The Piltdown forgery.* Oxford, England: Oxford University Press.
Weiss, M. L., & Mann, A. E. (1990). *Human biology and behavior* (5th ed.). Boston: Little, Brown.
Wells, S. (2002). *The journey of man: A genetic odyssey.* Princeton, NJ: Princeton University Press.
Werner, D. (1990). *Amazon journey.* Englewood Cliffs, NJ: Prentice-Hall.
Wheeler, P. (1993). Human ancestors walked tall, stayed cool. *Natural History 102* (8), 65–66.
Whelehan, P. (1985). Review of incest, a biosocial view. *American Anthropologist 87,* 678.
White, D. R. (1988). Rethinking polygyny: Co-wives, codes, and cultural systems. *Current Anthropology 29,* 529–572.
White, L. (1949). *The science of culture: A study of man and civilization.* New York: Farrar, Straus.
White, L. (1959). *The evolution of culture: The development of civilization to the fall of Rome.* New York: McGraw-Hill.
White, M. (2001). *Historical atlas of the twentieth century.* http://users.erols.com/mwhite28/20centry.htm
White, R. (2003). *Prehistoric art: The symbolic journey of humankind.* New York: Abrams.
White, T., Asfaw, B., Degusta, D., Gilbert, H., Richards, G., Suwa, G., & Howell, F. C. (2003). Pleistocene *Homo sapiens* from the Middle Awash, Ethiopia. *Nature 423,* 742–747.
White, T. D. (1979). Evolutionary implications of Pliocene hominid footprints. *Science 208,* 175–176.
White, T. D. (2003). Early hominids—diversity or distortion? *Science 299,* 1994–1997.
White, T. D., Asfaw, B., Beyne, Y., Haile-Selassie, Y., Lovejoy, C. O., Suwa, G., & Wolde Gabriel, G. (2009, October). *Ardipithecus ramidus* and the paleobiology of early hominids. *Science 326* (5949), 64, 75–86.
White, T. D., & Toth, N. (2000). Cutmarks on a Plio-Pleistocene hominid from Sterkfontein, South Africa. *American Journal of Physical Anthropology 111,* 579–584.
Whitehead, B. D., & Popenoe, D. (2004). *The state of our unions: The social health of marriage in America 2004.* Rutgers, NJ: Rutgers University National Marriage Project.
Whitehead, N., & Ferguson, R. B. (Eds.). (1992). *War in the tribal zone.* Santa Fe: School of American Research.
Whitehead, N. L., & Ferguson, R. B. (1993, November). Deceptive stereotypes about tribal warfare. *Chronicle of Higher Education,* A48.
Whiting, B. B. (Ed.). (1963). *Six cultures: Studies of child rearing.* New York: Wiley.
Whiting, J.W.M., & Child, I. L. (1953). *Child training and personality: A cross-cultural study.* New Haven, CT: Yale University Press.
Whiting, J.W.M., Sodergem, J. A., & Stigler, S. M. (1982). Winter temperature as a constraint to the migration of preindustrial peoples. *American Anthropologist 84,* 289.
Whorf, B. (1941). The relation of habitual thought and behavior to language. In L. Spier, A. I. Hallowell, & S. S. Newman (Eds.), *Language, culture, and personality: Essays in memory of Edward Sapir* (pp. 75–93). Menasha, WI: Sapir Memorial Publication Fund.
Whyte, A.L.H. (2005). Human evolution in Polynesia. *Human Biology 77* (2), 157–177.
Wiley, A. S. (2004). *An ecology of high-altitude infancy: A biocultural perspective.* Cambridge, England: Cambridge University Press.
Wilk, R. R. (1996). *Economics and cultures: An introduction to economic anthropology.* Boulder, CO: Westview.
Wilkie, D. S., & Curran, B. (1993). Historical trends in forager and farmer exchange in the Ituri rain forest of northeastern Zaïre. *Human Ecology 21* (4), 389–417.
Willey, G. R. (1966). *An introduction to American archaeology: Vol. 1. North America.* Englewood Cliffs, NJ: Prentice-Hall.
Willey, G. R. (1971). *An introduction to American archaeology, Vol. 2: South America.* Englewood Cliffs, NJ: Prentice-Hall.
Williams, F. (2005, January 9). Toxic breast milk? *New York Times Magazine.*
Williamson, R. K. (1995). The blessed curse: Spirituality and sexual difference as viewed by Euramerican and Native American cultures. *The College News 18* (4).
Wills, C. (1994). The skin we're in. *Discover 15* (11), 79.
Wilson, A. K., & Sarich, V. M. (1969). A molecular time scale for human evolution. *Proceedings of the National Academy of Science 63,* 1,089–1,093.
Wingert, P. (1965). *Primitive art: Its tradition and styles.* New York: World.
Winick, C. (Ed.). (1970). *Dictionary of anthropology.* Totowa, NJ: Littlefield, Adams.
Wirsing, R. L. (1985). The health of traditional societies and the effects of acculturation. *Current Anthropology 26* (3), 303–322.
Wittfogel, K. A. (1957). *Oriental despotism, a comparative study of total power.* New Haven, CT: Yale University Press.
Wolf, E. R. (1966). *Peasants.* Englewood Cliffs, NJ: Prentice-Hall.
Wolf, E. R. (1969). *Peasant wars of the twentieth century.* New York: Harper & Row.
Wolf, E. R. (1982). *Europe and the people without history.* Berkeley: University of California Press.
Wolf, E. R. (1999). *Envisioning power: Ideologies of dominance and crisis.* Berkeley: University of California Press.
Wolf, E. R., & Hansen, E. C. (1972). *The human condition in Latin America.* New York: Oxford University Press.
Wolf, E. R., & Trager, G. L. (1971). Hortense Powdermaker 1900–1970. *American Anthropologist 73* (3), 784.
Wolf, M. (1985). *Revolution postponed: Women in contemporary China.* Stanford, CA: Stanford University Press.
Wolffe, R., Ramirez, J., & Bartholet, J. (2008, March 31). *Newsweek.*
Wolfson, H. (2000, January 22). Polygamists make the Christian connection. *Burlington Free Press,* 2c.
Wolpoff, M. H. (1993). Evolution in *Homo erectus:* The question of stasis. In R. L. Ciochon & J. G. Fleagle (Eds.), *The human evolution source book.* Englewood Cliffs, NJ: Prentice-Hall.
Wolpoff, M. H. (1993). Multiregional evolution: The fossil alternative to Eden. In R. L. Ciochon & J. G. Fleagle (Eds.), *The human evolution source book.* Englewood Cliffs, NJ: Prentice-Hall.
Wolpoff, M. (1996). *Australopithecus:* A new look at an old ancestor. *General Anthropology 3* (1), 2.
Wolpoff, M., & Caspari, R. (1997). *Race and human evolution: A fatal attraction.* New York: Simon & Schuster.
Wolpoff, M. H., Wu, X. Z., & Thorne, A. G. (1984). Modern *Homo sapiens* origins: A general theory of hominid evolution involving fossil evidence from east Asia. In F. H. Smith and F. Spencer (Eds.), *The origins of modern humans* (pp. 411–483). New York: Alan R. Liss.
Wood, B., & Aiello, L. C. (1998). Taxonomic and functional implications of mandibular scaling in early hominines. *American Journal of Physical Anthropology 105,* 523–538.
Wood, B., Wood, C., & Konigsberg, L. (1994). *Paranthropus boisei:* An example of evolutionary stasis? *American Journal of Physical Anthropology 95,* 117–136.
Woolfson, P. (1972). Language, thought, and culture. In V. P. Clark, P. A. Escholz, & A. F. Rosa (Eds.), *Language.* New York: St. Martin's.
World almanac. (2004). New York: Press Publishing.
World Bank. www.worldbank.org/poverty
World Bank Development Indicators. (2008).
World Health Organization. http://www.who.int/about/definition/en
World Health Organization. (2003). *Global strategy on infant and young child feeding.* Geneva: Author.
World Health Organization. (2004). Statistical information system.
World Meteorological Organization. (2003). Increasing heat waves and other health hazards. greenpeaceusa.org/climate/index.fpl/7096/article/907.html

World Travel & Tourism Council. www.wttc.org
Worsley, P. (1957). *The trumpet shall sound: A study of "cargo" cults in Melanesia.* London: Macgibbon & Kee.
Worsley, P. (1959). Cargo cults. *Scientific American 200* (May), 117–128.
Wrangham, R., & Peterson, D. (1996). *Demonic males.* Boston: Houghton Mifflin.
Wulff, R. M., & Fiske, S. J. (1987). *Anthropological praxis: Translating knowledge into action.* Boulder, CO: Westview.
Xinhua News Agency. (2009, May 9). Canton Fair wraps up with export orders down 17 percent. *China Daily.*
Yip, M. (2002). *Tone.* New York: Cambridge University Press.
Young, A. (1981). The creation of medical knowledge: Some problems in interpretation. *Social Science and Medicine 17,*1205–1211.
Young, W. (Ed.). (2000). Kimball award winner. *Anthropology News 41* (8), 29.
Zeder, M. A., & Hesse, B. (2000). The initial domestication of goats (*Capra hircus*) in the Zagros Mountains 10,000 years ago. *Science 287,* 2254–2257.
Zeresenay, A., Spoor, F., Kimbel, W. H., Bobe, R., Geraads, D., Reed, D., & Wynn, J. G. (2006). A juvenile early hominin skeleton from Dikika, Ethiopia. *Nature 443,* 296–301.
Zihlman, A. (2001). *The human evolution coloring book.* New York: Harper Resources.
Zilhão, J. (2000). Fate of the Neandertals. *Archaeology 53* (4), 30.
Zimmer, C. (1999). New date for the dawn of dream time. *Science 284,* 1243.
Zimmer, C. (2001). *Evolution: The triumph of an idea.* New York: HarperCollins.
Zimmer, C. (2005) *Smithsonian intimate guide to human origins.* New York: HarperCollins.
Zohary, D., & Hopf, M. (1993). *Domestication of plants in the Old World* (2nd ed.). Oxford: Clarenden.
Zuckerman, P. (2005). Atheism: Contemporary rates and patterns. In M. Martin (Ed.), *The Cambridge companion to atheism.* Cambridge, England: Cambridge University Press.

Photo Credits

CHAPTER 1

p. 2: © New York Times/Stephanie Sinclair/VII Photo Agency; **p. 4:** © Documentary Educational Resources; **p. 6 (left):** © Michael Newman/PhotoEdit; **p. 6 (right):** © Marie-Stenzel/National Geographic Image Collection; **p. 9:** © Associated Press; **p. 10:** © AP Photo/Rodrigo Abd; **p. 12:** © Jeff Schonberg 2009; **p. 14:** © Living Tongues Institute; **p. 17 (above right):** National Anthropological Archives Smithsonian Museum 1895 Neg # 02871000; **p. 17 (below left):** Bildarchiv Preussischer Kulturbesitz/Art Resource, NY; **p. 19:** © Kerry Cullinan; **p. 22:** © The Canadian Press/Kevin Frayer; **p. 23 (left):** © Associated Press; **p. 23 (right):** © K. Bhagya Prakash in *Frontline* Vol 19, issue 7, March 30–April 12, 2002

CHAPTER 2

p. 26: © Imagemore Co., Ltd./Corbis; **p. 29:** From Lindauer Bilderbogen no. 5 edited by Frederich Boer, Jan Thorbecke Verlag Sigmaringen West Germany; **p. 30 (left):** © Yvette Pigeon; **p. 30 (right):** © BIOS Huguet Pierre/Peter Arnold, Inc.; **p. 31 (left):** © Fritz Polking/Peter Arnold, Inc.; **p. 31 (right):** © Dana Walrath; **p. 33:** © Vittorio Luzzati/National Portrait Gallery, London; **p. 36:** Courtesy of Rayna Rapp; **p. 40:** By Jonathan Marks (2000) "98% Alike: What Our Similarity to Apes Tell Us about Our Understanding Genetics." *The Chronicle of Higher Education,* May 12; **p. 42:** 20th Century Fox/The Kobal Collection/Hayes, Kerry; **p. 44:** © Marcia Inhorn; **p. 46:** © Camille Tokerud/Getty Images; **p. 47:** Otorohanga Zoological Society; **p. 48:** © Meckes/Ottawa/Photo Researchers, Inc.

CHAPTER 3

p. 52: © Steve Bloom Images/Alamy; **p. 55:** Courtesy of Michele L. Goldsmith; Photograph © Katherine Hope; **p. 57:** © Peter Arnold, Inc.; **p. 62:** © Tom Brakefield/Corbis; **p. 63:** © Cheng Min/Xinhua/Landov; **p. 66 (left):** © blickwirkel/Alamy; **p. 66 (right):** © Kevin Schafer/Peter Arnold, Inc.; **p. 67:** © Danita Delimont/Alamy; **p. 68:** © Inga Arndt/Minden Pictures; **p. 69:** © dbimages/Alamy; **p. 70:** © Gerard Lacz/Peter Arnold, Inc.; **p. 71:** © Jay Ullal; **p. 72 (left):** © 2005 Jim West/The Image Works; **p. 72 (right):** © Population Media Center, www.populationmedia.org; **p. 73:** © Martin Bennett/Alamy; **p. 74:** © AWF/Paul Thomson

CHAPTER 4

p. 76: Courtesy of Save the Chimps, the world's largest sanctuary for rescued chimpanzees. (www.savethechimps.org); **p. 79:** © Paul van Gaalen/zefa/Corbis; **p. 81 (left):** © Michael Nichols/National Geographic Image Collection; **p. 81 (right):** Bunataro Imanishi; **p. 82:** © Amy Parish/Anthro-Photo; **p. 84:** © Gunter Ziesler/Peter Arnold, Inc.; **p. 85:** © Biosphere/Gunther Michel/Peter Arnold, Inc.; **p. 86 (left):** © John Guistina; **p. 86 (right):** © Danita Delimont/Alamy; **p. 89:** © Tim Davis/Corbis; **p. 90:** © Bob Willingham; **p. 91:** The Great Ape Trust, photo courtesy of Sue Savage-Rumbaugh; **p. 92:** © age footstock/SuperStock; **p. 93:** © Martin Harvey/Peter Arnold, Inc.

CHAPTER 5

p. 98: © John Warburton-Lee Photography/Alamy; **p. 101:** © AP Images; **p. 102:** © Javier Trueba/Madrid Scientific Films; **p. 104:** Courtesy of Anne Jensen and Glenn Sheehan; **p. 106 (left):** © Charles Walker/Topfoto/The Image Works; **p. 106 (right):** © WaterFrame/Alamy; **p. 108:** © John Crock; **p. 111 (above):** © British Museum/Art Resource, NY; **p. 111 (below):** © University of Pennsylvania Museum From *Tikal, A Handbook of the Ancient Maya Ruins* by William R. Coe, 1967 #153371; **p. 112:** © AFP/Getty Images; **p. 113:** © Kenneth Garrett/National Geographic Image Collection; **p. 115:** © Eurelios/Photo Researchers, Inc.; **p. 117:** © University of Pennsylvania Museum # CX61-4-123

CHAPTER 6

p. 122: Courtesy of PLoS; **p. 125 (left):** © David Bygott/Kibuyu Partners; **p. 125 (right):** © Nishan Bingham; **p. 126:** © David Scharf/Photo Researchers, Inc.; **p. 128 (left):** © Wolfgang Kaehler/Corbis; **p. 128 (right):** © Pete Saloutos/Corbis; **p. 132 (left):** The Kobal Collection/Hammer; **p. 132 (right):** © Nishan Bingham; **p. 135:** Courtesy of PLoS; **p. 137 (right):** © David Begun; **p. 138:** The Natural History Museum, London; **p. 139:** Roger Ressmeyer/Corbis; **p. 141 (left):** Michel Brunet; **p. 141 (right):** © Orban, Thierry/Corbis Sygma

CHAPTER 7

p. 144: © T. White Inc.; **p. 147 (left):** Andrew Hill/Anthro-Photo; **p. 148:** © T. White, Inc.; **p. 149:** © Melville Bell Grosvenor/National Geographic Image Collection; **p. 150:** Pascal Goetgheluck/Photo Researchers, Inc.; **p. 151:** Discovery of the Pittdown Man in 1911, Cooke, Arthur Clarke (1867–1951)/Geological Society, London, UK/The Bridgeman Art Library; **p. 153:** AP Photo/Richard Drew; **p. 155:** VILEM BISCHOF/AFP/Getty Images; **p. 156:** © Kristin Mosher/Danita Delimont. All Rights Reserved; **p. 158:** © Dr. Fred Spoon/National Museums of Kenya; **p. 160:** © John Reader/Photo Researchers, Inc.; **p. 161:** © T. White, 1998; **p. 165:** Aztec Tlazolteotl. Photographed by Man Ray (1890–1976) © Artists Rights Society (ARS), NY. Statuette of Ixcuina, Mexican Goddess of Maternity. 1890–1941. Gelatin silver print, 9-1/16 × 6-7/8″ (23 × 17.4 cm). Gift of James Thrall Soby (204.1991) Digital image © The Museum of Modern Art/Licensed by SCALA/Art Resource, NY

CHAPTER 8

p. 172: © Javier Trueba/Madrid Scientific Films; **p. 175:** © 1999 David L. Brill; **p. 176:** © The Field Museum Neg A102513c; **p. 178:** © J & B Photos/Animals, Animals; **p. 184:** National Museums of Kenya; **p. 185:** © John Reader/Photo Researchers, Inc.; **p. 187:** © Michael S. Yamashita/Corbis; **p. 192:** © PhotoDisc/Getty Images; **p. 193:** Mary Evans Picture Library/Alamy; **p. 194:** © Paul Jaminski/UM Photo Services; **p. 195:** © The Natural History Museum, London; **p. 196 (left & right):** © William A. Haviland; **p. 199:** Courtesy of Marcel Otte

CHAPTER 9

p. 202: Photographer: H. Jensen/Copyright © University of Tubingen; **p. 204:** Jonesfilm/Warner Bros/The Kobal Collection; **p. 205:** © David L. Brill; **p. 207 (above):** Pascal Goetgheluck/Photo Researchers, Inc.; **p. 207 (below):** © 2001 David L. Brill/Brill Atlanta; **p. 208 (below):** © 1988 David L. Brill; **p. 214 (left):** Gianni Dagli Orti/Corbis; **p. 214 (right):** Réunion de Musées Nationaux/Art Resource, NY; **p. 216:** Rock painting of a bull and horses, c. 17,000 BC, Prehistoric/Caves of Lascaux, Dordogne, France/The Bridgeman Art Library/copyright status: out of copyright; **p. 217:** © John van Hasselt/Corbis Sygma; **p. 218:** © Jean Vertut; **p. 221:** © Goran Burenhult; **p. 223:** © Aunty Beryl Carmichael

CHAPTER 10

p. 228: © Tavid Bingham and Amory Ledyard; **p. 232:** © Tian chao—Imaginechina/AP Images; **p. 237:** © Sepp Seitz; **p. 238:** © maggiegowan.co.uk/Alamy; **p. 239:** © Harvey Finkle; **p. 241:** © Dr. Bruno Glaser Universitat Bayreuth; **p. 242:** © Bettmann/Corbis; **p. 243 (left):** © Dennis MacDonald/PhotoEdit; **p. 243 (right):** © Irven DeVore/Anthro/Photo; **p. 245 (left):** © UPPA/Photoshot; **p. 245 (right):** © Jim Richardson/Corbis; **p. 247:** © John Kerkhoven; **pp. 248 & 249:** © Alan H. Goodman, Hampshire College

CHAPTER 11

p. 252: © Aladin Abdel Naby/Reuters/Landov; **p. 254:** © Getty Images; **p. 256 (left):** © William A. Haviland; **p. 256 (right):** © Image Source/Getty Images; **p. 259:** © Nishan Bingham;

p. 260: © Anita de Laguna Haviland; **p. 262:** Rolex Awards for Excellence, Susan Gray; **p. 263:** Photo by Andrew Snavely of Dobra Tea; **p. 264:** © Robert Holmes/Corbis; **p. 265 (left):** © Angel Franco/The New York Times; **p. 265 (right):** © AFP/Getty Images; **p. 269:** © Tavid Bingham; **p. 271:** © Cahokia Mounds State Historic Site; **p. 272:** © AFT/Getty Images

CHAPTER 12

p. 276: © Xinhua/Photoshot; **p. 279 (above):** Courtesy of Wellcome Library, London; **p. 279 (below):** Missouri History Museum St. Louis; **p. 280:** Courtesy of Robert T. Jackson; **p. 281:** © Laurence Dutton/Getty Images; **p. 282 (left):** © AP Photo/Eugene Hoshiko; **p. 282 (right):** © Schalkwijik/Art Resource, NY; **p. 283:** © blickwinkel/Alamy; **p. 285:** © W. David Powell; **p. 288:** From *Journal of Heredity* "Post-natal growth disparity in monozygotic twins," Komai, T. and Fukuoka, G. 25:423–430 Oct 1934; **p. 290:** © Steve Elmore; **p. 291:** © Terrol Dew Johnson; **p. 292:** © Charles O. Cecil/Alamy; **p. 295:** © Michael Coyne/Getty Images

CHAPTER 13

p. 298: Lok Samiti (translation: People's Committee) of Mehdigani, India. Photograph by Nandlal Master; **p. 300:** © Corbis/Sygma; **p. 302:** © Kriss Snibbe/Staff Photo Harvard News Office; **p. 304:** © Reuters/Mike Segar/Landov; **p. 306 (left):** © Topham/The Image Works; **p. 306 (right):** © Ronnie Kaufman/Corbis; **p. 308 (left & right):** Population Media Center, www.polulationmedia.org; **p. 309:** © Reza/Webistan/Corbis; **p. 313:** With permission from Alberta Heritage Foundation for Medical Research. Artist: Carla Andrew; **p. 317 (left):** © Allison Wright/Corbis; **p. 317 (right):** © AP Photo/Caritas Hong Kong, Kahn Zellweger, HO; **p. 319:** Courtesy of Dr. Elizabeth A. Guillette; **p. 320:** © Sarah Blake Johnson

Index

Italic page numbers indicate charts, figures, and maps.